Methods for
Business Research

JOHN B. KERVIN
University of Toronto

HarperCollins*Publishers*

Sponsoring Editor: Debra Riegert
Development Editor: Susan Hull
Project Editor: Claire M. Caterer
Design Supervisor: Dorothy Bungert
Text and Cover Design: Armen Kojoyian
Production Administrator: Paula Keller
Compositor: ComCom Division of Haddon Craftsmen, Inc.
Printer and Binder: R. R. Donnelley & Sons Company
Cover Printer: The Lehigh Press, Inc.

Methods for Business Research

StatPac is a registered trademark of Walonick Associates, Inc. The owner's manual and software are copyrighted by David S. Walonick. More information may be obtained by contacting Walonick Associates, Inc., 6500 Nicollet Avenue S., Minneapolis, MN 55423.

SPSS/PC+ is a trademark of SPSS Inc. For more information on SPSS products, contact the Marketing Department, SPSS Inc., 444 N. Michigan Avenue, Chicago, IL 60611 (Tel: 312/329-3500).

Library of Congress Cataloging-in-Publication Data
Kervin, John B.
    Methods for business research / John B. Kervin.
      p.   cm.
    Includes bibliographical references and index.
    ISBN 0-06-043636-0 (student edition)
    ISBN 0-06-500690-9 (teacher edition)
    1. Industrial management—Research. 2. Industrial management—
Statistical methods. 3. Business—Research—Methodology.
I. Title.
HD30.4K47 1992
650'.072—dc20   91-27132
                                        CIP

95 9 8 7 6 5 4 3 2

Contents

*The Lighter Side of Research, Summary, Where Are We Now?, Discussion Issues and Assignments, and Further Reading appear at the end of every chapter.

PART TWO
Research Design 83

CHAPTER 3
Unit of Analysis and Basic Designs 84

CHAPTER 4
Specific Research Designs 116

CHAPTER 5
Variables and Data Sources 156

CHAPTER 9
Measurement II:
Questionnaires and Interviews   301

CHAPTER 10
Methodologies I: Introduction and
Available Data Studies   345

CHAPTER 11
Methodologies II: Pilot Projects, Evaluation Studies, and Field Experiments 378

CHAPTER 12
Methodologies III: Surveys 417

PART FOUR
Data Analysis and Reporting 455

CHAPTER 13
Data Preparation 456

CHAPTER 14
Preliminary Data Analysis 489

CHAPTER 15
Descriptive and Univariate Analysis   530

CHAPTER 16
Relationships and Group Differences: Bivariate Analysis   543

Preface

Performance. Competitiveness. Globalization. In the current economic climate (and the foreseeable future) these terms underline the importance of *business research* for organizational effectiveness. More than ever before managers face decisions that require reliable information and a clear understanding of the firm's situation. Business research provides this information and understanding; it makes possible better decisions in marketing, operations, personnel, finance, accounting, public relations, and other functional areas. Research is now an essential business tool, and the demand for graduates who can handle business research projects continues to grow. This text will help business students meet that demand and confront the challenges of today and tomorrow.

The text is appropriate for MBA and senior undergraduate business research courses, as well as courses in applied organization research. While an elementary knowledge of statistics is helpful, it isn't necessary; the text includes enough material to introduce students to the basic concepts.

OVERALL PHILOSOPHY OF THIS TEXT

I approached the writing of this text with four paramount goals:

- *Complete Up-to-the-Minute Coverage.* The text provides highly readable coverage of the full range of topics encompassed by current-day business research, from surveys to time series, from data analysis on the office microcomputer to advice for choosing business-oriented statistical software, from the expensive and elegant experimental design to quick-and-dirty data-cleaning shortcuts.

- *Business Focus.* This text recognizes the particular problems faced by *business* researchers, such as time constraints, organization politics, and data limitations. It begins with business needs as a premise; it doesn't try to adapt the methods of other disciplines. The focus is on solving business problems, not testing theories. For example, an entire chapter, Chapter 2, addresses the task of translating a business problem into a well-defined research problem.

- *Ethical Issues.* You'll find discussed here a wide variety of the ethical issues and dilemmas that business researchers face, such as gathering and using information about employees and reporting bad news to managers who don't want to hear it.

- *Practical Problem-Solving Approach.* The text offers a wealth of practical suggestions and procedures for evaluating, purchasing, and conducting business research *without* sacrificing the theoretical foundations. It combines the best of theory and practice without being a "cookbook." Like other business activities, research encounters problems that need solving, and a knowledge of the basics spawns better solutions.

Above all, this text should enable students both to *consume* and *produce* research: to appreciate the role of research in business problem solving and decision making, to purchase and evaluate consultants' research products, and to plan and carry out small to medium-sized projects on their own.

ORGANIZATION

Chapters are organized to follow the sequence of decisions in business research. Part One includes an introduction to the field and the formulation of research problems, a task which is often problematic in business research. Part Two deals with research design decisions: unit of analysis, basic design, specific design, variables and data sources, and sampling. Part Three involves measurement and data gathering, including a chapter devoted to questionnaires and interviews, plus a chapter on each of the three major data-gathering methodologies in business research: available or secondary data; pilot projects, evaluation studies, and other field experiments; and surveys. The final part of the text covers data analysis and reporting, beginning with data preparation and preliminary analysis. It includes a chapter on multivariate analysis of relationships and group differences, and time series. Part Four ends with a chapter on drafting recommendations and report writing.

SPECIAL FEATURES AND TOPICS

The text offers special features and emphasizes special topics to help meet the four goals discussed previously.

How to Do a Literature Review.   Chapter 2 offers a set of guidelines for conducting an effective and efficient review of the literature. It points out exactly what two objectives (important variables, and useful measures and methods) the literature review is supposed to accomplish and gives concrete suggestions for meeting these objectives.

Data Analysis on Computers.   Recognizing that today's managers use computers and software packages for data analysis, the data-analysis chapters (13 through 17) emphasize quality of input, selecting the appropriate statistical technique for the problem, and correctly interpreting the output. Guidelines for selecting software are included.

Multivariate Statistics.   In Chapter 17 the text emphasizes the *logic* of multivariate data analysis, including a readily understood introduction to the idea of statistical control. Rather than formulas and derivations, it stresses the importance of understanding the assumptions of various statistical tests and the *consequences of their violation.* It teaches how to use the output of multivariate analysis to answer research questions in a way that produces effective solutions and recommendations for business problems. An end-of-chapter appendix introduces causal modeling.

Sampling Theory and Inferential Statistics.   These topics, fundamental to understanding sampling and statistics, are introduced in a highly readable fashion in Appendix A. Topics that often puzzle students, such as the sampling distribution, are given special attention in an extended, easy-to-follow example.

Questionnaires and Data Collection Forms.   Examples from actual student projects are provided in Appendix D. In Appendix C you'll find a list of commonly used response categories for survey studies.

Running a Project.   Appendix E deals with the planning and administration of a research project, including budgeting, deciding whether to do the project in-house, writing the proposal and getting approvals, and hiring and training research personnel.

PEDAGOGY

The text provides an array of pedagogical tools to assist instructors and motivate the interest and involvement of students.

Research Skills Boxes.   Special boxes teach the craft of research, such as how to draw a random sample, pretest a questionnaire or interview, administer placebo treatments, and check for nonresponse bias. These boxes are identified by the icon at right.

Focus on Research Boxes.   These boxes provide background on selected topics, such as business research today, causal inference and alternative explanations, and the finite population correction.

Research Issues Boxes.   A series of boxes discusses current issues in business research, including the use of volunteers, the controversy over significance tests versus effect size, and the debate concerning ordinal variables treated as if they were quantitative.

Research Ethics Boxes.   Research ethics boxes throughout the text address the ethical issues and dilemmas researchers face at each stage of research, from detecting potential ethical problems at the beginning, to the ethics of interviews, to the misuse of graphics in research reports.

Continuing Case Examples.   Throughout the text two extended case studies allow students to follow the problems and decisions of a project from start to finish. The Campbell Switch and the Moving Sound cases show how researchers cope with the problems that arise at each stage of their projects. Campbell Switch is a medium-sized firm that produces switches and similar components for home appliances and industrial machinery. Moving Sound is a new, small company that sells records, cassettes, and compact discs from buses. Data sets for the two cases are available for students to analyze on microcomputers.

Short Case Examples.   A wealth of small case examples illustrate points of research methodology. Most of the examples, from firms such as Kellogg-Salada, General Electric, Radio Shack, Imperial Oil, Merrill Lynch, and Domtar, are drawn from real-life research situations faced by the author and his students. The examples cover human resource management, production, marketing, finance, accounting, and other business areas.

Easy-to-Find Marginal Definitions.   Definitions of key terms are provided in the margins of the text, as well as in a comprehensive end-of-text glossary.

Suggestions for Researchers.   Also in the margins you'll find practical suggestions to help researchers work efficiently and avoid pitfalls. For example, save time by using a copy of the questionnaire as a codebook, and take it to the computer whenever you do data analysis.

Optional Advanced Topic Sections.   Those portions of the text that present advanced material are lightly shaded and titled "Advanced Topic" to allow instructors to adapt the text to courses of different lengths and levels of sophistication. Examples include aggregate data in Chapter 3, pooled time series in Chapter 4, sampling in small populations in Chapter 7, multitrait and multimethod validity checks in Chapter 8, and casual modeling in Chapter 17.

Lighter Side of Research. Each chapter ends with a touch of humor to show that research also has a lighter side.

Summary and "Where Are We Now?" Also at the close of each chapter is a summary and a brief section that reviews just where the reader is at that point in the research process sequence and what lies immediately ahead. This helps students retain the continuity of the research endeavor, and not get lost in the details.

Discussion Issues and Assignments. Another end-of-chapter feature is a list of discussion topics and short exercises, providing students an opportunity to actively debate and practice the various steps of the business research endeavor. Students can do the exercises individually or in groups. Learning by doing keeps students interested, informed, and motivated.

Further Readings. The final end-of-chapter feature is a brief annotated list of references to allow instructors and students to pursue selected topics in more detail.

SUPPLEMENTS

Instructor's Manual and Test Bank with Transparency Masters. Written by the author, the manual is organized by chapter to help the instructor prepare relevant and thought-provoking presentations that convey the essentials and excitement of an ongoing research project. It suggests alternative course organizations and assignment schedules to match students' level of sophistication and the course length. The chapter contents include lecture objectives and outlines, supplementary lecture material, advice for teaching difficult concepts, 75 transparency masters, in-class exercises, suggestions for student projects, answers/comments to the "Discussion Issues and Assignments" items at the end of each chapter in the student text, and a bank of 20 to 30 multiple-choice, fill-in, and short-answer test questions for each chapter. Answers to test questions are keyed to specific pages in the text to help instructors in those important "post-mortem" review sessions.

TestMaster Diskette. This computer program allows instructors to assemble their own customized tests from the items included in the test bank. If desired, test questions can be viewed on the screen and can be edited, saved, and printed. In addition, instructors can add questions or even create their own item banks of test questions, which may include graphics. A real time saver, it is available for the IBM PC and compatibles.

Data Sets Diskette. Two data sets, one for each of the extended cases, are available to instructors on one 5¼-inch diskette included in the Instructor's Edition and available for student distribution. The data represent the "results" obtained by the continuing case researchers whose progress students have been following in the text. The diskette includes the raw data (in ASCII format), data definition information, and an explanatory README file. The data can easily be imported to, and analyzed on, a wide variety of spreadsheet and statistical software packages.

Grades. Free to adopters, this computerized grade-keeping and classroom management package maintains data for up to 200 students. It is available for the IBM PC and compatibles.

ACKNOWLEDGMENTS

Recognizing that it's often the students who teach instructors, I would like particularly to acknowledge the scores of students whose research, blood, sweat, tears, and triumphs are reflected in these pages. I'm also grateful to those staff members at HarperCollins who were helpful and encouraging, as well as my colleagues Noah Meltz, Frank Reid, Jeff Reitz, and Gerry Swartz. The text has also been greatly enhanced by the comments and suggestions of the text reviewers:

D. Ray Bagby	Baylor University
J.K. Bandyopadhaya	Central Michigan University
Janice M. Beyer	University of Texas–Austin
John S. Carroll	MIT–Sloan School
Angelo DeNisi	Rutgers University
Gerald Ferris	University of Illinois–Champaign-Urbana
Robert Gatewood	University of Georgia
Jim Grimm	Illinois State University
Marcella Kocar	Central Michigan University
Michael S. Lane	West Virginia University
Ed J. Manton	Eastern Texas State University
Bob Newberry	University of Wisconsin–La Crosse
Sukgoo Pak	University of Wisconsin–La Crosse
Marjorie Platt	Northeastern University
Neal Schmitt	Michigan State University

Finally, I want especially to thank Marika for her help with every phase of this text, and Susannah, whose sacrifice of daddy-time helped make this project possible.

John Kervin

PART ONE

Business Research and Research Problems

An introduction to business research and an examination of how business problems and questions become research problems and questions.

CHAPTER 1

What Is Business Research?

CHAPTER OBJECTIVES

- How does business research relate to the management function?
- How is it different from other kinds of research?
- What are its general methods?
- What are the typical stages of a business research project?
- What are the different types of business research?
- How do you assess its quality?
- What ethical problems does it encounter?

CHAPTER OUTLINE

BUSINESS RESEARCH AND THE MANAGEMENT FUNCTION
BUSINESS RESEARCH IN CONTEXT
THE METHODS OF BUSINESS RESEARCH
THE PURPOSES OF BUSINESS RESEARCH
WHAT MAKES GOOD BUSINESS RESEARCH?
ETHICAL PROBLEMS IN BUSINESS RESEARCH
IDENTIFYING THREATS TO ETHICAL RESEARCH

*T*his book is about business research.

A healthy functioning organization demands sound decision making and effective problem solving. Good decisions require relevant information; good solutions need thorough understanding of problems. Business research is a systematic method for obtaining information. It also provides the understanding of a problem's causes necessary for effective solutions. In short, business research is an important *tool* organizations use to gather information about business-related issues.

The Montgomery Metals example (Box 1.1) gives us a preliminary glimpse of the nature of business research. Note the following points:

- Business research frequently (though not always) focuses on people and their behavior or attitudes.

- It involves a specific question, decision, or problem facing a specific organization.

- It obtains information about the question, decision, or problem and often tests ideas about the causes of a problem.

- It is a systematic way of achieving the understanding and information necessary for some decision or action.

Business research is a practical, applied-research tool for obtaining the information that organizations need to answer questions and solve business problems.

BUSINESS RESEARCH AND THE MANAGEMENT FUNCTION

According to business publications, modern managers are making increasing use of business research. As Box 1.2 shows, this growth is due in part to the increasing availability of easy-to-use statistical analysis on microcomputers.

What Kinds of Organizations Use It?

Many kinds of organizations use business research. Sam's Corner Drugstore surveys customers about the products and services they want to find there. Black and Decker studies ways of reducing employee turnover. Texaco compares the accuracy of different accounting indicators of financial health.

Nonprofit organizations also carry out business research. A union local surveys its members about their feelings on job sharing. A symphony orchestra asks subscribers about their music preferences. Charities, cultural organizations, political parties, and in fact *any* goal-directed organization can use business research. It isn't just for business firms.

BOX 1.1
FOCUS ON RESEARCH

Business Research at Montgomery Metals

"Dammit!" CRASH!

The phone slams down. Pencils and paper clips jump. Outside the general manager's office secretaries smile and assistants shudder. There's another problem in the Cleveland plant of Montgomery Metals.

"That's the fifth time this month our day shift production has stalled! What am I going to do with those blinkety-blank furnaces? Argh!"

Harry Anderson quickly fires off an angry memo to the engineering department and turns to other matters.

Coincidentally, 1,200 miles away at Montgomery's Denver plant, a similar problem has arisen.

"Hmmm," murmurs Frank Morgan, the general manager, looking over the most recent production records. "We'd better research this one. Looks like it could mean trouble. I'll spend some time on this one myself, and use one of the people in Personnel to help with the legwork."

He summarizes the problem for Tom Harper, from Personnel.

"Production levels on the day shift are down again. One superintendent blames the new furnace timers, another thinks it may be the new employees. Perhaps there's been a breakdown in training. My hunch is that it's a 'people' problem, which is why I called you in to help. Anyway, we're going to research the problem, find out what's causing it, then figure out what we can do about it."

Morgan talks over the problem with two of the foremen. Harper checks the production records, discusses the problem with a few employees from each of the day and afternoon shifts, and gets the furnace records from engineering.

On the basis of their investigation, they conclude that the cause of the problem may be any one of four different factors: faulty materials, employee attitudes or abilities, furnace problems, or inadequate supervision. They agree that research will be required to test which factor is the primary cause. Harper devises a brief statement of the research problem ("To discover the causes of productivity differences between the day and afternoon shifts in the low-alloy furnace department") and comes up with a short list of seven specific research questions.

It is decided that Harper should spend some time observing what happens on each shift. On the basis of these observations, Harper gathers data both from company records and from a series of short interviews with a sample of 25 workers on each shift. These data are entered into the office microcomputer and analyzed using an SPSS/PC+ statistical software package.

Harper then writes up the results and his recommendations and presents them to Morgan. Together they discuss their implications.

As a result of their discussion, some new guidelines are written for the supervisors, two personnel changes are made, and day shift production is soon up to target levels. Meanwhile, at the Cleveland plant, the engineers have told Anderson it's a "supervisor problem," and production has stalled yet again.

What Functional Areas Use It?

As well as everyday decisions, managers are responsible for solving a range of administrative problems, from the shop floor ("Absenteeism is up again!") to a major financial decision ("Should we buy out our public stockholders?"), to the once-in-a-lifetime marketing nightmare ("Some maniac is tampering

BOX 1.2
FOCUS ON RESEARCH

Business Research Today

Business research is a rapidly growing activity. Much of the recent growth is due to the increasing involvement in research by managers themselves. Traditionally the bulk of business research has been conducted by external consulting firms and in-house research departments, but that picture is changing.

The expanding research role of managers is due to a number of factors.

- *Microcomputers.* Greater numbers of managers now have the computing capacity for sophisticated data analysis sitting on their desks, thanks to the widespread use of microcomputers in the office.
- *Software.* Recent advances in software for micros make even statistics user friendly. Packages such as SPSS/PC+, StatPac, NCSS (Number Cruncher), and Systat offer a wide variety of statistical procedures in an easy-to-use format, with

documentation geared to both the experienced and the neophyte. (As well as research, some of these packages can be used for statistical quality control—SQC.) Other software, such as project management programs, make it easier than ever to administer in-house research.

- *Sophistication.* The increasing sophistication of better educated managers and their growing familiarity with other business-oriented software (especially spreadsheets and database systems) makes them more willing to try their own statistical analysis.

The combination of these factors has resulted in more managers able to carry out or direct a wide variety of research projects on their own. Today's managers are insisting on the kinds of information and answers that business research provides, and in many cases they are able to get the information and answers themselves.

---

with our headache capsules!"). They need information to solve these problems, as well as for the everyday decisions and questions.

Business research provides information and solutions. Managers use it in many functional areas of the organization, including

- Marketing and promotion decisions
- Personnel issues such as hiring, training, and compensation
- Employee-management relations and industrial relations
- Public opinion about the organization, its products, or services
- Accounting techniques and indicators
- Human resource utilization and planning
- Individual and work-group productivity
- Work procedures and organization
- Organizational goals and performance

- Organizational change and development
- Consumer behavior and preferences
- Implementation of new technology and reactions to it
- Intraorganizational conflict
- Financial issues and investment decisions
- The organization's political and economic environment (including government policies and actions, and relations with other organizations)
- Fund-raising, membership recruitment, and maintenance in nonprofit organizations

The Montgomery Metals example in Box 1.1 illustrates business research in the area of work force productivity.

When Do Managers Use It?

When do managers need business research? What are the alternatives?

Managers with enough information and understanding about the problem or question they face do *not* need business research, particularly if they have experience with similar situations or are intimately familiar with details of the particular problem. In such circumstances, "management by hunch" is very cost effective; knowing when to rely on hunches is a distinguishing characteristic of good managers.

However, there are times when existing information is inadequate. The decision may be just too important, the question too complex, the causes of a problem unknown, or a hunch too uncertain. In these circumstances, business research obtains the needed information, makes specific predictions, or generates and *tests* hunches and ideas about what's happening in the situation. It reduces the chances of poor decisions and ineffective action.

Important Decisions. Business research is most useful when decisions and problems have important long-term implications, involve substantial uncertainty, and can't be solved by purely technical or routine means. These conditions are likely to be found at three different levels of organizational decision making.

- At the highest level, *strategic planning* often requires business research. Introducing a new product, making a takeover bid, initiating internal reorganization, or undertaking a new venture are examples of strategic planning decisions which often benefit from business research.

- Lower level *tactical decisions* involving the choice of alternative means to accomplish organizational goals may also require business research. Choosing alternative marketing approaches, deciding whether to introduce quality circles, evaluating different accounting procedures, and determining how to increase membership are examples of such needs.

- *Nonroutine operational problems* often require business research. Such problems involve more than day-to-day adjustments to changing organizational circumstances. For example, deciding how much overtime is needed to finish a project on time is normally a routine problem not needing research. On the other hand, dealing with union objections to the allotment of overtime is not a routine matter and might necessitate research for an effective solution that satisfies both sides.

Complex Problems.   Management by hunch works best in relatively simple and straightforward situations. Hunches are usually limited to characteristics of a group (e.g., "I think most of our employees favor flexible work hours" or "I know our absenteeism level is too high") and simple two-variable relationships ("I suspect the younger men have higher absenteeism levels" or "Absenteeism seems to be higher during hunting season" or "The new costing software has lost us seven contracts!").

Complex problems, however, involve a multitude of factors. Unfortunately, we seldom think in multivariate terms (relationships involving three or more factors), particularly when the relationships are complex. For example, it is unlikely that most managers' hunches would match the following conclusions from a research study of absenteeism.

CASE EXAMPLE

This study concludes that our absenteeism problem is strongly related to two factors: (1) employees' hunting activity and (2) weather.

With respect to hunting, our employees fall into two categories: those who hunt regularly during hunting season and those who hunt rarely or never.

For our nonhunting employees, the absenteeism pattern among younger men is several short absences, and for older employees fewer but longer absences. The older employees are more likely to be absent for medical reasons. For our hunting employees, at all age levels the pattern is many short absences, particularly Mondays and Fridays.

Therefore, to be most effective, our absenteeism-reduction program should focus on employees with a high number of short absences, and it should begin before the hunting season.

Although hunting season has an impact on absenteeism, bad weather has an even stronger effect: it accounts for three times as many one-day absences. Further, in bad weather employees who live 10 miles or more from the plant are more than twice as likely to be absent as those who live closer. However, employees with a working spouse and children under school age are only slightly more likely to be absent than other employees.

Therefore, we should investigate the possibility of alternative transportation arrangements in bad weather for all our more distant employees, not just those with children.

Unknown Causes.   Business research helps organizations identify the causal processes, or driving forces underlying trends and problems. An understanding of causes is crucial for finding effective solutions. For example, a decline in productivity may be due to new procedures, new management, poor labor relations, equipment or supply problems, or seasonal factors (such as influenza). Unless the most important causal processes are identified, the organization may take the wrong action. Business research can save money. (As we see in future chapters, inferences about causality are almost always elusive and open to question. Business researchers choose their research designs and their data analysis with at least one eye on the problem of inferring causality.)

Unverified Hunches.   An important limitation of management-by-hunch is that we often don't realize when our hunches are wrong. In part this is just human nature. We are all subject to selective perception, distortion, and rationalization as defenses for our mistaken decisions. As a result, our hunches are seldom subject to close scrutiny and systematic testing. In addition, feedback on a particular decision or action may be limited, or a problem situation may improve spontaneously or because of some factor we aren't even aware of. The effect of all this is that we often never know whether a hunch was right. Business research, however, systematically gathers and analyzes the evidence and provides the information that not only increases the chance of a correct decision, but also allows us to verify that our actions are having the desired effect.

In summary, business research is useful when we face important decisions or complex problems, when we want to understand underlying causal processes, and when we need to know with some certainty whether our hunches are correct.

BUSINESS RESEARCH IN CONTEXT

To better understand the nature of business research, let us locate it in the context of research in general and compare it with other kinds of research activity. We examine the following distinctions:

• Basic and applied research

• Within applied research: general and specific applied research

• Also within applied research: policy and organization research

We also compare specific and general organization research.

The term *research* has no single widely accepted definition. For our purposes, we define it on page 9.

Our definition covers a vast range of activities, purposes, and topics. It includes the pursuit of butterflies to South America in quest of their migration patterns and the testing of truck tires to determine their wearing properties and time to failure. Where in this range does business research fit? We start with the most fundamental distinction: basic and applied research.

Research is the process of systematically gathering and analyzing information in order to gain knowledge and understanding.

Basic and Applied Research

All research can be placed on a continuum representing the general objectives and intended audience of the work. At one end is *basic* research, at the other is *applied*. We can further divide this continuum into three categories by distinguishing between *general applied*, which occupies the approximate middle of the continuum, and *specific applied*, which takes the end position. As we see, business research is found in the specific applied category. Table 1.1 summarizes the differences among these three categories of research activity.

Basic Research. The results of basic research contribute to general laws and theories expressing our knowledge and understanding of the universe, including the behavior of individuals, groups, and organizations. Although often fascinating, research of this kind is carried out without any expectation that the results should be immediately useful. Here is an example of a law from basic small groups research:

An individual's power and prestige status within a group will determine his or her influence and his or her share of speaking opportunities.

Researchers and theorists assume that the laws and theories examined in basic research hold universally, within scope conditions set or implied by the theory. For example, Michels' (1959) "iron law of oligarchy" states that in all voluntary organizations (the scope condition) leadership tends to develop oligarchic tendencies. As long as the scope conditions are met, Michels' law is assumed to apply in all times and places.[1] If researchers find a circumstance in which it does not function, then either the law itself or its scope conditions must be altered. Within these conditions, basic researchers assume that their findings are generalizable.

Research results are **generalized** to the extent that the researcher believes them to be applicable to cases or situations beyond the set of cases specifically examined in the research.

Specific Applied Research. Specific applied research contributes to immediate decisions and actions. It provides information or understanding about a particular issue or problem facing an individual, group, organization, or government. It is expressly directed to needs and goals, and its results are expected to be useful and relevant.

Specific applied research results are sometimes generalized to other circumstances (although not to the "universe" as in basic research). For example,

---

[1]Hempel and Oppenheim (1960) call such results or lawlike statements "universal conditionals," meaning that they apply universally within certain conditions.

TABLE 1.1 ■ COMPARISON OF BASIC AND APPLIED RESEARCH

	Basic	**General Applied**	**Specific Applied**
Objectives	Knowledge expressed in general laws and theories	Understanding relevant issues, based on general theories	Information for immediate decisions and actions
Source of Research Topics	Unresolved theoretical questions; issues raised by previous research; unexplained phenomena	Same as "basic," plus widespread interest in an issue	Need to take action or make a decision related to needs and goals
Who Does the Research?	Academics	Academics; governments; large organizations*	Governments; organizations; consultants; research institutes
Source of Funds	Governments; foundations	Governments; foundations; large organizations*	Governments; social agencies; public and private organizations
Research Methods	Based on the scientific model of rigorous hypothesis testing	Based on the scientific model, but often less rigorous	Vary widely from very rigorous to quick-and-dirty
Determinants of Choice of Methods	Topic and research problem; resources and constraints; theoretical and research paradigm	Topic and research problem; resources and constraints; importance of problem; desired generalization	Topic and research problem; resources and constraints; importance of problem
Major Concerns	Validity; universality	Validity; relevance; applicable to similar situations	Validity; relevance; cost-benefit ratio

*Some general applied research is funded or carried out by private groups, such as the Russell Sage Foundation. Bell Laboratories is an example of a business organization which has carried out significant general applied research in social psychology.

a drug treatment program tested and found to be successful in one city may be introduced in similar cities, but the results are not assumed to apply to other countries. With other projects, little or no generalization occurs. For example, the cause of a rash of accidents in a particular trucking firm is not assumed to exist in any other companies.

General Applied Research.   In between basic and specific applied research is a body of research with both basic and applied features. This research is usually associated with those academic subfields that address more practical questions and issues, such as organizational sociology, administrative theory, or organizational behavior (psychology). General applied research combines both theory building and testing with a focus on issues of general interest to governments and organizations.

CASE EXAMPLE

A recent article by D. Quinn Mills (1985), entitled "Seniority Versus Ability in Promotion Decisions," is an example of general applied research in the area of compensation:

> This study tests the empirical validity of the proposition that longer service employees are paid more than others because they are more productive. This relationship—the positive slope of the age-earnings profile—is generally attributed to the accumulation of human capital by senior employees. Experience is held to be a significant source of investment by people in themselves and, therefore, a powerful determinant of earnings. Promotion systems in American industry, it has been argued, reflect the increasing contribution of experienced employees to productivity.

In this case, the source of the research problem is both human capital theory and recent research findings, the objective is to test a very general hypothesis (". . . longer service employees are paid more than others because they are more productive"), and the implicit boundaries of the research problem are very broad (Western industrialized countries).

Basic and Applied Research Methodology.   Most basic research employs a scientific model marked by a rigorous testing of hypotheses. Although specific methods vary across disciplines, the same fundamental principles apply in the physical, biological, behavioral, and social sciences. (One important difference among these disciplines is that in the latter two, research techniques normally take into account the awareness of individuals that they are being studied.) Perhaps because almost all basic research is carried out in universities, most courses in research methods teach this kind of research.

Basic researchers choose specific techniques on the basis of research topic and problem, available resources and constraints (such as money, personnel, and data access or availability), and the research paradigm in which they are working. For example, the network of researchers studying polarization in group decision making uses the same theoretical approach and variations on the same experimental procedures.

In contrast to basic research, the methods of specific applied research vary widely. Some projects are as rigorous as basic research (or *more* rigorous when millions of dollars depend on a decision). In other instances researchers use so-called quick-and-dirty methods to save time and money. Shortcuts are an important element of much specific applied research, rather than a weakness. The researcher's objective is to *satisfice* rather than *maximize:* the objective is research with enough validity to do the job at the lowest price. (An example is the use of quota samples, discussed in Chapter 6.)

In specific applied research, the choice of methods is affected by what's at stake (as well as the topic, resources, and constraints). The more critical a problem the less time the manager has to find a solution; the more money involved in a decision, the more resources the manager likely has to make it. When time is short, researchers often use time-saving methods such as quasi-experimental designs, available data, and telephone interviews. When resources are greater, true experimental designs, specially gathered data, and personal interviews may be employed.

Overall, the methods of general applied research lie between basic and specific applied, but are normally closer to the former.

Policy and Organization Research

Our third distinction involves the two major subjects of applied research activity: policy and organizations. The first includes issues relevant to the health and functioning of society and its citizens; the second (which includes business research) concerns the health and functioning of organizations. Before we turn to organization research, we look briefly at research involving social policies.

Policy Research.   Policy research entails the planning or evaluation of legislation, policies, or programs to deal with social problems and issues of public policy. It is often called "social research" or "public policy research." It may deal with social problems and issues in a *general* way, with results applicable to many different jurisdictions (e.g., states, provinces). Alternatively, the research may focus on a *specific* policy question for a particular government or agency.

Because social policies represent the context in which organizations operate, the results of policy research are often of interest to managers. Government policies may affect the skill and educational level of the work force, the costs of financing new projects, the general business climate, restrictions on the activities of tax-exempt organizations, and other aspects of business. Examples of policy research include

• Efforts to find the extent and causes of social problems such as drug abuse, poverty, highway accidents, and unemployment.

- Economic forecasting (e.g., next year's GNP growth and inflation rates).

- Economic analysis (e.g., the economic impact of free-trade legislation).

- Program evaluation (e.g., effectiveness of a drug control measure).

- Environmental and social impact analysis (e.g., effects of a new industrial waste disposal facility).

Governments at all levels, from municipal to federal, carry out policy research. So do various nongovernmental bodies, including social agencies, community groups (for example, in planning recreational services), and interest groups and other organizations that want to influence government decisions and find support for their arguments.

The methods of policy research (such as the use of quasi-experimental designs for program evaluation) are now taught in many courses in the social sciences and economics. While policy research is not our focus, many of the topics we discuss are relevant to this type of applied research, including data gathering and analysis techniques.

Organization Research. Within the applied area, the major alternative to policy research is research that deals with organizations. In particular, organization research, like policy research, can be either general or specific.

General and Specific Organization Research

Within the broad field of organization research we can distinguish the categories *general* and *specific*. Both focus on the functioning and effectiveness of organizations. The first studies organizations as a universal phenomenon; the second concentrates on the information or problem-solving needs of a specific organization. Business research falls into the second category.

General Organization Research. This type of research is a subcategory of general applied research. Its results are expected to be useful, but they are not limited to a single organization. Instead, it tests theories of organizational functioning and behavior which are generalized to a wide variety of associations, groups, corporations, societies, and other collectivities. Examples of general organization research include

- An investigation of a theoretical model of attitudinal and behavioral consequences for employees of plant closings. (Kinicki and Bruning, 1982)

- A comparison of the efficacy of two different predictors of advertising response—the immediate initial reaction to an advertisement. (Zinkhan and Martin, 1983)

- A study of how well managers and union officials were able to predict employees' preferences among collective bargaining issues. (Howells and Brosnan, 1972)

- A study of the accounting decisions made by 64 firms proposing to buy out public stockholders, to see how they handled the conflict of interest involved. (DeAngelo, 1986).

CASE EXAMPLE

Birnbaum and Wong (1985) recently published an article in *Administrative Science Quarterly* that demonstrates researchers' concern with generalization when they conduct general organization research. The study tests the relative effectiveness of culture-free and culture-bound explanations for the choice of organizational structure. The research surveyed 93 Hong Kong Chinese managerial employees. The authors report that

> Work satisfaction was examined with relation to organizational structure (centralization, vertical and horizontal differentiation, and formalization), controlling for job structure (significance, feedback, variety, identity, and autonomy of the job), and individual attributes (sex, age, tenure, education, and cosmopolitanism). The culture-free hypothesis was supported, except for the managers' preference for centralized decision making.[2]

Birnbaum and Wong generalize their results to the *culture-free* theory of organizational structure, a theory applying to almost all organizations. Thus, rather than pertaining to some specific organization or area, the research tests a theory which is, within its scope conditions, universally applicable.

Many of the problems faced in general research on organizations are similar to those encountered in business research. For example, we discuss surveys of organizational informants, sampling organizations and their subunits, and using available data from organizational records. These and other techniques are used in both business and general organization research.

Specific Organization Research. In specific organization research, the researcher seeks results useful and relevant for a particular organization. Business research is one form of specific organization research.

One of the major differences between general and specific organization research is the degree to which results are generalized. In business research, results are often based on a sample of cases drawn from the situation of interest. While business researchers sometimes generalize their results beyond this situation, the general practice is not to assume that the findings hold elsewhere. For example, the attitudes of 100 carefully selected employees may be generalized to a firm's entire work force, but the researcher is not interested in drawing conclusions about employees outside the firm.

Thus compared to general organization research, generalizing results is less a problem in most specific organization research because differences between the sample and the rest of the situation of interest are normally small.

[2]Reprinted from "Organizational Structure of Multinational Banks in Hong Kong from a Culture-free Perspective" by P. H. Birnbaum and G. Y. Y. Wong published in *Administrative Science Quarterly* 30 (1985) by permission of *Administrative Science Quarterly*. Copyright 1985 by *Administrative Science Quarterly*.

Marketing research is an exception; a researcher may want to assume that the attitudes of a sample of potential buyers in one city are the same in all areas in which the product or service is available. Such assumptions are often highly problematic, and market researchers are very concerned about valid generalization.

Who Does the Research? Another important difference between general and specific organization research is who initiates and carries it out. University academics conceive and conduct most general organization research; these researchers are found in the fields of organizational behavior, marketing, industrial and organizational psychology, administration theory, management science, accounting, finance, industrial relations, and industrial and organizational sociology.

Specific organization research, on the other hand, is normally initiated by an organization needing information for decision making or seeking to solve a problem. The organization employs in-house managers or researchers or an outside consulting firm to conduct it. Some academic researchers occasionally act as research consultants, although they often regard such work as less prestigious than basic research or more general applied research.

Audience for Results. Yet another difference is the audience to whom research results are reported. Researchers distribute the results of general organization research to a wide community of academics and fellow researchers through academic journals and conferences. The results reach business and management through journals, seminars, and workshops targeted to these groups.

In comparison, business researchers report exclusively to the organization for which the research is carried out. The organization usually distributes internally a few copies of the report. Occasionally, with the consent of management, a researcher publishes a shortened version of the results in the belief that others with similar specific problems may be interested in the methods or findings.

CASE EXAMPLE

W. A. McGeveran, Jr., in an article entitled "Meditation at the Telephone Company," published in the *Wharton Magazine* (1984), reported business research designed to evaluate a meditation program at the New York Telephone Company. A pilot project divided 154 participants into four conditions, three using different meditation methods and the fourth serving as a control group. Tests were administered before, during, and after the program. Positive results were shown in particular for one type of meditation, and employees reported less stress and greater efficiency.

Although this research was intended for the use of management at New York Telephone, the author believes his results may be useful for other firms.

Table 1.2 summarizes the differences between general and specific organization research. Unfortunately, we do not have convenient terms to distinguish the two. For example, the term *business research* is sometimes used to refer to general research of interest to businesses, or research that examines the ways in which businesses function in general. To avoid any confusion, such research is here referred to as *organization research.* Only a close examination of any particular research report indicates whether it is about organizations in general or focused on a specific problem in a specific organization.

Business and Other Types of Specific Organization Research. Within the category of specific organization research we can identify three major research activities. Business research is one, and the functional areas in which it is applied we just described. Organizations undertake operations and product research as well. *Operations research* involves the development of production and distribution systems that maximize productivity and minimize costs in the face of multiple operational constraints. It leans heavily on mathematical models of production, distribution, and other system processes. *Product research* (often called research and development) seeks to de-

TABLE 1.2 ■ GENERAL AND SPECIFIC ORGANIZATION RESEARCH

	General Organization Research	Specific Organization Research
Focus	Laws and theories of how organizations operate	The specific needs and problems of a particular organization
Problem of Generalization	Very important	Ranges from unimportant to very important
Who Does the Research	Mostly academics	Organization managers; in-house research departments; external consultants
Audience	Broad: journals and books read by other academics, applied researchers, managers	Narrow: reports for management usually read by only a few managers or other researchers

velop new products or to improve the effectiveness of existing products. It normally involves engineering and the application of new scientific discoveries. Because they both involve highly specialized techniques, we do not cover operations and product research in this text.

In summary, compared to other kinds of research, business research

- Is specific applied, rather than general applied or basic.

- Concerns organizations rather than social or public policy issues.

- Involves the needs of a specific organization rather than organizations in general.

- Deals with organizational areas other than operations or product development.

Making Use of General Organization Research

As you might expect, a close relationship exists between general organization research and business research. Many business researchers apply the findings, methods, and measures of the former to their own research designs. In particular, the results of general organization research suggest important factors to include in business research. Similarly, general organization researchers are often concerned with making their work relevant to business researchers as well as to the development of organizational theory (see Lawler et al., 1985).

General organization research also contributes to management practices directly, as well as through business research. Many managers make profitable use of the general research findings reported in business journals such as *The Wharton Magazine* and *The Harvard Business Review*, as well as more academic journals such as *The Accounting Review, Administrative Science Quarterly, Decision Sciences,* and the *Journal of Consumer Research.*

CASE EXAMPLE

An article by Gorn and Weinberg (1984) published in the *Journal of Consumer Research* illustrates general organization research with implications for managerial decision making. Entitled "The Impact of Comparative Advertising on Perception and Attitude: Some Positive Findings," the article reports a test of the impact of comparative versus noncomparative advertising using three types of products—cigarettes, golf balls, and toothpaste. Comparative advertising resulted in lesser brands being perceived as more similar to the leading brand.

An article by Barnes (1978) appearing in *Accounting and Business Research* has implications for organizations considering hostile takeovers. The report, entitled "The Effect of a Merger on the Share Price of the Attacker," suggests that the pattern of share prices prior to and following a merger or takeover may vary from country to country.

The overall context of business research and its relationships to other kinds of research are summarized in Figure 1.1. The dashed arrow in the figure indicates the contribution to business research of general organization research.

THE METHODS OF BUSINESS RESEARCH

The methods of business research have their roots in the social sciences, particularly economics, social psychology, sociology, and political science. Its three major methodologies are surveys, field experiments (often in the form of pilot projects), and the analysis of available or secondary data such as production records and financial statistics. All these methodologies are also used in basic social science research.

However, business research methods are also different from those found in other kinds of applied and basic research in the social sciences. Let us consider first the common thread tying all this research activity together—the scientific method—and then examine how business research is different.

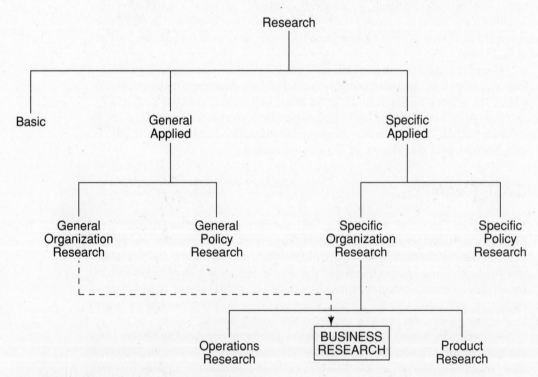

FIGURE 1.1 The Context of Business Research

The Scientific Method

Almost all research is based on the **scientific method:** a set of procedures used to gain knowledge and understanding. While there is no single definition of these procedures, and they vary from discipline to discipline, you can think of the scientific method as a set of principles guiding research activity:

- The application of scientific method is intended to both (1) find general *propositions* (lawlike statements about phenomena), and (2) apply these propositions to explain or understand specific events or conditions.

- Scientific propositions contain abstract **concepts**—precisely defined terms used to label phenomena or characteristics of phenomena. Most propositions relate one concept to another ("The greater the stock price volatility [first concept], the smaller the proportion of pension fund investors [second concept]"). Careful measurement of concepts (finding observable verifiable indicators of a phenomenon or characteristic) is crucial for science.

- The process of finding general propositions involves both *induction* and *deduction.* It begins with the repeated observation of similar *facts* (for example, a researcher counts 28 short strikes, 24 of them in large firms, and 14 long strikes, 12 of them in small ones). These facts lead to the induction of *empirical generalizations* ("Larger firms tend to have shorter strikes"). These empirical generalizations are then logically related to more general propositions, or *theories* ("The greater resources required for maintaining membership mobilization make it more difficult for large groups to maintain prolonged collective action"). Finally, these propositions and theories are tested by deducing more specific *hypotheses* from them ("Because firms A, B, and C are smaller than D, E, and F, their strikes should last longer"), and testing the hypotheses with more facts ("Strike lengths for the six firms are, respectively, 21, 13, 18, 12, 4, and 6 days").

- The essence of science is the use of *empirical evidence* to test hypotheses. Empirical evidence consists of facts that are objective, observable (directly or indirectly), and verifiable. This means that tests are replicable—another researcher using the same procedures should arrive at the same conclusion.

- In scientific method, hypotheses must be *falsifiable.* That is, it must be possible to find empirical evidence that disproves them.

- To the extent that observed facts are consistent with a hypothesis, confidence in the theory or proposition from which the hypothesis is deduced is increased.

- Scientific understanding is the explanation of some event or condition on the basis of its deduction from one or more general propositions ("If internally promoted new managers are generally less likely to be innovative, that explains why George is not very innovative.") Nonscientific explanations include both empathetic understanding ("I know why he sold short because I know how he's feeling") and appeals to higher or divine authority ("The product failed because God willed it").

As much as possible, business researchers strive to be scientific, particularly in the use of empirical evidence and falsifiable research hypotheses. However, they are seldom interested in developing general propositions and theories. As we see later, they are much more likely to borrow and apply the propositions and theories of general organization research.

Methodological Differences

Business research methods differ from other research activities in basic or general organization research in two important ways: the variety of techniques researchers use and the problems and constraints they face.

Variety of Methodologies.   Business researchers have to be familiar with a much greater variety of data-gathering methodologies, designs, and statistical techniques than their counterparts in basic or general organization research.

- Data gathering varies with the purpose of the research and with the functional area of the organization in which it is carried out. For example, both surveys and field experiments are common in the areas of marketing and consumer behavior. The latter also employs controlled laboratory-setting experiments. Personal interview, telephone, and questionnaire surveys are used in personnel and work force research, as are studies based on records and other available data. Research in accounting and finance, on the other hand, uses available secondary data almost exclusively.

- Business research problems may require experimental or nonexperimental designs, with or without sampling. Marketing research often uses quasi-experimental designs, as do pilot projects in almost any area. Employee surveys require nonexperimental designs, as does most financial research.

- The problem, design, and data dictate the statistical techniques required, including analysis of variance, regression, and other procedures.

A competent business researcher is acquainted with all these methodologies, designs, and techniques.

Problems and Constraints.   Business researchers face problems and constraints not normally encountered by other researchers. For example, many projects face the problem of small sample size or incomplete experimental manipulation and randomization. Time pressure is usually much greater in business research, and this may dictate the use of shortcut methods. There is less time for pretesting and the refinement of measures and research instruments.

Another problem stems from the fact that much of business research is **internal** to an organization: surveys and pilot projects involve respondents and subjects inside the organization that is carrying out the research. Internal research results in measurement bias problems, since employees' answers are more likely to be slanted in the direction of telling management what it wants to hear.

To reflect the differences between business and other kinds of research, and the variations found within business research itself, we intentionally adopt as our starting point the unique and varied needs of business researchers. We do not begin with traditional research methods and attempt to adapt them to business research examples. Nevertheless, there are some important similarities, and in the pages that follow we discuss some of these similarities, as well as differences, between business research and the methods of basic research and policy research.

Stages in Business Research Projects

Most business research projects can be divided into twelve separate stages. The usual sequence of these stages is shown in Figure 1.2. The solid arrows represent the movement from stage to stage. The dashed arrows indicate the revision loops which occur when decisions or constraints at one stage necessitate a revision of the decisions of a previous stage.

I: Research Problem Stages

1. Obtain an initial statement of the business problem or question, and investigate it. This exploratory research stage normally involves interviews with key people in the organization, checking relevant records and documents, observing or talking with the people involved, and perhaps focus groups or an informal survey.

2. Translate the initial business problem into a research problem, and draft specific research questions to be answered. (A tentative decision to proceed is often made following this stage.)

II: Research Design Stages

3. Begin the research design by selecting a unit of analysis, a basic design, and a specific design. Constraints at this stage may necessitate a revision of the research problem.

4. Choose the variables for the research. Select data sources and the data-gathering methodology (e.g., a survey). Constraints here may require a revision of the unit of analysis or the specific design.

I Research Problem

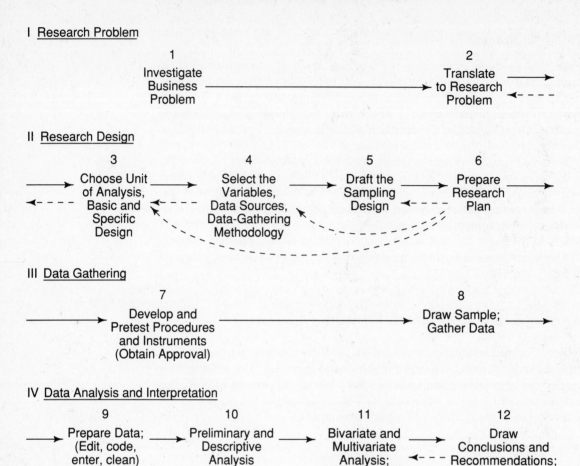

FIGURE I.2 Stages, Decisions, and Revision Loops in Business Research

5. Decide whether to sample, and draft the sampling design, including type and size of the sample.

6. Prepare the research plan (proposal), with cost estimates for materials, supplies, services, and other expenditures. Constraints may require revision of design decisions. Draft a time schedule for the research.

III: Data-Gathering Stages

7. Develop and pretest the measures, research instruments, and procedures. (The organization usually makes a final go-ahead decision at this time.)

8. Draw the sample. Gather the data.

IV: Data Analysis and Interpretation Stages

9. Prepare the data for analysis, which involves editing, coding, entering it into a computer, and cleaning up any errors.

10. Perform preliminary analysis, which includes checks of data accuracy, sample weighting, and the calculation of new variables, scales, and indices. Also carry out descriptive analysis for important variables.

11. Perform bivariate and multivariate analysis of relationships among variables. Conduct supplementary analysis of unanticipated findings.

12. Draw conclusions. Make recommendations relevant to the initial business decision or problem. Write the report.

To provide you with a step-by-step guide to conducting a business research project, chapters in this text follow the order of the research stages just listed. (The one exception is the material on research planning, budgeting, and administration. These topics are covered in Appendix E.)

THE PURPOSES OF BUSINESS RESEARCH

Managers use research for four distinct general purposes: description, prediction, evaluation, and explanation. As we see in subsequent chapters, the research purpose decision is important: it affects decisions about the research problem, research design, data-gathering methodology, and data analysis. Chapter 2 discusses the role of research purpose in research problem development. Here we discuss briefly the differences among the four general purposes.

Descriptive Research

Managers use descriptive research to get information about *characteristics* of the current situation. They may need this information to answer questions, to make decisions, or to determine whether a problem exists. The major concern in descriptive research is accuracy.

Examples of descriptive research questions include

- "How are our small appliance sales in California? What about New York?"

- "What's our absenteeism rate? Is it different in the three different offices? How does it compare with the competition?"

- "What's the average error in costing rates of return on our new product lines?"

Answers to the questions about appliance sales might require a look through a filing cabinet or a few long-distance telephone calls. The second problem might entail a more extensive research project requiring the examination of personnel records in three different locations. In addition, some research would be required to find rates in other firms. The research may be further complicated by the task of defining and measuring absenteeism (for example, are medical absences to be included?). The third question would require some analysis of available records.

CASE EXAMPLE

A firm specializing in elevator advertising decided to promote its services. The manager hired a researcher to find out what kinds of people were exposed to the company's advertising placards, which were placed in the elevators of high-rise buildings in major cities. The researcher discovered that a fairly high proportion of viewers had higher than average levels of education and income, that they were exposed to the placards on average five times a day, and that both aided and unaided medium recall levels were high. The firm used this information to market its advertising services.

In the field of consumer research, an example of descriptive work is the characterization of the public in terms of groups distinguished by their values and lifestyles, such as the "satisfied selves," "contented traditionalists," "worried traditionalists," and others. This research describes consumer subgroups in ways that are useful for advertisers seeking to market new products.

Prediction Research

Managers use prediction research to produce an estimate of what the situation will be like in the future. The research results in a **prediction model** derived from information about the past or present; the model in turn generates the prediction. The principal concern with prediction research is an accurate model. Two kinds of prediction research are useful to organizations: selection and forecasting.

Selection Prediction.   This type of prediction is used when managers must select from among a set of alternatives: job applicants, future plant sites, sales promotions, costing procedures, or other decision options.

- "Will this job applicant be a motivated, productive employee?"

- "Which city should we expand our Wonder-burger chain to next?"

The researcher constructs a prediction model of the desired outcome (employee productivity, burger sales, accounting errors) based on present information (current employees, current plant sites, recent costing projects). The characteristics of each alternative (job applicant, potential expansion city, costing procedure) are then inserted into the model, and the predicted outcome is calculated for that alternative. The manager chooses the alternative with the best outcome.

Forecasting Prediction.   Managers use forecasting to estimate future levels of sales, inventories, cash flow, demand for services, and other business parameters.

- "What's the average wage going to be next year for skilled mechanics in our industry, for firms of our size?"

- "How will the new part-time employee regulations affect our labor needs?"

- "If we relocate the plant to the other side of town, what will happen to absenteeism?"

- "What sales do you expect for the new line of jewelry?"

- "What will be the labor cost implications if mandatory retirement legislation is changed?"

Businesses often require this kind of research to help with strategic planning in marketing, finance, labor planning, product development, expansion, and the undertaking of major new projects. It is also an important function for nonprofit organizations.

Forecasting models differ from selection models in two respects. First, forecasting models are based on both present and past information, in order to identify trends. Second, the characteristics inserted into the model are estimates of their *future* values. For example, if the prediction model shows that mechanics' wages in the past have been affected by changes in the cost of living, then estimated increases in cost of living are used in the prediction model to forecast next year's wages.

Conditional Forecasts.   Managers also use forecasting prediction to assess the effects of a possible change in policy or procedure. To make these conditional forecasts of what would happen *if*, the researcher determines how the change might affect one or more predictor factors in the model. He or she then inserts these estimates into the model to calculate the predicted effect.

CASE EXAMPLE

The manager of a retail store is considering the implications of moving to a different location. One of the questions is whether absenteeism might increase because employees would have to travel longer distances to work. An absenteeism forecasting model shows absenteeism is related to distance from home to work. The manager estimates how much the proposed move would increase average travel distances (making allowances for those employees who might move), and uses that estimate to predict the effects of the new location on total absenteeism.

Evaluation Research

Managers use evaluation research to assess or audit whether a specific action, program, or policy has had the intended (or any) effect. Evaluation research includes both pilot projects and full-scale program implementations. The research results in a recommendation to extend, continue, revise, or end the program or policy. Good evaluation research also looks for unanticipated and unintended consequences of the organization's action, and tests whether some other factor might be responsible for any improvement in the situation. (If the action has *not yet taken place,* but an estimate of its impact is being sought, then the problem is one for prediction, not evaluation, research.) The major concern in evaluation research is to find an adequate comparison on which to base the evaluation.

- "Is our quality circles program producing the improved productivity we expected?"

- "Is the pilot project test of the new accounts receivable system showing any improvement in cash flow?"

- "How much have the new tax measures affected demand for our product?"

Our first example requires an examination of productivity records before and after the implementation of the quality circles program. This project might also look for other possible effects, such as reduced absenteeism and turnover. The second example involves a comparison of the departments using the new system with other departments still using the old method, or a comparison of before and after cash flows. The third example calls for an assessment of the effect on the business of an external government action, rather than an action of the business itself.

Explanatory Research

After a business problem has been identified, managers use explanatory research to find its causes.[3] The research generates and tests ideas about how and why the problem is occurring. It also suggests how and when the causal processes operate. With this understanding of the problem, the researcher can

---

[3]Explanatory differs from forecasting prediction in that it focuses on the *causes* that contribute to the current situation; the latter focuses on the *effects* of those causes in predicting what the situation will be like in the future.

make relevant recommendations for dealing with the problem. The major concern in explanatory research is the validity of its results.

- "How can we reduce our grievance rate?"

- "How can we improve productivity in the Pittsburgh plant to bring it up to the level of our Burnaby branch?"

- "Public reaction to our takeover bid is very negative. How can we improve our image?"

- "Why aren't they buying the new cake mix?"

- "We aren't getting enough members out to our monthly book club meetings!"

- "It seems to me we have a morale problem with our party workers in this campaign."

- "How can we reduce our union local's grievance costs without cutting the number of grievances we take up?"

The first example involves a survey of employees to determine what job factors and personal characteristics and attitudes are associated with higher grievance rates, so that a strategy for dealing with the problem can be developed. The second requires explanatory research to compare the two plants in order to try to find out what factors cause the difference, and what can be done in the problem plant. The third problem example entails a public opinion survey to find out why people feel as they do. The results will suggest points to stress in a public relations campaign. The fourth question might require the use of focus groups, observation, and in-depth interviews to discover attitudes about the problematic cake mix, followed by a survey or a field experiment to test the preliminary conclusions. The final three examples are management problems faced by not-for-profit organizations: a book club, a political campaign, and a union local.

The Research Purpose Sequence

The four general research purposes are often found in a natural sequence. First, descriptive research provides information about the current situation, or prediction research forecasts a future situation, either of which might indicate the existence of a problem for the organization. Second, explanatory research finds the causes of the problem and leads to recommendations to improve it. Finally, evaluation research determines whether the recommended action has actually resulted in improvement. As we see in Chapter 2, a fifth kind of general research purpose, **exploratory,** may precede any or all of these four.

WHAT MAKES GOOD BUSINESS RESEARCH?

Before they implement its recommendations, managers need to be able to assess the quality of a research project. Researchers, too, are concerned with assessing their efforts. An important purpose of this book is to teach you how to assess business research proposals and projects. The following chapters discuss many criteria in detail. For now it is enough to discuss how managers and researchers use the following three general criteria to judge a business research project:

- Research validity
- Relevance
- Cost-benefit ratio

Research Validity

Research validity is the extent to which findings and conclusions accurately represent what is really happening in the situation. For researchers, research validity is the most important of the three criteria. For managers, however, validity is often difficult to understand and assess. Many kinds of **research errors** threaten research validity, including inappropriate or weak designs, poor samples, inaccurate and misleading measurement, faulty research procedures, and poor choice of statistical tests. We discuss research errors, and ways of minimizing them, throughout the text.

To simplify the discussion, we divide research validity into three major components: research power, internal validity, and external validity.[4] These components are discussed briefly here and in more detail in Chapter 4.

Research Power. **Research power** is the capacity of a design, procedure, or statistical test to find a relationship that actually exists. It is reduced by unmeasured factors, poor measurement, and faulty statistical analysis. The importance of research power depends on the nature of the research problem. For example, a researcher who misses an important cause of high absenteeism has lost an opportunity to make a useful recommendation.

Internal Validity. **Internal validity** is the ability to draw accurate and legitimate conclusions about the group or sample actually studied. When it is low, findings may be wrong, or there may be alternative explanations for apparent causal relationships. Internal validity is threatened by faulty statistics,

---

[4]Both internal and external validity are terms normally applied to experimental and quasi-experimental research (Campbell and Stanley, 1963). Here we extend their use to all research methodologies as a way of assessing overall quality. Internal and external validity should not be confused with measurement validity, which is discussed in Chapter 8.

unmeasured variables, poor measurement, and other types of errors which allow alternative explanations for our findings. It is essential for all research; without internal validity, conclusions are meaningless. Thus internal validity is the most crucial of the three components of research validity.

External Validity. **External validity** is the ability to make valid generalizations from a sample. When it is low, researchers cannot legitimately draw conclusions about other people or situations beyond the specific time and place of a study, even though conclusions about the sample are correct. External validity is threatened by too small and unrepresentative samples and other errors. The importance of external validity varies from one research problem to another. It is of no concern in a study that examines every employee in the company and produces conclusions applied only to those employees; it is a major concern in market research that can study only a small fraction of all potential consumers.

Relevance

The second criterion, **relevance**, refers to the extent to which the research problem produces answers, information, or recommendations relevant to the actual business question, decision, or problem. To be effective, business research must address the pertinent issues. Factors leading to low relevance include failure to deal with underlying issues and causes, and getting sidetracked to less relevant questions or problems. For example, if a firm has an absenteeism problem caused by employee dissatisfaction with recent policy changes, but political pressures within the company force the researcher to ignore this underlying issue, the research problem and recommendations will suffer from inadequate relevance.

Relevance is best judged by managers and is usually their greatest concern. It is particularly critical at two stages of a project: (1) development of the research problem in the early stages and (2) drafting recommendations toward the end. As suggested in Figure 1.3, both these activities benefit from management input to ensure that results relate to the organization's real concerns and that recommendations are feasible given the organization's resources and constraints.

Cost-Benefit Ratio

The final criterion, *cost-benefit ratio,* is the degree to which the benefits of research outweigh the costs of doing it. Benefits are reduced by conclusions that are too tentative because of poor design or data-gathering decisions and unrealistic, impractical, or out-of-date recommendations. Costs are escalated by poor research administration, designs that are more elaborate than the problem requires, samples that are too large or too complex, and overanalysis of data.

FIGURE 1.3 The Manager-Researcher Relationship and the Research Process

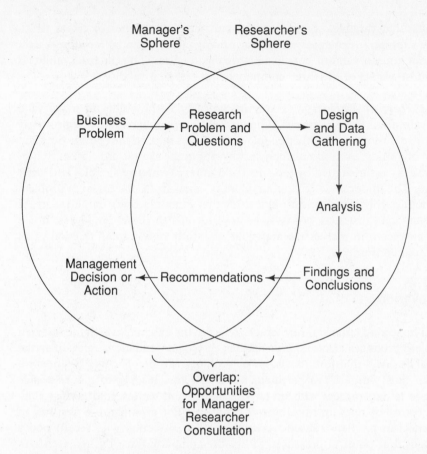

Managers' and Researchers' Concerns.   While research validity is the major concern of researchers and largely within their control, and relevance is the major concern of managers and a factor to which they can contribute substantially, the cost-benefit ratio of research occupies a more ambiguous position. From the managers' point of view, it is an important criterion (since the funds come from their budgets), difficult to calculate, and largely beyond control (since it depends heavily on the researchers' decisions). From the researchers' viewpoint, additional expenditures can often improve research validity. As a result, the cost-benefit ratio of a research project is always a potential point of friction between researchers and managers.

Estimating Costs and Benefits.   Researchers can usually estimate fairly accurately their costs: money, time, personnel and other resources, and opportunity costs. However, researchers and managers often have problems estimating the benefits of business research. They can readily assess the dollar value of reductions in labor costs or increases in sales or productivity, but the psychic benefits of a better work climate or less wear and tear on managers, for example, are difficult to determine. Their calculations of research benefits, therefore, always include subjective elements.

ADVANCED TOPIC

Utility Analysis.   Managers trying to decide whether to invest in research to help them make a strategic or tactical decision can often make use of **utility analysis** (also called decision analysis). It is a systematic, and somewhat subjective, procedure for assessing how helpful research information might be. Utility analysis also

- Helps managers weigh factors that might otherwise go unconsidered.
- Makes managers specify the assumptions underlying their decisions.
- At best, gives estimates of the benefits of conducting a specific research project.

The underlying principle of utility analysis is to compare the *expected utility* of a decision made without research to one based on research information. The analysis works best under certain conditions:

- The *action or decision options* facing managers are clearly defined.
- The situation in which the problem occurs is unknown, but can be readily expressed as a few possible *situation alternatives*. The manager can then attach estimated probabilities to these alternatives.
- The *utility* of a particular decision in a particular situation alternative can be readily estimated.
- *Research costs* can be reasonably well estimated.

These conditions are usually met for descriptive and prediction research, but not for evaluation or explanatory research. In both these types the benefits of research are much more difficult to calculate.

In evaluation research, the decision options are clear (continue, alter, or discontinue the program), but the utilities of continuing the program are unknown. The very purpose of research is to determine what these are, and whether they are truly a result of the program. In explanatory research, the decision options are unknown. The research is undertaken to generate viable options (potential solutions to the initial business problem).

Utility analysis is used most often in marketing research to decide between alternative strategies, but is applicable to many other management decisions, including capital investments, staffing, and the institution of new policies or programs, which meet the conditions we just listed. (See Box 1.3 for a discussion of utility analysis techniques.)

BOX 1.3
RESEARCH SKILLS

Utility Analysis and the Research Decision

Managers can use utility analysis to evaluate the potential benefits of a specific research project and help them decide whether to carry it out. A simple utility analysis of a potential project consists of six steps.

1. List the *situation alternatives* and *decision options* facing management (the strategic or tactical decision, not the decision whether to carry out research).

Best of Belgium is a small firm manufacturing and selling high-quality chocolates to upscale specialty and department stores. Management is considering whether to expand the present sales staff of seven by one or two more persons or to stay with the present staff levels (decision options). The decision depends on whether the market is saturated or demand is likely to grow for the product (situation alternatives).

2. Estimate the *dollar value utility* for each decision-situation combination. The dollar figures can be adjusted to take into account intangibles such as public relations, job satisfaction, the stress costs of union-management conflict, and the time it takes to complete the research.

For Best of Belgium management, the utilities represent thousands of dollars of profits, taking into account net sales and labor costs. For example, management assesses the utility of hiring no one, given low to moderate growth in the chocolate market, at $10,000.

(A simple nonresearch-based decision procedure you can use at this stage is the *minimax* rule: select the decision option that minimizes the maximum loss. This is a conservative approach to management,

most useful when resources are low and you want to avoid risk. For Best of Belgium, loss is minimized by hiring no new sales staff.)

3. Guess the *situation probabilities* for each of the situation alternatives.

The two situation alternatives for Best of Belgium are low-to-moderate growth (which management guesses at .6 probability) and substantial growth (.4 probability). The situation alternatives, decision options, and dollar value utilities (in thousands) that management assigns to each option-situation combination are shown in the first three columns of the table.

4. Calculate the *expected utility* of each decision option. Expected utility is a weighted average calculated for each decision option by multiplying each of the situation utilities associated with that option by the corresponding guessed probability of the situation's occurrence, and adding the products for all situation.

For example, for Best of Belgium, the expected utility for "no hires" is

$$(.6 \times \$10) + (.4 \times \$25) = \$16$$

(A second nonresearch-based decision procedure is to select the option with the highest expected utility. This approach is more venturesome than the minimax strategy. For Best of Belgium, the option with the highest expected utility ($23,000) is to hire one additional person.)

5. Since research would indicate which situation alternative was true, select the highest utility (the best decision option) for each situation alternative. Calculate the expected utility of these best utilities using the original guessed situation probabilities. The result represents the expected utility *using research information.*

If Best of Belgium carried out research that predicted moderate growth, the best decision would be to hire one salesperson, since this option has the greatest utility in that situation ($15 in the low to moderate growth column). Similarly, if the research predicted substantial growth, the best decision is to hire two, the option with the largest utility in that situation ($95). But since the research has not yet been done, management can only calculate the expected value of these two best utilities. The ex-

pected value of utilities using research is therefore

$$(.6 \times \$15) + (.4 \times \$95) = \$47$$

6. The difference in expected utilities between steps 4 and 5 represents the maximum amount that should be spent on research. Compare this difference with the estimated research costs to decide whether to proceed with research.

The difference in expected utilities, $24, is the maximum amount that Best of Belgium should spend on research. In other words, management should spend no more than $24,000 to find out what the market will be for their chocolates.

	SITUATION ALTERNATIVES				
	Low to Moderate Growth (P = .6)	Substan-tial Growth (P = .4)	Expected Utility: No Research	Expected Value: (Perfect Research)	Value of Research
Decision Options				$47	$ 47
No hires	$10	$25	$16		– 23
Hire one	$15	$35	$23		$ 24
Hire two	– 30	95	20		

The Manager and the Researcher

The manager's choice of researcher and the relationship between manager and researcher can both influence the caliber of research.

Choosing a Researcher. A manager faced with a question, decision, or problem that requires business research has four options:

- Hire an outside researcher or management consulting firm.

- Turn the research over to in-house research staff (if any).

- Assign it to subordinates under the manager's supervision.

- Carry out the research personally.

The choice is based on (1) the importance and complexity of the problem, (2) the resources of the organization and the manager (including time, money, and personnel), and (3) the manager's own level of research knowledge and experience. As Box 1.2 discussed, business research is increasingly being conducted or supervised by managers themselves. However, particularly in large-scale consumer and public opinion research, some projects can only be feasibly carried out by major firms such as Gallup, A.C. Nielsen, or Roper. Appendix E discusses in more detail the pros and cons of different researcher options.

The Manager-Researcher Relationship.   No matter who carries out the research, the relationship between manager and researcher is important to its success. This relationship is most formal when outside individuals or firms conduct the research and most informal when managers act as researchers.

The possibility of conflict between manager and researcher always exists (even when manager and researcher are the same person) because their interests conflict. The researcher's major concern is research validity; the manager's is relevance, and a potential source of conflict is the cost-benefit ratio.

The manager's concerns predominate at the beginning and end of the research process, as illustrated in Figure 1.3. The manager initiates the research with a business question, decision, or problem and applies the results in some decision or action. The researcher is responsible for the middle components of the process: the design and data gathering, the analysis, and the findings and conclusions.

In the most fruitful projects, manager-researcher collaboration occurs in the two areas in which their interests overlap: (1) specification of the research problem and questions early in the process and (2) formulation of recommendations near the end. Cost-effective, quality research requires coordination between manager and researcher in both areas. Without the manager's help, the researcher cannot specify a completely relevant research problem or make sound and feasible recommendations. Without the researcher's help, the manager cannot be sure of getting the quality of information the problem requires.

Coordination is easiest and most effective when the researcher-manager relationship is based on trust. Researchers must trust managers to disclose their long-term objectives, plans for the research results, and the political and other constraints and problems that might threaten the validity of the research. Managers must trust researchers to be sensitive to the needs and constraints of the organization and to keep research costs and time to a reasonable minimum.

To summarize, the conclusions and recommendations of good business research are valid, relevant to the organization's problem, and offer benefits that outweigh the costs of doing the research. One way of ensuring good research is to apply the appropriate criteria at each decision step in the research process to help choose the most efficient research problem, design, procedures, methods, and recommendations. You will encounter these criteria repeatedly in the following chapters.

ETHICAL PROBLEMS IN BUSINESS RESEARCH

Any type of research can be unethical and, as the media report from time to time, questionable practices can be found in research of all kinds. However, ethical conduct is often a greater problem in business research than in other kinds of research activity. The reasons have to do with research content, the researcher's power, and the scrutiny and invisibility of business research.

Research Content

Some business research deals with the behavior and performance of specific individuals. Its results are therefore potentially harmful

- To those in the organization whose behavior is considered unsuitable or whose performance is inadequate.

- To those outside the organization whose purchasing or other behavior and attitudes it seeks to influence and who might make purchasing decisions against their own interests.

New work techniques, procedures, or technology may have negative effects for employees, ranging from higher stress levels to unsafe working conditions. For example, universal product code readers at supermarket checkouts have been associated with carpal tunnel syndrome in cashiers. The syndrome is a muscular ailment resulting from the wrist movements required by the code readers. Similarly, market research may create needs and influence consumers to spend money better used for other purposes or to make purchases that may adversely affect their health. By comparison, general organization and basic research almost never have immediate implications for individuals. However, the content of other types of business research, such as accounting and finance research, is much less likely to have harmful effects on individuals.

Researchers' Power

The power discrepancy between managers and employees may contribute to ethical problems in *internal research,* research conducted inside the organization. When employees are the subjects or participants in business research, researchers enjoy greater power than they would in the case of **external research** involving individuals outside the organization, such as customers. For example, the option of refusing to participate may be curtailed for employees who fear negative reviews or loss of promotion. Often researchers themselves are subject to the authority of higher management when they wish to drop or modify ethically dubious research plans, but are prevented from doing so.

In some respects the power problem is also found in operations research. However, employees are better protected from the results of operations research; health and safety legislation, joint health and safety committees, and conscientious union representation act as safeguards and help maintain a balance of power. These checks and balances are often absent in business research.

Scrutiny of Research Plans

Business research plans are often less subject to scrutiny than other kinds of research activity. No independent body examines instruments, procedures, and practices. Within the organization, the major criteria are cost effectiveness and relevance, and only the research budget is likely to receive any close checking.

In comparison, basic and general organization research involving human subjects or respondents is largely conducted through universities, where ethics committees normally keep a close eye on research plans. In most universities, researchers have to submit their proposals to an ethics committee for approval before beginning a project. The existence of these committees reduces considerably, although not totally, the problems of ethical research in the basic sciences.

Invisibility

Finally, business research is often invisible to other researchers and to the general public. Only a few members of the organization may know that a research project is being carried out and what its objectives are. The problem is even greater if the research relies on files and records and the research and analysis are done in house rather than carried out by a management consulting firm.

In the area of marketing, the quest for understanding human motivations may invade consumers' privacy, but because of the greater visibility of this kind of research (since its participants are drawn from the general public), market research practices are probably subject to fewer ethical problems than other kinds of business research.

In comparison,

- Basic research and general organization research are frequently known to other researchers because results are reported at conferences and in journals, and research proposals are examined by other researchers before funds are granted.

- Policy research conducted by or for governments is subject to political constraints as a result of the higher visibility of such research under democratic governments. Unethical research practices are inhibited in part because of the political cost of their discovery and publicity. Some governments also use a form of ethics committee scrutiny for research they commission.

• Product research may produce new products with the potential for harmful effects. However, ethical problems of this kind are reduced by the potential for adverse media attention and public disapproval. Because product research that yields questionable goods and services can be very costly to an organization, the likelihood of ethical lapses is usually less than in business research.

As a result of these four features of business research (its content, the researcher's power, the lack of scrutiny, and invisibility), those who perform it must be particularly sensitive to ethical questions and issues. We now turn to the question of how to identify potential ethical problems.

IDENTIFYING THREATS TO ETHICAL RESEARCH

Ethical research appears at first to be an abstract and difficult objective. However, the matter of ethical practice really boils down to two issues:

• Is there an ethical problem?

• If so, what can I do about it?

You can recognize threats to ethical research by answering four simple and specific questions. These are questions you should ask, and continue to ask, as the research progresses and as each research decision is made. When combined with self-honesty and a measure of common sense, these points will serve as guidelines to help you identify ethically dubious situations. Box 1.4 summarizes the four questions, together with some techniques for ensuring ethical research.

Harm to Participants: Informed Consent

Will the research process harm participants or those about whom information is gathered (indirect participants)?
 The research process may harm respondents and subjects in one of two ways: the act of gathering data and the misuse of that data.

 Harm During Data Gathering. Interviews or questionnaires may be uncomfortable, embarrassing, or even painful if difficult or highly emotional subjects are discussed. (For example, a person whose marriage has recently ended may be very upset by questions about marital status and child-care

BOX 1.4
RESEARCH ETHICS

Questions to Detect Ethical Problems

Ask yourself the following four questions to detect potential ethical problems in your research. With each question some solutions are suggested.

1. Will the research process harm participants or those about whom information is gathered (indirect participants)?

   - Be sensitive to possibly painful questions and topics
   - Obtain participation through informed consent
   - Use identification codes
   - Restrict access to research files
2. Are the findings of this research likely to cause harm to others not involved in the research?
   - Be sensitive to risks: Apply the test of accepted risk (are the risks within a normally accepted range?)
   - Know who will use the results, and for what purpose
   - Know consequences of inappropriate methods
3. Are you violating accepted research practice in conducting the research and data analysis, and drawing conclusions?
   - Resist pressures to use faulty methodology
   - Anticipate the possibility of unfavorable results
4. Are you violating community standards of conduct?
   - Ensure your methods would stand up to close public scrutiny

arrangements.) The researcher must be convinced that the potential harm to respondents is neither substantial nor long-lived, and that the benefits of the research are likely to outweigh the respondents' discomfort. (Note that in business research, the benefits of the research to society are so indirect as to be discounted; the whole point of the research is to benefit the organization. At the same time, however, the individual as an employee may also benefit through better working conditions or a more secure job as a result of improved business performance, and the individual consumer may benefit through improved products or services.)

Informed Consent. The problem is compounded if participation in the research is not totally voluntary. Active participation in a research study should be voluntary and based on **informed consent**: full disclosure of the research objectives and an opportunity to decline without penalty. This kind of up-front honesty and openness often increases the quality of the respondent's participation and information. If participation is not voluntary, the researcher should be doubly aware of the possible negative effects of participation.

Note that employees of an organization are particularly subject to pressure to cooperate in that organization's business research. Managers may (unintentionally) imply that failure to do so will hinder the respondent's career, promotion chances, or job security.

If informed consent is not possible, perhaps because knowledge of the study's true purpose would result in distorted answers or behavior, the alternative is to use deception. Most typically this involves a less threatening *cover story*. In such cases, ethical research requires that immediately after their participation respondents be **debriefed**: given an explanation of both the study's true purpose and why the deception was necessary. However, immediate debriefing sometimes runs the risk of **contamination**: participants tell other potential participants of the study's deception and true purpose. If contamination cannot be prevented, the explanation may be provided at the conclusion of the study, although this is less desirable from an ethical point of view. Whenever deception is used, it is particularly important that the effects of the deception on participants be questioned. Are they likely to be upset, angry, or feel used? A well-thought-out explanation will help minimize such negative reactions.

Harm Resulting from Data Misuse. Misuse of information is the second potential harm that participants may suffer. Misuse can affect both those who participate directly and those whose role is indirect. The latter group includes those whose files and records provide data for the research and the business as a whole.

In many cases, information about an individual may harm that person if it becomes known to others. At the least, privacy may be invaded in the use of available records such as personnel files. More seriously, information may be used for purposes other than the original research and affect the individual's reputation, friendships, career, and life chances both within and outside of the organization. Similarly, information about a business, if it becomes known to competitors, may well lead to problems for that business.

To avoid the misuse of data, researchers should ensure that access to research files is limited and that procedures such as identification codes are used to protect respondents' anonymity. Outside research consultants should be particularly aware of their obligation to keep not only data, but in many cases even the *identity* of a client, confidential.

Harm to Others: Accepted Risk

Are the findings of this research likely to cause harm to others not involved in the research?

The possibility of harm to others is a particularly difficult threat to ethical research, since it is often impossible to foresee how conclusions might be used or who might be affected. It is made more problematic because the application of results is often out of the researcher's hands. Since it is usually possible to find, somehow, somewhere, someone who might be disadvantaged by the research results, it is impossible to avoid all potential harm. An interpretation of this ethical threat that is both practical and fair is to apply the test of **accepted risk**:

> *The researcher should avoid both probable and plausible damage to individuals and organizations* beyond the risks these others normally accept in the course of work and everyday life.

Thus research that aims to raise a firm's productivity and increase its market share at the expense of the competition is not unethical. Competition in the marketplace is an accepted and everyday risk. However, research that seeks to break a union and unfairly (or illegally) deprive employees of a legitimate and legal right to act collectively is clearly unethical. While unions accept conflict with management as part of their existence, their survival as organizations is legally a matter for employees, not management, to decide.

The question of the effect of research results arises most often when the good of the organization is balanced against possible harm to an individual. For example, research might conclude that a department would work more effectively if a supervisor were transferred elsewhere. The concept of accepted risk can help the researcher to decide whether there is an ethical issue. Employees, in accepting employment, accept some risk of transfer or dismissal for failure to perform at normal accepted organizational standards. On the other hand, it would be unethical to obtain information about someone's sexual orientation or religious beliefs and have it be used as a basis for personnel decisions. This misuse of information fails the test of accepted risk.

Violation of Accepted Research Practice

Is the researcher violating accepted research practice in conducting the research and data analysis and drawing conclusions?

The threat to ethical research of violating accepted research practice is somewhat like asking whether the researcher is honest with himself or herself, with those for whom the research is conducted, and about the standard practices of research among researchers. It represents the obligation of the researcher to his or her manager and of the consultant to the client. It covers obviously unacceptable practices such as falsified data. It also includes such borderline behaviors as representing relationships to be more significant than they are, using doubtful statistical procedures or inappropriate tests without warning about the possibility of erroneous conclusions, and presenting conclusions not fully supported by the data.

The best protections against this threat to ethical research are (1) to know what accepted practice is and the likely consequences of violating it and (2) to resist pressure to use inappropriate methods. If the latter is difficult, then the consequences of their use for the conclusions and recommendations should be pointed out clearly and forcefully. The following chapters have a great deal to say about appropriate and inappropriate methods.

A problem occasionally arises when the researcher is the bearer of bad tidings. The temptation to soften unfavorable results must be rejected. In many cases, the problem can be avoided by discussing beforehand all possible results, good and bad, so that the organization is forewarned. (This problem is discussed in Chapter 18, which deals with reporting research results.)

Violation of Community Standards

Are community standards of conduct being violated?
As well as general research standards, researchers are governed by their obligation to observe everyday community standards of conduct, including honesty, fairness, and the treatment of others with respect and consideration. For example, if information is given in confidence, that confidence should be maintained. If there are two sides to an issue, then a fair interview question will recognize that fact and not attempt to lead the respondent or load the question.

In some cases the requirements of research seem to run counter to these everyday standards. For example, it may be necessary to place identifying marks on an apparently anonymous questionnaire in order to match the data with other material from personnel records. In such instances, it is particularly important to adhere to the spirit of community norms. Although the identity of the "anonymous" respondent is known to the researcher, this information should be carefully guarded (preferably under lock and key) and every effort made to ensure that it remains confidential.

Another variation of ethical problems under the issue of standards of fairness has to do with the purposeful withholding of some benefit (e.g., longer coffee breaks) from one group while supplying it to another in order to examine its effects. This is an infrequent, and usually a temporary, problem in business research. (Chapter 4 describes how this problem can be partially overcome through research design.)

One effective way of resisting this threat to ethical research is to ask yourself whether your research procedures would stand up to extensive public scrutiny. (Picture yourself on *60 Minutes*!)

What Can You Do?

Unfortunately, there is no simple prescription for what to do if you find yourself in an ethically questionable research situation you are unable to correct on your own initiative. In business research, the difficulty is compounded because of the link between the researcher and the organization: your own prestige, future promotion, or even job may be on the line.

- You should point out the ethical problems and suggest that unethical research is often poor research. Respondents or clients who are harmed can damage a researcher's reputation. Recommendations based on suspect findings lead to ineffective actions that, in the long run, are more costly.

- As with many of life's problems, talking it over with someone else may help to clarify the situation and your alternatives, particularly if you can discuss it with another researcher from outside the organization.

- Dissociation from the project is an ultimate alternative, but occasionally this action is not feasible. In such cases the issue moves from the arena of research to that of organizational politics and personal ethics.

- Perhaps best of all is to anticipate ethical problems before the research is initiated. Use prevention rather than relying on finding a cure.

■ *The Lighter Side of Research*

If all economists were laid end to end, they would not reach a conclusion.

George Bernard Shaw

When you take stuff from one writer, it's plagiarism; but when you take it from many writers, it's research.

Wilson Mizner

Lots of folks confuse bad management with destiny.

Frank McKinney Hubbard

Advertising agency: 85 percent confusion and 15 percent commission.

Fred Allen

Summary

To answer the question, "What *is* business research?" this chapter used a variety of approaches: the Montgomery Metals scenario, a list of the functional areas in organizations that make use of business research, and a discussion of when managers turn to research for help. In addition, we described the relation of business research to other kinds of research activity and discussed their similarities and differences. The chapter also outlined the four general purposes of business research (description, prediction, evaluation, and explanation) and the stages of a business research project.

We covered the three criteria for evaluating the quality of any business research project (research validity, relevance, and cost-benefit ratio), and the ethical problems you might encounter when you carry it out: harm to direct or indirect participants, harm to others not involved in the research, and violation of accepted research practices or community standards of conduct.

Where Are We Now?

With our examination of the nature of business research complete, we're ready to consider how to do it and how to evaluate others' research efforts. This objective begins with the next chapter—the investigation of the initial business problem and its translation to a research problem.

Discussion Issues and Assignments

1. Find an example of general applied research (administration theory or organizational behavior) in *Administrative Science Quarterly* or a similar journal. Analyze the differences between this example and what a piece of business research might focus on in terms of (1) the audience for the report, (2) the target populations to which results apply and (3) who carried out the research. Also, compare this example with an example of policy research (check the government documents section of your library for a policy research report).

2. You're a manager with a problem. What criteria should you consider in deciding whether to (1) do the research yourself, (2) call in a management consulting firm, or (3) call in an academic to carry out the research? (If you answer, "It depends," on what does it depend?)

3. Take a manager to lunch and ask him or her about an organization problem he or she faces. Discuss the possibilities for business research. Is there a budget? Is there time? Is there somebody who could carry it out?

4. Compare the table of contents of this text with (a) a text in psychology or sociology research methods and (b) a text specializing in market research methods. Note the similarities and differences. Skim through two chapters (one from each text) that appear to be similar and two that are evidently different. What appear to be the greatest differences?

5. Imagine that Tom Harper's survey of employees (see Box 1.1) reveals that day shift productivity is low because the general manager, Harry Anderson, recently ordered a cutback on coffee breaks, informal chatter, and smoking in the department, rules that are largely ignored during the afternoon shift, since management seldom shows up on the shop floor. Role-play the ethical dilemma faced by Harper as he reports to Anderson.

6. Discuss with a commerce or business administration faculty member whose field is marketing where he or she gets ideas for research project topics. What constraints are there on the choice of topics? How would this compare with a market researcher working within a company? Working in a market research firm?

Further Reading

For a look at business research:

Cascio, W. F. 1982. *Costing Human Resources: The Financial Impact of Behavior in Organizations.* Boston: Kent.

> Strictly speaking, this book isn't about research but about measurement. It offers methods for estimating the value in dollars of personnel programs and other organizational actions or problems (e.g., turnover, absenteeism, employee smoking). Such measures open new avenues for business research.

Cascio, W. F. 1986. *Managing Human Resources.* New York: McGraw-Hill.

> Provides excellent examples of the role business research can play in the human resource management area.

Churchill, G. A., Jr. 1983. *Marketing Research* (3rd ed.). Chicago: Dryden.

> A classic text in a subfield of business research. Worth browsing through to compare the concerns of market research with those of other areas of business research.

Montgomery, D. C., L. A. Johnson, and J. S. Gardiner. 1990. *Forecasting and Time Series Analysis* (2nd ed.). New York: McGraw-Hill.

> A good introduction to forecasting prediction. It discusses the uses of forecasting and explains the use of time-series models, which are important in financial and other areas of business research.

Rothman, J. 1980. *Using Research in Organizations.* Beverly Hills: Sage.

> An excellent examination of the relationship and communication between manager and researcher and how better utilization of research can benefit the organization.

General organization research of relevance to managers:

Bateman, T. S., and G. R. Ferris. 1984. *Method & Analysis in Organizational Research.* Reston, VA: Reston.

> A good discussion of current research issues in general organization research. Some excellent examples of this type of general applied research.

Dyer, L., and D. P. Schwab. 1980. "Personnel/Human Resource Business Research." Chapter 5 in *Industrial Relations Research in the 1970s.* Madison, WI: Industrial Relations Research Association.

> An excellent summary of general applied research results in the area of work force behavior. It includes four topics of interest to management: job satisfaction, performance, turnover, and absenteeism.

An introduction to applied social policy research:

Judd, C. M., E. R. Smith, and L. H. Kidder. 1991. *Research Methods in Social Relations* (6th ed.). New York: Holt.

> A classic text on policy research. Provides an excellent insight into the methods and issues in policy research from a psychological and sociological point of view.

An introduction to operations research:

Render, B., and R. M. Stair, Jr. 1985. *Quantitative Analysis for Management* (2nd ed.).
Boston: Allyn & Bacon.
    A highly readable introduction to operations research and quantitative
analysis showing how this technique also contributes to managerial decision
making.

CHAPTER 2

Translating Business Problems to Research Problems

CHAPTER OBJECTIVES

- What is meant by the term *research problem*?
- Why do researchers need to define a research problem?
- How does a researcher go about translating a business problem into a research problem?
- What obstacles might prevent a good translation?

CHAPTER OUTLINE

OBJECTIVE: THE RESEARCH PROBLEM
STEP ONE: INVESTIGATE THE BUSINESS PROBLEM
STEP TWO: DETERMINE THE GENERAL RESEARCH PURPOSE
STEP THREE: SPECIFY THE VARIABLES
STEP FOUR: IDENTIFY RESEARCH BOUNDARIES
STEP FIVE: STATE RESEARCH PROBLEM AND RESEARCH QUESTIONS
OBSTACLES TO A RELEVANT RESEARCH PROBLEM

T he first and most important stage in business research is to translate the initial business problem or question to a research problem.

The *business problem* is the manager's first expression of the information needed, the question to be answered, or the problem to be solved: "What's our absenteeism rate?" "Is the public relations campaign working?" "Why aren't they buying our cake mix?" It is the starting point for business research. This chapter focuses on the process of translating the business problem to a research problem.

OBJECTIVE: THE RESEARCH PROBLEM

What *is* a research problem? What does one look like?

Harper's memo (Box 2.1) is pretty typical of a well-defined research problem. First, it is clear and concise. Good business research problems seldom take more than a sentence or two. Second, it makes clear the general research purpose ("To discover the causes . . ."). As we saw in Chapter 1, other common purposes are to describe, to predict, and to evaluate. Third, the statement includes the key variable on which the research will focus ("productivity"). Fourth, it makes clear the specific boundaries of the research problem (". . . the day and afternoon shifts in the low-alloy furnace department"). Finally, the research problem is accompanied by a list of research questions. These questions specify which other variables and issues associated with the research problem are to be investigated.

Before turning to the process of translating the business problem to a research problem, we address the questions of why translation is necessary and the benefits of a well-thought-out research problem.

A **research problem** is a brief statement indicating the general purpose, the key variable(s), and the boundaries of the research. It is usually accompanied by a set of specific **research questions** concerning aspects of the key variable and its relationships with other variables.

Why Translate the Business Problem?

The translation process is vital, no matter what the scale of the research: from a small quick-and-dirty project to a large-scale, high-profile study. Researchers gain three specific benefits when they translate business problems to research problems: problem clarity and completeness, an initial list of variables, and the possibility of finding an answer without having to do the full research project.

Translation may be minimal if the purpose of the research is descriptive: to provide the answer to a well-defined question. More translation is required in order to provide relevant information for a business decision with prediction

BOX 2.1

FOCUS ON RESEARCH

The Productivity Problem at Montgomery Metals

MONTGOMERY METALS—DENVER PLANT

Memo To: Frank Morgan, General Manager
From: Tom Harper, Personnel
Re: The day shift productivity problem

Here's my draft of the research problem:
  Objective: To discover the causes of productivity differences between the day and afternoon shifts in the low-alloy furnace department. In particular:

1. Why is only the low-alloy operation affected?

2. Are there other symptoms, such as absenteeism, turnover, etc.?

3. To what extent is the problem one of waste?

4. Is the cause one of differences in the source or quality of materials?

5. Is there something about the work force itself that accounts for the difference between shifts (skills, training, work attitudes, etc.)?

6. Are there differences in the way the furnaces are set up, repaired, serviced, etc., between the two shifts that might account for the differences?

7. Are there differences in the supervision (level, style, etc.) that might account for the differences?

Let me know if there's anything you want to add before we start gathering the data.

or evaluation research. Finally, a great deal of translation is necessary if the purpose of the research is to solve a business problem.

Clarity and Completeness.   In its initial form, a business problem is almost always vague and incomplete. It may focus on the wrong issues, it may be based on faulty assumptions, or it may misstate entirely the nature of the problem. If defined by someone too close to the situation, the initial version will miss important aspects because of hidden assumptions about the way the organization works. This is the familiar "can't see the forest for the trees" syndrome. On the other hand, if posed by someone too far from the situation, it will miss important subtleties.

A carefully translated research problem results in research more likely to meet the organization's true needs. The gains in clarity and completeness help ensure *relevance*.

List of Variables. The original statement of a business problem seldom specifies the content of the research: it doesn't list the variables the research is to include. An important part of the translation process is to state the research problem in terms of variables. For example, "gender" and "number of cars ever purchased" are variables that are attributes of persons and vary from person to person. "Size" and "net profit" are variables pertinent to business firms; the second varies over time within the same firm. "Duration" and "whether violent" are attributes of strikes.

Each variable takes on two or more values. There are only two possible values of "gender" (male, female) and "whether violent" (yes, no), but "number of cars" could range from none to perhaps a hundred or more for a wealthy eccentric, and "net profit" has an enormous number of possible values, both positive and negative.

Researchers classify or measure people or things according to the values of their attribute variables. For example, the number of cars ever owned by Bill, Sam, and Sue is 3, 1, and 4, respectively.

If an attribute takes only one value within a population, it is a *constant*. Note that a variable for one population may be a constant in another. For example, if we are conducting research in a union with only female members, then gender is not a variable as far as the population of union members is concerned.

Except in descriptive research, the researcher is primarily interested in relationships connecting pairs of variables. Researchers often distinguish between independent and dependent variables. For example, it is believed that the size of a firm affects its frequency of strikes; the larger the firm, the more often its employees are likely to strike. Similarly, age is thought to be a cause of job satisfaction, with older workers more likely to be satisfied with their jobs than younger workers. In these examples, firm size and age are independent variables, and strike frequency and job satisfaction are dependent variables.

Independent variables are also called predictor, explanatory, and exogenous variables; dependent variables are also known as criterion and endogenous variables. Note that while it is often convenient to treat variables as if they were causally related, establishing true causality is much more complicated, as we discuss in Chapter 3.

Variables that are related, but about which no assumption is made as to which is the cause and which the effect, are called **correlates**. The researcher may be unsure which is the cause, or may not care. Correlate variables are frequently used in prediction research. For example, the chance of being

A **variable** is an attribute or characteristic of an entity (person, group, firm, event, or object) that varies (i.e., has two or more different values) either across entities or within the same entity over time.

An **independent variable** is one that is treated as a cause of one or more other variables.

A **dependent variable** is one that is treated as an effect of one or more independent variables. Its value depends on the values of the independent variables.

promoted to foreman may be predicted by a worker's absenteeism record without a researcher needing to know whether high absenteeism causes a lack of promotion (the supervisor doesn't consider the employee to be dependable), or the lack of promotion has led to high absenteeism (the employee has become less committed to his job).

One of the advantages of a translation phase is that it generates the variables and relationships tested in following phases of the research. One cannot predict labor force needs, evaluate a sick-leave benefit plan, or explain a decline in footwear sales without knowing what variables might be associated with these phenomena. These potential associations and explanations are rarely found in the original statement of the business problem; instead, they have to be actively sought by translating the business problem into a sound research problem.

Avoiding Unnecessary Research. The translation stage may save the time and effort of having to do the research in the first place! A researcher may uncover a suitable preexisting answer to the business problem, or even find that there is actually *no* problem to solve.

For these reasons, the initial business problem needs translation into a feasible and relevant research problem. (Occasionally, an initial problem will even lead to two or more separate research problems.) The resulting research problem is more likely to address the real difficulties faced by the organization. Translation is doubly important if the manager who poses the business problem in the first place is also the researcher. It will force him or her to assess hidden assumptions.

CASE EXAMPLE

The union of teaching assistants at a major university asked a researcher to investigate why their members had narrowly rejected the leadership's call to strike over an administration contract offer. In translating and investigating this organization problem, the researcher found that the real issue had little to do with the content of the university administration's proposal. Instead, the vote was a result of members' perceptions of the union leadership and the union as largely irrelevant to teaching assistants, a view particularly held by members in the physical and life sciences.

Translation Difficulties

Translation can't be taken for granted. Unless undertaken deliberately and carefully, translation is likely to be unconscious, partial, and poor. Unfortunately, translating the initial problem is not often recognized as a distinct part of applied research. The process is vague; there is no widely recognized procedure for developing or evaluating a sound research problem.

The major reason for this omission is probably that most methodological and statistical procedures are developed in *basic* research, where the formulation of a research problem is much simpler and less problematic than in applied research. Researchers are usually conducting what is called *normal science*—examining one small aspect of an existing research problem. Research hypotheses usually flow directly from previous empirical or theoretical efforts.

In contrast, business researchers normally begin with a misleading or vaguely stated practical problem or question. The problem needs translation in order for research to proceed.[1] Basic researchers, not facing the translation problem, have therefore not developed procedures to deal with it. The suggestions and framework presented in this chapter are an attempt to fill this gap.

Role of the Research Problem

A well-translated research problem serves three important functions for a project: guiding design decisions, keeping research on track, and providing a framework for solving problems that arise in the course of the research.

A Guide for Design Decisions. Design decisions are an important part of research. Design choices must suit both the availability of data and resources and the research problem. A well-defined research problem helps ensure the most appropriate choice of unit of analysis, basic and specific design, variables, data sources, data-gathering techniques, sample size and type, measures, and statistical analysis. It really is the foundation on which research rests.

In turn, design decisions may also affect the research problem. Often a problem must be revised (as shown in Figure 1.2) because of constraints discovered during the research design phase. The better formulated the research problem, the easier it will be to see the implications of a design change.

A Target. A well-thought-out research problem helps the researcher avoid straying into intriguing but irrelevant side paths. Every researcher faces the temptation of exploring side issues, whether by gathering additional data or analyzing other interesting but irrelevant relationships. These excursions cost time and money; a good research problem will help keep a project on track.

A Guide for Problem Solving. In the course of any project, the researcher faces a wide variety of minor problems: "Can I use a cheaper sample?" "Should I include this variable?" "Which measure is better?" "How should I code the answers to this question?" "What significance level should I use for this statistical test?"

The answers to such questions become more apparent when the researcher can step back and ask, "What am I really after, anyway?" The answer

---

[1]See Lazarsfeld and Reitz, *An Introduction to Applied Sociology* (1975), for an excellent analysis of the problems involved in the translation process.

to this question is summarized, clearly and succinctly, in the research problem and research questions.

In summary, a sound research problem helps the researcher keep an eye on the big picture, which otherwise gets lost in the minutiae of research details. The research problem is an essential guide for relevant and cost-effective research. Without it, the researcher wastes money on misdirected activity that takes longer and produces vague and irrelevant solutions to the wrong problem. The research problem is the foundation for all the research decisions that follow and the thread that ties together the stages of the business research process.

The Translation Process

There are five steps in the translation process:

1. Investigate the business problem.

2. Determine the general purpose of the research.

3. Specify the key variable and other variables.

4. Identify the research boundaries.

5. State the research problem and research questions.

We now examine these in turn.

STEP ONE: INVESTIGATE THE BUSINESS PROBLEM

Treat the first statement of the business problem with a certain amount of skepticism, even if you make it yourself, and definitely when it's presented by a beleaguered manager. Assume that the problem is more complex and less obvious than it appears. Then try to unearth and clarify the *real* problem or question. Sometimes, particularly in descriptive research, you won't have to dig far. At other times, especially in explanatory research, your investigation will reveal unsuspected dimensions and aspects of the problem.

Exploratory Research.   The investigation step involves *exploratory research:* it seeks the important elements and dimensions of the problem and generates possible explanations for it. Exploratory research is much less structured than research for other purposes. It relies on subjective methods and analysis, including in-depth interviews, observation, and the evaluation of existing reports and documents. It may utilize a **case study**: the intensive examination of a single instance of a phenomenon. (In basic and general applied research, exploratory research is often used on its own; it is a fifth general research purpose. In business research, it is always combined with one of the other four research purposes.)

Because researchers immerse themselves in the business problem, the investigation step also has some characteristics of *qualitative research* (see Box 2.2).

Formative and Summative Evaluation. If the problem calls for evaluation research, the investigation phase corresponds to what is called **formative evaluation** (Judd, Smith, and Kidder, 1991). This kind of evaluation concentrates on the question of how, or through what process, a program or policy is working, rather than its outcome. It is often carried out early in the life of a program. The assessment of the results of a program is called **summative evaluation**. Good evaluation research includes both types of activity: (1) the investigation or formative evaluation phase and (2) the testing of the ideas generated in the first phase (including the outcome of the program)—the summative evaluation phase.

Investigation Procedures

Investigating a business problem is a combination of good management practice (listening, digesting, analyzing) and detective work (poking, probing, checking). The researcher asks,

- Why is this a problem, or why is this question being raised?

- Who says it's a problem?

- For whom is it a problem (and for whom is it not a problem)?

- When and where did this become a problem?

- What are the possible reasons, causes, solutions, or answers?

Investigation procedures in business research include interviews, examining organization documents, observation, focus groups, exploratory surveys, and reviews of external materials (including literature reviews).

Interviews. Researchers usually begin their investigation with interviews. The most important interviewees are those who perceive a problem and those who are apparently part of the problem. Also useful are interviews with those who have had experience with similar problems (perhaps other researchers, or managers in other organizations). For complicated issues, it may be necessary to meet several times with the manager who initiates the research. Successive meetings will help to establish a sufficiently high level of trust so that the manager's long-range objectives, concerns, and fears can be expressed. Rapport between manager and researcher is important for the formulation of

BOX 2.2
RESEARCH ISSUES

Quantitative Versus Qualitative Research

A long-simmering conflict in applied research has again been a recent focus of attention (e.g., Bateman and Ferris, 1984; the December 1979 issue of *Administrative Science Quarterly*). On one side of the conflict are those who favor quantitative research with a scientific emphasis, formal hypotheses, and rigorous statistical procedures. On the other side are those who argue for qualitative methods, which provide a more subjective and personal understanding of the phenomenon to be studied.

Allport (1937) made a similar distinction between *nomothetic* and *idiographic* approaches to research. The former seeks to establish general laws through scientific testing; the latter seeks to understand a specific, particular event by getting "inside" it. Quantitative techniques are best suited to the former, qualitative to the latter.

Luthans and Davis (1982) state that business researchers are more likely than others to adopt an idiographic approach. The problems of business research, because they are specific and unique to a particular organization at a particular time, appear to require a subjective approach. However, when the decisions involved represent important policies and substantial amounts of money, this understanding must be *tested* by more rigorous, objective means. We argue, therefore, that business research requires both qualitative and quantitative approaches: the former in an exploratory phase to generate understanding and ideas, the latter to test these ideas in order to recommend with confidence effective decisions and actions.

a good research problem that takes all the organization's considerations into account. Good rapport takes time to cultivate.

CASE EXAMPLE

One plant of a major breakfast food manufacturer was faced with an absenteeism problem. The corporation's head office asked a researcher to examine the problem. As part of his investigation, the researcher met briefly with the production manager in order to find out why absenteeism was perceived as a problem. Among the questions he asked was whether the problem was excessive labor costs to pay overtime to the employees filling in for absent workers, or whether it was production lines being shut down because of insufficient employees. No direct answer was provided. It wasn't until a later meeting that the researcher learned there were no absenteeism standards or guidelines for the plant or the corporation. In a third interview, the manager mentioned several possible reasons for the absenteeism levels, including unpleasant working conditions (a cold freezer room and a very noisy waffle room) and misuse of the company's sick leave benefit program.

Organization Documents. At the same time that interviews are conducted, the researcher should be on the lookout for any related internal reports, memos, and documents. The report of a similar problem in the past, the memo a supervisor sent his boss warning of a problem, or the written suggestion an employee submitted—these kinds of documents often shed light on critical aspects of the business problem.

Organizational records are also important sources of information about the existence and nature of a problem. Sales, absenteeism, accounts receivable, financial, or production records, for example, may help establish whether there really is a problem and how serious it is.

Observation. Another useful procedure for some problems is to observe the work, sales, or other relevant situation. There are two major approaches to observation:

- An observer watches the situation, but does not take part in the activity. The observation may be either overt, known to those observed (for example, watching a work group on the factory floor while stationed nearby with a clipboard and stopwatch), or covert (for example, a hidden observer watching customers' buying behavior).

- A **participant observer** actually takes part in the activity he or she is observing. For example, a researcher investigating point-of-sale promotional material works a few days as a sales clerk. This kind of observation may also be overt or covert, depending on whether the persons observed know they are being watched by the researcher in their midst. Participant observation provides a better feel for the activity, but may interfere with the group's normal behavior, especially if overt.

Covert observation is less likely to affect the behavior of those being watched, but it does raise ethical problems of deception similar to those discussed in Chapter 1. (See Chapters 5 and 11 for further discussion of observation as a way of gathering data.)

Focus Groups. Sometimes the researcher needs to learn the feelings and opinions of those directly involved in the problem or situation, such as consumers or employees. **Focus groups** are a common technique in consumer research. A group leader spends about two hours discussing the product or service with a handful of paid volunteers. In many cases the participants are fairly homogeneous (e.g., all women, or all roughly the same age, or the same socioeconomic background).

To help achieve a casual atmosphere, coffee, juice, and light food such as sandwiches are usually provided. The discussion is only slightly structured by the group leader, who asks questions to cover a predetermined set of topics and ensures that all group members participate. A skilled leader is important to make sure that one or two individuals don't dominate the conversation and to draw out opinions that individuals may be reluctant to express. Group sessions are often recorded or videotaped, and when focus groups are conducted by market research firms, the client's representatives may watch from behind one-way mirrors.

Exploratory Surveys.   Another way of getting at feelings and opinions is to conduct a small informal survey. Exploratory surveys use open-ended questions that invite respondents to discuss their experiences and attitudes. Interview surveys are best for getting feelings on complicated topics; sensitive issues are best pursued with questionnaires. Both techniques may produce ideas relevant to the original business problem; these ideas can then be examined and tested by more rigorous methods. (Survey measurement and methods are discussed in Chapters 9 and 12.)

SUGGESTION

Don't begin your literature review until your investigation of the business problem is almost complete. This will help you to focus your search and save valuable research time.

SUGGESTION

Keep a record of important articles you find in your literature review. You will want to return to them for help in making design decisions. Photocopy any articles that seem very important, and make your summary notes on the first page. For other important articles, photocopy the first page (with publication information so you can cite the article correctly). This page usually includes a summary of the paper.

Review of External Materials.   A final source to investigate for information about the business problem is external written material originating outside the organization. Two kinds of material should be examined: (1) summary statistics and other descriptive sources providing background material relevant to the organizational problem and (2) reports of others' research on related topics (most of which will be general organization research).

This step of the investigation provides four benefits:

- *Problem definition and conceptualization.* Background material or general organization research may suggest different and fruitful approaches to the business problem.

- *Variables.* Others' research may suggest important variables to include in the project, either as controls or as confounding and spurious factors. (These kinds of variables are discussed later in this chapter and in Chapter 5.)

- *Methods and measures.* Investigation may produce useful measures and methods to incorporate into your research design.

- *The possibility of an immediate solution.* The search for background material may provide information that will help to solve the problem or answer the question without any further research. For example, the search may uncover a program, or an evaluation, that suits the organization's needs. Based on this information, the researcher can move immediately to specific recommendations.

The importance of a literature review cannot be overemphasized. Taking advantage of what other researchers have done can increase both the cost-benefit ratio (by saving time) and research validity (by ensuring that no significant variable is unintentionally omitted). Unfortunately, most managers and some researchers often feel there isn't time for a literature review. As a result they often reinvent the wheel or miss important variables that might lead to better decisions and solutions.

Box 2.3 offers specific suggestions for conducting an effective review of general organization and business research. It also lists some of the sources to consider for this stage of the problem investigation.

Finally, note that investigation of the business problem serves another important purpose. When the data analysis is over, and the researcher has drawn conclusions from the findings, he or she will return to the results of the

(*text continues on page 60*)

BOX 2.3
RESEARCH SKILLS

Conducting an Effective Literature Review

1. *Be clear about what you're looking for.* You definitely don't want to know everything that's been done on your topic; this is not a Ph.D. dissertation you're writing! Instead, you want to meet two specific, limited objectives:

First, what can the literature suggest in terms of other variables related to your key variable? For example, if you find an article that reports a relationship between age and job satisfaction (your key variable) has been established, then include age as one of your other variables.

Second, what can the literature suggest in terms of how to conduct the research? Are there existing measures of your variables (or questionnaire items, or scales) that other researchers have devised and tested? If they're relevant, you can save time and increase validity by adopting them. What does other research suggest for your own research design and procedures?

2. *Focus on the appropriate literature.* The material you want to review consists of reports of general organization or business research. Such reports are applicable to a wide variety of organizations and situations in such areas as marketing, accounting, finance, human resource management, industrial relations, organizational change, and so on. The reports are found in two types of sources: those written for academics and researchers, and those intended for a business audience. Managers may want to start with the second type, but if you're making research decisions, you should be reviewing relevant material in the first. Other business research directly relevant to your problem is usually difficult to locate. Don't ignore research reports written for other organizations if you find them, but it usually isn't worth the effort trying to track them down.

3. *Organize your search to be efficient.* Further on we suggest some sources for your literature review.

Start with indices and abstracts, such as *The Business Index* or *Psychological Abstracts,* in areas relevant to your problem. These works contain concise descriptions of journal articles from a number of periodicals, organized by topics and *key words.* Some are available through on-line computer databases which you can access through a terminal or personal computer. Some of the more useful abstracts are indicated here, as well as a few of the journals relevant to business research. However, do not start your literature review by thumbing through journals; you'll waste a great deal of your time!

4. *Look for key words in the indices or abstracts that relate to your key variable or important other variables.* These key words are also useful in computerized literature searches. In the Campbell Switch example (Box 2.4), George might look for such topics as absenteeism and turnover in the business-oriented abstracts and for such key words as motivation, job satisfaction, and technological change in the researcher-oriented abstracts. After you find a relevant abstract containing a key word, consult the specific article. Then check the author's references to other studies for additional reports to consult. Begin by looking for summary and review articles, and reports of meta-analysis (which summarize the results and relationships found in a number of individual research studies).

5. *Don't do too little, or too much.* The review doesn't have to be thorough: you don't need to find every relevant article or report, and going back more than five years is probably unnecessary for most projects. However, you should be convinced that all relevant major variables with a potential relationship to your key variable have been considered.

INFORMATION SOURCES FOR PROBLEM INVESTIGATION

Use library sources to investigate the initial business problem and to unearth potentially important variables to include in your research. (Note: this list does not include sources of published data for available and secondary data studies. For such sources, see Box 10.1.)

Abstracts and Indexes

Abstracts and indexes don't contain the information you want, but they tell you where you can find it for specific topics in general business and organization research. Abstracts also provide brief summaries of what's in each item. Some of these indexes are also available in laserdisk form, so that rather than looking up headings and key words in which you're interested, you can use a computer to help your search.

Accountant's Index

American Statistics Index

Applied Science and Technology Index

The Business Index

Business Periodicals Index

Current Contents in the Social Behavioral Sciences

Dissertation Abstracts International

Encyclopedia of Business Information Sources

Index of Economic Articles in Journals and Collective Volumes

"Marketing Abstracts" in Journal of Marketing

New York Times Index

Psychological Abstracts

Social Sciences Citation Index

Social Sciences Index

Sociological Abstracts

Statistical Reference Index

Wall Street Journal Index

Computerized On-Line Services

Computerized services can bring the information you want directly to your microcomputer. Most contain a variety of different databases. These services are very useful when you want information about other firms, industries, business climate, economic indicators, and other general facts. As well as information for problem investigation, many also provide available or secondary data for certain business research problems, such as share prices for financial research and time-series data on competing firms.

You'll need a modem to connect with an information-source computer, and you'll have to pay membership, connect time, or other charges. For a general index of on-line services, consult *Directory of On-Line Information Resources*, Knowledge Industry Publications, Inc., 701 Westchester Avenue, White Plains, NY 10604. Among the major services of use to business researchers are

COMPUSERVE

DIALOG

DJNR (Dow Jones)

INFO GLOBE (Canada)

KNOWLEDGE INDEX

ORBIT

THE SOURCE

Market Research Firms

Many major market research firms supply to their clients, on a regular basis, information about market conditions. Costs for most clients are in the range of $10,000 to $50,000. These firms also produce specialized reports on particular topics. In other words, you can hire a market research firm to help you with your exploratory problem investigation. (Of course, these firms will also be glad to carry out most or all of the research.)

Directories, Dissertations, Yearbooks

County and City Data Book

Directory of National and International Labor Unions in the United States

Duignan, P., and A. Rabushka (eds.). 1980. *The United States in the 1980s.* Stanford: Hoover Institution Press.

Economic Almanac

Fortune Magazine Directory of 500 Largest Corporations

Labor Fact Book

Moody's Industrial Manual

Poor's Register of Directors and Executives

Rand McNally's International Bankers' Directory

Special Labor Force Reports, Bureau of Labor Statistics. (a series of reports, some of which are relevant for general business and organization research)

Statistical Abstract of the United States

U.S. Census of Manufacturers

Business Journals

Check the indexes of these business journals for items relating to your business problem. Journal articles also suggest research designs and variables to include in your project.

Academy of Management Journal

Academy of Management Review

American Opinion

Business History Review

Business and Society Review

California Management Review

Futures

Harvard Business Review

Journal of Business Research

Journal of Consumer Research

Journal of Economic Issues

Journal of Human Resources

Journal of Management

Journal of Marketing Research

Management Science

Organizational Dynamics

Personnel

Personnel Psychology

Public Policy

Quarterly Review of Economics and Business

Sloan Management Review

Technology and Culture

The Economist

Academic Journals and Reviews

The following journals and reviews provide articles and summary essays on business-related topics from the perspective of the academic disciplines of psychology, economics, sociology, and political science.

Administrative Science Quarterly

American Behavioral Scientist

American Economic Review

American Economist

American Journal of Economics and Sociology

Canadian Journal of Economics

Human Relations

Industrial and Labor Relations Review

Journal of Applied Psychology

Journal of Personality and Social Psychology

Journal of Social Psychology

Organizational Behavior and Human Decision Processes

Organization Science

Personnel Psychology

Public Opinion Quarterly

Social Psychology Quarterly

Dunnette, M. 1983. *Handbook of Industrial and Organizational Psychology.* New York: Wiley.

Katz, D., R. L. Kahn, and J. S. Adams (eds.). 1980. *The Study of Organizations.* San Francisco: Jossey-Bass.

Lindzey, G., and E. Aronson. 1985. *The Handbook of Social Psychology* (2 vols.). New York: Random House.

Nystrom, Paul C., and William H. Starbuck (eds.). 1981. *Handbook of Organizational Design.* New York: Oxford University Press.

original investigation to help formulate relevant and effective recommendations. (Problem investigation is an important part of the research described in Box 2.4. This extended case continues throughout the book.)

What to Look For

During the investigation, researchers should look specifically for underlying problems, triggering problems, constraints, and motivations.

Underlying Problems.   People are often reluctant or unable to recognize the basic, underlying causes of problems. It is human nature to assume that the visible and obvious symptom *is* the problem. Since one problem usually leads to another, the second to a third, and so on, the researcher must work backward to find the original problem. Failure to get to the basic cause may result in research and recommendations that deal only with symptoms, rather than the underlying problem.

Triggering Problems.   Alternatively, managers may pay too much attention to what they assume is the underlying problem and ignore the actual triggering problem which brought in the researcher. This often happens when there is internal political conflict in the organization. Ignoring the triggering problem may lead researchers and managers away from optimal solutions.

Constraints.   Third, identify any constraints on the solution to the business problem. There are almost always certain responses or actions that will be ruled out for economic, political, ethical, or other reasons. For example, a harsh response to alleged abuse of sick leave provisions might stop the abuse, but the negative impact on upcoming negotiations with the union makes it an unwise option. Similarly, an evaluation of the sales success of a new product may suggest that it be dropped immediately, but the substantial support it has

BOX 2.4
CAMPBELL SWITCH: A CONTINUING CASE

Part One: The Turnover Problem

"George!"

George Newman, a newly minted MBA still in his first month at Campbell Switch, stops his hurried pace past the open office door of his boss, Walt Ryan.

"We're having a problem with turnover at the new plant. Too many of the seasoned guys we moved from the old Concord plant are quitting or asking for transfers back. I want you to get a handle on the problem. Let me know what you think should be done. Fast!"

George has his first business research assignment.

In further conversations with his boss, George learns that 4 older employees have quit and 11 more have applied for transfers in the past two months. The new Ajax plant, just out of town, has only been in operation about four or five months. It was specially designed to produce a new line of touch-sensitive switches, and older skilled employees were moved from the nearby Concord plant to help bring productivity up to maximum levels in the shortest possible time. Walt doesn't know what rate of turn-

over the four employee quits represent, or exactly what the current rate is at other Campbell Switch plants.

George, desperately trying to recall his course notes in research methods, tells Walt he'll start looking into the problem immediately. Walt tells him to put his other projects on the back burner and to give this one top priority.

"We need those guys if we're ever going to make our production targets. We can't afford to lose 'em!"

Two days later, having found and reviewed his business research course notes, George has talked with two of the Ajax plant foremen, one 36-year-old shop floor employee who has already given notice and three other workers, two older, one younger. He has located a dusty report on Concord plant turnover written eight years ago, and asked the personnel department to give him the turnover rates and transfer requests in both plants, by department (just in case it's a localized problem) since the Ajax plant opened. George has begun to investigate the initial business problem.

CASE EXAMPLE

A researcher was told that the business problem in a large multinational corporation was an increase in the rejection of transfers among scientific and technical staff. Management regarded the problem as important because promotions in the corporation were generally linked to geographical moves. Management asked the researcher to study the effects of transfers on employees from two-career families in which both spouses hold full-time jobs. Management assumed that such individuals would be less mobile in accepting corporate transfers.

After doing some investigating, the researcher found quite a different triggering problem. Older managers who had worked their way up by accepting transfers along with their promotions (often to less desirable locations) were angry. They saw younger executives with two-career families turning down transfers because of their spouses' jobs, but being promoted anyway. This discovery shifted the focus of the research from the two-career families to the reactions of the older managers to changing corporate practices.

received from a senior executive makes it more likely that revisions to the product or its marketing are the only acceptable recommendations. A union local might wish to cut its grievance arbitration costs, but for political and ethical reasons it cannot reduce the number of grievances it pursues to the arbitration stage.

Motivations.   Finally, clearly establish the motivations underlying the request for research help. It sometimes happens that business research is motivated by office politics; more frequently, a major research effort fails to provide what a manager really wants because his or her real reasons weren't made clear. One way to get to underlying motives is to ask, repeatedly, "So what?" (or, more politely, "Why is this important?") until satisfied that the underlying motivations are clearly understood.

CASE EXAMPLE

The manager at the mill of a large pulp and paper firm asked to have a new weekly indemnity program evaluated. On investigation, the researcher found that the manager was already aware that sick leave claims had declined. What the manager really wanted to know was not whether there was an improvement, but whether it was the new program or other factors (such as poor economic conditions and high unemployment) that were responsible for the improvement. If the program had not caused the reduction, the manager could afford to change some aspects of the program to which the union had objected, as concessions in the next round of bargaining with the union, in return for union concessions on working conditions.

Investigation Techniques

Following are two specific techniques you can use in your investigation interviews: hypothetical results and current situation versus desired standard.

Hypothetical Results.   Give management several hypothetical research results and ask what their reactions would be in each case. Their responses will indicate whether you're on the right track in grasping the real problem, and whether there are issues and difficulties you should explore further.

The hypothetical results need not be in statistical form. You can merely suggest major relationships or possible findings. For example:

"What if we find that sales are 22 percent lower in the Mississippi region?"

"How would you react to finding that married women with children were not at all the source of high absenteeism levels?"

BOX 2.5
CAMPBELL SWITCH: A CONTINUING CASE
Part Two: Investigating the Problem

"Doodling again, George?" Roberta Wright, an energetic addition to the personnel department at Campbell Switch about a year before George was hired (and from a competing business school), stands smiling in his office doorway.

"Why, uh, Roberta," George stammers, slightly flustered. "I guess my mind is wandering. I'm trying to explore all the angles of the project Ryan assigned me yesterday. And believe me, it isn't easy!"

"What's this all about? I heard Walt was turning blue over the number of experienced employees quitting at the Ajax plant. And no wonder. It costs a lot more to hire and train replacements than you'd realize."

"That's the problem, or rather the symptom, all right," replies George. "Ryan is under a lot of pressure to get production up by the end of the year. He wants a fast answer to the problem. If you've got a

minute, let me tell you what I've got so far."

Roberta nods, and takes the other chair that George has managed to squeeze into his modest office. George explains what he has discovered.

"We've got an annualized turnover rate of 9.8 percent at the Ajax plant. At the Concord plant, the comparable rate is 1.5 percent. The problem is mostly older skilled employees leaving, as you said. Turns out that almost all the quits are former Concord plant people. And not only that, absenteeism is on the increase too. It's almost twice as high as Concord."

"But what's an acceptable level? The Concord rate?"

"I assume so," says George. "All in all, it certainly sounds like something's going on at Ajax. The turnover is just the tip of the iceberg." He continues to describe the results of his investigation to Roberta.

"What more would you need to know if we find that interest coverage is the most important factor related to planned capital spending among your new target clients?"

This technique also helps managers to clarify their own view of the problem, their assumptions, and their underlying concerns. (For more information on this technique, read Andreasen, 1985.)

Current Situation Versus Desired Standard. Interpret the initial business problem as the difference between the current situation and some desired standard, goal, or objective (see Box 2.5). The research problem then becomes a question of finding what the desired standard is, plus the answer to one of the following questions:

- What is the current situation? *(Descriptive research)*

- What will it be in the future? *(Prediction research)*

- What accounts for the difference between situation and standard? *(Explanatory research)*

- Has a particular policy or program narrowed the gap? *(Evaluation research)*

Measures of the current (or future) situation become dependent variables. Independent variables are causes of the situation, including policies or programs being evaluated.

The use of this framework raises other useful questions for investigation:

- Who sets the standard? Is it appropriate? Are there other possible standards?

- Is the information about the current situation accurate? Is there really a difference between current situation and standard (i.e., is there *really* a problem?).

STEP TWO: DETERMINE THE GENERAL RESEARCH PURPOSE

The second step in translating a business problem to a research problem is to identify which of the four general research purposes the problem involves: description, prediction, evaluation, or explanation. This step is important because purpose affects both design decisions and the choice of other variables to be included in the research. It usually isn't difficult to specify which purpose a problem entails. The differences are clearly seen by applying the situation-versus-standard technique.

Descriptive Research

If management only seeks information about the current situation, the general purpose is descriptive research. ("How are sales of our diet margarine doing?" "How do supervisors feel about the new collective agreement provisions on job posting?") Business questions and decisions often require this kind of information. Descriptive research is also used to obtain simple comparisons and breakdowns that help describe the situation ("How does production compare across plants? What are the total sales in each region?") Examples of descriptive research projects include a survey of other firms' benefit plans, a report on the extent of nonpayment of union dues, and a report on the proportion of employees who want flexible working hours.

Prediction Research

If a *prediction model* must be devised in order to make a projection, then prediction research is called for. In *selection prediction,* the model is used to select which option will be most beneficial to the organization (e.g., selecting which job applicant will have the highest level of productivity, selecting which investment will produce the greatest yield). In *forecasting prediction,* the model forecasts what the future situation will be (or might be if other characteristics change in certain ways). For example, a manager might want to predict future sales given certain assumptions about the economy. The task in prediction research is to find and test the best model that describes the *current* situation and then use it to predict the future.

This kind of research is often involved in strategic planning. Examples of selection prediction include choosing new employees and new retail outlet locations and organizing drive targets for a union. Examples of forecasting prediction include economic forecasting, sales forecasts, estimates of labor force needs, and matching inventory to seasonal and cyclical demand.

Note that if the initial question asks for predictions that do *not* require a model, the general purpose is simple descriptive research. For example, a questionnaire survey to ask people what they think might happen is descriptive research that describes what the sample thinks about the future. Similarly, a survey of plant managers' plans for the future (e.g., capital investments in the next fiscal year) is also descriptive research.

Evaluation Research

Evaluation research is usually easy to identify: the problem is to evaluate an existing organization action, program, or policy undertaken to improve some situation or solve some problem ("Is our Quality of Work Life program producing the improved productivity we expected?"). A good evaluation project seeks answers to all three of the following questions:

- Has the situation improved since the action?
- Was it the action, or something else, that improved the situation?
- Did the action have any other unforeseen consequences?

In addition, management may want to find out *how* the policy or program actually operated to cause an improvement (formative evaluation). Knowing the actual process may suggest a simpler or cheaper version of the action.

A common type of evaluation research is the **pilot project.** Examples include a preliminary test in one magazine of a proposed print media campaign, an evaluation in one region of a new package design for beer cartons, a six-month trial of new financial management software, and a trial run of flexible work hours in one department of a government agency. However, full-scale programs which cover the entire organization or sales population can also be evaluated.

Explanatory Research

Any research that asks for recommended solutions to a problem is likely to be explanatory research. Such research generates and tests potential causal relationships between explanatory variables and the situation. It is used to explain why the current situation is different from the desired standard ("Why is our union losing members?"). It usually focuses on variables that the organization can do something about in order to improve the situation and thus improve or end the problem.

Examples of explanatory research projects include a study of why customers purchase one brand of ice cream rather than another, an examination of why employees are rejecting a profit-sharing plan, an analysis of what factors affect the quality of financing decisions, and a survey of why managers feel uneasy about the introduction of computers to their departments.

Combining Descriptive and Explanatory Research. Some confusion occasionally arises because of the apparent combination of descriptive with evaluation or explanatory research. For example, the business problem "Are sales on target, and if not, why not?" involves both descriptive research ("Are sales on target?") and explanatory research ("Why not?").

In such cases, researchers usually treat the business problem as two separate but linked research problems. The nature of the second will depend on the answer to the first, but in designing the descriptive research, the researcher is aware of the possibility of follow-up explanatory research and tries to gather data that will serve both purposes.

Linking two related research problems saves time and money, but the researcher and manager should be aware that if the first project produces unanticipated results, they'll have to gather additional data. For example, if it is found that sales are below expectations only in large metropolitan areas, subsequent attention will focus on the characteristics that differentiate such markets from the rest of the country. It is unlikely that this information would have been gathered in the descriptive project.

As Box 2.6 suggests, identifying general purpose is usually not a difficult task.

STEP THREE: SPECIFY THE VARIABLES

Once the general research purpose has been identified, the next step in the translation is to specify the variables involved in the research. This step involves two parts. The first is to identify the key variable on which the research will focus. The second is to make a preliminary list of other variables potentially related to the key variable.

Key Variable

We discussed dependent and independent variables earlier. To help specify the research problem, it is very useful to use a different scheme to classify variables: key and primary.

BOX 2.6

CAMPBELL SWITCH: A CONTINUING CASE

Part Three: An Explanatory Research Project

George Newman reports his initial findings to his boss, Walt Ryan. There appears to be a real morale problem at the Ajax plant, and it is affecting not just turnover, but also absenteeism and transfer requests. The problem seems to be limited to older employees, and it may have something to do with working conditions at the new plant.

"Which is odd," remarks George, "since I know the plant was designed with the most up-to-date equipment and amenities, like controlled sound levels, and modern lighting, and . . ."

"So research it!" growls Ryan. "And I noticed Wright in your office this morning. Better bring her in on it. Help speed things up. Use the research budget for any expenses, but check with me first if they're major. Give me your report in two weeks."

Back in his office, waiting for Roberta, George puts his feet up on his desk to help him think through the problem, even though he has to wedge his chair into a corner to do it. One thing is immediately clear. The purpose of this research is to find the reason for the increase in turnover and the other symptoms. This is obviously explanatory research. And the next step is to get Roberta's help in identifying variables and finishing the problem investigation.

The key variable represents that characteristic or attribute in the situation which is the focus of the research and the basis of the business problem or question. The point of all except descriptive research is to attempt to verify what other variables are related to it (as causes, effects, or correlates) and how. Testing its relationships with other variables is the major focus of data analysis. Knowledge of these relationships leads to research conclusions and recommendations.

Some examples of key variables are

- Level of diesel engine sales.
- Return on investment for each separate product line.
- Machine shop productivity.
- Absenteeism.
- The new sick leave program.
- Proportion of potato chip purchases involving more than one bag.

The information gathered during the investigation of the business problem suggests the most appropriate key variable. As Table 2.1 shows, the choice also depends on the general research purpose. Note that in evaluation research the key variable is the action taken to improve the situation (an independent variable); in explanatory research it is that aspect of the situation which needs improving (a dependent variable).

Frequently an explanatory research project involves two or more related key variables. In the Campbell Switch example, turnover rates is an obvious

> The **key variable** is the variable central to the research problem. The key variable is a *dependent* variable in prediction and explanatory research, but an *independent* variable in evaluation research.

TABLE 2.1 ■ SPECIFYING THE KEY VARIABLE

Research Purpose	Key Variable	Example
Descriptive	The aspect of the situation about which more information is wanted.	"What's our absenteeism rate?" *Key variable:* absenteeism rate
		"What kind of sick leave benefits are other firms offering?" *Key variable:* sick leave plan contents
Prediction	The aspect of the situation that is to be predicted (dependent variable)	"What sales do you expect for steel piping next quarter?" *Key variable:* value of sales
		"What will happen to membership levels if we raise the fee by $10?" *Key variable:* proportion of membership renewals
Evaluation	The action, program, or policy to be evaluated (independent variable)	"Is the new agency doing a better job for us?" *Key variable:* advertising agency (former or new)
		"Is the QWL program really improving productivity?" *Key variable:* QWL program (before or after implementation)
Explanatory	The aspect of the situation to be explained or for which causes are sought (dependent variable)	"Why are we losing so many grievances?" *Key variable:* arbitration outcome
		"We've got to improve sales on the West Coast!" *Key variable:* value of West Coast sales

key variable, but absenteeism and turnover requests are also apparently being affected. It is likely that whatever is causing turnover is also a cause of the other two symptoms. In this example, all three could be used as key variables in the research.

If two or more potential key variables are largely unrelated, it may be easier to divide the business problem into several subprojects, each with a different key variable.

Primary Variables

After the key variable has been specified, the next step in the translation process is a preliminary list of **primary variables** to be included in the research.

Primary variables specify what relationships the research is to investigate.

> A **primary variable** is one that is related to the key variable and of major interest to the researcher.

- In *prediction research,* primary variables are possible *predictors* of the key variable. For example, sales at potential ice cream parlor sites (a key dependent variable) might be predicted by traffic flow, proximity of recreation facilities, and availability of parking (primary independent variables).

- In *evaluation research,* primary variables represent plausible *effects* of the action being evaluated (the key variable). They are indicators of situations (such as cash flow or productivity) the business is attempting to improve. For example, a new punch clock system (key independent variable) might affect employee productivity, employee morale, supervisor morale, and payroll department productivity (primary dependent variables).

- In *explanatory research,* primary variables represent potential *causes* of the key variable. Primary variables often represent aspects of the organization that can be influenced or changed (such as accounting procedures, marketing strategies, or hiring policies). For example, management may want to test whether poor sales (key variable) is the result of a new sales manager, recent staff transfers, stiffer competition in the region, less demand for the product, a reduced advertising budget, or a general economic downturn (primary independent variables).

As Harper's memo indicates (Box 2.1), the specific research questions that accompany the general statement of the research problem incorporate the primary variables Harper believes should be investigated.

Finding the Primary Variables

Where do primary variables come from? The two major sources are the internal investigation of the business problem and the literature review of relevant research. Other sources include the opinions of experts and consultants and examples of available secondary data.

SUGGESTION

Try explaining the problem to someone who is *unfamiliar* with it. Having to explain it may help you think of other aspects and variables that should be considered.

SUGGESTION

If your literature review shows one or two persons have done a great deal of work on an area you're researching, it is worth considering a telephone call or other contact to get advice. To save *their* time, describe your situation concisely and ask specific questions.

Initial Investigation. The internal investigation of the business problem is the major source of primary variables. Interviews, organization documents, observation, focus groups, and informal surveys will suggest or imply a number of variables relevant to the business problem. Pay attention to your own intuition and the hunches of those you talk with, especially strategically situated individuals and persons directly involved in the problem. In interviews, it helps to ask directly, "What do you think causes it (the problem)?" Replies may suggest potential primary variables.

Review of Literature and Other Sources. Part of the investigation includes a review of background literature and others' research reports in general business and organization research. This review is a second important source of primary variables. Look for supported hypotheses and significant relationships with substantial effect sizes (such as correlations).

Experts. A third source for identifying potentially relevant primary variables is to consult whatever experts are available, including individuals in other organizations and, if possible, management consulting firms. Experts can save time by suggesting variables to include, potential explanations to test, and research strategies to consider.

Samples of Available Secondary Data. If the research is likely to use available secondary data, such as production records or membership files, examine some samples. You may find information on primary variables that would be useful to include in the research. For example, for a study of why an organization was losing many salary arbitrations the researcher examined a few arbitration briefs. He noticed that some were poorly written, with many spelling and grammatical errors. On the chance that these errors might subtly influence an arbitrator, he decided to include "quality of presentation" as a variable.

How Many Variables?

The number of primary variables at this preliminary stage of the research depends in part on the general research purpose.

- Descriptive research involves no primary variables. However, the results often include **breakdowns** of information by geographic or demographic factors (e.g., number of sales staff broken down by gender and region).

- Prediction research normally uses no more than about a dozen primary predictor variables in a prediction model. However, many more than this may be examined in order to find the best model.

- In evaluation research the primary variables represent indicators of the situation that the policy or program (the key variable) was designed to improve. Normally there would only be a handful of such variables.

- Explanatory research normally involves the greatest number of primary variables, including all potentially important causes of the key dependent variable. In extreme instances, this could involve 100 or more variables.

At this stage of the research, the objective is to include any primary variables that appear to be relevant. During the research design stage, other variables will be added to this preliminary list, and inappropriate and unmeasurable variables will be dropped. Thus, we discuss variables in more detail in Chapter 5.

STEP FOUR: IDENTIFY RESEARCH BOUNDARIES

The specification of *research boundaries* is an important part of translating a business problem to a research problem. Boundaries indicate both the extent of the business problem and the people, events, or things to which the research applies. They refer not just to the people, events, or things from which data is gathered, but to the larger set of them to which the results are to be generalized. Research boundaries are the third component of the research problem statement (together with the general purpose and key variable). As we see in the next few chapters, research boundaries are important for choosing samples and comparison groups.

Boundaries and General Research Purpose

Research boundaries are fairly easy to identify in descriptive and prediction research. They indicate the persons, events, or things about which information is desired or about which a prediction is to be made.

Evaluation Research.   The identification of boundaries is slightly more complicated in evaluation research. The initial research boundary includes the intended target of the policy or program being evaluated. However, the research design will often require a comparison or control group not exposed to the organization action. In order to evaluate the action's effects, this second group will also have to be included within the research boundaries.

Explanatory Research.   Research boundaries are often difficult to determine in explanatory research. However, both the extent and assumed causes of the business problem may suggest appropriate boundaries.

The initial business problem as presented to the researcher usually includes at least one problem location, for example a particular department or plant. This location may represent the research boundaries. However, managers are not often aware of the extent of a problem; it may or may not exist in other locations. As part of the investigation, check whether the problem has been noticed elsewhere, and if so, whether these other locations should logically be included in the research. For example, a branch plant with the same problem would almost certainly be included, but a competitor facing the same problem would normally be omitted. Likewise, if the problem occurs in another location, but is not severe enough to raise any concern there, it may be decided that the second location lies outside the research boundaries.

The potential causes that managers and others suggest often imply research boundaries. When interviewees compare occurrences of the problem with situations in which it doesn't occur, they suggest that something about the occurrence locations is causing the problem. For example, if complaints about appraisal interviews are largely confined to one region, something about that region (such as a unique management practice) may be the cause. That region thus represents a logical research boundary, at least initially. Of course, if comparison groups or regions are added to the design, the research boundaries expand accordingly.

Types of Boundaries

Research boundaries can be specified on five different dimensions. Any single research problem may incorporate two or more of them.

Structural Boundaries. The most common method of establishing problem boundaries is to designate a set of individuals or groups identified by their structural role in the organization. For example, a problem might involve shipping department employees, or all production departments, or a union local, or a particular product.

Common Characteristics. A second way to specify boundaries is by the common characteristics of individuals, groups, decisions, or other actions affected by the problem. For example, female employees may have greater absenteeism, or a problem in overtime costs might be restricted to small departments. Financial reporting practices for only particular types of transactions may be of interest, with that type of transaction representing a research boundary.

Geographical Boundaries. A third dimension for specifying problem boundaries is geography, with reference to regions or other geographical entities. For example, one particular region may have a problem with sales staff, or a firm may have a public relations problem in large urban areas, but not in towns or smaller cities.

Technology Boundaries. The boundaries of still other problems may be identified in terms of the technology or work process used. For example, the installation of new word processors in certain offices may be associated with morale problems in those locations, or a new accounting procedure may be identified as the problem.

Temporal Boundaries.   Finally, the researcher should also look for time-related boundaries to a problem. This is often useful when the research is about decisions, sales, or other business actions. When was the problem first perceived? As well as calendar time, boundaries of this kind may be linked to procedural or technological change ("Our troubles began with the new punch presses") or organizational change ("Our troubles began with the new plant manager"). Temporal boundaries are also involved in prediction research where they indicate the limit of the time period for which the prediction is to be made.

STEP FIVE: STATE RESEARCH PROBLEM AND RESEARCH QUESTIONS

The final step of the translation process pulls together the results of the four previous steps (investigation, purpose, variables, and boundaries). The result is a *general statement* of the research problem and a set of *specific research questions*.

The statement of the research problem, as noted earlier, involves three components:

- The general research purpose (for example, explanatory).
- The key variable (for example, sales levels).
- The problem boundaries (for example, older employees).

The research problem thus indicates the overall focus and objective of the research: to explain the sales levels of older employees.

The research questions suggest specific aspects of the problem to be investigated and ideas to be tested. These questions are distilled from the results of the researcher's investigation of the business problem.

Types of Research Questions

Specific research questions fall into three categories: questions concerning the primary variables, questions about additional key variables, and questions pertaining to the research boundaries.

Questions About Primary Variables.   The most common type of research questions incorporate the primary variables that emerge in the translation process. These questions specify the relationships between the key and primary variables that the research is to test (for example, "Are seasonal variations in sales important?" "Are there gender differences in absenteeism rates?"). (In basic and general applied research, these research questions would be translated to formal falsifiable hypotheses. In business research this formalization is not necessary. However, when it comes time to carry out certain statistical tests, research questions must be converted to *null hypotheses.*)

In explanatory research, researchers usually add a question to focus on the *relative impact* of the causes: "Which factors have the greatest impact on (the key variable) when all other causes are controlled for?"

Key Variable Questions.   The second kind of research questions concerns key variables. They may present additional key variables to be investigated (for example, "Are turnover rates showing the same pattern?"). They may also suggest alternative measures of a key variable (for example, "What's the relationship between VCR sales as a proportion of the number of units available in the store, and sales as a proportion of the number of potential buyers entering the store?").

Boundary Questions.   These questions involve the research boundaries and are usually included when the researcher is unsure of the boundaries of the business problem. They may propose other cases to be investigated or may seek to determine temporal or other boundaries of the problem (for example, "When did absenteeism levels begin to rise? Is it a problem in all job categories?"). Boundary questions are the least common specific research questions.

The Role of Intuition

SUGGESTION

Write out and keep handy a copy of the research problem. Refer to it whenever a problem or question arises, particularly in coding and editing stages. Tack it to the wall over your desk!

Intuition *does* have a place in rigorous and scientific research! The research questions should reflect plausible hunches, suspicions, and suggestions of those involved with or knowledgeable about the business problem. Researchers should add to these their own intuition and ideas. If they suspect that a particular variable no one else has mentioned may be important, they ought to include it. They should not hesitate to include issues and variables they believe the client or manager will be interested in or find useful, even though he or she may not have raised them or even thought of them.

As is now evident, there are substantial differences between the manager's initial expression of the business problem and the researcher's statement of the research problem. The former is generally stated in terms of a problem in organizational effectiveness or a need for information; the latter is both broader and more specific. It is broader in that it goes beyond the immediate perceptions expressed in the business problem and more specific in the inclusion of particular variables and relationships to be examined and tested. Table 2.2 provides two examples.

TABLE 2.2 ■ EXAMPLES OF PROBLEM TRANSLATION

Initial Problem	Research Problem and Research Questions
Evaluation Research Example	
Is our new quality circles program working?	To investigate the impact of the quality circles program in the shipping department. a. Has the program reduced absenteeism and turnover? b. Has the program increased productivity? c. Has the program had any negative consequences?
Explanatory Research Example	
Why can't we get people out to union meetings or even social events?	To determine the causes of low levels of membership participation in the activities of union local 789. a. Is high job satisfaction among the members related to low participation levels? b. Is dissatisfaction with union officers' performance the cause? c. Are there different levels of participation by gender and by age group? d. Has membership participation dropped off over the past decade? Has there been a general trend among the members to be less interested in union affairs? e. Is membership participation affected by close hard-fought union elections? f. Is membership participation improved only when the members believe that they are not getting a fair deal in the contract? Does it depend on their knowing what workers at nearby plants are getting? g. Is participation reduced when workers get married, or have children and have less spare time, or is it increased because they have a greater need for income, benefits, and job security?

OBSTACLES TO A RELEVANT RESEARCH PROBLEM

The objective of the translation process is to move from the business problem to a clear and well-defined research problem. Of the three business research criteria (validity, relevance, cost-benefit ratio), the criterion most affected by researcher's efforts at this stage is *relevance*. The research problem must be relevant to management's real needs. (As well as relevance, the definition of a research problem raises certain ethical issues. See Box 2.7.)

A number of obstacles can prevent the formulation of a relevant research problem. These obstacles can result in missed or inappropriate variables that don't represent the real problem or research within the wrong problem boundaries.

Political and Personal Factors

The first set of obstacles are political and personal factors. It is the nature of organizations that their members, departments, branch plants, congregations (and in general any subgroups) are often in some degree of competition or conflict with one another, friendly or otherwise. When these individuals or groups have something at stake, or feel threatened in some way, their perceptions or interpretations of a problem may be affected. They may deny a problem exists or perceive one where none exists. More likely, they will have slightly distorted views of the nature, extent, or cause of a problem.

When the plant manager in Pittsburgh says that the problem with Denver is poor work scheduling (implying poor management), and the plant manager in Denver says that the local work force is just not reliable, both remarks should be considered as starting points rather than statements of the real problem or its causes. Similarly, when the president of a book club complains about membership turnout at meetings, her opinion may be colored by the impending annual election of club officers.

The best guard against distortions of this kind is to find out what the persons interviewed have at stake, what they hope to gain, and what they fear they might lose. This often takes some degree of interviewing skills, as suggested in Box 2.8.

Distorted Perceptions

Even without their own interests and hidden agendas, people with different backgrounds or in different situations perceive reality in different ways. Consequently, a researcher may have difficulty determining the real state of affairs. For example, what an older manager may see as a normal rate of union grievances, a younger one may see as a problem involving too many disciplinary grievances. This calls for some further investigation.

SUGGESTION

Make sure that the manager or client reads the research problem carefully. Ask for input at this time in order to avoid wasted time and effort later. This is also a good time to alert management to the possibility of unfavorable or unpleasant results. They can be phrased as hypothetical answers to the research questions. Ask what action management would take if these particular answers were found.

BOX 2.7
RESEARCH ETHICS
The Ethics of Problem Definition

The first stage of a research project—translating the business problem into a well-defined research problem—represents the researcher's first and best opportunity to anticipate potential ethical problems. In particular, the researcher (and manager) should apply the second, third, and fourth ethics questions discussed in Chapter 1.

- *Harm to others:* Some hard thinking about the underlying problem and business objectives should suggest whether the results are likely to be harmful to other persons or organizations. Use the test of *accepted risk.*
- *Violations of accepted research practice:* The researcher has an ethical obligation to the manager

to indicate whether a research project is feasible or whether the results are likely to be so tentative as to be worthless. It is unethical to accept an assignment or commission knowing that the results are highly unlikely to satisfy the manager's needs. (However, sometimes this isn't evident until the researcher has attempted a research design.)

- *Violations of community standards of conduct:* The manager has an ethical obligation to the researcher to disclose as fully as possible the nature of the question, decision, or problem facing the business. Such disclosure is necessary for a concise and relevant research problem and for efficient and effective research.

- What *is* the real current situation?

- *Who* says so?

- How do they know?

- Could their perception be biased in any way?

Even statistics and written records may be biased or erroneous or may not be a good indicator of the situation of interest. For example, the number of grievances filed is sometimes used as an indicator of employer-employee relations. A sudden high level of grievances, however, may be only the result of a new person recording the information and including informal grievances that were previously unrecorded.

To avoid a distorted view of the situation, it is wise to consider the other's frame of reference. What values and norms are important? What position does he or she occupy in the organization? How does he or she define events?

Uncertain and Inappropriate Standards

A third obstacle, particularly in evaluation and explanatory research, is that the standard against which the current situation is judged is either difficult to determine or inappropriate. Misperceptions and biases about standards are even more prevalent than differing opinions about the current situation, and

BOX 2.8

CAMPBELL SWITCH: A CONTINUING CASE

Part Four: Interviews at the Ajax Plant

"So you don't even think there's a problem?"

"Not much of one. Nothing we can't lick. Can't see what Ryan's so het up about, anyway. You're just wasting your time."

"You don't know if your absenteeism is higher in just one department, or in the whole plant?"

"What absenteeism? Just a few of the guys off sick. There's nothing wrong around here."

George is having some trouble interviewing one of the Ajax plant supervisors. On the suggestion of an experienced industrial relations manager he met at the regional Personnel Association, he and Roberta are trying to find the boundaries of the Ajax plant problem. He notices that Roberta has finished her interview and is approaching the supervisor's office.

"Hi! They tell me there's a coffeepot in here!" Roberta enters, pours herself a cup, and asks, "How's it going?"

"Uh, this is Roberta Wright, who's working with me on this. Roberta, this is Sam Goodman, one of the production supervisors here at Ajax."

Roberta shakes his hand. "I've heard about you. They tell me that you're the one who's been working out a lot of the bugs here."

"Well," Sam grins, "maybe they're just exaggerating a bit now."

George suddenly gets a thoughtful look on his face and pushes his chair back a few inches, as Roberta continues.

"No, really, I was just talking to Bill Turner, and he told me what you've done so far. Tell me, where did they go wrong here?"

"Now that you mention it, we do have a fair bit of troubles, especially in a couple of departments. I tell you. . . ."

Later, leaving the plant, George asks Roberta how she managed to charm Sam.

"That wasn't charm, and don't give me any of that sexist stuff. That was good interviewing, and being aware of things from his point of view. My conversation with Turner suggested that Goodman is getting a lot of pressure from higher up to make sure things run smoothly here. You've got to see it from his viewpoint, and then find out what he thinks is happening and why. A trick I learned in my business research course."

As they climb into George's car, he remarks, "Say, that must have been a pretty good course you took. What text did you say you used?"

it is very likely that different individuals will define the desired situation in different ways. As part of the investigation of the business problem, ask,

- What is the desired situation?

- Who set this objective?

- Is there really a problem? If so, is it the same problem initially described?

A related obstacle is the inappropriate standard. What a member of the organization sees as a target may not be a suitable standard against which to compare the current situation. Don't always accept at face value those statements about what would be right for the organization. Ask yourself and others

BOX 2.9

CAMPBELL SWITCH: A CONTINUING CASE

Part Five: A Research Problem Draft

"Check this out, will you?"

George hands Roberta a draft of the memo outlining the research problem for Ryan's approval.

TO: Walt Ryan
FROM: George Newman
RE: Draft of research problem re Ajax plant

Briefly, our research objective is to isolate the cause(s) of high levels of turnover, absenteeism, and transfer requests that began at the Ajax plant about a month after its start-up.

The research should address the following specific issues:

- How much relationship is there among turnover, absenteeism, and transfer requests? Do they appear to be the results of the same cause(s)?
- Are these increases typical of the period following a new plant start-up?

- Is there any trend to the increases that indicates things may be getting worse, or improving?
- Are all employees and all departments equally affected?
- Are there differences among the different types of absenteeism (excused versus nonexcused, short versus long, medical versus other, Monday or Friday versus midweek) that might suggest medical causes, or job dissatisfaction, or job stress?
- How are the following factors related to turnover, absenteeism, and transfer requests: foreman, type and adequacy of supervision, quality and supply of materials, type of machinery, machinery problems, nature of the job, intrinsic satisfaction of the job, wages and benefits, hours of work and other working conditions, plant conditions, employee characteristics including age, gender, seniority, experience, education, and previous job?

whether the standard is realistic. (A complete draft of a research problem, illustrating this and other obstacles, can be found in Box 2.9.)

CASE EXAMPLE

A researcher for a firm producing automobile parts was told by the recently hired personnel manager that the business problem was too high a grievance rate. As evidence for the problem, he told her that the rate for the current year was 10 percent while last year's rate was 4 percent. The researcher was asked to find the reason for the sudden increase, since contract negotiations with the union were coming up in a few months. Looking through company records, she found that grievance rates for the preceding five years were 12 percent, 8 percent, 10 percent, 11 percent, and 4 percent, respectively. She concluded that last year's rate was an anomaly and therefore an inappropriate standard or objective. Although the personnel manager was curious about what had happened the previous year, he realized that this would represent a substantially different research problem than the one initially given to the researcher. He decided not to pursue the problem any further.

Assumed Causes

A fourth obstacle to a relevant research problem is the *assumed cause.* Sometimes management will present a researcher with an initial statement of the business problem that includes its presumed origin, accompanied by an expressed need to correct it. The relevant current situation and desired standard are usually left unspecified. As well as determining the real nature of the problem, the researcher must ask whether the cause assumed by management is the real, or the only, cause of the problem.

With enough investigation and attention to these potential problems, the result will be a concise summary of the research problem (see Box 2.9).

■ *The Lighter Side of Research*

Evaluation research: Research conducted in an organization having a surplus of cash. Acceptance of the findings is dependent upon the congruence between the reality and the dream.

Hypothesis: A prediction based on theory formulated after an experiment is performed designed to account for the ludicrous series of events which have taken place. (Woodman, 1979)

Summary

For relevant business research, translation of the initial business problem into a sound research problem is essential. Translation begins with an investigation of the business problem utilizing interviews, organization documents, observation, focus groups, exploratory surveys, and external data sources of background information. Researchers look for underlying problems, triggering problems, constraints, and motivations underlying the research. Two useful techniques are to ask managers how they would respond to hypothetical results and to reinterpret the problem as current versus desired situation.

On the basis of their investigation, researchers can identify the general purpose of the research: descriptive, prediction (either selection or forecasting), evaluation, or explanatory.

The next step in the translation is to specify the key and primary variables, relying on the results of the initial investigation, discussions with experts, and a literature review. Next, define the boundaries of the problem. These boundaries may be structural, geographical, technological, temporal, or based on shared characteristics of the people, events, or things studied.

The translation phase ends with a statement of the research problem and the specific research questions. The research problem includes the general purpose of the research, the key variable(s), and the problem boundaries. The research questions deal with the relationships between the key variable and primary variables, alternative and additional key variables, and the boundaries of the research.

A good translation increases the relevance of the research problem by avoiding misinterpretation due to personal and political factors, distorted perceptions, uncertain and inappropriate standards, and assumed causes.

Where Are We Now?

With the statement of the research problem, you now have a specific research objective. The next task is to plan how to meet that objective: research design. Chapters 3 through 7 deal with the task of research design and the decisions it involves.

Discussion Issues and Assignments

1. Compare the obstacles to a clear research problem that might be found in basic research with those you might encounter in business research.
2. Find an example of business research and try to recreate the research problem. Specifically, identify the general research purpose, key variable, problem boundaries, and other variables.
3. If possible, contact a management consultant and discuss with him or her a recent business problem and how it was translated to a research problem. How much of the process was done consciously and formally? How much was intuitive?
4. Talk to a university or college administrator (dean, department head) about an administrative problem he or she faces and would research if the time or money were available. Translate it to a research problem.
5. Discuss how research on a topic such as declining enrollments in humanities courses might go through a natural evolution of research objectives, beginning with descriptive research and ending with evaluation. What would be the specific objective at each stage?

Further Reading

Lazarsfeld, P., and J. Reitz. 1975. *An Introduction to Applied Sociology.* New York: Elsevier.
>   Although focused on policy research, this book contains an excellent analysis of the translation process.
Posavac, E., and R. G. Carey. 1989. *Program Evaluation: Methods and Case Studies.* Englewood Cliffs, NJ: Prentice Hall.
>   This text applies specifically to organization programs and policies. Chapters 2 and 5 deal with problem investigation in evaluation research.
Williams, A. 1983. "Personnel Research and Organizational Decision Making" in A. Williams, ed. *Using Personnel Research.* Aldershot, England: Gower.

A good discussion of the relationship of applied business research to decision making and some of the difficulties of formulating research problems.

Wolf, F. M. 1986. *Meta-Analysis: Quantitative Methods for Research Synthesis.* Beverly Hills: Sage.

A good examination of the nature, methods, and problems encountered in meta-analysis. Worth looking at if you want to use the results of meta-analytic literature reviews.

PART TWO

Research Design

A look at the design decisions researchers make in planning how to get information to answer research problems and questions.

CHAPTER 3

Unit of Analysis and Basic Designs

CHAPTER OBJECTIVES

- What are the design decisions a researcher must make?
- What are the differences in units and levels of analysis?
- What do you need to know to infer that one factor causes another?
- How well does each basic design support causal inference?

CHAPTER OUTLINE

ELEMENTS OF RESEARCH DESIGN
THE UNIT OF ANALYSIS
CHOOSING THE UNIT OF ANALYSIS
THE THREE BASIC DESIGNS
CRITERIA FOR CAUSAL INFERENCE
BASIC DESIGNS AND CAUSAL INFERENCE
CHOOSING A BASIC DESIGN

nce you know where you want to go, you've got to plan how to get there. The previous chapter dealt with the task of defining the objective: the research problem. The five chapters in this part consider the next task: the research design.

ELEMENTS OF RESEARCH DESIGN

A **research design** is a plan for gathering data. It involves the selection of cases, variables, and data sources.

As the definition implies, all research design reduces to three questions:

- Which *cases* do I gather data about? (e.g., which employees, consumers, plants, union locals, etc. The employee Jean Smith is a case in a study of employees; the purchase of 24 boxes of computer paper is a case in an analysis of financial transactions.)

- Which *variables* do I gather information on? (e.g., age, gender, seniority, job satisfaction, etc.)

- What *data sources* am I going to get information from? (e.g., talk to employees, ask supervisors, examine production records, etc.)

A **case** is a single element or instance of the objects of the research about which the researcher gathers information.

Researchers need to answer these questions whatever their general purpose: description, prediction, evaluation, or explanation. *P.64 – P.65*

The distinction between cases and variables is easy to see. Picture research data in the form of a special table called a *data matrix*. The rows of the matrix represent the cases of the research, one case to each row. The columns represent the variables (the items of information to be gathered about each case). Table 3.1 is an example of a data matrix with five cases (each case a different person) and three variables: make of car, number of cars ever owned, and age. The data, which fill the body of the matrix, represent information on each variable for each case.

Research design is the process of specifying the rows and columns of the data matrix and choosing data sources for the information to fill up the matrix. At the completion of the research design stage, researchers know what cases (rows) will be included in the data matrix, what variables (columns) they want information about, and the data sources from which information will be gathered to fill the body of the data matrix.

Case Selection Decisions

The choice of cases can be further broken down into a set of decisions the researcher must make:

TABLE 3.1 ■ CASES AND VARIABLES: THE DATA MATRIX

Cases	Variables		
	Make of Present Car	Number of Cars Ever Owned	Age
George	Ford	2	24
Ellen	GM	1	22
Bill	Toyota	6	47
Susan	GM	3	38
Frank	Chrysler	1	29

Chapter 3, 4 {

- Most appropriate unit of analysis

- Basic design (true experiment, quasi-experiment, nonexperiment)

- Specific research design (which control, comparison, and sample groups; which measurement points)

Chapter 6, 7 {

- Whether to sample; which type and size of sample

SUGGESTION

As you plan your research, consider the data matrix you want to end up with. What will the cases (rows) be? What about the variables (columns)?

This chapter considers the first two of these decisions. Specific research designs are discussed in Chapter 4 and sampling decisions in Chapters 6 and 7. (Chapter 5 deals with variables and data source decisions.)

Terminology: Observations. Researchers usually gather data about a number of cases. Sometimes, however, they collect data about a single case, measured repeatedly. For example, the end-of-month value of inventory for one firm is recorded each month for a 24-month period. In this instance, the researcher has 24 *observations* based on one case.

THE UNIT OF ANALYSIS

The **unit of analysis** is the *kind* of case to which the variables and research problem pertain and about which data are gathered and analyzed.

The first design decision is to select the appropriate unit of analysis for the research project. Here are some examples of typical units of analysis in business research:

- An employee

- A VCR buyer

- A work group in an assembly plant

- A branch plant of a multinational corporation

- A purchasing decision

- A costing project

- A union-management relationship

- A state or province

The majority of research projects utilize just one unit of analysis and gather data on the attributes of a set of cases of that type (e.g., 300 employees or 1,800 purchasing decisions). If the research problem calls for more than one unit of analysis (e.g., employees and departments), researchers normally carry out separate data analysis for each (and sometimes use separate data-gathering methods).

Unit of Analysis Options

Business researchers generally use one or more of the following six units of analysis:

- An individual person

- An event

- An object

- A body of individuals (includes groups and organizations)

- A relationship

- An aggregate

The first three are the most common choices; the last two are the most complex.

The Individual.   In the simplest and most common unit of analysis in business research, each person (e.g., union member, customer, management trainee) represents one case.

The Event.   Business problems frequently require the choice of an event as the unit of analysis. For example, a firm's production department used the emergency incident as the unit of analysis in an examination of the variables affecting response time to emergencies. Other examples include the church sermon (do length and content affect offerings?), the purchase of a major appliance (what determines the buyer's choice of model?), and the union representation vote (what determines outcome?). Each event represents one case, and the data consist of the attributes of each event, such as when it occurred, its duration, perceived causes, outcome, effects, and who was involved. In service industries, the products provided by firms can often be treated as events (e.g., legal cases for a law firm).

The Object.   On occasion, particularly in quality control problems and operations research, an object such as a product or machine may be chosen as the unit of analysis. Each object represents one case.

In business research, however, we are more often interested in people's relationships to, or use of, objects. In such instances, the individual may be a better unit of analysis than the object. For example, in market research to examine how consumers use their new home computers, it would be more logical to examine a sample of purchasers rather than a sample of computers. Another alternative choice to the object is the event involving the object, such as a purchasing decision or a machinery breakdown.

The Body.   Another common unit of analysis is the body of persons: any group, administrative subunit, or organization consisting of two or more persons with an internal structure (a regular pattern of interaction). Examples include the committee, the department, the plant, and the retail outlet.

Each body represents one case. The researcher gathers data about the attributes of each body, such as its size, aspects of its structure, and measures of its performance.

It is important not to mistake attributes of individuals for attributes of bodies. For example, a committee does not have an education, a gender, or an opinion. However, individual attributes can be *combined* to make group or organization attributes by using averages, percentages, and proportions. Thus a committee can be characterized by the average age of its members, by the percentage female, or by the proportion preferring coffee to tea.

The Relationship.   For certain problems the best unit of analysis is the relationship between two (or more) individuals or bodies. Each relationship represents one case. For example, a study of union-management relations gathered data on attributes of each union-management pair, including the length of their relationship, number of strikes, frequency of joint committee meetings, and whether their collective agreement covered technological change.

Note two features of the relationship as a unit of analysis.

- Attributes of the individuals (or bodies) in a relationship can also be used as attributes of the relationship. For example, in a customer-retailer relationship, the age of the retailer and the income of the customer can be treated as relationship variables.

- An individual or body may be part of more than one relationship. In a study of manager-employee relations, each manager was part of a number of relationships, each with a different employee. As a result, each manager appeared in several cases.

The Aggregate.   Sometimes the most suitable unit of analysis is an aggregate, a collection of undifferentiated individuals or bodies with no internal structure. For example, individuals are aggregated into census districts, and firms are aggregated into industries and regions. Each aggregation (census district, industry, region) represents a case. Data are gathered on attributes of each aggregation (e.g., the size, proportion of rental housing units, and average income of each census district). Financial research often uses aggregates (the country, an industry) as a unit of analysis.

Do not confuse the attributes of the individuals or bodies composing an aggregate with the attributes of the aggregate itself. A census district has no brand preference; a region has no firm size. However, as we saw for bodies, the use of averages, percentages, and proportions will convert data from the individual, group, or organization level to the aggregate level. For example, size is an attribute of a firm; average firm size is the corresponding attribute of an industry or a region.

Levels of Analysis

Researchers often speak of the *level* of a unit of analysis. In general, higher level units are composed of sets of units from lower levels and have both greater size and greater complexity.

- At the lowest level are simple units such as objects, individuals, and events.

- At intermediate levels are found more complex units including bodies (such as a firm), simple aggregates (such as a theater audience), and relationships between individual persons (such as between the owner of a used car and the person who wants to buy it).

- At the highest level are units of analysis consisting of complex relationships (such as a firm and its supplier), aggregates of bodies (such as an industry), and large aggregates of individuals (such as a state).

These different levels of analysis are illustrated in Figure 3.1.

The importance of levels of analysis will become clear later when we discuss (in Chapter 5) how variables that pertain to one level can be converted to variables at another. In addition, researchers may encounter problems making inferences about relationships at a lower level of analysis using data from a higher level.

CHOOSING THE UNIT OF ANALYSIS

While the choice of the unit of analysis is normally straightforward, it occasionally presents difficulties even for experienced researchers. Keep in mind the following three points:

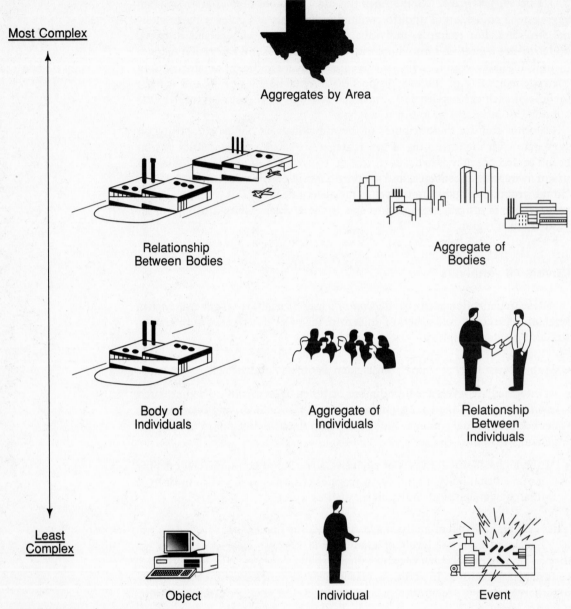

FIGURE 3.1 Levels of Analysis

- The unit of analysis must be *relevant* to the research problem.

- It must be *consistent* over the key variable and all primary variables.

- To increase research validity, it should provide *enough cases or observations* for statistical analysis.

SUGGESTION

A general rule of thumb is to select a unit of analysis at as low a level as possible. Another is to select the unit at the level where decisions are being made (individuals, committees, departments, etc.).

Relevance

The unit of analysis must fit the research problem. Inspect the key variable and the research questions that deal with primary variables. What kind of unit do they pertain to? Are the variables attributes of individuals, bodies, events, or other kinds of units? At what level is the phenomenon of interest actually happening?

Because the key variable alone may not suggest the best unit of analysis, pay particular attention to the research questions. For example, the key variable "absenteeism" might refer to individuals, to bodies (e.g., departmental absenteeism rates), or to events (e.g., incidents of absenteeism). Use the specific research questions (as shown in Table 3.2) to resolve the issue.

TABLE 3.2 ■ CHOOSING A RELEVANT UNIT OF ANALYSIS: AN EXAMPLE WITH THE KEY VARIABLE "ABSENTEEISM"

Research Question	Variables	Unit of Analysis
"Are women employees with children at home more likely to be absent?"	Individual absence rate Gender Marital status Number of children Ages of children	Employee
"Are absenteeism rates higher in the larger departments because of poorer working conditions?"	Department absenteeism rate Department size Department working conditions	Department
"Is our problem mainly one-day Monday and Friday absences of younger employees?"	Length of absence Day of week of first day of absence period Age of the employee who is absent	Each absence

CASE EXAMPLE

A government ministry was worried that hiring decisions had been biased in favor of individuals who had held temporary appointments previously with the ministry, to the disadvantage of more competent "outside" applicants. The researcher was faced with several options for her unit of analysis: the individual winning each position, the individual applicant, or the hiring decision event. Although applicants would have provided more cases, she decided to use the hiring decision and to include as its attributes the number and nature of applicants, as well as certain characteristics of the winner. She felt that the organization problem really focused on the hiring process and that her recommendations should concentrate on the decision-making event itself.

Evaluation Research.   The unit of analysis in evaluation research is slightly more complicated. The unit is the *target* of the program or policy to be evaluated; it is not the program or policy itself. For example, a new accounting method is intended to improve the cash flow of *branch plants,* a new public relations office is set up to improve corporate media coverage in *news items,* and a new accident awareness program is targeted to *employees.*

The research questions in evaluation research are particularly important because they indicate who or what the target is. The primary dependent variables in the research questions will pertain to attributes of the target.

CASE EXAMPLE

A small food manufacturer wanted to develop a new package to improve point-of-sale response to an upscale frozen food product featuring wild rice. After a review of existing research on package design and consumer attitudes, a new package was designed and tried out in several selected regions. The marketing manager then wanted to evaluate the impact of the new, more costly packaging. The key variable for the evaluation research was "packaging design" and the research questions included, "Is brand awareness higher as a result of the new packaging?" and "Is the new packaging triggering more purchase decisions?" These questions required information about the perceptions and behavior of individual shoppers. The grocery store shopper was chosen as the unit of analysis.

Consistency

In order to analyze data, the unit of analysis must be consistent among the key and primary variables in the research questions. Just as you cannot compare apples and oranges, you cannot analyze data consisting of variables from different levels of analysis. (In some instances, however, data can be converted upward or downward from one level to another. See Chapter 5.)

Where the research questions imply more than one unit of analysis, the researcher has two options.

BOX 3.1
CAMPBELL SWITCH: A CONTINUING CASE

Part Six: Choosing the Unit of Analysis

"You're here! Your message said you had good news!"

Roberta, carrying a squash racquet and sports bag, is in early and surprised to see George already at work. Judging from the cups on his desk, he's already on his third coffee.

"Yup! We got the go-ahead on the Ajax project from Ryan. He liked the memo. Wants a proposal on his desk by the end of the week. Complete with budget and work schedule. The works."

"You sound excited."

"Yeah, I really could get to like this stuff. Why don't you drop your gear and give me a hand?"

"Good idea, but let's move to my office. If I bring my bag in here, there won't be room for me."

In her office, Roberta suggests that they first work out the research design and then consider the proposal.

"That's exactly what I'm doing now," George says. "The first problem is what to focus on. We could just concentrate on each absence, but because there's so much else going on, we'll miss it if we just look at absences."

"So look at employees instead."

"Exactly. Use the employee as the unit of analysis. We'll get data about each employee."

"And test which of our hunches about the causes of the problem are true," adds Roberta. "If you look through the research questions on your memo, they all make sense at the individual employee level."

"So that's settled," says George, stretching out his legs. "Boy, you sure have room to spare in here."

1. Revise the list of primary variables and reword the research questions so that they all pertain to a single unit of analysis.

2. If this proves impossible because it neglects important aspects of the business problem, carry out a separate analysis for each unit of analysis. For example, analyze separately the questions about accountants (individuals) and the questions about costing estimates (events).

For example, the two research questions, "Is the employee's grievance rate related to job content?" and "Is the type of grievance related to job content?" imply different units of analysis: the employee and the grievance. You could change the second question to read, "Are employees in certain job categories more likely to file grievances of certain types?", or you could conduct separate analyses of data about employees and data about grievance submissions. Each analysis would require its own key variable, measured at the appropriate unit of analysis.

Number of Cases or Observations

If relevance and consistency are both about the same for several possible units of analysis, choose the unit that will provide the most cases or observations. (See Box 3.1.) The validity of statistical conclusions is generally greater with a larger number of cases, and in particular small numbers of cases or observations can provide only very tentative conclusions. For example, a researcher studying teaching effectiveness in a private school could use the class (22 cases), the individual teacher (34 cases), or the student (344 cases) as her unit of analysis. Since relevance was similar for all three options, and consistency was not a problem, she chose the student as her unit in order to obtain better statistical analysis.

As shown in Box 3.1 on page 93, it is frequently the case in business research that all three criteria are met with individuals as the unit of analysis.

ADVANCED TOPIC

Research at the "Wrong" Level: Aggregate Data

Occasionally researchers have to settle for a second-best unit of analysis. This sometimes happens with published or statistical data that are available only for a higher level of analysis than the researcher wants. For example, Ashenfelter and Johnson (1969) used data on the strike activity of *industries* to draw conclusions about strikes in *firms*. Such data are called **aggregate data.**

The principal reason for using aggregate level data is their ready availability at low cost compared to the difficulty of finding lower level information. However, these data encounter two problems: causal inference and relevance.

Causal Inference. Analysis at one level, when applied to a lower level, risks errors in causal inference. Causal relationships found at an aggregate level do not necessarily hold at a lower level. This problem is known as **aggregation bias,** and if the aggregation has a geographical basis, the bias that may result is referred to as the *ecological fallacy* (Robinson, 1950).

A change in level of analysis may even reverse the direction of causality between two variables. At the individual level, an employee's skill determines the wages he or she receives; at the aggregate level of the firm, the average wage paid by the firm determines the kind of employees it can attract, including their level of skill. Inferences based on the analysis of aggregate data must therefore be made with caution (Langbein and Lichtman, 1978).

Relevance. A second problem with aggregate data is that the relevance of the research may be impaired. Conclusions and recommendations based on a higher level of analysis may not apply as directly to the organization's problem or question. Aggregate data may not reflect the level of analysis at which the phenomenon of interest is occurring or the level at which decisions are made.

For these reasons, whenever possible the unit of analysis should correspond to the level at which the researcher wants to draw conclusions.

THE THREE BASIC DESIGNS

Following the selection of unit of analysis, the second design decision is a **basic design.** Researchers have three basic designs to choose from:

1. • true experimental
2. • quasi-experimental
3. • nonexperimental[1]

The basic design affects a researcher's ability to investigate relationships, particularly causal ones. It determines the quality of the researcher's test of whether a relationship exists (in prediction research) and, if it does, whether it is a true causal relationship (in evaluation and explanatory research).

Descriptive Research. Because descriptive research does not involve relationships between two or more variables, *no basic design choice is necessary.* For example, determining average return on total equity for a set of franchise operations requires no investigation of relationships among variables.

Descriptive research often breaks down key variable data by demographic categories (e.g., sales by region, productivity by gender) but it does not investigate the causal or correlational relationships between the key variable and the breakdown categories. Such an effort would become explanatory or prediction research.

We begin with a brief description of each of the three types of basic designs, and then we consider how well each of them supports causal inference.

True Experimental Designs

Compared to the other basic designs, true experimental designs have two distinguishing characteristics:

SUGGESTION

If you're doing descriptive research, once you've made your unit of analysis decision you can proceed directly to variable decisions (Chapter 5) and sampling decisions (Chapters 6 and 7).

[1]Unfortunately, the term *experiment* is used in two different ways. First, it refers to a type of *design* featuring manipulated variables. Second, it refers to the data-gathering *methodology* of projects using this design. To reduce the confusion, we use the term *true experiment* to refer to the design and *experiment* to refer to the methodology. This chapter discusses true experimental designs. The techniques and procedures of experimental research are discussed in Chapter 11. Similarly, following Cook and Campbell (1979), we use the term *nonexperimental design* rather than the frequently found *correlational design* to avoid the ambiguities they catalog.

- One or more manipulated independent variables

- Random assignment of cases to experimental groups

The elemental true experiment consists of cases randomly assigned to two experimental groups. The researcher administers a treatment (representing one value of the manipulated independent variable) to one group (the treatment condition) and leaves the other as a control group. The researcher compares the groups to see whether the treatment had any effect. In practice, researchers often use three or more groups, with each receiving a slightly different treatment.

CASE EXAMPLE

A market researcher decides that a pilot project is needed to evaluate which of three different television commercials (A, B, or C) is most effective. From a list of people interested in participating in this kind of research, she randomly chooses three groups of 24 people each. One at a time, in random order, participants watch 20 minutes of television consisting of 16 minutes of a comedy show and four commercials. The 20 minutes are identical for all three conditions except that one of the four commercials is commercial A, B, or C, depending on the condition. The test commercial is always shown at the 11-minute mark. The other three commercials are for noncompeting products. After the viewing session, the participants fill out a brief questionnaire. Then they are interviewed about their recall of the commercials and their reactions to the commercial being tested. On the basis of her analysis of the results, the market researcher suggests that commercial B be adopted for use in an upcoming advertising campaign.

Manipulated Independent Variable(s)

Business researchers or managers manipulate independent variables either of two ways:

- *By creating or changing a situation.* For example, a union can change the situation by altering its strike pay policy in randomly selected locals. Members in the treatment locals are paid for hours of picket duty rather than by number of dependents.

- *By using differential treatment of individuals or bodies.* A corporation can impose differential treatment by dictating new accounting procedures for half its subsidiaries in order to evaluate the new methods.

In both, management or the researcher causes the independent variable to vary over a given set of cases in a manner that he or she controls.

Not all independent variables can be manipulated. For example, you can't dictate a person's gender. For these variables, the researcher must take values as they occur naturally among the cases. Other variables are theoretically manipulable, but their change is too disruptive, too expensive, or not feasible for other reasons. For example, a firm cannot be allotted a poor sales year in order to examine the effect on employee morale. In both these instances, researchers use nonexperimental basic designs. Among the variables that *can* be manipulated are rules, policies, procedures, and decisions over which management or researchers have control.

Random Assignment to Experimental Groups. Researchers use random assignment to create equivalent experimental groups. The logic behind its use is straightforward. If it were possible to find cases that were identical in all respects, the researcher could expose one case to the first treatment, another to the second, and so on. Then *any* difference observed among the cases would *have* to be a result of the different treatments.

However, since equivalent *cases* are virtually impossible to find, the researcher attempts to create equivalent *groups* of cases. He or she randomly assigns individual cases to experimental groups (conditions), one condition for each value of the manipulated independent variable. As long as the groups contain enough cases, the chance achieved by random assignment ensures that the average case in one condition is equivalent to the average case in another, thus achieving equivalent conditions. This means that any differences found between experimental *groups* following the manipulation are highly unlikely to be the result of preexisting differences in the groups. Note that random assignment can be carried out only in conjunction with a manipulated independent variable (think of "gender" again).

Within business research, true experimental designs are most commonly found in consumer research, since other functional areas frequently have difficulty achieving both manipulation and random assignment of cases.

② Quasi-Experimental Designs

Compared to true experimental designs, quasi-experimental designs have the following distinguishing characteristics:

- One or more manipulated independent variables

- No random assignment of cases to groups

The basic quasi-experiment consists of a group of cases that has been selected (not randomly) for a manipulated treatment and a convenient nonequivalent comparison group. The researcher compares the groups to see whether the treatment had any effect.

CASE EXAMPLE

A firm with branch plants in several states wanted to assess the impact of "equal pay for work of equal value" legislation in effect in two of the states in which the firm is located. The four plants in these two states were compared with six other plants in states without equal pay legislation. The comparison plants were chosen because of their similarity to the four original plants with respect to technology, size, and urban location. The job category was selected as the unit of analysis. The major dependent variables were ratios of women to men applying for jobs, ratios of women employed, rates of pay for women compared to men, and numbers of complaints or grievances over pay rates. A number of control variables were also measured. For each of the ten plants in the study, annual measures on all variables were obtained for three years prior to the first equal pay legislation (in state M), and for two years following the most recent legislation (in state N), a total period of seven years.

Like true experiments, quasi-experiments have one or more manipulated independent variables. A manipulation may be initiated by some party outside the organization, such as a government change in taxation legislation. **Natural experiments** involve situations that occur by chance, such as snowstorms and natural disasters. Because cases are not randomly assigned, natural experiments are equivalent to quasi-experiments.

Nonequivalent Comparison Groups. Instead of the random assignment of cases to conditions found in true experiments, quasi-experimental designs often begin with a group that has received (or is about to receive) some treatment. The researcher then looks for an existing or ad hoc comparison group as similar as possible to the treatment group. Because of the lack of random assignment, the comparison group is not equivalent to the treatment group. Also, the researcher normally has no control over which group is "treated."

For example, to pilot test a quality circles program a comparison group could be created in several ways.

- Compare employees included in the program with other employees not included.

- Use the group as its own comparison, and compare performance or other data gathered prior to the program with results after it has been in place.

- If all employees are included in the program, look for a similar plant (in terms of industry, products, size, union status, etc.) without a program and use it as a comparison group.

Quasi-experimental designs are encountered fairly frequently in evaluation research, since change is often manipulated, but random assignment of cases is usually difficult to achieve.

Nonexperimental Designs

Compared to the other two basic designs, nonexperimental designs are marked by the following characteristics:

- No manipulated independent variables
- No random assignment of cases to groups

The essential nonexperimental design involves a set of cases about which data are gathered. These cases are not randomly assigned to groups. No variables are manipulated; the researcher accepts the values that occur naturally among the cases. The researcher then examines the data to see what variables may be interrelated.

CASE EXAMPLE

A large public utility undertook a survey to find out what employees thought of the company and management and why. Questionnaires were distributed to 2,000 randomly chosen employees, 500 in each of the four major divisions of the corporation. A total of 1,774 employees responded. The results showed that, although there were major differences among departments and between men and women, the most important factor determining an employee's attitudes was the nature of the supervision provided by his or her immediate supervisor.

The designs just described are very common in business research and are the basis of almost all employee and consumer surveys.

Table 3.3 summarizes the fundamental differences among the three types of basic designs.

CRITERIA FOR CAUSAL INFERENCE

Researchers base their choice of a basic design on a number of factors. Often the most important consideration is how confidently they can make causal inferences. In other words, researchers seek the design that will allow them to conclude with most confidence that an observed relationship between two variables is causal, that is, that X really does cause Y.

- Evaluation and explanatory research require causal inference. Errors in inferring causality (or the lack of it) can lead to costly mistakes in conclusions and recommendations.

TABLE 3.3 ■ THE FUNDAMENTAL DIFFERENCES IN BASIC DESIGNS

	True Experimental Designs	Quasi-Experimental Designs	Non-experimental Designs
Manipulation of Important Independent Variable(s)	Yes	Yes	No
Random Assignment of Cases to Conditions	Yes	No	No

- Prediction research models require only the inference of covariation: researchers need not know the direction of causality or whether some third factor is responsible for an apparent relationship.

Causal inferences are generally strongest in true experimental designs and weakest in nonexperimental designs. To understand why, let us examine first what we mean by a causal relationship. We then consider how well each of the basic designs handles causal inference.

Criteria for Causality. In order to conclude that X is a cause of Y, three criteria have to be met:

- Covariation

- Time order

- No extraneous variables

Many researchers add a fourth criterion for causality: a plausible explanation. We now examine these four criteria in turn.

Covariation

Covariation is the first criterion for being able to infer that variable X causes variable Y. If a researcher wants to test whether X causes Y, he or she first determines whether X and Y covary.

The presence of covariation is established through observing the behavior of the variables or with a statistical test of association. For example, a researcher notes that

- Employees with greater seniority generally have higher productivity.

- Employees with higher levels of education have higher productivity.

- Employees who take longer coffee breaks have higher productivity.

For each of these relationships, the researcher has met the first criterion, covariation, for inferring that seniority, education, and length of coffee breaks all cause productivity.

Antecedent Variation. A prerequisite for covariation between X and Y is that each of the variables has to vary among cases or observations. If they vary together systematically, covariation exists. If they don't, there is no covariation. But without some variation in both variables, covariation is impossible. In other words, neither X nor Y can be a *constant.*

The most important variation is antecedent: variation in the independent variable or potential cause. As long as the independent variable varies, a causal relationship will produce variation in the dependent variable.

In evaluation research the boundaries of the initial problem, as presented to the researcher, often embrace only target cases, for example, employees involved in a new sick leave benefits program. Since all employees have been included in the program, there is no antecedent variation within these boundaries. In such circumstances, the researcher must enlarge the problem boundaries to include an existing group (which might be preprogram records) to serve as a comparison group and provide the necessary variation.

The lack of antecedent variation in prediction or explanatory research can sometimes lead to questionable conclusions. One may find, for example, that X does not vary, even though Y does. For example, in a group composed entirely of males, income may range from $20,000 to $30,000. Clearly, gender is unrelated to (variations in) income *for this group.* However, it would be wrong to conclude that, in general, gender is unrelated to income. Failure to understand this important point can lead to embarrassing conclusions.

Covariation between two variables, X and Y, occurs when X varies systematically with Y over cases or over time. As one increases the other increases, or decreases, or behaves in some orderly fashion.

Antecedent variation is existing or prior variation in the independent variable, either through manipulation by the researcher or naturally occurring variation among the researcher's cases or observations.

CASE EXAMPLE

Recent research has found that the effect of campaign advertising on the outcome of federal elections is insignificant—the two variables are just not related. This does not mean, as some journalists immediately concluded, that advertising has no effect and can therefore be eliminated, thus saving candidates considerable amounts of money. What it does mean is that, among the elections studied, the *differences* in spending between the two major parties were not related to *differences* in outcomes. Most likely, this was because the spending levels for those cases included in the research were fairly similar and didn't vary a great deal from one party to the other. However, common sense tells us that if one party stopped all advertising, the effect would probably be very noticeable!

Dependent Variable Variation. Variation in the dependent variable is less an issue. Of course, for a causal relationship the dependent variable must also vary. However, explanatory and prediction research begin with known or strongly anticipated variation in the dependent variable. The researcher gathers data to test which other variables covary with this variable and whether the relationships are causal.[2]

Evaluation research, on the other hand, begins with known variation in the independent variable (the manipulated program or policy). The issue is whether there *is* variation in the dependent variable and whether the program or policy is the cause.

Time Order

Time order is the second criterion for causality. Causes must precede effects; if X causes Y, then X must precede Y.

The time order of two variables is often obvious. For example, a person's gender precedes his or her job satisfaction. In such instances, time order is said to be established *theoretically*. In other situations, the time order of two variables is much more ambiguous. For example, attitudes may cause behaviors or vice versa. The time-order criterion becomes particularly complicated when dealing with anticipated effects, but the same principle holds: the anticipation must precede its effect.

In the three productivity examples cited, it is clear that time order is obvious only for the variable "education." For this example, theoretical time order is judged sufficient to establish that education level precedes work performance. For the other two examples,

- High productivity may cause seniority because employees with low productivity are weeded out of the organization (through no bonuses, assignment to less pleasant tasks, etc.).

- High productivity may cause longer coffee breaks because the efficiency of highly productive workers means they can afford to spend more time at their breaks and still maintain satisfactory productivity levels.

An **extraneous variable** is one which is related to both the independent variable (X) and dependent variable (Y) in such a manner that it produces the covariation between X and Y, rather than X causing Y.

In each of these examples, some other nontheoretical way of ruling out reversed causality has to be found.

No Extraneous Variables

The absence of any plausible extraneous variable is the third criterion for causal inference. In other words, the covariation between supposed cause and

[2]Explanations offered for phenomena (dependent variables) with no visible variation tend to be teleological. An example is the ancient explanation for gravity. The question "Why do things fall to earth?" was answered, "They belong there." Because gravity didn't vary, it was difficult to imagine what might cause it. For an interesting discussion of how social researchers deal with this issue, see Lieberson, 1985.

effect must not be the result of some other factor or condition E related to both X and Y.

CASE EXAMPLE

A researcher studied strike activity among firms in the auto parts industry. She noticed that whether a firm requested a mediator to help settle contract negotiations prior to a strike (X) and the amount of picket line violence when there was a strike (Y) appeared to covary. It seemed that a prestrike mediator "caused" picket line violence. However, the researcher suspected an extraneous variable: both X and Y were caused by the climate of labor relations at the firm (E). Poor labor relations might cause a firm to be more likely to call in a mediator rather than try to settle contract differences on its own. Likewise poor labor relations might cause violence on the picket line.

In this case example, the third factor "labor relations" may be a cause of both the independent variable "mediator" and the dependent variable "picket line violence." If this is the case, and there is no real direct causal connection between X and Y, the observed covariation between X and Y is said to be **spurious.** The dependent and independent variables only appear to covary because both change systematically with variations in the extraneous variable.

When an extraneous variable E is not a direct cause of the independent variable X, but only covaries with it, the extraneous variable is said to **confound** the apparent relationship between X and Y.

CASE EXAMPLE

A researcher evaluated the impact on sales of two different promotion schemes for a newly released record. Scheme A was given a one-week trial in Philadelphia; scheme B in Baltimore during the same week. The results showed clearly superior sales in Philadelphia during the week of the promotion. However, the researcher noted a possible confounding factor. A heavy snowfall in Baltimore during the promotion week might have reduced sales there.

In this case example, the variable "weather" covaries with the variable "promotion scheme" (good weather is associated with scheme A and poor weather with scheme B), but weather obviously does not cause which promotion scheme is tried in which city. Weather is therefore a confounding factor, and the relationship between scheme and sales is confounded.

Note that for both spurious and confounded relationships, the extraneous factor E causes the dependent variable. However, it may either cause, or only covary with, the independent variable. Figure 3.2 diagrams how extraneous variables lead to both spurious and confounding relationships.

Returning to the earlier three examples, the possibility of an extraneous variable, "foreman's experience," is clear in the productivity and coffee break

FIGURE 3.2
Extraneous
Variables: Spurious
and Confounded
Relationships

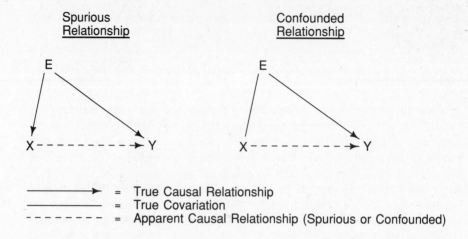

example. Perhaps foremen with more experience know how to motivate their workers to achieve high levels of productivity and also give their employees more discretion over scheduling their own time. Thus when work pressures are low, their employees take longer coffee breaks. However, the breaks have no direct causal relationship to the higher productivity of these workers. The extraneous variable "foreman's experience" causes both.

A researcher confronted with a possible extraneous variable E has to find some way of ruling out a spurious or confounded relationship before he or she can infer a causal relationship between X and Y.

As these examples show, *covariation is not enough to establish causation.* Not only must the relationship meet the time-order criterion, but the researcher must also attempt to rule out the existence of as many extraneous variables as possible. The more *alternative explanations* for the observed covariation can be ruled out, the stronger the inference of causality between X and Y (see Box 3.2).

Plausible Explanation

Some researchers add a fourth criterion for causality: there must be a plausible reason for the linkage between cause and effect. In other words, we must have an explanation for *how* X causes Y (Walizer and Wiener, 1978).

The researcher can normally supply a satisfactory explanation of the causal mechanism, and the investigation of such a mechanism is frequently built into the research design with intervening variables (discussed in Chapter 5).

BASIC DESIGNS AND CAUSAL INFERENCE

The preceding pages have discussed the criteria for causal inference. Let us now compare how the three basic designs fare in allowing the researcher to rule out alternative explanations based on time order (reversed causality) and

BOX 3.2
FOCUS ON RESEARCH
Causal Inference and Alternative Explanations

If two variables X and Y appear to covary, and the researcher would like to infer that X causes Y, he or she must check the remaining two causal criteria: time order and extraneous variables. This check really involves ruling out *alternative explanations* for the initial observed covariation between X and Y.

Alternative explanations for covariation between X and Y can take three different forms:

1. X does not really covary with Y *(erroneous covariation).*

2. They covary, but Y causes X *(reversed causality).*

3. They covary, but X and Y are both related to an *extraneous variable,* E, and there is no direct causal link between X and Y.

The first (erroneous covariation) can occur because of weak design, faulty statistical tests, or failure to remove distortions in the data. (We deal with this type of alternative explanation when we discuss specific designs and data analysis.)

The second and third represent alternative explanations for true covariation between X and Y. To eliminate the possibilities of reversed causality and spuriousness and confounding because of an extraneous variable, researchers use a battery of methods including research design, research procedures, and statistical tests.

Note that researchers cannot always rule out reversed causality, and they are never totally sure that all possible extraneous variables have been considered. Therefore, rather than "demonstrating causality" it is more realistic to talk of "ruling out alternative explanations." The more alternative explanations a researcher can reject, the stronger the inference that X causes Y. In short, *causal inference is a matter of degree.*

---

extraneous variables. We also consider other advantages and disadvantages of each of the designs.

Table 3.4 summarizes how well each of the basic designs meets the three major criteria of causality: covariation, time order, and no plausible spurious or confounding extraneous variables.

True Experimental Designs

Of the three basic designs, true experiments are best at establishing causality.

Covariation.   Because the independent variable is manipulated and antecedent variation is guaranteed, true experiments have little trouble establishing covariation if a relationship is truly causal.

Time Order.   Reversed causality is readily ruled out in true experimental designs. Manipulation of the independent variable establishes unequivocally the time order of variables: the manipulated variable comes before its observed effects.

TABLE 3.4 ■ CAUSALITY AND THE THREE BASIC RESEARCH DESIGNS

	True Experimental Designs	Quasi-Experimental Designs	Non-experimental Designs
Establishes Covariation	Yes, created by researcher	Yes, created by researcher	Usually, but may be a problem with antecedent variation
Establishes Time Order	Yes, through manipulated independent variable	Yes, through manipulated independent variable	Only theoretical time order
Design Eliminates Spurious Relationships	Yes	Most (the reason for manipulation may produce spuriousness)	No
Design Eliminates Confounded Relationships	Most	Some	No

Extraneous Variables. True experiments generally rule out spurious relationships and most confounded relationships. This occurs because of the combination of manipulation and random assignment.

When the researcher (or manager) randomly determines which cases receive which treatment, no other factor E can cause the manipulated independent variable. The researcher (or manager) is the sole cause. Thus the design rules out spurious relationships. As a result, the researcher does not have to anticipate which potential extraneous variables might produce spuriousness.

Confounding factors are also unlikely, although there is the possibility that some unanticipated chance event may occur in one condition and not in others and lead to differences in results between conditions. Thus the researcher must look for possible confounding variables accidentally associated with the manipulated independent variable.

Advantages. The major advantage of true experiments is the increased confidence they lend to inferences of causality. For important decisions with a great deal at stake, the added degree of certainty can be a significant factor. A second advantage is that they involve manipulated change and are therefore more directly related to management practice. Managers frequently implement or evaluate a change intended to improve the organization. True experimental designs lend themselves readily to planned and purposeful change.

Problems. The major problem is that random assignment is often not feasible. For example, in a field experiment to test advertising campaigns, it is impossible to assign randomly television viewers to different channels where different commercials are being aired. At best, one could randomly select different cities to view different commercials, a quasi-experimental design.

A second problem is that it may be unethical to provide only some of the study population with a valued benefit or "treatment," while withholding it from others. For example, a test of whether a program would increase employee morale might require giving prepaid medical plan benefits to some randomly selected employees, but not others. This action would raise ethical problems, to say nothing of the possible reactions of the deprived employees. (Chapter 4 suggests some design variations to deal with this problem.)

A third problem is that the statistics used with true experimental designs place a practical limit on the number of independent variables that a single study can handle. The limit is about ten. Finally, as we see in the chapters on specific designs and data analysis, the generalizability of results from true experiments in business research is usually limited.

Quasi-Experimental Designs

Quasi-experimental designs lie between true- and nonexperiments in their capacity to establish causality.

Covariation. Like true experiments, the independent variable in a quasi-experimental design is manipulated, and antecedent variation is guaranteed. This means that covariation is generally easy to detect if a relationship is truly causal.

Time Order. The manipulation of the independent variable assures the researcher that the cause precedes the effect, ruling out reversed causality.

Extraneous Variables. In quasi-experiments, with manipulated variables but no random assignment, there is a real possibility of extraneous variables causing spurious relationships. For example, the person manipulating the independent variable may be reacting to some other factor. This is frequently the case in evaluation research when a new program or policy is implemented because of some perceived problem. Thus a rise in the accident rate may prompt management to institute new safety policies. Although "safety policy" is a manipulated variable, it is caused by "accident rate." This leaves open the possibility of "accident rate" as an extraneous variable.

Confounding extraneous variables are an even greater threat. For example, when a new manager institutes a procedural change, productivity results could be due to the change or to the extraneous variable "new manager." Some characteristic of the manager, or just the fact of having someone new in the position, may be the true cause of any changes in productivity. Also, the fact that the comparison group is not equivalent to the treatment group means that some preexisting difference between the groups may confound the results.

Advantages and Disadvantages.   Quasi-experimental designs retain many of the benefits of true experiments while contending with the conditions that often exist in applied research generally and in business research in particular. As a result, many of their advantages and disadvantages lie midway between true experimental and nonexperimental designs, as shown in Table 3.5. These designs often represent a compromise between feasibility and ruling out spurious and confounding extraneous variables. As Box 3.3 suggests, they are often the only practical option in business evaluation research.

Nonexperimental Designs

Of the three basic designs, causal inferences are weakest with nonexperimental designs.

TABLE 3.5 ■ ADVANTAGES AND DISADVANTAGES OF EACH BASIC DESIGN

	True Experimental Designs	Quasi-Experimental Designs	Non-experimental Designs
Strength of Causal Inferences	Strong	Moderate	Weak, must be supplemented with multivariate analysis
Problems of Feasibility	Can be substantial	Slight or moderate	Not usually a problem
Ethical Problems with Manipulation	Sometimes	Less often	No manipulation
Design Easily Incorporates Organizational Change	Yes	Yes	No, but can be handled with multivariate statistics
Generalizability of Results	Moderate	Higher	Highest
Limit to Number of Independent Variables	Usually about 10	Usually about 20	Hundreds

BOX 3.3
MOVING SOUND: A CONTINUING CASE

Part One: Options for an Advertising Pilot Project

"It's been a while, ole buddy!"

"Sure has, Pete! Grab a beer and tell me how things are." George has a visitor—an old friend from business school has dropped over on a Saturday afternoon.

"Well, I guess they're pretty different from your situation up there at Campbell Switch. You probably have your own secretary, big office and all."

"Not all that big," mutters George.

"Got my first market research project. Not a lot of money for it, but really interesting. The folks I work for, Moving Sound, are operating on a shoestring, but if it flies we'll be in great shape."

"Let's see, you're selling records and tapes from old buses, isn't that right?"

"Right. Fifteen of them now at 12 colleges. We park near campuses and set up shop. Low overhead, easy access, and high visibility."

"I remember. Pink and orange buses. But what's the research?" asks George.

"Right now, we only advertise in campus papers. The question is, should we try some local television commercials around the shows students watch? You know, grade B movies, soaps, rock videos, stuff like that. Expensive, though, so we're going for a pilot project to see how it works."

"Sounds reasonable."

"My big problem is that I'd like to use an experimental design, but I just can't see any way to get it. I can't randomly pick one student to see the commercial and another not."

"And how would you know the effect, Pete, whether they bought something because of the commercial? Without random assignment, you're in trouble. Seems to me you've got problems with students as your unit of analysis if you do an experiment."

"Good point. The alternative is each bus location as the unit. But we don't have enough buses to create equivalent experimental groups, and my boss says there isn't enough money for commercials in more than two cities."

"Looks like you're going to have some kind of quasi-experimental design. How much time has he given you to do this?"

"It's she, not he. Sharon Dobbs. And the commercial will be ready in two weeks."

"Ouch!"

Covariation. Nonexperimental designs sometimes encounter a problem of insufficient antecedent variation. The researcher usually relies on knowledge, or a strong expectation, of variation on important independent variables. But if the researcher is wrong, the research may be useless. It is possible to select cases that, by chance, have little or no variation in some potentially important independent variable. For example, one could draw a sample in which all employees have about the same level of education. Without antecedent variation, there is no way of knowing whether education might be related to productivity, the dependent variable.

Fortunately, antecedent variation is not lacking in most business research. In fact, it is often part of the initial business problem (e.g., "Training methods are hurting sales" or "Sick leave benefit costs are higher in one plant than another"). If researchers find there isn't enough antecedent variation in the original problem boundaries, they normally expand them by adding a comparison sample or an additional time point (as we discuss in Chapter 4 on specific designs). In short, researchers using nonexperimental designs have to pay more attention to the problem of antecedent variation.

Time Order.   This criterion can also be a problem in nonexperimental designs. Researchers can rule out reversed causality only on a theoretical basis. When time order is theoretically ambiguous (such as whether an attitude causes a behavior or vice versa) researchers have no way of resolving that ambiguity.

Extraneous Variables.   Nonexperimental designs, lacking manipulated variables and random assignment, cannot rule out any spurious or confounding extraneous variables on the basis of the design alone. The effects of such variables must be controlled in other ways, typically through multivariate statistical analysis.

Advantages.   The major advantage of nonexperimental designs is their feasibility. They can be carried out in almost any situation, since they require neither manipulable variables nor random assignment. The number of independent variables that can be included is limited mostly by the fatigue of data collection. These designs are also high in generalizability compared to other basic designs, given appropriate sampling procedures.

Problems.   Their disadvantages include weaker causal inferences than other designs, particularly in ruling out spurious and confounding extraneous variables. By their nature, they do not lend themselves to evaluations of organizational change as readily as other basic designs, although some specific design alternatives partially overcome this problem. However, they are ideal for prediction research, which does not require causal inferences.

Table 3.5 summarizes the major advantages of each of the three basic designs for business research. Now that we have discussed the major differences among the three kinds of basic designs, let us consider the process of choosing the most appropriate basic design for the research project. (Note that within each of the three basic designs, different variations are used to rule out other threats to causal inference. Chapter 4 examines these design variations.)

CHOOSING A BASIC DESIGN

The selection of a basic design (true, quasi-, or nonexperimental) is the researcher's second design decision. The decision is based on the following four factors:

- The project's *general research purpose*
- Whether there is a *manipulable independent variable*

- Whether the researcher can find or create a suitable *comparison group*

- Whether it is possible to *randomly assign* cases to conditions

Let's examine each of these factors in turn.

General Research Purpose

The research purpose indicates whether a researcher needs to make causal inferences. If so, experimental designs are preferred. While neither descriptive research nor prediction research require causal inferences, both evaluation and explanatory research do.

- In *descriptive* research, relationships between variables are not even examined. In this sense, descriptive research projects have *no* basic design.

- *Prediction* research models do not require causal relationships; the inability to rule out spuriousness and confounding is not important. As a result, prediction research normally employs nonexperimental designs.

- In *evaluation* research, causal inference is normally very important. Before additional money is committed, the researcher must determine whether the program, policy, or pilot project caused an improvement, or whether the improvement is a result of other factors. Thus researchers prefer true or quasi-experimental designs for evaluation research and pilot projects.

- *Explanatory* research also requires causal inference. However, it is generally more difficult to meet the conditions required for experimental designs in this kind of research. As we see, the most common basic designs for explanatory projects are nonexperimental.

Manipulable Independent Variable

A true or quasi-experimental design is only possible when the researcher has one or more manipulable independent variables.

- In *evaluation* research, the program or policy to be evaluated has been manipulated already, or is soon to be. Thus this factor is seldom a problem in evaluation projects.

- For *explanatory* research it is often difficult to find a primary variable that can be manipulated without considerable expense or disruption to the business. Also, the search for causes very often includes a large number of independent variables. (The more manipulated variables, the greater the size and cost of a research project.) Thus these two conditions severely restrict the use of experimental designs in explanatory projects. However, if a research problem focuses on only one or two important independent variables and if at least one of them is manipulable, a researcher may choose a true or quasi-experimental design.

Existing Comparison Group

A requirement for a quasi-experimental design is the existence of an adequate comparison group, similar to the treatment group in as many respects as possible except for the manipulated variable.

SUGGESTION

If the situation contains two or more groups that naturally invite comparisons, you will probably use a quasi-experimental design if the comparison is on an independent variable and a nonexperimental design if it is on a dependent variable.

- In most evaluation research, manipulation of the key independent variable provides a comparison group: those included in the program or policy to be evaluated are compared either with those excluded or with themselves prior to the manipulation. A problem occurs if *all* individuals or units receive the manipulation and if there is no before data to make possible a before-after comparison. Because there is no comparison group, a quasi-experimental design is ruled out.

An alert researcher can achieve better research results by acting early to ensure a comparison group whenever the organization considers a new program or some change in an existing program. Ideally, the researcher can obtain both *before* data (through a survey or organization records) and a comparison group (by ensuring that only some parts of the organization are exposed to the change). Chapter 4 offers specific suggestions for such designs.

SUGGESTION

The quickest way to choose between a true and quasi-experimental design is to ask how readily you can randomly assign individual cases (persons, groups, firms, etc.) to the different levels of your manipulated independent variable without fear of too much contamination between the conditions or groups.

Possibility of Random Assignment

A true experimental design requires random assignment of cases to conditions to create control or experimental groups. This is often difficult with individuals inside an organization, but there are two circumstances in which random assignment should be considered:

- Instead of individuals, assign *intact groups* of cases (such as entire work teams, departments, offices, committees, and so on) to experimental conditions. For example, different work groups of employees can be randomly assigned to different coffee break treatments. Those work groups randomly assigned to condition A take one long break; the groups in condition B receive three short breaks. If there are enough intact groups, a true experimental design is both feasible and desirable.

An **intact group** is a preexisting interrelated group of cases, such as the employees (cases) in a work team (intact group).

- In projects that deal with individuals or bodies external to the business, it may be possible to employ random assignment. Consumer researchers do this by randomly showing subjects different forms of commercials, packaging, print advertisements, pricing, and other sales inducements. Clients could be randomly assigned to different reminder programs for overdue accounts receivable. Different purchasing procedures could be used with randomly assigned vendors.

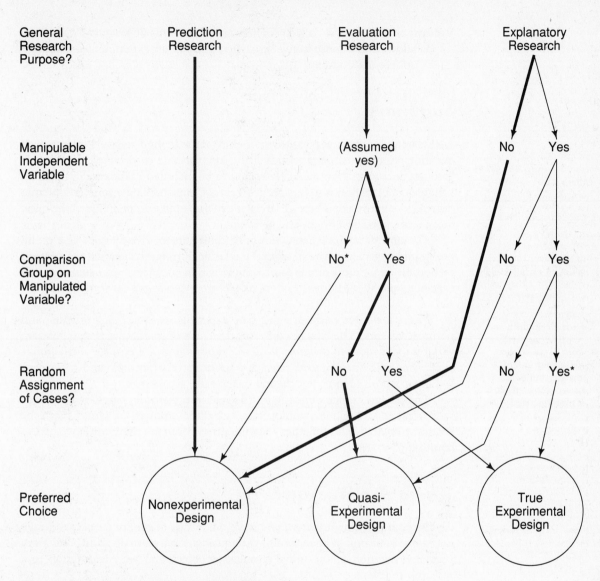

*This option is relatively rare in business research.

FIGURE 3.3 Factors in the Choice of a Basic Research Design

A decision tree illustrating these four factors is shown in Figure 3.3. The heavy lines indicate the most typical design choices in business research.

■ *The Lighter Side of Research*

Correlational study: The last two words of the phrase, "It is only a . . ."

Randomization: The assignment of subjects to conditions in an experiment according to some preconceived plan. Randomness, like chastity, is more often claimed than maintained.

Volunteer Subject: A college sophomore who, of his or her own free will, is allowed to choose between participating in an experiment or failing a course. (Woodman, 1979)

Summary

A research design is a plan for gathering data to find answers to research questions and to test ideas relating the key variable to primary variables. It involves decisions about which cases are to be included in the research, which variables information is to be sought for, and from which data sources information is to be gathered. The case decisions include the unit of analysis, the basic design, the specific design, and sampling.

The unit of analysis can be an individual person, a body such as a group or organization, an event, an object, a relationship, or an aggregate of persons or bodies. It should be relevant to the research problem, consistent over all variables, and should provide enough cases or observations for statistical analysis.

There are three basic designs: true experiments, quasi-experiments, and nonexperiments. The designs differ in their use of manipulated independent variables and random assignment. True experiments are best for causal inference; they rule out reversed causality, spurious relationships, and most confounding factors. Nonexperimental designs are weakest.

The design choice depends on the research purpose, whether the major independent variable is manipulable, whether comparison groups can be found or created, and whether individual cases can be randomly assigned to conditions.

SUGGESTION

It helps to have a clear statement of the research problem and research questions in front of you as you make your unit of analysis and basic design decisions. Post it over your desk.

Where Are We Now?

At this point in your research, you have made two of the fundamental design decisions: your unit of analysis and your basic design. Both decisions flow from your investigation of the initial business problem and your translation to a research problem.

As you continue the process of designing your research, the design decisions to come (specific design, variables, sampling) will build on, and relate to, your choice of unit of analysis and basic design.

Discussion Issues and Assignments

1. Check through recent issues of *Forbes* or similar magazines for articles reporting the success of specific organizations. Imagine doing evaluation research to check the report: pick a unit of analysis and a basic design appropriate for your evaluation. What would you need in the way of access to available data or employees in order to carry out the research? Compare your choices and answers with other students.

2. From any published source (*Wall Street Journal,* local newspaper, *TV Guide,* etc.) select three or four causal statements. Evaluate the extent to which the statements appear to meet the criteria of causality, paying particular attention to plausible spurious and confounding variables.

3. Debate the issue of the fourth criterion for causality. Is it really necessary? What about the causal conclusions you find in publications such as the *National Enquirer?*

4. If the circumstances in a firm were such that you could use a true experimental design, would you always want to? In general terms, when would you not?

5. Here is a small data matrix. As a test of your research imagination, how many plausible units of analysis and variables can you come up with that are consistent with the data? (Example: units are campus clubs, variable 1 is "size," 2 is "months since formation," etc.)

	VARIABLE 1	VARIABLE 2	VARIABLE 3	VARIABLE 4
Case 1	large	27	$284	no
Case 2	small	12	$ 47	yes
Case 3	small	18	$ 52	no
Case 4	medium	28	$112	no
Case 5	large	44	$ 88	yes
Case 6	small	8	$ 71	yes

6. Find the case example in this chapter in which data from a lower level of analysis is used as a characteristic of cases at a higher level. Make up two more examples of your own.

Further Reading

Cook, T. D., and D. T. Campbell. 1979. *Quasi-Experimentation: Design & Analysis Issues for Field Settings.* Boston: Houghton Mifflin.

Chapter 1 is an excellent discussion of the history and problems of the concept of causality and its relationship to experimental and quasi-experimental designs.

Langbein, L. I., and A. J. Lichtman. 1978. *Ecological Inference.* Beverly Hills: Sage.

A relatively advanced treatment of the problem of using data from one level of analysis to draw inferences at another.

Mitchell, M., and J. Jolley. 1988. *Research Design Explained.* New York: Holt.

A psychology text, but it has lots of useful information on true experimental and quasi-experimental designs and procedures.

Tsoukas, H. 1989. "The Validity of Idiographic Research Explanations." *Academy of Management Review* 14:551-561.

An interesting alternative view of causality and how to infer it using research procedures very different from the basic designs discussed here.

CHAPTER 4

Specific Research Designs

CHAPTER OBJECTIVES

- What makes one specific research design different from another?
- What are the research validity problems that researchers have to contend with?
- What are the most typical specific designs in business research? When are they used? What research validity problems are encountered?

CHAPTER OUTLINE

DIFFERENCES AMONG SPECIFIC DESIGNS
SPECIFIC DESIGNS AND RESEARCH VALIDITY
TRUE EXPERIMENT DESIGNS
QUASI-EXPERIMENT DESIGNS
NONEXPERIMENT DESIGNS
CHOOSING THE RIGHT RESEARCH DESIGN

Business research takes place in an imperfect world. Not enough time, not enough resources, late starts, problems with manipulations and measures—these are just some of the constraints researchers face as they design their projects.

- A researcher is called in to evaluate a company-wide safety program implemented five years ago. Unfortunately, the present measure of accident rates was implemented at the same time, and no comparable measure is available for the preceding period.

- A researcher is looking at effects of cash flow problems in certain profit centers. Unfortunately, there are only five such centers, not enough for any statistical analysis.

The previous chapter discussed the three basic designs: true experiment, quasi-experiment, and nonexperiment. Once the basic design is chosen, the researcher's next task is to select the best possible **specific research design** given the constraints the research faces.

DIFFERENCES AMONG SPECIFIC DESIGNS

Specific designs differ from one another in three ways:

- The *number of groups* of cases
- The *nature* of the groups: how they were formed
- The *time points* at which cases are measured

Number of Groups

The logic that researchers use to draw conclusions is based on two general approaches. The first is to compare two or more groups of cases. For example, do workers in older established plants have higher job satisfaction than employees in newer, more modern plants? The second is to look for covariation within a single group of cases. For example, is the age of an employee related to his or her job satisfaction?

- Some research designs use two or more distinct groups (typical of true and quasi-experimental designs).

SUGGESTION

When budgeting, consider the rough cost of adding a comparison group or sample to a single group design as a 40 percent increase in the total research budget.

- Other designs use only a single group of cases. The group may even consist of only one case that is measured at regular time periods (e.g., monthly sales).
- Still other research uses a single group divided into subgroups (typical in nonexperimental survey research when a sample of cases is divided into subsamples, such as male and female consumers).

Nature of Groups

Even though two specific designs have the same number of groups, the groups may differ in how the researcher formed or found them. The possibilities include random assignment, matching cases, matching groups, intact groups, and random selection.

Random Assignment.   As discussed in the previous chapter, groups formed by random assignment are the fundamental basis of true experiments. If one group is subjected to a new policy or program, it is called a *treatment group,* and the others are *control groups.* If different versions of some program are given to all groups, researchers use the more general term *experimental group.*

Matching Cases.   In true experimental designs, random assignment to experimental groups is sometimes combined with matching to ensure even greater initial equivalence among groups. Researchers match cases on important variables, such as gender and income, and then randomly assign cases within each matched set. For example, in a study with three experimental conditions, 30 employees are divided into 10 sets of three persons each, with the three in each set matched on age. The three are then randomly assigned, one to each of the three different experimental conditions of the study.

Matching Groups.   In quasi-experimental designs, researchers often look for an existing *comparison group* that matches as closely as possible the group which receives the treatment. This procedure sometimes takes perseverance and ingenuity. Occasionally several comparison groups are necessary.

Intact Groups.   Managers are often willing to allow an experimental design as long as all employees in a work group, team, or department are treated alike to avoid scheduling disruptions or other problems. In other words, random assignment of individuals is precluded, but random assignment of *intact groups* is allowed. Chapter 11 (pilot projects and field experiments) discusses in more detail the problems of using such groups.

Random Selection.   The cases used in nonexperimental designs are often randomly selected from some larger population (such as 100 mergers from all mergers in the country last year). Such groups of cases are called

samples, and when two or more are used in a study, they are called *subsamples* (such as 50 friendly mergers and 50 hostile takeovers). We discuss sampling in Chapters 6 and 7.

Measurement Time Points

In many specific designs the researcher gathers data from each case at more than one time point. These **repeated-measure designs** are particularly useful for assessing trends and changes over time, and for establishing the time order of variables in order to rule out reversed causality. They range from simple before-and-after designs with two measurement time points to designs that measure a case dozens of times over many months or years.

SPECIFIC DESIGNS AND RESEARCH VALIDITY

Researchers try to select a specific design that will maximize research validity within the time, cost, and data constraints of their research situation. They select the number and nature of groups and the number of measurement time points that will eliminate as many as possible of the threats to research validity.

Before we look at typical business research designs and how they deal with threats to research validity, we step back and take a broad look at these threats in general terms.[1] Then we turn to the specific designs and see which threats can be eliminated or reduced through design choices. Note that research design alone does not eliminate all threats: measurement and data gathering, as well as data preparation and statistical analysis, also present threats to research validity.

Research validity comprises three components: research power, internal validity, and external validity. We now look at each of these components and its threats in turn. To make the following material easier to understand, the threats are diagramed in Figure 4.1.

Threats to Research Power

Adequate research power is the first requirement for research validity. Low research power means the researcher mistakenly concludes that a particular relationship doesn't exist when it actually does. Threats to research power include the following:

[1]The following material is adapted from Cook and Campbell (1979) and extended to cover nonexperimental designs.

FIGURE 4.1
Threats to Research Validity

Lack of Research Power
(Result: "True" relationships are missed.)

Insufficient variation in dependent or independent variable	Uncontrolled or unmeasured variable related to dependent variable ("noise")	Random measurement error (unreliability); haphazard variations in procedure	Weak statistical test (type II error); too few cases

Lack of Internal Validity
(Result: Alternative explanations for apparent causal relationships are not ruled out; conclusions about characteristics or covariation relationships are inaccurate.)

Uncontrolled or unmeasured extraneous variable related to both dependent and independent variables (spuriousness, confounding)	Spontaneous change in dependent variable (maturation, spontaneous regression)	Faulty measures and procedures (validity and bias)	Violating test assumptions; outliers and other problem data; faulty assumptions about causal direction

Lack of External Validity
(Result: A characteristic, covariation, or causal relationship is erroneously generalized to the target population.)

Case selection error	Statistical test (Type I error)	Cause interacts with research constant, procedure, or measure	Change to tested program or policy following pilot test

- Designs or measures that don't yield enough variation in the relationship's variables.

- Designs that don't control or measure influential variables related to the dependent variable.

- Poor measurement and faulty procedures that introduce unwanted noise and variation into the data.

- Weak statistical tests that are unable to detect an existing relationship. (This is the "Type II error" of statistical tests; see Chapter 15.) Too few cases can have the same effect.

Research power is the capacity of a researcher's design, procedures, and data analysis to discover covariation relationships that actually exist.

Research Power and Specific Designs. The first threat can often be reduced by choosing an appropriate design. Sufficient variation is often a matter of selecting a group that will have the necessary variation among its members or choosing a manipulation with enough impact to create sufficient variation. (Sufficient variation is discussed in more detail in Chapter 5.)

Unmeasured and uncontrolled variables are a more serious problem because typically the phenomena studied in business research have many causes. For example, absenteeism is probably causally related to gender, age, marital status, job satisfaction, overall happiness, work-related values and beliefs, health, blood sugar level, weather, season, family problems, the movies on television the night before, supervisor's personality, disputes with co-workers, and a range of other factors. All these variables cause variation in the dependent variable—absenteeism.

If important causes of a dependent variable are uncontrolled, research power is reduced. The variation they cause in the dependent variable (sometimes referred to as *noise*) may cloak the variation due to the independent variable of interest, which will make it more difficult to detect covariation due to a particular independent variable. In other words, the design will not be *sensitive* to this covariation. Therefore, even though researchers are not interested in most of the causes of a particular dependent variable, they must take them into account.

Variables can be controlled either (1) through design or (2) by measuring them and including them in statistical analysis.

- In true and quasi-experiments, researchers can control these other independent variables by adding one or two of the most influential ones to the initial design. The result is known as a **factorial** or **blocked design.** These designs add more groups to the research. A second alternative is to use a design that holds a variable constant (for example, study only large firms or male employees).

- In nonexperimental designs, researchers can control by adding one or more comparison subsamples to the design. (However, control through measurement and multivariate analysis is much more common in nonexperimental research.)

Factorial and Blocked Designs

In true and quasi-experiments, factorial and blocked designs consist of variables added to the initial design to control their variation. If the additional variables are manipulable, the result is a factorial design; if they are not, the result is a blocked design.

A factorial design comprises two or more independent variables, both of which are manipulated. Each combination of their values constitutes an experimental condition.

A researcher is investigating the impact of three different sales training programs. The initial design involves one manipulated variable: the training program. The variable has three values (levels): programs A, B, and C. To increase research power, the researcher decides to control two additional variables and add them to the design: sales team size (small and large) and team composition (all males, all females, and mixed). Both these variables are manipulated by the researcher as she forms sales teams. The result is a 3 × 2 × 3 factorial design with 18 conditions and "sales team" as the unit of analysis. One condition is "small all-male teams from training program A"; another is "large mixed-gender teams from training program C," and so on. The design is fully crossed since each value of each variable is combined with each value of the other variables.

A blocked design is logically similar, except that not all variables are manipulable. Each value (level) of the nonmanipulable variable (or each combination of values if there is more than one nonmanipulable variable) represents a block, and the initial design is repeated within each block.

Another researcher manipulates both training programs and bonus schemes for production department foremen to assess their effect on productivity. There are two levels of the training program (A and B) and two bonus schemes (C and D). To this initial design he adds two nonmanipulable control variables: gender (two levels) and age (three levels: younger, middle, and older foremen). The result is six blocks (e.g., younger males, older females, etc.). The 2 × 2 initial design (training program by bonus scheme) is repeated in each of the six blocks. The result is 24 experimental conditions.

(In practice, researchers try to avoid large numbers of conditions in their experiments. Six or eight is often regarded as a practical maximum.)

Threats to Internal Validity

A conclusion about a group characteristic, or a covariation or causal relationship, has **internal validity** to the extent that it is accurate *among the cases analyzed.* Plausible alternative explanations for the conclusion can be ruled out.

Internal validity is the most important component of research validity. Without internal validity, conclusions and recommendations are misleading and worthless. It is essential for all research purposes, from descriptive to explanatory. Low internal validity reduces the accuracy of conclusions about group characteristics in descriptive research and covariation relationships in prediction research. The most challenging threats to internal validity, however, are those that threaten causal inferences in evaluation and explanatory research.

Internal validity is threatened by eight factors that may produce apparent covariation between X and Y in the absence of a real causal relationship. These factors are summarized in Box 4.1. They fall into four broad categories:

• Threats due to unmeasured or uncontrolled independent variables *(extraneous variables)* related to both the dependent and a primary independent variable. Extraneous variables cause either **spuriousness** or **confounding** and are thus threats to causal inference as described in Chapter 3.

BOX 4.1
FOCUS ON RESEARCH
Threats to Internal Validity

UNMEASURED OR UNCONTROLLED EXTRANEOUS VARIABLES

1. *Spuriousness.* A third factor (extraneous variable) causes both X and Y, making the resulting covariation between X and Y falsely appear to be a causal relationship.

2. *Confounding.* An extraneous variable whose variation accidentally coincides with variation in X is the true cause of Y. Confounding variables include events, mortality, and group characteristics.

SPONTANEOUS CHANGE IN DEPENDENT VARIABLE

3. *Maturation.* The spontaneous growth or development of a case, rather than a change in X, causes variation in Y.

4. *Spontaneous Regression.* A second measurement is likely to be closer to the group mean than the first, regardless of any manipulation. This change, rather than X, causes variation in Y.

RESEARCH PROCEDURES

5. *Procedure Effects.* Research procedures and the act of measurement itself may cause unintended variation in Y.

6. *Procedure Changes.* If procedures, including the act of measuring, change during data gathering, or not all cases are dealt with or measured alike, the procedural or measurement differences may be the cause of variations in Y.

DATA ANALYSIS

7. *Statistical Tests.* A misused statistical test, because of violated assumptions or problem data, may falsely indicate that X and Y covary when they don't.

8. *Causal Direction.* Instead of X causing Y, Y actually causes X. Causality may even operate in both directions (reciprocal causation).

• Threats that result from spontaneous changes in the dependent variable: **maturation** and **spontaneous regression.**

• Threats due to poor measurement and research procedures: **procedure effects** and **procedure changes.**

• Threats arising from data analysis: **violating statistical test assumptions**, data with **outliers** (cases with unusually high or low values) and other problems, and *reversed causation* and other faulty assumptions about **causal direction.**

1. *Spuriousness.* Spuriousness (a third variable is a cause of both the independent and the dependent) is often a problem in nonexperimental designs and

occasionally in quasi-experiments. The solutions for eliminating spuriousness include

- using a true experimental design (random assignment).

- measuring all potential extraneous variables and testing for spuriousness with multivariate analysis.

2. *Confounding.* Confounding is a potential problem in all three basic research designs. It occurs when a third factor is associated with both the independent variable of interest and the dependent variable. This makes it difficult to determine whether the independent variable or the confounding factor is affecting the dependent variable.

There are three major ways confounding factors occur: events, mortality, and group characteristics.

Confounding events occur simultaneously with the manipulation of, or change in, an independent variable. An obvious solution is to include a comparison sample or group that is also affected by the confounding event but differs on the independent variable. However, this solution won't work if only one group or subsample is affected by the event. In experimental designs confounding events are called **history effects** when they affect all conditions and **local history** when they affect only some conditions.

The only solution for confounding events is to be aware of their possibility (see Box 4.2). If you detect one that threatens internal validity, take one or both of these steps:

- If it doesn't affect all cases to the same degree, include a measure of the potential confounding event so that its effect may be eliminated statistically during analysis. However, if the extraneous variable correlates perfectly with the independent variable, you will be unable to assess its separate effect and thus rule out the possibility of a confounded relationship.

- Add to your design a comparison group or sample not affected by the confounding event.

- Repeat the measurement for the confounded group at a later time.

Mortality is a second threat to internal validity that confounds an independent variable of interest. It refers to the loss of cases *with certain characteristics* from one experimental group. This could occur between the measurement points or between treatment and measurement.

The loss of just certain kinds of cases (as opposed to random attrition of cases) confounds an X-Y relationship in an experiment, since the originally equivalent or similar groups are no longer similar. Thus the independent variable X is related to this confounding characteristic, leaving the researcher uncertain about the real cause of any observed group differences.

BOX 4.2
MOVING SOUND: A CONTINUING CASE

Part Two: Confounding Variables

"The way I figure it, one major problem is going to be confounding variables. Things that happen on campus, or in the news, or maybe even tests and exams. Even the weather!" Peter Grant is explaining his test of the Moving Sound commercial to George over lunch.

"Yes, that really could affect sales and confound the effects of the commercial. By the way, do sales go down or up during exams?"

"Up, of course."

"And I guess there are bound to be differences between the site you choose for the test and the comparison sites."

"You bet. Different colleges go for different types of stuff, once you get past the current hits. We've even got a couple of buses that we have to stock with extra country and western." He shudders.

"Now just a minute." George gives him a playful punch on the shoulder. "Nothing wrong with that. Why I remember Tammy Wynette got me through accounting."

"No accounting for taste, forgive the pun," Pete retorts. "Anyway, you can see the problem."

CASE EXAMPLE

An experimental test of a new office word processing software program randomly assigned 38 corporate offices to the treatment and control groups, 19 in each. However secretaries in 9 of the 19 offices in the treatment group found the new software difficult to use. The secretaries in these offices had to type many tables for technical reports, a task that was awkward and time consuming with the new software and resulted in decreased productivity. They abandoned the experiment and went back to using the old programs. However, the remaining 10 offices in the treatment group, which did not make use of technical tables, continued to use the new software. At the conclusion of the pilot project the researcher announced that productivity had sharply increased in the treatment group offices. However, a more experienced researcher suspected the effects of attrition, obtained measures of productivity for the offices that dropped out, and concluded that overall the new software lowered productivity, but that in offices which did not use technical tables, productivity increased. As a result, management introduced the new software only to those kinds of offices.

Two ways of handling confounding because of mortality threats to internal validity include:

- Use of multiple measurement points to permit analysis of effects of changes in group composition.

- Procedures to reduce attrition (rewards, encouragement).

Confounding characteristics occur when comparison groups or subsamples inadvertently have an unintended difference on some attribute. Thus this attribute is confounded with the *intended* difference between the groups (the independent variable of interest).

CASE EXAMPLE

A researcher studying job attitudes drew a sample of employees with low seniority levels who had been with the company less than two years. She also drew a comparison sample of employees with high seniority. However, the high seniority sample, unlike the other, was composed mostly of highly skilled employees.

In this example skill level is confounded with seniority. Any observed differences between two groups could be a result of the first rather than the second.

This problem can occur easily in quasi- and nonexperimental designs, where it is often difficult to find comparison groups or samples that are equivalent in all respects to the treatment group or primary sample.

Solutions to the problem of confounded characteristics include

- Careful selection of comparison groups and samples to minimize differences, or the use of several comparison groups that differ from the treatment group in different ways.

- Measurement of suspected group differences so their effects can be calculated and controlled statistically.

3. Maturation. This threat to internal validity affects any designs with two or more measurement points or with measurement following treatment. Individuals grow more experienced and become more accustomed to new situations; groups grow more efficient as they learn to work together; firms learn to adapt to legislation. Thus growth and change within a case, rather than a change in X, may cause changes in Y. For example, an improvement in sales following the introduction of a product change may be a result of the increasing skill of sales staff rather than greater appeal of the product.

The solutions to maturation threats to interval validity include the following:

- Use a comparison group (doesn't completely remove the threat because one group may change more quickly as a result of some confounding characteristic, such as an age or gender difference.)

- In true and quasi-experimental designs, use two or more measurement points prior to any manipulated change in the independent variable of interest, in order to determine whether maturation rates are comparable between groups.

4. Spontaneous Regression. This is another example of spontaneous change in Y that falsely appears to be related to variation in X. It affects designs with two or more measurement points.

Here is a brief explanation of how spontaneous regression works. Because of the random measurement error that most variables have, the second time you measure a case you are likely to find a slightly different result from the first. Furthermore, the second measurement of an extreme case is more likely to be closer to the group mean. For example, if a group of consumers has an average preference rating for a cheese product of 4.5 on a 10-point scale, and one of the group gave a response of 8.9, chances are that if she were asked a second time, her answer would be somewhat less than 8.9. The more extreme the initial result, the greater the tendency of a second measure to regress toward the mean. Notice that this regression occurs even if nothing else happens between the two measurement points. For this reason, we call it *spontaneous regression.*

This threat to internal validity, also known as *statistical regression,* or *regression toward the mean,* can make a program appear to be successful when spontaneous regression alone accounts for the improvement.

CASE EXAMPLE

A firm that manufactures frozen foods experienced an unusually high accident rate one quarter. The increase prompted management to institute a new safety program. Accidents decreased the following quarter, but a researcher was able to determine that the improvement was entirely the result of spontaneous regression, not the consequence of the safety program. In other words, the measure (number of accidents) of the variable "accident proneness" spontaneously regressed from its extreme value. The safety program was continued in a reduced and less costly form.

The solutions for this threat are

- Use more measurement points to find the true baseline against which the effects of a change can be compared.

- Use a comparison group or sample.

5. Procedure Effects. Research procedures and the act of measurement may cause unintended changes in the dependent variable Y. These effects are particularly troublesome when the effect covaries with an important independent variable, thus confounding the results.

Several examples illustrate the wide variety of procedure effects:

- A poorly worded question biases respondents' answers to a questionnaire. The questionnaire suffers from *measurement bias* (discussed in Chapter 8).

- Volunteers in an experiment which shows them several television commercials notice that the research assistant becomes particularly interested when one of the commercials begins. They pay more attention to that commercial. This tendency is an example of *experimenter effect* (see Chapter 11).

- Future interviewees are told about the research by friends who have just been interviewed. The friends tell them their personal interpretations of what the study is about. This phenomenon is known as *contamination* (Chapter 11).

- Members of a work team become aware that a researcher is observing them and making notes. They stop chatting and give the appearance of being intent on their jobs. The observation is an *obtrusive,* or *reactive measure* (Chapter 8).

Other procedure effects include

- The *testing effect* found in repeated measure designs when participants become familiar with the questions, and this familiarity, rather than some other independent variable X, changes their responses.

- The *Hawthorne effect* in experimental studies when people react to the novelty of being studied rather than the actual treatment.

Cook and Campbell (1979) mention three other procedure effects relevant to true and quasi-experimental designs in business research.

- *Compensatory equalization of treatments* occurs when authorities perceive that a treatment is beneficial to one group and attempt to compensate persons in other groups for their disadvantage. In doing so, they reduce the original differences between the groups created by the researcher's manipulation.

- *Compensatory rivalry* is a threat to internal validity when members of groups not receiving a treatment try harder to produce the same effect as those receiving it, thus blurring differences between the groups on the dependent variable.

- *Resentful demoralization* happens when respondents receiving what they perceive as less desirable treatments react with withdrawal or hostility, leading to unintended effects on Y.

Solutions to the problem require, first of all, sensitivity on the part of researchers. Otherwise, procedure effects can be reduced through

- The use of nonreactive or unobtrusive measures.

- Separation of comparison groups to avoid contamination.

- The addition to the design of a comparison group with no pretest.

- Attempts to measure procedure effects and eliminate them statistically.

The chapters on measurement and data-gathering (Chapters 8 through 12) discuss other ways researchers can reduce procedure effects.

6. *Procedure Changes.* Like the people they study, researchers also tend to change over the course of a study. They become both more skilled and more bored with what they're doing, and so they add refinements and changes to procedures and measures. These changes mean that different cases or observations are dealt with or measured differently, and these differences may affect Y.

CASE EXAMPLE

A team of interviewers conducting a marketing study systematically visited 11 cities in turn, interviewing randomly selected heads of households. As the study progressed, they grew more skilled at asking for respondents' income. As a result, they got fewer upwardly biased answers as they moved from the initial cities to those at the end of the study. Data analysis showed, not surprisingly, some significant differences in income among cities. However, the real intercity differences could not be separated from the procedure change.

The type of procedure change just described is called *instrumentation*. It is a threat to internal validity with measures that rely on subjective or highly skilled judgments by researchers or that involve sensitive questions.

Solutions to procedure change research errors include

- As much as possible, using identical procedures and measures for all cases.

- Careful training of research personnel.

- Designs to detect and measure the effect of procedure changes.

- A measure indicating the sequence in which other measurements were made, to be included in the multivariate analysis.

- Detection of differences among research personnel by recording (as a variable) which interviewer or researcher was responsible for each case, and including this variable in the multivariate analysis.

7. *Statistical Tests.* The misuse of a statistical test can lead to the erroneous conclusion that X covaries with Y when it actually doesn't (a Type I error), or the extent of covariation is stronger than it actually is. The two most common errors are

- Violating the assumptions underlying a statistical test.
- Not checking the data for unusual cases that might distort the results of measures of association.

The best precautions are awareness of pitfalls in statistical analysis and how to avoid them, and an examination of each variable's distribution.

8. Causal Direction. Instead of X causing Y, it may be that the direction of causality is actually reversed, with Y causing X. (We encountered this threat to internal validity in our discussion of causal criteria in Chapter 3.)

CASE EXAMPLE

In a survey of employees following a strike, a researcher found that unfavorable attitudes toward the employer were associated with taking part in strike activities such as picketing and rallies. The attitudes were presumed to be the cause of the strike-related behavior, but closer analysis of the data showed that, for most employees, participation in the strike activities began for social support reasons and brought about a change in attitudes.

In other cases, causation between X and Y may work in both directions: Each causes the other. This *reciprocal causation* is difficult to detect without repeated measurement designs.

Faulty assumptions about causal direction are normally a threat only in nonexperimental research. To avoid it,

- Examine closely your assumptions about the time order of variables, particularly behaviors and attitudes.
- Use designs with two or more measurement points.

Internal Validity and Specific Research Designs. In general, internal validity is greatest for true experimental designs and weakest with nonexperimental designs. The more groups and measurement time points in a specific design, the greater internal validity is likely to be.

As we've seen, not all the threats we have described are applicable to all kinds of designs. Spontaneous regression threats, for example, only affect designs with repeated measures, and spuriousness is ruled out when groups are formed by random assignment.

Threats to External Validity

External validity is the final component of research validity. It is essential when a researcher wants to generalize findings. Note that a conclusion may have low external validity even though its internal validity is high.

Characteristics and Relationships.   On the whole, the generalization of characteristics is more problematic than the generalization of relationships. Whether the generalization is to future circumstances or to other cases, characteristics tend to change more quickly than the causal processes that underlie relationships. For example, the proportion of employees satisfied with wages will change from month to month, or plant to plant, more quickly than the causal processes that lead to wage satisfaction. We wouldn't be surprised to see the proportion vary from .65 to .75 in the space of a month, but we expect that perceptions of relative status, for example, will almost always be related to wage satisfaction. For this reason, external validity is a paramount concern in descriptive research, since it deals with characteristics rather than relationships.

Threats to external validity fall into four groups, as shown in Box 4.3.

1. Case Selection Error. The way cases are sampled, chosen, or self-selected for the research will limit generalizability if these cases are not representative of the population of interest. A relationship between X and Y for these cases may not hold for others. In other words, some characteristic of the cases in the research, which is not found in the population, may combine or interact with X to produce Y; in the absence of this characteristic X has a different or no effect on Y.

The following examples illustrate case selection threats to external validity:

- An experiment on effectiveness of print ads randomly assigned volunteers to four conditions, one for each advertisement. Although one ad proved to be most effective among the volunteers, it failed to produce the expected response when used in a nationally distributed magazine. Volunteers are more likely to be risk seekers or people who are bored and want a change of routine. Both seem more likely to respond positively to very dramatic advertising than the average consumer.

- A questionnaire sent to a random sample of union local presidents showed that they believed general union-management relations in the near future would be peaceful. However, the local presidents responding to a questionnaire are more likely to be those with the time to respond because of quiet industrial relations, compared to presidents of locals in high-conflict situations who have little time for what they perceive as low-priority activities.

- Similarly, plants with no major problems in sales, production, or other areas are more likely to participate in research initiated by the head office.

A conclusion about characteristics, covariation, or causal relationship has **external validity** to the extent that it can be applied to cases and situations beyond those specifically examined in the research.

BOX 4.3
FOCUS ON RESEARCH
Threats to External Validity

1. *Case Selection Error.* The way cases are sampled, chosen, or self-selected limits generalizability because these cases are different from the population of interest.

2. *Statistical Test Error.* A statistical test erroneously indicates that a relationship is not due to random chance when in fact it is.

3. *Cause Interacts with Research Constant, Procedure, or Measure.* When a cause X only operates in the presence of some condition or circumstance (a factor held constant in the design, a research procedure, or a particular measure), the researcher erroneously generalizes that it is X alone, rather than the combination of X and the condition, that causes Y.

4. *Changes to Program or Policy.* Following a pilot test, a program or policy is altered before implementation in the wider population, or the manner of implementation is changed.

There are several steps that can be taken to reduce case selection errors that threaten external validity.

- Encourage broad participation in the study to reduce self-selection and nonresponse. A variety of techniques are available, including rewards and callbacks.

- Keep the time and effort cost of participating in the research low. For example, use shorter questionnaires and interviews.

- Ensure that samples are representative. (Sampling threats to external validity are discussed in Chapter 6.)

2. *Statistical Test Error.* With respect to external validity, statistical tests indicate whether a particular relationship may just be the result of chance. The researcher may select a statistical test that biases the results toward finding a significant relationship when such a conclusion is unwarranted. (Researchers call this Type I error: See Chapter 15)

3. *Cause Interacts with Research Constant, Procedure, or Measure.* Researchers may erroneously generalize a finding beyond the cases in a study because the cause they deal with only "operates" in conjunction with some specific constant, procedure, or measure used in their project. Beyond the boundaries of the study, however, and in the absence of this interacting factor, the cause does not operate as the researcher believes.

By design, researchers often hold certain factors constant in their research. They don't allow variation on those factors. For example, a study of lobbying success might be limited to state legislatures and exclude federal lobbying, or consumer research on cookie preferences might be restricted to women. "State legislatures" and "women" are examples of *research constants*.

While this strategy increases research power by eliminating a source of variation the researcher isn't interested in, it may reduce external validity. Outside the research boundaries, the research constant, when allowed to vary, might combine or interact with X to affect Y. For example, the relationship between age and cookie preferences might be very different for males and females (perhaps because of diet concerns). This interaction between age and gender (cause and research constant) limits the generalizability of the research findings to women.

In general, the external validity of a conclusion that X causes Y may be limited to those situations with the same value of the research constant. Without the variable at that "constant" value, the relationship might be very different or disappear entirely.

This threat to external validity can also occur with variables beyond the researcher's control, as long as the variable is a constant *during* the research.

CASE EXAMPLE

A researcher conducted a comparison of broadcast versus print media advertising. When the study was replicated two years later, she found very different results. She concluded that, because the first study was carried out during the year of a presidential election, the participants had been sensitized by interesting and important current news events. In the absence of the presidential campaign, there was no relationship between medium and public response.

Here are some suggestions to counter this threat to external validity:

- To increase research power, don't hold constant any factors that vary widely in the target population to which you'll want to generalize your results.

- Be sensitive to inadvertent research constants. (This is a problem with much of the social-psychological research on college students and research that is carried out on males and unthinkingly generalized to females.)

- Be aware of particular events or situations that may interact with important independent variables. If you notice any, the research should be repeated at a time or location in which the event or situation is absent.

In most business research, the researcher cannot avoid dealing with participants or data. Unfortunately, sometimes the results are a combination of both an independent variable and some research procedure or measurement. In other words, the independent variable interacts with measurement or other procedures to produce the dependent variable. Without the procedure, the relationship between independent and dependent variable would not exist or would be different.

CASE EXAMPLE

A researcher examined managers' opinions about performance appraisals in a government department. He found that younger managers were much more likely to approve of performance appraisal interviews. However, he suspected a sensitizing effect of the questionnaire title, "Performance Appraisals, Promotions, and Fairness." Further research with telephone interviews and a different sample showed, in the absence of the title, no relationship between attitudes and age.

A pretest, the particular setting of the research, the cover letter to a mailed questionnaire, or some other aspect of the procedure may interact with X to affect Y.

Sorting out the effects of procedures is difficult at best. Here are some steps you can take:

- Scrutinize closely all procedures and measures.

- For surveys, use instrument pretests (not to be confused with measurement pretests) to find how respondents interpret questions and whether their interpretations are affected by earlier questions.

- Although expensive, replication of the research with different procedures and measures is an effective way of eliminating this threat to external validity.

4. *Changes to Program or Policy.* This threat is a potential problem in evaluation research and pilot projects using true or quasi-experimental designs. If, following a successful pilot test, a program or policy is altered before it is implemented in the wider population, or the manner of implementation is changed, the X_1 examined in the pilot test is not the same as the X_2 representing the revised program or policy. Thus conclusions about X_1 and Y may not apply to X_2 and Y.

CASE EXAMPLE

An absenteeism program included rewards for low absenteeism and interviews for those with frequent short absences. The program successfully reduced absenteeism in a pilot project and was then implemented throughout the firm, but without the follow-up interviews, which were thought to be too costly. The program failed to deliver the anticipated results.

One solution for this threat to external validity is to anticipate possible alternative manipulations and try to include them in the research.

External Validity and Specific Designs. Three aspects of specific designs can have appreciable effects on external validity:

- Pretest measures may sensitize participants and limit generalization to individuals who have been pretested.

- Nonrepresentative comparison groups in quasi-experimental designs make generalization uncertain.

- Groups or samples chosen to incorporate research constants may also limit generalization.

TRUE EXPERIMENT DESIGNS

The next three sections are intended to help you with your specific design decision. They describe a variety of designs in each of the three basic design categories. We begin with an explanation of the symbols used to diagram the specific designs, and then examine three of the most commonly used true experimental designs found in business research.

Symbols Used in the Specific Design Diagrams

Each line represents a different subsample or comparison group or experimental condition. The symbols in each line are shown in their time sequence, left to right.

X   An experimental manipulation. X_i represents the manipulation of category "i" of the independent variable X. (A second independent variable is represented by W.)

M   A measurement point. Different letter subscripts (e.g., M_A, M_B) indicate different measures of the same concept. Different number subscripts (e.g., M_1, M_2) indicate measures of different variables.

R   Group is formed by random assignment of cases.

---- A broken line separating two lines indicates that they are comparison subsamples, or nonequivalent groups in a quasi-experimental design.

m   The measure of a single case.

Consider this example:

$$R \quad M \quad X_1 \quad M$$
$$R \qquad\quad X_2 \quad M$$

Both groups are first formed through random assignment. The first group is then measured prior to being treated to form category 1 of the manipulated variable X. The second group has no prior measurement and receives the treatment corresponding to category 2. Both groups are measured following the manipulation.

Pretest-Posttest Control Group Design

The most frequently used true experimental design, pretest-posttest with a control group involves two groups formed by random assignment of cases and two measurement time points. A pretest measure provides additional evidence of experimental group equivalence.

The design can be represented as follows:

$$R \quad M \quad X_1 \quad M$$
$$R \quad M \quad X_2 \quad M$$

It can easily be extended to experiments with an independent variable having more than two values:

$$R \quad M \quad X_1 \quad M$$
$$R \quad M \quad X_2 \quad M$$
$$R \quad M \quad X_3 \quad M$$

Use: Pretest-posttest with a control group is often regarded as the ideal experimental design, although it is subject to some threats to research validity. It requires both pretest measurement and random assignment, which are generally difficult to find outside of consumer behavior experiments.

Example: A pilot test of the impact of a sales training videotape for a firm's sales staff to decide whether to use the videotape nationwide. In particular, the video is intended to improve ability to sell to newly appointed purchasing managers who tend to be very cautious. All sales staff in one division are asked to indicate which of their sales and attempted sales in the previous month were to purchasing managers who had held that position for four months or less. Using this information, a measure of sales performance to new managers is calculated (M). Then, one at a time, randomly assigned sales staff are shown 50 minutes of either the videotape (X_1) or nonrelated video material (X_2). Sales performance to new managers is measured again for the following month (M). Notice that each case produces two variables: pretest sales performance and posttest sales performance.

Alternatively, the design could be used to evaluate three different training videotapes $(X_1, X_2, \text{and } X_3)$.

Research Validity: This is among the better designs for minimizing threats to internal validity. Spuriousness is avoided (it's a true experimental design).

Confounding is minimized by running cases one at a time in random order. Any event is likely to affect only a few cases or, if prolonged, both conditions equally so that the control group can detect it. The control group and pretest allow the researcher to check for maturation, spontaneous regression, and procedure changes.

The only likely threats to internal validity are procedure effects and the misuse of statistical procedures. The major threat of the former kind is that sales staff will discuss among themselves the content of the training video. This contamination might diffuse the video's effects or lead to special efforts on the part of those in the nontraining group to match any gains made by the training group. The nontraining group might also distort their sales data or report new managers who fail to buy as "old" ones. Procedure effects from the pretest and case selection (sales staff from one particular division) may reduce external validity.

Variations: Typically a researcher will also measure several control variables. For example, including one or more quantitative control variables results in a design in which data are analyzed using analysis of covariance.

Posttest-Only Control Group Design

This design has two randomly assigned groups but only one measurement point following the manipulation.

$$\mathbf{R} \quad \mathbf{X_1} \quad \mathbf{M}$$
$$\mathbf{R} \quad \mathbf{X_2} \quad \mathbf{M}$$

Use: Often used when a pretest might have a procedure effect by "sensitizing" cases to the subsequent manipulation. This design is especially useful when the dependent variable is individual feelings or attitudes.

Example: In the training videotape example, the act of asking sales staff about their sales to new managers could result in a procedure effect. To prevent this, the equivalence of groups is achieved through random assignment but not verified with a pretest.

Research Validity: This design is open to confounding characteristics and maturation threats to internal validity. On the other hand, it prevents sensitizing procedure effects resulting from pretest measures and thus offers greater external validity.

Factorial and Blocked Designs

These designs are simple extensions of the previous experimental designs, with other independent variables added. If these other variables are manipulated, the result is a *factorial design*; if they're not, the design is *blocked*. For example, when an additional variable W with 2 categories is added to the pretest-posttest control group design, the result is

$$R \quad M \quad X_1 W_1 \quad M$$

$$R \quad M \quad X_1 W_2 \quad M$$

$$R \quad M \quad X_2 W_1 \quad M$$

$$R \quad M \quad X_2 W_2 \quad M$$

Notice that each condition is treated with a different combination of categories of the independent variables X and W.

Use: Used to either (1) examine joint effects of several variables together or (2) to increase research power by controlling one or more other independent variables.

Example: In the training videotape example, an additional factor might be exposure to a follow-up interview (W). The result is a 2×2 fully crossed design (2 levels of "video" and 2 levels of "interview").

Research Validity: Helps increase research power, since another important variable is controlled for.

QUASI-EXPERIMENT DESIGNS

Quasi-experimental designs fall into two classes:

• Those using one or more nonequivalent groups of cases for comparison.

• Those using a series of measurements of each case before and after the manipulation of the independent variable. These designs are called **interrupted time series.**

Pretest-Posttest Comparison Group Design

This often-used design features two nonequivalent groups and two measurement points.

$$M \quad X_1 \quad M$$
$$\overline{M \quad X_2 \quad M}$$

It is similar to the pretest-posttest control group true experimental design, except that the groups are not equivalent (no random assignment), as indicated by the broken line.

Use: Whenever random assignment can't be used, but manipulation is required or desired.

Example: In the training video example, management decides to show the video to all sales staff in a single office. The researcher selects a similar office (in terms of size and market conditions) as the comparison group to watch nontraining video material.

Research Validity: Confounding and maturation are particular problems because the two groups are not equivalent. As with all comparison group designs, external validity largely depends on the representativeness of treatment and comparison groups.

Comparison Group with Multiple Pretests

This specific design also uses two nonequivalent comparison groups, but employs two or more measurement points before the manipulation of the independent variable.

$$\begin{array}{cccc} \mathbf{M} & \mathbf{M} & \mathbf{X_1} & \mathbf{M} \\ \hline \mathbf{M} & \mathbf{M} & \mathbf{X_2} & \mathbf{M} \end{array}$$

Use: Very useful if maturation, procedure changes, or spontaneous regression are strongly suspected as threats to research validity. It is particularly useful if group differences might interact with any of these, such as one group gaining experience faster than another.

Example: In the video training example, it might happen that the two offices representing the best (or only) choice of comparison groups differ noticeably in the average age, and thus sales experience, of their sales staff. The use of this design will help to determine if ability to sell to new managers is changing at a different rate in the two groups.

Research Validity: The only major threat to internal validity in this design is confounding.

Comparison Group with Posttest Only

This weak design has two nonequivalent comparison groups but only one measurement point.

$$\begin{array}{cc} \mathbf{X_1} & \mathbf{M} \\ \hline \mathbf{X_2} & \mathbf{M} \end{array}$$

Use: Often used when the researcher begins work after the manipulation of the dependent variable has taken place and *no* pretest or proxy pretest is available. For this reason, it is sometimes called an *ex post facto* design.[2]

---

[2]Early researchers attempted to overcome the limitations of ex post facto designs by matching cases among the two groups. Current practice (thanks to computers) is to use the variables previously employed to match cases as control variables in multivariate analysis.

Research Validity: The lack of information about the equivalence of the comparison group threatens any conclusions about the effect of the manipulation. There are many alternative explanations for any observed differences between groups, including prior group differences, confounding variables, and maturation, spontaneous regression, and procedure changes. If the manipulation is done by someone other than the researcher, spuriousness may also be a problem.

This weak design can often be strengthened by adding additional comparison groups to control for alternative explanations:

$$X_1 \quad M$$
$$X_2 \quad M$$
$$X_2 \quad M$$
$$X_2 \quad M$$

CASE EXAMPLE

A life insurance firm adopted a pay equity policy for its head office female employees and, about a year later, asked a researcher to evaluate the effect of the policy on the job satisfaction of its women employees. The researcher realized that no pretest was possible, and that the obvious comparison group, males at the office, was hardly equivalent prior to the equity policy. She arranged for two additional comparison groups, a sample of females and one of males at the head office of an insurance firm without a pay equity policy, in return for the results of the research. With these four comparison groups she compared male-female differences in job satisfaction at the two firms, ruling out sex alone as a confounding variable.

Pretest-Posttest with No Comparison Group

This design is also very weak. It involves two measurement points, but only a single group.

$$M \quad X \quad M$$

Use: Used only when a policy is implemented in an isolated situation where no comparison group exists and no set of repeated measures is available. Fortunately, these circumstances are relatively rare. In general, even a poor comparison group is better than no comparison group at all.

Research Validity: This design is subject to many threats to internal and external validity. Only spuriousness and reversed causality are unlikely.

Example: In the following case example, a research design that at first seems to be without a comparison group is augmented with a group that allows the researcher to rule out at least some threats to internal validity.

CASE EXAMPLE

An evaluation of a new weekly indemnity program in a pulp and paper company was made difficult because the program was introduced for all mill employees simultaneously. However, the researcher noted that "woods" employees of the same firm, though working under vastly different conditions, came from the same local areas, were also unionized, and were subject to the same economic conditions. She used the "woods" employees as a comparison group, comparing the cost of weekly indemnity benefits for the two groups before and after the new program took effect in the mill.

Interrupted Time Series

This design uses only a single case with repeated measures of the dependent variable before and after the manipulation.

$$\mathbf{m \quad m \ldots m \quad X \quad m \quad m \ldots m}$$

The logic of time-series designs is that, if the manipulation of X has an effect, the pattern following the manipulation should be different from that prior to it.

Use: A good design to consider when there is no comparison group and only one case (or a group for which only aggregate data, such as office productivity) is available.

Example: The researcher in the previous video training example repeats the study for another firm. However, in this company there are only five sales staff, and data are available only for the staff as a whole. The researcher gathers from company records monthly data on sales to new managers for the preceding 12 months, runs the training program, and continues to collect sales data for another 8 months.

Research Validity: This design allows the researcher to test for the effect of trends representing maturation, procedure changes, and spontaneous regression as alternative explanations. However, confounding variables (especially events and mortality) and procedure effects remain as potential threats to research validity. In some cases, these threats are lessened if the period between observations is relatively small (but at the cost of possible procedure effects).

Variation: When there is more than one case available to receive the treatment (but too few to form experimental and comparison groups), researchers can make use of *pooled time series*. This permits some comparisons among the cases and also increases the number of observations.

$$\mathbf{M \quad M \ldots M \quad X \quad M \quad M \ldots M}$$

(Pooled time series are discussed in more detail later under nonexperimental designs.)

Interrupted Time Series with a Comparison Group

This design is identical to the previous pooled time series, with the addition of a comparison group. Here X_2 normally represents a group being excluded from a new program or policy manipulation.

$$M \quad M \ldots M \quad X_1 \quad M \quad M \ldots M$$
$$\overline{M \quad M \ldots M \quad X_2 \quad M \quad M \ldots M}$$

Use: A good design when comparison groups can be located but they are too small in size to permit simpler pretest-posttest designs. Repeated observations substitute for lack of cases. This design can also be used with only two cases.

Example: This design would be a good choice in the video training example if the researcher particularly wanted to rule out cyclical and seasonal effects on sales.

Research Validity: This design is considerably stronger than the previous one because of the addition of a nonequivalent comparison group. The comparison group reduces much of the threat of confounding factors; although group differences may be an alternative explanation, the pattern shown by the time series should make it possible to rule out much of this threat as long as the groups are reasonably alike (see Box 4.4).

NONEXPERIMENT DESIGNS

SUGGESTION

If you're not sure about enough antecedent variation within the research problem boundaries of a nonexperimental design, assume the worst! Either check it out, or choose a design variation to guarantee enough variation.

Researchers use two general types of nonexperiment designs.

• **Cross-sectional** designs use data gathered at a single measurement point.

• **Longitudinal** designs use two or more measurement time points.

Notice that no Xs appear in the nonexperimental design diagrams here. The reason is that no variables are manipulated in these designs.

Single Sample Cross-Sectional Design

This is the simplest and most common of all nonexperimental designs. M_n represents the measurement of n different variables (as opposed to just a dependent variable).

$$M_n$$

BOX 4.4
MOVING SOUND: A CONTINUING CASE

Part Three: The Research Design

"So that's what I recommend, Pete." George sips his coffee and tries to ignore the check a waiter has just placed on the table.

"An interrupted time series with a comparison group. Why?"

"First of all, you need more cases than just the three or four campuses. Using repeated observations substitutes for those cases. It also takes care of some of the threats to internal validity. For example, as long as you stay away from end of term, you won't find all the tests coming at the same time. And even if they do, you've got the comparison group."

"But what if the weather's lousy when we run the commercial?"

"If you think that weather's an important factor, then pick a comparison group close to the test campus, so that the same weather affects them both. But my bet is that there are other factors to control for that are much more important than the weather."

"What about this idea? We run the commercial at two different test sites, and we have a comparison site for each one."

"Even better. That could also help control for differences between campuses."

"Hmm. This is looking good. And by the way, let me pick up the tab."

"Glad to help. Now, let's talk about how to choose the test sites. And I want to think over how we might hand out questionnaires to customers."

Oblivious to the hovering waiter, they continue to plan Pete's research for Moving Sound.

There are no manipulated variables, no comparison groups, and no repeated measures.

Use: This design is used for most selection prediction research and much explanatory research. Because there are no manipulations or design controls, it best captures the amount of covariation occurring in the target population.

Research Validity: Reversed causality, spuriousness, and confounding are all potential problems with this design. Procedure effects involved in data gathering can also threaten internal validity.

Another problem with this design is the possibility of low research power because of a **truncated sample.**

Truncated Samples

A truncated sample is one in which certain types of cases from the population of interest are systematically omitted, such as poorly performing stocks (because the companies have gone bankrupt) or problem employees (they've been fired). As a result, such samples normally have one or more variables with limited variation (e.g., "stock performance," "presence of employee problems"). These variables will often show little covariation with other variables. Even if there is a substantial relationship between X and Y in the population as a whole, a truncated sample with limited variation on either X or Y will produce a much smaller *(attenuated)* relationship, or none at all.

CASE EXAMPLE

A firm was interested in the effect of leadership ability on job tenure among management. It wanted to test whether good leaders became more committed to the firm and stayed longer. Because most middle and lower level managers were busy preparing budget estimates, a sample of upper management executives was chosen for the research. This truncated sample had a limited range of leadership ability because the upper managers *all* tended to have fairly high levels of leadership. As shown in the figure, the researcher found that there wasn't enough variation in leadership within the sample to explain any variation in job tenure.

While a clear trend line relationship is apparent for the population of all managers, there is no evident trend for the group of upper managers alone: the M characters form an almost circular cluster.

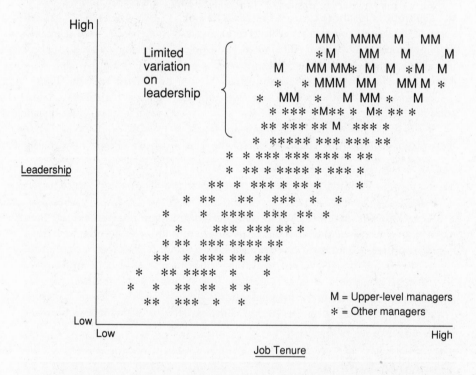

The problem of truncated samples is most prevalent in prediction selection research when a prediction model is based on a limited range of cases. For example, imagine that your firm decides to base its hiring on applicants' scores on several ability and aptitude tests that you think will predict productivity. If you attempt to develop a prediction model for the test scores and productivity using existing employees, you are very likely to find attenuated relationships between the test scores and productivity. This happens because these employees represent a limited range of abilities; most of those with low levels of ability were never hired or have been dismissed.

One solution to the problem is to use a comparison sample cross-sectional design and choose the comparison sample from a different range of the truncated variable. Statistical solutions to truncated sample problems are also available, but beyond the scope of this text (e.g., Berk, 1983).

Comparison Sample Cross-Sectional Design

This design includes samples from two or more distinct groups.

$$\frac{M_n}{M_n}$$

Use: This is the second most common design in nonexperimental research. Business researchers employ it

- to make direct comparisons among two or more distinct groups of interest.

- to provide antecedent variation in an independent variable of interest.

- to provide dependent variable variation in selection prediction research when the dependent variable has a limited range within the group of interest.

- to provide dependent variable variation in explanatory research when the organization problem is a uniformly high (or low) level of some behavior.

- with stratified samples. (Sample stratification is discussed in Chapter 6.)

If researchers suspect a lack of variation on an important variable, they often gather some preliminary data to help them decide whether to add a comparison sample to the research design.

CASE EXAMPLE

A researcher working for a political party wanted to target particular new party members for further political work by estimating their political commitment. She planned to develop a prediction model on the basis of commitment's relationship with age, gender, marital status, and other factors. However, the model would not be accurate if based on present members, all of whom were highly committed. (Those with low commitment had either quit or been persuaded to leave.) She drew a comparison sample of lapsed members to obtain enough antecedent variation for the variable "commitment."

Research Validity: Comparison samples help ensure sufficient research power, but suffer from the same threats to internal validity as single sample designs.

The Cohort Design

This is a variation of the comparison sample design, used to compare groups at different stages of some experience. The researcher draws comparison samples from *cohorts,* groups of individuals who represent different stages of progression through an organization or system. The members of each cohort group begin at the same time and progress together.

$$
\begin{array}{ll}
M_n & \\
\hline
M_n & (M_n) \\
\hline
M_n & \qquad (M_n) \\
\end{array}
$$

The measurement points in parentheses indicate that each group is assumed to reflect a different stage, or time point, although all groups are actually measured at the same time.

CASE EXAMPLE

The dean of a business college asked a researcher to study the effectiveness of a compressed 18-month executive training program. The program admitted a new cohort of student trainees each six months. The researcher took samples of students in the first six months, the second six months, and the final six months of their programs. By comparing the three cohorts he drew conclusions about the efficacy of the training program in improving management skills and altering job attitudes.

Use: Researchers use this design when the preferred panel design (discussed later) is not possible. It is much faster to complete, since it requires only one measurement time point.

Research Validity: The major threats to internal validity include confounding and maturation.

The Trend Design

This design gathers data at two or more measurement points, using a different sample at each point. The number of measurement points is usually only two or three, but may extend to a dozen or more.

$$
\begin{array}{llll}
M_n & & & \\
\hline
& M_n & & \\
\hline
& & M_n & \\
\hline
& & & M_n \\
\end{array}
$$

Use: Provides a picture of trends over time without using repeated measures on the same cases. This design is frequently found in public opinion research and consumer surveys.

Research Validity: A trend design helps eliminate two threats to internal validity: reversed causality and procedure effects due to repeated measures. It is subject to threats from confounding events, group differences, maturation, procedure changes, and spontaneous regression.

The Panel Design

Panel designs are similar to trend designs, but measurement is repeated on the *same* sample of cases instead of separate samples.

$$M_n \qquad M_n \qquad M_n \qquad M_n$$

Each case serves as its own "control," as in pretest-posttest experimental designs. The number of measurement points ranges from two to a dozen or more, but is usually fairly small.

Use: Frequently found in market research, particularly media audience surveys. A major advantage over trend designs is that it tracks the response changes of individual cases rather than just changes in population averages and proportions. This allows the researcher to identify the causes of changes in individual attitudes and behaviors (see Box 4.5).

Research Validity: Compared to trend designs, panel designs reduce group-difference confounding threats to internal validity.

Variation: A variation of panel designs used in political and consumer surveys replaces a small proportion of the panel at each measurement point. For example, in a monthly survey panel of 1,000 members, 200 new respondents are added each month and 200 dropped. Each respondent stays in for five months. This modification reduces respondent fatigue and thus provides more accurate estimates.

The Time-Series Design

This common design is based on repeated observations of a single case:

$$m_n \qquad m_n \qquad m_n \qquad m_n \cdots m_n \qquad m_n \qquad m_n \qquad m_n$$

Because more than one variable is involved and the focus is relationships among variables, the design is sometimes called *concomitant time series*.

Use: Researchers use time-series designs in three circumstances:

• When the research problem deals with variation over time rather than across cases.

BOX 4.5
RESEARCH ISSUES
Panel Versus Trend Designs

Tables A and B represent two sets of hypothetical data from a study of job satisfaction. Satisfaction is measured at two time points and categorized as either high or low.

Trend designs provide information only about population distributions at each measurement time point. This is equivalent to the row and column totals (called *marginals*) of the table. Thus a trend design would tell you that at time one, 25 of the sample of 100 employees had high job satisfaction, and at time two this number of employees had increased to 30.

The advantage of a panel design is that different individual transition rates may give the same marginal distribution and therefore the same trend results.

Panel designs, however, also provide information on the number of individual transitions between levels of job satisfaction occurring between the two measurement points. This information is found in the cells of the table, which show that 3 employees moved from high to low satisfaction while 8 moved from low to high.

Table B shows a situation in which 18 employees declined in job satisfaction, while 23 increased, and yet the population distributions (marginals) at each measurement time point are the same as in Table A. Clearly, the situation is much more unstable in situation B, information that only a panel design could provide.

TABLE A

		Time 2		
		High	Low	
	High	22	3	25
Time 1	Low	8	67	75
		30	70	100

- Conclusion from trend design:
  Job satisfaction increased from 25 to 30

- Conclusion from panel design:
  3 decreased but 8 increased in job satisfaction

TABLE B

		Time 2		
		High	Low	
	High	7	18	25
Time 1	Low	23	52	75
		30	70	100

- Conclusion from trend design:
  Job satisfaction increased from 25 to 30

- Conclusion from panel design:
  18 decreased but 23 increased in job satisfaction.

- To generate forecasting prediction models.

- When the researcher's only data source is repeated measures available data.

Example: A time-series design helps explain variations in monthly sales as a result of monthly changes in variables such as advertising budget, number of sales staff, number of loss leader specials, and indicators of economic conditions in the community.

Research Validity: Statistical problems frequently arise in time-series designs because observations are not independent, and may be serially correlated. (These problems are discussed in Chapter 15.) Spuriousness, confounding, and procedure effects can also threaten internal validity.

Variation: A time series with only one variable is called a *trend time series*. Researchers use it to predict future values of the variable by extrapolating from previous values of the same variable. This type of prediction does not make use of a prediction model based on relationships. It is a more sophisticated type of descriptive research.

ADVANCED TOPIC

Pooled Time Series. An important variation of the time-series design is **pooled time series**. This design is used when time-series data are available for more than one case.

$$m_n \quad m_n \quad m_n \quad m_n \quad \cdots \quad m_n \quad m_n \quad m_n \quad m_n$$
$$m_n \quad m_n \quad m_n \quad m_n \quad \cdots \quad m_n \quad m_n \quad m_n \quad m_n$$
$$\vdots$$
$$m_n \quad m_n \quad m_n \quad m_n \quad \cdots \quad m_n \quad m_n \quad m_n \quad m_n$$
$$m_n \quad m_n \quad m_n \quad m_n \quad \cdots \quad m_n \quad m_n \quad m_n \quad m_n$$

It combines features of both cross sectional and time series. Its use is largely restricted to explanatory research.

While the pooled time series appears similar to a panel design, the two are different, in that pooled time series normally comprise many measurement points and a relatively small number of cases, whereas panel designs feature a small number of measurement time points and a large number of cases.

There is also a difference in the emphasis of the researcher. Panel designs are generally employed to locate short-term trends and changes and to isolate the time-order differences of causes and effects. Pooled time-series designs are used to examine longer term trends and the different effects of cross-sectional and time-related variables.

Cross-Sectional Versus Time-Series Designs

It is important to note that cross-sectional and time-series designs do not explain the same kind of variation. Recall that a covariation relationship between X and Y is really the *variation in X* associated with the *variation in Y*.

- Cross-sectional variation is the differences among cases, and cross-sectional designs explain why one case is different from another.

- Time-series variation is the difference in the same case from one time to another, and time-series designs explain differences over time in one case.

Variables associated with one kind of variation are not necessarily associated with the other. For example, the causes of variations over time in gross sales for one store are likely to be very different from the causes of variations across stores in the same region.

- "Weather" is likely to be strongly related to variations in gross sales over time within the same store, but only weakly to variations across stores.

- "Store size" is one of the strongest causes of variations in gross sales across stores, but would vary little or not at all over time within the same store.

For this reason, researchers must be careful to pick the type of design, cross sectional or time series, that best suits the research problem.

The Retrospective Panel Design

In this design, researchers ask respondents for their *recollections* of behavior or attitudes at previous times (represented by parentheses), rather than actually taking measures at those times.

$$(\mathbf{M_n}) \quad (\mathbf{M_n}) \quad (\mathbf{M_n}) \quad (\mathbf{M_n}) \quad \mathbf{M_n}$$

Use: When repeated measures are needed, but there is no available data and no time to wait for future measures, this design is a fast and inexpensive way to mimic a true panel design.

Research Validity: The retrospective panel design suffers from obvious problems of measurement bias in respondents' recall. This is particularly the case when attitudes are being studied; recollections of behavior tend to be slightly better. Nevertheless, it often offers advantages over single sample designs that concentrate on present attitudes and behaviors.

BOX 4.6

RESEARCH ETHICS

Choosing a Specific Design

Management researchers seldom enjoy the luxury of the best design. Compromise is essential, but compromises raise questions of ethics. The researcher's commitment to "best professional practice" (the third ethics question discussed in Chapter 1) must be balanced against time and costs.

To choose the best *ethical* research design, follow these six steps:

1. Begin with the basic and specific design that seems most appropriate and relevant to your *research problem*. In particular, consider problem boundaries: do they suggest a natural group or sample?

2. Consider threats to *research power* and *internal validity*. List them, together with a rough estimate of their likelihood and their potential impact, and modify the design accordingly. For example, you may have to deal with a probable contamination problem or the fact that a pretest is impossible. Among specific designs, validity tends to increase with more comparison groups, more equivalent comparison groups, more measurement time points, and larger numbers of cases.

3. Appraise threats to *external validity* in your research. What threats exist, how serious is their impact, and how likely are they? Again, list them and modify the design as required.

4. Consider *nonmonetary constraints,* such as political and ethical problems, access to data sources, and data quality. Take into account organizational practices and norms. For example, can intact groups be split up for random assignment without disrupting production schedules? Again, revise the design to reduce these problems.

5. Consider the *cost of data gathering* in terms of money, personnel, and time. In general, more comparison groups and more measurement time points lead to greater costs. Designs with more than one measurement point take longer (although this isn't a drawback in most time-series designs using secondary data). Weigh this against your estimate of how useful the research results will be in both monetary and nonmonetary terms, short and long run, as you determined in your initial investigation of the problem. What's at stake? What is the cost of a faulty conclusion and a wrong recommendation? Modify the design as required.

6. Finally, go back and recheck the internal and external validity of the design you are now considering. The more important the problem, the more importance has to be attached to research validity. This is equivalent to asking, "What's at stake? How important is it that the research conclusions be correct? What would the wrong recommendation cost in the short term? In the long term?" Keep in mind that you may have to revise the unit of analysis or even the research problem itself.

BOX 4.7
CAMPBELL SWITCH: A CONTINUING CASE

Part Seven: George and Roberta's Specific Design

"I guess it does seem to be a little roomier."

"Sure it is. I just turned the desk a little this way, so my chair can edge back into the corner, and there we are. Room to meet!"

"Well, if you say so." Roberta looks a little doubtful. "But this research design looks good to me. Let's see if we've got all the angles covered."

"Comparison samples of employees from the two plants. It's consistent with the research problem, since employees are our unit of analysis. And we know that access to the files and to the employees themselves won't be a problem. Ryan really wants this solved, and now we have Sam Goodman at the Ajax plant on our side."

"It's not bad for internal and external validity, either. We'll have to watch out for procedure effects, though. The employees at Ajax are a little sensitive about this whole problem."

"It's also optimal in terms of time and money," says George. "And the two of us can take care of it really quickly. Is there anything else you can think of?"

The two continue to evaluate their specific design choice.

CHOOSING THE RIGHT RESEARCH DESIGN

Selecting a design is always a tradeoff between validity and cost considerations. Box 4.6 offers some suggestions for coping with the ethical dilemmas of selecting a specific design for your research. (Also check Box 4.7.)

The most typical design for *descriptive* and *prediction* research is a single sample nonexperimental design; alternatives will seldom be necessary. The most typical designs for *evaluation* research are the pretest-posttest comparison group and the interrupted time series with comparison group. For *explanatory* research, the most typical designs are single sample and comparison sample designs.

Note that the designs discussed in this chapter are not the only alternatives. Other researchers have developed ad hoc designs that deal with specific organizational constraints, and their reports are often worth study (e.g., Campbell, 1969; Cook and Campbell, 1979; Evans, 1975).

SUGGESTION

If you find it necessary to revise the research problem because the design required by the first draft is unattainable, be sure to discuss the implications with management to ensure that the results will still be relevant to the organization's problem.

◼ *The Lighter Side of Research*

Artifact: The only true fact in an experiment.

Control group: A group having some vague resemblance to an experimental group. In the ideal control group, neither flood, fire, nor famine will cause any change. . . .

Experimenter effects: All the effects in an experiment.

Field experiment: An experiment which should have been done in the laboratory.

Laboratory experiment: An experiment more appropriately suited for field research. (Woodman, 1979)

Summary

Each basic design (true experiment, quasi-experiment, nonexperiment) has a number of variations employing different combinations of groups and measurement time points. These specific designs differ in the degree of research power and internal and external validity they offer. Researchers try to select the design that best meets situational and organizational constraints and particular threats to research validity.

Research power is the capacity of a design to detect relationships that really exist. Internal validity is high when a design allows you to rule out many alternative explanations for a relationship. External validity is high when a design produces results that can be readily generalized beyond the specific cases involved in the research.

The choice of a specific design is based on the research problem, threats to research validity, situational constraints, and the cost-benefit ratio of the research results.

Where Are We Now?

With the choice of a specific design, we have finished about a third of our research design decisions. These decisions specify what groups of cases will comprise the data matrix we will eventually analyze.

The next task, and the topic of the next chapter, is to choose the variables we will incorporate in our research. Following this, we complete the research design by selecting a sample design (Chapters 6 and 7), which indicates how we will choose the specific cases from our actual target population.

Discussion Issues and Assignments

1. University courses are sometimes marketed in response to changes in demand. Choose a course and obtain both course descriptions (instructors' handouts are best, college calendars and brochures are a substitute) and enrollment figures (try the registrar) for the past five or ten years. Look for a change in the course content or structure following a year or two of low enrollments. Could any subsequent improvement in enrollment be explained as spontaneous regression rather than the change in marketing (course description)?

2. A dog food commercial is tested in Salt Lake City, Palm Beach, and

Calgary. Telephone interviews on the day following evening television exposure find high levels of day-after recall in the first and third locations. The researchers conclude that the commercial is not effective in communities with very high average incomes. What threats to external validity might reduce the generalizability of this finding?

3. "In general, if you're looking for greater internal validity in business research, add additional comparison groups to your design rather than additional measurement points." Debate this statement.

4. Select five research articles from journals such as *Administrative Science Quarterly, Accounting Review, Management Science, Accounting and Business Research, Decision Sciences,* and so on. Identify the specific design each uses.

5. From the same five articles, select two and state the principal causal relationship in which the author is interested. Think of a plausible alternative explanation for it. Did the author choose a design that rules out this alternative explanation, and if so, how is it ruled out? Can you think of a better design, if time and money were not a constraint?

6. Recall the last job you had (summer employment, job before the present one). From your point of view, what was the major researchable problem facing that employer? What kind of design would you use to research it?

Further Reading

Campbell, D. T. 1969. "Reforms as Experiments." *The American Psychologist* 24:409–429.

> A thought-provoking article with some innovative application of quasi-experimental designs to help overcome political problems in evaluation research.

Cook, T. D., and D. T. Campbell. 1979. *Quasi-Experimentation: Design & Analysis Issues for Field Settings.* Boston: Houghton Mifflin.

> A fuller treatment of true and quasi-experimental designs and more innovative solutions to particular problems in finding comparison groups.

Kimberly, J. R. 1980. "Data Aggregation in Organizational Research: The Temporal Dimension." *Organizational Studies* 1:367–377.

> A useful discussion of the problem of selecting time measurement points in longitudinal designs. Some of the discussion is also applicable to quasi-experimental studies with repeated measures.

Miller, D. C. 1991. *Handbook of Research Design and Social Measurement* (5th ed.). Newbury Park, CA: Sage.

> A good general reference that may help with specific research and design problems.

Seashore, S. E. 1984. "Field Experiments with Formal Organizations." In T.S. Bateman and G.R. Ferris (eds.), *Methods and Analysis in Organizational Research.* Reston, VA: Reston.

> A seminal discussion of the dilemmas and strategies of conducting experiments in organizations.

Spector, P. E. 1981. *Research Designs.* Beverly Hills: Sage.

> Treats a number of specific designs, together with the statistical analyses most appropriate for each. Most useful for true and quasi-experimental designs.

Warwick, D. P., and C. A. Lininger. 1975. *The Sample Survey: Theory and Practice.* New York: McGraw-Hill.

A good discussion of longitudinal and panel designs in nonexperimental research.

Winer, B. J. 1971. *Statistical Principles in Experimental Design.* New York: McGraw-Hill.

This is the classic work on true experimental designs and the statistical analysis of the data each produces.

CHAPTER 5

Variables and Data Sources

CHAPTER OBJECTIVES

- What are the kinds of variables researchers deal with?
- How does a researcher decide which variables to include in the research?
- From what data sources can a researcher get information corresponding to the variables?

CHAPTER OUTLINE

TYPES OF VARIABLES
DESIGN-RELATED VARIABLES
DROPPING PROBLEM VARIABLES
DATA SOURCES
CHOOSING DATA SOURCES AND VARIABLES

usiness researchers use a wide range of variables in their projects:

- The evaluation of a health and safety program gathered data on 12 variables, including employee's age, gender, seniority, job classification, marital status, number of accidents, type of accidents, and five other personal and job-related characteristics. The researcher obtained the data from three different company files: personnel, payroll, and accident reports.

- An explanatory investigation of consumer behavior for a breakfast cereal manufacturer gathered data with a questionnaire. The questionnaire provided information on 143 variables, including breakfast and morning habits, family purchasing behavior, and personal, family, and demographic data.

The choice of variables begins with the preliminary list that's part of the researcher's investigation of the original business problem. This list is then revised to obtain a consistent unit of analysis for all the variables, as discussed in Chapters 2 and 3.

The objective now is a final list of variables. To make your variable decisions, you'll also have to decide on data sources. The list of variables is the information you want about each case; the data sources represent where you'll get it. The two decisions are interrelated: variables affect the choice of data source, and data source affects the choice of variables. A data source with the information you want may be too costly, unreliable, or time consuming. Another more feasible data source won't include all your variables. Because of this interdependence, the decisions about variables and data sources are normally made in conjunction with one another.

We begin by considering how variables are related to one another and identifying six basic types of relationships.

TYPES OF VARIABLES

For all but descriptive research, the researcher begins with two different types of variables: dependent and independent. The whole point of the research is to examine relationships between one or more key or primary independents, and one or more key or primary dependents. The researcher usually has no trouble identifying these variables: they are implied or specified in the research problem.

But other variables may affect the relationship between any independent-dependent X-Y pair. If researchers want to know what's happening between X and Y, they must include these other variables in the research design. Our first question, then, is how can other variables affect an X-Y relationship? Once we've answered this question, we only have to anticipate these effects and include the appropriate variables in the design.

In all, we can identify six different types of variables based on how a variable relates to other variables. Each variable in a project belongs to one or more of these types (but not all research includes all six types). The types are as follows:

Dependent (key or primary)

Independent (key or primary)

Control

Extraneous

Intervening

Interacting

Listing and categorizing variables accomplishes two objectives:

- It provides a check on the specific research questions in your research problem; all but control variables should appear in the research questions.

- It helps your data analysis by identifying the kinds of relationships among variables you will want to analyze.

Key or Primary Dependent Variables

The dependent variable is the one you treat as an *effect* of one or more independent variables. The dependent variable is your *key* variable in *prediction* and *explanatory* research; it represents the phenomena you want to predict or explain. Dependent variables are the *primary* variables in *evaluation* research; they represent the consequences of the program or policy being evaluated.

- You expect a new training program for sales staff to improve sales volume. You also believe that it might improve repeat sales, customer relations, word-of-mouth leads, and customer recommendations. All of these effects are primary dependent variables in this evaluation research project.

Key or Primary Independent Variables

Independent variables are those you treat as *causes* of the phenomenon you want to explain or predict. In *prediction research,* primary independent variables are those to be tested for inclusion in the forecasting or selection model.

- In a selection problem you test whether the time an employee stays with the firm before seeking another job (the key dependent variable) can be predicted from the employee's age, marital status, number of children, education, years at last job, and self-esteem. All these factors are primary independent variables.

- To develop a forecasting model for predicting next season's ski resort vacationer days (the number of paying guests times the average length of stay), you include the primary independent variables advertising budget, ski lift ticket price, ski lodge room price, and the number of days below 25°F.

In *evaluation research*, the key independent variable represents the policy or program to be assessed.

In *explanatory* research, independent variables represent the primary potential causes of the phenomenon to be explained.

- You want to test whether business volume at your circus is down because of competition from television, poor advertising, media reports of pickpockets on the circus grounds, or people's beliefs that circuses mistreat animals. Each of these four factors is included in the design as a primary independent variable.

The diagrams in Figure 5.1 illustrate the relationship of independent to dependent variables in prediction, evaluation, and explanatory research. The independent variables are uppercase; the dependents are boldface. Causal relationships are indicated by arrows, and covariation relationships by lines. These arrows and lines represent the expected relationships the researcher wants to test. Note that the diagrams show prediction tests for covariation relationships, evaluation and explanatory test for causal relationships.

Control Variables

Control variables are other possible causal variables included in the research. They normally have little or no intrinsic interest for the researcher. For example, Christmas season retail sales are affected by the amount of snowfall. But in explanatory research to find ways of increasing sales, snowfall would be treated as a control, rather than a primary variable, since there is little the retailer can do about it.

Why include control variables? There are three reasons, all related to the fact that they affect the dependent variable:

- They allow researchers to control and adjust for their effects (using multivariate analysis) in order to *see more clearly the effects of key or primary independent variables*. This increases research power and make it easier to detect true relationships.

FIGURE 5.1
Dependent and
Independent
Variables

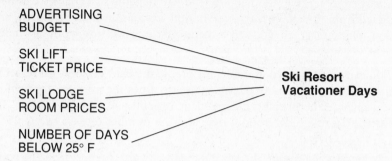

Prediction Research

ADVERTISING
BUDGET

SKI LIFT
TICKET PRICE

SKI LODGE
ROOM PRICES

NUMBER OF DAYS
BELOW 25° F

**Ski Resort
Vacationer Days**

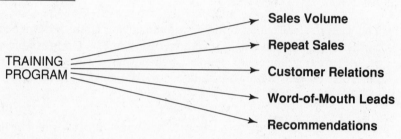

Evaluation Research

TRAINING
PROGRAM

Sales Volume

Repeat Sales

Customer Relations

Word-of-Mouth Leads

Recommendations

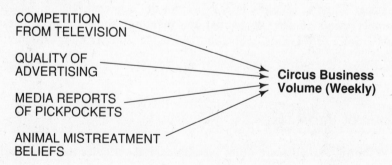

Explanatory Research

COMPETITION
FROM TELEVISION

QUALITY OF
ADVERTISING

MEDIA REPORTS
OF PICKPOCKETS

ANIMAL MISTREATMENT
BELIEFS

**Circus Business
Volume (Weekly)**

- They enable the researcher to *assess more accurately the relative impact of each primary independent variable* compared to as many other causes as possible.

- They *help prevent erroneous conclusions* about the impact or causal role of a variable because of the effect of an unmeasured variable. A control variable *may* turn out to be an extraneous variable or may have some other complex effect that, if not measured and controlled, would distort conclusions.

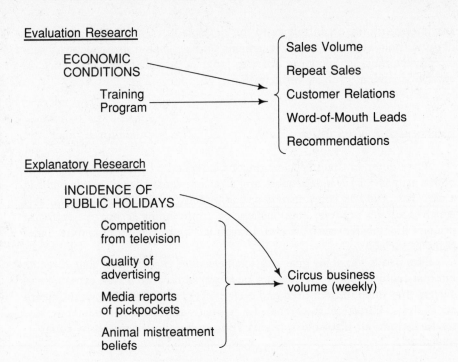

FIGURE 5.2 Control Variables

Figure 5.2 illustrates the addition of a control variable (shown uppercase) to the evaluation and explanatory situations shown previously in Figure 5.1. (Large brackets represent a set of variables, each of which has the same relationship to one or more other variables.)

Prediction Research.   Prediction models do not include control variables as defined earlier. None of the three reasons just cited for including control variables apply to prediction research, since the researcher is not interested in the effects of any particular variable. The task in prediction research is to find the set or combination of variables that makes the most efficient prediction. The only distinction the researcher makes among the primary (predictor) variables is whether their relationship to the dependent variable is strong enough to warrant inclusion in the prediction model.

Evaluation Research.   In evaluation research, control variables include all other potential causes of the primary dependent variables. Before assessing the impact of a new program or policy, researchers control for, and statistically remove, the effects of these other causes. In the example in Figure 5.2, the control variable "economic conditions," a potential cause of sales volume, is included so that its effect can be removed to show more clearly the impact of the training program.

Explanatory Research.   In explanatory research, control variables include environmental and situational variables beyond the control of, or of less interest to, the organization. In the example in Figure 5.2, the incidence of public holidays is beyond management's influence, but its impact on circus attendance must be known in order to judge accurately the relative effect of each independent primary variable.

Extraneous Variables

As we noted in Chapter 3, extraneous independent variables are related to both a primary or key independent and a key or primary dependent variable in a way that produces spuriousness or confounding. (An independent variable which does *not* produce spuriousness or confounding is just a control or primary independent variable even though it may be related to another independent variable.)

Extraneous variables give rise to alternative explanations that threaten internal validity. When they cannot be removed through a true experimental design, they must be measured and their effects controlled through multivariate analysis. Therefore, researchers using quasi- and nonexperimental designs try to include all plausible spurious and confounding extraneous variables related to

- The key independent variable in evaluation research.

- Any primary independent variable in explanatory research.

Extraneous variables that affect only control variables, however, are generally ignored, since the issue of whether a control variable's effects are true causes or extraneous ones is less important. Such extraneous variables are simply treated as other control variables (since they are still related to the dependent variable).

Figure 5.3 illustrates the addition of potential extraneous variables (shown in uppercase letters) to the evaluation and explanatory research examples from the two previous figures. The relationship for which the extraneous variable is an alternative explanation is shown with a dotted line and question mark.

In the evaluation research example, the variable "new manager" is included to test for a possible confounding effect: a new sales manager entered the firm at the time the training program began.

In the explanatory research example, the extraneous variable "urban/rural" allows the researcher to test for a spurious relationship. The covariation between "beliefs about animal mistreatment" and "business volume" may be spurious. Whether the circus is in an urban or rural location might cause both: city dwellers may have less time to come to the circus (because of competing attractions), and their beliefs may be a result of their lack of familiarity with animals.

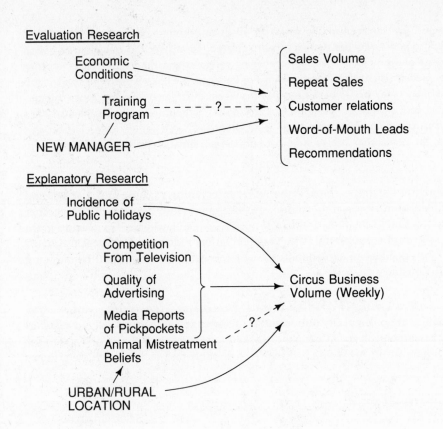

FIGURE 5.3
Extraneous Variables

Intervening Variables

Researchers are often interested in the causal mechanisms or processes at work in a situation. For this reason, they frequently include intervening variables in their research. Intervening variables (also called **mediating variables**) explain why the independent variable affects the dependent variable and help a researcher understand the original relationship. For example, a consumer researcher investigating why a new package leads to greater sales finds the mediating variable "optic attention." The color and design of the new package trigger more optic nerves, thus capturing the consumer's attention. "Optic attention" explains why the new package has higher sales.

An **intervening variable** (V) is a third variable located, temporally and causally, between an independent and a dependent variable. It explains the relationship between X and Y by suggesting a causal process linking them: X causes V which causes Y.

CASE EXAMPLE

In a study of 22 offices in a corporation, a researcher finds a relationship between the size of the office staff and office employees' job satisfaction. As it stands, this finding is interesting but vaguely dissatisfying, particularly if management wants to increase job satisfaction. To make an effective recommendation, the researcher needs to know why the two factors are related. To answer this question, he has to suggest one or more possible intervening variables and then test to see whether they mediate the original relationship. For instance, the linkage between size and job satisfaction may occur because office managers in larger offices are more bureaucratic and slower to respond to employees' complaints and problems. Thus "bureaucratic complaint handling" is a potential intervening variable. To test this idea, the researcher has to have data on the potential mediating variable.

Figure 5.4 illustrates the addition of an intervening variable in the evaluation and explanatory research examples from the previous figures. The researcher suspects that "sensitivity to buyers' needs" explains why the training program for sales staff is successful. The variable "effort required by viewer/customer" is to be tested as an explanation for why television viewing might be reducing circus business.

Intervening Variables and Business Research. Intervening variables are particularly important to business research, especially in _explanatory_ research projects. When you're asked to recommend a remedial action for an organization problem, it often isn't enough just to know which primary

FIGURE 5.4
Intervening Variables

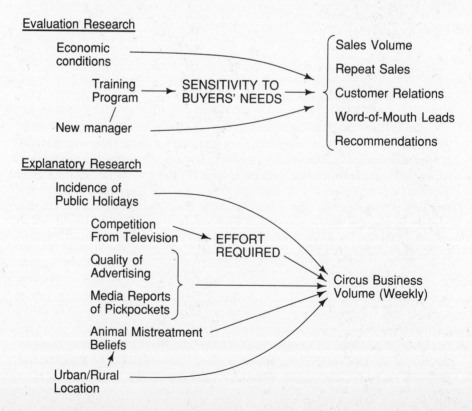

variable has the most impact on the key variable. You'll need to know the causal mechanism or process through which it operates.

For example, knowing only that office size is related to employees' job satisfaction isn't enough to produce a sound recommendation. A program to improve the handling of office workers' grievances will have little effect if the major intervening variable is the scope of employees' jobs. Thus, for research undertaken to deal with organization problems, understanding the causal process is essential, and this means testing intervening variables.

Intervening variables are sometimes important in *evaluation* research, particularly when a pilot project is found to be successful. Knowing why it works (through what intervening variables) is important in deciding whether to extend it throughout the organization, and whether it is likely to have the same effect if it is altered in some particular way. Intervening variables in evaluation research are therefore a way of testing the results of **formative evaluation,** the study of how programs and policies bring about their effects.

Coming Up with Intervening Variables. Sometimes inexperienced researchers have difficulty thinking of potential intervening variables. Three techniques are useful:

- As you develop the rationale for each primary or key independent variable, ask yourself *how* and *why* it is related to the dependent variable.

- In your literature review, check other research results for potential mediating effects.

- Whenever someone in the initial investigation suggests a cause, ask "Why?" or "How would that work?"

Note these other points about the use and testing of intervening variables:

- They require a leap of faith. Intervening variables are included in research to test for the explanation of a relationship, which itself has to be tested for. In effect, you are asking, "*If* variable X is found to cause Y, then what variable M might mediate that relationship?"

- You can test a chain of two or more intervening variables within a single X-Y relationship. For example, a sales training program may produce more customer recommendations because sales staff are more sensitive to buyers' needs, which in turn increases the trust buyers feel toward the salesperson. This trust, in turn, increases recommendations to other buyers because buyers are more likely to recommend someone they trust in order to maintain their own credibility and reputation. The result is three intervening variables:

Sales training program	→	Sensitivity to buyers' needs	→	Buyers' trust	→	Buyers' need to maintain credibility	→	Recommendations to other buyers

- How far should you extend a chain? In general, continue until you feel you would know enough to recommend a solution to the organization problem.

- An independent variable may affect a dependent variable both directly and indirectly through a mediating variable. (A *direct effect* between two variables is one with no intervening variable; an *indirect effect* is one that operates through one or more intervening variables.)

- A frequent problem is that data on potential intervening variables are unavailable. Many mediating variables involve attitudes, beliefs, and perceptions. However, only questionnaires and interviews can reliably provide this information. Observation and available data sources seldom provide measures of such variables.

Intervening variables that mediate control variables are normally ignored, since these causal relationships are less important.

Alternative Intervening Variables. Researchers sometimes include alternative intervening variables for a relationship and then test to see which ones mediate it. They may find two or more, each representing a different causal process. In the preceding case example, alternative causal paths for the relationship between office size and job satisfaction include the following:

- Workers in large offices are more specialized and have less variety in their jobs, which leads to low satisfaction (intervening variable = "scope of job").

- Workers in large offices see many others just like themselves and come to feel that they don't play an important part in the organization (intervening variable = "perceived importance").

- Workers in large offices have less access to management to make complaints and suggest changes (intervening variable = "perceived influence").

Occasionally you may find it difficult to anticipate the direction of a relationship; an increase in the independent variable might plausibly cause either an increase or a decrease in the dependent variable. For example, you might be able to think of good reasons why older employees would be both more likely and less likely to support a strike. This suggests that two causal processes might be operating in the relationship *in opposite directions*. To test this possibility, include an intervening variable to represent each opposing process. You can then determine (with multivariate analysis) which has the greater impact on the dependent variable.

Interacting Variables

Interacting variables have the most complex relationship with other variables. There are two types: moderator variables and interaction effects.

Moderator Variables. Moderator variables affect how a primary or key independent variable covaries with the dependent. For example, the length of a television commercial may affect viewer recall *except* during sports programs, when there is no effect. The moderator variable "type of programming" affects the length-recall relationship.

Moderator variables can affect an X-Y relationship in four ways: existence, strength, shape, and direction. However, they normally exert no direct effect of their own on the dependent variable. (If an interacting variable has its own direct effect on the dependent, it is generally treated as an interaction effect rather than a moderator variable.)

The *existence* of a causal relationship may be limited to certain situations. For example, a relationship between plant size and job satisfaction may exist only for assembly line technology and not for batch or continuous flow production. The variable "type of technology" is a moderator variable: it affects *when*, *where*, or *for whom* a given relationship holds. Only when the technology is assembly line does plant size affect job satisfaction; otherwise, the causal process does not operate.[1] In other words, *as the moderator variable M varies, the X-Y relationship turns "on" and "off."*

The *strength* of a relationship may vary from one circumstance to another. For example, a study finds that the relationship between number of dependent children and willingness to strike is fairly strong among men, but weaker among women employees. The moderator variable "gender" determines the impact the number of an employee's children exerts on his or her willingness to strike. *As the moderator variable M varies, the strength of the X-Y relationship changes.*

Some causal relationships have a different *form* in different subgroups or situations. For example, wage increases may be linearly related to productivity gains for skilled employees, but curvilinearly related for unskilled employees. As Figure 5.5 shows, the relationship is a straight line for skilled employees, but for unskilled workers, continuing increases in wages lead to increasingly smaller improvements in productivity. In other words, "employee skill level" moderates the form of the relationship between wages and productivity. More generally, *as the moderator variable M varies, the shape of the X-Y relationship changes.*

In some instances the *direction* of a relationship may be reversed from one group to another. For example, research shows that a crowded meeting room (compared to a large, uncrowded one) produces more competitiveness in males but less in females (Freedman et al., 1972). The interacting variable "gender" affects the direction of the relationship between room density and competitiveness. This kind of moderator variable effect can make it appear that there is no X-Y relationship when there are really two opposing relationships. For example, a group composed of equal numbers of males and females would show no overall change in competitiveness in moving from a small to a large room. *As the moderator variable M varies, the direction of the X-Y relationship changes.*

A **moderator variable** (M) affects the degree or form of the relationship between an independent and dependent variable: M affects X-Y.

---

[1]This is an oversimplified example. The effects of plant and work-group size are complicated and not entirely understood.

FIGURE 5.5
Moderator Variable
Affecting the Form
of a Relationship

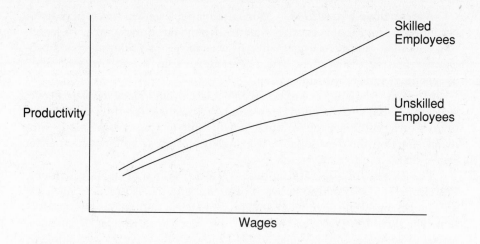

Interaction Effects.   The second type of interacting variables involve what are commonly called interaction effects. An interaction effect occurs when two primary independent variables have, in combination, a joint effect different than the sum of their individual effects. This kind of interaction is called *nonadditivity.*

An **interaction effect** is the result of two independent variables combining in a nonadditive manner to cause the dependent variable.

CASE EXAMPLE

A researcher observed that in one plant females have 5 percent more absenteeism than males, and younger workers have 10 percent more absenteeism than older workers. He expected these two effects to add to 15 percent higher absenteeism for younger females compared to older males (the effect of being female plus the effect of being younger). However, he found the difference between younger females and older males is actually 25 percent. He concluded that there was an interaction effect between gender and age.

In this example the effects of gender and age are nonadditive. There is something qualitatively different about the category "younger females" that leads to more absenteeism than would be predicted on the basis of just gender and age. (It might be having young children at home who need extra care.)
  Interaction effects differ from moderator variables in two important ways:

• Moderator variables normally have no direct effect on the dependent variable, but interaction effects involve two primary variables that may have direct as well as interaction effects. (Their direct effects are also known as *main effects.*)

• Moderator variables are included in the research only to test for a potential moderating effect. The primary independent variables in an interaction effect are included because the researcher believes their direct effects to be important.

Figure 5.6 illustrates the addition of a potential moderator variable to the earlier evaluation example and an interaction effect in the explanatory example. The moderator variable is shown with an arrow directed to the line of the X-Y relationship that it moderates. The interaction effect is shown with the causal arrows of the two independent variables joining (like the letter *Y* lying on its side).

In the evaluation research portion, the researcher suspects that "gender" moderates the relationship between "sales staff training program" and "sensitivity." If female sales staff are already sensitive to buyers' needs, the program will have no effect on their sensitivity.

Evaluation Research

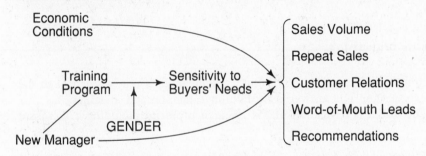

FIGURE 5.6
Moderator Variables and Interaction Effects

Explanatory Research

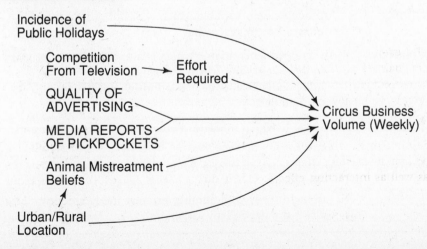

In the explanatory research example, the researcher expects that "quality of advertising" will interact with "media reports of pickpockets": if advertising quality is high, the report of a few pickpocket incidents (compared to none or many) will actually enhance business volume.

Interacting Variables and Business Research. Moderating variables are important in business research because they indicate the boundaries and limitations of particular effects. Knowing these boundaries can improve recommendations in evaluation and explanatory research. You can tell for what groups or situations a program will have the desired impact or a particular cause has a significant effect. Moderator variables also alert management to the possible need for different programs or policies for different groups or different types of employees.

Interaction effects also lead to more useful recommendations. Knowing interaction effects tells you under what circumstances a cause will have a greater-than-expected impact.

All six types of variables are summarized in Table 5.1.

Finding Variables

How then does a researcher find variables of each type to include in the research design? The answer is twofold: investigation and imagination.

The initial investigation of the research problem, including a literature

TABLE 5.1 ■ TYPES OF VARIABLES BY RELATIONSHIPS AMONG VARIABLES

Dependent	An "effect" of a primary or key independent variable
Independent	A "cause" of a key or primary dependent variable
Control	An independent variable which is of little or no intrinsic interest to the researcher
Extraneous	An independent variable which is also related to a primary independent, and which makes the independent-dependent relationship spurious or confounded
Intervening	A variable which mediates between the independent and dependent; it represents a causal process linking them
Interacting	A variable which affects the independent-dependent *relationship,* or a primary independent which combines nonadditively with another primary independent to affect the dependent variable

review, will indicate variables which are thought to, or have been found to, relate to the dependent variable. If they are not primary independents, they might be included as control or extraneous variables. Similarly, previous research might suggest intervening variables related to causal processes, or interacting variables, which the researcher can include.

The second way of finding variables is to use your "research imagination." Think about the processes going on. What else might cause the dependent variable? How might the primary or key independent variables operate on the dependent? Are there any groups or situations in which the process might not work? Are there any combinations of variables which might affect the dependent variable in special ways?

Generating Interacting Variables.

Like intervening variables, interacting variables are sometimes difficult to anticipate as you plan your research. Here are some suggestions:

- Ask yourself, while you're constructing a rationale for each independent variable (primary or key), whether you expect its relationship with the dependent variable to be the same for all groups and situations in your research. If not, add a moderator variable to test for potential differences in the relationship among groups or situations.

- Check back over your notes from your investigation of the initial problem. What differences did there seem to be among groups, plants, or situations that otherwise wouldn't make it into your list of variables? Such differences suggest moderator variables.

- Can you imagine any circumstances in which two primary independent variables may combine to produce a greater-than-expected (or less-than-expected) interaction effect? Your literature review may suggest some possibilities.

Tests for moderator variables also require an anticipatory leap of faith. You must add any potential moderating variables to your design even before you know there is an X-Y relationship to moderate because it is very costly to gather additional data once the analysis has begun.

The situation is easier for interaction effects involving primary or control variables. These factors will already be in your list of variables because you want to test their direct effects.

Complicated interaction effects involving three or more independent variables are possible, but seldom anticipated or tested for in business research. The data analysis of interaction effects is discussed in Chapter 17.

Rationales.

In the process of finding variables to include in the design, researchers usually formulate *rationales* for each of the variables they consider using. A rationale is a brief statement indicating why a particular variable is included in the research. It includes:

- What other variable(s) in the research it is related to.

- Why the variable is expected to relate to these other variables.

- The nature and direction of the expected relationship. A relationship's direction is *positive* if, as X increases, Y also increases. It is *negative* if, as X increases, Y decreases (and vice versa).

The major sources for variable rationales are the investigation of the initial problem and the literature review.

CASE EXAMPLE

The manager of a family-oriented ski resort carried out some market research in order to determine what changes he should make to increase his sales. He believed that one of the important factors in determining whether people would come to his resort was the "ages of skiers' children." The rationale, based on his own experience, was that as children grow older, their parents' needs change from instruction and child-care facilities to challenging hills and socializing opportunities for their teenage children.

Rationales serve three purposes:

- They help you decide whether a variable is really relevant or should be dropped from your list because it is unrelated to any dependent variable.

- They help you identify what role each variable plays in your research, that is, what type it is.

- The process of working out rationales may help you think of additional variables for the research.

DESIGN-RELATED VARIABLES

To deal with particular problems and constraints, research designs may require the addition of design-related variables. These include group identifiers, repeated measure, lagged, retrospective, structural, and contextual variables.

Group Identifiers

When a specific design involves two or more distinct groups or subsamples, the researcher must be able to identify to which group each case belongs.

Group identifier variables are usually independent variables; on rare occasions in nonexperimental research subsamples are chosen on a dependent variable.

- In experimental designs, group identification is normally captured by the value of the manipulated independent variable. This variable defines which condition a case is in; no further group identifier is needed.

- In quasi-experimental designs with only one comparison group, the value of the manipulated variable serves as a group identifier. However, if two or more comparison groups are used, you'll need to add a variable to indicate which group a case belongs to. For example, if one office tries new accounting procedures, and three other offices are selected as comparison groups, you would add the variable "office" as a group identifier.

- In nonexperimental designs, each subsample will have to be identified. If this isn't captured by an existing variable, add the variable "sample" to indicate to which sample each case belongs.

Repeated Measure Variables

Many specific designs involve repeated measures: information on the same variable is gathered from the same case at two or more time points. Researchers handle this information in one of two ways:

- Designs with just a few measurement points treat the information from repeated measures as separate *variables* (e.g., pretest-posttest designs). Any type of variable (dependent to interacting) can be measured repeatedly.

- Time-series designs with many more measurement points treat the information from repeated measures as separate cases, or **observations.**

For example, a pretest-posttest study of consumers' gasoline buying, measured before and after a major advertising campaign, would include the variables "prior brand choice," "after brand choice," "prior average purchase," "after average purchase," and so on, for each characteristic measured both before and after the campaign. For characteristics that don't change (such as gender), only one variable (and one measurement) is needed.

Time Series.   In time-series designs, each case or observation represents information from one of a series of measurement points (such as weekly, monthly, quarterly, or annual observations). Since each variable is recorded at each time point, and each time point is equivalent to one case, the number of variables is the same, no matter how many times the measurements are repeated. Additional measures add more observations, not more variables. However, you must add a variable to indicate the time point, or period, of each observation. Thus, time-series designs do not need variables representing each repeated measure, but they must always include a variable for "time."

ADVANCED TOPIC

Lagged and Leading Variables

In time-series designs, researchers use data from different time points to help establish causal time order. A researcher might want to demonstrate, for example, that "return on assets" is related to "cash flow" at a previous time, or that "advertising expenditures" are related to "sales" in a subsequent period.

This presents a problem during data analysis, however, since analysis is based on a comparison of cases or observations. All the data pertaining to an observation must be present in the variables for that observation. However, the data on previous cash flow or subsequent sales are in *different* observations. To overcome this restriction, researchers construct lagged or leading variables.

For example, in a marketing study the observation for the month of July contains variables representing total sales, advertising expenses, and hours of business for that month, together with a lagged variable giving the advertising expenses of the *previous* month. The lagged variable is "previous month's advertising." Any type of variable can be lagged or led.

Lagged variables are useful when you believe that a particular cause takes some time to have an effect, and you therefore want to measure the causal variable at an earlier time point. Leading variables are useful when anticipation of a future situation affects behavior and decisions. The future situation itself is used as a measure of the anticipated future situation, and thus the cause is measured at a later time point.

A **lagged variable** is a variable representing some attribute or characteristic at a previous measurement time point. It is constructed from variables in previous observations. A **leading variable** is the value of a variable at a subsequent time.

CASE EXAMPLE

The research design in a company's study of its union-management relations called for quarterly observations of the firm using company records and files as data sources. A number of variables were measured for each quarter, including the key variable, the quarterly grievance rate. Because the researcher suspected that the grievance rate in any quarter would be affected if there were an election of new shop stewards in the previous quarter, he included a lagged variable to indicate whether or not such an election took place in the preceding time period.

A lagged or leading variable can be inserted in time-series designs in two different ways:

- Add it to the list of variables and treat it as simply another variable during data collection (e.g., "previous month's inventory").

- Make use of a data analysis program (such as SPSS/PC+ or STATPAC) that will automatically create such variables from the data in earlier or later observations.

The latter technique is preferable, since it allows you to test different amounts of lagging and reduces clerical errors.

Retrospective Variables

As we noted in Chapter 3, researchers need to establish a cause-before-effect time order to make valid causal inferences. However, achieving time-order differences between variables is difficult in nonexperimental cross-sectional designs with only a single measurement time point, such as consumer or employee surveys.

One solution is to include **retrospective variables** in questionnaires or interviews. These variables ask respondents to recall behaviors, attitudes, or situations at an earlier time. In general, information about easily recalled behaviors is more reliable than information about past attitudes or perceptions. Any kind of variable can be measured retrospectively.

Retrospective variables in surveys are subject to bias and are influenced by a respondent's present attitudes and beliefs. However, half a loaf is better than none, and retrospective variables provide a slightly stronger basis for causal inferences than variables based solely on present behaviors and attitudes. (Chapter 9 discusses measurement problems associated with recall.)

Structural Variables

As we discussed in Chapter 3, all variables must pertain to the same unit of analysis. However, in some instances it is useful to include variables that make use of information drawn from a lower level of analysis. Structural variables indicate something about the internal structure of each case. They are usually independent or control variables.

The values of a **structural variable** are the means, proportions, or ratios of variables originally measured at a lower level of analysis.

CASE EXAMPLE

A researcher studying work groups, with the group as the unit of analysis, used two structural variables based on a brief questionnaire sent to each member of each work group. She defined the first, "work group morale," as the average of the individual employee's morale levels in each work group. Calculating the average converted the individual-level variable ("employee morale") to a group-level variable ("work group morale"). The second, "gender composition," she defined as the proportion of women in the group. Calculating the proportion for each group converted the individual-level variable "gender" to a group-level variable. She then tested whether group composition, group size, and group morale affected group productivity.

Business researchers often use structural variables. Research problems frequently require units of analysis at a level higher than the individual employee, such as departments, firms, and regions.

Structural variables require data first gathered at a lower level of analysis and then aggregated to the level at which the rest of the research is taking place. Such data often impose considerable additional costs on the research, particularly when the researcher uses interviews or questionnaires.

Contextual Variables

The values of a **contextual variable** represent the different contexts or circumstances shared by subsets of cases.

Contextual variables involve information from a higher level of analysis, usually bodies or aggregates. Like structural variables, contextual variables occur frequently in business research and are usually independent or control variables. However, they do not usually entail extra data-gathering costs.

CASE EXAMPLE

A researcher studied the reactions to technological change and workplace hazards of 823 employees in all seven plants of a firm. She included the contextual variable "plant" in the research because she believed that employees' attitudes might be affected by the conditions and organizational culture of each plant.

In this example, the variable "plant" has seven categories, one for each plant; all employees in the same plant are assigned the same category.

Other common contextual variables are the shift and department (for individual employees), region, industry, and other organizational and geographical aggregates.

Design-related variables are summarized in Table 5.2. They are best added to the list of variables once a tentative specific design has been chosen (see Box 5.1).

DROPPING PROBLEM VARIABLES

Once a researcher has assembled a reasonable list of variables, including those necessitated by the specific research design, he or she must check for problem variables which must be dropped from the list. This includes variables with insufficient variation and those for which data of acceptable quality are unavailable or too costly.

T A B L E 5 . 2 ■ VARIABLES REQUIRED BY THE RESEARCH DESIGN

Group Identifiers	A variable that indicates to which experimental or comparison group, or subsample, each case belongs
Repeated Measures	In pretest-posttest and similar designs, a set of variables, each of which indicates the measure of the same variable but at different times
Time	In time-series designs, a variable that indicates the measurement time point for each observation
Lagged and Leading Variables	In time-series designs, variables that indicate the value of a variable at a previous or subsequent time
Retrospective Variables	Respondents are asked about earlier time periods
Structural Variables	Means, proportions, or ratios of variables at a lower level of analysis
Contextual Variables	Variables representing different contexts or circumstances shared by subsets of cases, representing higher levels of analysis

Variables with Insufficient Variation

A variable without sufficient variation cannot covary with any other variable. If your research purpose involves relationships among variables (as it does for prediction, evaluation, and explanatory research) such variables are not much help. You can safely drop them from your research.

Before you exclude a variable from your research, however, consider whether there is any way of increasing the variation by adding other cases to your design. As we discussed in Chapter 3, this usually involves another comparison group or sample. This step is normally taken only if the variable is fairly important and research resources and time are plentiful.

Assessing Variation. Usually a researcher has only a vague idea of how much variation there is in any particular variable. However, for variables with two or three categories, preliminary information or a quick check of a small sample of cases may be enough to tell.

How much variation is enough? As a rule of thumb, if more than 85

BOX 5.1
CAMPBELL SWITCH: A CONTINUING CASE

Part Eight: Choosing Variables

George is sitting at his desk, sipping coffee, and devising rationales for the variables that he and Roberta have come up with. With the aid of his notes, he recalls conversations over the past few days.

Walter Ryan (his boss): "We're having a problem with turnover. . . ."

George and Roberta early on tagged "turnover" as a key dependent variable and have since added "absenteeism" and "transfer requests." Turnovers they have defined as nonretirement quits, and absenteeism has been subdivided into a number of variables, including number of days and number of incidents for each employee, and for each incident whether excused, whether medical, length, and days of week absent. George reminds himself that the variables pertaining to each absence incident are structural and will have to be aggregated for each individual employee.

Walter again: ". . . at the new Ajax plant." "Plant" is certainly one of the primary variables, capturing the effects of the new plant startup. It is also, George notes, a contextual variable picking up variation not caused by the variables at the employee level. And both "department" and "foreman" are other primary contextual variables to test whether different groups of employees might be feeling different effects. George notes that either of these might also be treated as a potential interaction variable.

George also recalls that job dissatisfaction seemed to be a recurrent theme. This makes sense, since all the key variables are indicators of job dissatisfaction. He adds it as an intervening variable.

All three workers and one of the foremen had commented on the new machinery in the plant, which could certainly be part of the problem. And since not all the machinery there is the same kind, George categorizes "type of machine" as a primary variable representing the machine the employee works at.

But why might machinery lead to turnovers? George checks his notes. Two workers had mentioned breakdowns. Perhaps the breakdowns that happen with new machinery are frustrating the operators. But two foremen had mentioned that the new machinery was particularly easy to learn and to operate. In fact, on their recommendation some units had also been installed in the Ajax plant. George adds "machine breakdowns" and "ease of operation" as intervening variables.

Sam Goodman, a supervisor, had mentioned another possibility. Sam thought that the machine layout and work flow gave employees less chance to talk to one another because workers are stationed further apart than with the old machines in the Ajax plant. It occurs to George that if the men found the plant a cold and unfriendly place to work, it might lead to dissatisfaction and lower morale. He adds "opportunities to socialize" as an intervening variable relating type of machine to job dissatisfaction.

"But why only older employees?" That sounds like an interaction effect, George decides. "But where would it fit in?"

Taking another sip of his now cold coffee, George continues working on his list of variables.

percent of the cases fall into one category of a variable (e.g., skilled as opposed to semiskilled and unskilled employees), chances are that the variation will be insufficient. If more than 90 percent fall into one category, the variable is very likely to prove unusable. This rule, however, can be relaxed for experimental studies, very important variables, and large samples. If in doubt, keep the variable in the research so that data can be gathered and the real amount of variation determined.

Variables with Inadequate Data

One other kind of problem variable can be dropped from your design: variables for which no data of adequate quality are available. Before you can make this decision, however, you have to consider the selection of data sources.

DATA SOURCES

As we noted earlier, variables determine the data sources you need, and data sources determine the variables for which you can get information. We now turn to the second element of this interrelated pair of research design decisions: the data source.

Business researchers use five different types of data sources:

- Individual self-reports

- Inside informants

- Outside observers

- Researcher observations

- Available (secondary) data

A comparison of these sources is shown in Table 5.3.

Individual Self-Reports

The most frequently used data source is to ask the people who are the objects of the research (such as consumers or employees) for information about themselves. The result is self-report data. It is gathered by questionnaires or interviews.

The major advantage of this data source is that it provides the broadest range of variables, including attitudes and perceptions. The major disadvantages are that it is often more costly in time, money, and personnel, and the information gathered is sometimes subject to bias. Nevertheless, this data source can provide very high-quality data on a large number of topics.

Aggregated Data. By definition, self-report data consists of information about individuals. If the unit of analysis is a group, organization, relationship, or aggregate, the researcher must aggregate the individual self-reports up

TABLE 5.3 ■ COMPARISON OF DATA SOURCES

	Individual Self-Reports	Inside Informants	Outside Observers	Researcher Observation	Available Data
Appropriate Units of Analysis	Individual, Body, Relationship, Aggregate	Body, Relationship, Aggregate	Any	Any	Any
Data Quality	Moderate to very high	Moderate to high	Moderate to high	High	Varies widely
Range of Variables	Broadest	Fairly high	Moderate	Limited	Limited
Data-Gathering Costs	High	Moderate	Low to moderate	Low	Low

to the appropriate level of analysis. For example, the self-reported individual data on the variable "number of children" are aggregated to the department-level variable "average number of children." Similarly, when data are gathered from both supervisor and employee in a study of supervisor-employee relationships, the self-reported data on the variable "age" are aggregated to the relationship variable "age difference."

Inside Informants

An **informant** is a selected individual who belongs to a group, organization, relationship, or aggregate of interest to the researcher. The researcher asks the informant for information about the body, relationship, or aggregate to which he or she belongs.[2] Informants provide information about the entire case rather than just themselves.

Informants are not often used as the sole data source in business research. Most researchers use them to supplement data from other sources. Data from informants is gathered with a questionnaire or interview.

CASE EXAMPLE

A researcher studied salary distortions and pay inequities among 86 departments of a major stock brokerage firm. The departments were spread across 33 different cities. An important variable for her research was the degree to which each department's salaries were affected by local labor market conditions in its town or city. In

---

[2]The term *informant* is sometimes misunderstood. Informants are seldom cloak-and-dagger informers. They are usually official representatives or organization members who have the authority, experience, and access to information desired by the researcher.

BOX 5.2
RESEARCH SKILLS
Choosing Organization Informants

When you are choosing informants from among members of an organization, here are four important considerations to keep in mind:

- Does the potential informant have *adequate knowledge* about the case to provide information on all the variables of interest to the researcher? In some instances, several informants may be required. For example, a CEO might provide general information about company performance, and a personnel manager about employee relations practices.
- Can you *obtain access* to this person? The higher

in the organization, the more difficult it is to obtain access because of competing demands on a manager's time.
- Will this person be *willing and able* to provide the information? One problem with lower status members of organizations is that they often lack the authority to provide researchers with the information they desire. The more bureaucratic the organization, the greater this problem.
- Is the person's *information likely to be biased?* For example, public relations officials are less likely to provide information that might put the organization in an unfavorable light.

telephone interviews she asked each department head to rate his or her department's salary levels as "highly," "moderately," or "not very much" affected by local conditions.

Informants are sometimes an alternative to self-report data from members of the body, relationship, or aggregate. Using informants is faster and cheaper, but data quality may be less for some variables. However, if the informant is selected carefully, the data quality may be just as great unless attitudes and beliefs are important research variables. In such cases, the researcher will obtain better data from a sample of members of each body or aggregate, or from all members of a relationship.

In other instances, informants are the only data source. For example, information about company policy, sales, size, and other characteristics is usually available only from an informant who works for the company (see Box 5.2). Typical informants in business research include committee chairmen, department heads, personnel managers, CEOs, and shop stewards.

Outside Observers

An outside observer is a person knowledgeable about some unit of analysis of interest to the researcher (another person, an organization, event, object, relationship, or aggregate) but not a member of the body, relationship, or aggregate. This category includes both experts (such as a financial analyst familiar with the firms in an industry), and nonexperts who are in a position to observe what's happening (the employee operating a punch press at the time it breaks down). Outside observers may be knowledgeable about just one, several, or all cases in the research.

CASE EXAMPLE

In the study of stock brokerage pay inequities in the preceding case example, the researcher wanted to be sure of her measure of effects of local labor market conditions on salaries. She met with a personnel department manager knowledgeable about salary structures and asked him to rate how much each of the 86 departments' salaries were affected: "highly," "moderately," or "not very much."

In this example, although the personnel department manager is a member of the firm, he is an "outside observer" with respect to each of the 86 departments (except his own).

Researchers often use outside observers as data sources for events and objects. They generally gather this data with interviews, although questionnaires are sometimes used when they consult many observers. The cost of data gathering is generally low, particularly when an observer provides information about many cases.

An observer is likely to know less about a case than an informant, but his or her information is less likely to be biased, since there is little self-interest involved. Thus this data source provides information on fewer variables, but data quality may be higher.

Researcher Observation

Researchers occasionally gather their own data by observing individuals, bodies, events, or objects (for example, consumer behavior at the point of purchase, work teams on the plant floor, sales meetings, or cars coming off the production line).

The major drawbacks of researcher observation are the time it takes and the limited range of variables for which information can be secured. For example, attitudes and opinions cannot be measured using this data source.

For some research problems, however, researcher observation is the most appropriate data source and often the only way to gather certain kinds of information. For example, research on customer purchasing behavior, committee decision making, and work-group productivity may need information that can only be reliably gained through observation.

Another advantage of researcher observation is that, if carried out unobtrusively, it reduces procedure threats to internal validity. Asking supervisors how they treat women employees might lead to biased answers; watching how they treat women provides more accurate information. In general, the

BOX 5.3
RESEARCH SKILLS

Observing

If you are gathering data through observation, consider the following points:

- Will you be able to obtain information on the variables you want? Observation limits the researcher to the visible behavior of people and objects. Other variables, such as attitudes and perceptions, can only be inferred from an individual's observable verbal and nonverbal behavior. For this reason, observation is often combined with other data-gathering methods, such as secondary data or response data.
- Can you get access to the situations you want to observe, at the times you want to observe

them? Will the individuals or objects you want to observe necessarily be there at those times, or will the events of interest necessarily happen?
- What might be the effects on the individuals being observed of their awareness that they are being studied? If the observation is intended to be unobtrusive, what would be the effect if the observation were discovered?
- How much time will it take to complete enough observations to provide sufficient and accurate information? Observation, particularly of behaviors that happen only occasionally, can be very time consuming.

quality of data gathered through researcher observation is likely to be relatively high.

The varieties of observational methods and the problems researchers must deal with when using this data source are discussed in Chapter 8. Box 5.3 suggests other considerations researchers ponder when deciding whether to use observation.

Available Data

Business researchers often make use of information from secondary data sources. Next to individual self-reports, available data is the most common data source in business research. Because it is almost always the least costly way of obtaining information, it is generally the first data source to be considered.

Available data come in an enormous variety of forms, including

- Personnel, production, sales, maintenance, and other company records; sales orders.

- Data gathered in other research projects, such as responses to previous consumer, public opinion, and employee surveys.

- Census and other government data in printed form or on computer tapes.

- Internal organization communications, such as notes, letters, and memos.

Available data (also called **secondary data**) is information generated or gathered by persons or agencies other than the researcher for purposes other than the researcher's specific project.

BOX 5.4
RESEARCH SKILLS

Using Available Data Sources

If you are considering an available data source, here are a number of questions to weigh:

- Are both the variables and the cases in the available data appropriate for the research problem? Ensure that the data source covers all the cases you want. Often records exist for only a subset of cases. For example, a union keeps records of grievances that go to arbitration, but no records are kept of grievances settled before the arbitration stage.
- Are the data available for each individual case, and not averaged, percentaged, or otherwise aggregated? If they are aggregated, as is often the case with reports of previous research, you may have information at the wrong level of analysis.

- If you plan to combine available data with data from other sources, is there sufficient information to identify each case? For example, if information from personnel records is to be combined with questionnaire responses, you will need to be able to match George Brown's questionnaire with his personnel file.
- If the available data do not cover all the variables, so that additional data sources are necessary, would it be more cost efficient to obtain all the data from these other sources, since you have to use them anyway? For example, if you have to use a questionnaire, it may be easier to get information about age, gender, and seniority through the questionnaire rather than to go through personnel files and match them to questionnaires.

- Documents that record the deliberations and decisions of groups or organizations, such as meeting minutes.
- Media accounts, including newspaper reports and television videotapes.
- Reports of committees; annual company reports.
- Transcripts of hearings; briefs and submissions.
- Industry statistics and reports.
- Application forms (for employment, membership, etc.).

In many instances, the data are in electronic form within a computer, such as spreadsheets or databases.

Information of this kind can exist for any unit of analysis, from individuals to objects. However, because someone else determined what to ask or observe, you are likely to find that the variables you want are not always present in the data set, or are not measured in the way you would prefer. Furthermore, because someone else gathered the data the quality is beyond your control. The data may be good or very poor.

If you believe that available data exist that might be relevant to your research, you must determine whether you can gain access to them and to what extent they will provide information about the variables you want for the cases you want (see Box 5.4). Techniques for use with available data, and problems encountered with its use, are discussed in Chapter 10 on available data studies.

Aggregate Data. A problem sometimes faced by business researchers is that available data are obtainable only at an aggregate level, such as industry sales or regional strikes. Alternatively, access to a preferred data source at the desired level of analysis may be prohibitively expensive, time consuming, or impossible.

In these circumstances, researchers have to revise the research problem to reflect the aggregate unit of analysis for which they have data. For example, instead of the individual employee, the problem may have to be framed in terms of a committee or department. Productivity information in a factory may be available only for work groups, not for individual workers.

As discussed in Chapter 3, research using data at one level to analyze phenomena at a lower level encounters relevance and validity problems and should be undertaken with caution.

CHOOSING DATA SOURCES AND VARIABLES

Having looked at types of variables and data sources, we can now examine the process of making the interrelated design decisions involving both. The researcher's first task is to determine which data sources are available. The next problem is to select one or more of them.

Selecting a Data Source

When choosing from among several potential data sources, researchers consider both data availability and data quality. Ethical issues often enter the picture as well (Box 5.5).

The first concern is how many of the researcher's variables each potential data source can provide. For example, personnel files usually contain background demographic information, but not data on job satisfaction attitudes. If a particular source is missing information on certain variables, the researcher either drops those variables from the design or adds another data source.

The second question is which data source provides the best quality data. Researchers look for the following three characteristics:

- Data that are accurate: no guessing or rough estimates.

- Data that are unbiased: information is not intentionally (or unintentionally) distorted.

- Data that provide information for each case: no cases for which data are missing or unobtainable.

BOX 5.5
RESEARCH ETHICS
Data Sources

Each type of data source raises potential ethical problems, and in selecting one or more data sources, the researcher must consider the ethical dimension as well as validity, relevance, and cost.

- Gathering information by *individual self-reports,* particularly if it is personal or sensitive, might subject the individuals to undue stress. (See Chapters 9 and 12.)
- The risk with *inside informants* is that they provide confidential data or invade the personal privacy of others in the organization. You should always

check how the informant obtains the information.
- *Outside observers* raise relatively few ethical problems compared to other data sources.
- The technique of *researcher observation* raises issues of invasion of privacy. (These problems are discussed in Chapter 11.)
- The use of *available data* about individuals, such as personnel files, might also raise invasion of privacy issues. In some jurisdictions there is a legal requirement that the individual's permission be obtained before accessing available data about him or her. Check.

Table 5.4 summarizes the data quality you can expect for each combination of data source and unit of analysis. As the table suggests, outside observers are poor sources of information about individuals' feelings and attitudes unless they are close to those individuals. However, even spouses often misjudge the

T A B L E 5 . 4 ■ DATA SOURCES AND TYPICAL DATA QUALITY FOR THE DIFFERENT UNITS OF ANALYSIS

	Individual Self-Reports	Inside Informants	Outside Observers	Researcher Observation	Available Data
Individual	a		b or c	b	b
Body (Group or Organization)	a or b	a	b	b	b
Relationship	a or b	b	c	b	c
Aggregate	a	a	b	c	b
Event			b	a	b
Object			b	a	b

a = Good possibility of high data quality
b = Moderate data quality, some important information likely to be unavailable
c = Many important factors likely to be unavailable

feelings and opinions of their partners. With a few exceptions, such as embarrassing or self-prejudicing material, the best source of information about individuals is self-reports.

Researcher observations provide the best information about events and objects. Available data and outside observers don't provide data of the same quality, since these sources may fail to note information important to your research problem.

Multiple Sources. To cover all the variables in a research design, the researcher may need to adopt two or more data sources. For example, he or she might combine productivity records, personnel file data, and an interview or questionnaire. Multiple techniques and sources add to the costs of research, but can significantly enhance its relevance and validity.

Whenever multiple sources are used, the researcher must ensure that all cases are identified with a common *identifier variable,* so that information for a case from one source can be matched with information about the same case from another source.

Selecting Variables

Researchers face two competing concerns in their choice of variables:

- For conclusions to be statistically and logically valid, the research design must include *all* causes of the dependent variable. Omitting important variables results in misleading conclusions and recommendations. (Inexperienced researchers sometimes mistakenly discard variables that the organization can't change, believing them to be irrelevant.)

- Cost, time, personnel, and measurement constraints put practical limits on the variables you can include. Too many variables may reduce the overall accuracy of the research (for example, people get bored with long questionnaires). Other variables are impractical. For example, employees' blood sugar levels affect productivity, but measuring this variable is seldom feasible. Data for yet other variables may require an unreasonable investment given the potential research benefits.

The rule of thumb is to include all variables that are plausibly related to the dependent variable and for which data sources and measurement are practical. Drop only

- Variables with insufficient variation.

- Confounded independent variables.

- Variables for which your data source provides inadequate information. (For very important variables, however, poor data may be better than no data at all.)

SUGGESTION

Any variable likely to have a substantial relationship with the major dependent variable(s) should be included, whether or not it has intrinsic interest for the organization.

BOX 5.6

MOVING SOUND: A CONTINUING CASE

Part Four: An Additional Data Source

Peter Grant picks up the phone at his desk in the Moving Sound warehouse. "Yeah?"

"Pete, this is George. I've got a great idea for your evaluation project."

"Let's hear it. I was just checking over the script for the TV commercial. Not bad for community college students. They're in the media arts program."

"Students? I guess you're getting a good price."

"Actually, it's a project assignment for one of their courses. We just pay production costs."

"Figures. Anyway, here's my idea. As well as the secondary data, that's the weekly sales records, I think we should use another data source and cover additional variables. How about a postbroadcast survey at both test and comparison sites?"

"How would that work?"

"We'd hand out questionnaires to customers and ask things such as whether they've been there before, how they first heard of Moving Sound, how it compares to other record stores, and so on. You could get a lot of useful data to help interpret whatever shows up with the sales figures."

"What do we need to do?"

"First we should get together and figure what variables to include in the questionnaire. Or maybe it should be a mini-interview. But we need to discuss variables. Sex, age, shopping habits . . ."

"Why don't I drop by your apartment after dinner?"

"OK. And you can try out my new muffin recipe."

"Oh." He pauses. "How about I just bring doughnuts instead?"

SUGGESTION

When deciding whether to drop a variable, keep in mind that, because of data-gathering costs, the total number of variables is most crucial for questionnaires or interviews, less important for observation, and least important for available data.

• Variables for which the costs of data gathering outweigh the anticipated benefits of greater research validity. Ultimately the importance of the research to the organization will determine what resources are made available, and thus what data sources and variables the research can utilize.

As the last point suggests, decisions about data sources and variables are often made in tandem (Box 5.6).

Defining Variables.   Once variables are selected, researchers should ensure that each is clearly defined. Clear definitions are important in order to understand what concept each variable represents and to enable the researcher to choose the best measure for each variable.

Definitions are not a problem for variables such as "gender" or "age," but attributes like "satisfaction" and "size" are vague. Box 5.7 discusses some useful techniques for defining variables.

Research Model Sketch.   Often it is useful to get an overall picture of your variables and their expected relationships by sketching a research model (see Figure 5.6). Such a sketch is a concise statement of what will be examined in the research (see Box 5.8). Together with the statement of the

BOX 5.7
RESEARCH SKILLS
Defining Variables

Check back to the original and underlying organization problem. For example, if your problem focuses on absenteeism you will certainly have a variable by that name. But are you really interested in all kinds of absenteeism, or will a more restrictive definition serve you better (e.g., short-term absences)? Does the problem relate more to total number of days absent or number of absence incidents (a single incident may include any number of consecutive work days)? If productivity losses are the underlying problem, perhaps you should focus on medical absences (since they tend to be of longer duration and cost the firm more in lost productivity) or unplanned absences (since foremen can't foresee them and arrange for replacement workers).

Ask yourself what particular aspect of the variable causes (or is caused by) the key variable. This question will help you to isolate the important component of a vague variable. For example, "customer satisfaction" is vague, but "repeat purchase" is specific and concentrates on the important element of customer satisfaction from the point of view of the organization: the customer likes the product enough to buy it on subsequent occasions.

Make sure the name you give each variable makes clear what it is that's varying. For example, "children" is vague; it could mean either "whether respondent has any children" or "number of children." In particular, don't call a variable by one of its categories; for example, "married" is a category, "marital status" is the variable.

research problem, the research model is an excellent guide for data analysis and report writing.

Unmeasured Variables

What happens if an independent variable cannot be included in the research design? This is the problem of unmeasured (or, in experimental designs, uncontrolled) variables. Unmeasured variables threaten both research power and internal validity.

Effects on Research Power. If an independent variable causally related to the dependent variable is unmeasured or not incorporated into the specific design, its variation is said to be "uncontrolled." The portion of the variation in the dependent variable linked to the unmeasured independent variable cannot be statistically controlled. This uncontrolled variation in the dependent variable, if excessive, makes it more difficult to detect the relationships of other measured variables to the dependent variable. The effect is analogous to having a conversation at a crowded party, compared to talking in a quiet library. When the "noise" (or the proportion of total variation) produced by unmeasured variables is great, only the strongest effects are likely to be detected. In other words, research power is low.

BOX 5.8
CAMPBELL SWITCH: A CONTINUING CASE

Part Nine: George and Roberta's Research Model

George has joined Roberta to pool their ideas on variables for the research design.

"I know you think that women wouldn't quit because of machine breakdowns," Roberta explains, "but we can't test it because there's not enough variation. Only 3 of the 122 workers there are women."

"O.K., so we drop it. And we have to combine 'department' and 'foreman' because they're perfectly correlated contextual variables."

"Here's my first sketch of the research model showing how they relate to the key variables," Roberta says, indicating a sheet on her desk. "My problem is that I know 'seniority' is an important variable, but I'm just not sure where it fits. It could affect job satisfaction directly, or it could be a moderating variable affecting the relationship between one of the other factors and quitting."

"Let me have a look," George says, moving around to Roberta's side. He studies the sketch, then picks up a pencil and points. "What if you just add it here, as a control variable. After all, if you're in doubt, that's the safest way to treat it for the time being, and nothing's lost. We can try the other possibilities during the data analysis. And it's likely to be related to 'age.'"

"That would make the research model look like this." Roberta sketches the diagram shown below.

"Not bad. Most of this will come from the questionnaires. Some, like machine breakdown data, we can get from company records. And we'll confirm the socializing opportunities by observing the machine layout in the plant." For the next hour, Roberta and George sketch, discard, and retry several possibilities as they continue with their variable design decisions.

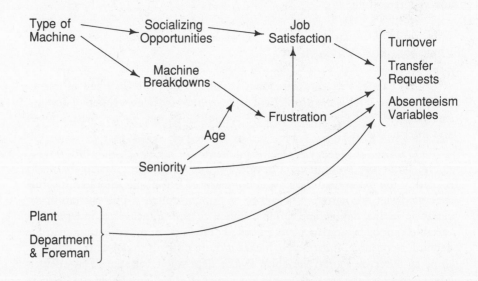

Effects on Internal Validity. Spurious and confounded relationships and groups are a major threat to internal validity. Researchers normally eliminate these threats by controlling the extraneous variables that produce them. This control may be through research design (such as true experiments) or by measuring a potential extraneous variable and including it in multivariate analysis. Remember, it is impossible to detect and remove the effect of an extraneous variable if it is unmeasured.

CASE EXAMPLE

A researcher was assigned the task of investigating the reasons for rising numbers of dismissals among young employees in a small fast-food restaurant chain. Available data for an eight-year period were gathered from 23 outlets in two provinces. The researcher concluded that the reason for increased dismissals seemed to be that, when the chain reached a certain size, discharges increased, perhaps because less able managers were then being hired or managers were forced to hire less committed employees. Unfortunately, the researcher failed to note that discharges for drunkenness showed a sharp increase in the year the legal drinking age dropped from 21 to 18. Subsequent reanalysis, prompted by the questions of the personnel relations manager, showed that the legislation coincided with a major increase in discharges.

Unmeasured variables are inevitable in all research. Researchers can never anticipate, or measure, all potential causes of any dependent variable. But, within the constraints of time, money, and feasibility, they try. The fewer the number of important variables that remain unmeasured, the more valid the research.

■ *The Lighter Side of Research*

Methodologically unsound: Using methodology with which I am unfamiliar.

Participant observation: A method of gathering data somewhat analogous in degree of objectivity to taking notes while playing outside linebacker.

Validity: There are many types of validity. The distinctions among them are boring. Suffice it to say validity issues may be summarized as being chiefly remarkable for the unfair, unrealistic constraints which they place upon the creativity and imagination of the researcher. (Woodman, 1979)

Summary

The selection of variables for the research design begins with the key and primary dependent and independent variables. Then, based on the problem investigation and literature, additional variables are added: control, extraneous, intervening, and interacting. It is a good idea to provide rationales for these additional variables.

Then consider the need for any design-related variables: group identifiers, repeated measure, time, lagged, leading, retrospective, structural, and contextual. Problem variables include those with insufficient variation, confounded, and inadequate data availability. If the problems cannot be solved, the variables are dropped from the design. Follow these steps when selecting variables:

1. List key and primary dependent and independent variables as part of your investigation of the initial problem and research problem formulation.

2. Revise these variables to ensure they are consistent with the unit of analysis.

3. Add control, extraneous, intervening, and interacting variables as suggested by the literature review and "research imagination." Provide rationales.

4. Add any variables required by your specific design: group identifiers, repeated measures, time, lagged and leading, retrospective, structural, contextual.

5. Discard problem variables

- With insufficient variation.

- Confounded with another variable (substitute proxy variable if possible).

- For which adequate data cannot be obtained.

- For which the costs of data gathering outweigh the potential benefits of the information.

6. Provide clear definitions.

Select data sources from the following options: individual self-reports, inside informants, outside observers, researcher observations, and available data. Business research projects often make use of multiple data sources. In extreme situations, aggregate data at a higher level unit of analysis may have to be used, despite the risk of aggregation bias.

Where Are We Now?

At this stage of the research, the design or planning is almost finished. The major case selection decisions which specify the rows of the data matrix (unit of analysis, basic design, and specific design) are complete. The variable selection decisions defining the columns of the data matrix have also been made. In addition, you have chosen your data sources for these variables.

One more step remains in the process of research design. If there are more cases than needed within the research boundaries, you will want to draw a sample. Sampling is covered in the next two chapters. Following that, we turn to the process and problems of measurement and gathering data.

Discussion Issues and Assignments

1. Select three research articles from journals such as those mentioned in discussion issue number 4 of Chapter 4. List the variables used in the research and classify them as to type (e.g., key dependent, primary independent, control, etc.). What data sources were used? What alternative sources might have been better, and what constraints might have prevented their being used?

2. Imagine you are commissioned to study factors affecting enrollments in different courses. The course is to be the unit of analysis. What contextual variables might be relevant to the research? What structural variables?

3. The following conclusions are wrong. Each is based on an observed relationship, but an alternative explanation for the relationship is its true cause. What alternative explanations (extraneous variables creating spurious or confounded relationships) can you think of for the following conclusions:

- There are more cats per person in high-traffic downtown areas than in the suburbs because per capita sales of kitty litter are higher in those locations.

- Canadian workers are more likely to strike than American because Canada's annual workdays lost to strikes per 100,000 workers is higher than in the United States.

- Work-group productivity is higher on the day than the night shift because workers have trouble adapting to working at night.

4. A hypothetical research project discovered the following in interviews with 75 recently hired MBA graduates:

> In deciding which job offer to accept, MBA graduates of schools located in major metropolitan areas are often faced with the choice of taking a job in the same city or moving to another location, often at a higher salary. What are the implications for careers? The researchers found that women seem to do better than men if they move. Women appear to be more able to adjust quickly to a new location, to develop a support system of new friends and social groups, and to establish a household on an operating basis (finding a laundromat, doctor, and a garage for car repairs). Men, on the other hand, perhaps because of the belief about male independence, are less able to accomplish these things, and their careers seem to be slower in getting off the ground as a result, whereas if they remain in the same city, this disadvantage disappears.

List and classify the variables. Are there any interacting variables? If so, what kind? Are there any intervening variables?

5. Treat a management consultant to lunch (it could be an instructor in the Business School or someone working in a private firm). Talk about his or her preferences for using available data or questionnaires and interviews. Do you think that some people naturally seem to prefer one form of data gathering over another? Why?

Further Reading

Osigweh, C., and A. B. Yg. 1989. "Concept Fallibility in Organizational Science." *Academy of Management Review* 14:579–594.

>A discussion of the pitfalls in formulating and using concepts, highly relevant to the use and definition of variables in business research.

Peters, L. H., E. J. O'Connor, and S. L. Wise. 1984. "The Specification and Testing of Useful Moderator Variable Hypotheses." In T. S. Bateman and G. R. Ferris (eds.), *Method and Analysis in Organizational Research.* Reston, VA: Reston.

>An insightful and somewhat advanced discussion of how to interpret and analyze interacting variables.

Webb, E., and K. E. Weick. 1979. "Unobtrusive Measures in Organizational Theory: A Reminder." *Administrative Science Quarterly* 24: 650–659.

>The authors review interesting alternatives to self-report data sources for research in organizations.

CHAPTER 6

An Introduction to Sampling

CHAPTER OBJECTIVES

- How does a researcher go about getting a sample?
- What are the most common types of samples in business research?
- What are the similarities and differences among types of samples?

CHAPTER OUTLINE

THE SAMPLING PROCESS
PROBABILITY SAMPLES
NONPROBABILITY SAMPLES

esearchers often sample. So do managers.

Back at Montgomery Metals, Harry Anderson is wondering whether the foremen are going to like the new training program that the head office is planning. He has doubts. But is he right? Harry jumps up and heads for the plant floor to ask some foremen. He first looks for Abe and Sam, since he and they often see eye to eye on plant matters. Harry explains the program and asks what they think. Sam, after some initial wavering, seems to share Harry's doubts. So does Abe. Harry also talks with three other foremen who seem not to be too busy at the time. In all, four of the five don't like the program, and Harry fires off a memo to the head office, predicting trouble with the foremen over the training program.

A **sample** is part of a population selected to represent the whole and used to estimate its characteristics.

A **population** is the entire set of cases (often called elements) for which the characteristics are to be estimated, and to which the research conclusions will apply.

Harry is sampling—estimating the reactions of all Montgomery Metals foremen on the basis of five foremen's opinions. Sampling is the final design decision. The sample design is a plan for choosing which cases from the population are to be measured. Analysis of the sample results in *estimates* of population characteristics, such as the average age of Montgomery Metals foremen or the relationship between a foreman's age and his opinion about the new training program. Good samples are *representative* and produce good estimates; bad samples (such as Harry's) don't include representative cases and thus produce poor estimates.

We normally associate sampling with surveys. In business research, however, sampling is used in all kinds of research including pilot projects and evaluation studies. Unlike basic and general applied research, business research is always relevant to a specific population, time, and place.[1] If we cannot measure all the elements in that time and place, we sample.

THE SAMPLING PROCESS

The sampling process is a series of four steps that begins with the population specified by the boundaries of the research problem. The first two steps take place at the population level, the third and fourth involve samples.

Population:	1. **Target population**
	2. **Sampling frame (sampled population)**
Sample:	3. **Initial sample**
	4. **Achieved sample**

We examine each of these steps in turn.

---

[1]Basic research, by comparison, applies to the *universe* of situations falling within the general scope conditions of the theory being tested, such as *all* task-oriented groups or *all* continuous process technology firms (Webster and Kervin, 1971).

Target Population

Researchers take the first step in sampling when they specify research boundaries as part of the research problem. These boundaries delineate the target population. They may have been revised in the design stage to include any control or comparison groups required by the specific design.

The target population must be defined precisely enough to allow the researcher to judge whether any potential case is to be included. This often requires thinking back to what the research problem is all about. For example, if the research problem boundaries include all employees of a manufacturing firm, the researcher needs to decide what "employee" means:

The **target population** is the total set of cases lying within the research problem boundaries. These are the cases about which the researcher hopes to draw conclusions.

- Does it include supervisors? Middle management?

- Are part-timers included? Those still in their probationary period? On disciplinary suspension?

- What about contracted-out work performed on site, such as cleaners?

When necessary, the target population also specifies temporal boundaries and time periods for repeated measures.

Table 6.1 provides some examples of target populations. Note that the population may be *internal* to the organization (its employees, departments, or sales) or *external* to it (its present or potential customers, other firms in the industry.) As we see, these two different research locations—internal and external—lead to different concerns and constraints in sample designs for business research. For internal research you may be able to specify the exact number of cases in the target population, but this is unlikely for most external research.

Target populations often delete particular groups that are too difficult to include or don't logically fit the research problem. Common examples of such deletions are individuals found in jails, hospitals, or other institutions, and persons in military service.

CASE EXAMPLE

The research boundaries for a marketing pilot project carried out for a soft drink manufacturer specified all potential young adult consumers living in Roanoke, Virginia. The researcher selected a target population defined as persons 18 to 25 years of age at any time during the month of the study, living within the boundaries of Roanoke, Salem, and Vinton, excluding institutions (such as jails and hospitals). The question of whether a given person fell into the target population could be addressed on the basis of that person's birth date and place of residence.

Target populations also exclude geographical areas that would be too expensive or time consuming to sample. Alaska and Hawaii are often excluded

TABLE 6.1 ■ PROBLEM BOUNDARIES, UNIT OF ANALYSIS, AND TARGET POPULATION

Problem Boundaries	Unit of Analysis	Target Population
Descriptive Research: "How are our recent West Coast small appliance sales?"		
Place: California, Oregon, and Washington *Time:* past six months	The weekly sales of each appliance model in each retail outlet (an event)	20,202 weekly sales totals (21 models, 37 outlets, 26 weeks)
Prediction Research: "Based on the past five years, how many employees in our Midwest plants will take early retirement this coming year?"		
Place: three Midwest plants *Time:* past five years	The plant	60 observations (3 plants, with data from each quarter for five years)
Evaluation Research: "What impact is the new quality circles program having on productivity?"		
Place: the 13 departments included in the program and the 23 not included *Time:* since program implemented	The employee	1,865 employees
Explanatory Research: "What do people think about our bank, and why do they or don't they use it?"		
Place: Rochester, N.Y. *Time:* present	The adult individual	Approximately 600,000 adults 18 years old or over living in Rochester

from national surveys in the United States, and the Yukon and Northwest Territories from Canadian studies. Similarly, overseas employees may be omitted from an employee survey.

Sampling Frame

The second step in the sampling process is to obtain or specify a sampling frame. The sampling frame is a necessary part of the sampling process. It designates the *sampled population* (sometimes called the frame population).

Business researchers usually find one of three situations:

- A frame list is readily available.
- There is no single frame list but partial lists are known of, or can be compiled.
- There are no lists at all.

Sampling Frame Lists. A fairly accurate frame list is often available for internal business research. For example, personnel records and other organization documents provide good sampling frames, although they are seldom without minor errors. The most useful frame lists contain additional information, such as a list of individuals with data on gender and occupation or a list of retail outlets with the number of employees in each. This information is often helpful in drawing a more efficient or cost-efficient sample.

Compiling Partial Lists. When there is no single list of the population cases, it may be possible to compile one by adding together sublists. For example, a charitable organization may not have a single list of members, but each regional office has a list of all chapters in the region, and each chapter can provide a list of its members. This method of list construction can be very time consuming when the target population is large and dispersed.

Frame Procedures. Sometimes a complete list of cases is unavailable and compiling partial lists is too costly. This happens frequently in external research such as surveys of consumers, potential clients and customers, and possible employees. In this situation the researcher has to rely on a frame procedure. Three such procedures are described in Box 6.1: multiphase sampling, area sampling, and on-site selection.

CASE EXAMPLE

An organization of environmental activists was interested in the opinions of those members who participated in political campaigns. They used a multiphase sample frame procedure to sample members. The first phase involved sampling 1,000 members, using membership lists as a sampling frame. These members were tele-

SUGGESTION

When specifying your target population, avoid too complicated a definition. It will require more extensive (and expensive) screening.

A **sampling frame** is (1) a list of all cases in the target population (a *frame list*) or (2) a set of procedures for obtaining a sample of cases from the target population (a *frame procedure*).

BOX 6.1
RESEARCH SKILLS

Sampling Frame Procedures

The following three sampling frame procedures are useful when frame lists are unavailable or not feasible.

Multiphase Sampling. Use this procedure when the target population is an unusual subset of some larger group for which a frame list *is* available.

1. Draw a large first phase sample from the frame list.

2. Gather information from this sample to indicate whether each case falls into the target population. (If you also gather additional information such as gender or age, you may be able to improve the efficiency of the sample through stratification, discussed later).

3. Use this information to construct a frame list for the target population. Draw the second sample. (This is permissible because a random sample of a random sample results in another random sample.)

Area Sampling. This procedure makes use of the fact that almost all persons, groups, or organizations are associated with a specific geographical location. Persons, for example, may be found at their residence or, if appropriate to the research problem, at their place of employment.

1. Instead of sampling cases directly, sample *areas* using lists of locations such as census documents and maps.

2. Select some or all of the appropriate cases at that location for the sample.

Area sampling procedures are common in marketing and other external research.

On-Site Selection. Use this option when all cases are at, or pass through, one location. Specify a set of procedures to choose cases at the location. Examples of frame procedures include

- Handing out questionnaires to every tenth employee leaving the plant.
- Asking every fiftieth customer entering a store for an interview.
- Noting the registration number of every sixth sailboat passing between two buoys. (Gather data later from government small-craft registration records.)

phoned and asked the extent of their political involvement. Of the 228 indicating high levels of involvement, a second phase sample of 40 was selected for personal interviews.

Box 6.2 discusses some of the lists available for sampling frames or as the bases of area sample frame procedures.

BOX 6.2
FOCUS ON RESEARCH
Sampling Frame Lists

INTERNAL RESEARCH

Employee Lists: Usually excellent and up to date, especially if generated from payroll data.

Lists of Organization Members: Often out-of-date. Many organizations update their lists only annually, producing both under and overcoverage.

Lists of Departments, Plants, Outlets: Usually very good, particularly if taken from organizational charts. On the other hand, it is usually much more difficult to get a complete list of temporary structures within organizations, such as committees and task forces.

Events: Usually fairly good, particularly when organization policy and decisions are involved and a number of persons take part (such as shareholder meetings and rounds of collective bargaining).

EXTERNAL RESEARCH

Client and Customer Lists: Their quality depends on who assembles them. Accounting departments normally provide better lists than sales staff.

Telephone Directories: Not very good because directories are systematically biased by age, income, and race. For example, lower income persons without telephones, upper middle income families with unlisted numbers, and persons in more mobile occupations who have just moved and don't yet have a listing are all underrepresented. Techniques that add random numbers to the selected listings overcome most of these biases, for example,

Randomly selected listing:	266-3849
Added random number:	+ 137
Number actually called:	266-3986

There are, however, other problems. For example, families with children and higher incomes who have a separate line for the teenagers are overrepresented.

Random Digit Dialing (RDD): An improvement over telephone directories, but reaches a high proportion of nonusable numbers. Many calls will be wasted; Schuman and Kalton (1985) estimate that just over one-fifth of all possible telephone numbers are residential. However, *cleaned lists* are commercially available that remove many of the commercial or unused numbers.

Mailing Lists: A wide variety of mailing and membership lists are available from mailing list brokers, and the degree to which they fit your target population will vary widely. The use of two or more lists carries a strong possibility of duplication.

Lists of Organizations: Not used very often in business research (although widely used in research on organizations). A good place to start is the *Standard and Poor's Register of Corporations.*

FOR AREA SAMPLING

Firms That Do Survey Research, Marketing and Public Opinion Surveys: Usually have their own well-organized network of area sampling sites and personnel, together with sampling experts. Many can carry out either regional or national surveys.

Census Publications: Very good, especially for the metropolitan areas that have been divided into census tracts. The *County and City Data Book* is a good source of demographic information for selecting clusters.

Initial Sample

The third step of the sampling process is to draw the initial sample. To produce an accurate estimate of the population characteristics, researchers want their samples to be representative of the population.

Achieved Sample

An **achieved sample** is the set of cases about which the researcher actually obtains data for analysis.

The initial sample is the set of cases about which you want data; the achieved sample is what you get. The initial and achieved sample may be different because the latter omits

- Cases the researcher was not able to contact (no telephone, no current address, moved, quit, transferred, retired, died, etc.).

- Cases that refused to participate in the research.

- Cases that provided incomplete or otherwise unusable information.

Screening is the procedure researchers use to examine cases and delete those that do not belong in the target population.

Screening. Initial and achieved sample will also be different if the researcher screens out cases. Screening is necessary when a sampling frame list includes some unwanted cases. Rather than discard the frame, the researcher draws a sample, gathers data, and then screens out the cases he or she doesn't want. The disadvantage is that time and money are spent gathering some unusable data. The advantage is that much time and money can be saved by avoiding a frame procedure.

Enumerations

An **enumeration** (or *census*) of a population gathers data from each case in the target population.

Not all business research projects require a sample. Under certain circumstances (discussed in Chapter 7), researchers may choose to enumerate rather than sample. Enumerations require a target population and a sampling frame. They gather information from every case in the sampling frame list (or frame procedure). Thus an enumeration omits the third step of the sampling process; there is no initial sample. The achieved sample, if all goes well, is the same as the target population.

Two potential problem points for an enumeration are

- Differences between the target population and the sampling frame because of an inadequate frame that misses cases.

- Differences between the target population and the achieved sample because of missing, refused, or incomplete data.

Having looked at the sampling process in general terms, we now turn to the different types of samples found in business research.

PROBABILITY SAMPLES

Researchers and statisticians have developed different types of samples to meet the requirements of accuracy and economy in different situations. The major distinction among types is between probability and nonprobability samples. Probability samples offer two major advantages over nonprobability samples.

The first advantage of probability samples is that they allow us not only to make estimates about the population, but also to estimate the precision of our estimates—how wrong we're likely to be. This is a very useful characteristic for managers and others who are relying on research results to help them decide how to spend large sums of money!

Estimates of precision are based on **inferential statistics.** The classical logic of statistical inference is based on the examination of all possible samples that might be drawn, given a particular population (known as the sampling distribution).[2] This and related concepts are discussed in Appendix A.

The second advantage of probability samples is that their random selection procedures produce more accurate estimates. The choice of specific cases is dictated strictly by chance rather than the whim of a researcher.

In short, probability samples are not only more accurate, but tell us how accurate we are.

The most common probability samples used in business research are the following:

- Simple random

- Systematic

- Stratified

- Cluster and multistage

Simple random and systematic samples are alternative ways of selecting cases. Stratified, cluster, and multistage samples are ways of structuring the target population *before* the selection of cases, in order to improve precision or reduce costs. In many cases two or more types are combined, such as a systematic, stratified, multistage sample.

> A **probability sample** is based on random selection with each case in the population having a known nonzero probability of being selected.

Simple Random Samples

A simple random sample has two defining features:

- All cases in the population have an equal chance of appearing in the sample.

- All possible samples of a given size n (i.e., all possible combinations of n cases) have an equal chance of being selected.

[2]An alternative approach, based on Bayesian statistical theory, considers all possible populations that might exist given a particular sample (Frankel, 1983).

A sample of cases or observations is **independent** when the selection of one case doesn't affect the chance of selection for any other case.

The most important characteristic of simple random samples is that observations are independent. Because the assumption of independent observations underlies most of our statistical procedures and tests, the simple random sample is regarded as the "basic" sample; other types all violate the assumption of independent observations to some degree.[3] Although not often used in business research, simple random samples provide a convenient point of comparison for other sample designs. Most researchers draw a simple random sample with a frame list, as described in Box 6.3. Variations include

- Using a computer to generate the random numbers.

- Drawing cases, such as clients or employees, randomly from a computerized database.

CASE EXAMPLE

In a study of nurses' attitudes toward 12-hour shifts, a researcher drew a simple random sample of 100 of the 1,210 nurses in a major hospital. He first obtained a listing of all nurses containing their names and employee numbers. The five-digit employee numbers ranged from 70244 to 84002. Most of these numbers (about 91 percent) were inactive (they referred to nurses no longer working at the hospital); the remaining numbers referred to employed nurses. Using a computer program, he generated 2,000 random 5-digit numbers between 70244 and 84002, inclusive. He then used these numbers to select nurses for the sample. It took 1,088 random numbers to get 100 numbers that matched valid employee numbers.

Each nurse had the same chance of being drawn (100/1,210) and all possible combinations of 100 nurses had the same chance of forming a sample.

Systematic Samples

Simple random samples can be time consuming to draw, particularly when the frame list is long or the sample is large. It is faster simply to select every ith case. For example, for a sample of 50 names from a list of 5,000, pick every 100th name. This idea is the basis of systematic sampling; the procedure is described in Box 6.3. Systematic samples are the most common procedure for selecting cases in business research.

- They save time whenever a researcher has a frame list.

- They are more convenient with frame procedures, such as interviewing every ith person passing through a door or tucking a questionnaire into every ith pay envelope (see Box 6.4).

- They are particularly helpful with arrays of secondary data (such as a filing cabinet of customer files or 3-by-5 cards of equipment breakdown reports).

[3]As we see later in discussing the finite population correction, even simple random samples frequently violate the assumption of independence, but in a way that doesn't matter for most research situations.

BOX 6.3
RESEARCH SKILLS
Random Sampling Procedures

I. USING A TABLE OF RANDOM NUMBERS

Required

- A table of random numbers. Three pages of random numbers can be found in Appendix B. A book of random numbers can be found in most college libraries (Rand Corporation, 1955).
- A list of cases in the target population (your sampling frame). You'll need to know approximately how many cases are on the list.
- The sample size you want. (Sample size is discussed in Chapter 7.)

Steps

1. Determine how many digits you need in your random numbers. (For example, a list with 2,883 names will require 4-digit numbers, ranging from 0001 to 2883.) *All* the numbers you draw must have the same number of digits.

2. Number the cases on the list, if they are not prenumbered. It isn't necessary to write a number beside each case. Every tenth one will do, or, if you're careful and the list is many pages long, only the first and last numbers of the cases on each page. The trick is to write in only as many numbers as you'll need to find easily the case corresponding to any random number that comes up.

3. If the cases are already numbered, you may either use those numbers or renumber the list yourself. If there are many "missing" numbers in the sequence, or the number of digits you'd need is too great, then renumbering might well be worth the extra time. For example, a list of 100 names numbered between 109824 and 886590 would require going through an enormous number of six-digit random numbers in order to find valid ones. Of course, if the first few or last few digits are all the same, you can ignore them. For example, treat 103711 to 103959 as 711 to 959.

4. Determine n, the size of the sample you want. Include corrections for

- the proportion of cases to be screened out.
- the proportion of nonresponses you expect.

5. Decide how to reduce the proportion of invalid numbers you'll draw. (A *valid* number is one that corresponds to a case in the sampling frame and hasn't come up previously.) For example, if you had a list of exactly 100 names, numbered 1 to 100, you might decide to select 3-digit numbers, since 100 has three digits. Unfortunately, this means that about 90 percent of all the numbers you select (from 101 to 999) won't correspond to a case, and you'll have to skip them. To save time, decide beforehand to treat the number 100 as "00." This will allow you to use just two-digit numbers, and all of them will be valid.

Another trick is to use substitutes for the first digit. For example, if your case numbers run from 0001 to 1882, the only valid first digits will be 0 (for 0001 to 0999) and 1 (from 1000 to 1882). To prevent skipping all numbers starting with 2 up to 9, decide beforehand to treat all even-numbered first digits (0, 2, 4, 6, 8) as "0," and all odd-numbered first digits as "1." For example, the random number 7662 would be treated as 1662. This will substantially reduce the proportion of invalid numbers you'll draw. Just make sure that you have the same number of substitutes for each first digit. (If the required first digits are 0, 1, and 2: Use 3 and 6 for 0, 4 and 7 for 1, and 5 and 8 for 2, and skip all numbers starting with the digit 9.)

6. Decide whether you're going to read the digits in the random number table across or down. Note that they come in blocks of five 5-digit numbers for easier reading. If you need numbers greater or less than five digits, ignore the spaces between blocks. (You can actually read them in any pattern you wish, as long as you're consistent.)

7. Select a starting point. An easy way is to close your eyes and apply a pencil point to the page. Start where the pencil lands. (This isn't strictly random, but the method is more than good enough for business research.)

8. Read the first number (e.g., 7002). Check whether it's valid. If so, find the corresponding case, and *mark it* as being in the sample (as long as it isn't one that's supposed to be screened out at this stage). If you select a case that's already been chosen, don't include it again in the sample. (In technical terms, business research sampling is almost always without replacement.) Draw another random number and continue; *don't* pick the next case on the list (this violates the assumption of independently drawn cases). Keep track of how many cases have been chosen, and continue until you have enough.

9. For *stratified sampling* (defined later): when all the strata are on the same list (e.g., males and females identified by gender on the list itself), keep separate track of the numbers of males and females you have. When you have enough of one group, ignore any further random numbers that correspond to cases in that group.

If the proportion of one group on the list is relatively low compared to others (less than 20 percent), you'll save time if you mark and number them separately (use a different colored ink for each stratum) and draw each subsample separately.

2. SYSTEMATIC SAMPLING

Required

- A table of random numbers.
- The frame list, array of data, or location in which cases are to be selected using frame procedures.
- The sample size you want. (Sample size is discussed in Chapter 7.)
- A calculator will help.

Steps

1. Determine N, the number of cases in your frame. If this can only be approximated, it is probably better to underestimate than overestimate. This will result in a larger rather than a smaller sample (because of a smaller selection interval).

2. Determine n, the size of sample you want. Include corrections for

- the proportion of invalid cases you expect to draw (such as cases to be screened out).
- the proportion of nonresponses you expect.

3. Calculate *i*, the **selection interval**: $i = N/n$. Ignore any remainder (for example, if $N = 1,000$ and $n = 90$, $N/n = 11.11$ and $i = 11$).

4. Select a random starting number *r* between 1 and *i* inclusive.

5. Starting with the *r*th case, pick every *i*th case for the sample. If a selection is invalid, ignore it and go on to the next *i*th case. Do *not* skip the invalid case and take the one next to it. Also, don't skip invalid cases as you're counting. (Both practices overrepresent cases following invalid cases.)

6. If your selection interval is small, or N is known only approximately, you may end up with a few too many cases. If you don't want the extras, delete them *randomly* (use either a systematic or a simple random sample).

If you know N, you can calculate to within one case how many extras you will have (extras = $N/i - n$), and delete them systematically as you go along. For example, if you want a sample of 200, and choose 5 extras, the 5 cases to be deleted are a subsample of the 205, with a selection interval of $205/5 = 41$. Pick a random starting point, say 25, and then ignore the 25th case you select and every 41st case after that.

7. Systematic sampling can also be based on measures as well as counts. For example, a drawer of file cards measures 16 and one-quarter inches, equivalent to 65 quarter inches (small units are best, such as quarter inches or millimeters). To get a sample of 10, the sampling interval is $65/10 = 6.5$ or 6 quarter inches. Select a starting card within the first six quarter inches, and then pick a card every sixth quarter inch. (Of course, if some cards are thicker than others, the sample will be biased in favor of those cards, and this technique shouldn't be used.)

A variation of this technique can be used for frame lists on computer printout or similar pages, as long as there are an equal number of cases on each page. Determine how many cases you need on each page. Randomly select distances from the top of the page, and use those same distances on each page. For example, if you need three cases per page, your distances might be 7.4, 18.9, and 22.3 millimeters from the top edge. If the resulting sample is slightly too large, drop randomly selected cases.

BOX 6.4
MOVING SOUND: A CONTINUING CASE
Part Five: A Systematic Sample

"Sharon wasn't thrilled at first, but I convinced her that we'll get a much better test if we run the commercial on two campuses. So which two? Ah, here comes the hot dog cart now! You'll love their chili dogs!"

Pete is treating George to lunch again.

A little later, wiping mustard from his chin and taking some papers from the case beside him on the park bench, George begins. "The way I see it, each test location is going to be matched with a comparison location. You've got 12 campuses."

"But three of them have two buses."

"That shouldn't matter, since you're really interested in percentage sales increases at each location, not total sales. You won't be changing the number of buses during the test period, I hope."

"No plans for that," Pete reassures him. "But when we interview customers, isn't that going to take a lot of time?"

"Maybe not. The way I see it, you probably want a systematic sample. There's no sampling frame list, so you'll have to do it on the spot with a frame procedure. . . ."

"Whoa there. This stuff is all new to me. I'm in music, remember?"

"You're also in marketing, old buddy, and you should learn this stuff. A systematic sample is just about the cheapest way to get a random sample you can generalize from safely."

"I hear you. Cheapest. Sounds good."

"And here's how you do it. Basically, you'll just choose every tenth or twelfth person—we'll figure that out later—who walks into the bus. They're the ones you interview. And give the follow-up questionnaire to."

"I get it. All we have to do is count customers as they walk in."

"Right."

"This is looking good. We have a terrific double data source—a short interview and they get a questionnaire to take home. This systematic sampling procedure sounds straightforward. We're in business! How about another chili dog for the research consultant?"

CASE EXAMPLE

A manager conducting a study of absenteeism among hourly workers used field procedures to draw a sample of 150 workers from the personnel file cards of all

2,642 hourly employees in the plant. The cards were arranged alphabetically in file drawers. To get a sample of 150, she calculated that she would have to draw every 17th card (2,642/150 = 17.6). She then selected a starting number between 1 and 17 from a table of random numbers: 12. With this starting point, and a selection interval of 17, she chose the 12th card, then the 17th card after that, the 17th card after that one, and so on. The result was a sample of 155 employees. Because time was short, she randomly deleted 5 cases to obtain a sample of 150.

Sampling Error.   With a systematic sample, each case in the population has a known and equal probability of being chosen, but not all combinations of cases are possible. For example, two contiguous cases could not appear in the same sample. Despite this violation of independent selection, business researchers can treat systematic samples as if they were simple random samples with the same degree of sampling error.

When cases are listed or arrayed by groups, such as personnel cards arranged by department, and the sampling interval is sufficiently small, a systematic sample will decrease sampling error. Because of this *implicit stratification* (see discussion of stratified sampling), all groups are proportionally represented. The result is more precise estimates. (*Precision* and *sampling error* are discussed in Appendix A.)

Stratified Samples

Stratified samples divide the population into groups, or *strata,* and draw a separate subsample from each stratum. Thus, rather than a procedure for selecting cases (like simple random and systematic sampling), stratified samples are a way of structuring the target population *prior* to drawing a sample.

Researchers use stratified sampling to reduce sampling error in four situations:

- The target population has natural homogeneous subgroups.

- The population distribution is skewed on an important variable.

- A small subgroup is to be compared with larger ones.

- The researcher is using several sampling frames or data sources.

Homogeneous Subgroups.   Some populations can be divided into naturally occurring homogeneous subgroups (such as males and females, or skilled and unskilled employees) on some variable related to the key or primary dependent variable. Researchers stratify by taking a subsample from each subgroup.

Such a stratified sample has less sampling error than a simple random sample of the same size because it eliminates many potential unrepresentative samples. For example, if you select a subsample of males and a subsample of females, you eliminate all those possible total samples with few males or few females. (This principle is illustrated in Appendix A.) The effect is often multiplied, since other variables are usually related to the stratified variable, and thus potential distortions of these variables are also avoided. For example, stratifying on "seniority" would also tend to stratify on the variable "age."

The more homogeneous the strata (subgroups), the more precision a stratified sample offers. In most cases, researchers with stratified samples choose to reduce sample size (and thus research costs) while keeping the same level of precision that a simple random sample would have provided.

Skewed Population Distributions.

Sometimes important independent variables have highly skewed distributions: some cases have values much greater than most of the population. This happens frequently in business research using higher levels of analysis (e.g., departments, plants). Stratified sampling can help assure representative samples with skewed variables.

An example is the distribution of weekly sales shown in Figure 6.1. Sales of the top three outlets are substantially higher than the rest of the population. A representative sample should include one of these stores, but the chances of a sample missing all three are fairly high. (For a sample of size six the probability is .40.)

To guarantee a representative sample, stratify on the skewed variable "sales." Divide the outlets into two strata: the three "high" and the 21 "not-high" weekly sales. If a sample of one-third is taken from each stratum, the resulting stratified sample of eight will have less sampling error and more precision than a simple random sample of the same size.

The underlying principle is the same as for homogeneous subgroups: the elimination of unrepresentative samples. The difference is that stratification is based on arbitrary rather than naturally occurring subgroups.

Comparisons with Small Subgroups.

Some specific research designs involve a category independent variable with both very small and very large categories. For example, male diaper buyers are vastly outnumbered by women. A simple random sample would result in many women and few men. The problem with this is that, because sampling error is inversely related to sample size, the sampling error of the male subsample will be too great. As a

FIGURE 6.1
A Skewed Distribution of 24 Retail Outlets' Weekly Sales

$18,664	$29,882	$33,588
20,998	29,980	34,219
21,811	30,295	35,968
27,261	31,824	36,101
27,380	32,054	37,925
28,012	32,106	**45,024**
28,454	32,845	**49,752**
29,809	33,251	**60,963**

result, a comparison between men and women diaper buyers will not be accurate.

One solution is to draw a very large sample to ensure a small sampling error in the smaller subsample of men. If males are 5 percent of the diaper buyers, it would require a sample size of 500 to get about 25 men. This is a lot of effort for a few cases!

A better solution is *nonproportional* stratified sampling: the sample is stratified on the groups to be compared, and a different sampling fraction is used in each subsample. If women diaper buyers are sampled at 2.6 percent and men at 50 percent, the result is a stratified sample of about equal numbers of women and men. Relative to women, male diaper buyers are intentionally *oversampled*.

The **sampling fraction** is the ratio of the number of cases in the sample (or subsample) to the number in the target population (or subpopulation).

Multiple Frames and Data Sources.

Occasionally researchers require more than one sampling frame or different data sources for different parts of the population. For example, one group of consumers may be systematically sampled from a frame list while a second requires cluster sampling, or detailed records are available for employees in an Employee Involvement Program but a comparison group of nonparticipating employees must be surveyed by questionnaire.

Stratified sampling is a useful way of dealing with different levels of sampling error and different sampling fractions associated with the different frames or data sources. Treat the cases from each frame or data source as a separate stratum.

Stratified Sampling Decisions.

Researchers using stratified samples are faced with a set of decisions, including whether to stratify proportionally, allocating sample size among strata, and how many dimensions to stratify on.

1. Proportional or nonproportional stratification?

- *Proportional* stratified sampling is most common in descriptive and prediction research when the population has homogeneous subgroups or a skewed distribution. It provides population estimates with the lowest sampling error.

- *Nonproportional* stratified samples are used when comparisons are to be made among groups, and one or more are relatively small. It is most likely in evaluation and explanatory research. Each group represents a different level of a key or primary independent variable.

2. Which variables to stratify?

Samples can be stratified on two or more variables, as long as they are all related to the dependent variable (otherwise there is little point in stratification). It is tempting to overstratify. Avoid it. One or two variables are generally sufficient for most business research problems.

- Too many strata will increase the costs of drawing samples and contacting cases, since much more screening will be required to locate required cases.

- It may be difficult or impossible to estimate the population size of each stratum (in order to calculate sampling fractions).

3. How to allocate total sample size among strata?

  Researchers using stratified samples must decide what size subsamples to draw.

- *Proportional:* Use the same sampling fraction in all strata. Allocation is determined solely by the size of the total sample. (Sample size calculation is discussed in Chapter 7.)

- *Nonproportional:* If the purpose is to compare subgroups, sampling error is normally lowest when each subsample is equal in size (Sudman, 1983).

(Other criteria are sometimes used to allocate total sample size in nonproportional stratified sampling using different sampling frames or data sources. The alternatives include differences in variation among the strata and differences in data-gathering costs. These methods are beyond the scope of this text: consult a sampling text for further information, e.g., Frankel, 1983; Kish, 1965; Sudman, 1976.)

CASE EXAMPLE

A market researcher wants to compare older well-off consumers (a group representing only a small proportion of the population) with other age and income groups. He decides to stratify on the two dimensions of age (three levels) and income (two levels). His sampling design consists of the following six strata:

Under 21, household income less than $50,000

21 to 59, household income less than $50,000

Over 59, household income less than $50,000

Under 21, household income $50,000 or more

21 to 59, household income $50,000 or more

Over 59, household income $50,000 or more

ADVANCED TOPIC

Stratifying on a Dependent Variable. In most instances researchers stratify samples on an independent variable. For example, a survey of customer satisfaction stratifies customers on annual purchase volume (an independent control variable), and an evaluation of quality circles treats the test and comparison departments (the independent key variable) as separate strata.

Business researchers occasionally stratify on a dependent variable. When this happens it usually involves a comparison sample cross-sectional design (discussed in Chapter 4) in which the samples represent different values of the dependent variable. For example, the researcher compares samples of low- and high-productivity employees. Stratification on dependent variables requires caution to ensure that comparisons are made across subsamples (Blalock, 1979) or that the analysis uses symmetric measures of association. (Symmetric measures of association, unlike asymmetric measures, give the same result no matter which variable is the dependent.) The problem is illustrated in Box 6.5.

Calculations and Statistics.   Strictly speaking, statistical tests based on simple random samples are technically inappropriate for stratified samples. The necessary adjustments (such as estimates for population variance) can be complicated, but fortunately they are seldom required for most business research.[4] The use of uncorrected statistical tests normally presents no practical problems other than results that are slightly conservative.

If you pool nonproportional subsamples to make estimates for the entire population, you must weight the cases. For example, if you gather equal-sized subsamples of males and females from a population with only 10 percent males, you'll have to upweight each female case (multiply it by 1.8) and downweight each male (multiply it by 0.2) to return them to the correct population proportions. Note that, after weighting, sample size *must remain the same.* Weighting is simple with most computer statistical packages. (See Chapter 14.)

Weighting involves multiplying each case by a factor representing its contribution to the sample so that some cases "count" more than others. It is used with nonproportional sampling to return each subsample's proportion of the total sample to its corresponding proportion in the population.

Cluster and Multistage Samples

Cluster and multistage sampling divide the population into clusters—naturally occurring sets of cases that are physically or administratively close together. For example, people are clustered into cities, branch plants, retail outlets, church congregations, and union locals. Each cluster represents a *primary sampling unit* (PSU) to distinguish it from the unit of analysis.

• In **cluster sampling,** the researcher draws a sample of clusters and gathers data from (or about) *all* cases in the chosen clusters. Each cluster (and each case in the sample) has an equal probability of being chosen. If some clusters are very large or very different from others, clusters may be stratified before the primary sampling is performed.

[4]When precision and costs are of greater concern, as in some external research, consult a sampling text such as Frankel, 1983, or Kish, 1965.

BOX 6.5
RESEARCH ISSUES

Nonproportional Stratifying on a Dependent Variable

Nonproportional stratification on a dependent variable can lead to distorted results if the researcher uses asymmetric measures of association or fails to limit comparisons only to those between subsamples (instead of between categories of the independent variable, as would normally be the case in analysis).

Consider this example: A plant has a work force of 1,200, of whom 1,000 are males and 220 have low levels of productivity. The distribution looks like this:

		Males	Females
Productivity	Low	200	20
	High	800	180

Productivity is related to gender: 20 percent of males but only 10 percent of females have low productivity, for a 10 percent difference.

The researcher, who is unaware of this relationship, draws a nonproportional stratified sample on the basis of the dependent variable, productivity. He draws a 50 percent sample of those with low productivity, and a 10 percent sample of those with high productivity. The distribution he gets looks like this:

		Males	Females
Productivity	Low	100	10
	High	80	18

In this table 56 percent of males and 36 percent of females have low productivity, for a 20 percent difference. The percentage difference, an asymmetric measure of association, *doubled* as a result of nonproportional sampling on the dependent variable.

- **Multistage sampling** involves two or more rounds of sampling. In the simplest situation the researcher draws a sample of clusters and then samples the cases within each chosen cluster before gathering data. In more complicated designs, he or she further subdivides each selected cluster into subclusters (secondary sampling units), and draws a sample of subclusters within each cluster. The selected subclusters are further divided into tertiary sampling units, and so on until in the final stage samples of cases or clusters of cases are drawn. The sampling of clusters at any stage (and of cases in the final stage) may be stratified and carried out with either simple random or systematic sampling. The process of multistage sampling can be very complex and often requires expert advice.

Like stratified samples, cluster and multistage samples structure the population before a sample is drawn. The structuring is based on geographical location (area sampling) rather than on characteristics of the population as in stratified sampling. Cluster and multistage sampling are used to save time and money in two situations:

- Sampling frame lists are unavailable or too costly.

- A project calls for personal interviews from widely dispersed respondents or available data stored in widely dispersed locations.

Sampling Frame Lists. Frame lists of all cases in the population often cost too much to obtain or compile. The alternative is cluster and multistage sampling from a map (or list) of locations. An actual list of cases (or a frame procedure) is needed only for the final stage of multistage sampling, and not at all in cluster sampling.

Scattered Interviews. When a population is geographically dispersed, contacting randomly chosen cases for personal interviews can be very costly, particularly if one or more callbacks are required. For example, interviews with 100 employees spread throughout the continental United States (four in New York City, one in Denver, two in Seattle, one in Boise, one in Charlotte, etc.) would be expensive and time consuming. Clustering cases together saves on travel time and provides better administrative control.

CASE EXAMPLE

A market research firm established a consumer panel to evaluate new food products. The firm created the panel using a multistage sample. In the first stage, they chose eight states stratified by region (Northeast, South, North Central, and West). Within each state, they selected three counties or metropolitan areas. In the third stage, they picked four census tracts in each metropolitan area and one community in each county. The fourth and fifth stages involved sampling the blocks and dwelling units in the census tracts and communities. Each selected dwelling unit was then contacted. In the sixth stage a person randomly chosen from among the adults living in the dwelling unit was asked to participate in the testing panel. The sample design used the following lists:

- The states in each of four census regions (government lists)

- The counties and metropolitan areas in 8 selected states (government lists)

- The census tracts and communities in 16 metropolitan areas and 8 counties (government maps)

- The blocks in 64 census tracts and 8 communities (government or commercial maps or lists)

- The dwelling unit addresses in 216 selected blocks (commercial lists supplemented by researcher field counts as required)

- A field count of the adults living in 1,080 homes (compiled by interviewers)

Only in the last two stages did the researchers carry out any field listing or counting; in the final stage they used a frame procedure for selecting individuals. No list of individuals was required at all.

Researchers are most likely to use cluster or multistage sampling in external research, such as market research or public opinion surveys. Occasionally they need it in internal research. For example, interviews with employees in a chain of 210 jug milk outlets are much cheaper with cluster sampling.

ADVANCED TOPICS

Sampling Error, Heterogeneity, and Number of Clusters. Sampling error in cluster and multistage samples is almost always greater than a simple random sample of the same size. Because cases are not selected independently, those within a cluster are likely to be more homogeneous than cases in different clusters. Twenty-eight employees at a McDonald's in Boston are more likely to have attitudes and interests in common with each other than 28 employees chosen randomly from all McDonald's outlets in the country. Warwick and Lininger (1975) estimate that on average the sampling error of a cluster sample is about 1.5 times that of a simple random sample of the same size.

- One frequent solution to the greater sampling error is a larger sample. This improves precision and the cost is usually much less than the alternative of a smaller but nonclustered sample.

- A second solution is to divide the population into clusters that are internally heterogeneous. However, this is often difficult to do and still retain the rationale for cluster sampling: reduce data-gathering costs with cases located close together.

- A third option is to control the number of clusters. In cluster sampling, sampling error is lowest with a large number of small clusters (since all cases within each chosen cluster are included). In multistage samples, on the other hand, sampling error is less with a few large heterogeneous PSUs (Satin and Shastry, 1983).

Calculations and Statistics. A problem in cluster sampling is controlling sample size. Clusters usually vary in size, but all clusters normally have the same probability of selection. (Calculations are simpler when all clusters, and thus all cases, have the same probability of selection. Because no weighting of cases is required, such samples are called *self-weighting.*) Consequently, the sample size depends on which clusters are chosen: a sample of three large clusters will have more cases than a sample of three small clusters.

Unfortunately, the precision of estimates based on cluster samples is subject to error when sample size varies, an error which increases with the variation in size among clusters. From a practical point of view, however, this error is normally disregarded in all business research except when very precise estimates are needed in descriptive research. A partial solution to the problem of controlling sample size, and minimizing the error of precision estimates, is to stratify clusters on size.

In multistage sampling, sample size can be controlled while still allowing each case an equal chance of selection. This is achieved by selecting the primary sampling unit clusters with probabilities proportional to the size of each cluster. The complexity of calculations increases when cases are stratified within each cluster (as might be required in a complex sample design), and subsample size varies as well. The error produced by this subsample size variation is, like that for cluster samples, usually small enough to be ignored.

A second problem with cluster and multistage samples is that statistical tests intended for simple random samples are inappropriate. The errors that result are likely to be substantial and to lead to the conclusion that a relationship is significant when it really isn't (Blalock, 1979). On the other hand, the corrections required in order to use the tests tend to be complicated. In practice, this problem can be partially overcome by choosing lower (more conservative) levels of alpha (such as .01 instead of .05). If your research requires a well-specified degree of precision, consult a text in sampling theory or an expert in sampling.

NONPROBABILITY SAMPLES

Business researchers frequently don't have the time or resources to select cases using a strictly random procedure (such as a table of random numbers). Instead they use procedures that produce nonprobability samples.

A **nonprobability sample** is one in which the probability of a given case being selected from the population is unknown and may be zero.

The advantage of nonprobability samples is cost; drawing the sample and gathering the data are usually very inexpensive. The major drawbacks are two:

- They tend to be nonrepresentative.

- The precision of estimates cannot be estimated, since sampling error is unknown.[5]

Some types of nonprobability samples are more nonrepresentative than others. However, the accuracy and precision of estimates are always problematic; the researcher can only rely on subjective judgement (Frankel, 1983), aided wherever possible by a comparison of the sample with known characteristics of the target population.

[5]Thus, while measures of association are appropriate and common in many nonprobability samples, tests of significance are inappropriate and problematic (see Appendix A). There is an important exception that psychology students often wonder about. Laboratory experiments use convenience samples of whatever students are handy or can be persuaded (with grades or other inducements) to volunteer as subjects. Yet these studies use significance tests (usually analysis of variance F tests). Is this legitimate? Yes. These experiments, like random samples, *do* have a random basis: the random assignment of students to experimental conditions. In these studies, the significance tests consider whether any observed differences could be due to *assignment error,* which is equivalent to *sampling error* in probability samples.

Uses.   Despite their disadvantages, many research objectives can be met effectively with a nonprobability sample.

- *Exploring a problem.* The use of nonprobability samples is frequent in the problem investigation phase of research. Examples: the difficulties employees are having understanding a new benefit plan; whether retailers are having problems with the promotion scheme for a new product.

- *Finding behavior patterns and types.* Examples: patterns of absenteeism (many short absences, a few long periods, or Friday-Monday patterns); types of membership support for the union local (everyday participant, crisis supporter, opposing faction).

- *The range of a variable.* Examples: the range of customer opinions about a change in banking hours—is the reaction extreme, or did the change make only a slight difference?

- *Preliminary checks.* Nonprobability samples can provide quick and inexpensive checks of new products, programs, or procedures. If a substantial portion of respondents in a nonprobability sample react negatively, it is unlikely that the results will be very different with a probability sample. If, on the other hand, problems seem to be few, then a follow-up with a probability sample is warranted.[6]

- *Examining relationships.* While nonprobability samples are not good for descriptive research estimates of population characteristics (such as average weekly retail sales), they are often sufficient for the investigation of relationships. Deciding the presence or absence of a causal process requires less accuracy than the estimation of a population mean or proportion. (This is part of the reasoning behind the development and extensive use of quota samples in marketing research.)

In general, if you don't plan to use a statistical test to assess the precision of an estimate, you may not need a probability sample. On the other hand, you can't make intelligent use of the results of a significance test with a nonprobability sample.

Types.   Different types of nonprobability samples vary in the amount of time and other resources they require and the amount of control the researcher exercises over the selection of cases. The more control, the more representative the sample and the more accurate the estimates.

The most common types of nonprobability samples of use to business researchers, in order of increasing researcher control, are as follows:

---

[6]The principle underlying this use can be extended to other situations where a cheap but less accurate version of a test is available, as well as a more expensive accurate one. Decide which kind of error is more important: concluding that the product is good when it's not, or that it's not good when it is. In this example, the researcher decides that the first is more important, so that if the cheap test shows that the product is good, he double-checks with the expensive test to make sure that the firm doesn't market a faulty product (a mistake which is worse than deciding to improve a good product before marketing it). On the other hand, if the test shows that the product is bad, he decides on further improvements without resorting to the more expensive test.

- Convenience sample
- Self-selection sample
- Snowball sample
- Judgment sample
- Quota sample

Convenience Samples

Convenience samples are the easiest samples to draw: the researcher simply gathers data from whatever cases are conveniently close by. This includes employees on the shop floor (particularly if they don't appear to be busy at the moment), students in the hall, people on street corners, and the first few files in a filing cabinet.

Cases appear in convenience samples because of where they are at a particular time. Since few people wander around randomly, and where people (and things) are found is a result of habits, gender, occupation, and other characteristics, the sample is usually very nonrepresentative, and the accuracy of estimates is always in doubt.

- These problems are less important if the population is highly homogeneous, since there's less opportunity for error. (Drawing blood, for example, is a convenience sample: the nurse selects a convenient artery. It works because blood is highly homogeneous; one cc. is much like another.)

- Convenience samples often provide suggestive results leading to more structured research. Managers use them to find out whether there are any initial problems with a product, process, or program.

Self-Selection Samples

When researchers allow individuals to choose whether to take part in the research, the result is a self-selection sample. To be effective, researchers must ensure that each potential member of the target population has an opportunity to participate. For example, they might flood the target population with questionnaires.

Respondents appear in self-selection samples because of their feelings or opinions about an issue. What the researcher gets, of course, is an unrepresentative sample. In other forms of sampling, self-selection is minimized as much as possible. For example, organizational employees or members who volunteer to take part in research are much more likely to be committed to the organization and its objectives than are members of the population.

Self-selection samples, on the other hand, make use of this unrepresentativeness; for some kinds of research problems, *it may be just what the researcher wants!* For example, self-selection samples are good at getting responses from people who are excited about an issue, have a related problem, or who, in general, find the topic to be salient or important. Information from these kinds of persons is often used to formulate product ideas or workplace improvements, which are then tested more systematically. These samples provide a good idea of the extremes of opinion on an issue by overrepresenting those for whom it is important. (Depending on the issue, overall variation in the sample may be less than in the general population, a trait common in samples of volunteers.)

Beside the intentional unrepresentativeness a researcher may want, the major advantage of self-selection samples is that they are cheap. The major drawback, as with all nonprobability samples, is that the researcher has little idea how representative the sample is. For this reason, researchers use large sampling fractions, or a substantial sample size, to increase the chances of a minority opinion showing up. It is important, as with all nonprobability samples, to compare the sample to known characteristics of the population.

The researcher controls the content of the sample by where the topic is publicized and where questionnaires or other opportunities to take part are distributed. Methods of distribution are varied:

- Hand out questionnaires or stuff them into mailboxes.

- Ask people in selected locations if they can spare a few minutes to talk about a specific consumer product.

- Advertise widely a telephone number for people to call about a specific issue (a reversal of the normal method of telephone interviewing).

Snowball Samples

Snowball sampling is a useful technique when the research involves cases with fairly uncommon characteristics, experiences, or attitudes. It is especially useful when informal networks of respondents share these characteristics.

The researcher begins by finding a few respondents fitting the target population specifications. After data gathering, the researcher asks each one to suggest others who have the same characteristics. These respondents, in turn, suggest others. The sample snowballs: the researcher draws it as he or she gathers data. For example, a researcher asks union members who feel they've been discriminated against in job promotions for the names of other members who feel the same way.

Respondents appear in snowball samples because their specific experiences or characteristics are known to other respondents. (Compare this with self-selection samples, where inclusion is totally the decision of the respondent.) The problems of representativeness are substantial: respondents are most likely to know and mention other potential respondents similar to themselves. A comparison of the sample with known population characteristics is important. Another problem is that snowball samples may require considerable time and effort to track down recommended respondents.

SUGGESTION

If you use a large self-selection or other nonprobability sample with a high likelihood of nonrepresentativeness, it is often useful to draw a small random sample at the same time. The random sample provides a rough but useful baseline against which to compare the estimates from the nonprobability sample.

Judgment Samples

In a judgment sample, researchers select "typical" cases, relying on their own opinions. Cases appear in the sample because researchers judge them to be representative. Unlike self-selection and convenience samples, inclusion in the sample is not up to respondents themselves or a result of their general characteristics and habits; researchers exercise a much greater level of control over the content of the sample. (A related nonprobability procedure is the *expert sample,* in which researchers rely on the judgment of one or more experts about which cases are typical.)

One problem with judgment samples is that they frequently contain too many cases grouped at what the "judge" sees as the mean of the population. Atypical cases are underrepresented. The result is often an acceptable estimate of the mean, but too low an estimate of population variance. Larger sample sizes are not likely to overcome this defect.

Despite this problem, judgment samples can be very useful. They require few resources and are often used in pretests of questionnaires and other instruments and in market research focus groups. When combined with quota sampling, the low variance problem is substantially reduced. A final, but important, advantage is that when a sample must be very small (10 or 15 cases), a judgment sample is likely to be *more* representative than a probability sample, because of the latter's large sampling error.

Quota Samples

In quota sampling, the researcher establishes quotas for the number of cases having certain characteristics, for example, 10 respondents in each of the following categories: male under 30, female under 30, male 30 or over, and female 30 or over. Interviewers then find "typical" respondents within each category.

The quota sample is the most representative of all nonprobability samples. It combines the principles of stratified and judgment sampling. Like strata, the quota categories help ensure a more representative sample by ensuring a broad range of cases. Within the categories, however, cases are not selected randomly; interviewers must use their own judgment about the representativeness of a potential respondent within the category.

Because they deal effectively with the representativeness problem affecting nonprobability samples, quota samples are often used to study relationships in explanatory and evaluation research. However, because sampling error and precision remain unknown, they are not very effective for descriptive research (which estimates population averages and proportions).

Respondents appear in quota samples because they meet quota specifications of age, gender, or other characteristics and because they are judged to be typical. Compared to other nonprobability samples, the researcher exercises a substantial degree of control over the content of the sample (for this reason

BOX 6.6

CAMPBELL SWITCH: A CONTINUING CASE

Part Ten: George and Roberta Plan a Sample

"All right," says George, "now that we have a specific design and a list of variables, what kind of sample are we going to use?" He reaches for the only cup with coffee still left in it.

"I always liked quota samples myself," replies Roberta, deftly snatching the cup away before George can reach it. "That's mine."

"Oh, sorry. But I think this ought to be a probability sample. Much better for estimating accuracy."

"But we haven't got much time. Quota samples are faster."

"That's true. And speaking of time, I'm going to get another coffee. Want a fresh one?"

When George returns, Roberta looks up from some notes. "I've jotted down the pros and cons of quota and random samples, George. I'd say for this project, you may be right. We won't save much time with a quota sample because of the screening we'd have to do. And we have a good accurate sampling frame right here in Personnel."

"All right!" says George, looking pleased. "You do take cream only, don't you?" He sits down and the meeting continues.

---

such samples are sometimes called *purposive*). Very sophisticated forms of quota sampling are often used in market research because of the substantial savings to be made (see Box 6.6). These researchers often use stratification, multistage sampling, and random selection procedures in all but the final sampling stage.

Researchers usually combine two or more quota variables to form categories, and specify category quotas for interviewers to meet. For example, three levels of age, two levels of sex, and three levels of income generate 18 categories. The researcher decides on the number of cases to be found for each category by examining that category's population distribution: if 18 percent of the population are women aged 21 to 34 earning less than $15,000 a year, then 18 percent of the total sample size is assigned to that quota category. This practice, however, can lead to procedure problems (see Box 6.7).

Distribution Quotas. With more than three quota variables, researchers normally relax the requirements by specifying *distribution quotas* (rather than category quotas). Targets are given for the entire sample, rather than for categories. For example, the research could specify that, of 120 cases:

gender	60 must be males
age	41 must be under age 25
income	17 must earn under $12,000
	28 between $12,000 and $19,999

SUGGESTION

For explanatory research, when time or funds are meager, give serious consideration to a quota sample.

BOX 6.7
RESEARCH ETHICS

Quota Samples

It is not unknown to have interviewers bend the ethics of good research practice when using quota samples with many categories. The problem arises as the project nears its end and most categories are filled. By that time, interviewers have to screen many individuals to find those needed to fill the few remaining quotas.

The temptation to cheat by substituting close cases is inevitable and understandable. However,

this practice can seriously undermine sample representativeness and lead to erroneous conclusions. To avoid it, make sure interviewers understand the possible consequences of stretching quota definitions, and make sure that project planning builds in enough time for these hard-to-find final cases to be located. It also helps to telephone a sample of respondents to verify interviews and quota placement (see Chapter 12).

	47 between $20,000 and $29,999
	28 must earn $30,000 or more
dwelling	76 must live in rental units
job	29 must hold white-collar jobs

Distribution quotas are usually selected to represent known or estimated proportions of the characteristics in the target population.

■ *The Lighter Side of Research*

Sample: A unique collection of subjects having virtually no chance of being representative of the population from which it was drawn. This shortcoming is trivial and is generally ignored.

Subject: Mankind's equivalent of the white rat. A victim of science. (Woodman, 1979)

Summary

A sample is part of a population selected to represent the whole and used to estimate its characteristics. Researchers try to obtain representative samples in order to make accurate estimates of population characteristics.

The sampling process begins with the target population specified by the research problem boundaries. Researchers then choose a sampling frame: one or more lists of cases in the target population or a procedure for selecting cases. Using the sample frame, they then draw an initial sample of cases and gather data. The cases for which they obtain usable data is the achieved sample. If sampling procedures are unbiased and other research errors have been kept to a minimum, the achieved sample is highly representative of the target population.

Probability samples employ random selection procedures (simple random or systematic sampling) that allow researchers to use inferential statistics to test the significance of results. Some probability samples (stratified, cluster, and multistage) structure the population to increase accuracy or reduce costs.

Nonprobability samples are faster and cheaper, but don't permit statistical tests of significance and measures of precision. They include, in order of the researcher's control over sample content, convenience, self-selection, snowball, judgment, and quota samples.

Where Are We Now?

This chapter completes an introduction to the sampling process and the different types of samples used in business research. In the next chapter we consider the criteria and process for choosing a sample design. At that point, the design decisions will be complete.

Discussion Issues and Assignments

1. Here is an exercise in sample design decision making. The printer, who is considering a subsequent edition of this text, wants to know how many italicized words it contains. Choose the type of sample you would use to arrive at an estimate. Also consider the population, target population, your choice of sampling frame, sampling procedure, and whether to stratify.

2. Contact a marketing research firm and offer to take their research design expert to lunch. Ask about the sample designs they use for large projects. Get details about a recent project, and determine what type of sample it was. Why did they choose it? Would you have chosen the same kind?

3. Together with one or two other students, devise a cluster or multistage sampling design to survey (with a questionnaire) student attitudes toward the campus bookstore. Consider what groups are homogeneous and what a suitable cluster might be.

4. Repeat the exercise in question 3, but plan a self-selection sample.

5. Devise a quota sample for interviews with faculty members about the campus bookstore. What variables would you use to establish quotas? What additional instructions would you give interviewers?

6. In what ways do systematic, stratified, and cluster samples violate the assumption of independent observations?

Further Reading

Deming, W. E. 1960. *Sample Design in Business Research*. New York: Wiley.

   This is the classic work for sampling designs and decision making in business research.

Dutka, S., and L. R. Frankel. 1990. "Misuses and Abuses of Statistical Techniques in Market Research Surveys." *Chance* 3:14, 18-23.

A highly readable discussion of common errors involving sampling frames business researchers commit, and how to correct them.

Satin, A., and W. Shastry. 1983. *Survey Sampling: A Non-Mathematical Guide.* Ottawa: Statistics Canada.

An excellent introduction to the more complex issues of survey sampling. Highly readable and very clear.

CHAPTER 7

Selecting a Sample Design

CHAPTER OBJECTIVES

- What are the criteria of a good sample?
- When and why should we sample?
- What type of sample should we use?
- How large should our sample be?

CHAPTER OUTLINE

WHAT MAKES A GOOD SAMPLE?
SELECTION BIAS
SAMPLE OR ENUMERATE?
SELECTING THE RIGHT SAMPLE TYPE
CHOOSING THE RIGHT SAMPLE SIZE

usiness researchers use a wide variety of sample types and sizes:

- From the personnel records of all 12,492 hourly employees of a major steel mill (the population), a researcher selects every 50th file and copies information on absenteeism and tardiness. She then sends questionnaires to the 249 employees in the sample.

- A union local draws a sample of 50 members each from the four different plants it represents. Names are selected so that half are males and half are females.

- A researcher draws a sample of 35 recent mergers and acquisitions from among those reported in the past 12 months in the *Wall Street Journal.*

- A researcher contacts by telephone a sample of 300 households on the day following the broadcast of a test version of a television commercial. The sample is drawn through random digit dialing. A comparison sample is drawn in a city that did not see the commercial.

- An interviewer contacts 100 households in each of 11 major cities. He choose ten areas in each city, two blocks in each area, and five households on each block. He interviews the principal food shopper about brand preference.

- Researchers working for a marketing firm approach individuals in a shopping center, asking them to look at some magazine advertisements and answer some questions. They test 10 persons in each of 12 different categories (e.g., male over 40 earning more than $30,000 annually; female 18 to 24, earning less than $12,000, etc.). Half the persons in each category are shown version A of the advertisement; the other half are shown version B.

What determines the type of sample researchers choose? How do they know how big to make it? Why do they sample in the first place, rather than enumerate?

WHAT MAKES A GOOD SAMPLE?

Good samples meet two criteria: (1) for a reasonable cost, they (2) provide sufficiently accurate estimates. We apply these two criteria to each of the three sampling design decisions discussed in this chapter.

Sampling Costs

Samples vary widely in the time, money, and personnel they require. Different types of samples differ in the costs of (1) drawing the sample, (2) gathering data from the sample cases, and (3) analyzing the data. Smaller samples are cheaper to draw and save on data-gathering and analysis costs. In general, the cheaper the sample the less accurate the estimates. However, there are a number of exceptions, as we discuss later when we consider the choice of sample type and sample size. We also look at the issue of costs in more detail when we discuss sample size.

Accuracy

Although the researcher never actually knows it, there is a *true* value for every population characteristic that a sample estimates. Among employees in a plant, there is a true average age and a true level of association between age and job satisfaction. The difference between the estimate and the true value is the accuracy of the estimate.

Accuracy is affected both by the choice of cases for the sample and by how carefully those cases are measured. Measurement error is the topic of the next chapter; the focus here is case selection, that is, how *representative* the sample is of the target population from which it is drawn. The fewer case selection errors, the more accurate the estimates and the greater the *external validity* of the conclusions.

Case selection errors fall into three categories:

- *Sampling error:* Even when we use strict random procedures, the element of chance can produce an unrepresentative initial sample.[1]

- *Selection bias:* If faulty sampling procedures systematically underrepresent (or overrepresent) certain kinds of cases, the sample doesn't truly reflect the population. In other words, certain kinds of cases are more likely to be omitted from the initial sample.

- *Missing cases bias:* If cases that cannot be found, or that refuse to participate, or for which data are unusable are systematically different from cases in the sample, the sample will be unrepresentative. In other words, certain kinds of cases, although in the initial sample, are omitted from the achieved sample. (Since missing cases bias results from data-gathering rather than sampling procedures, we postpone its discussion to following chapters.)

An *unbiased* sample is one with a low level of selection and missing cases bias. We first examine sampling error and sampling costs and then look at selection bias. Then we focus on the three sampling design decisions.

Sampling Error

Researchers normally try to choose designs that minimize sampling error. Sampling error is the inaccuracy that results because of the luck of the draw

---

[1]The term *random* as used in sampling does not mean haphazard. It means *occurring strictly by chance,* involving procedures that ensure no causes other than chance determine the outcome.

and is present in all estimates based on random samples. For example, even with strict random procedures you might draw a sample of 10 cards from a well-shuffled 52-card deck and find that 8 of them are hearts. Based on this sample, your estimate of the proportion of hearts in the population is .8, rather different from the true population proportion of .25. (For those whose statistics are a little rusty, the concept of sampling error is explained in Appendix A.)

The smaller the sampling error, the greater the precision of your estimates. Sampling error and precision are attributes of estimates, not of samples. The same sample might give a precise estimate for one variable but a very imprecise one for another, depending on the variability of each variable in the population.

Even with purely random and totally unbiased selection procedures, researchers are always somewhat unsure of their estimates because of sampling error. The advantage of random sampling is that it allows researchers to *estimate the precision of their estimates*. As a result, researchers can see the effect of different sample sizes and types on precision.

In summary, a good sample is reasonable in cost and provides accurate estimates through low sampling error and low selection and missing cases bias. The next section discusses how sampling procedures affect selection bias. Then we consider the three sampling design decisions: whether to sample, sample type, and sample size.

The **precision** of an estimate is the inverse of the sampling error associated with that estimate.

SUGGESTION

If you undertake a major external research project (e.g., marketing or public opinion survey), you will almost always save time and money by securing professional help with sample design, particularly if you are considering area probability sampling methods.

SELECTION BIAS

Harry's selection of foremen (Chapter 6) was selection biased on at least two counts: his choice of Abe and Sam was based on their relationship, and his choice of the other foremen was based on their availability. Thus both foremen who tend to agree with Harry and foremen who are not too busy were overrepresented in his sample.

Selection bias has its source in the procedures used to select cases for the sample. Some sources of selection bias are fairly obvious and therefore easy to prevent. Others are so subtle that inexperienced researchers are often not aware of them.

Handing questionnaires to the first 50 employees leaving the plant at the end of their shift introduces an obvious bias. Such a sample is likely to overrepresent those with little commitment to their jobs, or those with important interests outside of work that play a significant role in their lives. Their attitudes about the implementation of new technology are likely to be very different from those of the last 50 employees to leave. Handing questionnaires to every tenth employee eliminates much of the selection bias, but the resulting sample still underrepresents those who are more likely to be absent and those working overtime. Mailing questionnaires to every tenth employee on the payroll list would overcome these biases, but might miss recently hired or transferred employees.

By contrast, missing cases bias has its sources in the researcher's failure to obtain data from cases that are systematically different. In other words, certain kinds of cases in the initial sample are underrepresented in the achieved sample.

We now consider specific sources of selection bias. This kind of bias occurs in the target population, sampling frame, and initial sample phases of the sampling process. (Missing cases bias, discussed later, occurs in the data-gathering phase that results in the achieved sample.)

The Sampling Frame

Selection bias is present whenever the sampling frame differs systematically from the target population. This stage of the sampling procedure is often a major source of selection bias. Because a frame list may have gaps, errors, or out-of-date information, or a frame procedure may miss some cases, the sampled population doesn't necessarily correspond to the target population. If the differences are systematic, so that certain types of cases are under- or over-represented, selection bias is present and will lead to inaccurate estimates. On the other hand, if the differences are few and not systematic the effects will be minimal.

Three kinds of selection errors occur in sampling frames: undercoverage, overcoverage, and duplication.

Undercoverage.   Undercoverage is the omission of cases that belong in the target population. It is serious for two reasons.

- It is normally impossible to recover these cases and get them into the frame.
- These omissions tend to be systematic rather than random, and thus increase selection bias. For example, telephone directories don't include unlisted numbers, the majority of which are requested by households with high income.

If a frame list carries additional information (such as gender or age), you can check for undercoverage before data gathering by comparing a sample from the frame to known characteristics of the target population (such as gender ratio or average age). If undercoverage is severe, it may be possible to supplement the sample with a second frame and a stratified sample design, one stratum from each frame.

Overcoverage.   Overcoverage occurs when the sampling frame includes cases that don't belong in the target population. This error is less serious, since these cases can usually be screened out at one or more of three stages:

- As the sample is drawn from the sampling frame, if the frame includes appropriate screening information

- As cases in the sample are contacted, if the screening information is readily available at the time of contact

- As the data are prepared for analysis, provided that the screening information has been gathered

The later the screening, the more costly it tends to be. Research that focuses on special subgroups often involves extensive screening.

CASE EXAMPLE

A researcher investigates the responses of female employees to alternative pay-equity policies their employer is considering. From the sampling frame (a list of employees), he screens out cases with obvious male names. For a subsample contacted by telephone, he screens out males with an initial question about the employee's gender. For a second subsample to whom questionnaires are sent, screening is performed as questionnaires are returned, using a question asking for the respondent's gender.

Duplication. A duplicate is the second or subsequent entry of the same case in a sampling frame (list or procedure). This type of selection error occurs

- When record keeping is poor (common in the membership lists of voluntary organizations).

- When two or more lists are combined to create a single frame list.

- When a case goes through frame procedures twice (an employee leaves the plant, returns for a forgotten lunch pail, and leaves again, each time picking up a questionnaire at the plant gate).

Duplication produces selection bias when cases with characteristics that increase their chances of showing up on two or more lists are systematically overrepresented. For example, recently promoted and transferred employees may be listed in two organization departments or individuals with higher education who subscribe to many magazines will appear on many mailing lists.

If duplication is a possibility, first check to see how many duplicates are present in the sample. Then you can (1) ignore the problem if it's minor and unsystematic, (2) delete all duplicate entries from the frame lists (leaving the first entry), or (3) correct the problem by compensating for duplicated entries (see Box 7.1). Note that both solutions 2 and 3 require that you go back to the sampling frame list. You cannot deal with duplication from the sample alone. Nor can you just drop second and subsequent appearances of a duplicate case from the sample—the overrepresentation problem will remain.

BOX 7.1
RESEARCH SKILLS

Compensating for Duplicate Cases

The following procedure eliminates the selection bias that occurs when the same case appears more than once in a sampling frame.

1. Check each case in the sample to see if it appears on more than one frame list. This is easiest if the sample can be arranged in some numerical or alphabetical order and is easier still if the frame is in some order.

2. If a case appears twice on a frame list, or on more than two lists, determine the number of times it appears.

3. *Downweight* that case: multiply each occurrence of the case *in the sample* by a factor that reduces its contribution to the sample. The downweighting factor is $1/L$ where L is the total number of times the case appears *in the frame list.* (With statistics packages such as SPSS/PC+ and STAT-PAC, downweighting is easily accomplished by an IF statement to identify the case ID, and statements giving the weighting factor and weight command.)

The result of downweighting is to give all cases in the sample an equal probability of having been selected. Note that this procedure does not involve removing duplicate cases from the sample.

CASE EXAMPLE

A student wanted to obtain detailed evaluations of the instructor in a large class. He obtained a class list to use as a sampling frame, intending to mail questionnaires to the selected students. The list contained 644 names. Of those, unknown to the student, 18 had already dropped the course and, more seriously, the names of 55 students auditing the course were not included on the class list. Four students who registered late were mistakenly listed twice. When these problems became evident, the student corrected his sampling frame with a revised class list provided by the instructor, based on students who had written the most recent test and those who had requested permission to audit.

SUGGESTION

An important part of your report will be a discussion of the adequacy of the sample. Keep a file of the problems you encounter (administration, selection bias in the target population or frame, missing cases, processing) to help write that section. This discussion is important in informing the reader of the limits of generalizability (external validity) of your conclusions and recommendations.

The Initial Sample

The initial sample, obtained by drawing the sample from the frame, normally produces little selection bias. If the researcher uses a table of random numbers correctly (see Chapter 6) or carries out a correct systematic sampling procedure, there will be few systematic errors. Although a clerical error during screening might drop cases that ought to be included, most errors at this stage tend to be random and are not likely to result in selection bias.

Selection Bias in Systematic Samples

When cases are listed or arrayed in rank order or periodically, a systematic sample may be biased.

Rank Order Arrays.   A systematic sample of cases ranked on an important variable produces selection bias. The greater the random starting number, the higher the average value of the sample will be.

For example, Figure 7.1 shows the same ranked set of retail outlets discussed in the previous chapter. The stores are listed in order of increasing weekly sales. The starting number for a systematic sample of 6 of the 24 outlets determines the average weekly sales for the sample:

- A starting number of 1 selects a sample that estimates average weekly sales of $29,916.

- For a starting number of 4 the estimate is $36,535.

Ranked lists will result in substantial under- or overestimation when the selection interval is large and the variable used to rank the cases has high variance. If an array of this kind cannot be shuffled, then a simple random sample is preferable, or the sample should be stratified.

Periodic Arrays.   A second source of selection bias occurs when the frame list or data array is *periodic* (that is, every kth case has some unique feature), and the selection interval i is a multiple of k.

For example, consider employee cards filed by work groups (each group having ten employees) with the first card in the group being the leader's. A systematic sample with a selection interval of 30 would contain either no group leaders or all group leaders. A more common example is data arrayed in pairs, such as briefs presented to an interest arbitration hearing. Each management

FIGURE 7.1
A Skewed
Distribution of
Retail Outlets'
Weekly Sales

$18,664	$29,882	$33,588
20,998	29,980	34,219
21,811	30,295	35,968
27,261	31,824	36,101
27,380	32,054	37,925
28,012	32,106	45,024
28,454	32,845	49,752
29,809	33,251	60,963

Average sales, systematic sample of size 6 (sampling interval = 4):

Starting with first case: $29,916

Starting with fourth case: $36,535

brief is followed by the corresponding union's brief. An even-numbered selection interval would result in a sample of only management or only union briefs. Periodic lists are relatively rare, however, and a quick check is usually enough to indicate whether a problem might arise.

SAMPLE OR ENUMERATE?

To sample or enumerate is the first of the three sampling design decisions. The three factors to consider in choosing between a sample and an enumeration are accuracy, costs, and measurement effects. (We discuss a fourth consideration, population size, when we examine the sample size decision.)

Accuracy

At first it seems obvious that estimates based on enumerations must be more accurate than those based on samples. However, a sample of reasonable size and an enumeration may be almost equally accurate, and in some cases samples are *more* accurate.

The accuracy of samples is affected by sampling error, selection bias, missing cases bias, and measurement error. The accuracy of enumerations is affected only by missing cases bias and measurement error. Sampling error and selection bias are eliminated because there is no sampling procedure. Missing cases bias remains a problem because the researcher may still be unable to contact cases, they refuse to participate, or the data are unusable.

Because enumerations must gather data from many cases, they frequently use large numbers of relatively poorly trained interviewers and other staff. These people are more prone to make interviewing and clerical mistakes that produce measurement error. Sample surveys typically use smaller, better trained, and more closely administered staff. Missing cases bias is often more prevalent in enumerations because personnel have neither the time nor training for effective follow-ups. In surveys, on the other hand, three or four callbacks to reduce missing cases bias are not uncommon.

In some instances, then, the greater measurement error and missing cases bias in an enumeration may more than offset the elimination of sampling error and selection bias, particularly when data are gathered through interviews or questionnaires. As a result, samples may provide *more* accuracy than enumerations.

Costs

The cost of an enumeration in time, money, and personnel often makes it impractical. Costs decline substantially when only a fraction of cases are investigated. Time is often very important in business research; decisions are required quickly. For example, there usually isn't time to evaluate an advertising campaign with an enumeration.

On the other hand, when data-gathering costs are small or negligible, sampling provides little or no savings. For example, if data are already in the computer (such as a database of employees or customers) the *only* advantage to sampling is to lower the data-analysis costs of using expensive statistical procedures, which require relatively large amounts of computer time.

Measurement Effects

When the act of measuring destroys or alters a case, sampling is necessary to avoid eradicating the population or changing it in undesirable ways. An obvious example is quality control testing. Researchers cannot test all tires to the point of failure, but with careful sampling researchers can make accurate estimates about a large batch of tires on the basis of a few tests. Similarly, employees interviewed about problems with their foreman are thereafter more sensitive to the possibility of such problems. If management doesn't want the entire work force population sensitized by reactive measurements, sampling is the solution.

SELECTING THE RIGHT SAMPLE TYPE

Once you've decided to sample, the next decision is to select the sample type. The differences among probability samples are summarized in Table 7.1; the differences among nonprobability samples in Table 7.2. In order to select the appropriate type of sample, researchers weigh the relative importance of accuracy and costs.

Accuracy

The original organization problem, together with the results of your investigation, will indicate how accurate your estimates must be.

- The more at stake in the decisions that management is going to base on research results, the more accuracy you need. Decisions affecting the health and existence of the organization require more accuracy than efforts at fine-tuning organizational procedures.

- The general research purpose also determines the amount of accuracy you require.

TABLE 7.1 ■ COMPARISON OF PROBABILITY SAMPLES

	Simple Random	Systematic	Stratified	Cluster and Multistage
Cost of Drawing Sample	High if large sample, long or no frame list (unless computerized)	Low	Low if subgroup lists available	Very low, since no frame list required
Costs of Interview Data Gathering	High if sample is dispersed	High if sample is dispersed	High if sample is dispersed and much screening required	Reduced substantially
Sampling Error (Efficiency) Compared to Simple Random Sample	—	Unchanged or reduced	Reduced	Usually increased
Possibility of Inherent Selection Bias	No	Yes, if cases arrayed periodically or ranked	No	Some, depending on how homogeneous clusters are
Effect on Statistics and Calculations (Compared to Simple Random Sample)	—	Usually too small to be a concern	Better comparisons across subgroups; may need to reweight non-proportional strata; test results somewhat conservative; some adjustments are complicated	Adjustments can be very complex; with no adjustments, significance tests are too liberal and substantial errors are possible
Special Concerns	High cost	Periodic or ranked data	Overstratifying	Need for heterogeneous clusters

T A B L E 7.2 ■ COMPARISON OF NONPROBABILITY SAMPLES

	Convenience	Self-Selection	Snowball	Judgment	Quota
Researcher Control over Sample Content	Very low	Low	Low to moderate	Moderate	Moderately high
Costs of Drawing Sample and Interview Data Gathering	Very low	Low	Moderate	Moderate	Moderately high to moderate
Possibility of Inherent Selection Bias	Very high	High, but self-selected	High, but cases have desired characteristic	Moderately high	Moderate to low
Major Advantage	Good for highly homogeneous populations	Good for exploratory examination of people's problems	Good for finding cases otherwise hard to locate	Fairly accurate for population means; good for very small samples	Inexpensive alternative to probability sampling

Research Purpose and Need for Accuracy. Descriptive research such as public opinion surveys and market research normally requires fairly accurate estimates of population means and proportions.

CASE EXAMPLE

A market researcher was called in to carry out descriptive research for a firm selling esoteric breakfast cereal. The company wanted a precise estimate of the increase in market share resulting from a recent price reduction of 50 cents. The firm planned to use the results in deciding whether to continue or end the promotion. They told the researcher that the decision could hinge on as little as one half percent change in share, and the cost of being wrong could be very high.

Prediction research of either the selection or forecasting type usually requires somewhat less accuracy. Organizations realize that other unmeasured factors always affect the performance of a selected case. For forecasting prediction in particular, the estimates of future values of variables inserted into the prediction model are often more prone to error than the prediction model the research generates.

Explanatory and evaluation research involving estimates of relationships among variables typically require moderate levels of accuracy.

CASE EXAMPLE

The manager of a bank in a large midwestern city had a problem with employees showing up late for work at many of its branches. She initiated an explanatory research project to estimate the impact of employees' transportation problems on tardiness. She decided that if the research found that public transportation delays were a statistically significant cause contributing to more than 25 percent of tardiness incidents, the bank would institute a program to encourage and assist car pooling among employees. She realized that research costs could be kept low because she needed only modest accuracy for the decision. The cost of an estimate being out by as much as 5 percent would not matter a great deal.

For research in the exploratory stage of grappling with a problem or seeking a preliminary evaluation, accuracy may be less important than obtaining a range of responses. In such cases, sampling error is normally not a concern, and moderate levels of selection bias are tolerable.

Accuracy and Type of Sample. Having determined how much accuracy you need, you can choose the type of sample most likely to provide it at the least cost. As Figure 7.2 shows, accuracy is determined by a variety of factors, only some of which are in turn affected by sample size and type.

- If accuracy is of minor importance a nonprobability sample will generally be enough for your needs. Table 7.2 suggests some differences in researcher control and selection bias among nonprobability samples.

- When accuracy is moderately important, a nonprobability judgment or quota sample might be sufficient as long as you don't require statistical tests of significance.

- If you plan to use significance tests to estimate the precision of estimates, or if you need a high level of accuracy, a probability sample is necessary.

All probability samples offer less selection bias than nonprobability samples, but differ in their efficiency. When one type of sample produces less sampling error and more precision than another of the same size, it is said to be a more efficient sample. Table 7.1 indicates the relative efficiency of probability samples. If efficiency is a paramount concern, a stratified sample is likely to be the best choice.

The **efficiency** of a sample is its level of precision relative to its size.

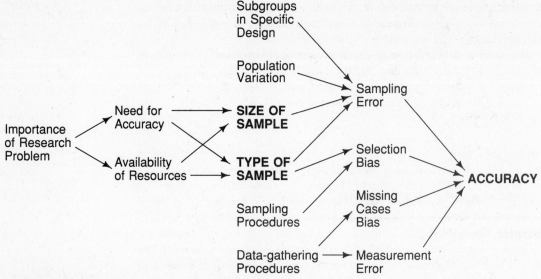

FIGURE 7.2 Factors Affecting Accuracy of Estimates

Accuracy and Sampling Procedures. For all types of samples, both probability and nonprobability, careful procedures can improve the quality of samples.

- Obtain the best sampling frame list possible, and check it for errors, duplications, and omissions to reduce selection bias.

- Use data-gathering techniques that reduce missing cases bias. Techniques for reducing nonresponse bias in sample surveys are discussed in Chapter 12. These methods also apply to field experiments that employ samples and questionnaires or interviews.

- Always try to assess the extent of missing cases bias. (See Chapter 12 for suggestions on estimating missing cases bias in surveys.)

- In nonprobability samples, exercise as much control as possible over the selection of cases. Be sure researchers are well instructed as to what constitutes an acceptable case. This will help avoid too many friends, relatives, and close substitutions appearing in the sample.

Costs

Different types of samples entail different research costs. When (1) the standard error cannot be estimated or (2) you use nonprobability samples, compare samples of different types on the costs of drawing a sample, gathering data, and data analysis. To estimate these costs, consider

- The time required.

- The personnel needs.

- The time and cost of providing training.

- Transportation and communication costs.

- Supervision and administration costs.

- Need for, and cost of, sampling and statistical consultants.

(More information on cost estimates and project administration is provided in Appendix E.)

Cost of Drawing a Sample. When drawn from a frame list or an array of data (such as a file drawer), systematic samples are much faster than simple random samples. When there is no easily accessible sampling frame list, cluster and multistage area samples substantially lower the costs of drawing samples.

Among nonprobability samples, convenience and self-selection samples are the cheapest to draw, followed by snowball and judgment samples. Quota samples are the most expensive and time consuming; complex quota samples with a great deal of screening can cost more to draw than simple probability samples.

Costs of Data Gathering. The costs of data gathering through interviews or questionnaires distributed by hand (including administration costs) vary substantially among the different types of samples. Convenience samples are the cheapest; stratified samples the most expensive (when screening is required). For mailed questionnaire surveys and available data studies, cost differences among sample types are fairly small by comparison. The costs of field experiments depend to a large extent on the nature of the manipulated variable, so that differences in types of samples have relatively little impact.

Cluster and multistage samples lower the costs of data gathering. Even when sample size is increased to compensate for larger sampling error, the costs of the larger sample are usually outweighed by the savings in data-gathering costs (see Box 7.2). When data must be gathered through interviews or observation, but research resources are minimal, a quota sample is often the best choice; data-gathering costs are low and the careful selection of cases within quotas can minimize selection bias, although precision remains unknown.

Costs of Data Analysis. Complex sample designs usually mean complex statistical analysis. In particular, when stratification is combined with area sampling, data analysis is a potential cost consideration; the services of a statistical consultant will be necessary if a high level of precision is required. Consultants increase costs but are essential in producing cost-effective results.

BOX 7.2
MOVING SOUND: A CONTINUING CASE

Part Six: Stratifying the Sample

"How's the pizza slice?" Pete is treating George to another lunch.

"It'll do. Now what do you think of this sampling design? It's a stratified cluster sample for looking at sales records. I've divided your locations into two strata. You've got buses at four relatively big-city campuses, and eight in smaller cities and towns. You randomly pick a pair from each stratum, and then flip a coin to see which one in each pair gets the test commercial. Then you check sales records before and after."

"That controls for the city size, which is certainly related to lots of campus culture variables. What about the weather?"

"You can't control everything. You know what they say, 'Everybody talks about it. . . .' "

"OK, OK. But how does this fit in with the systematic sampling of customers you were talking about last time? You know, we systematically sample people coming into the bus in both the test and comparison locations, and ask them if this is the first time they've been there, how they first heard about us, and we can also get some feedback on what they like and don't like. This way, we can see whether the commercial is bringing in a different type of customer."

"For the customer data source you do both. The stratified part divides up your target population into groups, and then you sample in two stages: randomly picking locations and then systematically sampling customers. That makes a stratified multistage sample, using systematic frame procedures. The design is a bit weak—posttest only—but we've got to make do with what we've got. And the cost is good. That means low, Pete! Together with the sales records, you should get a good evaluation of the TV commercial."

"Great stuff! Now how about a coffee? There's a stand just around the corner. . . ."

Market research firms and public opinion polls that specialize in complicated national samples often have experts on staff.

In summary, when other factors (such as precision) are equal,

- Systematic samples are cheaper than simple random samples.
- Cluster and multistage samples are cheaper than unstructured samples (especially when data sources are dispersed).
- Stratified samples are cheaper than unstratified.

CHOOSING THE RIGHT SAMPLE SIZE

Like the choice of a sample type, the decision about sample size is based on the need for accuracy and the availability of research resources. Because both affect sampling error (as shown in Figure 7.2), researchers make both type and size decisions at the same time; if one factor increases sampling error the other can offset it.

Accuracy

Sample size affects accuracy. In probability samples size is related to sampling error. In nonprobability samples size is related to the effects of the haphazard processes by which cases are selected. Increases in sample size reduce sampling error and nonrepresentativeness due to haphazard choice; but increases in size do not affect selection or missing cases bias.

The importance of sample size for accurate estimates is shown in Figure 7.3. The figure shows two estimates, a population mean and a correlation coefficient, taken at sample sizes from 5 to 350, in increments of five. As sample size increases, the estimates show less fluctuation and more stability. Many of the estimates based on small sample sizes are wildly inaccurate.

Sample Size and Sampling Error.   An illustration of the effect of sample size on sampling error is included in Appendix A. The relationship between sample size and sampling error is not direct: to cut the standard error in half requires a quadrupling of sample size. Therefore, each time another 100 cases are added to the sample, the reduction of the sampling error decreases. Sooner or later a point is reached beyond which additions to sample size aren't worth the cost.

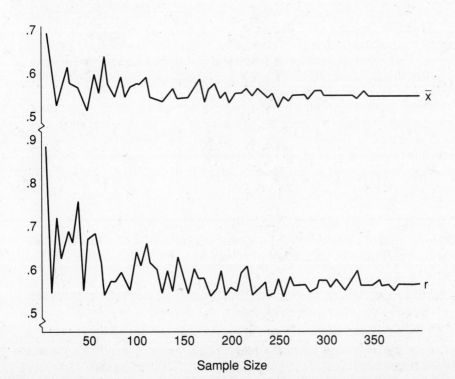

FIGURE 7.3 Stability of Estimates and Sample Size

As Figure 7.2 shows, sampling error is also determined by population variation and the type of sample. As a result, sample size can be adjusted to compensate for these other factors when they increase or decrease sampling error.

Population Variation and Sample Size.

The variation of a variable in the population will affect the sampling error of that variable in the sample. The more homogeneous the population, the smaller the sampling error and the smaller the sample size needed for accurate estimates. For example, if you want to evaluate the taste of a new soft drink, you don't need to try a large random sample. With current manufacturing methods, homogeneity of the product is very high, and a sample of one or two cans will very likely be enough to give you an accurate taste test. At the extreme, the estimate of a variable with no variation (a constant) will have no sampling error.

For many variables, higher level units of analysis (such as work groups, departments, branch plants) tend to have much more variation than is found among individuals (Sudman, 1983:186). For example, variation in size among stores is much greater than variation among individual incomes. For such units, larger samples are often needed to attain satisfactory levels of accuracy. On the other hand, careful stratification can reduce these sample sizes, as can the use of a finite population correction (discussed later). This point is particularly important for business research, which frequently uses higher level units of analysis.

Specific Design and Sample Size.

Many specific designs involve control or comparison groups, with analysis focused on comparisons between groups. This is always true for experimental and quasi-experimental designs, and often in nonexperimental designs (for example, comparison sample cross-sectional designs and cohort designs).

When researchers compare groups, the subsample from each group must be large enough for accurate estimates of that group's characteristics. In other words, it is not the total sample size that matters but the size of each subsample. As a result, the total sample size for designs with comparison and control groups is considerably larger than for designs without subgroup comparisons.

Sample Type and Sample Size.

Because they vary in efficiency, different types of samples require different sample sizes to achieve the same degree of accuracy. In particular,

- Stratified samples can use smaller sample sizes because they have smaller sampling error (unless, as noted earlier, the purpose is to compare across groups or strata).

- Cluster and multistage samples produce higher levels of sampling error and need larger samples.

Population Size and Sample Size

It is commonly thought that to get an accurate estimate, the larger the population, the larger the sample size must be. In fact, *population size is almost unrelated to the sample size needed for a given level of accuracy.* The only exception occurs when populations are very small; then sample sizes may be reduced without loss of precision. To see why, we now examine the effects of large and small populations on the accuracy of sample estimates.

Large Populations and Sample Size. Many nonresearchers instinctively believe that the sampling fraction determines accuracy: a sample of 2,000 from a population of 20,000 is as accurate as a sample of 200 from a population of 2,000. Both have a sampling fraction of 1/10.

The truth, however, is that the relative size of sample and population is much less important than the absolute size of the sample itself. In other words, sampling error (the aspect of accuracy at issue) depends much more on sample size than on the sampling fraction. As a result, larger populations do *not* require proportionately larger samples.

> The **sampling fraction** of a sample is its size n divided by the target population size N: n/N.

To see the relationship of sample size, sample fraction, and sampling error, consider the equation for the *standard error,* the measure of sampling error:

$$SE = \sigma \, \frac{1}{\sqrt{n}} \, \sqrt{1-f}$$

where:
   σ is the standard deviation of some characteristic in the population
   n is the sample size
   f is the sampling fraction n/N.

The right-hand side of this equation contains three factors.

- The first factor is the population standard deviation, a measure of variability in the population (and therefore a constant for whatever sample size we choose, since the population doesn't change).

- The second factor contains n, the size of the sample.

- The third factor contains f, the sampling fraction.

This equation allows us to compare the relative impact of sample size and sampling fraction on sampling error by comparing the effect of changes in the second and third factors. See Box 7.3.

As the box example demonstrates, *compared to sampling fraction, sample size has much more impact on sampling error.* In other words, for large populations we can safely ignore population size and concentrate on the effects of sample size in attempting to reduce our sampling error. A sample of 1,000 will be almost as accurate for a population of 100,000 as for a population of 10,000.

BOX 7.3
RESEARCH ISSUES

Comparison of Sample Size and Sampling Fraction Effects

A brewing company's employees are divided into five groups (from upper management to unskilled employees). The groups vary in size from 100 to 2,700, with a total population of 5,000. You plan to draw five corresponding subsamples. You want to have both low sampling error (measured by standard error) and about the same sampling error in each of the five subsamples. You can afford to survey only 250 cases. The question is how to allocate the 250 cases among the groups.

- If you allocate solely on the basis of *sampling fraction,* you will use the same fraction (250/5,000 = 1/20) for each group.
- If you allocate solely on the basis of *sample size,* you'll assign the same size sample (n = 50) to each group.

The table shows the standard error for each subsample under each allocation rule (assuming a population standard deviation of 1.0).

As the table shows, varying the sample size (with a constant sampling fraction) results in much greater variation in the standard error, from .08 for unskilled to .44 for management employees. However, changing the sampling fraction (with a constant sample size of 50) results in only a small variation in standard error, from .10 for management to .14 for unskilled employees.

In other words, when we want maximum accuracy (minimum standard error) in all subsamples, we pay more attention to sample size than sampling fraction.

Group	Size	CHANGING SAMPLE SIZE, CONSTANT SAMPLING FRACTION		CHANGING SAMPLING FRACTION, CONSTANT SAMPLE SIZE	
		n	SE	n	SE
Management	100	5	.44	50	.10
Staff	200	10	.31	50	.12
Clerical	500	25	.19	50	.13
Skilled	1,500	75	.11	50	.14
Unskilled	2,700	135	.08	50	.14

The sampling fraction may be large or small; what matters most is the sample size.

ADVANCED TOPIC

Small Populations and Sample Size.   Very small populations of 200 or less are not unusual in business research, especially with internal projects. In such situations, even moderately sized samples (of 25 to 50) produce relatively large sampling fractions.

Common sense suggests that when the sampling fraction is large, sampling error should be small, even with a small sample size. There are fewer opportunities for really unrepresentative samples when a large proportion of the cases are going to be in whatever sample is chosen. There is very little sampling error when the sample is almost as large as the population, and an enumeration has no sampling error at all.

When sampling fractions are large (one-tenth or more), researchers can reduce the size of the sample needed to achieve a given level of sampling error. The amount of the reduction is related to the *finite population correction* (see Box 7.4). The procedure for reducing sample size when f is large is shown in Box 7.5.

The Cost of Additional Cases

The choice of sample size is also affected by the costs of gathering data and preparing it for analysis (editing, coding, data entry). These costs have two components, one fixed and the other varying with sample size. The cost of each *additional* case varies (for example, it is usually less in internal research), but the following figures provide rough estimates:

Available data:	$1–$5
Telephone interviews:	$5–$15
Face-to-face home interviews:	$25–$75

The costs of drawing a sample and analyzing the data also increase with sample size, but these costs tend to be relatively small.

Larger samples take more time, and in some research situations time is more important than money. In these instances, estimate the time required to collect and process each additional case.

Rough Guidelines for Sample Size

As sample size increases, population estimates show less fluctuation because of declining sampling error. Because this increase in stability is gradual (as shown earlier in Figure 7.3), there is no acceptable minimum standard size.

BOX 7.4

FOCUS ON RESEARCH

Finite Population Correction

Researchers normally draw samples in such a way that the same case doesn't show up in a sample more than once. (This procedure is known as *sampling without replacement*). However, statistical tests are based on the assumption that cases in the sample are drawn independently: knowing the identity of one case doesn't tell us anything about the identity of other cases in the sample. Obviously, if we sample without replacement, we know that the same case *can't* appear again, and the assumption of independence is violated.

As a result, when we sample without replacement our results contain errors because of the violation of the assumption of independence.

- When the sampling fraction is small we can safely ignore these errors. Below one-twentieth, the chances of a case showing up more than once even if we did sample with replacement are too small to worry about. Thus sampling fractions of .05 or less are normally no cause for concern, and we make no adjustments to our statistical results.

- With sampling fractions larger than .05, the finite population correction may be applied to adjust for these errors.
  - For most research the correction is ignored when f is less than .20.
  - For more precise estimates, especially in important descriptive research, the correction may be applied to statistical results when f is greater than .10, or in extreme cases, f is greater than .05.

The finite population correction is

$$\sqrt{1 - f}$$

This is equivalent to the square root of the *unsampled* fraction of the population. (Notice that it is also the third factor in the formula given earlier for the standard error.)

If the finite population correction is used to reduce sample size, it should also be applied to statistical tests. Details of its use are given in Appendix A.

SUGGESTION

If you're using available data, take a preliminary look at 20 randomly selected cases to estimate how many might be incomplete. Any more than one means that you should increase your sample size correspondingly to compensate for cases you won't be able to use.

Thus researchers must estimate the minimum sample size in terms of the level of accuracy required for each project on an ad hoc basis.

There are basically two methods for estimating minimum sample size. The first is approximate, based on aspects of the research design, the population, and the researcher's needs. The second is more exact and is based on projected statistical tests to be used and the results anticipated. Box 7.6 offers guidelines for making rough estimates of needed sample size that, for most business research projects, will be more than adequate.

ADVANCED TOPIC

Exact Estimates of Sample Size

The general procedure for making an exact estimate of sample size is to use a statistical formula and solve for n, making assumptions about the other

BOX 7.5
RESEARCH SKILLS

Reducing Sample Size When Sampling Fraction Is Large

It can easily be shown that the finite population correction modifies the original sample size estimate as follows:

$$n_c = \frac{n\,N}{n + N}$$

where:

n_c is the corrected sample size
n is the original sample size
N is the population size.

The reduction (and cost savings) can be substantial. For example, for a population of 200 an original sample of 150 can be reduced to 86 with no loss of precision when the correction is applied.

- Consider using the correction whenever the sampling fraction is greater than one-tenth.
- When the population is less than 100, you should seriously consider an enumeration of the entire population to save the time and effort of sampling.
- If the population is below 40, an enumeration is mandatory.
- When sample size is reduced in this way, statistical calculations must incorporate the finite population correction (as discussed in Appendix A), otherwise statistical tests will be too conservative.

terms in the equation. The calculations are carried out for one or two variables, usually the most important ones in the research or ones for which population variability can be estimated. Box 7.6 shows two different sets of calculations for exact estimates, based on the formulas for confidence intervals and correlation coefficients.

Exact estimates of sample size are complicated by three major difficulties:

- You need to know, or guess fairly closely, the population variation (standard deviation) of the variable you use.

- If you gather data with interviews or questionnaires, you have to guess accurately what proportion of individuals in your sample of cases will refuse or provide unusable data. Even in available data studies, you need to know what proportion of the records will be incomplete and unusable. As a guide, some typical survey response rates are given in Table 7.3 on page 251. (Response rates are discussed in detail in Chapter 12.)

- You need to know the *design effect:* how the sample design (stratified, cluster, or multistage) will affect sampling error and thus the required sample size. (Exact calculations of design effect are beyond the scope of this text. As a rough rule of thumb, Warwick and Lininger estimate that the standard error of cluster and multistage samples is about 1.5 times that of simple random samples of the same size.) The calculations presented in Box 7.6 apply to simple and systematic random samples.

Because of these difficulties, many researchers use only rough estimates of minimum sample size (see Box 7.7).

BOX 7.6
RESEARCH SKILLS
Estimating Sample Size

ROUGH GUIDELINES FOR SELECTING SAMPLE SIZE

Begin with these suggested minimum sample sizes for business research:[1]

- A well-controlled *true experiment* design: 20 cases in each condition.
- A *quasi-experiment* (typical pilot project or evaluation study), when the main analysis is a comparison of two or more groups: 40 cases in each group.
- A *nonexperimental* design (typical survey) with a single sample: 80 to 100 cases.
- A *nonexperimental* design (e.g., survey) with two or more *comparison subsamples,* when the main analysis is a comparison across subsamples: 50 to 80 cases in each subsample. (If the comparison is a minor part of the research, 25 to 50 cases will usually suffice.)

Then revise your initial sample size according to the following conditions:

- If a group or subgroup has fairly high variation on the most important variables, increase the group sample size by 50 percent or more. If a group or subgroup is particularly homogeneous, the size can be lowered slightly (maximum of 10 percent).
- If you are going to use only tabular analysis, multiply your sample size by the ratio:

$$\frac{\text{(number of cells in the main table)}}{4}$$

[1]Others have suggested smaller sample size guidelines (e.g., Cowles, 1974, suggests 35 as a rule of thumb), but very small samples, following the central limit theorem, are much more likely to have nonnormal sampling distributions. As a result, the assumptions of normality underlying many statistical tests are more likely to be violated.

(For example, if your main table has six cells, multiply the sample size by 6/4, or 1.5.)

- If you are using control variables in tabular analysis, take this into account in calculating the number of cells. (For example, if the dependent variable has two categories, the independent three, and a control variable three, you would have $2 \times 3 \times 3 = 18$ cells and would need to multiply your initial sample size by $18/4 = 4.5$.)
- If you anticipate a missing cases rate (nonresponse, noncontacts, unusable cases) greater than 10 percent, increase the sample size to correspond to the anticipated rate (see Table 7.3).
- If you plan to use more than five primary or control variables simultaneously in an analysis (e.g., regression), increase the sample size by 5 percent for each variable over the fifth, up to 50 percent. (For example, a project using 13 primary and control variables would increase sample size by 40 percent.)
- If you use a cluster sample or multistage sampling procedure, double your sample size.
- If you use a proportional stratified sample, and the strata are fairly homogeneous relative to the population, decrease the sample size by a maximum of 20 percent.
- If the sampling fraction is greater than .25, calculate the corrected sample size (based on the finite population correction): $nc = nN/(n + N)$. Do not reduce sample sizes much below the rough guidelines suggested here.

ESTIMATING SAMPLE SIZE BASED ON CONFIDENCE INTERVALS

Confidence intervals are an indication of the precision of estimates of population means and proportions and are common in descriptive research. The more precise the estimate, the narrower the confidence interval (see Chapter 15).

If you make assumptions about the response rate and population variation, you can use the confidence interval formula to calculate the sample size needed to obtain a desired degree of precision at a selected level of significance. The following example is based on research to find the average age and other demographic characteristics of home computer users. The example assumptions and guesses are given in brackets.

1. Select a variable on which to base the sample size estimation. [age]

2. Select:

- Alpha level for significance [.05]
- Desired precision interval [± 2 yrs (= 4 yrs)]

3. Guess:

- Target population standard deviation[2] [12 years]
- Response rate [.75]

4. Formula:[3]

$$\mu = \overline{X} \pm Z \frac{s}{\sqrt{n}}$$

where:

μ = population mean
$\overline{X}$ = sample mean
s = population standard deviation
Z = value of Z corresponding to the desired alpha (from a table of areas under the normal curve in standard deviation units, two-tailed).

[2]A useful rule of thumb is that the standard deviation is about one-sixth of the range. If the group is small, one-fourth of the range will be more accurate.
[3]This formula gives a confidence interval for the population mean. With a related formula, the population proportion can also be used to calculate required sample size.

5. Rearranged in terms of n:

$$n = \left(\frac{2Zs}{precision\ interval} \right)^2$$

6. Calculated example:

$$= \left(\frac{2 \times 1.96 \times 12}{4} \right)^2 = 138$$

7. Correcting for estimated nonresponse rate to give required sample size:

$$138 \times \frac{1}{.75} = 184$$

ESTIMATING SAMPLE SIZE BASED ON CORRELATION COEFFICIENTS

The most common statistical procedure used in nondescriptive research is regression. For the sake of simplicity, sample size estimates can be based on the formula for testing the significance of a correlation coefficient (which is equivalent to a test of the significance of a regression coefficient). Example assumptions are shown in brackets.

1. Select two variables on which to base the sample size estimation.

[X = age]
[Y = hours per week computing]

2. Select:

- Alpha level for significance   [.05]
- Strength of relationship required to assume significance   [r = .30]

3. Guess:

Response rate   [.80]

4. Formula:

$$t = r \sqrt{\frac{n - 2}{1 - r^2}}$$

where:
r = correlation coefficient
t = value of t corresponding to the desired alpha (from a table of the one-tailed t distribution, since the direction of the relationship is predicted).

5. Rearranged in terms of n:

$$n = \left(\frac{t}{r}\right)^2 (1 - r^2) + 2$$

6. Calculated example
a. with maximum degrees of freedom (df):

$$= \left(\frac{1.65}{.30}\right)^2 (1 - .09) + 2 = 30$$

b. with df revised to preliminary result above:

$$= \left(\frac{1.70}{.30}\right)^2 (1 - .09) + 2 = 31$$

7. Correcting for estimated nonresponse to give required sample size:

$$31 \times \frac{1}{.80} = 39$$

BOX 7.7

CAMPBELL SWITCH: A CONTINUING CASE

Part Eleven: Selecting Sample Size

"We obviously have to sample employees at the Concord plant—there are 1,626 of them. We don't need a cluster sample for the questionnaire. A systematic sample with the payroll list as a sampling frame will do it quickest. Money's not going to be a problem here."

Roberta stirs her coffee, declining a sugar packet from the collection George keeps in his desk. "That's true, George, but what about the sample size?"

George pauses. "I'm not sure."

"We want the same precision in each subsample. While the means for absenteeism and turnover are different in the two plants, there's no reason to suspect that the variations are different. . . ."

". . . and so both samples should be the same size," George interrupts.

"And that reduces the question to the sample size for the Ajax plant," says Roberta. "And since there are only 122 employees there, we should enumerate all of them."

George is not convinced. He argues that, by his rough estimates, the minimum sample size at Ajax only need be about 80, since variation is not high and nonresponse should be pretty small. "What's more," he adds, "even this can be reduced. Let's see, I figured it out last night. Here it is. The finite population correction would reduce the 80 to a sample size of 48. So let's take a sample of 50."

"So far so good," says Roberta, "but you've got to take into account the number of variables we'll be using. In all, we've got about 17 control or primary variables. This means that your 80 should be increased to. . . ." She does some calculating. "We would increase it by 35 percent, which brings it to 108."

George does some figuring of his own. "The fpc correction reduces that to 57."

"So you want to sample 60 in each group."

"Not quite. There's no finite population correction for the Concord sample."

"So we sample 60 at Ajax and round it off to 110 at Concord. Problem is, 60 at Ajax is still about half the population. That means everybody will know what's going on, and half of them will feel left out. There'll be less fuss if we simply enumerate them all. The cost isn't that much greater. That means 122 at Ajax and 110 at Concord."

"I'll drink to that," says George. "Hey, I baked some carrot and raisin muffins last night. Want to try one?"

T A B L E 7 . 3 ■ TYPICAL RESPONSE RATES

For interviews with callbacks	
Internal research	70–95%
External research	50–80
For questionnaires with reminders	
Internal research	60–80%
External research	30–70

■ *The Lighter Side of Research*

Tests of Significance: A ritual performed by worshippers of a Deity known as the "God of Significant Differences." The failure of this illustrious Personage to appear in the results of an experiment, even after painstaking observance of the proper rites, has been known to occasion attacks of acute temptation. (Woodman, 1979)

"Given only a table of random numbers, prove that a random sample of parametric statistical techniques would take the form of the normal distribution."

—J. Price (1986), "A Comprehensive Exam for Students in Introductory Psychology"

Summary

The sample design portion of the research design involves three decisions: whether to sample, the type of sample to use, and the sample size. All decisions are made on the basis of two criteria: accuracy (which includes both selection bias and sampling error) and cost.

Selection bias results when sampling procedures systematically select too many or too few of certain types of cases. Sampling error is the chance element present in all random sampling procedures. The more each is reduced, the more representative the sample and the more accurate the estimates of population characteristics.

Once the decision to sample has been made, the type of sample is chosen on the basis of the accuracy required by the research problem and by the available resources.

The sample size decision is affected by the variation in the population, the specific research design, and the type of sample, but not by the population size

SUGGESTION

While the choice of sample type and size is important, keep in mind that errors of measurement (such as faulty questionnaire wording) are generally a much greater threat to the accuracy of estimates and the overall validity of business research. In other words, don't overemphasize sampling design at the expense of data gathering.

(unless the population is very small). The smallest acceptable sample size can be estimated using either exact procedures based on statistical formulas or rough guidelines adjusted for features of the population, sample, and analysis.

Where Are We Now?

The design portion of the research is now complete. We have specified the basic and specific design and the form of the data matrix. We know how many and what kinds of cases will make up the rows of the matrix and which variables will constitute the columns.

The next step is to gather the data. We must choose procedures for measuring our variables and for contacting cases and obtaining information. The next section includes chapters on measurement and on data gathering through surveys, field experiments and observation, and the use of available data sources.

Discussion Issues and Assignments

1. One use of nonprobability samples is as a preliminary check of a new program. This is what Harry Anderson does at Montgomery Metals (in the example at the beginning of Chapter 6). What's wrong with Harry's nonprobability sample? How could it be improved?

2. For question 1 from Chapter 6, discuss sources of selection bias and sample size.

3. Carry out the sampling plan you worked out in question 1 of Chapter 6 and question 2 here. Time yourself. Compare your estimate with other students. To what extent are the differences the result of the sampling design and procedures? Sample size and sampling error? Whose was least costly (i.e., took the least time)?

4. Using the guidelines, choose a sample size for the sampling problem in question 5 of Chapter 6. What nonresponse rate would you expect?

5. Repeat question 4 using the exact estimate methods for selecting sample size. What differences among sizes do you find using the different methods? What does this suggest?

Further Reading

Berk, R. A. 1983. "An Introduction to Sample Selection Bias in Sociological Data." *American Sociological Review* 48:386–398.

    Berk's article reviews recent work in selection bias, including material relevant to truncated samples.

Deming, W. E. 1960. *Sample Design in Business Research.* New York: Wiley.

    A classic that offers many examples of sampling in business research, both internal and external.

Frankel, M. 1983. "Sampling Theory." In P. H. Rossi, J. D. Wright, and A. B. Anderson (eds.), *Handbook of Survey Research*. Orlando: Academic Press.

> Frankel provides a good discussion of basic and advanced topics in sampling theory. He also offers an excellent bibliography of other sources.

Sudman, S. 1976. *Applied Sampling*. New York: Academic Press.

> Readable, practical, and useful for anyone engaged in research.

Warwick, D. P., and C. A. Lininger. 1975. *The Sample Survey: Theory and Practice*. New York: McGraw-Hill.

> The authors work through an excellent example of a multistage area sample.

PART THREE

Measurement and Data Gathering

The three major types of data-gathering methodologies found in business research and the measurement techniques they use.

CHAPTER 8

Measurement I: General Issues

CHAPTER OBJECTIVES

- What's the difference between concepts, variables, and measures?
- How is measurement an operation?
- What makes a measure good, and how do you choose among alternative measures?
- How do you combine measures to form indexes and scales?
- Should you develop your own measures?

CHAPTER OUTLINE

THE NATURE OF MEASUREMENT
MEASUREMENT VALIDITY
MEASUREMENT ERROR
SOURCES OF MEASUREMENT ERROR
LEVEL OF MEASUREMENT
COST OF MEASUREMENT
MULTIPLE-ITEM SCALES AND INDEXES
MEASUREMENT ISSUES AND PROBLEMS

T his chapter is the first of five involving measurement and data gathering. New researchers often underestimate measurement problems. They concentrate on complex research designs and new statistical techniques, but the most refined design and the most sophisticated statistics won't produce a silk purse of meaning from a sow's ear of measures. The adage is true: "Garbage in, garbage out!"

Good measurement pays a number of dividends for research validity:

- It produces more accurate estimates.

- It increases internal validity by reducing alternative explanations based on bias.

- It increases research power by decreasing random measurement error.

- It increases research power by making possible more powerful statistical tests.

This chapter covers general issues in the selection and development of measures for all five data sources: self-reports, inside informants, outside observers, observation, and available data. The first three sources produce *response* data (since information is gathered through individual's responses to questionnaires or interviews), the fourth and fifth produce observation data and secondary data. Chapter 9 is devoted to measurement with questionnaires and interviews, since these survey techniques present special measurement problems.

THE NATURE OF MEASUREMENT

Every variable in your study needs at least one measure. The measure specifies exactly what information you are going to gather to represent that particular variable.

For example, for the variable "skill level" you assign the number "0" to unskilled employees and "1" to skilled employees. You base your assignment on employees' job class information found in personnel files (the data source) and a list of skilled job classes found in the company's collective agreement. As part of the same project, you also assign to each case a two-digit number corresponding to the year of the employee's birth, for example, "56" means "born in 1956."

Measurement is the process of assigning numbers to cases.[1] The numbers represent characteristics of the cases, and the assignment of numbers follows specified rules that match characteristics with numbers.

[1]For certain kinds of variables, letters or other symbols, rather than numbers, can be assigned to cases.

Concepts, Variables, and Measures

Concepts, variables, and measures represent increasingly concrete representations of the ideas we are studying.

Concepts are the basic ideas we have about the characteristics of individuals, bodies, events, objects, relationships, and aggregates. Concepts are broad and abstract. The most useful ones, such as "social conflict" and "organizational complexity," have explanatory power: they seem to be useful in helping us to organize and understand our experiences and observations.

Variables are the expression of these ideas in terms of something that varies across cases or changes over time. Sometimes this variation is clearly implied in the concept, and we use the same term for both concept and variable (for example, "gender"). At other times, we have to specify what it is that varies. For example, "number of managerial levels" is a variable reflecting one aspect of the concept "organizational complexity." It may take several variables to capture all aspects of a concept. For example, "organizational complexity" is also reflected in the variables "number of subunits" and "number of functions."

Measures designate the operations we carry out to determine what category or amount of a variable a case possesses. We may use several different measures of the same variable, particularly when the right value isn't obvious. For example, we typically measure the variable "job satisfaction" with a set of specific questions.

Measures are specific, concrete, and narrow definitions of variables. Concepts are general, abstract, and broad ideas about characteristics and phenomena. Variables fall in between.

To illustrate the differences, look at the example of "absenteeism." At the most general level, "absenteeism" is a broad concept; it implies the idea of being away from some situation for which there is an expectation of attendance. It could refer to work, school, or even family life.

To convert the concept of absenteeism to a variable, we specify that something varies. This is accomplished by referring to "level of absenteeism" or "absenteeism rate." The implication is that the level or rate can vary.

We can improve the variable by specifying to what unit of analysis the variation pertains, for example, "individual absenteeism rates," or "department absenteeism levels." We can further refine the variable by specifying which of several possible types of absenteeism we want to focus on, for example, "department nonmedical absenteeism rates."

To convert the variable to a measure requires even more specificity: the operation to be carried out for gathering the information and the rule for assigning numbers.

> *Individual levels of absenteeism are measured by calculating the total number of days absent from July 1 to December 31 for which no doctor's certificate was provided, as recorded in columns 8 to 13 on employee time sheets.*

This statement is much more specific—it indicates what kind of absenteeism is being measured, over what period, where the information comes from, and what the numbers used to measure absenteeism actually represent (number of days).

When response data are used, information is gathered by asking questions in an interview or on a questionnaire. The measure is the question item itself:

> *How many working days were you absent from the beginning of the year to the end of last month? Of those, how many were* not *covered by a doctor's certificate?*

In this example, the measures of "absenteeism" exclude absences for medical reasons (defined as those for which a doctor's certificate is submitted). But this isn't the only possible measure. For some research problems, a measure including medical absences might be more appropriate. How can you tell which measure you need? This is the problem of measurement validity, one of the criteria for evaluating measures we discuss shortly.

Evaluating Measures

Since there is always more than one way to measure any variable, a researcher tries to construct the best measure (or measures) for each variable.

- In a questionnaire he could use either of the following wordings to measure the variable "age."

  > *How old are you?*
  > *In what year were you born?*

- For measuring firm performance, she could determine sales, profits, efficiency (output per work hour), the annual increase in any of these, or some other indicator.

Researchers evaluate their measures at three stages. As they develop data-gathering procedures and instruments, they construct and consider alternative measures. Second, as they pretest procedures and instruments, they try to improve measures that appear to be flawed. Third, once all the data are gathered, researchers construct scales from multiple items and refine measures to obtain the best measure possible.

To evaluate measures, researchers use four major criteria:

- Measurement validity

- Measurement error (unreliability and bias)

- Level of measurement

- Cost

We now examine these four in turn.

SUGGESTION

Today's statistical software packages and microcomputers have increased enormously the capacity for organizations to conduct their own applied research. To make sure that these gains translate to more valid research, *invest the time saved by computers in improvements to measurement.*

BOX 8.1
FOCUS ON RESEARCH

Terminology: The Different Types of Validity

Research validity is the total validity of a project: are the conclusions accurate? It includes the other three types of validity:

Internal validity refers to a relationship between two variables observed among the cases actually measured: is it genuine, or is there an alternative explanation for what you observe?

External validity also refers to a relationship between two variables: can it be generalized beyond the measured cases to a target population?

Measurement validity (often called validity) refers to the relationship between a concept and its measure: does the measure reflect the intended concept? Measurement validity is assessed two ways:

- *Theoretical validity* is a subjective approach to determining measurement validity. It includes *face validity* and *content validity*.
- *Empirical validity* is a more objective approach to appraising measurement validity. It includes *criterion validity* and *construct validity*.

MEASUREMENT VALIDITY

Measurement validity is the extent to which a measure reflects or captures the concept of interest to the researcher.

The term *validity* crops up a lot in research. You've already encountered the expressions *research validity, internal validity,* and *external validity.* We now add the term *measurement validity.* Measurement validity is often called just *validity.* Here we use the term *measurement validity* to avoid confusion with other kinds of validity. As well as the three just mentioned, we encounter even more types of validity later. The differences among all these validities are summarized in Box 8.1.

The effects of low measurement validity are

- *Erroneous estimates* of case or population characteristics, since you are estimating the wrong concept (the one measured instead of the one intended). A firm's score on a measure of cash flow doesn't capture the real fiscal fitness of the organization.

- Any relationship you find using an invalid measure is *not the one you think you have.* Instead, the relationship involves some other concept that corresponds only partially to the concept you intended. Thus lack of measurement validity reduces internal validity by providing alternative explanations for any findings.

- You may *fail to find a relationship* which really exists because you are measuring the wrong concept. Thus low measurement validity also reduces research power.

Types of Measurement Validity

There are two major ways in which a measure may be invalid: undercoverage and overcoverage.

Undercoverage.   A measure may not capture all (or even any) facets of the intended concept. For example, the concept of organization size includes such aspects as value of total sales, total production, number of employees, and equity. A measure of organization size based only on total sales will miss the other aspects. Whether undercoverage is a serious error depends on the research problem and which aspects the researcher needs to measure.

Overcoverage.   A measure may capture both the intended concept and other unintended concepts. This kind of measurement invalidity is more common. Measures of behaviors and attitudes often tap other unintended dimensions. For example, a measure of attitudes about the employer also picks up the employee's feeling about his or her fellow workers. Likewise, when the intended concept is "unexcused absences" (those not approved in advance by management), a measure of absenteeism that includes requested days off (an excused absence) has low measurement validity because it taps more than the desired characteristic.

Proxy Variables.   Overcoverage is a particular problem with proxy variables. A proxy typically represents many other characteristics in addition to the one for which it is a stand-in. For example, if the desired concept is "annual production" but the proxy is "amount of product shipped," the error in the measure is "what's left in inventory minus the previous year-end inventory." The extent of this error is subject to immediate market factors to a greater extent than is "annual production." These immediate factors are the overcoverage in this measure. Similarly, if "number of grievances in the department" is used as a proxy for quality of supervision in that department, the measure also reflects physical working conditions, relationships among the workers themselves, and other factors.

The same problem can be found in contextual variables: many aspects of the context are reflected in a single variable. For example, the contextual variable "plant" in a survey of employees captures such factors as plant management, local employment conditions, age of the plant, and other factors affecting how pleasant a place it is to work.

ADVANCED TOPIC

Computed Variables.   Researchers often construct new variables in the course of their analysis by calculating ratios or otherwise combining two or more measures. Even though the original measures have high levels of validity, the computed variable result may have low measurement validity.

CASE EXAMPLE

A researcher studied the effects of union power in newspaper publishing companies, focusing on productivity and the implementation of new technology. She wanted a measure of the potential extent of union power. Her first such measure was computed as the proportion of all employees who were union members. Both "number of employees" and "number of union members" were valid measures. However, the computed measure turned out not to be related to factors she expected it to correlate with. She computed a second, more valid measure: the proportion of all production employees who were union members.

This case example demonstrates a problem of overcoverage measurement validity in the computed variable.

Assessing Measurement Validity

There are two basic ways of assessing the validity of a measure:

- **Theoretical validity:** You judge to what extent the measure appears to reflect the intended concept. This is a subjective approach to measurement validity.

- **Empirical validity:** You examine how the measure of the concept correlates with other measures of the same concept, or with different concepts. This is a more objective approach to measurement validity.

Researchers normally assess theoretical validity while devising their measures and empirical validity after they have data that allow them to calculate relationships among measures of the same variable. Note that validity can never be known for certain, but these assessments can strengthen your confidence in the validity of a particular measure. Table 8.1 on page 265 summarizes the different checks for measurement validity.

Theoretical Validity

Researchers assess theoretical validity by examining the face validity and content validity of their measures.

Face Validity.   This is the basic approach for determining theoretical validity. The question is whether, on the face of it, the measure reflects the intended concept or variable. To ensure maximum face validity, examine your measure in light of

- *Your research problem.* A well-specified research problem should suggest whether a particular measure captures the concepts and ideas you want. In particular, review the research questions in which the intended variable appears.

- *Definition of the variable.* A well-defined variable will also suggest which of several measures is likely to have the highest face validity.

This examination should also confirm that your definition and use of each variable is consistent. If not, you will have to include additional variables and construct measures for them.

Another tactic is to obtain judgments about face validity from experts who know something about the phenomenon being measured. (This is often a good time for you to consult with the manager involved.)

Content Validity. Also subjective but somewhat more systematic than face validity is content validity. It is most used for assessing multiple-item measures. List all possible aspects of the concept and judge which of these will be picked up by the items that comprise the measure. The more of them it covers, the greater the measure's content validity. In other words, ensure that the measure contains a representative sample of the many meanings associated with the concept.

For example, job satisfaction consists of satisfaction with income, benefits and other extrinsic rewards, intrinsic aspects of the job, the work setting, co-workers, the variety and challenge of job content, and other aspects. A job satisfaction measure with high content validity would include most or all of these facets of the concept.

Empirical Validity

There are two kinds of empirical validity checks: criterion and construct. Each is based on examining how well a new measure correlates with some other measure.

Criterion Validity. This approach to measurement validity checks the relationship of the new measure with a criterion. The criterion is another variable that represents exactly the concept the researcher is interested in. It is assumed or known that the criterion itself is measured with high validity and low measurement error. When the measure to be assessed involves an attitude, the criterion is often a behavior expected from those having that particular attitude. For example, a questionnaire measure of employee attitudes toward unions should correlate highly with how the employee votes in a union certification election. To check the measure, a researcher would compare how employees answered the questionnaire with how they voted.

- When the criterion is measured at the same time as the new measure, the researcher is said to be checking **concurrent validity.** For example, a questionnaire asks consumers what they think about a particular brand of soft drink and how often in the past month they have purchased it.

- When the criterion is a behavior or condition measured some time after the new measure is administered, the assessment is known as **predictive validity.** For example, a researcher compares the results of a pencil-and-paper measure of potential employee productivity given to new employees with their productivity six months later.

The stronger the relationship between the measure and the criterion, the greater the measurement validity.

Why bother with criterion validity when you can use the presumably more valid criterion as your measure?

- The criterion may be much more expensive and time consuming to measure.

- The criterion may not be known until some time in the future.

- The criterion may be difficult to measure, may occur only intermittently, or may sensitize respondents.

In the first and third circumstances, you could carry out a separate small preliminary study to test the criterion validity of a measure, and then use only the validated measure in the major study.

CASE EXAMPLE

A researcher wanted to validate a new questionnaire measure of union attitudes by asking respondents to report how they had voted in the most recent union certification election (the criterion). However, he feared that respondents would give biased reports of their voting because of a bandwagon effect—more would report voting for the winning side than actually did. Instead he conducted a preliminary study in a plant just about to have a certification vote. He compared the results of the actual vote with respondents' attitudes. He found that the distribution of attitudes, measured just prior to the vote, corresponded closely with the results of the vote. With this validation of his new measure, he proceeded with the major study, mailing questionnaires to employees in 87 plants.

Construct Validity.   Researchers using multiple-item scales usually attempt to assess the construct validity of their measures. Constructs are the underlying theoretical ideas supposedly represented by the items. Checking for construct validity involves the answers to two questions.

- Is more than one construct represented in the measure? The researcher examines the relationships among the items and may drop one or more items to improve the measure and represent better the desired constructs.

T A B L E 8 . 1 ■ ASSESSING MEASUREMENT VALIDITY

Theoretical Validity Techniques

Assessment is based on the researcher's judgment. There are two techniques:

Face Validity:	Measure's validity is judged on overall impression.
Content Validity:	Validity is judged on basis of how many aspects of the concept are reflected in the measure.

Empirical Validity Techniques

Assessment is based on the measure's relationships with other measures or variables. There are two major groups of techniques:

Criterion Validity:	Checks relationship with a criterion measure that accurately reflects the concept. There are two types:
Concurrent Validity:	Criterion is measured at the same time.
Predictive Validity:	Criterion is predicted and measured in the future.
Construct Validity:	Checks relationships involving the theoretical ideas underlying the measure. There are two general procedures:
Interitem Relationships:	Used with multiple-item measures; checks (for example with factor analysis of the items comprising the measure) whether they reflect one (or more) desired dimensions.
Hypothesized Relationships:	Checks correlations with the measures of other concepts hypothesized to be related to the concept of interest. There are two subtypes:
Convergent Validity:	Significant correlations are hypothesized: the concepts should be related.
Discriminant Validity:	No correlations are hypothesized: the concepts should not be related.

• Are the constructs in the measure the intended ones? The researcher first examines the theory behind the concept to determine other variables or concepts it should be related to. He or she then generates and tests hypotheses about these relationships, using the new measure of the concept and well-known and accepted measures of the other concepts and variables. If the relationships appear as predicted, the new measure is assumed to capture the intended constructs. For example, a researcher believes a measure of "brand anxiety" (a fictitious concept) should be related to "frequency of brand changes"; she checks whether such a relationship exists. Researchers also use this procedure to check the measurement validity of single-item measures.

Both criterion and construct validity assessments examine relationships involving the measure to be assessed. The difference is that for criterion validity both measure and criterion involve the same underlying concept; for construct validity the relationship is between two different concepts that are theoretically hypothesized to be linked.

Convergent and Discriminant Validity.

A more sophisticated version of construct validity recognizes that not only should a valid measure correlate with variables with which a relationship is expected, but it should *not* correlate with variables with which no relationship is expected (Campbell and Fiske, 1959). If "brand anxiety" correlates as expected with frequency of brand changes and recall of commercial content, the measure of brand anxiety is said to have convergent validity. If it does not correlate with other concepts with which no relationship is predicted, such as brand recognition and impulse buying, it has discriminant validity. Similarly, we would expect a measure of union attitudes not to be highly related to productivity.

ADVANCED TOPIC

Multitrait-Multimethod Validity Checks.

Confidence in the validity of a measure is further increased if it shows consistent relationships with other variables ("multitraits") when measured with a variety of different data-gathering techniques ("multimethods"). For example, brand anxiety might be measured by observing consumer behavior, conducting personal or telephone interviews, distributing questionnaires, or examining cash register tapes. The more consistently brand anxiety correlates as predicted with other concepts (frequency of brand changes, recall of commercial content) across different measurement modes, the greater its measurement validity. (Details and examples can be found in Campbell and Fiske, 1959, and Bohrnstedt, 1983.)

MEASUREMENT ERROR

Measurement error is the second criterion for assessing potential measures. When asked their age, people may give the wrong answer for several reasons, such as vanity, poor memory, or desire to meet some age requirement (e.g., drinking age, pension). These mistakes, whether intentional or not, constitute measurement error.

We can divide measurement error into two types: measurement bias and unreliability.[3] Diagrammatically,

| Reported value of variable | = | "True" value of variable | + | Measurement bias (systematic error | + | Unreliability (random error) |

Measurement error is the difference between the "true" value and the measured value of a variable.[2]

Measurement Bias and Unreliability

A measure is **biased** if there is a systematic difference between the true and recorded values, so that the error is almost all in one direction. There are two kinds of bias associated with measures:

- **Measurement bias** is a systematic distortion in the value of a variable. For example, age may be measured in such a way that it is always underreported. In general, socially desirable behaviors tend to be overreported, particularly in response data.

- **Item nonresponse bias** is a systematic failure to obtain information for a variable from certain kinds of cases. For example, if older women are more likely not to answer a question about age, the average age of women in the sample will be underestimated.

Researchers normally refer to both these kinds of errors as *measurement bias* (or simply "bias").

A measurement has low **reliability** if there is a substantial random difference between the true and recorded values. For example, a study of airline passengers found that they were as likely wildly to overrate as underrate their true feelings about a particular airline. (The researcher made the mistake of asking questions as passengers were disembarking and in a hurry to find luggage and transportation.) Similarly, a measure is unreliable if repeated measures of the same characteristic for the same case would produce different

[2]Some measurement theorists question whether there is always a "true" value. For our purposes we assume that there is, since we can then include *bias* in our discussion of measurement error. We also assume that for objective information (such as organization size) it's easier to find the true value than for beliefs and attitudes. For further discussion, see Bohrnstedt, 1983.

[3]Sometimes systematic measurement bias is considered as a problem in validity. Treating it as measurement error, however, allows us to consider ways of reducing bias together with ways of increasing reliability.

results. If the same passenger was asked about the same airline on five successive days and gave five different answers, the measure would be unreliable. The less the recorded values fluctuate around the "true" values, the more reliable a measure is.

A biased measure can be highly reliable. If every store manager in a chain inflates true sales figures by exactly $10,000 (a systematic upward bias) and the figures don't fluctuate in any other way from "true" sales, the result is a highly reliable, though biased, measure. In a sense, you can rely on the sales managers to inflate their figures, and if you know the amount of sales inflation, you can determine the true sales.

Variance and Measurement Error. Do not assume that high variance in a variable necessarily indicates high levels of random noise because of an unreliable measure. High variance may also be due to high variation among cases in the sample, variation accurately captured by the measure.[4] Similarly, low variance can indicate either low variation among cases or measurement bias. For example, employees responding to a questionnaire on substance abuse are likely to underreport such behaviors. The result of this bias will be much lower variance than actually exists in the sample.

Reliability and Validity. Reliability and measurement validity are related. A measure cannot be valid if it is not reliable; but a reliable measure isn't necessarily a valid one. For example, a measure of consumer behavior that fluctuates randomly, and therefore has low reliability, cannot give a valid measure of the behavior because the correspondence between the concept and the measure is low. However, a measure with little fluctuation (high reliability) isn't valid if what it measures reliably doesn't correspond to the intended concept. Thus measurement validity implies reliability, but not the other way around.

Effects of Measurement Error

Measurement error produces four kinds of distortions:

1. Distorted estimates of sample and population characteristics (such as average income or gender ratio).

2. Erroneous conclusion that a relationship among variables exists in the sample (such as the relationship between income and job satisfaction) when it actually doesn't.[5]

---

[4]When we speak of sample here we mean the *achieved sample* of cases for which the researcher has data, rather than the *initial sample* from which data was sought.

[5]An erroneous conclusion that a relationship exists in the population when it actually doesn't (even though it's in the sample) is a consequence of case selection error rather than measurement error (see Chapter 4).

3. Erroneous conclusion that a relationship doesn't exist in the sample when it actually does.

4. Erroneous conclusion that a relationship doesn't exist in the population when it actually does.

Measurement bias usually produces the first two effects and sometimes the third; unreliability often leads to the third and fourth.

Effects of Measurement Bias.

Effects of Measurement Bias.   Biased measures always lead to distorted estimates of sample and population characteristics. If departments underreport waste or overreport time spent training new employees, your conclusions about average waste and training time are going to be wrong. This is true whether all or just some cases produce biased data. (This is the first effect in the preceding list.)

In certain circumstances measurement bias can lead to erroneous conclusions about relationships (and thus reduce internal validity). This happens when the measure is biased for particular subgroups or cases with certain characteristics, rather than cases randomly spread throughout the sample.

CASE EXAMPLE

A researcher studied cheating and honesty among college students. She provided a situation in which students taking a test could easily cheat by looking at a "dropped" answer sheet. Through surreptitiously observing students' behavior, she found that males and females were equally likely to cheat. However, on a questionnaire administered two weeks later, males underreported incidents of cheating while females reported accurately. If she had relied on the questionnaire data alone, she would have concluded wrongly that there is a relationship between gender and cheating.

The case just cited is an example of the second effect, illustrating how measurement bias can threaten internal validity. Similarly, lower level managers (a group more likely to be competing for promotions) are more likely than middle managers to give favorable responses to questions about attitudes toward the firm, even though the two groups' true attitudes are identical. As a result, analysis of the data shows a false correlation between job status and attitude.

On some occasions measurement bias hides a difference. This occurs when some subgroups of cases bias their responses to suggest similarities with other groups when they are really different. For example, if younger car buyers report that they spend more time researching options before the purchase than they actually do, and older buyers report accurately that they spend considerable time in such research, you will fail to find a relationship between age and research effort when there really is one. (This is an example of the third effect, and it results in lower research power, since a true relationship goes un-detected.)

Bias from Item Nonresponse.   As discussed earlier, this type of measurement bias occurs when data for a variable (item) is not available from, or is withheld by, some cases in the sample. (If the variable was missing for most or all cases, you would drop it from your analysis.) As long as the cases with missing data are randomly distributed throughout the achieved sample, you can justifiably generalize from the subset of cases with complete data (the valid-answer cases) to the cases in the achieved sample. However, if those cases for which data for the item is missing are systematically different, either on true values of the unreported variable or other characteristics, the result is item nonresponse bias.

CASE EXAMPLE

A questionnaire survey of shopping patterns in The Beaches, a trendy residential and business area of Toronto, asked respondents how much of their clothing and food shopping was done in the area. The researcher noticed a relatively high proportion (34 percent) of blank and "Don't Know" answers for these questions. He tele-phoned 12 of the nonresponse cases for those items and found that they had been embarrassed to admit that they shopped elsewhere, particularly since local mer-chants were mounting a campaign to encourage residents to support area busi-nesses. All 12 respondents had left the item blank or answered "Don't Know" rather than admit to shopping elsewhere. On the basis of the valid-answer cases, the researcher had concluded that about 38 percent of respondents shopped regularly in The Beaches. If he assumed that all the item nonresponses were really "No's," the percentage declined to 25 percent.

Measurement bias due to item nonresponse can lead to both distorted esti-mates, as in the case example, and erroneous conclusions about relationships.

Effects of Unreliability.   When measuring a single case, unreliability means that the researcher cannot have much confidence in his or her result. An unreliable measure of "takeover susceptibility" doesn't really help manage-ment know whether they must take protective action.

On the other hand, estimates of sample and population characteristics are only slightly affected by unreliability. With a large enough sample the random errors cancel one another out leaving a relatively accurate estimate. (However, the *precision* of estimates is reduced.) Similarly, the noise introduced by unreli-able measures does not produce erroneous relationships where none actually exist in the sample.

The major effect of unreliability is to increase variation and thus *obscure true relationships* so that researchers mistakenly conclude that they don't exist. This can happen either in analysis of the sample data (the third effect in the list) or while generalizing to the population (the fourth effect). In other words, unreliability *reduces* the true correlation between two variables and makes otherwise significant relationships appear statistically insignificant. In short, unreliability reduces research power.

Although both kinds of measurement error are important in all kinds of research, the relative attention given to bias and reliability varies.

- In descriptive and prediction research, more attention is paid to bias, since it has a greater impact on population estimates.

- In explanatory and evaluation research, more effort is made to increase reliability, since it has a greater impact on relationships.

Poor measurement validity and measurement error always distort the results of measuring a single case. Table 8.2 summarizes their effects in measuring population characteristics and relationships.

Assessing Measurement Bias

Assessments of measurement bias are usually subjective. Such assessments are similar to judgments of face validity; you must consider whether a measure is likely to produce biased data. For example, formal accident reports may systematically underestimate the rate of accidents in a plant, and estimating accident rates with these available data would result in biased measures.

Where there is an available, objective criterion measure, the extent of bias can be readily calculated by comparing the measure with the criterion (in a manner similar to *concurrent criterion validity,* as discussed earlier).

With response data, some objective assessments of bias are possible by including in the same questionnaire or interview different measures of the same variables. For example, if you suspect respondents might be more likely to answer "Yes" to a question regardless of their true opinions, you can add a "reversed" form of the question at another place in the instrument:

Initial form:

Do you think that promotions in this company are difficult to get?

Reversed form:

Are people promoted readily in this firm?

Assessing Reliability

The reliability of measures is determined in two general ways: stability and equivalence.

T A B L E 8 . 2 ■ EFFECTS OF LOW MEASUREMENT VALIDITY AND MEASUREMENT ERROR

	Population Estimates	Internal Validity	Research Power
Low Measurement Validity	You estimate the wrong population characteristic (the one actually measured instead of the one you intended).	You draw conclusions about the wrong relationship (the one with the concept actually measured instead of the one you intended).	You fail to find a relationship that really exists because you are measuring the wrong concept.
Measurement Bias	Your estimate of the population characteristic is distorted.	You mistakenly conclude that a relationship exists when it actually doesn't.	You mistakenly conclude that no relationship exists when it actually does (somewhat rare).
Unreliability	Slight errors in accuracy of your estimate (more if sample size is small). Major effect is loss of precision of your estimate.	No effects. Random error is unlikely to produce an illusory relationship that doesn't really exist.	You conclude that there is no relationship in the sample or in the population when the true relationship is cloaked by high variance due to measurement error. Correlations are attenuated.

Stability.   If you measure a variable at two time points, the correlation between the two measures provides an estimate of the reliability of the measure. The logic of the *test-retest* method, as it is known, is that only random fluctuations cause the differences of results within each case. In the absence of such random fluctuations, a measure is reliable.

CASE EXAMPLE

A researcher wanted to measure the extent of socializing behavior among members of work crews. The initial measure was obtained by counting the number of times members spoke to one another in a randomly selected 15-minute period. However, test-retest assessment showed that this measure was highly unreliable. In one period crew members would talk a great deal, in the retest period members of the same crew might not speak at all. The researcher developed a second measure: how many members of each work crew ate lunch together. Test-retest assessment showed this measure to be highly stable; certain members of each crew invariably ate lunch with one another.

The degree to which a measure is stable is indicated by the correlation of the test and retest measures. A perfect correlation (1.0) indicates a high level of reliability; a low correlation suggests that a better measure is needed.

There are problems with a stability approach to reliability, particularly for response data.

- People remember, or try to be consistent with, their earlier responses to questions.

- The sources of measurement error might be similar or identical each time, so that you aren't getting a true picture of the range of random fluctuation (e.g., asking employees how they feel about their jobs on two successive Mondays, instead of a Monday and a Thursday).

- The case itself may have undergone an actual change, so that differences in measurement reflect more than just unreliability.

Assessments of reliability based on stability must take these possibilities into account.[6]

Equivalence.   Researchers use this approach to assessing reliability when there are two or more different measures of the same variable. For example, if you believe that "number of hourly employees" and "net sales" are both equally valid indicators of the concept "organization size," you can assess the reliability of these measures by determining how well they correlate. Similarly, if two researchers both measure or rate the same behavior, reliability can be checked by seeing to what extent their measures agree. This *interrater reliability* is particularly useful with observation measurements.

The equivalence approach is especially important in multiple-item scales, where it is often used to assess the reliability of a scale. Techniques for assessing reliability based on the equivalence approach are discussed in Chapter 14.

Intergroup Differences.   A measure that is reliable for one group of cases may be less reliable for another. For example, males but not females may respond reliably to questions about career goals. Therefore, reliability estimates of measures should be constructed not only for the entire sample, but

[6]Measurement theorists have devised a number of approaches to deal with these problems. See Bohrnstedt, 1983.

also for subsamples that represent important breakdowns in the analysis: age groups, gender, race or ethnicity, and so on, wherever there is any reason to believe that a measure may be more or less effective with one group than another. In most cases, because subsamples are smaller than the overall sample, reliability for subgroups will be less than that for the total sample.

SOURCES OF MEASUREMENT ERROR

There are many reasons why a measurement operation may fail to result in an accurately recorded value. As shown in Figure 8.1, we can divide the

FIGURE 8.1 Sources of Measurement Error

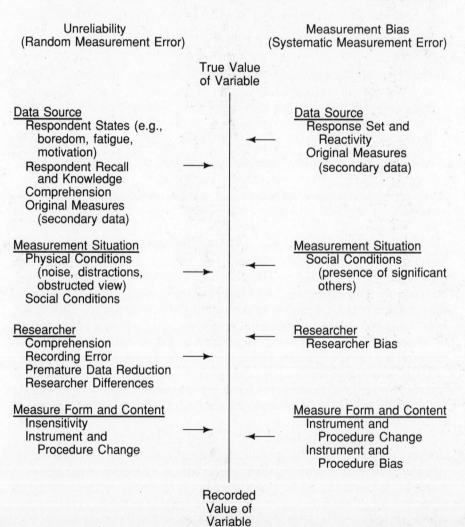

Unreliability (Random Measurement Error)	True Value of Variable	Measurement Bias (Systematic Measurement Error)
Data Source Respondent States (e.g., boredom, fatigue, motivation) Respondent Recall and Knowledge Comprehension Original Measures (secondary data)		**Data Source** Response Set and Reactivity Original Measures (secondary data)
Measurement Situation Physical Conditions (noise, distractions, obstructed view) Social Conditions		**Measurement Situation** Social Conditions (presence of significant others)
Researcher Comprehension Recording Error Premature Data Reduction Researcher Differences		**Researcher** Researcher Bias
Measure Form and Content Insensitivity Instrument and Procedure Change		**Measure Form and Content** Instrument and Procedure Change Instrument and Procedure Bias

Recorded Value of Variable

many sources of unreliability and bias into four categories according to whether the error is attributable to the data source, the measurement situation, the researcher, or the measure's form and content. In order to reduce measurement error, a researcher must be familiar with each of these sources and how it contributes to erroneous measures.

To illustrate these four sources, consider how measurement error may occur. Imagine the following three measurement operations:

- Susan Green, a consumer, is marking her answer to a questionnaire item about ketchup preferences.

- As part of a field experiment evaluating autonomous work groups, Bill Smith is observing the amount of "socializing" in a plant floor work group using a form to record type and duration of "socializing" activity.

- Jill Martin, a researcher, is collecting the quarterly sales performance figures of the educational software division of a company, using a data sheet to record sales information from summary sheets in company files.

In each of these three examples we can imagine potential measurement errors.

Data Source Errors

The data source is the immediate person(s) or object(s) from which information is gathered:

- Susan Green

- The seven members of the work group

- One of the 248 sales performance summary sheets

Some of the important data-source causes of measurement error include respondent states and recall, acquiescence, comprehension, reactivity, and, for available data, errors in the original data gathering. (Although many of these errors are the indirect result of a faulty measurement instrument or operation, the immediate origin of the error is the data source.)

Respondent States. Fatigue, boredom, and low levels of interest and commitment to the research produce unreliability in response data. If Susan Green is tired from a busy day at the office, she will not devote much thought and attention to her answers.

Respondent Recall and Knowledge. Respondents' memory problems affect the reliability of response data. Susan may not be able to remember when or where she last bought a bottle of ketchup. She may not know in what store the last bottle was purchased if her husband bought it.

Comprehension.   When respondents or experimental subjects have problems understanding the measurement operation, such as questionnaire wording or experimental instructions, reliability suffers. Comprehension problems can be due to intelligence levels, language difficulty, or limited experience with research and researchers. Susan may become confused when asked to list up to seven qualities she associates with ketchup ("It makes me think of blood" or "I like it not too thick").

Response Set and Reactivity.   A response set is a tendency to answer a question in a particular way, regardless of the correct answer. *Acquiescence,* for example, is the tendency to agree. Susan may be inclined to answer "yes" to a question asking whether she feels ketchup is an important food.

When respondents alter their behavior or answers because they are aware of being measured, the measure is *reactive.* Measurement anxiety may lead to more "don't know" responses or constrained behavior. Social desirability is the tendency to answer or behave in a way that puts the data source in a good light. The work-group members, seeing the researcher, may adopt a "hard-at-work" posture and reduce social conversation. Both response set and reactivity produce measurement bias.

SUGGESTION

To reduce measurement errors from response data sources, place yourself in the position of a respondent and imagine possible reactions to a particular question.

Original Measures.   Errors in the way that available data were originally gathered (by response or observation) can produce bias or unreliability. The summary sheet may include clerical errors as data were transferred from other documents, or a different person may have filled out the sheet during the regular clerk's vacation, using a different method for calculating net sales.

Measurement Situation Errors

The measurement situation is the physical and social setting in which the measurement operation is carried out:

- The dining room table where Susan Green is filling out the questionnaire at 8:15 P.M.

- The trim department where the group is working in the Akron plant from 10 to 11 A.M. Wednesday morning

- A desk in the corner of the sales department office near the filing cabinet containing past sales summary sheets, where the researcher is gathering data at 2:42 in the afternoon

Measurement errors associated with the situation can be divided into physical and social conditions.

Physical Conditions.   Noise and other distractions (such as TV) can lead to unreliability. The data source or the researcher may have trouble concentrating. In interview situations, respondent and interviewer may have trouble hearing questions and answers. Other physical conditions may also reduce reliability. Low lighting levels make it difficult to read data; an obstructed view can hinder observation. Uncomfortable seating can make it difficult to concentrate on the research task. The absence of bathroom facilities in field research can lead to hurried observations and interviews!

Social Conditions.   Other persons in the measurement situation (such as fellow employees, supervisors, and family members) can produce bias. Individuals notice the presence of important and powerful others and alter their behavior to others' expectations. With questionnaires or interviews, responses may be altered to take into account the known opinions of these persons. Similarly for observation measurement, a work group with a supervisor nearby is likely to behave differently than in his or her absence.

These errors are likely to be systematic rather than random. However, some reliability losses may occur as well. In interviews, respondents might be unwilling to admit not knowing or having no opinion. The guesses they give instead diminish reliability.

Researcher Errors

The researchers include both those directly gathering the data and others associated with the research.

- The editor and coder who code Susan Green's questionnaire, the keypunch operator who enters the data into the computer, and the researcher responsible for cleaning the data

- The observer watching the seven members of the work group, the editor and coder who code the data collection form, the keypuncher, and the data cleaner

- The researcher transferring data from summary sheet to data collection form, the editor, coder, keypuncher, data cleaner, and the researcher who combines these data with other company records already in the computer

Some of the important researcher-related causes of measurement error include comprehension and recording errors, premature data manipulation, and researcher differences and bias.

Comprehension Error.   If an interviewer, observer, or other data collector misunderstands or misinterprets the responses, behavior, or information of a data source, reliability suffers. Comprehension errors stem from the ability, intelligence, training, or experience of the researcher. Interviewers and observers with different backgrounds (race, ethnicity, gender, or social status) may misinterpret answers or behaviors. The work-group observer, who is from a different social background, misinterprets one worker's striking another on the shoulder as a sign of hostility instead of respect. (The observer doesn't hear the worker say, "Way to go!")

Recording Error.

Whenever data is recorded or transferred, there is a danger of recording error. Such errors threaten reliability. There are a number of reasons why researchers may record information erroneously. Researcher states (boredom, fatigue, low commitment to the research) can produce recording errors. A tired coder misreads one of Susan's responses, coding "Likes ketchup on potato chips" instead of "Likes ketchup on eggs."

Poor training and low ability may also produce errors. An interviewer with poor memory is another source of recording errors through failure to recall the first part of a respondent's answer to a question.

Premature Computations.

In recording information for available data studies and coding interviews, questionnaires, and data collection forms, researchers are often tempted to compute and record new variables. For example, the starting and ending dates for a strike may be used to compute "strike duration." Similarly, the data on the number of males and number of females may be combined to compute "gender ratio." The starting and ending dates and the numbers of males and females are themselves not recorded—only the newly computed variables.

This practice is unfortunate in two respects.

- As long as the original variables are recorded, the computer can do the calculations much faster and with no errors. The possibility of errors when researchers calculate ratios and change scores while gathering data is relatively high. These errors contribute to lack of reliability.

- Important information can be lost. This is especially the case in recording data in designs with two or more measurement points.

Measuring Change.

A frequent problem in longitudinal or repeated-measure designs is how to measure change between two successive time points. For example, a researcher with information on sales of pens wants to know whether changes in advertising expenditures correlate with pen sales. His options are to record

- *Level* of pen sales and advertising expenditures in each period between time points (e.g., pen sales were 128,000 units in February).

- *Change* in levels of sales and expenditures between time points (e.g., pen sales declined 31,000 units in February).

- *Rate of change* in level of sales and expenditures between time points (e.g., pen sales declined 19.5 percent in February).

The first option is the preferred. In general, you have more flexibility in your analysis if you measure and record the *levels* of each variable at each time point.

You can then have the computer calculate change scores or rates of change. The analysis of levels is usually preferable to the analysis of change scores, which can lead to erroneous conclusions.

Researcher Differences. Different researchers usually follow slightly different procedures or interpret slightly differently the definitions of key terms. For example, an observer watching a work group excludes most of the nonverbal communication in her measure of socializing activity. Another observer with a different group includes nonverbal communication. These differences, which are compounded by poor training and ambiguous or incomplete instructions, are responsible for the resulting random error.

Researcher Bias. Research personnel are often aware of the aims and hypothesis of a study and may inadvertently distort data to confirm the hypothesis. The result is measurement bias. Interviewers and observers may hear or see, and thus record, what they expect to hear or see. The work-group observer may be more likely to code the same interaction behavior as task-related in the experimental autonomous work groups than in the comparison groups.

Researcher bias is most likely when information is ambiguous and requires interpretation before being recorded. It is also more likely with poorly trained personnel.

Errors Due to Measure Form and Content

Each measurement operation involves form and content, such as the layout and meaning of instructions that the respondent or researcher is following.

- The questionnaire asks Susan Green to rank, from among those listed, her three favorite brands of ketchup. She selects Hunt's and Heinz, and makes no third choice.

- Following instructions on the check sheet, the observer, using a stopwatch, counts 12 minutes, 21 seconds of socializing time within the work group between 10 and 11 A.M.

- On the data collection form, the researcher writes "24380" in one column to indicate that sales of software for the first quarter of 1988 totaled $24,380 in the Northern California region.

The most important form and content sources of measurement error include insensitivity and instrument effects (bias and changes in instruments and procedures).

Insensitivity. Insensitive measures are those that don't pick up existing variations in the sample. It is a common problem in measures that categorize data or responses.

CASE EXAMPLE

A questionnaire item asking employees how far they traveled to work offered the following three response categories:

less than 10 miles   [   ]
10 to 20 miles   [   ]
more than 20 miles [   ]

The categories had worked well for a sample of employees drawn from a large urban area. However, for a study of employees of a pulp mill located in a small town, they failed to detect any substantial differences among employees. Subsequent inquiry revealed that almost all employees lived within 2 miles of the workplace. Most respondents therefore marked the first category, and the item was not sensitive to variations among employees.

Lack of sensitivity produces a form of unreliability, except that instead of too much random variation in the data, there is not enough variation of any kind. For example, Susan Green and almost all other respondents, asked whether they use ketchup "once a month or more" or "less than once a month," indicate the former.

SUGGESTION

If you suspect there will be relatively little variation in an important variable, and that your measure may be too insensitive to pick it up, use several different measures to increase the probability that at least one of them will provide sufficient variation.

Instrument and Procedure Change. Changes to the form or content of measures during the course of research can reduce or increase bias and random error. This includes changes to definitions, data collection forms, check sheets, question items, questionnaires, and interview schedules.

If the changes result in better measurement, they are probably worth making as long as the cases measured with the old procedures are not otherwise systematically different from those measured with the new. If, however, the two groups of cases are systematically different (for example, if a questionnaire were revised following a survey in one plant prior to surveying the second plant) the bias produced by the change presents a major threat to internal validity.

Instrument and Procedure Bias. The wording or response format of a question may be a source of bias in response data. The preceding questions in a questionnaire or interview may also have an effect on how the respondent interprets and answers a question. Similarly, the appearance and layout of a questionnaire can also produce bias. These errors, which occur in both questionnaires and interviews, are discussed in detail in Chapter 9.

Other measurement procedures inadvertently introduce systematic bias into the data. For example, researchers sometimes round numerical available data to fewer significant figures as they transfer it. If done incorrectly, rounding can introduce bias into the data (see Box 8.2).

BOX 8.2
RESEARCH ISSUES:

Rounding Errors

Bank rounding, in which numbers ending in 5 are always rounded up (e.g., 4.25 becomes 4.3) introduces a small but systematic bias into your data. Since more final digits are rounded up (5, 6, 7, 8, 9) than down (1, 2, 3, 4), the mean is distorted upward as well.

To avoid this bias, **statistical rounding** adopts the convention of rounding to the nearest even number. Thus 4.25 becomes 4.2 and 4.35 becomes 4.4. Overall it is assumed that the ratio of even to odd second-last digits is close to unity, so that as many numbers are rounded down as up. This procedure eliminates systematic bias in rounding.

In summary, there are many rocks in the shoals of measurement error. What can you do to navigate through with the least damage? The following four chapters discuss specific suggestions for reducing measurement error with the different data-gathering techniques. Before turning to those suggestions, however, we continue with more general issues in measurement. One other point must be mentioned: the ethical problem that researchers encounter in their attempts to reduce measurement error (see Box 8.3).

LEVEL OF MEASUREMENT

Level of measurement is the third criterion to consider in selecting measures for your variables. Before we turn to a description of the different measurement levels, we discuss what we mean by the term and why it's important.

Measures produce data coded into numbers. For example,

- We measure the variable "gender" in two categories, which we might code so that "1" means female and "2" means male.

- We measure a respondent's level of job satisfaction in five categories labeled "very low," "low," "so-so," "high," "very high," and assign the codes "1" to "5."

- We measure the number of times an employee was late for work in the past month and code using the actual number ("2" means late two times).

Not all these numbers can be treated the same way. In each of the three examples, we see instinctively that the numbers mean different things. It's clear that in the first example, the choice of numbers is totally arbitrary. Females could easily be coded "3" or "0" or "22." In the second, the assignment of

SUGGESTION

In trying to maximize measurement validity, pay more attention to measurement form and content, such as question wording. It affects validity much more than other aspects of the measurement: data source, situation, and researcher. By comparison, reliability and bias are much more affected by all four elements of measurement.

BOX 8.3
RESEARCH ETHICS
Controlling Measurement Error

Researchers encounter potential ethical problems whenever they seek to reduce or control measurement error. This conflict is inevitable, since improvement to measurement is achieved by exercising *control* over the measurement situation. However, this control may conflict with the interests of the data source, particularly in interviews.

For example, a researcher conducting an interview in a respondent's home will normally seek to remove other individuals from the room, turn off the television set, and otherwise remove physical and social distractions from the situation. However, these actions impinge on the respondent's right to enjoyment of his or her property.

The ethical researcher ensures that a respondent's consent is obtained before attempts are made to control the situation. This usually entails explaining the nature and purpose of the research. An added benefit is that, if well done, such explanations also increase respondents' attention and motivation, which further reduce measurement errors.

---

numbers seems more limited. It would make less sense to code the five categories as "1, 7, 4, 25, 11." In the third example, there are even more restrictions. We wouldn't likely code two absences as "5." In each of the examples, the numbers mean something different.

Measurement theory deals with the relationships between the measures we use and the properties of the numbers produced by those measures. Traditionally, researchers have found it useful to distinguish four different sets of properties or levels of measurement: nominal, ordinal, interval, and ratio.[7] In this typology, nominal is the lowest, ratio the highest.

The **level of measurement** for a variable indicates how the numbers assigned to cases as part of the measurement operation can be interpreted.

Level of measurement is important for three reasons:

- Higher levels of measurement allow us to see more accurately the relationships between variables.

- Higher levels of measurement allow us to use more powerful statistical tests.[8] These tests increase research power.

- Higher levels of measurement convey more information by making finer discriminations between cases. This increased sensitivity adds to research power.

---

[7]These are not the only possibilities. Mathematical psychologists and others working in the field of measurement theory have suggested other measurement levels (e.g., Pfanzagl, 1968).

[8]Actually, you can use any statistical test you like with any level of measurement you have, since the numbers themselves don't know what they mean or where they come from. The issue is whether the numbers fit the statistical assumptions of the test, such as errors being independent and normally distributed with homogeneous variance (Gaito, 1980). The validity of your *interpretation* of the results of a test rests on whether statistical assumptions are violated, not on the level of measurement. However, some levels of measurement are more likely to meet these assumptions than others.

The discussion of measurement levels here distinguishes dichotomies as a separate level and divides ordinal into category ordinal and ranked ordinal levels. These two changes result in six useful levels for business research:

Dichotomous   (lowest level)

Nominal

Category Ordinal

Ranked Ordinal

Interval

Ratio   (highest level)

(We will find the two additions very useful when it comes time to choose statistics for data analysis.)

Terminology Note.   Measurement levels are also called measurement scales (e.g., nominal scales, interval scales). We avoid that terminology here to prevent confusion with two other meanings of "scale": multiple-item measures and the response formats used in questionnaires and interviews.

Nominal Measures

Nominal-level measures consist of a set of categories to which cases are allocated as part of the measurement operation. Each category represents a different characteristic, attribute, or quality. (Variables with nominal-level measures are often called *qualitative*.)

The numbers assigned to categories are arbitrary, have only symbolic value, and are there for convenience. For example, for the variable "marital status" with three categories you might assign the following numbers:

1 = "single, never married"

2 = "married or cohabiting"

3 = "divorced, separated, or widowed"

Alternatively, you could assign the numbers 7, 12, and 3 to the categories, the letters S, M, and D, or the symbols @, #, and *.

The numbers used to represent categories in nominal level measures cannot be manipulated mathematically; all you can say is that cases with the same number share the same characteristic.

Examples of variables measured at the nominal level include industry, region of the country, ethnicity, field of study, plant location, union local, and type of safety program. As you can see, nominal-level measures are frequent in business research.

The measurement rules for allocating cases to categories are discussed in Box 8.4.

Category Ordinal

Category ordinal measures involve a small set of categories which are ordered in terms of the amount of some characteristic or quality. For example, consumers testing a new brand of toothpaste are asked to respond to its flavor using the categories "Really disliked it," "Didn't like it much," "Liked it somewhat," and "Liked it very much."

The numbers assigned to category ordinal categories are more restricted than for nominal: they must be in numerical order.[9] Thus for the toothpaste example the numbers assigned to the categories could be 1 to 4, or 1, 3, 12, and 59. Other than this, the numbers are symbolic and arbitrary, like nominal measures. The only mathematical operations that can be performed with these numbers involve inequalities, such as $1 < 2$ or $59 > 12$.

Because category ordinal measures have only a small number of categories, many cases are tied and fall into the same category. For example, of 250 consumers responding in the toothpaste test, 54 indicate that they "Liked it somewhat."

Category ordinal measures convey more information than nominal measures. Whereas nominal measures only place cases in different categories, category ordinal measures also tell us whether a case has more or less of some attribute relative to other cases. How much more or less, however, we cannot tell with category ordinal measures.

Examples of category ordinal measures include occupational categories (ranked in terms of amounts of social status) and attitudinal questions of many kinds. Measures at the category ordinal level are particularly frequent in response data. For many variables, including attitudes and opinions, we can get no higher levels of measurement without resorting to multiple-item measures.

Ranked Ordinal

Ranked ordinal measures don't employ categories. Instead, a different number is assigned to *each case* representing its ranking on some characteristic or dimension. For example, a supervisor may rank all 27 employees in her section on "leadership potential." The highest is ranked "1" and the lowest "27" (or vice versa).

Ranked ordinal measures are ordered, like category ordinal measures, but provide much more information because each case is distinguished from all others, that is, the cases are uniquely ranked. We know whether a case has less or more of an attribute compared to any other particular case. While there may

---

[9]Technically, even this requirement is not essential. However, it is convenient and avoids problems: statistical programs will produce erroneous results if the category numbers are not in appropriate numerical order.

BOX 8.4
RESEARCH SKILLS

Choosing Categories for Category Measures

Category measures require that you choose the categories to which cases are to be assigned as part of the measurement operation. The categories must reflect those differences among cases relevant to your research problem.

For some variables the categories are obvious. This is particularly true for natural dichotomies such as gender. For other variables, you can use widely accepted categories as long as they are relevant to your purpose. Appendix C offers examples of some of these categories, such as marital status and occupation. Chapter 9 gives other examples of response categories for questionnaires and interviews.

For some variables, however, you have to develop the categories yourself. As you do, keep the following principles in mind:

- *The categories must be mutually exclusive.* To avoid ambiguity, each case must be assignable to only one category. For example, the categories for the question, "Where did you buy your last *TV Guide*: department store, supermarket, shopping center, or other location?" are ambiguous about how to classify a department store located in a shopping center. Similarly, the two income categories "$5,000 to $10,000" and "$10,000 to $15,000" overlap at $10,000.
- *The categories must be exhaustive.* You must anticipate, and provide categories for, all possible classifications. The easiest way of doing this is to include a residual category for all cases not otherwise classified (e.g., ". . . or other location"). The danger with this solution is that a residual category will not distinguish among cases that ought to be differentiated. For example, the categories "supermarket," "department store," and "other" don't distinguish among drugstores, convenience stores, and bookstores as places where consumers may purchase *TV Guide*. Exhaustive

categories are a particular problem for questions about ethnic background and occupation.

- *Avoid unnecessary categories* irrelevant to your research problem and research questions. It is a waste of research time to make unnecessary distinctions among cases. In a study of where consumers buy books, it may be important to distinguish between chain and independent bookstores, but it is unlikely to be useful to distinguish between bookstores with high and low levels of employee turnover.
- Ensure that *categories match research questions.* For example, in this set of categories

    1 = single, never married
    2 = married or cohabiting
    3 = divorced, separated, or widowed

a person who had been cohabiting with another in a relationship that has ended would technically fall into category 1. However, research focusing on individuals whose relationships have ended requires a measure that would classify such persons in category 3.

- *Limit classifications to one dimension,* unless there is a good reason to do otherwise. For example, classify bookstores on size and on ownership in two separate variables rather than combining the two dimensions into one variable ("large independent," "small chain," etc.).

Categories must also be *sensitive* to the level of variation in your target population. In general, the greater the differentiation a measure provides, the more information it yields. This fact has important implications for both the content and number of categories in category measures.

- *Content:* Unless a variable has natural division points (such as gender or occupation) categories should be constructed so that they are unlikely to contain a large proportion of cases. Try to spread the cases over several categories. For example, if most respondents work in small plants (less than 100 employees), the following categories of plant size will not differentiate very well among them:

1–99
100–499
500–999
1,000–4,999
5,000 and over

A better set of categories would be:

1–9
10–24
25–49
50–99
100–199
200–499
500–999
1,000 or more

- *Number:* The greater the number of categories, the more sensitive the measure is likely to be. Of course, the number of categories for some variables, such as gender, is limited by the nature of the variable itself.

be ties (two or more cases with the same rank), they are relatively few, unlike category ordinal measures (in which all cases in the same category are tied).

The mathematical operations we can perform with ranked ordinal measures are limited to orders, for example, $27 < 28$ (where 1 is lowest). This is similar to category ordinal measures; the advantage of ranked ordinal measures is that there are many more different numbers (ranks).

Do not confuse ranked ordinal measures (which rank cases) with questions that ask *respondents* to rank things (such as brands of soap). In these instances, it is not *cases* which are ranked; rather each case ranks some other set of objects. (The answers to such ranking questions are numbers representing *category ordinal* measures. For each brand variable, the ordered categories are "first brand choice," "second brand choice," and so on.)

Ranked ordinal measures are rankings of the cases themselves, usually through the judgments of one person who assesses and ranks all cases in the sample. His or her judgments represent the measurement operation. For example, an expert might rank the attractiveness of 100 different investment options, or an instructor the management potential of 84 employees. For this reason, ranked ordinal scores are unlikely to be used with large samples where there are too many cases to rank.

Ranked ordinal measures are not often used in business research.

- There is a limit to the sample size or the number of cases a single person can rank.

- In many instances a better level of measurement (interval or ratio) is available. For example, compared to an expert's rank order judgment of investment potential, the net value increase of an investment option conveys more information.

Examples of ranked ordinal measures for business research include unions ranked by rate of membership growth, management trainees ranked in terms of management potential, and firms ranked by level of strike activity.

Interval Measures

Like ranked ordinal measures, interval measures assign a number to each case, and the numbers indicate the relative amount of some characteristic. In addition, the interval or difference between two successive numbers is the same. Thus the *intervals between numbers* have meaning: the interval between two cases can be compared to the interval between another pair of cases. For example, calendar time is an interval measure. The difference (time period) between 1950 and 1970 is exactly the same as between 1920 and 1940 and exactly half the difference between 1810 and 1850.

This kind of measure adds metrical information. The numbers now represent some unit of measure, such as degrees or years, over and above their relative ranking. The mathematical operations we can perform with interval measures allow us to compare and equate *intervals:*

$$1970 - 1950 = 1940 - 1920 = \tfrac{1}{2}(1850 - 1810).$$

We cannot, however, mathematically divide or multiply the individual measures. It makes no sense to say that the year 995 is half of the year 1990.

There are actually few variables in business research measured at the interval level. Any variables measured beyond the ranked ordinal level are likely to utilize ratio measurement. Although most test scores (such as a scale measuring job satisfaction) are treated as interval data, some methodologists argue that this is inappropriate. The real test is whether equal intervals have the same significance (e.g., does a job performance test score difference between 50 and 60 have the same meaning as the difference between scores of 80 and 90).

Ratio Measures

A ratio measure is identical to an interval one with the addition of a natural zero point, or origin, which indicates total absence of the characteristic. By comparison, the zero point in an interval level measure is arbitrary. For example, it makes sense to talk of zero sales or zero union members (ratio measures) but not of a zero calendar time or zero intelligence (even though an IQ test may produce a score of zero, this doesn't truly represent a total lack of intelligence).

The natural origin makes it possible to compare absolute amounts of a characteristic. The mathematical operations we can perform with ratio measures include multiplication, division, and ratios of the actual measures. For example, an employee absent for 10 days has twice the absenteeism of one absent for 5 days. We can determine the ratio of male to female employees from two variables: number of males and number of females. The ratio characteristic allows us to compute statistics such as geometric and harmonic means, and other statistics in which a variable shows up in the numerator and denominator of a statistic, including coefficients of variation.

Ratio and interval measures can both include more than one case with the same number or value. Most of these ties are a result of rounding. For example, if we measure age in years, then any large sample will have a number of people tied (e.g., at age 22). On the other hand, if we measure age in days (e.g., Susan is 22 years 46 days old), the number of ties would be considerably fewer.

Many variables in business research are measured with ratio measures. This includes all counts (such as number of grievances in the past year), all rates (such as sales per 100 employees), and other variables such as income, seniority, age, monthly sales, price, and duration of strikes.

Dichotomies

A *dichotomy* is simply a measure with only two categories. For example, we categorize cases on the variable "gender" as either "male" or "female." Similarly, the union membership of employees is either "union member" or "nonmember." Other variables that are not natural dichotomies can always be collapsed into one. For example, age can be collapsed into "young" and "old," wage rates into "high" and "low," and toothpaste attitudes into "like" and "don't like."

Dichotomies have an interesting property: they can be treated like other levels of measurement. Consider a dichotomous measure (such as "gender") with the numbers zero and one assigned to the categories.

- The dichotomy can be regarded as a nominal measure, since the two categories reflect different characteristics or attributes. The "0" and "1" here have symbolic value.

- It can be considered a category ordinal measure, since it can be interpreted as one category (the one coded "1") having more of an attribute than the other (coded "0"). For example, "male" has more of the characteristic maleness than "female," "union member" has more of the characteristic "union membership" than "nonmember," and "young" has more of the characteristic youth than "old."

- It can be treated as an interval measure. Since there are only two numbers, "0" and "1," we can ignore the criterion of equal intervals between numbers.

- It can be treated as a ratio measure. The "0" is a natural zero point meaning none or absence of the characteristic (e.g., maleness or favorable opinion of toothpaste); the "1" means presence of the characteristic. This is how dichotomies are used as dummy variables in regression equations. (You can also think of the numbers as representing *proportions* of the characteristic with only two levels allowed: all or none.)

As a result of this property of dichotomies, we can use them with statistics that would normally be restricted to interval and ratio measures. Such statistics have greater statistical power, and their use increases research power.

The disadvantage of dichotomies is that, for any variables which are not natural dichotomies (gender is, age isn't), collapsing to achieve a dichotomy loses a great deal of information. Consider the loss of sensitivity when age is reduced to just "young" and "old."

Table 8.3 summarizes and compares the six levels of measurement. As the preceding discussion suggests, ratio measures are preferred where possible (see Box 8.5).

Category and Quantitative Measures

For convenience we can group our six levels of measurement into three classes: category, ranked, and quantitative measures. The distinction is very useful when it comes time to carry out statistical analysis.

- Nominal and category ordinal levels are called *category* measures, since the measurement operation assigns cases to categories.

- Ranked ordinal measures fall between category and quantitative measures.

- Interval and ratio measures are often referred to as *quantitative,* since each number indicates a specific quantity of some attribute, characteristic, event, or object.

- Dichotomies can be treated as either category or quantitative measures. The choice usually depends on which statistical test the researcher is using.

T A B L E 8.3 ■ COMPARISON OF LEVELS OF MEASUREMENT

	Establishes Differences Among Cases	Orders Differences Among Cases	Uniquely Orders Differences Among Cases (Few Ties)	Equal Interval Differences Among Cases	Natural Origin
Nominal	x				
Category Ordinal	x	x			
Ranked Ordinal	x	x	x		
Interval	x	x	x	x	
Ratio	x	x	x	x	x
Dichoto- mous	x	x			sometimes assumed

BOX 8.5
MOVING SOUND: A CONTINUING CASE
Part Seven: Improving Level of Measurement

"You don't like my question?"

"Don't take it personally, Pete, but we can do better."

George and Pete are drafting questions for the mini-interview and questionnaire they plan to use for the Moving Sound project. They want to evaluate the impact of a television commercial on record sales.

"So what's wrong with it?"

"You need a higher level of measurement. Go for a ratio measure."

"So what have I got now?"

"Ordinal categories. You're asking them how many records they bought in the past month. And you give them four categories: 'none,' 'one to three,' 'four to ten,' and 'more than ten.' Those are four categories in order of magnitude."

"So?"

"You get more usable information if you just ask the exact number. Sure, you'll get some unreliability because they may not remember exactly. But you'll gain much more by having a ratio level measure."

"I see. We try for the measures that get the most information."

"Right. Ratio measures are better than interval, which are better than ordinal, which beat nominal."

"What's an interval measure?"

"Funny you should ask. We hardly ever use them. Although we often treat scales as if they were interval, or even ratio measures."

"Forget I asked, George."

Pete ponders for a moment. "So how about this: 'How many records have you purchased any time in the last four weeks?' "

"Better. Much better."

The question construction continues.

COST OF MEASUREMENT

The fourth and final criterion for evaluating measures is their cost. Some measurement operations can be very costly in time or money. For example, a questionnaire that asks respondents where they live, and then requires the researcher to calculate the distance from home to work, is a time-consuming measure. (However, like most measures, technology can sometimes reduce the time involved. See Box 8.6.)

As another example, consider the measurement operation: "Observe the amount of time each employee spends in nonproductive behavior each day for a week." Depending on the number of employees involved, it might take an extraordinary amount of time to gain this information. Further, it is likely that the researcher will be noticed and that this itself will bias the employees' behavior.

Some measurement costs may be hidden. For example, a complex measurement operation may require a great deal of training for researchers to carry it out reliably. This training is costly in time and money. Interviews with complex skip patterns are the most common culprit. In general, the easier the measurement operation, the lower the cost.

BOX 8.6
RESEARCH SKILLS
Measuring Distance with an Opisometer

In some studies variables representing distances have to be measured, for example, the distance from each employee's home to place of work. A quick method for making such measures is to obtain the employees' street addresses, and use a map and *opisometer.*

The opisometer is a pen- or diallike instrument with a small wheel on the bottom. As it rolls over the map's surface, the wheel measures the distance in inches or centimeters. Using the map's scale, you can convert the distance to miles (or kilometers) or, if all cases are measured on the same map, you can enter just the inches (or centimeters) as your variable.

When you calculate the cost of a particular measure, consider both the time to collect it and the time to analyze it. In particular, open-ended response categories on questionnaires can require much more time to code and analyze than forced-choice questions. Also keep in mind that cost alone is not the only consideration: cost must be weighed against the benefit of including a particular variable in your analysis or a particularly accurate measure of the variable.

MULTIPLE-ITEM SCALES AND INDEXES

Researchers often combine several items measuring the same concept into a single measure in order to improve the quality of their measurement. There are two kinds of multiple-item measures: scales and indexes. The major difference is how closely related the component items are. Job satisfaction is usually measured with a scale of several items that capture satisfaction toward various aspects of the job, including peers, supervision, and intrinsic and extrinsic rewards. An index of socioeconomic status combines the concepts income, occupational status, and level of education. Similarly, the consumer price index is a measure that combines prices for a carefully chosen sample of consumer goods and services. An index of workplace climate might combine the variables grievance rate, absenteeism rate, productivity, and turnover.

Because they reflect a single variable, we expect the items in a scale to be more closely related to one another than the items in an index. Scales and indexes also differ in other respects:

A **scale** is a combination of individual measures of the same variable, each measure reflecting a different aspect of the variable.

An **index** is a combination of individual measures of different variables or concepts that are combined to represent a new concept.

• Scales are used primarily to increase reliability; indexes are used to increase measurement validity (e.g., the consumer price index combines the prices of a large number of consumer items).

- Scales are used predominately in questionnaires and interviews, especially to measure attitudes, opinions, and beliefs. Indexes are used in all kinds of data-gathering techniques.

- The construction of scales is generally more systematic than index construction and involves statistical tests.

- Scale items are usually category level measures, whereas an index may combine both category and quantitative items.

Specific examples of different types of scales are presented in Chapter 9. Here we discuss the general aspects of multiple-item measures.

Advantages of Multiple-Item Measures

Multiple-item measures offer two major benefits: greater reliability and greater measurement validity.

Reliability.   When you combine several items, their random measurement errors tend to cancel out. This leaves a more accurate estimate of the true value than you would get using just a single item. For example, Table 8.4 shows a consumer's "true feelings" and actual answers to six questions about a product. (Note that in real research we seldom, if ever, know "true feelings.") As the table shows, there is some random error (unreliability) associated with the answer given to each question. Because some errors are negative and others positive, the sum of errors tends to be small relative to the sum of true opinions. If just the first item were used, the error would be 20 percent of the score. When the six items are used, the error is only 7 percent of the total score. In other words, multiple-item measures are more reliable. (Researchers must avoid the temptation, however, to include too many items—see Box 8.7.)

The less reliable each of the individual items, the more of them are needed to achieve a given level of reliability. Multiple-item measures not only increase reliability, but they also make it easier to assess the reliability of the measure (as we see in Chapter 14).

Measurement Validity.   When a concept is complex and has a number of related dimensions, multiple items are necessary in order to tap all those dimensions. For example, the concept of organizational centralization includes the dimensions of autonomy, CEO span of control, worker-supervisor ratio, middle management participation in decision making, and others. A multiple-item measure of centralization will do a better job of capturing all these aspects than just a single question about centralization, which might overemphasize one particular aspect. The result is a more valid measure.

TABLE 8.4■ ILLUSTRATION OF RELIABILITY IMPROVEMENT WITH MULTIPLE ITEMS

	"True Feeling"	Actual Response to Question	Random Error	Percentage Error
Single-Item Measure				
"Overall, how satisfied were you with the training course? Answer from 7 (extremely satisfied) to 1 (extremely unsatisfied)."				
	4	5	+1	20%
Multiple-Item Measure				
". . . with the quality of instruction. . . ."				
	5	7	+2	
". . . with the opportunities to participate. . . ."				
	3	2	−1	
". . . with the time scheduling. . . ."				
	4	4	0	
". . . with the feedback. . . ."				
	5	3	−2	
". . . with the instructional aids. . . ."				
	4	6	+2	
". . . with the relevance of materials. . . ."				
	6	7	+1	
SCALE TOTAL	27	29	+2	7%

Choosing and Combining Items

Researchers using multiple-item measures must consider these questions:

- Which items should be included in the measure? Which set of items best achieves the objectives of the measure?

- What relative weight should be accorded to each item? Should each item be weighted equally, or should some contribute more than others to the final measure?

Scales. When developing a new scale, researchers normally decide which items to include after data have been gathered. They almost always assign equal weights to each item.

BOX 8.7
CAMPBELL SWITCH: A CONTINUING CASE
Part Twelve: A Scale Construction Disagreement

"It'll work, I tell you!"

"No it won't! They'll get bored. They won't answer it, or they'll just answer anything."

"It's worked before. They do it all the time!"

"Yeah, but they do it in laboratories, and we don't have one here."

"That doesn't mean it wouldn't work."

". . . and they have to pay them to do it. Or promise them grades."

George and Roberta are having a slight disagreement over the length of the job satisfaction scale they want to include in their questionnaire.

"Well, I took a psychology course, and I was a subject in some research projects. I didn't feel put upon by any questionnaire scale."

"You wouldn't. But you understood the purpose."

"Right. Your reliability goes up enormously as you add more items. So we want reliability, right? So let's go with the 20-item scale."

"But let's be practical, Roberta. That's the difference between business research and psych experiments. We should only go for as much as we need. And I say five items is enough. One for each component we want: the task, working conditions, supervision, co-workers, and equipment."

"But if an item's biased, we're really in trouble. Let's at least have two items for each component."

George pauses. "Hmm. That's not a bad idea. Insurance. And insurance *is* practical. Ten items it is."

They select which ten, and move on to the next measure.

The usual practice is to include a large number of items in the questionnaire or interview, and then to analyze them to select those that produce the most reliable scale. The construction of individual items follows the principles outlined in Chapter 9. It is important to ensure that the items for a scale are carefully written and pretested. They should cover as many aspects of the concept or phenomenon as possible and be written so that the respondent will not be uncertain about the frame of reference. It doesn't hurt to have experts in the area evaluate your potential scale items.

Indexes.   Researchers usually judge which items to include in an index on the basis of face and content validity. Such decisions, unlike the situation for scales, are made prior to data gathering. However, a check of item interrelationships prior to data analysis may sometimes result in some modification to an index.

Items in indexes are often assigned different weights according to the researcher's a priori idea of their relative importance. Also, if the metric is different for each item, some weighting procedure is necessary to avoid giving the most weight to the item with the largest numerical scores.

The techniques for index and scale construction—combining and weighting items to achieve an overall scale or index score—are described in Chapter 14. The same chapter includes methods for assessing the reliability and validity of multiple-item measures.

MEASUREMENT ISSUES AND PROBLEMS

We have already dealt in this chapter with a number of general issues and problems in measurement. We turn now to three additional topics: existing measures, standardized measures, and pretesting.

New Or Existing Measures?

Rather than take the time to construct a new measure, you can often find a measure that has already been developed and used. An existing measure offers four advantages:

- *Cost:* It saves the time and money it takes to develop and test your own measure.

- *Comparability:* It makes it possible for you to compare your results with the study using the original measure.

- *Validity:* It enables you to check the validity of some of your other measures. Compare the relationships between these measures and the existing measure with the relationships found in the original study.

- *Reliability:* If the existing measure is a scale, its reliability may have been tested and reported.

Your literature review includes a search for existing measures that may be useful for your project. You should also consult publications that describe existing measures, particularly scales and attitude measures. These works often include information on validity and reliability. Box 8.8 lists a few examples of these publications.

Whenever you use or adapt an existing measure, consider the population and situation in which it was originally employed. Is the measure appropriate for your target population and general circumstances? If not, you may have to make adjustments to it or discard it altogether. Keep in mind that the more changes you make, the less you can assume that a measure's validity and reliability remain unchanged.

Standardized Measures

Standardization of the measurement operation is an important way of reducing both unreliability and bias in all measurement modes. Common standardization practices include

BOX 8.8
FOCUS ON RESEARCH

Some Sources for Existing Measures

Cook, J., S. J. Hepworth, T. D. Wall, and P. B. Warr. 1981. *The Experience of Work.* New York: Academic Press. This source provides information on 249 work-related measures.

Miller, D. 1991. *Handbook of Research Design and Social Measurement* (5th ed.). Newbury Park, CA: Sage. Contains information on a number of useful scales and indices.

Robinson, J. P., R. Athanasiou, and K. B. Head. 1969. *Measures of Occupational Attitudes and Occupational Characteristics.* Ann Arbor: Institute for Social Research.

Robinson, J. P., and P. R. Shaver. 1973. *Measures of Social Psychological Attitudes.* Ann Arbor: Institute for Social Research.

Seashore, S. E., E. E. Lawler III, P. H. Mirvis, and C. Cammann. 1983. *Assessing Organizational Change.* New York: Wiley. This book suggests many measures for a wide variety of organizational phenomena.

Shaw, M. E., and J. M. Wright. 1967. *Scales for the Measurement of Attitudes.* New York: McGraw-Hill.

Smith, P. C., L. M. Kendall, and C. L. Hulin. 1969. *The Measurement of Satisfaction in Work and Retirement.* Chicago: Rand-McNally. This source contains a description of the Job Description Index.

Sudman, S., and N. M. Bradburn. 1982. *Asking Questions.* San Francisco: Jossey-Bass. Chapter 7 suggests standardized wordings for demographic questions.

Thomsen, D. J. 1981. *Handbook of Quantitative Methods Applied in Personnel.* Pacific Palisades, CA: Compensation Institute.

Webb, J. W., D. T. Campbell, R. D. Schwartz, and L. Sechrest. 1966. *Unobtrusive Measures: Nonreactive Research in the Social Sciences.* Chicago: Rand McNally. Contains suggestions for a variety of nonreactive measures.

- Written procedures and instructions.

- Data collection forms and checklists.

- Using the same measurement setting for all cases.

A **standardized measure** is structured so that each case is subjected to the same measurement operation.

Because standardization holds constant many aspects of the measurement operation, there are fewer uncontrolled causal factors operating and therefore less random noise in the recorded values. This means that reliability and research power are both increased. For example, using the same wording and color of questionnaire paper eliminates any variation from those sources.

Standardization also reduces measurement bias. If all interviewers read the same wording, they are less likely to bias respondents' answers. If an observation check sheet describes exactly what behaviors to count, there is less room for subjective interpretation on the part of the observer. When measures are standardized, researchers' own biases are less likely to color what data are recorded.

Pretesting

Pretesting is important for research quality. It is a practice well worth the additional time and cost and should only be bypassed for minor projects of little importance, tight budgets, and looming time constraints. (Don't confuse

BOX 8.9
RESEARCH SKILLS
Multiple Pretesting

For the most effective pretesting, utilize two or more of the following five stages:

1. Ask colleagues (fellow students, managers, etc.) to review your measures, instruments, and procedures. They should evaluate both form and content.
2. Solicit comments from friends and relatives who know neither the research area nor anything about research methods. Again, ask them to comment on both form and content.
3. Ask persons knowledgeable in the area (experts) about the content of your measures.
4. Ask experienced researchers to comment on the form of your measures and instruments.
5. Conduct a field test: gather data from a small sample of cases similar to your target population, or try your measures, instruments, and procedures in the actual situation (or as close as you can get to it, if contamination might be a problem).

Only the field test stage will provide you with accurate information on the time it takes to complete the data gathering for each case. You can then use this information to refine estimates of research costs.

If the field test results in major changes to the measurement operation, it should be pretested and evaluated again before moving to the data collection phase. (The following four chapters discuss in more detail the pretesting of measures, instruments, and research procedures.)

"pretesting" with the "pretest measures" that precede the manipulation in experimental and quasi-experimental designs.)

We often think of pretesting as refining question wording for a survey. In fact, pretesting must be much broader than this.

- Pretesting is important in *all* methodologies; field experiments and available data studies as well as surveys need pretesting.

- Pretesting includes not just measures but instrument format and research procedures as well.

Pretesting of measures, instruments, and procedures is normally carried out at the same time, although if major measurement problems are anticipated, pretests of measures might be done first. When you conduct your pretests, consider the stages discussed in Box 8.9.

Pretesting Measures. Measurement pretests check for possible measurement error from *data sources* (Do respondents become bored or hostile? Are available data complete and legible?), *researchers* (Can they follow interview instructions? Do they make mistakes recording observations?), and *measurement form and content* (Is the measure sensitive enough? Is it biased?). In some instances a pretest will include alternative measures to discover which one works best.

A **pretest** is a preliminary evaluation performed so that changes can be made to improve research quality. It is carried out before the major data gathering begins.

SUGGESTION

Don't underestimate the usefulness of managers in assessing the face validity of new questionnaire or interview items. In fact, managers should be routinely included as one of your pretest sources.

SUGGESTION

How many cases are needed for a field pretest? A rough rule of thumb is a minimum of ten for available data. Where there are potential contamination problems, as in internal business research, the number should also be kept small (but an absolute minimum of ten). For external marketing research, practitioners recommend from 25 to 75 (Converse and Presser, 1986).

Checking the sensitivity (particularly of dependent variables in explanatory studies) is one of the most important aspects of measurement pretesting. If there is no variation in the dependent variable, there is nothing to explain. An insensitive measure, if uncorrected, can make useless at least one variable and possibly threaten the entire study.

CASE EXAMPLE

A survey of turnover among nurses asked how satisfied they were with their jobs. The researcher used five categories, ranging from "very satisfied" to "very dissatisfied." The pretest showed that 84 percent of the nurses were selecting the "very dissatisfied" category. To improve the sensitivity of this variable, the researcher added three additional related attitude measures. Additional pretesting showed that the four-item scale provided much greater sensitivity than the original single item.

■ *The Lighter Side of Research*

Reliable: Sometimes capable of giving the same results. (Woodman, 1979)

"All raters rated all students, with a [reliability] of .57, which was deemed acceptable on the grounds that it would be a pain to do it over."

—Schwartz, 1986

Summary

This chapter examined general principles underlying measurement in business research. Measurement is an operation making use of operational definitions of concepts and variables. The operation follows rules for assigning numbers to represent characteristics of the cases.

Researchers use four criteria to evaluate measures: validity, measurement error, measurement level, and cost.

A measure is valid to the extent it reflects the concept or variable the researcher wants to measure. Validity is assessed through both theoretical and empirical methods. The former includes subjective judgments about face and content validity. The latter investigates relationships (1) between the measure and a criterion (criterion validity), (2) among the items that constitute a multiple-item measure, and (3) between the measure and other variables that the researcher hypothesizes to be related to the measured variable (the second and third constitute construct validity).

Measurement error comes from four general sources: data source, measurement situation, researcher, and the measure itself. Researchers have to deal with two kinds of measurement error: bias (systematic error) and unreliability (random error). Bias is normally assessed by subjective methods similar to theoretical validity. Alternative question forms in response data can also indicate the presence of bias.

Reliability is assessed through either stability (test-retest) or equivalence-based procedures. The latter uses relationships among different forms of the measure, or composite items, to assess reliability.

The level of measurement has implications for the amount of information contained in a measure and the likelihood of its meeting the assumptions required for using different statistical tests. We can distinguish six different levels of measurement: nominal, category ordinal, ranked ordinal, interval, ratio, and dichotomies.

The final criterion, cost of measurement, includes the time and money required for training, measuring, and coding associated with a particular measure.

Researchers use multiple-item scales and indexes to improve the validity and reliability of their measures. Scales generally measure a single concept, and indexes combine several variables or concepts into a new one.

The chapter ends by pointing out the advantages of using existing measures, standardized measures, and pretesting.

Where Are We Now?

This chapter dealt with measurement in general terms. The next four chapters provide greater detail on measurement and data gathering. Questionnaires and interviews are covered in Chapters 9 and 12 (surveys), procedures involving available data in Chapter 10, and field experiments and pilot projects in Chapter 11.

Discussion Issues and Assignments

1. With a friend, during a coffee break unobtrusively select a sample of ten students in your class. Each of you should "measure" the age of each student through observation (of features, dress, etc.) and record your individual estimates. Then ask each of the ten his or her age, and record their answers. What is the intercoder reliability of your observation measures (i.e., the correlation between your estimates and your friend's)? Did the observation measures have high criterion validity (correlation with response data)? Was there any measurement bias in your observation measure? What about the "asking" measure?

2. Your class instructor for this course has a grading scheme that represents a measurement operation. What is it measuring? What's the theory behind the measure? Is it valid? Is there overcoverage or undercoverage? Is it reliable? Biased?

3. Think of three different measures to capture the "organizational effectiveness" of your college (school, faculty, department) student organization. Evaluate them. What are the greatest potential sources of measurement error?

4. Obtain a copy of a questionnaire or interview schedule used by a market

SUGGESTION

When you're trying to decide where to invest limited research time, keep in mind that measurement errors normally far outweigh inaccuracies due to sampling error. Measurement bias and poor reliability and validity are greater threats to research validity than small samples. A good pretest probably contributes more to research validity than a 50 percent increase in sample size.

research firm. Decide the level of measurement for each question. What numbers would you (or did they) assign to answers?

5. For two of the items on the questionnaire or interview from the previous question, discuss the concept and variables implied by the measure. Could the measure represent more than one concept?

6. From a review of research articles, find and compare two existing measures of some variable or concept on validity, level of measurement, reliability (if possible), and cost. What would you suggest to improve them? How would you evaluate your suggestion?

Further Reading

Bohrnstedt, G. W. 1983. "Measurement." Chapter 3 in P. H. Rossi, J. D. Wright, and A. B. Anderson (eds.), *Handbook of Survey Research*. Orlando: Academic Press.

A thorough discussion of measurement error, the mathematical expressions of reliability and validity, and their estimation.

Nunnally, J. C., Jr. 1970. *Introduction to Psychological Measurement*. New York: McGraw-Hill.

The classic introduction to the basics of measurement and psychological measures of abilities and attitudes.

Seashore, S. E., E. E. Lawler III, P. H. Mirvis, and C. Cammann. 1983. *Assessing Organizational Change*. New York: Wiley.

An excellent guide to measures of organizations and their members.

Webb, E. J., D. T. Campbell, R. D. Schwartz, and L. Sechrest. 1966. *Unobtrusive Measures: Nonreactive Research in the Social Sciences*. Chicago: Rand McNally.

Chapter 1 presents a very useful discussion of the problem of reactivity and some fascinating examples of measures that overcome it.

CHAPTER 9

Measurement II: Questionnaires and Interviews

CHAPTER OBJECTIVES

- How should a question be worded?

- How do we provide for the answer?

- What order should we use in asking questions?

- How should a questionnaire or interview schedule be laid out?

(You should also check the questionnaire examples in Appendix D.)

CHAPTER OUTLINE

QUESTION WORDING
RESPONSE FORMATS
QUESTION ORDER
INSTRUMENT FORMAT
REDUCING MEASUREMENT ERROR
SPECIAL PROBLEMS

A **questionnaire** is a self-administered measurement instrument for obtaining response data. It normally consists of one or more pages of questions and is often sent to respondents by mail.[2]

An **interview** is a series of questions posed by an interviewer to obtain response data. The interviewer normally uses an interview schedule of question items. The interview may take place face to face or by telephone.

Q uestionnaires and interviews are the most difficult measurement modes.[1] Unlike other modes, both the researcher and the data source have to agree on the meaning and intent of the measurement operation to get a valid measure.

Besides the validity problem, there are two other reasons for devoting a chapter exclusively to questionnaires and interviews:

- They are used in all types of research designs (true experiments, quasi-experiments, and nonexperiments). They are found in surveys, lab experiments, and field experiments. For example, a pilot project to evaluate a new purchasing system uses questionnaires to determine departmental reactions. In a laboratory experiment, subjects fill out questionnaires and are given debriefing interviews to check manipulated variables.

- They are more vulnerable to unreliability and measurement bias than other data-gathering techniques.

QUESTION WORDING

Good question wording is much more difficult than most people realize; it seems easy, but countless respondents have suffered through frustrating questionnaires and tiresome interviews, producing questionable data as a result.

Good question wording accomplishes several objectives:

- It ensures *measurement validity:* the question must measure what you want it to measure.

- It minimizes *measurement error:* bias and unreliability.

- It minimizes *item nonresponse* (respondents skip a question or answer "don't know" when they *do* know).

Measurement validity is the primary concern. Both researcher and respondent must share the same interpretation of a question and use the same *frame of reference* in asking and answering it. Many of the suggestions offered here concern respondents' perception and interpretation of questions. A very useful ability for you to cultivate as you develop question wording is to put yourself in the respondent's shoes and imagine what the respondent hears and thinks.

---

[1]The work in this chapter draws from a number of sources, including Converse and Presser (1986), Sudman and Bradburn (1982), and my own experience with scores of questionnaires, both good and bad.
[2]In this text the term *questionnaire* refers only to a self-administered instrument. The pages of questions used by interviewers is called an *interview* or *interview schedule.*

Factual and Attitude Questions

Before we discuss guidelines for good question wording, consider the distinction between two types of questions, factual and attitude. Factual questions ask for information about characteristics, behaviors, events, and experiences, such as

- gender (characteristic)

- brand of butter purchased most recently (behavior)

- number of employees hired last year (events)

- ever involved in an industrial accident (experience)

These questions can be asked about the respondents themselves or about other individuals or groups they know about.

Attitude questions ask about attitudes, beliefs, and feelings about such things as

- job satisfaction (attitude)

- necessity for protectionist legislation (belief)

- reactions to a training program (feelings)

In most instances, these questions can only be asked about the respondents themselves, although in some instances respondents are asked to report on others' feelings. Factual and attitude questions are associated with different major problems, as shown in Table 9.1.

Another important distinction involves attitude questions: they may be bipolar or unipolar.

Bipolar: *Do you favor restricting or strengthening unions' right to strike?*

Unipolar: *How strongly do you feel about restricting unions' right to strike: very strongly, somewhat, only mildly, or have no opinion?*

A **bipolar** question presents opposite alternatives to the respondent. By contrast, a unipolar question measures the presence or absence, or the degree of extremity, of an attitude.

TABLE 9.1 ■ FACTUAL AND ATTITUDE QUESTIONS: MAJOR AND MINOR CONCERNS

	Validity	Reliability	Measurement Bias	Item Nonresponse
Factual Questions	minor	minor	major	major
Attitude Questions	major	major	minor	minor

BOX 9.1
RESEARCH SKILLS

Writing Questions

I. Be clear and specific.

- Avoid vague and general words and phrases.
- Don't use ambiguous frequency terms.
- Ask about concrete instances, events, and options.
- Use specific alternatives.
- Establish a clear frame of reference.
- Make it clear to whom the question refers.
- Include response units in the question.
- Place screening and focus instructions before the question, response instructions after.

2. Use appropriate language.

- Consider respondents' education, intelligence, and experience.
- Use jargon and technical terms only for special groups.

3. Avoid condescending words and phrases.

- Avoid too many simple words and sentences and needless definition.
- Place term to be defined following the definition.

4. Emphasize.

- Use underlining instead of italics.

- Place key idea early in questionnaire, late in interview questions; in interviews, response options follow the question.

5. Keep it simple.

- Avoid passive voice and complex sentences.
- Avoid double-barreled questions.

6. Keep it brief.

- Use short attitude questions.
- Use longer factual questions when they require recall.

7. Keep it neutral.

- Avoid leading questions (exception: some factual questions).
- Avoid loaded questions.
- Use bipolar alternatives for single attitude questions.

8. Keep it relevant.

- Ask only questions applicable to the respondent.
- Justify questions that appear unrelated to the research.

Guidelines for Question Wording

Following are eight guidelines for question wording. Some of these apply to factual questions, some to attitude questions, and most apply to both. You can also use these guidelines to evaluate questions you are thinking of borrowing from other questionnaires and interviews. The guidelines are summarized in Box 9.1.

1. *Be Clear and Specific.*

a. Avoid vague and general words and phrases to make sure that your terms are understood in the same way by all respondents.

CASE EXAMPLE

The student counseling office of a university commissioned a survey of foreign students' perceptions of the help available to them for their problems. Among the primary variables the researcher included the number of persons each student respondent lived with and their relationships to the respondent. One question on the questionnaire asked, "How many other people do you live with?" An examination of the returned questionnaires indicated that the expression "live with" was interpreted in two different ways. Some respondents took it to mean "live in the same household," which was the meaning intended by the researcher. Other respondents interpreted "live with" as meaning "married or cohabiting." In addition, some respondents interpreted the phrase "other people" to mean those with whom they did not share a familial relationship or even, in some cases, a common ethnic background. Thus one respondent answered "none" to the question, but indicated in another question that she shared the same living quarters with two other students of the same ethnic background.

b. Whenever possible, don't use ambiguous frequency terms such as *usually, generally, often,* or *regularly,* especially in factual questions. If respondents guess or misinterpret the term, the result is greater measurement error. Instead, ask how many times in a specific period:

> *In the past two weeks, how many times did you shop at a corner store in your neighborhood?*

c. Respondents will answer more accurately when asked about specific, concrete instances, events, and options. Also, specific questions are better predictors of behavior than general questions (Converse and Presser, 1986). Instead of

> *Do you think this company needs more training programs?*

ask,

> *Do you think management of this plant should spend more, less, or about the same as they are now spending on training managers in management techniques?*

Specific questions are more sensitive. For example, when asked,

> *How do you generally get to work?*

only 2 percent reported walking and 1 percent bicycles. However, when the question was revised to read,

> *How did you come to work this morning?*

the percentages reporting walking and bicycling increased to 5 percent and 14 percent, respectively. In general, questions that ask for respondents' most common behavior will elicit less variation than questions asking for behaviors at specific times.

d. Attitude questions about general opinions should be phrased with *specific alternatives* to avoid having respondents generate and respond in terms of their own alternatives. Instead of,

> *Would you prefer a four-day work week with the same total hours as you work now?*

ask a question that standardizes the alternatives for all respondents:

> *Assuming you would work the same total number of hours as you work now, would you prefer a four-day work week or the present arrangement?*

or,

> *Assuming you would work the same total number of hours as you work now, would you prefer a four-day work week, or a flexible work schedule that lets you set your own hours, or the present arrangement?*

e. Establish a clear frame of reference or context for the question. Instead of,

> *What kind of union do you belong to?*

which can be answered in terms of size, sector, membership participation, power, militancy, and other dimensions, ask,

> *To what extent do members participate in decision making in your union?*

f. Make it clear to whom the question refers:

> *Does your firm have a policy about smoking in the workplace?*

> *Do you, yourself, approve of the recent pay equity legislation?*

g. For factual questions, mention the *response units* you want in the question itself. Instead of,

> *How far do you drive to work?*

ask,

> *How many miles do you drive to work?*

h. Put instructions in the appropriate place. In general, *screening instructions* and instructions to recall an event or focus on a specific topic precede the question; *response instructions* follow the question.

> PLEASE ANSWER IF YOU HAVE PURCHASED COFFEE BEANS
> IN THE PAST THREE WEEKS.
>
> *Thinking back to the store where you last purchased coffee beans, which of the following were true?*
>
> (CHECK THOSE THAT APPLY)
>
> *(a) Both packaged and loose coffee beans
> were visible*   [ ]
> *(b) You could see at least five different
> kinds of coffee beans*   [ ]
>   . . .
> *(f) You could detect the smell of coffee*   [ ]

2. Use Appropriate Language.

a. To make sure a question is understood, use words and phrases appropriate to respondents' education, intelligence, and experience (including both life experiences and familiarity with questionnaires and interviews). Use short and simple words rather than polysyllabic locutions of multifarious meanings (for example!).

b. Use jargon or technical terms only if you're sure respondents will understand and appreciate them. (For example, a business research survey of CEOs can and should use common business terms.) The same rule applies to slang and colloquialisms, which many respondents may not understand or may find inappropriate.

3. Avoid Condescending Words and Phrases.

a. Too many simple words and sentences, and definitions of terms they know perfectly well, can alienate respondents and lead to higher item nonresponse. Worse, respondents may throw out the whole questionnaire or break off the interview. Treat respondents with respect; avoid question wording that talks down to them.

b. If a term needs definition, Payne (1951) suggests that the term should follow, rather than precede, the definition. The result is less likely to seem condescending. For example,

> *Does your firm engage in regularly scheduled discussions with the union that could result in changes to the collective agreement in midterm; that is, does your firm engage in continuous bargaining?*

4. Emphasize.

a. Use underlining to call attention to key words and phrases that define the question or which differentiate it from other words and questions. (Don't use italics; they are not as noticeable and respondents often miss the emphasis.)

What do you believe your <u>foreman</u> thinks about the QWL program?

What do you believe your <u>fellow workers</u> think about the QWL program?

b. Arrange word order for emphasis and understanding. For questions that the respondent *reads* (i.e., a questionnaire), key ideas and qualifications should come early in the sentence; for questions that the respondent *hears* (i.e., an interview) they should come late.

Questionnaire: What does your <u>foreman</u> think about the QWL program, in your opinion?

Interview: People have different opinions about the QWL program. What do you believe your <u>foreman</u> thinks?

When an interviewer reads response options they must *follow* the key idea.

Some people feel that the economy will improve significantly in the next 12 months. Do you strongly agree, agree, disagree, or strongly disagree?

5. Keep It Simple.

a. Avoid the passive voice and complex, multiclause sentence structure. Questions should focus on one idea. Any complex idea should be broken down into several subquestions. Simplicity should prevail over the rules of grammar and punctuation when they result in awkward phrasing.

b. Avoid **double-barreled** items that ask two different questions or include two attitude objects in the same item:

Do you plan to leave your job and look for another one in the coming year?

   Yes   [   ]
   No   [   ]

Because the question seeks a "yes or no" response, it will miss respondents who could truthfully answer "yes and no" (e.g., leaving the job and taking early retirement). Any question having two possible ideas for respondents to focus on will have low measurement validity.

6. Keep It Brief.

For attitude measures, keep questions short. However, research shows that when factual questions require recall, longer questions give better results (Sudman and Bradburn, 1982).

For attitudes,

How successful was the management teamwork workshop?

but for facts,

> *A variety of workshops are available to middle-level managers. They deal with different management skills such as hiring, discipline, employee motivation, time management, handling conflict, and other topics. How many such workshops have you attended since January 1 of this year?*

On the other hand, too many questions like this one will make the instrument unbearable. Use long questions sparingly.

7. *Keep It Neutral.*

a. For attitude measures, avoid **leading questions** that are phrased to push the respondent in the direction of one particular answer:

> *Would you say that union leaders are responsible for most strikes?*

However, for factual questions a leading question may increase measurement validity. It can overcome the tendency to withhold accurate information because the answer is ego threatening or would violate social norms (Gorden, 1975). Thus a leading question *contrary* to public norms may help establish a situation in which the respondent can open up:

> *Most people take a day off work from time to time even though they don't have a valid reason. They want to do some work around the house, run errands, go fishing, or maybe they just don't feel like going in to work. How often in the past six months have you been absent without a valid reason?*

b. Avoid **loaded questions** that use emotion and slanted response categories:

> *Is the power of big business responsible for the problems of this country?*
> (emotionally laden terms)

> *Would you agree that people like you who read the* Toronto Telegram *have a better idea of what's happening than the average newspaper reader?*
> (an emotional appeal to prestige)

> *While on strike, did you spend your time picketing or doing other things?*
> (partial mention of alternatives)

Most people these days get their news from television rather than newspapers. Which do you prefer? (bandwagon effect)

c. For single attitude questions, avoid presenting respondents with a unipolar statement to which they are asked to agree or disagree. (This produces acquiescence, discussed later.) Instead, use **bipolar** alternatives:

Do you favor or oppose product-code scanning in supermarkets?

However, multiple-item scales such as the Likert scale can use unipolar items with the wording of some items reversed.

Do you think product-code scanning will lead to lower prices?

Do you think product-code scanning will end up costing you money on your food bill?

An alternative for interviews is to mention all response categories in the question.

With respect to product-code scanning instead of price stickers, are you strongly in favor, somewhat in favor, undecided, somewhat opposed, or strongly opposed?

SUGGESTION

As you check over question wording, make a separate pass for each of the criteria: clarity and specificity, appropriate and condescending language, emphasis, simplicity, brevity, neutrality, and relevance. This sounds like a lot of work, and it is—but it's easy to let poor wording slip by, and the result is unwanted measurement error and invalidity.

8. Keep It Relevant.

a. Respondents should find the question relevant; they shouldn't have to write in, "Not applicable." Avoid questions which assume that respondents have some characteristic or experience. For example, a respondent who is not a member of the union may be offended by a question that asks,

How often do you attend union meetings?

To avoid the problem, use **filter questions** that screen out inapplicable respondents and "skip" them to the next relevant question. Alternatively, include a "Not applicable" response category.

b. Avoid questions that the respondent can't relate to the ostensible purpose of the research. If the respondent cannot see why you're asking for income and education, for example, you increase the chance that these questions will not be answered. Use a comment such as the following to explain why you are asking what might otherwise appear to be irrelevant questions:

Here are a few background questions to help ensure our sample is representative of all employees.

RESPONSE FORMATS

As well as question wording, the researcher must also decide what format respondents will use to mark their responses: open or closed, and which type of closed response scale.

Closed and Open Formats

A closed format specifies categories for the response to a question. The respondent answers by selecting one (or sometimes more) of the categories. For example, to the question, "What is your gender?"

Male   [ ]
Female   [ ]

An open format requires a response in words and leaves the content and length of the reply up to the respondent. For example,

Interview: *Please tell me what you think about the company's performance appraisal policy.*

Questionnaire: *What is your gender?*_____

Responses may vary from a single word or number to a lengthy reply. Such questions are often called *closed-ended questions;* those with open formats are called *open-ended questions.*

Closed Response Formats.   The advantages of closed formats are many. A closed format is easier to code, takes less of the respondent's time, provides a uniform and standardized set of comparable responses, produces less bias with sensitive and embarrassing topics (by including the less socially desirable alternatives), and helps ensure that respondents use the researcher's frame of reference. In addition, closed formats in interviews make it easier for the interviewer to record answers and remove any unconscious bias in the interviewer's selection of what to record.

On the other hand, they don't get detailed or complex feelings and attitudes. They also assume that the respondent sees the question the same way the researcher does.

In questionnaires the respondent reads the response categories as part of the question. In interviews, the interviewer reads the categories aloud or hands a **response card** to the respondent (see Box 9.2). In telephone interviews, the interviewer can only read the response categories over the telephone unless information has been sent to the respondent beforehand.

BOX 9.2
FOCUS ON RESEARCH

Response Cards

Response cards (also called *show cards* or *flash cards*) are often used in interviews. Each card contains the response categories for one or more questions.

Their purpose is to help respondents keep in mind the response categories as the interviewer reads the question. The respondent then reads the appropriate number from the card to indicate which category he or she has chosen. Sudman and Bradburn (1982) recommend response cards whenever the number of categories is five or more or the categories have more complex names. Response cards also save time when a sequence of questions uses the same response categories; the interviewer doesn't have to read the categories after each item.

How frequently are you bothered by feeling that you have too little authority to carry out the responsibilities assigned to you?[1]

> 1. Never bothered
> 2. Rarely bothered
> 3. Sometimes bothered
> 4. Bothered rather often
> 5. Bothered nearly all the time
>
> 9. Does not apply

Select the number that best corresponds to your net monthly income, after taxes and deductions.

> 1. Less than $500
> 2. 500   to 999
> 3. 1,000 to 1,499
> 4. 1,500 to 1,999
> 5. 2,000 to 2,499
> 6. 2,500 to 2,999
> 7. 3,000 or more

The layout on the card should approximate the layout that the same response categories would have on a questionnaire. To reduce the number of cards interviewers must carry around, response scales for two different questions can be printed one on each side of a card.

[1]This example is adapted from Kahn's Index of Job-Related Tensions, as reported in Miller, 1991.

Open Response Formats.   Open formats are best for interviews in the exploratory stages of research, when the objective is to get some feeling for the phenomenon being investigated. They provide detailed answers that allow the researcher to examine how respondents themselves categorize the phenomenon. They are also useful when you're not sure what possible answers respondents might give to a question (for example, "What aspects of free trade worry you the most?"). Open response formats are also appropriate when the question calls for a short fill-in response (such as numbers, counts, and dates) and there are too many categories to list. An example is "Year of birth?"

A major disadvantage is that coding the information they provide is usually time consuming and expensive (see Chapter 13).

Open-Ended Response Units.   For fill-in replies, the choice of response units should be unambiguous. For example, Canadian respondents might answer the question, "How far do you drive to work?" in either miles or kilometers. The choice of units should also ensure that answers will be sufficiently sensitive. To accomplish these ends, specify the desired units for the response as part of the question or in the response categories. This avoids ambiguity and suggests the degree of accuracy you would like (to ensure sensitivity).

How long did you spend in total interviewing your most recent applicant for a middle-management position?

_____*hours*, _____*minutes*

Using Open-Ended Questions.   For questionnaires, open-ended questions that invite the respondent to give reasons or provide details are generally unsuccessful unless respondents identify fairly strongly with the objectives of the research or have strong feelings on the topic.

Interestingly, open-ended questions can sometimes produce less rich and varied information because respondents implicitly assume that certain topics are excluded.

CASE EXAMPLE

A survey of employees' reactions to flextime produced answers in terms of personal and family benefits concentrating on time. Many employees mentioned spending more time with their spouses and children and less time in rush-hour traffic. Relatively few employees talked about social costs or drawbacks with flextime. A follow-up questionnaire with response categories for "Less time spent in after-work socializing with friends" and "Not enough time to get settled before getting down to work" elicited these and other negative feelings that the open-ended question missed.

One alternative to open formats is a combined format question. It involves a closed-ended question with one of the response categories labeled "other." A respondent choosing that category is asked to specify his or her choice. However, only highly motivated and interested respondents seem to make use of an "other" category.

For interviews, Warwick and Lininger (1975) and others discuss an alternative to open-ended questions for checking the respondent's frame of reference and interpretation of the question. The technique is called **random probing**; it is a technique for checking *measurement validity*.

The procedure is to select randomly a few closed questions (different questions for each respondent). After getting the respondent's answer, ask,

Could you explain what you had in mind when you made that choice?

Then check to see whether the answer given by the respondent is consistent with the researcher's intention.

The random selection of questions is made before the interview. One simple method is to make a numbered list of the closed response questions. Then use a table of random numbers to select the specific questions to be probed in the forthcoming interview. For example, an interview schedule with 16 questions (some with several parts) and 25 closed items results in the following list:

Closed item	1	Question	1
	2		2a
	3		3a
	4		3b
	5		4
	. . . .		
	25		16

For each interview, three items are chosen randomly for probing. Before the interview, the researcher writes the letter *P* beside each question to be probed.

The random probe method does *not* work for questionnaires. Respondents are likely to find the question puzzling and to restate their answers or rephrase them only slightly.

To summarize, the choice of an open response format should be made after considering the purpose of the research, the time and effort the respondent will be willing to spend, the variable to be measured, and how much is known about possible responses.

Response Scales

Closed response formats use a wide variety of response scales. The most common types of response scales are

Choice scales

Categorizing scales:
   Checklists
   Category scales
   Sorting scales

Rating scales:
   Frequency, extremity, and intensity scales
   Likert scales
   Numeric rating scales
   Semantic differential scales

Ranking scales:
   Item ranking scales
   Grouped ranking/sorting scales

It's easy to confuse the terms *response scale* and *scale*. A response scale refers to the response format for a single question. A scale (as we noted in the previous chapter) is a multiple-item measure, a series of similar questions used to measure a single concept. The confusion comes about because some of the standard response scales (such as Likert and semantic differential) are used almost exclusively in multiple-item scales. However, there is no reason why any particular response scale couldn't be used for a single question by itself. Some standard questions and response scales for demographic and other variables are presented in Appendix C.

Choice Scales

This form is the most prevalent of all response scales. Respondents are simply asked to choose the most appropriate among several alternative options.

Do you:
[   ]   *own your home*
[   ]   *rent*

Choice scales result in nominal, category ordinal, or dichotomous level measures. To construct a choice scale, follow the guidelines in Box 8.4.

Categorizing Scales

Categorizing scales ask respondents to select the appropriate nominal level category for each of a *series* of items. They are used for both factual and attitude questions. There are three general forms of categorizing response scales used in business research: checklists, category scales, and sorting scales.

Checklists.   The most common categorizing scale is the checklist. The best checklist form asks the respondent to place each item in one of three categories, depending on how the item applies to the respondent.

Which of the following occurred in your last round of collective bargaining?

	Occurred	Didn't Occur	Don't Know
Union strike vote before contract expired	[ ]	[ ]	[ ]
Mediation	[ ]	[ ]	[ ]
. . .			
Strike	[ ]	[ ]	[ ]

SUGGESTION

Wherever possible, borrow or adapt an existing question and its response scale to save the time required to develop, test, and revise your own. This advice is doubly important when it comes to multiple-item scales, since constructing and validating a scale can be a highly technical and time-consuming task.

The response categories used in checklists vary widely and include "Yes/ No," "Applies/Doesn't apply," "Occurred/Didn't occur," "Like/Dislike," and others. A third category is normally included for instances in which respondents are unable to choose between the other two.

A mistake sometimes made in checklists is to use only the positive category, omitting the negative and the unable-to-answer options. This makes it difficult to interpret an unchecked response, which could indicate a negative answer, uncertainty, the item doesn't apply, or item nonresponse. To reduce the ambiguity, use all three categories: positive, negative, and "Don't know" (for factual questions) or "Uncertain" (for attitude questions).

Checklist response scales result in nominal or dichotomous level measures for each item in the list.

Category Scales.   These scales use the same logic as checklists, except that each item is placed into one of several categories.

In which type of store would you most prefer to shop for each of the following items? (PLEASE CHECK ONE TYPE OF STORE FOR EACH ITEM)

	Depart- ment Store	Drug- store	Corner Store	Spe- cialty Store	Other or Don't Know
Tooth- brush	[ ]	[ ]	[ ]	[ ]	[ ]
Camera film	[ ]	[ ]	[ ]	[ ]	[ ]
News magazine	[ ]	[ ]	[ ]	[ ]	[ ]
. . .					
Candy bar	[ ]	[ ]	[ ]	[ ]	[ ]

Again, the best scales include options representing no choice because of indecision, some other alternative, or the item is irrelevant to the respondent.

Data from category scales is usually at the nominal level of measurement.

Sorting Scales.   Sorting scales combine the logic of categorizing with a physical activity. They are used exclusively in face-to-face interviews. Respondents are handed a series of cards on which the items to be categorized are printed. The interviewer then asks the respondent to sort the cards into designated piles. These piles represent the sorting categories.

CASE EXAMPLE

A market researcher hired by a travel agency used a sorting technique to assess consumers' perceptions of various holiday destinations. A series of 25 cards were printed with the name of each destination and a small picture representing the place (e.g., a beach hotel in Hawaii, a tennis resort in the Catskills, an African sight-seeing safari). Respondents were asked to sort the cards into piles representing "Two weeks with my family," "Two weeks with just my spouse," and "Two weeks' dream vacation." They were then asked to sort the cards in the middle pile into two further piles: "Places to go in the winter" and "Places to go in the summer."

Sorting scales are useful for breaking the monotony of a long interview because they ask the respondent to act rather than speak. They normally result in a nominal or dichotomous level measure for each sorted item.

Rating Scales

Many scales ask respondents to rate items and behaviors rather than just categorize them. The rating may involve the frequency of a particular behavior, the extremity of feelings or opinion on a topic, or the intensity with which a position is held. Rating scales produce category ordinal measures.

Extremity and intensity are often highly correlated (those with extreme positions usually hold them fairly strongly), but this isn't necessarily the case (Converse and Presser, 1986). You should decide which aspect is more important and focus on that. If you want both extremity and intensity, use two questions, the first for extremity of position and a follow-up for intensity of feeling.

The most commonly used rating response scales in business research are general frequency, extremity, and intensity scales; Likert scales; numeric rating scales; and semantic differential scales.

Frequency, Extremity, and Intensity Scales. For attitude and factual questions, response options are often presented in terms of an ordinal scale of three or more categories to measure the intensity or frequency of an attitude or behavior.

In general, how often do you watch television news?

[ ]   *very often*

[ ]   *often*

[ ]   *sometimes*

[ ]   *rarely*

[ ]   *never*

The scale may be worded to measure the direction (positive or negative) as well as the extremity or intensity of an attitude.

How do you feel about your job?

very satisfied	[ ]
somewhat satisfied	[ ]
so-so	[ ]
somewhat dissatisfied	[ ]
very dissatisfied	[ ]
no opinion	[ ]

There doesn't seem much point in using a large number of response categories for intensity scales. The apparent gain in measurement accuracy is illusory, since respondents normally can't distinguish more than six or seven ordered category descriptions. (See Box 9.3 for some commonly used category labels.)

In bipolar questions, use the same number of categories on either side of the neutral midpoint to avoid confusing your respondents. If you expect many more respondents to choose one direction than the other, add an extra category to each side. Later during analysis you can collapse two or more adjacent categories if just a few respondents choose them.

Intensity and frequency scales result in a category ordinal measure for each rated item.

Likert Scales.   This is a specific form of intensity rating scale very frequently used in multiple-item measures of attitudes. The respondent is presented with a series of statements (usually ranging from 4 to about 20) and for each one chooses from among the categories:

[ ] *Strongly agree*
[ ] *Agree*
[ ] *Uncertain*
[ ] *Disagree*
[ ] *Strongly disagree*

(Sometimes the middle category is omitted to force a choice between agreeing and disagreeing.)

A score for each respondent is calculated by assigning numbers from "0" to "4" to the categories (taking care to reverse the numbers for reversed items), and then summing the item scores to get an overall score. For this reason, Likert scales are also called *summated rating scales*. Details for developing a

BOX 9.3
FOCUS ON RESEARCH

Commonly Used Category Labels for Intensity and Frequency Scales

Terms on the same line indicate approximately the same level of intensity or frequency. For a shorter scale, drop one or more of the categories.

General Adjectives (unipolar)

1 Very, Extremely, Strongly
2 Somewhat, Moderately, Fairly, Quite
3 Slightly, Weakly
4 Not very, Hardly
5 Not at all

satisfied
true
interesting
important
concerned
agree
etc.

Directional General Adjectives (bipolar)

1 Very, Extremely, Strongly, Definitely
2 Somewhat, Moderately, Fairly, Mostly
3 Slightly, Weakly
4 Neutral, Neither . . . nor . . . , Undecided, So-so, Not sure, Uncertain
5 Slightly, Weakly
6 Somewhat, Moderately, Fairly, Mostly
7 Very, Extremely, Strongly, Definitely

satisfied
true
etc.

dissatisfied
untrue
etc.

Directional Comparisons (bipolar)

1 Much better
2 Better
3 About the same
4 Worse
5 Much worse

Frequency (unipolar)

1 All the time, A great deal
2 Very often, Most of the time, Fairly often, Quite a lot
3 Often, Frequently
4 Sometimes, Some of the time, Not very much
5 Seldom, Hardly ever, Rarely
6 Never, Not at all

Evaluation (unipolar)

1 Excellent, Superb, Outstanding, Superior
2 Very good, Above average
3 Good, Fairly good
4 Fair, Average
5 Poor, Below average
6 Very poor, Not good at all, Awful

Likert-type scale are presented in Box 9.4. Likert scales typically do not include a "Don't know" category; the middle category picks up the "don't knows" as well as those with intermediate opinions. Likert scales also assume that each statement carries equal weight among respondents: a "disagree" on one item has the same impact as a "disagree" on another item worded in the same direction.

Although technically only an ordinal measure, summated Likert scale scores are often treated as interval data, especially in multivariate analysis.

BOX 9.4
RESEARCH SKILLS

Developing a Likert Scale

The development of a true Likert scale involves two steps:

- Creating scale items and gathering data
- Conducting an **item analysis** to eliminate the less useful items and arrive at the final scale

The first step begins before data gathering; the final step follows data gathering and is part of the researcher's preliminary analysis. In some instances the item analysis is omitted; the result is a Likert-type scale rather than a true Likert scale.

To develop the statements that comprise a Likert scale, researchers must use knowledge of the phenomenon, creativity, and imagination. Useful techniques are to derive some statements logically from others, to think of actions or attitudes associated with the main ideas, and to break the overall attitude object into its constituent aspects. (For example, satisfaction with one's supervisor includes his or her advice and suggestions, peremptory instructions, support, general manner, tolerance, flexibility, and so on.) Enlist the help of others in generating potential statements.

Once this brainstorming stage is over, carefully review and evaluate the statements to reject those that appear to have less face validity.

With the remaining items, reverse half of them so

that a disagreement on a reversed item is consistent with an agreement on a nonreversed item. For example,

The economy is basically sound.

High inflation is just around the corner. (reversed)

Researchers sometimes inadvertently include a negatively worded item in the question in an attempt to reverse the question content. If a respondent disagrees, the resulting double negative can often be confusing. For this reason, reversed items should not be worded as negatives. For example, instead of,

I do not expect unemployment rates to rise.

use,

I expect unemployment rates to stay the same or fall.

For true Likert scales the second step is item analysis once the data have been collected. The researcher's objective is to reject those items that fail to differentiate between those with low and high scores. Item analysis is described in Chapter 14.

Numeric Rating Scales. This type of rating scale is often used to measure the extremity and intensity of opinions. It overcomes the limitation on number of category descriptions (in Likert and other rating scales) by using words only to indicate the end categories (and sometimes the middle category). These labeled points are said to be *anchored*. Other points on the scale are represented by numbers:

How would you rate the taste of Princess peach jam?

Absolutely delicious				*Tasted awful*
1	2	3	4	5

An additional category for "Don't Know" responses can be added and should be slightly separated from the rest of the scale.

The result of a numeric rating scale is a category ordinal measure for each rated item.

Semantic Differential Scales.
Another variation of rating scales is the **semantic differential**. It is often used in consumer research to determine underlying attitudes, impressions, and psychological meanings of brands, packaging, and advertisements.

The respondent is asked to rate a single object or idea on a series of dimensions. Each dimension is represented by a line, with two bipolar adjectives anchoring the ends of the line. Each adjective pair represents a different dimension (such as good-bad) or characteristic (such as expensive-inexpensive) on which the concept is to be rated. If a characteristic has no opposite, absence of the characteristic is used as the other end point. The standard semantic differential scale has seven points or cells.

Think of a Moving Sound record store bus, and remember the last time you were in one. On the lines below, indicate how you feel about the store. Read the word or phrase at each end of a line and then PLACE A CHECK AT THAT POINT ON THE LINE WHICH BEST INDICATES YOUR FEELINGS. Then go on to the next line.

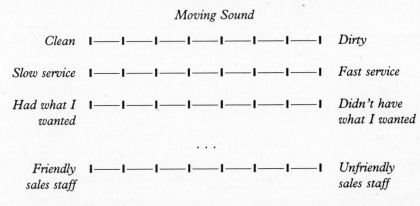

Instructions for semantic differential questions almost always include an example to show respondents what is wanted. Note that the positive adjectives are not all on one end. This makes it necessary for the respondent to read each line carefully and helps discourage a respondent from putting all the marks on one side under one another (a form of position bias, discussed later).

Like the Likert scale, a semantic differential can combine the results of a number of item pairs into an overall evaluation. The scale for each item pair is numbered from 1 to 7 with the positive end the highest. The individual ratings are then summed over all pairs. Unlike Likert scales, the item pairs are usually not subjected to an item analysis to eliminate pairs that don't differentiate.

Semantic differential results are also used in a different way to compare the profiles of two or more brands, packages, or advertisements. See Box 9.5.

BOX 9.5

RESEARCH SKILLS

Creating Semantic Differential Profiles

Semantic differential profiles are useful for exploring consumers' opinions of different brands, stores, packages, advertisements, or other objects.

First, develop a semantic differential scale with at least four or five item pairs, and gather data from a sample of consumers familiar with each of the two or more objects to be compared.

For each item pair, calculate the sample mean for each object. (If the data show much skewness, or you wish to treat the data as an ordinal rather than an interval measure, substitute the median for the mean.)

Adjust the scale so that the positive end of each item pair is on the right. Then mark each item scale with the mean (or median) point for each object. Draw a line connecting the first object's marks on each scale to obtain the profile for that object, and repeat for the remaining objects.

The profile for one object can then be compared with the profile for another.

The profiles show at a glance the strong and weak points for each object. They can suggest themes to emphasize in advertising and areas in which the object needs improving.

In the example for Moving Sound and Bigstore Records, you might conclude that Moving Sound should put some effort into the appearance of its stores, since there is a substantial difference between it and Bigstore Records. Sales staff are not perceived as very friendly, but there is no immediate need to improve this aspect as long as Bigstore Records is the only major competitor. Moving Sound should also stress low prices in its advertising.

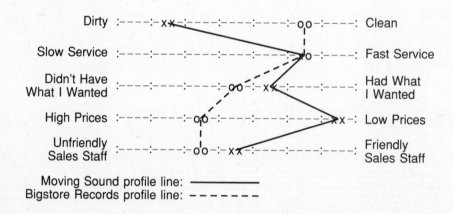

Moving Sound profile line: ————
Bigstore Records profile line: — — — — —

A variation of the semantic differential, called the *Stapel scale,* uses a single label in the middle of the scale, with ten points ranging from -5 to $+5$. Respondents who believe the term is not at all descriptive of the object would assign it a -5 score, and those who believe it is highly accurate would assign it $+5$. Stapel scales are easier to construct, since they don't require finding opposite words or phrases and their results are similar to those for semantic differential scales.

Measures from both semantic differential and Stapel scales are category ordinal level.

Ranking Scales

Ranking scales ask respondents to rank a list of items in terms of preference, familiarity, or some other attribute. Although ranking scales are generally more difficult for respondents than rating scales, the extra information they provide is often highly desired by researchers. They produce category ordinal measures (it is the items, not the cases, which are ranked, and many respondents will be given an item the same rank).

Ranking response scales are generally of two types: item and grouped.

Item Ranking Scales. These scales simply ask respondents to rank a series of items (e.g., presidential candidates, breakfast cereals) in terms of preference, familiarity, or some other aspect. The results are category ordinal measures for each item, with as many scale categories as there are items. For example, each item from a list of 12 is assigned to one of 12 categories ranging from "ranked first" to "ranked twelfth."

Ranking raises three problems:

- Respondents can only rank accurately when they can easily see or remember all the items. For face-to-face interviews, interviewers often use response cards. For telephone interviews, three or four items is normally the maximum.

- Each additional item adds appreciably to the time it takes to rank an entire list, since the number of possible comparisons increases sharply with each new item. Whether on cards or in a questionnaire, anything beyond seven or eight items often takes too much time and effort. The risk is an incomplete answer, item nonresponse, or (worst) the respondent abandons the interview or questionnaire.

- Respondents are often vague about the relative ranking of items in the middle range. They know what they like and what they don't like, but the rest is somewhat uncertain. The reliability for middle ranks is often poor.

A solution to the second and third problems, if more than eight items are involved, is to ask respondents to rank the top (and perhaps the bottom) three. This will take less time than ranking the entire list and allow you to include many more items in the question. It reduces the number of categories in the category ordinal measure and adds a new category: "unranked."

In your opinion, which of the following 15 stocks do you consider to be the investments with the greatest potential and the least potential?

PLEASE RANK THE 3 WITH <u>GREATEST</u> POTENTIAL, USING "1" FOR THE GREATEST, "2" FOR THE NEXT GREATEST, "3" FOR THE THIRD GREATEST. THEN RANK THE 3 WITH <u>LEAST</u> POTENTIAL, USING "13," "14," AND "15," WITH "15" FOR THE LEAST POTENTIAL OF ALL.

NCR	_____
Sara Lee	_____
Penn Central	_____
. . .	
Heinz pf	_____
Don't know	[ ]

Another solution for these problems is to use grouped ranking response scales.

Grouped Ranking Scales.   A different type of ranking scale asks respondents to classify each item in one of three or four ranked categories. This greatly reduces both the number of categories and the number of distinctions respondents are asked to make.

In your opinion, do each of the following 15 stocks have great potential, modest potential, or little potential?

FOR EACH STOCK, PLEASE CHECK ITS POTENTIAL.

	Great	Modest	Little	Don't Know
NCR	[ ]	[ ]	[ ]	[ ]
Sara Lee	[ ]	[ ]	[ ]	[ ]
Penn Central	[ ]	[ ]	[ ]	[ ]
. . .				
Heinz pf	[ ]	[ ]	[ ]	[ ]

This procedure produces less information than a simple ranking scale, but respondents can apply it to evaluate a much longer list of items.

This form of scale is equivalent to a categorizing scale with ordinal level categories. Consequently, a sorting technique can be used for this type of scale. For example, the vacation destination cards in the preceding case example could be sorted into "Places I'd love to go," "Places I feel so-so about," and "Places I don't really want to go."

A wide variety of other scales exist, most of which are now seldom used in business research because of methodological problems or the cost of developing them. They include Guttman scales (replaced by scales based on latent structure analysis), Thurstone equal-interval scales, and others. (For details, see McIver and Carmines, 1981.) Other techniques, such as multidimensional scaling analysis, are beyond the scope of this text.

Response Scale Issues

For response scales in general, there are three general points to consider: in what order to put the alternatives, whether to include a middle position, and how to record "no opinion" and "don't know" responses.

Order of Alternatives.   The order in which scale options are presented can affect answers and produce response bias. Experience suggests several ways to minimize order problems.

- For factual questions, list the response categories starting with the least socially desirable. This reduces the tendency to select the first category or to fail to read the entire list.

- For multiple-item intensity, frequency, and Likert scales, keep the same order of response categories throughout. Reversing the order confuses respondents. To reduce position bias, vary the item wording between positive and negative, not the response scale.

- For numeric rating and semantic differential scales, vary the position of the positive anchor phrases between left and right.

- A more general solution is to use two (or more) forms of the instrument, with forms randomly distributed across the sample. Each form contains a different order of response alternatives. This use of two or more forms to overcome response bias is known as the **split ballot** technique.

The Middle Position.   On bipolar attitude scales a middle position represents indifference, the inability to decide between two alternatives. Many researchers omit the middle position to force respondents to choose one alternative or another on the assumption that no respondent is perfectly neutral. This practice appears to be legitimate as long as there are enough categories (no fewer than six) to represent respondents with weak opinions. If there are only four categories, keep a middle option for those with weak opinions. There is evidence that this will not affect the overall ratio of those in favor to those opposed (Schuman and Presser, 1981).

"No Opinion."   While the middle position on a bipolar response scale allows respondents to indicate indifference in an attitude question, it will also pick up those respondents who have not thought about the issue enough to *have* an opinion. In other words, it doesn't differentiate between indifference (neutral opinion) and ignorance of the issue (no opinion).

If you want to make this distinction, and determine the size of the group with no opinion (as opposed to a neutral opinion), add a "No Opinion" category to the *end*. This position makes it clear that it is not the same as a neutral opinion. However, if the scale has no middle or neutral position, the "No Opinion" category will also pick up some of those who really have a neutral opinion.

With interviews, you can avoid the confusion between neutral and no opinion by following any "No Opinion" response with a probe to ensure that there is truly no opinion and that the respondent doesn't mean "Neutral" (or isn't just trying to avoid answering for reasons of social desirability).

Probing. Probing is an important skill for interviewers. It reduces measurement error and increases the validity of answers by ensuring that

- The respondent's frame of reference matches the researcher's.
- The respondent's answer is complete.
- The answer is understandable and codable.

Skilled interviewers must judge on the spur of the moment when an answer is inadequate and what probe to use. This requires close attention to what the respondent is saying, as well as a good understanding of the objectives of the research in general and the specific question in particular.

At the same time, the interviewer must not lead the respondent or suggest an answer (a form of measurement error due to the researcher).

Among the useful forms of probes are the following:

- *Pause* for three to five seconds, waiting expectantly as if you anticipate that the respondent will say more. This will apply some pressure to the respondent to amplify his or her previous remarks.

- *Rephrase* the question, emphasizing that you want to know what the *respondent* thinks, believes, or perceives.

- *Ask* for general clarification.

    Can you tell me what you have in mind?

- Ask a *follow-up question* using a key word the respondent used in his or her initial answer.

    You used the term . . .
    You say you . . . [did some action].

"Don't Know." When a questionnaire respondent gives no answer to a factual question, it means one of two things. Either the person legitimately doesn't know the answer or skips the question out of boredom, frustration, or resentment. You can safely assume the latter when the entire page is skipped, but a missing answer for one or two questions is ambiguous. To resolve this ambiguity, include a "Don't Know" category in response scales for factual questions.

This practice also relieves some of the embarrassment of not knowing by suggesting that it's a legitimate response. This can be a particular problem when surveying employees, who might otherwise find it awkward to admit ignorance and might fabricate an answer.

QUESTION ORDER

Careful attention to the order in which questions are asked is important for three reasons.

- A logical flow of questions helps guide respondents through the instrument with a minimum of confusion and frustration. Topics that are raised once should not be raised again later in the instrument.

- Asking the right question at the right time, especially the opening and closing questions, can increase respondents' commitment to the questionnaire or interview and reduce item nonresponse.

- The influence of earlier questions on the answers to later ones, known as *order effects,* can be reduced through attention to question sequence.

General Sequence

The general order of your questions should be based on the principle of *funneling* and the implicit logic of the variables. Include bridges and filter questions where necessary.

Funneling.   Arrange the questions on a particular topic in a funnel order. Begin with the most general ones and then move to increasingly specific items. This provides a natural focus for the respondent's thoughts as you move to the specific topics of interest. For example, ask first about the respondent's general satisfaction with his or her shopping experience, and then move to specific questions: number of brands stocked, availability of carts, and lengths of lines at the cash registers.

If you need to grab the respondent's attention for a topic to which he or she hasn't paid much attention, it might be necessary to start with a specific question and then move to more general ones. This inverted-funnel sequence forces respondents to move from specific to general attitude objects in a way that mirrors most everyday thinking—from the concrete to the abstract.

Implicit Logic.   In questionnaires, particularly, the sequence of questions should naturally follow the logic implicit in the topic. Failure to follow a logical pattern can frustrate and confuse respondents. For example, in a study of working conditions, ask first about conditions in the respondent's workplace, then about conditions in other settings the respondent may know about. Finish your questions on a topic before you switch to a new one.

If you are getting retrospective information about past behaviors or situations, work consistently backward or forward in time. For example, ask about the previous strike, then the one before that, and then the one previous to that.

Bridges.   *Bridges* are short phrases that introduce the next section of the questionnaire. They help to keep a smooth flow, break up the monotony of questions, and can help the respondent shift mental gears and adopt the desired frame of reference for the next set of questions.

Here are some questions about . . .

Next I'd like to ask you . . .

The next few questions deal with . . .

And now here are some questions about . . .

Filter Questions.   Not all questions will be relevant for all respondents. For example, informants in firms that have not undergone mergers should not be asked questions about middle-management reactions to a merger. To minimize respondent frustration with inapplicable items, use filter questions to determine whether a set of questions is relevant. If it is not, then skip the respondent to the next relevant item. See Box 9.6 for suggestions for handling skip patterns in questionnaires and interviews.

Order Effects

The order in which you ask questions can contribute substantially to measurement bias. In particular, two kinds of order effects tend to be a problem for attitude questions: framework persistence and cognitive consistency.

Framework Persistence.   Merely asking a question and presenting response categories provides the respondent with a framework for that question and subsequent ones (see Box 9.7). In particular, attitude questions will be interpreted as having attitude objects consistent with earlier questions. For example, a question about shopping preferences means that subsequent questions are likely to be interpreted as related to shopping experiences.

The careful choice of an initial question in each section of the questionnaire or interview can help ensure that respondents use the desired frame of reference for the entire section. On the other hand, it is important to signal a change in frame of reference. This can be done either with a carefully worded question or a bridge.

Cognitive Consistency.   Replies to earlier questions influence later responses because respondents attempt to be consistent, as well as accurate, in their answers. Especially when the question topics are similar, earlier opinions tend to color later ones.

To avoid respondents' attempts at consistency, separate questions referring to similar or related attitude objects. Unfortunately, this suggestion has two problems.

SUGGESTION

Don't number conditional follow-up questions. Respondents for whom a follow-up question is not applicable will be more likely to answer it if it has a number in sequence (for example "11" following "10" or "6b" following "6a"). Also indent such questions to set them off from the normal sequence. (For editing, coding, and data entry, conditional follow-up questions can be treated as having an implied letter suffix. For example, the follow-up question after "18" is "18a").

BOX 9.6
RESEARCH SKILLS

Writing Skip Instructions

In many interviews and questionnaires, not all respondents should be asked all questions. For example, respondents in their first job shouldn't be asked questions about previous jobs. *Filter questions* (e.g., "Is this your first job?") determine whether a subsequent set of questions is relevant to a respondent. *Skip instructions* direct the respondent to the next relevant question, depending on the answer to the filter question.

Good skip instructions help prevent respondent frustration. Poor skip instructions produce confusion and lead to inadvertent missing data. Time spent devising and pretesting skip patterns and instructions is usually time well invested.

There are two major types of skip instructions: "go-to" and graphic.

"GO-TO" SKIP INSTRUCTIONS

These skips are instructions conditional on the answer to a filter question. Sometimes an "if" condition replaces the filter question.

IF **YES**, GO TO QUESTION 17.

IF THIS IS YOUR FIRST PAID JOB, GO TO QUESTION 17.

This kind of skip works best with interviews. Interviewers can train and practice so that improper skips and missing data are largely avoided. Training also helps the interviewer follow skip patterns easily and without having an awkward break in the interview.

With questionnaires, however, a small proportion of the sample is sure to misread the instructions and either fill out (with some confusion) inappropriate questions or skip questions they should answer.

GRAPHIC SKIP INSTRUCTIONS

Graphic skips use arrows and boxes. They are generally easy to follow and can handle complex sequences. Check the example in Appendix D, and note how boxes are used to group questions.

The major disadvantage is that graphic skips take more space. They are also difficult when a large number of questions must be skipped; in that instance a combination of graphic and "go-to" skips is best.

SUGGESTIONS

- If skip patterns are complicated, work them out first with a flow chart.
- If large parts of the questionnaire will not be relevant for some respondents, consider using two different forms. If you cannot prescreen to ensure that respondents receive the proper questionnaire, send them both (in two different colors), with cover letter instructions on which questionnaire to complete.
- Avoid skip patterns that require an interviewer to go back and check a previous answer. This restriction does not apply to computer-assisted telephone interviews (CATI). CATI systems can be programmed so that answers from any previous question will influence the choice, the wording, or even the order, of subsequent questions.
- Pretest! Make *sure* the skip works properly and smoothly.

BOX 9.7
MOVING SOUND: A CONTINUING CASE

Part Eight: Order Effects

"Hey, Pete! What's that guy carrying? Is that the latest Tammy Wynette CD?"

Pete and George are working at Pete's desk in a corner of the warehouse, putting together the two survey instruments for their evaluation research.

"Calm down, George. Take it easy. Get back to this sensitizing problem."

George, with a last look at the departing disks, sits down again. "Well, what I was saying, because we have two different instruments, we have to be careful that what we ask in the short interview doesn't affect their answers to the take-home questionnaire."

"Like what?"

"For example, say the interviewer asks what problems they find buying records at Moving Sound, and then the questionnaire asks about the buses. They'll have had time to think about all kinds of problems. You're going to get more negative answers just because they're sensitized. Things they would never think about if they just answered the questionnaire item about the Moving Sound bus."

"So maybe the interview should just ask short factual questions. We leave the opinions for the questionnaire."

"That's a good way to handle it, Pete, though there still might be some other order effect."

"We just want the interview to get basic information about the commercial."

"And to get them interested enough to complete the questionnaire at home."

"Speaking of home, why don't you take along one of those CDs when we're done. Maybe the Tammy Wynette. Unless you'd prefer heavy metal?" He ducks an imaginary punch.

SUGGESTION

As you construct the questionnaire, keep each question on a separate sheet of paper. Make revisions on the same sheet, and if it will help, keep notes of the concept the question is designed to measure on the sheet. You can then shuffle the sheets to find the best order for questions.

- Questionnaire respondents may look up their previous answers, particularly if the instrument is short. The only solutions are to use highly specific questions and to word the second question so it appears to be different.

- Respondents find it frustrating to return to a topic they thought they had finished with, and frustrated respondents often don't finish questionnaires or lose interest in interviews. Use pretesting to find the best balance between item separation and respondent frustration.

General questions are more subject to order effects than those with very specific referents or attitude objects. Therefore, ask general attitude questions before specific ones.

On the whole, how do you feel about the new productivity campaign?

How do you feel about the scheduling of the work-team productivity meetings?

INSTRUMENT FORMAT

The general layout or format of your survey instrument is next in importance to question wording and order for assuring low item nonresponse.

- For *questionnaires,* a good layout with clear skip patterns looks easy and attractive. The respondent can follow the instructions and questions without hesitation. This reduces both total and item nonresponse.

- For *interviews,* good layout helps the interviewer avoid inadvertent item nonresponse because of accidentally skipped questions. It also allows the interviewer to maintain a smooth interview, record answers easily, and utilize probes where needed.

A well-planned format also takes into account the needs of editors and coders, leaving space for entering editors' comments and question codes.

Questionnaire Formats

Here are suggestions for questionnaire formats to help reduce item nonresponse and misunderstood questions.

Instructions.   Most general or focusing instructions will be part of a specific question, such as,

> *Think back to when you first came to work for Campbell Switch. How did you learn about the job opening?*

However, response instructions should appear in capital letters.

> *PLEASE RANK YOUR FIRST 3 CHOICES, BEGINNING WITH "1."*

Skip instructions should also be presented in capital letters and should immediately follow the response categories, rather than the question. Use positive wording for skip instructions (e.g., "IF YOU ANSWERED 'YES' . . ." rather than "IF YOU DID NOT ANSWER 'NO' . . .").

Response Categories.   For factual questions on a questionnaire, arrange response categories vertically, with the categories indented. Don't try to save space by using more than one column; the result will look too crowded, and some respondents will think you want an answer in each column.

Have respondents check a box (or circle a number if the questionnaire is

SUGGESTION

Don't start a question at the bottom of one page and continue it on the next. For questionnaires, the respondent must be able to move easily from the response categories back to the question for clarification. Interviewers should not have to turn pages in the middle of a question.

precoded—see Chapter 12). The box may be located either in front of or after the response option.

Female   [ ]
or
[ ]   *Female*

If you use numbers, put them after the response option to avoid confusion. If multiple answers are called for, add an appropriate instruction:

PLEASE CHECK AS MANY AS APPLY.

Attitude scale response categories may be presented either vertically (e.g., ranking scales) or horizontally (e.g., numerical rating scales).

Question Matrix.   A question matrix is the space-saving combination of two or more similar questions with identical response categories. Usually, the questions occupy the rows and the response categories the columns. This layout makes it relatively easy for respondents to answer a set of related questions.

	Strongly Agree	Agree	Disagree	Strongly Disagree
My supervisor knows how to deal with people.	1	2	3	4
My work is very boring.	1	2	3	4

Interview Formats

The layout of interview schedules is not as crucial as for questionnaires. However, good formatting helps prevent errors and facilitates smooth interviews. Following are some suggestions for formatting instructions and response categories.

SUGGESTION

Avoid hyphenations and right justification in questionnaires and interviews; reading a block of three or more lines is easier without them.

Instructions.   Instructions for the interviewer are easier to see if they are printed in capital letters. If space is a problem, put the instructions in a box so they won't be missed. Place instructions immediately *before* the relevant part of the question. For example, screening instructions precede a screening question. General probe instructions precede the response categories, and probe instructions for a specific category should appear next to the category.

Response Categories.   For interviews, the layout of response categories can be somewhat more compressed than in questionnaires, as long as the interviewer can read it easily. Two or even three columns can be used to save space. However, provide space for the interviewer to make a note of a respondent's relevant comments.

REDUCING MEASUREMENT ERROR

Several sources of measurement error associated with the data source represent particular problems for interviews and questionnaires. This section discusses three such sources: respondents' memory and knowledge, response set, and respondent states.

Memory and Knowledge Problems

Fallible memory and insufficient knowledge are the major sources of measurement error in factual questions.

- Many respondents will not know, will have forgotten, or will not be sure of the information you are asking for. The threat to measurement error is unreliability from guessing.

- Other respondents will recall events but *telescope* them forward (by reporting events as more recent than they actually are) or backward (reporting events as taking place earlier than they actually did). The danger here is biasing responses with systematic errors.

There are several strategies for reducing memory-induced measurement errors and ensuring more accurate replies.

- Ask a specific question about a specific behavior or event within a specific time period. Instead of

    Last month how many employees did you counsel?

ask,

    In the month of January, how many employees did you yourself counsel for drug-related problems?

- If you ask respondents to recall feelings and attitudes, give them specific targets. For example, instead of satisfaction with the previous job, ask about wages, supervision, co-workers, and other specifics.

- Add memory cues to the question by giving examples or specific options rather than leaving it open ended. The examples or list of items should be fairly exhaustive.

Which of the following topics were discussed at your last bargaining committee meeting?

	Discussed?		
	Yes	*No*	*?*
The union's strategy	[ ]	[ ]	[ ]
Union reactions to management demands	[ ]	[ ]	[ ]
. . .	*. . .*		
Resetting bargaining priorities	[ ]	[ ]	[ ]

Other (please specify): _____

- The less important the event or behavior, the shorter the time period respondents should be asked to recall.

- Reduce telescoping by avoiding too short a time period (e.g., last two days, last week). Two weeks to a month is usually best (Sudman and Bradburn, 1982).

- Ask respondents to consult organization or personal records. This is easiest with a questionnaire and most difficult with a telephone survey. Sudman and Bradburn suggest mailing a copy of the questionnaire and then telephoning at a prearranged time for the answers if records are involved.

- Make sure that respondents understand that "I don't know" or "I can't recall" are acceptable answers. This will reduce the tendency to give a poor or fabricated response just to satisfy the researcher.

Also consider the use of a **diary survey**: a form or booklet left with the respondent for a specific period of time. He or she fills it out on a daily basis (or hourly, or whenever an event occurs). A study of business telephone calls, for example, will obtain much more accurate information using diaries than by attempting to get respondents to remember their calls. Consult Sudman and Ferber (1979) for details of diary use in consumer research.

There is one circumstance in which a good memory is a problem. In repeated-measure designs using questionnaires and interviews, some questions will necessarily be repeated at each measurement point. Respondents will try to recall and duplicate their previous answers. (This is similar to the order effect in which respondents try to recall their answers to previous similar questions in the same instrument.) One solution is to build into the design sufficient time between measurement points and pretest to check the amount of recall. Another is to tell each respondent what he or she answered the last time, and ask whether there is now any change in his or her thinking.

The typical respondent's knowledge and perspective will vary from study to study. As a result, you must tailor your questions to the respondent's ability to understand and provide meaningful answers. For example, asking a union member,

Do you think the union should continue to hold national conventions every three years?

assumes knowledge of current practice, the reasons for it, and the issues involved in a change. For most rank-and-file members the question is not likely to be very meaningful, and neither is the answer. To avoid a lack of measurement validity, you must put yourself in the respondent's shoes and ask whether he or she is able to answer the question.

Response Set

Response set is a source of measurement bias in questionnaires and interviews. There are three types of systematic response sets: acquiescence, position bias, and social desirability. The first two lead to errors independent of the content of the question; the third is triggered by question content.

A **response set** is a tendency to answer a question in a systematic fashion unrelated to the "true" answer.

Acquiescence. Many factual and attitudinal questions are phrased so that respondents answer either "yes" or "no," "agree" or "disagree." Some solutions for this acquiescence are as follows:

Acquiescence is the tendency to answer "Yes" or "Agree" in response to a question.

- Repeat a reversed form of the question and compare the two answers. (This detects, but does not remove, acquiescence.)

- Reword the question substituting concrete options for "yes" and "no," or "agree" and "disagree." Instead of,

Do you agree or disagree that antiscab legislation would lead to more strikes?

ask,

Do you feel that antiscab legislation would lead to more strikes, fewer strikes, or would it stay about the same?

Position Bias. There are several forms of position bias which affect respondents' answers to questions with response scales.

In categorizing response scales, respondents have a tendency to avoid selecting the extreme top or bottom (or left or right) categories from a list if the options are numbered, no matter what the question content. However, if the options are unnumbered, the extreme categories are slightly more favored (Payne, 1951). One way to combat this is to number the options and add additional unlikely categories at each end. For example, a list of income categories should have a very low and a very high category at the extremes.

Another form of position bias is the tendency to select the second when presented with two options (Payne, 1951). (Interestingly, more people choose "heads" when asked "heads or tails?" Try it!) One solution is to use the split-ballot technique: two forms of the questionnaire or interview with positions reversed on all two-option questions. Half the sample is measured using one form, half using the other.

An alternative solution is to mix the order when the same two options appear in several similar questions. For example, in yes/no questions put "No" first in the first question, "Yes" first in the second question, and so on. The intention is to keep respondents from developing a habit of finding the "Yes" category first. The mixed formats force them to pause briefly before answering. However, when you use a multiple-item intensity, frequency, or Likert scale, keep the *same* order of response categories to avoid confusing respondents.

Semantic differentials, rating, and similar scales present another problem. Respondents tend to use their answer mark on the first scale item as an anchor and evaluate succeeding marks relative to that. This is another, more subtle, form of position bias. It can be partially overcome by varying the order of scale items so that positive options don't always appear on the same side. For categorizing scales in a matrix form, you can partly reduce this kind of position bias by using labels in addition to numbers to give meaning to the categories.

Social Desirability. If respondents feel that there is a preferred answer to a question, they are subject to pressure to choose the more socially acceptable response. Behaviors consistent with organizational or societal norms will be overreported, and those that represent some failing or weakness (including medical problems, addictions, and illness-related absenteeism) will be underreported.

Similarly, there is a tendency to tell the researcher what he or she wants to hear if the respondent learns who is sponsoring a consumer survey ("I *always* buy brand X!").

To reduce measurement bias from social desirability,

- Ask about specific recent or current actions rather than usual behavior.

- In two separate (but adjacent) questions, ask for both (1) the respondent's perceptions of the social norm or typical person, and (2) the respondent's own opinion or behavior.

- If the social desirability pressure is to answer "No," soften the question. Instead of,

    Did you have any accidents last month?

    ask,

    Did you happen to have any accidents last month?

- If the social desirability pressure is to answer "Yes," give equal weight to both possible answers. Instead of,

    Do you prefer to work on your own?

ask,

In business some people find it easy to work with others as a team, and some people find that they work better on their own. Which do you prefer, working with others or on your own?

Respondent States

Respondents can be tired or energetic, bored or interested, discouraged or motivated. Negative respondent states are a major source of both measurement error and nonresponse. Bored, tired, and discouraged respondents give abrupt and superficial answers. In some instances they will throw out the questionnaire or terminate the interview.

One objective in question and instrument design is to motivate respondents to want to help with the data gathering and to keep them from becoming tired or bored. Here are some suggestions:

- Shorten the instrument by removing all unnecessary or doubtful questions. Ask yourself, "Am I actually going to use this item in my analysis? Is it relevant to my research problem and research questions?" Shorter instruments have better response rates and less item nonresponse.

- Avoid repetitious questions.

- Avoid long lists of items in factual questions and lengthy attitude scales. What you gain in potential reliability with a lengthy scale will be more than offset by measurement error due to boredom.

- Change the pace by varying response formats and by interposing factual with attitude questions.

If an instrument is long, avoid teaching the respondent how to shorten it. For example, if you probe only negative answers, respondents will quickly learn to give positive responses!

Graphics.   A change of pace can also be achieved with pictures, particularly in consumer surveys of the general population. Use pictorial analogies for the response categories. Examples include "happy faces" to register satisfaction or dissatisfaction (from broadly smiling to deep frown), thermometers to indicate degree of approval (above and below zero for bipolar items), and dials (such as a car's gasoline gauge) for the amount of any unipolar attitude.

Another common graphic aid for bipolar intensity scales is to use a cartoon format showing two characters, one at each end of the scale, with the two bipolar statements in balloons above their heads. Of course, the two characters should be similar in age, gender, and other visible characteristics. In consumer research, pictures of the products about which opinions are being sought also provide a more interesting instrument. Be wary, however, of graphics in questionnaires for groups that might regard them as trivial or condescending. A survey of professional engineers shouldn't be using happy faces.

Motivation and Demanding Questions.   Some factual questions demand a great deal of time and effort from respondents. This is not necessarily bad, but you must make sure that respondents are sufficiently motivated to spend the time and effort on your behalf. Otherwise, such questions will elicit poor answers. For example, the question,

> *What are your annual transportation expenses involved in traveling to and from work?*

is almost impossible to answer without a great deal of time and calculation. (Note that the question is also ambiguous. Are insurance costs for an automobile to be included? Depreciation? Traffic tickets?)

To avoid measurement errors (as a result of guesses) and item nonresponse, make sure that respondents understand the purpose of the study, see it as relevant to themselves, and see the demanding question as highly pertinent to the study. Check levels of respondent motivation during the pretest.

SPECIAL PROBLEMS[3]

This section considers question wording in special problem situations: threatening and embarrassing questions, consumer surveys, and telephone interviews.

Threatening and Embarrassing Questions

Occasionally you'll need to ask respondents difficult factual questions either about themselves or about organizations for which they are serving as an informant.

To get more accurate information on how frequently an undesirable event or behavior occurs, use a long open-ended or fill-in question. Preface it with a question asking whether the event or behavior has ever occurred (Sudman and Bradburn, 1982):

> *From time to time firms are cited by the Labor Board for violations of the labor code. Has this ever happened with this firm?*
>
> *Yes* [ ]
> *No*   [ ]

[3]This section includes material adapted from Sudman and Bradburn (1982).

BOX 9.8
RESEARCH ETHICS
Threatening and Embarrassing Questions

Researchers sometimes forget just how uncomfortable respondents can become when faced with questions that might put them in a bad light or force them to reveal undesirable behaviors. Even a socially acceptable answer might make it seem that they have something unsavory to hide.

We now know how to word such questions to minimize threats to data quality. But what can't be taught, and what each researcher must ask himself or herself is whether such questions are absolutely necessary for the project at hand.

Go back to your research problem and research questions. Do you really need this piece of data? Could you justify it if confronted publicly? Subject yourself to the *60 Minutes* test!

IF "YES":

How often has this happened to this company since July of last year?

_____ *times*

Note that this question also distances the respondent from the event by referring to "this" firm instead of "your" firm. See Box 9.8.

Other strategies include

- Using a series of questions about undesirable behaviors and events, so that the impact of the particular question in which you're interested is lessened.

- Using a leading question, as described earlier (see Box 9.9).

When you want to get accurate information about *socially desirable* events or behaviors, phrase the question to ask about the most recent opportunity for the event or behavior. For example, as part of a survey of toothpaste use,

Some people don't get a chance to brush their teeth as often as they would like to, perhaps because they're too busy. Remembering yesterday, for instance, how many times did you brush your teeth?

_____ *times*

Consumer Surveys

The major problem in consumer surveys is obtaining sufficiently high response rates. General strategies for raising response rates are discussed in Chapter 12.

BOX 9.9
CAMPBELL SWITCH: A CONTINUING CASE

Part Thirteen: A Sensitive Question

"Let's go to your office. We seem to get more done than in mine."

"I think it's because you get cramps. You wedge yourself in and can't move. I think your office used to be a broom closet."

"Maybe that's why it smells of industrial cleanser."

George and Roberta are meeting to polish up some questionnaire items.

"How do you ask someone if he plans to quit?" George begins.

"Or she. I think you lead up to it. Don't put it early in the questionnaire. And you can use a leading question to counteract the tendency to deny you might want to leave."

"I thought that leading questions were a no-no."

"Usually yes. But sometimes they help overcome response bias to embarrassing or threatening questions."

"Well, what would it look like?"

"Let me see." Roberta spends a moment chewing the end of her pencil. "How about something like, 'A lot of people, when they find their work getting too stressful, start looking for another job. Have you given any thought to looking for a job elsewhere?'"

"Shouldn't we make that something like, 'In the past six months'?"

"Yes. It should be more specific. Good idea."

George enjoys the luxury of a good stretch, and the meeting continues.

Some of the general points just made merit additional emphasis in consumer research.

- Rating and ranking questions are important in consumer research. The respondent must be made to feel comfortable making evaluations. However, if the consumer guesses which brand is sponsoring the research, there is a chance of distorted results.

- Pay attention to time periods in order to get accurate recall and reporting of purchase, viewing, and other decisions.

    In the past week, that is, from Monday up to last Sunday, how often did you . . .

- Use screening questions to make sure the consumer buys the class of products or services you are researching.

- Questions about awareness of a product or company are best asked in face-to-face or telephone interviews where the respondent doesn't have time to look in the pantry or ask someone else.

- Check the reliability of answers to brand or company awareness questions by including a *sleeper option*—a brand not distributed or a company not known in the region.

Telephone Interviews

Interviews conducted over the telephone create special measurement problems because the respondent has to rely entirely on what he or she hears; there is no visual component to the measurement. Consider the following suggestions:

- Use response formats with no more than three or four options.

- If more than four items are to be ranked, use grouped ranking scales. Alternatively, send materials to respondents prior to the telephone interview.

- An alternative for ranking scales is to divide the question into two subquestions. The first subquestion asks the respondent to select only the four highest ranked items.

  > *I'm going to read a list of the features you might look for if you went shopping for a new television set. Please tell me which four features you think are most important. I'll read the list several times so you can pick the four most important features.*

  The second subquestion asks the respondent to rank-order only the four most important items selected in the first question. If you wish, this can be repeated to select and rank-order the four lowest ranked items.

- For rating scales, ask respondents to imagine a 12-inch ruler. Zero inches represents the lowest rating, 12 inches the highest, and 6 is right in the middle. (As usage becomes increasingly metric, this will have to be revised to a 10-centimeter scale with 5 as the midpoint.)

- Sudman and Bradburn (1982) suggest using *the telephone itself* as a visual aid for rating questions. Present instructions like the following:

  > *For the next few questions, I'm going to ask how much you like or dislike certain things. To answer these questions, I want you to look at the dial or touch-tone buttons on your telephone. Imagine that the numbers from "1" to "9" on your phone indicate how much you like or dislike something. The number "1" tells me that you dislike something very much. The number "9" at the other end means that you like it very much. The numbers in between tell me your feelings in between. The number "5" in the middle tells me that you're neutral, that you neither like nor dislike something.*

■ *The Lighter Side of Research*

The pollster's greatest ingenuity has been devoted to finding ways to ask embarrassing questions in nonembarrassing ways. We give here examples of a number of these techniques, as applied to the question, "Did you kill your wife?"

The Casual Approach: "Do you happen to have murdered your wife?"

The Everybody Approach: "As you know, many people have been killing their wives these days. Do you happened to have killed yours?"

The "Other People" Approach:
(a) Do you know any people who have murdered their wives?
(b) How about yourself?

—Barton, 1958

Summary

Questionnaires and interviews are the most common data-gathering techniques and are more subject to measurement error than others. They also suffer from validity problems, since both the researcher and the data source have to agree on the meaning and intent of the measurement operation.

To write good questions, follow these eight rules: (1) be clear and specific, (2) use appropriate language, (3) avoid condescending words and phrases, (4) emphasize, (5) keep it simple, (6) keep it brief, (7) keep it neutral, and (8) keep it relevant.

Response formats for questions can be open or closed. Closed formats are easier for both researchers and respondents and provide greater reliability and less measurement bias. Open formats are preferred in exploratory stages of research and usually provide richer data.

The response categories in a closed-ended question constitute a response scale. The four general types of response scales are choice, categorizing, rating, and ranking scales. Three of the problems that researchers must deal with when developing scales are (1) in what order to put the alternatives, (2) whether to include a middle position, and (3) how to record "no opinion" and "don't know" responses.

In any questionnaire and interview, the order in which questions are asked can affect data quality, measurement validity, and measurement error. Funneling and implicit logic are important principles in organizing a survey instrument; bridges, filter questions, and skips can make the questionnaire or interview progress more smoothly.

Three additional sources of measurement error have to be considered in questionnaires and interviews: (1) respondents' faulty memory and incomplete knowledge, (2) response set biases including acquiescence, position bias, and social desirability, and (3) negative respondent states including fatigue, boredom, and discouragement.

Where Are We Now?

With this chapter we have completed an examination of the measurement process in business research.

In the next three chapters we turn to the three major data-gathering methodologies: available data studies, field experiments, and surveys. The next chapter begins with a brief comparison of these three methodologies and then considers the issues involved in available data research.

Discussion Issues and Assignments

1. Divide the class into groups. Each group constructs three interview items (one factual, two attitude) for a survey of student satisfaction with the college bookstore. Each group develops its three questions in both a *good* version and a *poor* version. Each group then passes its *poor* versions to another group and attempts to improve the poor questions passed to it. The class discusses and votes on whether the *improved* version of each question is better than the *good* version developed by the original group. The group with the most winning questions (maximum of six) wins.

2. As a class project, construct an interview schedule to be administered to professors to gather data on the following two questions:

What factors determine their choice of textbook for a course?

Do differences among professors in these factors have more to do with course or professor characteristics?

Divide the class into groups and carry out the interviews, with different groups interviewing professors in different faculties, schools, or departments. The interviews should be short (maximum of 15 minutes); each student should conduct at least three. At the end, evaluate the interview schedule. If this were a pretest, what would you change?

3. Obtain a copy of a questionnaire or interview used by a market research firm. Evaluate the question wording, response format, question order, and instrument format. Suggest improvements.

4. Visit the sociology or psychology department and get copies of student research project questionnaires. Evaluate them. Find questions that threaten measurement invalidity, unreliability, or measurement bias. Suggest improvements.

5. Devise two short forms of an opinion questionnaire on "The best methods for assessing student performance and assigning grades." Use closed-ended questions in one form, open-ended in the other. Administer both forms in a class, one form to half the students (randomly selected), the other form to the other half. Compare the results from the two forms.

6. Repeat the exercise in question 5, but include in each form both a choice scale and a ranking scale question. Use different orders of scale items in the two forms. Compare the results for position bias.

Further Reading

In addition to these sources, consider browsing through journals that often report research on questionnaire design and survey methodology, such as *Advances in Consumer Research, Journal of Consumer Research, Journal of Marketing Research,* and *Public Opinion Quarterly.*

Dillman, D. 1978. *Mail and Telephone Surveys: The Total Design Method.* New York: Wiley.

   Dillman offers many suggestions for questionnaire measures and survey planning and strategy.

Gorden, R. L. 1975. *Interviewing: Strategy, Techniques, and Tactics.* Homewood, IL: Dorsey.

   An excellent and practical analysis of all types of interviewing. Very useful for anyone in research or management.

Koltko, M. E. 1989. "How Vagueness Can Ruin a Survey: Comment on Pope, Tabachnick, and Keith-Spiegel." *American Psychologist,* May: 845–846.

   Also check the original authors' following reply. For some questions, vague may be better!

McIver, J. P., and E. G. Carmines. 1981. *Unidimensional Scaling.* Beverly Hills: Sage.

   A good treatment of Likert and other types of scales, with an excellent example of item analysis of a Likert scale.

Miller, D. C. 1991. *Handbook of Research Design and Social Measurement* (5th ed.). Newbury Park, CA: Sage

   Contains much practical advice, an excellent review of sources, and examples of scales and measures useful for business research.

Payne, S. L. 1951. *The Art of Asking Questions.* Princeton: Princeton University Press.

   The classic treatment of question design. Payne's work marked a major advancement in survey research.

Sudman, S., and N. M. Bradburn. 1982. *Asking Questions: A Practical Guide to Questionnaire Design.* San Francisco: Jossey-Bass.

   Comprehensive and based on both experience and research. A really invaluable guide for both beginners and experienced survey researchers.

CHAPTER 10

Methodologies I: Introduction and Available Data Studies

CHAPTER OBJECTIVES

- What are the differences between surveys, field experiments, and available data studies? What are their respective strengths and weaknesses?

- What are the different types of available data and their advantages and disadvantages?

- How do researchers in available data studies organize and carry out data collection?

- What other problems do available data studies typically encounter? How are they solved?

CHAPTER OUTLINE

SURVEYS, FIELD EXPERIMENTS, AND AVAILABLE DATA STUDIES
AVAILABLE DATA STUDIES
ASSESSING AVAILABLE DATA
ACQUIRING AVAILABLE DATA
ISSUES AND PROBLEMS IN AVAILABLE DATA STUDIES

A manufacturer of chemical products decides to assess its safety program. The program has been in place for just over four years. A researcher in the personnel department conducts an available data study, examining accident records for all 12 plants over a ten-year period. He also examines company records for other factors that might affect accident rates and safety program administration, such as hiring of new employees, layoffs, and changes in management. The results of the research convince the director of personnel to begin looking for a new safety program.

An organizational psychologist suggests that a firm change its office layout from the open plan to one providing more privacy and individual lighting control for secretarial and clerical workers. She conducts a field experiment in which three of the seven floors of offices in the building are changed. She interviews employees and observes work patterns before and after the change. She also examines data on employee productivity. Based on her report, the firm converts the other four offices, and employee morale and productivity rise significantly.

A pharmaceutical company hires a market research firm to determine the likely demand for a new form of medication. The proposed product is intended for people who find it difficult to get back to sleep when they wake up in the night. The research firm conducts a survey involving face-to-face personal interviews with over 2,500 adult consumers in ten states. Among other questions, respondents are asked about their sleeping problems, what remedies they take now, and what they would like to see on the market. As a result of the research, the firm shelves its plans for developing the product.

The three examples of business research just described illustrate three different methodologies. As the term is generally used, a *methodology* is a particular combination of basic design and data source. Business researchers commonly use one of three major methodologies: surveys, field experiments (for evaluation studies and pilot projects), and available data studies.

Before we examine each in turn in the next three chapters, let's compare these major business research methodologies.

SURVEYS, FIELD EXPERIMENTS, AND AVAILABLE DATA STUDIES

Research activity can take many forms because projects differ in their basic design and type of data source. In theory, there are 15 different combinations of basic design:

- true experiment
- quasi-experiment
- nonexperiment

and data source:

- self-reports
- inside informants
- outside observers
- researcher observations
- available data

However, when we look at the work that business researchers carry out, we find that not all combinations of these elements are equally likely. In fact, three combinations predominate: surveys, field experiments, and available data studies (the latter includes studies using archival and secondary data).

Characteristic Design Decisions

Each of the three methodologies is characterized by typical design decisions, as shown in Table 10.1. As the table shows, there may be some overlap.

T A B L E   I 0 . I ■ TYPICAL DESIGN DECISIONS FOR SURVEYS, FIELD EXPERIMENTS, AND AVAILABLE DATA STUDIES

	Survey	**Field Experiment**	**Available Data Study**
Customary Basic Design	Nonexperiment	True or quasi-experiment	Non- or quasi-experiment
Unit of Analysis	Individual; body	Individual; body	Individual; body; event; aggregate
Most Common Specific Designs	Single sample; comparison sample	Comparison or control group; pretest-posttest	Single sample; time series; interrupted time series
Data Sources	Self-reports; inside informants	Self-reports; researcher's observations; available data	Available data
Sampling	Very often	Often	Occasionally

All three may use individuals as the unit of analysis, surveys and available data studies typically employ single sample specific designs, and both field experiments and available data studies make use of available data. Similarly, a survey may ask organization informants to return copies of organization documents (available data) along with a questionnaire.

Nevertheless, the combination of design decisions leads to three distinct methodologies. Each has a predominant design pattern. For example, surveys almost always involve a nonexperimental basic design, and available data studies rarely involve sampling.

Other Methodologies.   Surveys, field experiments, and available data studies are not the only methodologies used in business research. Chapter 2 discussed the use of *case studies* in the exploratory stages of examining a research problem. General applied researchers frequently use case studies in the initial phase of a larger project. The design features of case studies involve one, or just a few, cases, which are intensively examined using a variety of data-gathering techniques, including available documents, questionnaires, interviews, and observation.

Other methodologies are found much less frequently in business research. These include *observational studies* using a nonexperimental design and gathering data through observation and *laboratory experiments* gathering data through observation and questionnaires in a highly controlled laboratory setting.

Typical Research Errors

As well as design decisions, we can also compare the three major methodologies in terms of their typical research errors. Each is prone to certain types of errors that are irrelevant or only minor problems for the others. In Chapter 4, Figure 4.1 summarized the basic types of research error. Figure 10.1 is an expanded version of that figure, adding further detail about errors associated with extraneous variables, measurement, research procedures, sampling, and missing cases that threaten research power and internal and external validity. (In one respect, the figure summarizes everything that can possibly go wrong!)

For *surveys,* the major concerns are

- Measurement error. Both unreliability and biased errors are frequent, particularly for sensitive and recall questions because the measures are reactive and memories are fallible.

- Nonresponse bias. Refusals and noncontacts are major problems for survey researchers and often lead to unrepresentative samples.

- Problem data and reversed and reciprocal causality. Data peculiarities may lead to unjustified conclusions; nonexperimental designs sometimes leave cause and effect ambiguous.

FIGURE 10.1
Errors That Reduce Research Validity

Lack of Research Power   *("True" relationships are missed.)*

Insufficient variation in dependent or independent variable	Uncontrolled or unmeasured variable related to dependent variable ("noise")	Random measurement error (unreliability); haphazard variations in procedure	Weak statistical test (Type II error); too few cases

Lack of Internal Validity   *(Alternative explanations are not ruled out; conclusions about characteristics or covariation relationships are inaccurate.)*

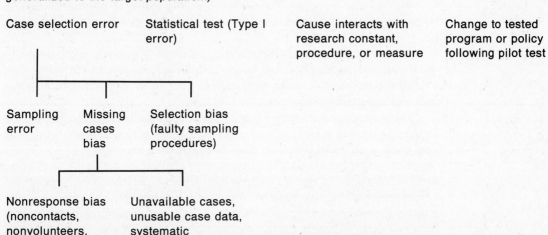

Uncontrolled or unmeasured extraneous variable related to both dependent and independent variables (spuriousness, confounding)

Spontaneous change in dependent variable (maturation, spontaneous regression)

Faulty measures and procedures (validity and bias)

Violating test assumptions; outliers and other problem data; faulty assumptions about causal direction

Spurious relationships

Confounding events, characteristics; mortality

Lack of measurement or manipulation validity

Measurement bias; researcher bias; response, item nonresponse bias; attrition bias

Procedure bias, experimenter bias

Lack of External Validity   *(A characteristic, covariation, or causal relationship is erroneously generalized to the target population.)*

Case selection error

Statistical test (Type I error)

Cause interacts with research constant, procedure, or measure

Change to tested program or policy following pilot test

Sampling error

Missing cases bias

Selection bias (faulty sampling procedures)

Nonresponse bias (noncontacts, nonvolunteers, refusals)

Unavailable cases, unusable case data, systematic attrition

For *field experiments and pilot projects,* the major problems are

- Finding unconfounded comparison groups, which will permit valid causal inferences.

- Spontaneous change in the dependent variable—particularly a problem in evaluation research.

- Procedure bias in manipulations or treatments. Interference by management or government officials is often the culprit.

- Changes to tested programs or policies following pilot tests. These changes, frequently made by management or government officials, threaten external validity.

For *available data studies,* the major difficulties are

- Unmeasured variables related to the dependent variable. Many sources of variation will be uncontrolled because the data contain no measures for them. This reduces research power.

- Spurious and confounded relationships. If the researcher cannot measure other potentially important variables, conclusions may be doubtful.

- Lack of measurement validity. Some measures won't match the intended concept because the data were gathered for other, often nonresearch, purposes.

- Selection bias, since data are often not available for the desired target population.

Research Purposes and Other Differences

We can also compare the methodologies in terms of the most common research purposes for which they are used and other aspects of research activity.

Table 10.2 summarizes the research purposes commonly associated with the three major methodologies. As the table shows, surveys and available data studies are the most versatile; field experiments are largely limited to evaluation and explanatory research.

Table 10.3 compares other aspects of the three methodologies. Surveys are frequently used in marketing and other forms of business research. Available data studies are more common than field experiments.

With respect to research validity, surveys are best for obtaining population estimates for specific variables and groups. Field experiments are superior for causal inference because they build in controls to eliminate alternative explanations that the other methodologies lack. The time and financial resources required depend largely on the size and complexity of the research, but in general available data studies take the least amount of time and field experiments the most, particularly when they involve before-and-after designs. The

TABLE 10.2 ■ METHODOLOGIES AND RESEARCH PURPOSES

	Survey	Field Experiment	Available Data Study
Exploratory Stages of Research	Yes	No	Yes
Descriptive Research	Yes	No	Yes
Prediction Research	Sometimes	No	Yes
Evaluation Research	Yes	Yes	Yes
Explanatory Research	Yes	Sometimes (market research)	Yes

TABLE 10.3 ■ COMPARISON OF SURVEYS, FIELD EXPERIMENTS, AND AVAILABLE DATA STUDIES

	Survey	Field Experiment	Available Data Study
Frequency of Use:			
Marketing and External Research	High	Moderate	Moderately low
Internal Business Research	High	Moderately low	High
Major Advantages	Best population estimates for specific variables and groups	Most valid causal inferences	Fastest and cheapest
Overall Validity	Moderate to high	Usually high	Moderate to high
Relevance of Research to Initial Problem	High	Usually high	Usually moderate
Cost	Moderate to high	Moderate to high	Low
Time Required	Intermediate	Most	Least

relevance of available data research to the original organization problem is usually lowest of the three.

In-House or Contract Out?   Another difference in the methodologies is whether researchers can gather their own data or must hire a research firm. With respect to business research, almost any firm or group can conduct a questionnaire survey, field experiment, or available data study. However, few firms conduct their own telephone or personal interview surveys, particularly for external research. These kinds of surveys are almost always contracted out to research firms.

Having compared the three methodologies, we now turn to two further questions:

- How do researchers using a particular methodology organize and carry out data collection?

- What problems does each methodology typically encounter? How are they solved?

We begin our examination of methodologies in this chapter with available data studies; the following two chapters consider field experiments and surveys.

AVAILABLE DATA STUDIES

Given what sometimes seems to be a paper flood of documents, records, statistics, government and other time series, and company files, it isn't surprising that business researchers make use of this information. We've seen its importance in the investigation stages of research, where it provides the variables and other information that help researchers formulate research problems, and sometimes even the answers to research questions. In this chapter we consider business research projects based *entirely* on available data. The most obvious examples are financial and economic research, but other kinds of problems also use available data.

CASE EXAMPLE

A personnel department researcher was asked to evaluate a new sick leave plan that had been in effect over a year. She decided to use available sources exclusively in order to save time and money, since the department had few funds for other kinds of data gathering. The Weekly Indemnity Register contained records of claimants, date and duration of disability, and level of payment. She used the Register as a sampling frame as well as a data source. She gathered additional data from personnel files and from weekly indemnity claim forms. She collected the data during a one-week period using collection forms she designed for the purpose. During the collection period, she checked with the salaries and benefits supervisor about any perceived discrepancies and irregularities. Two weekly indemnity cases who had not yet returned to work at the time of data collection were dropped from the sample and replaced with two randomly selected cases. She entered the data into the department's personal computer, merging it with the information from the already computerized personnel files. Using STATPAC software, she completed the data analysis in two days and took another day to write up the research report.

Previous parts of this text have discussed available data. Chapter 5 (variables) identified available data as one of five basic data sources. Chapter 8 discussed some principles of measurement relevant to available data. This chapter has discussed the relative advantages and disadvantages of available data studies compared to surveys and field experiments. We now consider in more detail the applications of available data studies and types of available data.

Available Data and Research Purpose

An available data study is often the preferred methodology for reasons of time and cost. Financial research, for example, would be impossible without available data from the government and other sources. It is also a highly adaptable methodology; it can be used for all research designs (true, quasi-, and nonexperiments) and for all four general research purposes (description, prediction, evaluation, and explanatory).

Descriptive and Prediction Research. These two general research purposes rely heavily on available data methodology, especially when the research problem requires information about past events or circumstances. For example, when the descriptive research purpose is to determine the performance of individuals or organizational subunits, researchers rely on sales, production, and other organization records. Forecasting models use almost no other methodology, since future performance or behavior is based on what has happened in the past. Many selection models are also built from available data (such as performance records), and in the personnel field appraisal models are often based on available data from written tests.

Evaluation Research. Available data studies are important and common in evaluation research because evaluation is often an afterthought once a program, policy, or project is in place. If researchers want to use pretest-posttest or time-series designs to evaluate these actions, they must find data from the past. Using questionnaires or interviews to ask people to recall what they did or felt some time ago is fraught with measurement error. A safer procedure is to rely on existing records for information about the past.

Explanatory Research. Researchers conducting explanatory projects use available data studies in a variety of circumstances:

- The research problem requires time-series data, that is, the variation to be explained is within the same unit or case over time. Going *back* in time with available data is easier and faster than planning a study to gather data now and at future time points.

- The research problem involves explaining some event or circumstance in the past. Available data are likely to provide the only information.

- The choice of unit of analysis allows only one, or at most a few, cases. When researchers can't make use of variation across cases, they focus on variations across time. (This usually necessitates changes to the research questions to make them relevant to longitudinal instead of cross-sectional variation.)

- The desired information is sensitive. Using questionnaires or interviews, or even researcher observations, might have unwanted measurement effects that bias the data. Available data studies are very unobtrusive.

- Good quality available data are accessible at much less cost than it would take to obtain comparable primary data.

Types of Available Data

Examples of available data include company records, government and other published statistics, questionnaires from previous research, and media reports such as news stories or stock quotations. They are distinguished from **primary data,** which researchers gather for themselves. (Other terms applied to available data include secondary data, existing data, archival data, and documents.)

Business researchers use available data of many kinds. These data can be divided into several types, each with its advantages and problems. Available data may come from a direct or indirect source and apply to either the organization or its components (internal) or the organization's environment (external).

Direct and Indirect Available Data Sources. Available data about a unit of analysis can be produced in either of two ways: directly by the unit itself or indirectly by some other person or agency.

- *Direct Available Data.* Individuals, groups, and firms produce a wide variety of data including letters, telegrams, memos, forms, applications, doodles, reports, requisitions, invoices, expense reports, and punch clock records. All of these provide information, sometimes considerable, about the person or body producing them.

- *Indirect Available Data.* Information and documents pertaining to a person or body but produced by a different person or body can take many forms.

A few examples are a secretary's meeting minutes, a foreman's productivity and absenteeism records for a work crew, newspaper and industry reports about firms, and census data.

Internal and External Available Data.   Internal data is information about the organization, its administrative subunits, or its members. They include personnel files, membership records, grievance forms, collective agreements, accident reports, and the like. They are usually gathered by the organization itself.

External available data is information about the organization's environment. They include data about clients and customers, other firms with which the organization has dealings, competitors in the industry, the economy and business climate, and the political and social environment in which the organization operates. Examples of such data are polls, labor force surveys, newsletters written by industry analysts, and arbitration hearing decisions. External data sources also include clipping services and market research information services.

These data are often gathered by outside persons or agencies for their own purposes. Sometimes they are gathered by the organization or some firm hired by the organization. For example, the questionnaires from a past marketing survey are external available data about consumers.

- *Internal Data.* Internal available data are used very frequently in business research. Usually, although not always, their existence is well known and access is easily obtained for the organization's own researchers.

- *External Data.* Business researchers frequently use external available data for consumer and marketing research problems and for strategic planning research. They can choose from a vast array of published and on-line data sets (see Box 10.1).

Raw, Compiled, and Research Data

Available data vary in how much they have been processed, screened, and analyzed. They range from the raw, not-yet-gathered, and unanalyzed to data that have been cleaned, compiled, aggregated, and reduced to summary statistics. In general, available data fall into one of three broad categories.

- *Raw data* is information that has undergone little or no processing. The materials may not have been assembled in one place and may not be in numerical form. Examples are committee meeting minutes, collective agreements, shopping lists, and corporate annual reports.

- *Compiled data* is information that has been assembled and reduced to a more digestible form. They are often summarized in tables, with case counts for different categories (e.g., males and females, firms by return on capital and return on common equity). Census data and sales reports are examples of such information. Published and on-line data are normally compiled.

BOX 10.1

FOCUS ON RESEARCH

Directories, Guides, Catalogs, and References for Published and On-Line Available Data

There are many data sets of published and on-line compiled data suitable for quantitative analysis. They cover many topics of interest to business researchers.

What follows is a list of directories and other works that provide information on these data sets. Most describe a number of different data sets and how to obtain them. (Note: This list does not include background information suitable for investigating the initial organization problem. For such sources, see Box 2.3.)

American Society for Information Science. *Computer-Readable Data Bases*. Washington, DC.

Capital Systems Group. *Directory of On-Line Information Resources*. Rockville, MD.

Congressional Information Service. *American Statistics Index*. Washington, DC.

Gale Research Company. *Encyclopedia of Business Information Sources*. Detroit, MI.

Gale Research Company. *Statistics Sources*. Detroit, MI. Check for the most recent edition.

Inter-University Consortium for Political and Social Re-search. (An enormous collection of research data sets.) Write Executive Director, ICPSR, P.O. Box 1248, Ann Arbor, MI 48106.

Kiecolt, K. J., and L. E. Nathan. 1985. *Secondary Analysis of Survey Data*. Beverly Hills: Sage.

Miller, D. C. 1991. *Handbook of Research Design and Social Measurement*. Newbury Park, CA: Sage.

Statistics Canada. *Selected Publications*. Ottawa, ON.

U.S. Bureau of the Census. *Catalog of United States Census Publications*. Washington, DC. Published quarterly.

U.S. Bureau of the Census. *1990 U.S. Census Users' Guide*. Washington, DC.

U.S. Bureau of Labor Statistics. *Handbook of Labor Statistics*. Department of Labor, Washington, DC.

U.S. Department of Commerce. *Measuring Markets: A Guide to the Use of Federal and State Statistical Data*. Washington, DC.

U.S. Department of Commerce. *Selected Publications to Aid Business and Industry*. Washington, DC.

U.S. Department of Commerce, National Technical Information Service. 1975. *Directory of Computerized Data Files and Related Software Available from Federal Agencies*. Springfield, VA.

U.S. Government Printing Office. *Monthly Catalog of U.S. Government Publications*. Washington, DC.

- *Research data* is information from a previous project, gathered by another researcher, usually for a different research purpose. They may exist in the form of (1) the original research instruments such as questionnaires or data collection forms or (2) the computer data matrix representing cases and variables. Some published data fall into this category.

The amount of prior preparation represents a trade-off for researchers in available data studies. On the one hand, the more preparation someone else has done, the less the researcher has to do. Research time and costs are highest with raw data, lowest with research data. On the other hand, more preparation means that someone else has made decisions about variables, measurement, coding, and analysis. These decisions are unlikely to be exactly the ones that a subsequent data user would make, and in some cases they may render the data useless for that user's purpose.

BOX 10.2
FOCUS ON RESEARCH
Secondary Analysis

Most available data are *compiled*—gathered as part of an organization's or government's ongoing record keeping, such as productivity records and census data. The initial purpose behind the collection of these data is to provide information.

However, business researchers sometimes make use of data from *previous research,* which were originally gathered for a particular research problem. Other researchers may then use the original research data for different research problems. Their examination of the original data to try to answer new and different research questions is called *secondary analysis.*

For example, an initial project involved a survey of employee day-care needs. This survey produced questionnaire data that the original researcher analyzed. Later, a second researcher analyzed the day-care questionnaire data to determine whether employees with children have higher absenteeism levels. (If the second researcher's problem is the same as the original researcher's, he or she is said to be *reanalyzing* the data.)

Raw Data.   The advantage of raw data is that the only screening they have undergone is the errors and exclusions of whoever produced the information in the first place. On the other hand, they require the most effort to prepare data for analysis. Often information in written form (such as memoranda) will require **content analysis** to reduce it to numbers suitable for statistical treatment. The procedure is analogous to coding answers to open-ended questionnaire items.

Compiled Data.   The major advantage of compiled data is that they require much less data preparation and preliminary analysis before they are ready to use. In many cases, such as most government statistics, information is obtainable *only* in compiled form. The major problem is that compiled data have often been aggregated—collapsed into geographical, administrative, or other categories—for summary purposes. If the level or basis of aggregation doesn't suit your research problem and unit of analysis, the data may be useless for your research problem.

Research Data.   These data place particular limitations on the research. They have already undergone a series of restrictive decisions: specific design, choice of variables and measures, and sample. Furthermore, information in data matrix form has been edited and coded using someone else's decisions. In the extreme instance, research data consisting only of summary statistics of the results of analysis incorporate all of the drawbacks just mentioned plus someone else's analysis decisions.

In spite of these restrictions, researchers can often gain valuable insights into organization and other problems by analyzing available research data. This activity is called **secondary analysis** (see Box 10.2). The major advan-

Secondary analysis is the analysis of available (secondary) research data originally gathered for a different project and purpose.

tage of research data is that they are likely to have few problems with measurement error and selection bias, provided that the original researcher was competent.

On the whole, most researchers prefer raw data because they can then control research validity. They can develop variables and measures relevant to their own research problems. They can check coding reliability and take other steps to ensure measurement and analysis quality.

ADVANCED TOPIC

Unusual Sources of Available Data

Occasionally an ingenious researcher will make use of an unusual available data source to solve a research problem. Although this happens more often in organization research, business researchers cannot afford to overlook any data that might address their research questions.

CASE EXAMPLE

Grusky (1963) examined the question of how rates of managerial change are related to the performance of organizations. Do organizations that change managers frequently do better or worse? To test his hypotheses on organizations that were approximately similar in organizational goals, size, and authority structure, Grusky used data from 16 major league baseball teams, from 1921 to 1958, omitting the 1942 to 1950 war and postwar period. He gathered data on team changes in field managers and team season-end standings. His sources included *The Official Encyclopedia of Baseball, Who's Who in Baseball, The Encyclopedia of Sports, 1958 Baseball Guide and Record Book,* and *Baseball Register.* The results show a strong inverse relationship between average team standing and rate of managerial succession.

Researchers with ingenuity and perseverance may find convenient available data that will serve as well as other data sources, for much less cost. For example,

• Attendance records: attendance during bad weather is an indicator of job commitment.

- Telephone bills: the median duration of long-distance telephone calls to customers and clients may be a measure of product problems. (Short calls maintain contacts; longer calls suggest customer problems.)

- Union newsletters: the relative attention given to current strikes and past successes and the amount of text and number of pictures of incumbent officials may shed light on political conflicts within the national (or regional) union office.

ASSESSING AVAILABLE DATA

The major research errors to which available data studies are susceptible stem from the quality of the data. For that reason, researchers normally spend some time investigating any potential data source. This investigation can save much wasted time, effort, or money spent acquiring or transferring the data (see Box 10.3). Investigation is doubly important when you have a choice of available data sources.

The results of your investigation help you assess a potential available data set on six important criteria:

- Unmeasured variables

- Measurement validity

- Reliability

- Measurement bias

- Coverage and unusable cases

- Cost-benefit ratio

We now examine these criteria in turn.

Unmeasured Variables

The number of variables in any available data source is usually limited. Compared to the dozens or hundreds of variables in a survey, an available data source may have 15 or fewer. Researchers will normally select a source because it includes the key and primary variables they want. However, the absence of control variables can, in some circumstances, present a difficulty.

The problem of unmeasured variables is seldom a concern in descriptive research. But for prediction, evaluation, and explanatory research, missing variables can threaten both research power (through uncontrolled noise) and internal validity (through confounded or spurious relationships).

SUGGESTION

Another reason for taking an early look at examples of potential available data is that they may suggest new variables to add to your design.

BOX 10.3
RESEARCH SKILLS

Investigating Available Data

To investigate a potential available data source, you'll need a few examples of cases, such as reports, forms, pages, or cards. Look them over for obvious problems: Are they legible? Complete? Do they contain the variables you want? Are there marks, codes, or other entries that will need interpreting? Are there obvious erasures and corrections, and if so, who made the changes and why?

Other useful investigation procedures:

- *Talk with the people who gather, process, and use the data.*
- Have procedures or processes changed? Are they identical for all data gatherers?
- How many different people are involved in data gathering?
- Are data collection procedures standardized and formalized (i.e., written and distributed to those who gather the data)?
- Is accuracy stressed? How likely are clerical and data input errors? Does anyone double-check the data?
- Do those who gather it see the data as perfunc-

tory or crucial? Do important matters like wages depend on the information?

- For compiled and research data, *obtain the documents that describe the data-gathering procedures* (and, for computer data, the codebook). Census statistics and data from other government sources often have accompanying notes that explain the data-gathering and sampling methods. Find out which cases are included in the data set and which are excluded.
- *Compare a small sample of the data* with one or more other available data sources containing the same variables. For example, is an employee's job classification as noted in the personnel files the same as the classification recorded in the payroll database? Alternatively, check the real situation. Locate the original data source and check a few facts with a telephone call. For example, call a few employees to verify their job classifications.
- *Find other research that has used the same available data.* What problems did those researchers find? Do their conclusions suggest measurement error or other difficulties?

CASE EXAMPLE

A researcher, using available data from personnel files, is trying to explain variations in productivity among employees. The files contain data on productivity and eight potential independent variables: age, seniority, absenteeism, job category, gender, height, weight, and marital status. (Productivity is measured by the most recent foreman's rating in each employee's file.)

The relationship of each variable to "employee productivity" and the interrelationships among the independent variables are shown in Figure 10.2. Each circle in the figure represents the *variation* in one variable. The top three circles (supervisor quality, job satisfaction, and equipment quality) are unmeasured variables. Where two circles overlap, the variables *covary*. The amount of overlap represents the amount of covariation or the extent of the relationship.

The figure shows which variables are related to the key dependent variable: employee productivity. Five of the measured variables covary slightly with productiv-

FIGURE 10.2 Case Example: The Effects of Unmeasured Variables

ity, and three do not. One, marital status, isn't related to any of the others. Altogether, the five independent variables overlap only slightly with productivity. They do not explain very much of the variation in productivity among employees. The unexplained variation in productivity represents noise.

The figure also shows how the three unmeasured variables (job satisfaction, quality of supervision, and equipment quality) relate to productivity. Had these been included in the available data, the researcher would be able to explain more of the variation in productivity among employees, since the total overlap with the dependent variable would have been increased.

If research power and internal validity are crucial and unmeasured variables appear to be a problem, researchers must seek alternative or additional available data sources. In some cases they may have to use questionnaires, interviews, or some other data source instead.

Measurement Validity

The most important criterion in evaluating potential available data is measurement validity. A common problem is that the measures don't quite match the variables or concepts researchers want. For example, the data may provide employees' "number of days absent" instead of "number of absence periods," or firms' "return on total equity" instead of "common equity."

Researchers using available data that lack measurement validity have an internal validity problem. They may think they have found a relationship involving one concept when they have really tested for a somewhat different relationship involving a slightly different concept. Research using proxy measures and contextual variables is particularly susceptible, since these measures represent many other characteristics besides the one in which the researcher is interested.

SUGGESTION

Always try to obtain copies of the instruments through which available data were gathered: forms, questionnaires, interview schedules, and so on. This will allow you to check the face validity of the measure and to make a rough approximation of measurement error (e.g., ambiguous or loaded questions).

Faulty Computed Variables.   Inappropriate computed variables in available data often lead to problems of measurement validity (Jacob, 1984). When a variable is computed from two or more unreported variables, the computation formula may produce an imprecise or misleading measure that the researcher cannot correct.

CASE EXAMPLE

A researcher was examining the effects of early retirements among firms in the financial industry using available data. The available research data from an earlier survey of firms in the industry provided a measure of early retirements in each firm: the number of retirees in the last fiscal year standardized per 1,000 employees. This variable was computed from two other variables: "number of early retirements" and "number of employees." Unfortunately neither of these variables was still available. The measure was misleading because a firm with many older employees who refused to take early retirement might produce the same early retirement rate as a firm with very few older employees all of whom retired early. The researcher realized that a more valid measure of early retirements would be to standardize the number of retirements per 1,000 *eligible* (for early retirement) employees. Unfortunately, information on eligible employees was also missing from the available data.

In this example, a poor choice of *denominator* for a measure of rates ("employees" instead of "eligible employees") will cloak variations in the numerator. In general, all elements in a computed variable should be as close as possible to the desired concepts. As well as having less measurement validity, faulty computed variables often show less variation than what exists in the population. This lowers measurement sensitivity and reduces research power.

Solutions.   Short of finding a better data source, there is no simple solution for low measurement validity in available data. As a first step, however, you should test the quality of the available measure (see Box 10.4). You should also assess measurement validity by examining relationships in the data for convergent or discriminant validity (see Box 8.1 in Chapter 8). If you find low validity, try to utilize two or three measures for your concept of interest, combining them into an index. Hopefully the index will cover the dimensions

BOX 10.4

RESEARCH SKILLS

Testing Available Data for Measurement Validity

If you have doubts about the measurement validity of a particular variable in an available data set, try to evaluate it. Although such tests are approximate and subjective, the information they provide is better than nothing. Use the following steps:

1. Find another data set containing both the available measure you want to test and a more precise measure of the variable you intend. For example, if the variable you want is net sales, but the available measure is only gross sales, find another data set containing both measures. (The case coverage and presence of other variables are not important in the "test" data set.)

2. Determine whether you could reasonably generalize a relationship from the test data set to the original available data. For example, if the test data with gross and net sales figures are from the same industry as the original available data you could likely generalize across regions, states, or even countries.

3. Calculate the level of association between the two measures in the test data (for example, a correlation coefficient).

4. Evaluate the relationship you found in step 3. If the correlation is high (a Pearson's *r* of .80 would be acceptable for most research situations), and generalization isn't a problem, you can use the available measure in the original available data with confidence. If it's low, you have to abandon the data or temper your conclusions.

Alternatively, if you can't locate a test data set, and if time and resources permit, gather a small sample of data on the two measures from your target population. You might do this with a telephone survey, for example. A sample size of 25 should be enough for most instances, although additional cases will give a more accurate estimate of the relationship. Then check the relationship as just described.

of the concept you have in mind, and the total overcoverage of other concepts will be relatively small.

Reliability

Reliability is the third criterion for evaluating available data. It is a common problem with indirect and internal available data and often unknown in external data.

Indirect Data.   When another person or agency produces information about an individual, department, organization, or some other unit of analysis, the data are more likely to be unreliable than if the unit produced the information itself. For example, a person's own shopping list is a more accurate indication of what he or she plans to purchase than a response to a questionnaire. The possibility of unreliability is compounded if different people collect the information under different circumstances so that the measurement operation is inconsistent.

Besides checking the data-gathering procedures, you must pay attention to the context in which the information is produced. Newspaper reporters writing about a union leader, for example, write to the level of the average reader: but the average reader of the *New York Times* is not the average reader of the *Baltimore News-American.* What gets reported in one may be omitted (or emphasized) in the other.

Internal Data.   Organizations are frequently inconsistent in measuring internal performance and other characteristics over time and across administrative units. Reliability is threatened in several ways:

- Inconsistent definitions and classifications (e.g., different departments measure "waste" or classify "type of absenteeism" in different ways).

- Changes in the personnel responsible for gathering and compiling the data. Persons differ in their commitment to accuracy and the energy they devote to resolving ambiguities in the data.

- Clerical errors as data pass through several hands. This is particularly so if the information is not seen as important and if no checks are built in to ensure accuracy as information passes through the organization.

External Data.   The reliability of external available data varies widely. It may be much greater or much less than the reliability of internal data produced by the organization itself.

External agencies that publish available data vary in the care they take with it. If the agency accepts data uncritically from organizations or individuals, using haphazard procedures and doubtful measures, reliability is likely to be poor. If the agency is careless about proofreading for typographical and other reporting errors, reliability will be worse. However, if a single agency gathers the information from individuals or organizations using a standardized form or questionnaire, error checks, and other procedures to ensure accuracy, reliability will likely be high. However, no researcher should ever take reliability for granted, even with census data.

CASE EXAMPLE

Coale and Stephan (1962) reported finding some anomalies in the 1950 U.S. census; for example, large numbers of widowed boys: at age 14, 1,670 boys were reported widows, compared to 630 at age 19. They investigated and hypothesized that columns on one punch card were punched one position to the right for several thousand cards. The result of the errors was that widowed and divorced middle-aged males were reported as boys, white children of heads of households became young Indians, and Indians were shown to have extremely large proportions of widowed and divorced members.

Checking and Reducing Unreliability.   The data set investigation (Box 10.4) should help uncover any reliability problems. It will tell you how consistent the measurement operation was across administrative units (such as departments) and over time.

One way to minimize clerical and compiling errors is to get your available data as close to the original source as possible. Avoid data summaries (e.g., the *Statistical Abstract of the United States*) except as reference sources of what available data might exist and where to get them. (Similarly, because they pass through fewer hands, raw data are preferable to compiled.)

Measurement Bias

Measurement bias is the fourth criterion to consider when selecting available data. It occurs in two circumstances:

- Deliberate and intentional distortions of data

- Changes to data-gathering procedures

Bias is more likely with internal data and information from direct sources and less likely with external data and indirect sources.

Deliberate Distortion.   Individuals and organizations may distort performance or other data to make effectiveness appear greater than it is. They may report inaccurate numbers or accurate numbers of misleading events or objects, or omit relevant information. For example,

- Foremen may ignore minor accidents in weekly accident reports for their departments.

- Supervisors can keep rejection rates low by reporting only the proportion of units rejected at the *final* inspection stage. Rejects prior to this stage are not included in the count, whether they are returned to the production process for correction or just discarded.

- Accounting procedures, such as the value of goodwill (Jacob, 1984), are an important source of potential bias in available financial data.

- Organizations may alter the data they present for external consumption. Figures in annual reports, for example, may downplay or ignore more negative aspects of performance.

Other distortion may be deliberate but not intended for any advantage. When individuals produce data for themselves, the information may be incomplete because some of it is unimportant or because recording it is unnecessary or time consuming. For example, appointment books often omit the regularly scheduled events for which an executive needs no reminding. Travel expense reports omit minor items or lump them under "miscellaneous." While not important for the individual, these omissions make the data less useful for a researcher, particularly if they are systematic and therefore potentially biased.

Changes to Data-Gathering Procedures. The data set investigation should look for any changes to data-gathering procedures. For example, a firm may have recently implemented new "improved" accident report forms.

When organizations, governments, or other data-gathering agencies change their measurement procedures, the result may be systematic bias. What actually happens is that the *amount* of bias changes. Remember that as long as the amount of measurement bias is constant, bias is only a problem for descriptive research; if all observations are equally biased, conclusions about relationships are unaffected. A new procedure, however, changes the amount of bias and poses a potential threat to internal validity.

CASE EXAMPLE

In 1975 the government of Canada revised the questionnaire used in the Canadian Labour Force Survey. The purpose was to obtain a more accurate measure of unemployment by counting only those persons who were actively searching for work. To accomplish this, the unemployment questions were reworded from the general

"What did this person do mostly last week? Did this person do anything else last week?"

to ask more specifically about job searching activity:

"In the past 6 months, what has . . . done to find work? In the past 4 weeks what has . . . done to find work?"

In addition the new measurement procedures required that actual methods of job seeking had to be reported. As a result of this change, unemployment rates in general decreased from 7.1 percent to 6.9 percent, and the rate for women increased dramatically from 6.4 percent to 8.1 percent. The reason for the latter is that women were more likely to identify themselves as homemakers when responding to a simple question about what they did, but were more willing to admit to job-seeking behavior when asked specifically what they had done to find work.

Solutions. Your data investigation can also help uncover potential problems with bias in your available data. Unfortunately, bias resulting from deliberate distortion is usually difficult to detect. Thus an important additional check is to compare measures in your available data with other data sets and with your expectations from common sense or experience. For example, if department accident rates seem particularly low, check against accident rates for similar organizations. If these are unavailable, compare the rates with data from an organization from which you would expect lower accident rates. If the comparison figures are not lower, you have some reason to suspect bias in the available data.

If the available data is reports or other communications (memos, notes, etc.) look for pressures on the original source to bias the data. Who is the target or audience? What is the topic? Similarly, examine the context in which the data are produced for possible bias pressures. For example, letters to spouses are likely to be quite different in content from letters to lovers. A memo to your boss on the sales trip may be different from the notation in your own travel diary.

To detect bias due to changes in measurement procedures, first note whether measurement operations, recording forms, definitions, or boundaries (e.g., two new departments added to turnover records) changed at any point. Then compare observations for that variable before and after the change. If there appear to be systematic differences, consider adjusting the data to remove the effects of those differences or including the change itself as a variable to be controlled in your multivariate analysis.

Coverage and Unusable Cases

The fifth criterion is which cases are included in the available data set. In particular, the researcher must determine (1) whether coverage is satisfactory and (2) whether unusable cases jeopardize external validity.

Coverage.   Coverage is a problem of external validity. It occurs when the cases in the available data set don't correspond to the desired target population. There are two kinds of coverage problems:

• The data include unwanted cases (overcoverage).

• The data omit needed cases (undercoverage).

If the data set comes with a description of the sample boundaries (e.g., all full-time hourly employees hired up to 12 days ago), you can easily identify coverage problems. If no description is available, you must investigate. Occasionally it may be difficult to detect the existence and extent of a coverage problem.

Once detected, overcoverage can be cured as long as the data contain variables that allow you to identify the unwanted cases. For example, if you want only skilled employees, the variable "job category" allows you to delete unskilled and semiskilled employees. Two other situations, however, present problems.

• The data include unwanted cases but no variables to identify and exclude them. You have a potential selection bias problem.

• The data omit significant numbers of desired cases (undercoverage), and the omissions are systematic. The problem is missing cases bias. For example, you may want data on all advertising agencies, but the data set contains only those with offices in more than one state or province.

In these situations you can only try to estimate the extent of bias and take it into account in your conclusions.

BOX 10.5
CAMPBELL SWITCH: A CONTINUING CASE

Part Fourteen: Going Through the Files

"These data collection sheets sure are a time saver."

George and Roberta are spending a Saturday morning collecting data from the personnel and payroll files at the Campbell Switch Concord Plant, where these data are kept.

"Here's another batch. No missing values for any of these cases." She hands three sheets of paper to George.

"Good. I'm missing the department for case 34. That's personnel number 146-265-72. I'll have Mrs. Beasley check it out on Monday."

"Just put a yellow sticker on it, and add it to the 'check' file."

"Right. And the file for Harrison is missing entirely. Probably one of the clerks has it. I'll check for that Monday too." He adds another note to the check file.

After a few minutes' more work, Roberta asks, "When we go to the Ajax plant to observe machine type and layout for socializing opportunities, how will we know which are the employees in the sample?"

"Probably the best way is to give the plant manager a list of the names we want in both plants and get him to point them out to us."

"Won't that arouse suspicions? Why don't we just get the foremen there to tell us what machines each one works on, and then we can have them point to work stations on a floor plan."

"That certainly sounds less intrusive. I wonder if there are any floor plans of Ajax around here. And I guess we need one for Concord, too. More help we need from Mrs. Beasley."

"And even if we only go to the foremen, I think we should do the observing a couple of days after the foremen hand out the questionnaires at the end of the shift. That way, if anyone sees us at the plant the questionnaires will already be distributed and most should be back."

"Good." George pours another cup of coffee. "Sure glad I brought this thermos along. Want another cup?"

Unusable Cases. Even if coverage is not a problem, bias can enter if some cases are systematically unusable.

CASE EXAMPLE

A firm in the auto parts industry had recently implemented a participative work-group structure, which gave employees increased autonomy for work scheduling and procedures. To overcome problems with foremen adapting to their new roles, the company also instituted a training program for foremen and supervisors. The company asked a researcher to evaluate the training program. The researcher used available data, including the weekly report cards on which foremen recorded both group production and their own comments about work-group progress and problems. She found that about a quarter of the foremen's records were incomplete or illegible, and it appeared from other data that these were from foremen having the most difficulty with the new work-group structure.

If unusable cases cannot be corrected, seek an alternative data source to obtain the information and prevent systematic bias and a loss of external validity. Perhaps you can telephone the people responsible for the illegible marks or missing notations, or send a brief questionnaire, or get help from someone else in the organization (see Box 10.5). Otherwise, you can only estimate the likely extent of bias and take it into account in drawing conclusions. (Note that this problem is similar in form to systematic attrition in field experiments.)

Cost-Benefit Ratio

The final criterion for assessing available data is a comparison of the cost of acquiring them with the benefits they contribute to the research.

Costs. The costs of available data can vary dramatically. Some data are virtually free, except for the cost of actually recording or transferring them. If the data already exist in a computer, the cost of moving them to your own facility may be extremely small (such as the price of a diskette). Other available data, such as information from a commercial data service or data bank, may be relatively expensive.

Benefits. To determine the benefits of a potential available data source, consider the importance for your research of the variables contained in the data.

- Primary variables are more important than controls.

- Control variables that are interrelated (and thus might produce spurious, confounding, or suppressor effects) are more important than controls that are related only to the dependent variable.

- Controls that are strongly related to the dependent variable are more important than controls that are only weakly related.

- If you are planning to combine data from two or more sources, each must have an *identifier variable* so that individual cases can be linked.

Of course, you can only guess at control variable relationships before you actually have the data, but your literature review (from the problem investigation stage of the research) should provide enough information to enable you to make an assessment.

You must also consider the worth of the data's quality as judged on the preceding five criteria: unmeasured variables, measurement validity, reliability, measurement bias, and coverage and unusable cases. Keep in mind, however, that for important variables poor data may be better than none.

ACQUIRING AVAILABLE DATA

Once you have located the available data and decided they are worth their cost, the next step is to plan how to acquire them. This step includes obtaining access to the data, generating measures, developing forms and procedures, and deciding whether and how to sample.

Access

The first problem most researchers must consider is access. Even internal business researchers may have access problems when they need data from departments whose heads are unwilling to surrender it. Often access is more a political than a research problem (see Box 10.6).

SUGGESTION

Start your quest for internal available data about an organization as high up the organizational ladder as possible. The dilemma is that higher level persons can grant access, but they often don't know what data the organization uses. Lower level managers know, but are often reluctant to grant access. Start by approaching upper-level managers for tentative access to look for information. Then go to lower level individuals to find what there is. Finally, clear the access through upper levels.

Measures

If your available data are raw, rather than compiled or from previous research, you'll have to develop measures for any information not in numerical form.

- Counts present no problem. For example, you can easily count the number of employees in each department from lists of employees.

- Category variables will require that you develop the appropriate set of categories for coding the data. Some are obvious (such as gender). Others are more difficult, and the choice of categories will have to take into account the research purpose and the nature of the data. General information about categories is presented in Chapter 8.

Forms and Procedures

Prior attention to forms and procedures often makes the difference between error-free and error-prone data gathering. For available data studies, it's generally a good idea to design and use your own data-gathering forms. Custom-designed forms save a great deal of time and reduce clerical errors. The same form can be used for

BOX 10.6
RESEARCH SKILLS

Getting Access to Available Data

Begin your request for access at the highest feasible level of the organization. This usually means you'll have to convince upper management of the utility and importance of the research.

- Permission for access from higher management is usually easier, since they don't have to justify the decision to superiors.
- In addition, higher management are more used to dealing with nonroutine issues and requests.

To transfer available data to your own office or computer may require a single short contact (if you are transferring data between computers on diskettes or via modems) or repeated lengthy visits (if you are transcribing information from files by hand).

Once you have access, use tact, courtesy, and common sense in your dealings with other organization personnel. Your presence alone will arouse some degree of anxiety and suspicion. To allay their concerns, let them know, within reason, what you're doing and why. It also doesn't hurt to ask for their help.

- Editing (resolving discrepancies and errors in the data).

- Recording already numeric data.

- Coding nonnumeric data to counts or categories.

- Entering data into the computer.

Editing and coding as you gather the data saves a great deal of time. You can also do your double checking on the spot. You'll need to develop a codebook first; see Chapter 13 for details. An example of a data collection form for an available data study is shown in Appendix D.

Often researchers combine available data from two or more sources or with data from another data-gathering technique, such as a questionnaire. In these instances, your form must include a provision for an identifier variable, a case identification code that will enable you to match the data for each case with the appropriate data from other sources. For example, the information from an individual's personnel records must be identified in such a way that it can be combined with information from the same individual's productivity records. This means that you may have to record the employee's name on the data collection form.

If you're transferring data from one computer to another for analysis, you won't need a data collection form. However, you will need a copy of the data set's codebook to make sense of the variables. Also make sure you obtain the necessary documentation describing the data's computer form (e.g., a Lotus or dBase file) and character set (e.g., ASCII, EBCDIC).

SUGGESTION

In some cases you can speed data gathering from summary documents (with many variables) by photocopying the relevant documents and writing your codes in the margins. The photocopies serve as your data collection forms.

SUGGESTION

Do not underestimate the amount of time it takes to move available data electronically. Typically, there are a number of bugs in any system for moving data through telephone lines via modems. Even if you overcome this by transferring data via diskette or tape, there may be problems with software that is partially incompatible. For example, dBase uses variable names ten characters long. SPSS/PC+ truncates these to eight characters. If, as a result of truncation, two or more variables have the same name, SPSS/PC+ drops the second and succeeding variables. Thus, for a time series of variables TURNOVER01, TURNOVER02, and so on, all but the first would be dropped! To avoid this problem, the variables have to be renamed prior to transfer.

Resolving Ambiguities. Your data-gathering procedures must include methods for resolving ambiguities and discrepancies. Sometimes records are illegible (e.g., does that scribble mean absent two days or seven days?). If possible, go back to the source to solve the problem (e.g., ask the foreman who made the notation). Another alternative is to check with the clerical or other staff who make use of the information and who may be familiar with the handwriting or shorthand. (See Chapter 13 for alternative ways of coding ambiguous data.)

Sampling Available Data

Because available data collection costs are generally much lower than for surveys and field experiments, it may seem odd that researchers would sample in available data studies. However, there are two circumstances that call for sampling to save money:

- When data are in raw form, coding and content analysis costs escalate sharply with increasing numbers of cases (although costs are still likely to be much less than for surveys and field experiments).

- When a researcher uses multivariate statistical procedures requiring relatively large amounts of time (such as certain variations of regression analysis), the costs of analysis rise significantly with more cases.

If you sample, decide on sample size using the procedures outlined in Chapter 7. If data are to be taken from two or more sources (e.g., production records and accident reports), determine which one offers the best sampling frame. Use that source for drawing the sample, and match it with cases from the other sources.

CASE EXAMPLE

A researcher conducting a study of management style and employees' reactions to the implementation of new technology used raw data from two sources. One source listed managers alphabetically by name. The second listed them by department. The researcher chose the second for his sampling frame, since it provided an implicit stratified sample if he used systematic sampling. Taking every ninth manager from the list ensured that no department would be over- or under-represented. The result was a sample with less sampling error than if the first source had been used to draw the sample. As a result, the researcher decided he could safely use a smaller sample.

Type of Sample. The decision about the type of sample for an available data study should take into account both the form and location in which the data are found.

- For data in a list or file drawer (probably the most common form of available data), the easiest sampling procedure is *systematic sampling*.

- If there are small but important (for analysis) subgroups in the population, use *nonproportional stratified sampling*. This type of sampling from file drawers and lists is more time consuming and requires more passes through the data set. For example, a study using warranty-questionnaire cards stratified buyers by gender. The researcher required one pass to choose every 10th female, and a second pass to select every 44th male. (There are ways to do this on one pass through the data, but they get fairly complicated and the chance of error is substantial.)

- When raw data are found in more than one location, *cluster sampling* is the most useful technique. For example, if you are getting employee data from filing cabinets in 24 different plants, you may want to consider each plant a cluster and draw a sample of plants. (If you then sample within each of the drawn plants, this becomes a *multistage sample*.)

- For data already in a computer, use *simple random* sampling. In many cases your computer's statistical program can draw a simple random sample for analysis. (For example, in SPSS/PC+ use the SAMPLE command.) If there are small but important subgroups, you should use *nonproportional stratified sampling* by carrying out a simple random sample on each stratum. Statistical packages with file-splitting or selection capabilities (such as STATPAC and SPSS/PC+) make this very easy to do. For subsequent analysis, weight the cases appropriately.

ISSUES AND PROBLEMS IN AVAILABLE DATA STUDIES

This chapter has already discussed a number of problems associated with available data studies. We conclude with an examination of two additional issues: pretesting and ethical concerns. (A closeup look at ethics can be found in Box 10.7.)

Pretesting Available Data

Available data studies present many fewer opportunities for the researcher's measurement errors because most such errors have already been made by the original data collectors and producers. However, pretesting the data-gathering forms and procedures can still provide important benefits and avoid further errors.

Researchers have two specific reasons for pretesting procedures and forms in available data studies:

BOX 10.7
RESEARCH ETHICS
Confidentiality and Available Data

Very often confidentiality is a condition for the use of available data. Information you gather from an organization could, if it became known to competitors or the public, severely compromise the organization. Similarly, information about individuals, if leaked, could seriously harm their reputations or promotion opportunities.

Promising confidentiality is one thing, but how do you ensure it? You should be prepared to show organization officials just how you'll restrict access to your records and maintain confidentiality.

Confidentiality procedures fall into two types.

• *Physically restrict access to the information.* Locked doors and filing cabinets are typical measures of this kind. Computer passwords are another physical restriction. Only researchers committed to maintaining confidentiality should be allowed access.

• *Disguise the identity information of each case* so that names and other obvious characteristics can't be detected without knowing the code or key. The codes, of course, must themselves be guarded against unauthorized access.

The major problem is that, in the excitement of analysis, or the pressure of deadlines, researchers become careless and leave raw data or computer output lying about where others can read it. The solution is to take confidentiality seriously and realize that your reputation as a researcher is at stake.

• To gather some data for the investigation and evaluation of unmeasured variables, measurement validity, reliability, measurement bias, coverage and unusable cases, and cost-benefit ratio of the data set.

• To ensure the data-gathering operation works smoothly.

Pretesting Procedures.   Begin by pretesting access to the data: are they where you thought they'd be? Are any data missing, and if so, how do you locate them? How will you get files or forms that employees are working with elsewhere?

Try collecting data from a few sample cases, on location under conditions similar to what you'll encounter. Note any conditions that might present a problem (e.g., heating, air conditioning, lighting, seating, noise or other distractions). Is there a pencil sharpener around? Erasers? A desk? A place to get coffee? Food? What assistance will be present to help you find files and decipher entries?

Pretesting Forms.   Check the data collection form. Is it clear? Does it provide enough space for comments and include enough information for on-location coding?

Don't neglect to pretest your measurement operations if you are using raw data. Are your categories sensitive enough? Do you have adequate rules for resolving ambiguities in the data?

Ethical Issues

Compared to other major methodologies, available data studies present the fewest ethical problems. The issue of confidentiality is the major concern most researchers are likely to encounter. See Box 10.7.

■ *The Lighter Side of Research*

Bias: The sugar in the gas tank of measurement. There are many sources of bias, which may be roughly categorized as (a) uncontrollable and (b) unknown. (Woodman, 1979)

M.I.S.: "Missing Information Syndrome." A common disease that strikes researchers using company information systems for research purposes. Sometimes known as "Management Information System."

Summary

We began by comparing the three major methodologies: surveys, field experiments, and available data studies. The basic differences among them are their characteristic design decisions, including basic design, data sources, data-gathering techniques, and use of sampling. The methodologies also differ in their most troublesome research errors, typical research purposes for which they are used, resource requirements, and other aspects.

The balance of the chapter examined available data research. Available data studies are common in business research. This methodology is used for all research purposes (descriptive, prediction, evaluation, explanatory) and basic designs (true and quasi-experiments, nonexperiments). Researchers may, with ingenuity, find unusual data sets for answering research questions.

Direct available data is what individuals or organizations produce themselves. Data produced by others is indirect. Available data about the organization is internal; information about the organization's environment is external available data.

Raw, compiled, and research data vary in the degree to which screening and other restrictions have been applied. Raw data take more effort to record and prepare for analysis (e.g., content analysis), but the results are likely to have higher measurement validity.

Available data suffer in particular from problems of unmeasured variables, measurement validity, and unknown measurement error. These problems occur in different degrees for different types of available data. Before using any available data set, investigate the potential for these problems as well as coverage, usable cases, and cost-benefit ratio. Balance the importance of the variables in the available data against the data quality and the cost of obtaining the information.

The most common type of sampling for available data is systematic. For data in multiple locations, cluster sampling can save time and money.

It is almost always beneficial to design your own data collection forms for available data studies. Data forms and procedures should make it possible for you to code, record, edit, and enter the data using a single form.

Where Are We Now?

We are now well into the topics of measurement and data gathering. This chapter discussed the first of the three major methodologies used in business research. The following two chapters discuss the other methodologies: field experiments and surveys.

Discussion Issues and Assignments

1. Visit an organization and find examples of two or more sources of internal data that might be used to measure the performance of individual employees or department heads. Assess and compare the sources for measurement validity and coverage.

2. Investigate the reliability of the stock quotations published in a local newspaper. What steps are taken to ensure accuracy?

3. Collect a dozen company annual reports. Evaluate them for potential bias in reports of performance. Develop a measure of performance for each company. Find an alternative data source that also provides performance-related information, and compare the report-based measures you developed with the second source.

4. Select three business-related news items of interest to the general public (e.g., a major merger, a business scandal). Buy copies of your local newspaper(s), *U.S.A. Today,* the *New York Times,* and the *Wall Street Journal.* Use content analysis to compare their reporting of the three items.

5. What unusual available data could you use to test the following hypothesis: The degree of improvement in organizational performance following technological change depends on management style. What problems of coverage and case selection do your data have?

6. Ask a faculty member for some old research data. Select a research problem different from the original one that you might investigate with the data. Evaluate the measurement and other problems you would encounter in doing so.

7. Your university's calendar (brochure) is a raw data source. How would you use content analysis to test the belief that sexy course titles have shorter course descriptions but draw larger enrollments? Approach your registrar for course enrollment figures and gather the data to test the relationships.

Further Reading

Holsti, O. R. 1969. *Content Analysis for the Social Sciences and Humanities.* Reading, MA: Addison-Wesley.

    A classic on this technique. A good introduction for researchers planning to use it.

Jacob, H. 1984. *Using Published Data: Errors and Remedies.* Beverly Hills: Sage.

    A useful guide to the often ignored problems inherent in published or on-line data sets. The author offers both solutions and cautions to these sources of measurement error and restrictions to generalizability.

Kiecolt, K. J., and L. E. Nathan. 1985. *Secondary Analysis of Survey Data.* Beverly Hills: Sage.

    A comprehensive guide to available research data and a good discussion of techniques and problems.

Webb, E. J., D. T. Campbell, R. D. Schwartz, and L. Sechrest. 1966. *Unobtrusive Measures: Nonreactive Research in the Social Sciences.* Chicago: Rand McNally.

    Chapters 3 and 4 offer useful suggestions and insights into gathering and using available data.

Weber, R. P. 1985. *Basic Content Analysis.* Beverly Hills: Sage.

    A short introduction to the techniques of content analysis. Weber offers some useful suggestions for increasing reliability.

CHAPTER 11

Methodologies II: Pilot Projects, Evaluation Studies, and Field Experiments

CHAPTER OBJECTIVES

- How are pilot projects, evaluation studies, and field experiments different from other experiments?

- How do researchers conducting field experiments choose groups and manipulate and measure variables?

- How do researchers measure by observing behavior?

- What problems does this methodology typically encounter? How do researchers solve them?

CHAPTER OUTLINE

CHOOSING EXPERIMENTAL GROUPS
MANIPULATION AND CONTROL PROCEDURES
MEASUREMENT IN FIELD EXPERIMENTS
RESEARCHER OBSERVATION
ISSUES AND PROBLEMS IN FIELD EXPERIMENTS

usiness researchers frequently make use of pilot projects, evaluation studies, and field experiments.

- **Pilot projects** are trial runs on a small scale of programs or policies before they are implemented across an organization. For example, a human resources manager decides to pilot test a new procedure for handling employee grievances, using 14 different departments located in the same plant.

- **Evaluation studies** attempt to assess existing programs or policies. For example, a pharmaceutical corporation conducts an evaluation study of an accounting procedure implemented four years ago.

- **Field experiments** refer to any study using an experimental design and carried out in a "real world" situation. They include carefully controlled experiments to look at the effects of particular variables (such as in consumer research). For example, an advertising agency carries out a field experiment comparing three different advertising approaches in six different cities on the East Coast.

All three use experimental designs. (For convenience, in this chapter we use the term *field experiment* to refer to all three variations. Thus a field experiment is any study using a true or quasi-experimental design in a natural setting rather than a created one.) Researchers using this methodology typically gather data with questionnaires, interviews, researcher observation, or by examining available data.

CASE EXAMPLE

A firm in the home-building industry hired a consultant to propose and test a procedure for increasing productivity. After exploratory work, the consultant suggested a pilot project: a temporary change in the procedure for assigning tradesmen to work teams. Under the old procedure, the foreman arbitrarily assigned two bricklayers to work together. He did the same with carpenters. The consultant suggested that the men select their preferred co-workers. To test this recommendation, he carried out a field experiment using two adjacent work sites in a housing project on the outskirts of Chicago. The two sites were separated by a highway so that there was little or no contact between workers on the different sites. Prior to the manipulation, the consultant administered a job satisfaction questionnaire and gathered data from company records on turnover rates, an index of labor costs, and an index of materials costs for the previous three months. Then, while pairs of carpenters and bricklayers in one site continued to work as before, workers in the other selected their own preferred co-worker. In other respects (weather, type and methods of construction, materials, etc.) the groups were identical. Over a second three-month period the consultant collected data on turnover, labor costs, and materials costs and measured job satisfaction. The group in which workers selected their co-workers proved to be superior on all four criteria (Van Zelst, 1952).

Laboratory Experiments. Laboratory experiments take place in artificial surroundings especially constructed for the purpose. In some cases the setting may be designed to look comfortable and realistic—a meeting room or a waiting room. In other instances no effort is made to disguise the setting.

The advantage of laboratory experiments is that they allow a much higher degree of control over other potential causes of the dependent variable, since so many factors can be held constant (e.g., lighting levels, time of day, instructions subjects receive, and so on.) On the other hand, laboratory experiments suffer from some disadvantages:

- Manipulation of the independent variable in a laboratory experiment is often weaker, so that treatment effects are more difficult to detect.

- The setting may interact with the manipulation to produce the observed results. For example, people may respond to commercials in a different way in a laboratory than they would in their own living rooms.

- Participants in a laboratory experiment are usually more aware of taking part in a research study and may act in the way they believe the researcher wants them to act *(demand effects).*

In short, laboratory experiments compared to field experiments are usually higher on internal validity, but lower on external validity. This is a problem when test results are to be generalized directly to a target population, but is less a problem when the experiment is conducted to examine a theory (Webster and Kervin, 1971). However, even in field experiments a study with one type of group (e.g., urban consumers) may not generalize readily to others (e.g., rural and small-town buyers).

Ethical issues are often less a problem in laboratory experiments, since subjects are aware that they are taking part in a study, and informed consent is usually obtained. Random assignment of persons to conditions is also much less a problem.

In the field of organization behavior, a significant amount of work is carried out in laboratory settings, almost all of it using random assignment and true experimental designs. However, the use of laboratory experiments for general applied research of this kind is a matter of current and continuing debate (e.g., Dobbins, Lane, and Steiner, 1988). The closest counterpart in business research is the booths that marketing firms set up in shopping centers to test television commercials and other advertising.

Besides the obvious difference in setting, field and laboratory experiments tend to differ in general objectives, research purpose, and basic design. These and other differences are summarized in Table 11.1.

Note that some business research occurs in laboratories. For example, consumer research often brings individuals into highly controlled settings to

T A B L E   I I . I ■ FIELD AND LABORATORY EXPERIMENTS COMPARED

	Field Experiments	Laboratory Experiments
Setting	Natural setting, used "as found" with little or no alteration	Artificial setting created for the purpose, but may be partially disguised to appear realistic
General Nature	Mostly business research, but some general organization research	Mostly general organization research, but some business (e.g., consumer) research
Most Typical Research Purpose	Evaluation research, some explanatory	Explanatory research
Most Frequent Basic Design	Quasi-experiment	True experiment
Techniques for Controlling Other Variables	Mostly statistical, some standardization	Random assignment, standardization, some statistical
Common Measurement Modes	Researcher observation, interviews, questionnaires, available data	Researcher observation, questionnaires

evaluate reactions to advertisements or products. Such studies are similar in most respects to traditional laboratory research. They generally use true experimental designs with random assignment and standardization.

CHOOSING EXPERIMENTAL GROUPS

The researcher's most crucial step in a field experiment is choosing the groups required for the specific research design. Box 11.1 gives the terminology for the types of groups used in field experiments. Most designs entail the comparison of two or more groups (especially pilot projects and controlled experiments) or the comparison of a group with itself before and after a manipulated change (especially evaluation studies). The quality of the experimental groups strongly affects the quality of the research.

BOX 11.1

FOCUS ON RESEARCH

Terminology: Groups in Field Experiments

Comparison group: In quasi-experimental designs, the "untreated" group or the group of cases receiving an alternative treatment. Cases are *not* randomly assigned to comparison groups.

Control group: In true experimental designs, the "untreated" group, or the group of cases receiving an alternative treatment. Cases are randomly assigned to control groups.

Experimental group: One of the groups in an experiment.

Intact group: A preexisting group of cases in which all members are treated alike, usually at the same time, as if they were a single case.

Treatment group: The group of cases receiving the treatment or the major manipulation.

The members of experimental groups are normally called *subjects*. However, in field experiments, particularly those with quasi-experimental designs without random assignment of cases, individuals are often called *participants*.

True Experiments. Whenever random assignment is possible, researchers give serious consideration to using a true experimental design. The advantages of true over quasi-experiments (reducing threats to internal validity by removing alternative explanations) are described in Chapters 3 and 4. The major disadvantage is the heightened possibility of communication between respondents in different conditions. Random assignment opens the possibility of two friends or co-workers being assigned to different experimental groups, so that individuals in one condition learn what is happening in others. (This problem is called *contamination* and is discussed later in the chapter.)

Quasi-Experiments. In business research the random assignment of cases to groups is often not possible:

- Someone other than the researcher selects which individuals or administrative units will receive the treatment.

- The treatment group consists of individuals who have volunteered for a new program or project.

- Everybody in the organization receives the treatment.

In such circumstances a quasi-experimental design is the only alternative.

Most business research field experiments involving employees or administrative units use quasi-experimental designs. However, when management permits the random assignment of individuals or units, true experimental designs are possible and preferred. When the research is external, such as consumer research field experiments, researchers frequently use true experimental designs.

Treatment and Control Groups in True Experiments

Researchers using true experimental designs must consider the selection of cases and random assignment procedures.

Selection of Cases.   Prior to random assignment researchers must consider the question of how the cases to be assigned are selected in the first place. This is a problem of external validity: are the individuals or groups selected for the study representative of the target population? Frequently a field experiment or pilot project in business research is to be generalized to a specific target population. For example, ten work teams are chosen to try a new production technique which, if it works, will be extended to hundreds of other teams. In this situation random procedures are required at two steps:

- Cases are chosen randomly from the target population.

- The chosen cases are randomly assigned to treatment and control groups.

Assignment Procedures.   Researchers should attempt to carry out random assignment themselves to ensure that it is truly random. Managers or other organization personnel, not realizing the importance of random assignment, may allocate individuals or groups on other grounds such as need, cost, or ease of administering the manipulation. Such nonrandom assignments threaten the internal validity of the research. Random assignment procedures are described in Box 11.2.

Comparison Groups for Quasi-Experiments

When random assignment of individuals or other cases to conditions is impossible, the researcher needs a quasi-experimental design. The task is to find or create one or more comparison groups that are as similar as possible to the treatment group(s). Finding an adequate comparison group often requires considerable ingenuity. Researchers may consider other administrative units, divisions of the company, or even other organizations.[1]

CASE EXAMPLE

Smith (1977), in a study of attendance and job satisfaction, took advantage of a freak severe snowstorm in Chicago as the manipulation of the variable "external impediment to attendance." The experimental group consisted of salaried employees in the Chicago headquarters of a merchandising corporation. For his comparison group, Smith used salaried employees of the company's office in New York, which had no

[1]For other examples and suggestions for comparison groups, review Cook and Campbell (1979) and Evans (1975).

BOX 11.2
RESEARCH SKILLS

Randomly Assigning Cases to Conditions

Random assignment of cases can be done with a coin, die, or table of random numbers. Once the experimental groups are identified,

1. Decide how many cases are to be included in each group.

2. Assign each case, one at a time, by flipping the coin (if two groups) or rolling the die (up to six groups).

3. As soon as one group is filled, no longer assign individuals to it. If you have only two groups, the remaining cases go into the second group. If you

have three or more groups, as soon as all but one are filled, the remaining cases are assigned to the incomplete group.

4. If you use a table of random numbers, first number each case, and then go through the table to select the numbers corresponding to first one group, then the next, and so on, until all groups are filled.

Do not put numbers on pieces of paper and pull them from a hat. This technique is not sufficiently random. Besides, it takes too much time.

storm the day of the Chicago snow squall. He compared cities on the correlation of job satisfaction and attendance on the day of the storm.

Designs with No Comparison Group. If you cannot find or create a comparison group, your specific design must be a single-group repeated-measure experiment. The most common is a pretest-posttest single-group design. Better is an interrupted time-series design with measures at several time points both before and after the manipulation, since this provides more protection against threats to internal validity.

Intact Groups

Researchers often make use of intact groups in field experiments, particularly with quasi-experimental designs. Their use in true experiment designs is normally associated with several difficulties.

Intact Groups in True Experiments. When the unit of analysis is an individual, the researcher often has the choice of breaking up an intact group to assign its members randomly to different conditions or assigning the group as a whole to one condition. The former preserves the requirements of experimental designs, but it also has disadvantages. The obvious one is contamination, but in addition the performance of the group may suffer if its members are separated at crucial times in order to undergo different experimental treatments. Both productivity and morale may suffer. Furthermore, the disruption is a confounding factor that threatens the internal validity of the experiment.

On the other hand, an intact group is easily assigned, and morale and productivity disruptions are fewer. This strategy, however, raises two serious problems:

- The *true* unit of analysis becomes the group rather than the individual. Individuals in the same group share group culture, work settings, interaction patterns, and other characteristics. The members' behaviors are not independent, and the assumption of independent observations is violated. Therefore, the group is the correct unit of analysis. However, this severely limits the degrees of freedom for statistical tests (see Chapter 16).

- When there are relatively few groups to be assigned, sampling error rises sharply, that is, experimental and control groups are likely to be very different despite the random assignment of intact groups.

For example, imagine that you want to test a new training program for sales staff. The staff are administratively grouped into six closely knit sales teams. If the teams differ substantially from one another (in size, experience, methods and tactics, success, or other characteristics) a random assignment of teams, three to each condition, is likely to produce treatment and control groups with large pretreatment differences. This will make it harder to draw valid conclusions about the effect of the treatment.

Preassignment Matching.   A workable solution for this sampling error problem is to *match and assign* the intact groups (see Box 11.3). While matching is subject to a number of problems (Mitchell and Jolley, 1988), its use with intact groups and aggregate units of analysis improves internal validity (Cook and Campbell, 1979).

CASE EXAMPLE

A provincial Ministry of Labor wanted to determine whether a new form for employee appraisals would lead to higher morale and greater productivity. The researcher's experimental design called for three conditions: one using the new procedure, one continuing with the old methods, and a third in which employee appraisals were discontinued. To avoid contamination effects, the researcher decided to use intact groups. Of the 11 departments in the ministry, 3 would use the new form, 3 would suspend employee appraisals, and the remaining 5 would continue with the old procedures. The researcher constructed three groups of three matched departments, taking into account the size of the department and the general nature of its work, in particular the amount of contact with the public. Within each group, one department was randomly assigned to each of the three conditions. Since the other two departments were somewhat unlike each other and the other nine in size and nature of work, the researcher decided to gather data from them but to exclude them from the formal analysis of the experiment.

BOX 11.3
RESEARCH SKILLS

Match-and-Assign Procedures for Intact Groups

1. Divide the intact groups into *matched sets,* with

- As many intact groups in each set as there are conditions in the study, and
- The groups in each set as similar as possible on either (1) as many important independent variables as possible, or (2) on pretest scores.

2. Deal with any leftover groups.

- If there were groups so different from the others that they couldn't be matched, you can either drop them from the experiment (at the risk of decreased external validity), or randomly assign them (but be prepared to consider their analysis separately).
- If the number of conditions doesn't divide evenly into the number of intact groups (e.g., with 3 conditions and 14 groups you will have 2 left over) add the extra groups to the sets they most closely match.

3. One set at a time, randomly assign the groups in the set to the conditions of the experiment, one intact group to each condition. If a set has extra groups, randomly assign those, one to each condition, until you run out of groups.

Example: Consider an experiment with three conditions (A, B, C) and nine intact groups (Group 1 to Group 9) varying in size (a primary independent variable).

The preliminary matching results in two sets and leftovers:

Set one (all large):   Groups 1, 4, 6

Set two (all small):   Groups 2, 5, 9

Leftovers: Groups 3, 7, 8

Group 3 is substantially different (extremely large) and cannot be matched. It is dropped. Groups 7 and 8 are both intermediate in size, but closer to the groups in set two. They are added to that set, giving

Set one: Groups 1, 4, 6

Set two: Groups 2, 5, 7, 8, 9

The groups in set one are randomly assigned to the three conditions:

Condition A: Group 4

Condition B: Group 6

Condition C: Group 1

The first three groups in set two are randomly assigned, producing

Condition A: Groups 4, 7

Condition B: Groups 6, 5

Condition C: Groups 1, 2

Finally, the remaining two intact groups in set two are randomly assigned, producing

Condition A: Groups 4, 7

Condition B: Groups 6, 5, 9

Condition C: Groups 1, 2, 8

Note that the same match-and-assign procedure can also be used when the unit of analysis is itself an *aggregate,* and there are relatively few units available for the field experiment (such as a study of government departments' hiring practices, with only five departments in the experiment).

Limited Number of Groups. The smaller the number of intact groups, the weaker the design and the greater the threats to internal validity. Like experimental conditions with small numbers of persons, the likelihood of achieving equivalent groups by random assignment drops sharply as the number of groups declines. When the number of groups is so small that you cannot match, a judgment assignment is preferred to random assignment. (This is analogous to the situation discussed in Chapter 7 in which a very small sample will have less sampling error if selected by judgment rather than by random procedures.) Assign groups to achieve what you believe will be the best balance among conditions. Technically, this is now a quasi-experimental design.

What if you have the extreme case, only as many intact groups as there are conditions? In this instance, even if you randomly assign groups to conditions, you do *not* have a true experimental design. The reason is that the purpose of random assignment is to help create equivalent experimental groups. However, if you have only two groups for two conditions, for example, even random assignment will not help to make them equivalent! Designs with one intact group per condition are quasi-experimental.

Intact Groups in Quasi-Experiments. The use of intact groups is very common in quasi-experimental designs in which no random assignment is attempted. Often someone other than the researcher decides which individuals are to receive the treatment. This person usually selects one or more intact administrative units such as work groups or departments. The researcher, in turn, normally finds that the most convenient comparison groups are also likely to be intact.

Problems in Group Selection

Several problems threaten the validity of field research at the stage of group selection. Two of the most important are volunteers and confounding characteristics.

Volunteers. On occasion, organizations ask their members to volunteer for pilot projects. The problem is that people who volunteer to take part in experiments are, in some respects, unlike other individuals. Therefore, the use of volunteers can threaten external and internal validity (see Box 11.4). To avoid relying on volunteers, consider using monetary or other incentives to encourage people to take part and to remain in the experiment. This is particularly important if one treatment is less desirable than another and participants in one condition are likely to be in contact with those in the other.

Confounding Group Characteristics. Confounding characteristics are variables on which experimental and comparison groups differ. *Group*

BOX 11.4
RESEARCH ISSUES:

Volunteers and Research Validity

In business research, the use of volunteers limits the generalizability of a pilot project or field experiment to people with similar "volunteer personalities." You cannot be sure that the same results would hold with nonvolunteers. (The volunteer problem is similar to that of self-selected samples, discussed in Chapter 6.)

It is likely that volunteers have more free time and are more open to new experiences. Rosenthal and Rosnow (1969) found that volunteers tend to be better educated and have higher occupational status and intelligence. They are also more eager for social approval.

The volunteer problem becomes one of *internal validity* if people volunteer specifically to participate in the *treatment* condition. This makes it impossible to use random assignment and means that the experimental and comparison groups will be different, at the very least, in terms of volunteer personalities.

However, volunteers are not without their advantages. They are less likely to drop out midway through the pilot project or field experiment. They are also likely to pay more attention to instructions. Unfortunately, these differences also seriously affect external validity: a relationship you find using volunteers may not show up with nonvolunteers.

composition differences at the individual level (such as age, experience, or gender ratio) or *group context* differences (such as working conditions or time together as a group) both threaten internal validity. Each confounding characteristic represents an alternative explanation for whatever differences between groups the research discovers. Confounding characteristics are normally eliminated by random assignment, so this problem is usually restricted to quasi-experiments. (Recall, however, that a *confounding event* threatens internal validity for both true and quasi-experimental designs.)

To reduce the problem, try to avoid comparison groups substantially different from the treatment group, particularly for group context characteristics. If differences can't be avoided, try to use several different comparison groups, each with some characteristics in common with, and some different from, the treatment group.

Another strategy is to measure, for each individual, the potentially confounding characteristics. For example, if the average seniority in the treatment group is higher than the comparison group, include a measure of seniority in the data. As long as these characteristics vary within the comparison group, you can control them statistically to determine and remove their confounding effects.

CASE EXAMPLE

A company opening a new plant asked a researcher to assess the effects on night-shift productivity of playing popular music in the plant. Management thought that it might help keep employees awake and alert. Management suggested that the music project could be tested by comparing productivity of the new plant with another plant in the same state.

The researcher pointed out several confounding factors. Employees in the new plant would be affected by the novelty of a new setting, as well as the breaking-in problems that new plants invariably undergo. The new plant was also to have a significantly younger work force compared to the older and more experienced workers in the comparison plant. As long as each plant was considered a single case, the researcher would be unable to separate the effects of the treatment from the effects of novelty, breaking-in problems, age, or experience. The researcher suggested that the study wait until productivity in the new plant had stabilized and that a nonmusic period of several months then precede the trial period (providing opportunities for pretest measures). She also suggested that the same procedure be carried out simultaneously at one of the other plants and that to remove the effects of age and experience, individual (rather than plantwide) measures of productivity would be needed (i.e., converting each plant to an experimental group of cases). She could then make use of measures of age and experience to control these factors.

MANIPULATION AND CONTROL PROCEDURES

After you have decided how to select or create the appropriate experimental groups, the next task is to prepare procedures for the experiment. These procedures include manipulating the treatment variable(s) and controlling extraneous factors and other sources of variation in the dependent variable.

Manipulating the Treatment

The treatment variable in a field experiment is the key independent variable the researcher (or some other agent) manipulates. If more than one treatment variable is manipulated, each experimental condition is a unique combination of categories of treatment variables. Each condition receives a different manipulation designed to create the appropriate levels of the independent variable(s) it represents.

Business researchers manipulate independent variables two different ways.

- *Situation change.* The researcher changes or creates a new situation. The different situations then reflect the different values of the independent variable. The manipulation may either (1) change a particular situation at one point in time to create the familiar before-after design (e.g., implement a quality circles program in a plant that previously had none) or (2) create several different situations simultaneously (e.g., establish three different training programs in three different company offices in order to compare their effectiveness).

- *Differential treatments.* The researcher treats different cases differently. The two or more different treatments represent the different values of the independent variable. For example, some employees may get a congratulatory letter after a successful sales effort; others get a verbal commendation.

In both situation change and differential treatments, the researcher causes the independent variable to vary over a given set of cases in a manner that he or she controls.

Not all variables can be manipulated. Nonmanipulable variables include three kinds of characteristics:

- Ascribed characteristics that cases have at genesis (e.g., gender of an individual; year of incorporation of a firm)

- Past experiences (e.g., a war veteran employee; turnover rate; total sales of a firm)

- Past choices (e.g., education; marital status; product mix of a firm)

If a variable cannot be manipulated, values must be taken as found among the cases. For example, since gender cannot be manipulated, the researcher must take males and females as they occur naturally in the population. For other variables, manipulation is theoretically possible but not feasible. For example, a firm could intentionally downsize or expand, but it is unlikely to alter its size at the request of a researcher.

CASE EXAMPLE

SUGGESTION

When examining consumer reactions to products, use *blind treatments,* in which subjects are not told the identity of products or other objects they are exposed to. This prevents prior knowledge of brand names and other beliefs or attitudes about a brand from affecting responses.

A researcher uses a field experiment to evaluate customer reaction to potential new packaging for a toothpaste. He plans to manipulate two variables: package color (dark red and light red) and package shape (two versions, A and B). The unit of analysis is the retail drugstore outlet; each store is to be stocked with one of the four color and shape combinations. In addition, the stores are blocked on three sales volume categories: small, medium, and large. The result is a field experiment with 12 conditions (2 colors × 2 shapes × 3 store categories). The researcher chooses 60 drugstores, 20 in each sales volume category. Within each category, he randomly assigns stores to conditions: five stores for each color and shape combination. The dependent variable is toothpaste sales in the three months following the manipulation (controlling statistically for sales in the previous three months).

Selecting the Manipulation. The researcher's task is to choose the best form and levels of manipulation. In many instances the correspondence between manipulation and concept is very clear. For example, the operationalization of a new absenteeism reduction program is the implementation of that program—its letters and interviews with high-absenteeism employees, point assignments, rewards for low absenteeism, and graded sanctions for excessive absenteeism. Business researchers have little discretion if someone else has selected a specific program or policy to be evaluated.

In other circumstances, however, devising the manipulation involves hard thinking about the concept. Deciding to manipulate "employee autonomy" might be very difficult. What does it mean? What would you do to create a situation with high levels of it? What about a situation with intermediate and with low levels?

In business research the problem is usually not so much operationalizing an abstract concept as deciding which of several treatment possibilities will provide the best pilot project or experimental manipulation. For example, a researcher must choose from among several different forms of sales training programs. Then he must choose treatment levels for the selected program: weekend, four-day, full week, or two-week training. If the researcher can't afford to include all the possibilities, he must choose on the basis of relevance, validity, and cost. Similar choices face the researcher evaluating safety policies, promotional mixes, or price structures, or any other policy or program alternatives.

In general, the time spent developing a sound manipulation is well invested. A poor manipulation produces ambiguous results of doubtful relevance; a good manipulation is the key to effective field experiments.

Experimental Control

In evaluation and explanatory projects, researchers try to control the effects of variables known to have an impact on the dependent variable, but that are not of primary interest. If left uncontrolled, the variation caused by these variables produces noise, which reduces research power. The more researchers can control such variables, the more easily they can detect existing relationships.

In field experiments, researchers try to control both *group composition* and *group context* characteristics.

Group Composition Controls.   Composition characteristic variables include attributes of individual cases, such as gender or age. In aggregate these attributes determine the composition of the experimental group. Composition characteristic variables in field experiments are controlled three ways. Each is illustrated here for the control variable "gender":

- *Selection of cases:* Choose only cases with a particular level of the composition characteristic. For example, run a field experiment with only male employees, so there is no variation of gender within conditions. (A major disadvantage of this method of control is that it seriously limits external validity.)

- *Research design:* Use factorial, blocked, or interrupted time-series designs. A factorial design adds a manipulated control variable. A blocked design is used when a category control variable cannot be manipulated (see Chapter 4). (For example, a study of the effect of incentives on sales performance used four conditions: all-male and all-female treatment and control groups. The effect of gender was then assessed and removed.) Interrupted time-series designs effectively hold constant many composition characteristics that don't change between measures of the group, including its gender composition.

- *Measurement:* Record naturally occurring fluctuations in the characteristic and use multivariate analysis to assess and remove its effects. For example, measure each person's gender and include it as a control variable in the analysis. The effect of gender can then be assessed and removed.

(Note that random assignment, which helps ensure equivalence across conditions in true experimental designs, does *not* control for the effects of other independent variables. For example, it ensures that approximately equal proportions of females appear in all groups, but it does not control for the effect of gender.)

Group Context Controls.   Context variables represent the environment of the experiment. If any of these factors are related to the dependent variable, the researcher should try to control them. For example, a researcher studying productivity might control for day of the week (since performance levels are often lower on Mondays and Fridays). Similarly, the researcher's tone of voice, clothing, gender, and gestures are also part of the context that can affect group members' behavior.

Context variables in field experiments are usually controlled through standardized settings and procedures. (In some circumstances, blocked designs and measurement are also used to control context characteristics.)

Standardization

Standardization is the structuring of an experimental situation so that all subjects or groups share the same experience, receive the same information, and are measured in the same way.

Chapter 8 discussed the standardization of measures. The same principle applies to experimental manipulations, settings, and procedures. Although generally associated with laboratory experiments where many factors are standardized (e.g., lighting, room temperature, content of verbal instructions), standardization is also utilized in field experiments, although to a lesser degree.

Standardization is easier and more effective when research personnel, rather than organization managers, administer the experiment. It is difficult when nonresearch personnel are responsible for giving instructions, explaining and implementing new programs, distributing questionnaires, and gathering other data.

Standardization generally takes place at two levels: the manipulation within each condition, and procedures and settings across conditions.

Standardized Manipulations. Field experimenters attempt to structure their experimental manipulations so that cases within the same condition will not receive unequal amounts or forms of treatment. For example, if some subjects hear an important phrase read twice or with more emphasis, or attend more training sessions than others in the same condition, they are more likely to respond to the manipulation. The resulting variation makes it more difficult to detect true differences between conditions and decreases research power.

Manipulations can be standardized several ways.

- If you are using intact groups, present instructions and explanations to the group as a whole.

- Read instructions and explanations from written scripts. This ensures that no points are missed or overemphasized.

- If the manipulation involves objects, check that their appearance is held constant *within* each condition. For example, if shelf height position of a supermarket product is the manipulated independent variable, keep shelf heights exactly the same within each condition so that the only differences are *across* conditions.

- Regulate and supervise procedures as much as possible. If you cannot take responsibility for implementing the treatment, train the people who are going to do it. Monitor the application of treatment programs or policies.

Standardization Across Conditions. Researchers also standardize settings and procedures across conditions by treating all cases as much alike as possible (except for the manipulated treatments). This reduces both noise and experimenter bias.

- If all subjects or groups are treated alike except for the manipulation, then random noise variations in their responses to the treatment will be reduced and true differences between experimental conditions will be easier to detect. In other words, standardization, like other forms of control, increases the power of an experiment.

- Standardization across conditions also reduces experimenter biases that occur when researchers unintentionally treat cases in different conditions differently *aside from* the intended manipulation. With standardization, participants are less likely to pick up the subtle cues that suggest what the researcher is expecting of them. (Experimenter bias is discussed in more detail later in the chapter.)

Standardized Settings. Hold constant the physical and temporal setting of a field experiment as much as possible. For the shelf height experiment example, other factors such as location of the shelf in the aisle, quantity and array of other nearby products, lighting level, and season should be as similar as possible across all conditions.

If you cannot standardize an important setting factor, measure it and use multivariate analysis as an alternative method of control. For the shelf height example, amount of traffic in the store, weather, and day of the week can be measured and controlled statistically during data analysis.

Standardized Procedures.

The same methods just suggested for manipulations can be applied to standardizing procedures across conditions: presentations to intact groups, written scripts, constant appearance of objects, and close supervision. Measurement procedures, too, should be uniform across conditions.

Researchers using laboratory experiments often standardize instructions by using audio- or videotape presentations. Sometimes these same techniques can be applied to field experiments, but more often the procedure in a comparison or control group, especially in business research, is simply business as usual. In such situations, standardization requires a minimum of instructions and explanations for the treatment group; the more unobtrusive the manipulation, the more similar the treatment and the comparison or control group.

Standardization and External Validity.

Ironically, standardizing a field experiment may decrease external validity. This can happen two ways.

First, a factor that is controlled through standardization (a "research constant") may interact with the manipulated variable to produce the observed effect. If the controlled factor were present at a different level, you would observe a different result, or perhaps no effect.

CASE EXAMPLE

A consumer study carried out in supermarkets used "shelf height of product" as the manipulated variable and controlled for "aisle position" by having the product always located at the end of an aisle. The results were called into question, however, by an industry consultant who suggested that shoppers, when rounding the end of an aisle, almost never look at the lower end shelves. However, they do gaze at lower shelf positions as they make their way up an aisle. A follow-up study confirmed the interaction effect: the relationship between shelf height and consumer response is different depending on whether the product is within an aisle or at the end of an aisle. In this case, standardization of aisle location reduced external validity: the initial results were only valid for end aisle positions.

Second, the relative importance of a particular causal factor compared to other causes will not be the same in the world outside a standardized experiment. Factors that are standardized in the field experiment may, in the outside world, wash out the effects of the manipulated factor. In other words, although you can generalize about the existence of a particular effect, you cannot generalize about the relative strength of that effect.

If generalization is important, consider repeating the experiment under different conditions, with different participants and manipulations. If you observe the same results, external validity will be much stronger.

Manipulation Problems

In addition to the problems of unequal treatments and reduced external validity, business research field experiments often encounter two other threats to research validity: interference and confounding events.

Interference in the Manipulation.   Managers who want to be fair to their employees are sometimes a problem. As soon as some individuals are treated differently from others, these managers may worry about the consequences of the difference and try to reduce them. They may tacitly decrease the treatment, or they may offer some compensatory treatment for the comparison or control group. Both reduce or obscure the difference between the groups and thus the impact of the manipulation. The result is a loss of research power.

CASE EXAMPLE

A government agency asked a researcher to evaluate the impact on morale and productivity of a flextime work schedule program. In a pilot project, employees in four departments were allowed to choose their own working hours, provided their hours added up to the standard 37 per week. Employees in comparison departments soon became aware of the project and complained to their managers about being excluded from the study. All managers of comparison group departments began to be much more lenient with employee absenteeism and requests for time off. Further, in response to subtle pressures from these managers, two department heads in the treatment group placed informal limits on the use of the flextime scheduling by suggesting that employees should leave no earlier than 3:30 and should be in the office every day of the week. About two weeks after the start of the project, the researcher had to call a meeting of department heads and managers and explain the need for maintaining differences between the experimental groups.

Confounding Events.   When an event involving one condition occurs at the same time as an experimental manipulation, it may not be possible to separate the effects of the event from the effects of the treatment. For example, if a new no fault absenteeism program is tested in one plant with another serving as the comparison group, and the treatment plant undergoes a layoff at the time of the manipulation, an improvement in absenteeism may be due to either the program or employees' fears of further layoffs.

Competitors can also confound the results of market and other external field experiments by changing the situation in the treatment or control areas. For example, a test of a new product is confounded when the competition cuts prices in the test area. The resulting poor sales of the new product may delay or prevent its introduction.

SUGGESTION

When nonresearchers must be involved in running a field experiment, make sure you provide adequate training and as much supervision as possible. Try to standardize manipulations, other procedures, and settings. For procedures taking place in remote locations, use a hot line so personnel can reach you whenever problems and anomalies arise. (They will!) Vigilance is the price of effective field research.

Confounded manipulations are notoriously difficult to deal with. One of the best safety measures is to test in several plants, regions, departments, or other sites. Researchers should also closely monitor the treatment and control sites for potentially confounding events and circumstances. If necessary, add additional comparison conditions to the design.

MEASUREMENT IN FIELD EXPERIMENTS

After selecting groups and preparing procedures, the next task is to choose the timing and nature of your measurements. In most field experiments, researchers gather data both before and after the manipulation. They usually measure three kinds of variables:

- Dependent variables representing the expected effect of the treatment. The major dependent variables are often called **criterion** variables (the term comes from psychology).

- Variables representing the independent variable manipulation.

- Control variables and potential extraneous variables. These variables are used in multivariate analysis in order to see more clearly the effect of the treatment and rule out spuriousness and confounding.

In addition, if researchers are interested in the causal process of the manipulation, they may measure intervening and interaction variables.

Business research field experiments use virtually all types of data sources and measurement modes. Questionnaires are very common. The use of available data and researcher observation is also frequent, and some studies employ personal interviews.

Pretest Measures

Pretest measures are made prior to manipulations. What is not so obvious is that pretest measures should be made before participants learn about the treatment, in order to avoid anticipatory responses.

What gets measured at the pretest stage? The most important are the dependent or criterion variables, in order to establish a baseline against which to compare posttest measures. In addition to dependent variables, you should also gather demographic and other information about each experimental group for two reasons:

- To determine how equivalent the groups are. This is particularly important in quasi-experimental designs in which randomization cannot be used to help achieve equivalent groups. If pretests show that the groups are wildly different, it is a good idea to begin again. With a true experiment, carry out another random assignment. Unfortunately, this luxury is not available in most quasi-experimental design studies, since the researcher has usually already selected the best available comparison group. The researcher will have to rely on multivariate analysis controls.

- To provide a baseline for assessing the possible effects of mortality—the loss of group members in the course of the experiment. The mortality problem in field experiments is discussed later.

Posttest Measures

For postmanipulation measures the most important issue is timing. Two criteria are important. First, researchers need to measure an effect near its point of maximum impact, in order to have a powerful test able to detect any effect. Second, researchers want to measure an effect as soon after the manipulation as possible in order to reduce opportunities for confounding events to occur and obscure the effect. These two time points do not always coincide. The researcher must then judge the best measurement time point, or (better) use several posttest measures.

For a single posttest measurement point, the timing of that measurement will depend on whether the anticipated effect of the manipulation is

- immediate or delayed.

- sudden or gradual.

- persistent or decaying.

These three dimensions are shown in Figure 11.1.

If an effect is immediate, sudden, and persistent (such as the effect on sales of a change in shelf height) the posttest measurement should be made fairly soon after the manipulation. At the other extreme, a complicated effect may be delayed, gradual, and decaying. For example, a sales training program may not show any effect for a week as new techniques are tried and digested, then lead to increased performance, and then show a decline as motivation declines, information is forgotten, and novelty wears off. Timing of the measurement is crucial in order to capture the effect close to its maximum impact.

For complex effects such as the preceding example, a better strategy is to use a *series* of posttest measures. If resources permit, multiple posttest measures are safer, provide more information about the nature of the manipulation's impact, and improve internal validity.

Manipulation Checks

Objectively, researchers in field experiments know the nature and level of the manipulated independent variables. However, they cannot always be sure

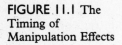

FIGURE 11.1 The Timing of Manipulation Effects

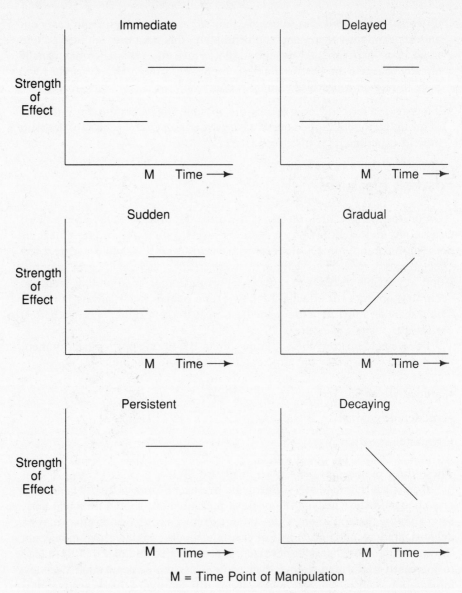

M = Time Point of Manipulation

that participants see their situations in the way the researcher intends. To determine subjects' perceptions, researchers carry out manipulation checks.

Manipulation checks are measures to determine whether participants are *aware* of manipulated variables. They verify the treatment and also make sure that the comparison or control group did not perceive any treatment. Such checks are particularly important if the manipulation involves a change in procedures or policies and if the change may be too small to be noticed (a weak manipulation). A case that fails the manipulation check is usually dropped from the analysis, since it does not represent a legitimate test of the manipulation.

BOX 11.5
MOVING SOUND: A CONTINUING CASE

Part Nine: Multiple Data Sources

"Run that by me again?"

"It's simple. We've got a field experiment here, right?"

"That much I understand. We're pilot testing our commercial. By the way, have you seen it yet? Terrific! Like a rock video."

"No. Maybe later. The point is, we've got several data sources for the pilot project. For the available data—that's weekly sales information—we've got ten weeks before and ten weeks after the commercial first airs, in two treatment locations, and two comparison locations."

"That's the interrupted time-series part of it. You expect an immediate but decaying effect, you said."

"Right. That's why the ten-week postbroadcast period. We'll look at the multiple posttest measures of sales, the criterion variable. We also measure some control variables, like weather, other stores' promotions, and campus events."

"Each bus manager has a check sheet to fill out for that information."

"That's the second source. Then we have the data from the interviews. This is a posttest only measure, but for both treatment and comparison groups."

"And don't forget the questionnaires. They're costing me about two hundred in CDs."

"Don't forget the return postage, printing, and all your other expenses."

"But at least the interviewers are cheap. Those staff people are really glad to get out of the office."

"Only the questionnaire measures the manipulation. It's our manipulation check. You want to know whether the commercial registered on the people who saw it."

"It sure did with me. Come on back to the office, I'll show it to you. We can grab some doughnuts on the way."

Manipulation checks usually employ questionnaires or interviews and are normally included in the posttest measures (see Box 11.5). In some instances it may be useful to carry out manipulation check measures at the pretest. For example, if a new safety program is to be introduced, do employees know about the old one, or even that there is such a program? The danger in pretest manipulation checks is that they sensitize participants to the following manipulation and posttest measures. Sensitization reduces external validity (and is discussed later in the chapter).

RESEARCHER OBSERVATION

Measurement by researcher observation is a data-gathering technique common in controlled field experiments. It is used to a lesser degree in pilot projects and evaluation studies. (Occasionally, nonexperimental studies also use observation measurement.) Observation data are usually combined with data from other sources.

SUGGESTION

Before your final design and measure decisions, review the specific data analysis you will use. Because analysis of data from field experiments is often more complicated than with surveys or available data studies, it pays to ensure that your design and measures will provide the data you need.

Observation is also useful in the initial investigation stage of research. Unstructured observation can provide useful clues to what's happening and what the research should focus on. A researcher who spends time in relevant settings, carefully observing what happens, is almost certain to gain insights that will improve the research. At this stage, the researcher should note both normal verbal and nonverbal behavior and reactions to events and circumstances that represent the organization's problem. Focus groups can be conducted in situations where the group members can be observed (one-way mirrors or videotaping). The members' reactions to the topic of discussion provide additional data about their feelings.

Observation in field experiments, however, tends to be much more structured, standardized, and systematic. Researchers use check sheets, stopwatches, and other aids.

- Traffic counts and work flow monitoring are examples of fairly simple structured observation measurement.

- Observation of purchasing decision behavior might be fairly complicated. For example, the observer records the following on a data collection form:
  amount of time customer spends at display of hand soaps
  customer's demographic characteristics (gender, approximate age, race)
  whether alone or accompanied by other adults or children
  number of different products touched
  number picked up and examined
  visible reactions (e.g., head shaking or nodding)
  brand actually purchased, if any

- Another variation is to have the researcher present a stimulus and observe how individuals react. For example, a researcher might visit a number of stores, dropping and breaking a bottle of ketchup in each one and observing both who cleans it up and how long it takes.

Problems and Advantages

The problems associated with researcher observation include measurement validity, measurement error, and cost.

Validity is a problem because what the researcher sees may be a poor indicator of the variable or concept of interest. For example, attitudes and beliefs are seldom straightforwardly expressed in behavior. Behavior at the bargaining table is seldom an accurate indication of how the chief union and management negotiators feel about one another!

A second problem is measurement error. Random error is likely when instructions for observational measurement are ambiguous or don't include procedures for resolving discrepancies. For example, if instructions don't specify how to code participation at a committee meeting if a person makes a motion and then withdraws it, one observer might record this as one participation act, another as two, and a third as no participation.

Biased measurement errors are also a problem. The observer may be tempted to impose his or her own interpretation on the observations. This is a problem when the behavior is ambiguous. When one employee punches another on the shoulder, is it anger, horseplay, or a sign of affection? This subjectivity can be overcome by using more structured observations (such as a behavior check sheet) and by training observers not to add their own interpretations.

A third problem is cost. Observation is generally time consuming and requires either the physical presence of a researcher (with attendant transportation costs) or the use of recording equipment.

Advantages.   Nevertheless, for some purposes observation is an ideal measurement method.

- It provides the best data about children's responses to products such as breakfast cereals and skateboards, since children are not often able to verbalize their feelings and opinions.

- When the unit of analysis is an event or object, the best data are often gained through researcher observation.

- Measures based on researcher observation are less likely to be subject to the biases of self-report data and information from informants and outside observers.

Observation Options

There are a wide range of observation options available to business researchers. We now consider further advantages and disadvantages of these observation alternatives.

Disguised/Undisguised.   Undisguised observation occurs when the persons or groups observed are aware of the observation. It is a reactive measure; the measurement operation is likely to affect the behavior. However, if observation continues for some time without any apparent ill effects, people become accustomed to it, and more normal behavior will eventually emerge. This is time consuming, however, and there is no assurance that procedure effects have been eliminated.

The major problem with disguised observation is ethical. It involves a clear invasion of privacy and often doesn't meet the criterion of accepted risk discussed in Chapter 1. In addition, if those observed become suspicious or learn about the observation, the research project may be effectively finished, and other repercussions may be serious. Managers seldom welcome such disruptions, and, combined with the ethical problems, business researchers should think carefully before undertaking disguised observation.

Participant/Nonparticipant.   The observer can choose to remain outside the action, or take part in it *(participant observation)*. For example, the observer could either watch or work as a member of a sales team.

Participant observation puts the observer in the midst of the action, but makes it more difficult to record observations, particularly if the observation is disguised. For this reason it is often limited to the initial investigation phase of business research. The advantage is that the observer's presence over a long period of time, even when undisguised, reassures the other individuals and makes it more likely that they'll behave naturally and talk freely about their own perceptions and problems.

Observation using data collection sheets, clipboards, instructions, and possibly stopwatches or other equipment is much easier in a nonparticipant mode.

Intermittent/Continuous.   As part of standardizing the measurement operation, the researcher must not only indicate specifically what is to be observed, but when. Observation can be intermittent or continuous. A sales clerk could be observed for 15 minutes each hour, an hour a day, or continuously all day.

Initial investigation observation is usually continuous for long periods of time, whereas data-gathering observation is undertaken at specific times. In other words, the behavior is sampled at designated times, either systematically (e.g., every half hour) or at randomly chosen times within a given period. For example, a research assistant could be instructed to count the number of sales clerks actively involved with customers at four times of day: 10:17, 11:42, 2:08, and 7:57.

Direct/Indirect.   The measurement modes used with observation can be direct and in person, or can make use of indirect methods based on mechanical or electronic technology. Such means include road traffic counters, television audience audiometers, and recordings using audiotape, film, or videotape. Indirect methods usually result in "hard copy" of the observed behavior, which can be examined closely, repeatedly, and systematically at the researcher's convenience. However, it is usually more expensive and sometimes awkward to put the necessary equipment in place. The researcher must also be prepared to deal with technical problems and equipment failure. Indirect observation is most common in marketing and consumer behavior research.

Action/Traces.   In some circumstances the researcher has a choice of watching the action or behavior of interest, or looking for *traces* of behaviors left behind. For example, metal shavings under a lathe indicate work rates, a waste bin shows how much waste material a group has produced, the number of shopping carts in a parking lot at closing time suggests how busy the store has been, garbage bags contain traces of the products people buy and use.

The major advantages of traces is that they are unobtrusive and nonreactive measures, and they are somewhat less subject to ethical problems (see Webb et al., 1966). The major problems are validity and other variables:

• What is observed is sometimes a poor indicator of the variable or concept of interest. For example, a large number of beer cans in household garbage could indicate either a high level of socializing and entertaining or the presence of one or more heavy drinkers.

- Information on other variables to relate to the trace data may be difficult to acquire. A researcher can check the ratio of popcorn containers to candy wrappers after a movie, but can't tell who bought what.

ISSUES AND PROBLEMS IN FIELD EXPERIMENTS

The preceding sections have discussed a number of the problems that business researchers encounter in field experiments. We now examine in more detail five procedure effects: experimenter bias, contamination, sensitization, mortality, and demand effects. We then turn to the importance of pretesting and some issues in organization politics and research ethics.

Experimenter Bias

With facial expressions, tone of voice, or other behaviors, a researcher can unintentionally communicate to subjects what responses he or she expects from them. Subjects pick up these expectations and act on them, and thus produce data to confirm the experimenter's hunches and hypotheses. **Experimenter bias,** as this phenomenon is known, adds an alternative explanation for any findings: are they due to the manipulation or to experimenter behaviors? Thus experimenter bias threatens internal validity.

One solution to the problem of experimenter bias was discussed earlier: standardization of procedures. A second solution is to minimize contact between researchers and participants, and where they must be in contact (for example, to give instructions) to use a **double-blind** design in which neither the subject nor the researcher knows which condition a subject is in or the identity of the product or other object being evaluated. For example, in a cola soft drink taste test neither taster nor researcher would be aware of which drink was in which glass. Double-blind procedures are not always possible in field experiments, but their use is recommended wherever feasible.

Contamination

Contamination is a procedural problem in many field experiments. It occurs when participants (especially in nontreatment groups) learn that they are treated differently from other groups or individuals (especially treatment groups). For example, employees in the shipping department learn about a new complaint procedure in the packaging department. The danger in contamination is that participants will act on this knowledge and thus distort the results of the experiment (Cook and Campbell, 1979).

- Contaminated participants may act to diffuse the treatment, that is, behave as if they, too, had been subject to the manipulation. This is particularly likely if you use a staged start design and persons in comparison groups know they are to receive the manipulation in the near future. Their behavior anticipates the treatment.

- Participants may resolve to try harder and make up for their perceived disadvantage (compensatory rivalry).

- They may act in ways to exaggerate differences between treatment and comparison groups. For example, their "resentful demoralization" (Cook and Campbell, 1979) at being excluded from the treatment might lower performance levels in the comparison group.

- They may generate pressures to curtail or end the experiment or strike back in ways that hinder the organization and threaten the experiment (such as sabotage).

Diffusion of treatment, anticipatory behavior, and compensatory rivalry all reduce intercondition differences and lower research power. Resentful demoralization represents an alternative explanation for any differences you find between treatment and nontreatment groups: are they due to the manipulation or to contamination?

Here are four suggestions for reducing the likelihood and consequences of contamination.

- Use widely separated treatment and nontreatment groups.

- Keep the manipulation as unobtrusive as possible.

- Don't compel participation, particularly if nontreatment might be seen as disadvantageous or costly. If participants are compelled to participate, as is often the case in internal business research, their hostility may increase contamination effects.

- Use **placebo treatments** in the control or comparison groups (see Box 11.6). This won't prevent communication, but will reduce resentful demoralization.

Sensitization

Measures or research procedures are **sensitizing** when they affect participants' subsequent behavior or responses.

Sensitization is a problem that threatens research validity.[2] A pretest or procedure threatens internal validity and research power when it, rather than the manipulation, affects posttest responses.

[2]Also known as *testing*. We prefer the term *sensitization*, since it may result from research procedures as well as measures.

BOX 11.6
RESEARCH SKILLS

Administering Placebo Treatments

Control and comparison groups are usually thought of as conditions in which no treatment is administered. However, when contamination is likely, researchers try to avoid having a group to which nothing happens. If members of a control or comparison group learn that another nearby group is receiving some attractive treatment, or even just more attention, the contamination may easily lead to major problems for researcher and managers.

The solution is to provide something for each group. This entails administering a *placebo treatment* to the control or comparison group. Placebo treat-

ments can be achieved by introducing some change that is actually irrelevant to the real purpose of the study. For example,

- While a new database accounting system software is tried in one department, a comparison department receives new word processing software.
- An accident prevention campaign mounted in the treatment plant is timed to coincide with a stop smoking campaign in the comparison plant.
- While some salesmen are sent to a one-week training course (the treatment), others are given a course in personal financial management.

CASE EXAMPLE

A researcher is asked to help evaluate a quality circles program. The program is to be implemented for all employees in a government office that processes welfare payments. He administers a job satisfaction measure one week prior to the beginning of the program and again five weeks later. The results show little improvement in job satisfaction. Puzzled, the researcher carries out some intensive follow-up interviews with eight randomly selected employees, and learns that they like the program and feel better about their jobs. It appears that, in the posttest measure, many employees tried to remember their earlier responses and strove for consistency rather than an accurate portrayal of their feelings. Others, following the pretest, became more aware of what they didn't like about their jobs, and this increasing awareness of job problems, rather than the quality circles program, was reflected in their posttest answers.

When sensitization interacts with the experimental treatment, external validity is threatened. This often happens in business research field experiments when pretest measures are highly visible. Questionnaires, interviews, or observers with clipboards indicate to employees that something is going on. Employees are then on the lookout for other events or circumstances that might explain it. The manipulation is often exactly such an event, and employees therefore pay more attention to it.

When a pretest measurement sensitizes participants to the following manipulation, the pretest increases the strength of the treatment. External validity

SUGGESTION

Avoid handouts (e.g., descriptions of a new program) in field experiments. They sensitize participants to their participation (especially by comparison with nonparticipants) and increase the risk of contamination if they vary among conditions.

is reduced because, without the pretest measure, the manipulation would not have shown the same impact. Thus a program or policy cannot be assumed to have the same impact elsewhere as in the pilot project unless it is accompanied by a sensitizing pretest.

To reduce sensitization:

- Make pretest measures and other procedures as unobtrusive as possible, for example, through the use of available data.

- Disguise the pretest so that it appears unrelated to the subsequent manipulation. For example, you can use a questionnaire that covers a wide range of topics, "burying" the measure in which you're interested.

- Augment your specific design. Remove the threat to internal validity with a design that employs a control or comparison group which receives the pretest but not the manipulation. Remove the threat to external validity with the more elaborate Solomon four-group design, in which two more groups are added, neither of which are pretested and one of which receives the manipulation.

Mortality

Because field experiments contact participants at a minimum of two time points (manipulation and posttest measure), mortality between contact points is always a potential problem.

Mortality (also known as *attrition*) is more likely in field experiments because they take place over longer time frames than the typical one- or two-hour laboratory experiment. This provides more opportunities for individuals or groups to leave the experiment.

Modest levels of *random mortality* (all participants are equally likely to drop out) are not a concern. However, two types of nonrandom mortality may present problems:

Mortality is the loss of cases from a study as participants or groups drop out because of boredom, anxiety, lack of time, illness, or other causes.

- **Systematic mortality:** Subjects with a particular characteristic are more likely to drop out.

- **Differential mortality:** Subjects are more likely to drop out of some conditions rather than others.

Systematic mortality threatens external validity. At best, it limits the extent of generalizability.

CASE EXAMPLE

A pilot project was devised to test a new computerized inventory control system for a company selling replacement auto parts. The experimental design called for 10 retail outlets, randomly selected from the 21 in the company, to use the new system for a six-month trial period while the rest continued with the old. Because of problems with employees adapting to the new hardware, three of the ten test outlets reverted to the old system in a matter of weeks. The researcher noted that the three were the largest outlets. He was forced to limit his conclusions about the benefits of the new system to small and mid-sized outlets. He also recommended special attention be given to system implementation in the larger stores.

At worst, when the systematic mortality characteristic is also related to the dependent variable, it reduces the accuracy of estimates of *population characteristics,* although not relationships in the population. When mortality is both systematic and differential, and the systematic mortality characteristic is also related to the dependent variable, the result is *mortality bias.* Severe mortality also reduces research power by reducing sample or condition size and making it more difficult to detect true relationships and differences.

Minimizing Mortality. To prevent or reduce mortality, *reduce participants' costs.* Make sure that your procedures are not too onerous or time consuming. Take into account participants' available time and level of interest. Show an appreciation for any disadvantages they may be suffering.

Provide intrinsic rewards. Motivate them to stay in the study by telling them of the practical importance of the study and its potential contribution to their own welfare.

Use *extrinsic incentives* to encourage people to continue in the experiment, such as financial bonuses or time off. Obviously, such incentives should not interfere with the manipulated treatment. Incentives are particularly important when one condition has more appeal than another and you are unable to avoid contamination. When this happens, individuals in the less attractive conditions are more prone to drop out.

Finally, it never hurts to contact dropouts for *exit interviews.* Try to find out why they left the experiment, and correct your procedures if possible (without changing the treatment in mid-study).

Demand Characteristics and the Hawthorne Effect

Demand characteristics are aspects of the experimental procedures or setting that suggest to participants what the purpose of the study is and how they are expected to behave (Orne, 1962). Particularly in laboratory studies, subjects search for clues about the nature of the study and their expected responses. The effects are similar to experimenter bias: subjects' behavior tends to confirm experimental hypotheses. Demand characteristics can be a potential problem in field experiments of consumer behavior. In experiments with employees, however, the participants are less likely to want to be "good subjects" even though it is usually clear what behavior the researcher is expecting (increased productivity, reduced absenteeism, etc.).

Hawthorne Effect.   Related to demand characteristics, but more important in field experiments, is the Hawthorne effect.

CASE EXAMPLE

Roethlisberger and Dickson (1939) conducted field experiments at the Hawthorne plant of Western Electric in Chicago to examine the effect of illumination levels on productivity. Over two and a half years, they found that as lighting was increased and decreased, productivity levels did not change in a corresponding way. Instead, productivity continued to rise, no matter what lighting manipulations the researchers employed. They finally concluded that the participants were reacting not to the manipulations, but to the fact that they were in an experiment and that someone was paying attention to them.

The effect that Roethlisberger and Dickson encountered is now known as the "Hawthorne effect," even though there is some dispute about whether such an effect operated in their subsequent field experiments at the same plant (Franke and Kaul, 1978). When participants are aware that they are participating in a study and appreciate the attention they receive as a result, their behavior is likely to show "desirable" changes. When these changes result from the fact of the study itself, rather than a specific manipulation, a Hawthorne effect has occurred.

Researchers reduce demand and Hawthorne effects by making their studies less obtrusive and by disguising their purposes in measures and procedures. The use of placebo treatments also avoids singling out one particular group for attention.

Pretesting the Procedures and Measures

Pretesting (in the sense of preliminary checks for measurement and procedure errors) is essential for field experiments, since research procedures are such an important part of this data-gathering methodology (e.g., assigning participants to conditions, introducing the manipulation, and measurement operations). Researchers must ensure that their procedures will operate smoothly before beginning the experiment, or measurement error is likely to be high.

- Check to ensure that the procedures for assigning participants or cases to conditions are truly random.

- Verify that contamination is kept to a minimum. If it is likely, how will you deal with it?

- Include all measurement procedures in the pretest, including manipulation checks. If observation measures are employed, is lighting adequate? Is field of vision blocked? Try observing and recording data in the real situation. Check distractions, noise levels, and the personal comfort of researchers. Make sure that measures are sufficiently sensitive.

- If you use written scripts, rehearse and check to make sure they are easily understood. Are all instructions clear and unambiguous?

- Also check the procedures you'll use if something goes wrong (such as significant mortality, participants become angry or upset, research personnel become ill, etc.).

SUGGESTION

Pretest your experimental procedures on at least five cases per condition to verify that measures and manipulations work as you intend. If all goes well, include the pretest cases in your data. Of course, they'll have to be discarded if you make substantial changes to the procedures.

Organization Politics

Business researchers carrying out field experiments within organizations must be sensitive to the realities of organization politics. While researchers normally gain permission for access by convincing higher level managers of the need for the research, it is important not to forget these two groups in the organization:

- Middle and lower level managers. They will worry that the research will interfere with their responsibilities. They may feel threatened that the results will make them look bad and harm their reputations in the organization. They often have an interest in seeing the research reach particular conclusions.

- Employees. The employees who are part of the experiment, often without their explicit consent, will wonder how the results may affect their job content and job security.

Because either group is capable of hindering or helping the research, researchers must take steps to communicate with both groups to avoid problems in the conduct of field experiments.

The importance of communication with these groups is increased because of the visibility of field experiment personnel. Compared to survey researchers (who may never even see a respondent), field experimenters are often much more visible around the organization (carrying out pretests and posttests, selecting experimental groups, administering the manipulations). This visibility may increase apprehension about the experiment.

Communication. To avoid problems with organizational politics, make sure you contact at least key members of each group and inform them of your objectives and methods. Pay particular attention to on-site supervisors, who often suffer from too much responsibility and too little power.

It may also be necessary to inform union officials. If you do, start at the top of the local hierarchy (the local president or the business agent), and then contact shop stewards (since politics are even more important in unions than in firms). Likewise, a study within the union might, in some cases, be threatening to managers who are uncertain of what is happening. Communicate with management in order to avoid unnecessary strains on union-management relations.

These steps will help lessen fear and resentment. Remember, change and uncertainty almost always produce anxiety, and anxiety often produces hostility. Communicate to avoid hostility that might interfere with the research.

Of course, communication is sometimes not enough. Be prepared to counter objections to your procedures and methodology. The best defense is scrupulous design and procedures and anticipation of any potential problem.

Managers with Vested Interests.   A related problem in business research is the manager seen as responsible for the experiment. When a change is considered, a new program is implemented, or a new procedure is tested, there is usually at least one person in the organization who is identified with that change and who therefore has a vested interest in positive results. At times, this can lead to subtle or even overt pressure to show beneficial consequences.

To respond to this pressure, the researcher should at least be aware of the possibility. A good strategy is to balance the picture by bringing other administrators into the research. Alternatively, talk the problem over with the manager, and make relative freedom to operate a condition of the work. Ultimately, invalid research results harm everyone.

Negative Results.   A major problem in business research is that no one likes the bearer of bad tidings. If your results are negative, you can often mitigate the bad news by suggesting what needs to be done to make the new program work as intended. (Reporting negative results is discussed in more detail in Chapter 18.)

Ethical Issues

The manipulation of variables leads to some particular ethical problems in field experiments. The issues include treatments withheld from some individuals or cases, whether and when to reveal the experimental manipulation to subjects, and stressful manipulations.

Withheld Treatments.   A major ethical and administrative problem in pilot projects and field experiments is withholding a desirable treatment from a comparison or control group. The withheld benefits may range from income (testing a new training program to improve sales performance, and thus commissions) to life chances (testing a new manufacturing procedure to reduce asbestosis).

The administrative problem is to prevent workers' reactions from hindering organizational goals. When health, security, or performance is affected, individuals are understandably upset when others gain an advantage. Particularly when the choice is arbitrary (as random assignment must be), granting

BOX 11.7
RESEARCH ETHICS
Withheld Treatments

Researchers have developed several solutions to the administrative and ethical problems of withheld treatments (Cook and Campbell, 1979).

- *Multiple treatments.* One solution is to use more than one treatment, so that each comparison group receives some potential benefit. Data analysis then compares the relative efficacy of the different treatments. To maintain a no-treatment baseline for comparison purposes, one comparison group can be given an irrelevant placebo treatment or a treatment intended to deal with a different problem.

- *Costly treatments.* The ethical problem is different when the cost of supplying every person or group with the treatment is more than the organization can bear. In this instance, the issue becomes one of how to distribute the benefit most fairly. Thus a lottery to assign individuals randomly to treat-

ment and control groups is much more acceptable.

- *Staged start designs.* Designs in which groups receive the beneficial treatment in different time stages (see Chapter 4) are another solution to the problem. This solution is particularly effective if the treatment is costly, available only in limited supplies, or if implementation is time consuming. Administrative problems are lessened if the non-treated group is assured that they will receive treatment later when resources permit. However, contamination is a problem with these designs, and some resentful demoralization remains as a threat to internal validity.

Cook and Campbell (1979) discuss other possibilities, such as distributing the benefit on the basis of need, which require more complicated statistical analysis.

some employees better working conditions or other opportunities is likely to arouse resentment.

The ethical problem is whether it is morally justifiable to differentiate among individuals by withholding desirable treatments from some. The answer depends to a large extent on two points:

- Whether the gains to the organization as a whole (including other employees, not just upper management and owners) from the experimental results outweigh the deprivations to the no-treatment cases.

- Whether the deprived no-treatment individuals can be given some other, or delayed, compensatory benefit.

The answers, unfortunately, are seldom easy (but see Box 11.7).

CASE EXAMPLE

Researchers evaluating a treatment procedure for discharged mental health patients received hostile media publicity because of a research design involving a withheld treatment. Half the 120 patients, chosen randomly, received rehabilitative supervision under a case manager who helped to provide housing, secure a job, and ensure adequate food and care. The other 60 were assigned to a clinical therapist who did not provide such services. The plight of patients in the control group came to public attention when officials in the mental health center at which the research was conducted complained to the media about homeless patients being ignored.

Revealing the True Experiment.   In field experiments, subjects often participate without knowing that research is being conducted. This practice raises three ethical questions:

- Is it necessary to tell individuals about the research in which they're participating?

- If so, is it necessary to tell them beforehand?

- If this isn't possible, must they be told afterward?

To answer the first question, apply the principle of *accepted risk* (discussed in Chapter 1). If the research is a legitimate and normal part of the organizational activity one encounters (e.g., while working for a firm or shopping in a department store), disclosure is not necessary. We know, as consumers, that our buying patterns are often monitored; we know, as employees, that management will examine our productivity and absenteeism records. However, if the research goes beyond accepted risk, disclosure and informed consent is an ethical necessity. We don't expect a researcher to follow us home from the shopping center in order to find out where we live, the size of our home, and whether we have children. When informed consent *is* required, it must be obtained prior to the subject's participation.

A further problem is that some experiments require deception to obtain valid responses. If participants knew the true nature of the study, their responses would be colored and biased. This raises the third question—later disclosure. If deception is necessary in research going beyond accepted risk, the researcher has a different obligation: **immediate disclosure debriefing.**

Disclosure debriefings place an important burden on the researcher. The explanation for the deception must be good enough to secure the cooperation of the subject. This cooperation is not for agreement to participate (for unwitting participation has already occurred), but for

- Agreement not to alert other potential subjects to the treatment.

- Agreement not to disrupt or hinder the continuation of the research (e.g., by complaining to the media).

Such debriefings are not easy, but they are essential ethically. The alternative of a mailed explanation once the research is over is ethically unacceptable for research not meeting the accepted risk or informed consent criteria.

Stressful Manipulations. A third ethical dilemma is the use of stressful experimental manipulations. The problem is that such manipulations may harm participants.

CASE EXAMPLE

The personnel department in an oil industry firm was responsible for selecting applicants for transfers to a new high-tech petroleum refining plant. The department researcher's assignment was to examine whether intensive interviews of applicants would provide better information to improve the personnel decision. Over a six-month period, 16 candidates for 13 transfers were given lengthy, in-depth, highly scrutinizing interviews, and 17 candidates were treated to the normal short interview procedure. The intensive interviews were highly stressful for most candidates.

Stressful treatments must meet the criteria of *accepted risk* and *informed consent.* If there is some fear that persons would decline to participate if told beforehand about the study, then an *immediate disclosure debriefing* is required.

An additional ethical issue is how to minimize the possibility of harm to participants in stressful manipulation conditions. This often requires that the researcher implement special procedures to safeguard subjects. Two such procedures are important.

• Monitor closely the behavior of subjects. At the first sign of excessive stress, their participation must be terminated. This means that, if you plan a stressful manipulation, you must hire adequately trained personnel (for example, a psychologist) who can judge when a subject's stress level is too high.

• Conclude each experimental session procedure with a debriefing interview that includes (1) a discussion of why the stressful manipulation was necessary and (2) therapy for those subjects who are upset, angry, or otherwise adversely affected by their participation. Often all that's necessary is to give upset subjects a chance to ventilate their feelings and frustrations. After such ventilation, most subjects will accept the necessity for the manipulation. In other cases, however, an intensive therapy session may be necessary. This procedure implies that your study must employ trained personnel who can provide the therapeutic counseling to restore troubled subjects to the same, or better, condition than they were when they entered the study.

Ethics and Observation. Observation carries its own set of ethical dilemmas. People do many things when they believe they are unobserved that they would be mortified to be seen doing in public. Most of these are utterly irrelevant to the research. Researchers must respect privacy and ignore these behaviors.

■ *The Lighter Side of Research*

Deception experiment: An experiment in which the researcher is pleased to believe that the true nature of the situation is unknown to the participants. Typically the only parties deceived are the funding agency and the journal editor.

Manipulation check: A handy device which allows the researcher to dispose of data from subjects who stubbornly refuse to conform to the experimenter's perception of reality. (Woodman, 1979)

Summary

Business researchers frequently design pilot projects and evaluation studies. Controlled field experiments, carried out in natural settings, are common in consumer and marketing research.

The first task facing field experimenters is to choose the groups needed for the designs they plan to use: control groups for true experiments with random assignment of cases to groups and comparison groups for quasi-experiments. Field experiments often use preexisting intact groups. Although easier to work with, intact groups present some problems that can be partially overcome in true experiments by matching and assigning.

Field experiments in business research face a number of problems. Those that reduce research power include weak manipulations, variation from uncontrolled variables, unequal treatments and other haphazard procedures, and contamination. Those that present alternative explanations and weaken internal validity include confounding group characteristics and events, sensitization, demand characteristics, and experimenter bias. Problems related to diminished external validity include mortality and the use of volunteers.

The solutions to these problems include standardization, manipulation checks, mortality checks, and pretesting procedures and measures. Above all, vigilance is important for valid field experimentation.

Political interference from organization personnel is a particular problem for field experiments in business research. Anticipation and communication are important to minimize it. Ethical issues confronting field experimenters include withheld treatments, revealing the true purpose of the experiment, and stressful manipulations. Some of these difficulties can be overcome with placebo treatments, particular designs, and therapeutic debriefing.

Where Are We Now?

We have now examined available data studies and field experiments, two of the three major data-gathering methodologies in business research. The next chapter considers surveys. Following the discussion of these three methodologies, we begin to look at data analysis.

Discussion Issues and Assignments

1. To illustrate the problems of randomly assigning small numbers of intact groups, randomly assign the following four coins to two different groups: penny, nickel, dime, quarter. How often do you get group total values that differ by more than 25 cents? If you match by nearest value (penny and nickel, dime and quarter) and randomly assign, what's the worst you can do? How often will you get this outcome?

2. Last year an instructor changed her course textbook in order to increase student satisfaction and comprehension of material. What methodology and data-gathering procedures would you use to evaluate the change? An instructor tells you that he wants to change his course textbook (different course!) next year for the same reasons. What methodology and data-gathering procedures would you use? Compare the two projects.

3. Go to a shopping center and look for people with clipboards doing consumer research. Talk to their supervisor about present and past projects. From among the projects, select one that you can identify as a field experiment. Determine its basic design (true or quasi-experimental) and its specific design. Did it use a pretest measure? A manipulation check? Were there any controls over experimenter bias? Did the researchers take any steps to increase research power? Evaluate its internal and external validity. Note: the supervisor may not know some of these terms; you'll have to do the translation.

4. Discuss the advantages and disadvantages of treating your methods class as an intact group taking part in an experiment. What if the experiment had to take place during class hours?

5. Your methods class is to be the treatment group in a quasi-experimental field experiment. The purpose is to evaluate a new system for taking notes during class. The system is said to greatly improve comprehension of new material. The manipulation is a two-hour training session. What's the best comparison group you can think of, and why? Identify confounding group composition and context factors. How could you control random variation? What form would you anticipate for the effect, and how would you time your posttest measures? What threats to internal and external validity would you anticipate, and how would you deal with them?

6. Would you use volunteers for the study in question 5? If so, how?

Further Reading

Bateman, T. S., and G. R. Ferris. 1984. *Method and Analysis in Organizational Research.* Reston, VA: Reston.

    An excellent section on field experiments in organization research. The book contains examples of both experimental and quasi-experimental designs useful for business researchers.

Cook, T. D., and D. T. Campbell. 1979. *Quasi-Experimentation: Design & Analysis Issues for Field Settings.* Boston: Houghton-Mifflin.

    This book is almost an essential accompaniment to all but the simplest of field experiments. It is an invaluable source of design and procedure suggestions. Chapter 8 in particular offers an excellent discussion of some major problems facing field researchers, including mortality and withholding treatment from control groups.

Sawyer, Alan. 1975. "Demand Artifacts in Laboratory Experiments in Consumer Research." *Journal of Consumer Research* 1:20–30.

Sawyer suggests methods for investigating and reducing demand effects in consumer research experiments, including the association between price and quality made by subjects.

Webb, E. J., D. T. Campbell, R. D. Schwartz, and L. Sechrest. 1966. *Unobtrusive Measures: Nonreactive Research in the Social Sciences.* Chicago: Rand McNally.

Chapters 5 and 6 provide a practical guide to unobtrusive observation.

Weubben, Paul, Bruce Straits, and Gary Schulman. 1974. *The Experiment as a Social Occasion.* Berkeley: Glendessary Press.

An informative discussion by the authors and others of the social psychological processes affecting subjects' behaviors in experiments. It helps remind us that experiments are not as easy as they appear to be.

CHAPTER 12

Methodologies III: Surveys

CHAPTER OBJECTIVES

- What types of surveys can business researchers use?
- What are the basic procedures for conducting each type?
- What are the problems that business researchers face when they conduct surveys?

CHAPTER OUTLINE

TYPES OF SURVEYS
CONDUCTING QUESTIONNAIRE SURVEYS
CONDUCTING INTERVIEW SURVEYS
SURVEY ISSUES AND PROBLEMS

I t's almost impossible to find a person who hasn't completed a consumer questionnaire or taken part in a marketing interview. It's almost as hard to find someone who hasn't thrown a mail survey into the garbage or refused a telephone interview.

Surveys typically involve *nonexperimental* designs and *self-reports* from a *sample* of cases. Common variations include surveys of informants (about their firms or departments) and enumerations of an entire target population. Surveys are so important in business research (particularly in marketing and sales, but also in employee management and other functional areas) that business researchers even conduct research on the conduct of surveys (Box 12.1).

TYPES OF SURVEYS

Business researchers commonly use three types of surveys, which vary in terms of how data are gathered:

- Questionnaire (including mail surveys)

- Personal interview

- Telephone interview

Each type of survey involves slightly different administrative techniques and has to deal with different problems. The relative advantages and disadvantages of the three types of surveys are summarized in Table 12.1. As the table shows, questionnaire surveys are usually lowest in cost and best for dealing with sensitive topics. Personal interviews provide the highest response rates and are best for dealing with complex topics. Telephone surveys take the least time to complete.

Costs. For reasons discussed later, the three types of surveys differ in their costs.

If your survey requires just a few questions (no more than a dozen or so), it is worth checking to see whether you can *piggy-back* those questions onto another survey. Piggy-backing means that your questions are added to the original questionnaire or interview schedule and administered along with the initial questions. The savings in data collection costs can be substantial.

Commercial polling firms often sell space for piggy-back questions on their national or regional polls. Some major corporations conduct fairly frequent employee surveys on which you might piggy-back for a share of the research costs. Once you have defined your target population, it is worth some effort to check into these and other piggy-backing possibilities.

The data you get back from a piggy-backed questionnaire can take several forms. At one extreme you'll be given the completed interview schedule or

BOX 12.1
FOCUS ON RESEARCH

Research on Survey Research

Not surprisingly, researchers have always been interested in research on research methods. Some important work was published in the early 1950s (e.g., Payne, 1951). Since the mid-1970s, however, the amount of research on research methods, particularly on surveys, has increased enormously. Both Sudman and Bradburn (1982) and Converse and Presser (1986) summarize results from these studies.

The topics of this research on survey research have been varied. They include the effects of systematic differences in question wording, question order, paper size and color, reminders of different forms (e.g., letters, postcards), different types of rewards and incentives, and other factors.

Much of this work was prompted by the growth of commercial survey firms, both in public opinion and marketing. It mirrors earlier work by social psychologists analyzing the methodology of laboratory experiments (e.g., Rosenthal and Rosnow, 1969).

---

questionnaire pages containing your questions. At the other extreme, you'll get a computer tape or diskette with the data coded (and perhaps cleaned) and ready for analysis. You might also get data on general demographic variables such as gender and age if any were included among the initial questions.

But there are drawbacks to piggy-backing:

- You are sharply limited in the number of questions you can use.

- You have no control over the data collection process. The data preparation (editing, coding, and cleaning) may also be out of your hands.

- The target sample may not correspond to what you want. If the problem is too broad a sample, rather than too narrow, you can eliminate the cases you don't want by adding a screening question.

- In some cases the survey owners will give you only the summary of responses for each of your questions. If so, further analysis will be impossible.

Errors.   The most common errors in surveys are measurement error, nonresponse bias, and to a lesser extent, sampling error. The first and third have been discussed in earlier chapters; we now take a moment to look at nonresponse bias. Then we consider to which errors each of the three types of surveys is susceptible.

Nonresponse is a form of missing cases. It occurs when people refuse a telephone or personal interview, throw away questionnaires unanswered, or are unavailable when the researcher tries to contact them (e.g., ill, away at work, on vacation, or moved to an unknown address). This nonresponse is *biased* when *cases with certain characteristics are more likely to be refusals or noncontacts.* In other words, the nonresponse cases are not randomly distributed within the sample, and certain types of cases are underrepresented. When

Nonresponse bias is the systematic underrepresentation of certain types of cases because of refusal or inability to participate or the researcher's inability to contact the case.

TABLE 12.1■ COMPARISON OF QUESTIONNAIRES, PERSONAL INTERVIEWS, AND TELEPHONE INTERVIEWS

	Questionnaire	Personal Interview	Telephone Interview
Cost	Lowest	Highest	Intermediate
Time Required to Gather Data	Intermediate	Intermediate or greatest	Least
Response Rate	Lowest	Highest	Intermediate
Nature of Nonresponse	Mostly refusals, some noncontacts if mailed questionnaire	Two-thirds refusals, one-third noncontacts	Mostly refusals and break-offs
Capacity for Assessing Extent of Nonresponse Bias	Poor	Good	Intermediate
Item Nonresponse	Can be high	Low	Low
Control of Measurement Situation	Poor	Good	Intermediate
Dealing with Sensitive Topics	Best	Intermediate	Worst
Dealing with Complex Topics	Poor	Good	Poor

nonresponse bias is substantial, external validity is low and generalization from the achieved sample to the target population is inappropriate.

CASE EXAMPLE

An association of 22 teaching hospitals asked a researcher to examine job sharing among nurses. She found that 18 of the hospitals had about 800 job-sharing nurses, with the proportion in each hospital varying from less than 1 percent to more than 15 percent.

The study was plagued with nonresponse problems. Because of union opposition, four of the hospitals declined to participate. Thus nurses in hospitals with unions opposed to job sharing or with poor labor-management relations were underrepresented. Response rates to the questionnaire were much higher in hospitals with a higher proportion of job sharers, so that nurses in hospitals in which job sharing was not a widely used option were also underrepresented. Finally, response rates were also lower for nurses on a two-week on, two-week off rotation, as opposed to those with half-day, half-week, or weekly rotations with their job-sharing partners. This probably occurred because these nurses were more likely to be absent during the week in which the questionnaires were distributed. The conclusions of the research were limited to job sharing in hospitals where it was a supported and popular practice and to job sharers on shorter rotations.

Errors and Type of Survey. Each of the three survey types is more prone to some of the research errors we've described than others. Questionnaire studies are highest on measurement error because of the lack of opportunity to probe or to explain the meaning of questions to respondents. They also have the highest levels of nonresponse bias because response rates are lower and because there is less opportunity to assess, and therefore correct for, bias of this kind.

Personal interview surveys tend to be highest in sampling error because they usually have smaller samples and often use cluster sampling. These characteristics, in turn, are due to the high cost per case of personal interviews. Because of the presence of an interviewer, these surveys are lowest in measurement error and nonresponse bias.

Telephone interview surveys are intermediate on measurement error and nonresponse bias. Because they involve simpler sampling designs, their sampling error is generally low as well. The time restrictions on telephone interviews mean that researchers may have to ignore potentially important variables. This is likely to introduce the errors associated with unmeasured variables.

Mailed Questionnaire Surveys

Questionnaire surveys vary from the one-page informal instrument to the lengthy questionnaire with prior contact by letter or telephone, visual aids to increase respondent interest and improve recall, and incentives and follow-ups to raise response rates.

Advantages. The major advantages of questionnaire surveys are as follows:

- The low cost of administration and personnel. If necessary, one person can conduct the entire study.

- They provide a more anonymous setting for threatening and embarrassing topics and produce less distortion than personal or telephone interviews. This advantage also holds for status-related questions such as income and education (Dillman, 1978; Scott, 1961; Wiseman, 1972).

- They make it easier to ask for information that the respondent must take time to gather. He or she can leave that question until later, ask someone else to get the information, or pause to get it in the middle of the questionnaire.

Disadvantages. The major disadvantages of questionnaire surveys are related to the researcher's lack of control over the measurement situation.

Because no interviewer is present, response rates for questionnaires tend to be lower than for personal or telephone surveys. The intended respondent may not be the one who answers. Order effects may appear when respondents answer questions out of sequence. The respondent may skip awkward or difficult questions, so item nonresponse is greater. It is difficult to explain and probe for opinions and understanding of complex issues.

Questionnaires take time to mail out and get returns. While you can readily calculate your response rate, you are seldom sure how much nonrespondents are biasing your results.

Questionnaires by Fax and Electronic Mail.   Fax (facsimile transmission) machines, which are now common in most offices, present a new way of combining telephone and questionnaire surveys of organizational members and informants. Use the telephone for an initial interview, then immediately afterward forward a questionnaire to collect further details. This technology promises to be very useful for business research. Similarly, electronic mail offers researchers the opportunity to survey organizational informants by sending a list of questions. Like fax, this is probably best done in conjunction with a prior telephone contact.

Personal Interviews

Personal interviews range from a few questions the consumer answers at the front door to longer sessions involving response cards, product samples, pauses to check family or organization records, and lengthy attitude scales. Survey interviews tend to be highly structured and to focus on one or a few well-defined topics. Overall response rates for personal interviews of the general population run around 70 percent. Rates tend to be lower in urban areas.

Advantages.   The personal contact of a face-to-face interview is best for

- Motivating respondents and building rapport.

- Adapting the interview to the situation. The interviewer can pick a convenient time or quiet setting and remove distractions.

- Handling complex topics and skip patterns. The interviewer can repeat questions that are not understood, probe to clarify answers, and use response cards and other aids to assist respondents.

- Carrying out multistage sampling. An interviewer can carry out the final sampling stages (such as selecting which house on the block or apartment in the building and which individual in the home).

- Assessing nonresponse bias. If the field interviewer can obtain some information about nonresponding cases, researchers can often assess the threat of nonresponse bias. (See discussion later in this chapter.)

Disadvantages.   Personal interviewing is the most expensive way of gathering data. The very involvement of interviewers is time consuming and costly since they must be hired, trained, and transported. The time required to locate respondents selected for the sample is often substantial.

The presence of an interviewer heightens the likelihood of social desirability bias and often makes respondents feel uncomfortable answering sensitive or status-related questions. The interviewer also introduces inadvertent unreliability and measurement bias by varying the phrasing or tone of questions, and by deciding what to record, what to probe, and what to omit.

Interviewers in turn are influenced by respondents; it is difficult to treat respondents identically when they may be powerful and wealthy, poor with little education, or tired, bored, or nervous.

Unstructured Interviews.   Unstructured interviews are used to probe respondents' feelings, perceptions, and personalities. They are often lengthy and unfocused and rely heavily on open response formats. They require well-trained interviewers able to establish a relatively high degree of rapport with respondents.

Survey researchers seldom use unstructured interviews, with two exceptions.

- They may use them in the exploratory stages of research, such as the preliminary examination of how consumers view various products and the meanings attached to certain symbolic words and pictures. These interviews generate the hypotheses or ideas to be tested in a subsequent survey.

- They occasionally use them in a follow-up phase. Unstructured interviews with a few respondents can explore in more detail some of the findings from the analysis of survey results. These interviews are useful for both developing recommendations and for generating hypotheses for further research. (This postsurvey phase is a useful combination of nomothetic and idiographic approaches.)

Focus Groups.   Focus groups are similar in some ways to unstructured interviews, and like them they are often used in the exploratory stages of a research project. The group leader uses his or her expertise and knowledge of group dynamics to draw out group members' feelings and perceptions. Sessions may begin with easy specific questions to warm up the group, and then move to broad general issues that allow participants to expand on their attitudes. The interaction is usually taped or videorecorded and may be observed by other researchers or clients through one-way mirrors.

Telephone Surveys

The last decade has seen an enormous increase in the use of telephone surveys, particularly for consumer and public opinion research, as North

Americans become more reluctant to let strangers into their homes. Telephone surveys range from small local projects to major studies using computerized equipment and long distance WATS-line (Wide Area Telephone Service) calls across the country.

Computer-Assisted Telephone Interviewing.   In the last few years telephone surveys have made increasing use of computer technology. CATI *(Computer-Assisted Telephone Interviewing)* systems operate with an interviewer seated at a computer keyboard and screen. The screen shows the questions the interviewer is to ask in order, and how to input the response directly into the computer via the keyboard. The interviewer wears a telephone headset (microphone and earpiece), which frees both hands for entering data.

The computer can be programmed to carry out a number of functions:

- Sampling

- Keeping track of cell counts for quota sampling

- Automatic dialing and random dialing

- Reminding interviewers about optimum calling times (for different time zones) and callbacks

- Presenting introductory statement, questions, bridging sentences, and closing remarks

- Recording answers (interviewer types responses on keyboard)

- Checking the answers on-line for both illegitimate codes (range checks) and illogical or inconsistent codes

- Following skip patterns based on respondent's previous answers

- Introducing random prompts

- Changing question wording on the basis of previous responses

- Randomly changing order of questions or response categories (to overcome response bias effects)

- Tabulating answers and updating the tabulations as interviews are completed

- Carrying out statistical calculations on the data, such as cross-tabulations

Many survey firms now use CATI systems. The advantages are numerous:

- Better data quality because of fewer interviewer errors, elimination of coding errors, and more control over interviewers.

- Faster results because of instantaneous on-line data entry and cleaning.

- More reliable data because the interviewer can immediately resolve discrepancies (which the computer identifies) while the respondent is still on the line.

- Cost savings (once the capital investment in equipment and software has been made) because of the omission of editing, coding, and keypunching as separate operations. CATI-based studies can also be costed very accurately.

A final advantage of CATI systems is that they greatly facilitate research on research. Respondents can easily be assigned randomly to alternative question wordings or question orders, with the computer automatically recording which wording or order was used. This kind of work is important for market and other research firms that mount many studies every year.

The typical CATI system consists of ten or more interviewer work stations, each with telephone equipment and a microcomputer linked to a central micro acting as a file server.

The benefits of microcomputers are not limited to telephone surveys. Similar programs are also used to help administer personal interview surveys by keeping track of interviews, callbacks, and other details.

Advantages.　Telephone surveys fall between questionnaire and personal interview surveys with respect to

- Cost. In general, telephone surveys with long-distance calling cost more than questionnaire surveys, but less than half of a corresponding personal interview survey.

- Nonresponse information. They rank between personal interviews and questionnaires in the researcher's ability to collect information relevant to possible nonresponse bias.

- Control over the measurement situation. Control is greater than for questionnaire surveys, but less than in personal interviews.

Compared to both other types, telephone surveys are superior with respect to a number of issues:

- Speed of results. Research projects using telephone surveys can be completed in two or three weeks. Research firms using CATI systems get results even more quickly.

CASE EXAMPLE

When the Tylenol tampering incident hit the news in 1986, McNeil Labs, a subsidiary of Johnson and Johnson, had to act quickly. (Several packages of Tylenol capsules had been surreptitiously opened and cyanide added.) McNeil commissioned Burke Marketing Services to design and execute a national sample survey, to be completed within a four-hour period, to assess consumer reaction to the tampering. Burke used a quota sample of 275 interviews. Because Burke was using a CATI system, the results were available on time. McNeil was able to give a press conference the afternoon of the survey day to announce that they would withdraw the product.

- Complexity of questionnaire design. With the help of CATI systems, researchers can use extremely complicated skip patterns and alternative question wordings.

- Cost of contact attempts. Telephone surveys are least likely to suffer from nonresponse because the respondent can't be contacted. Callbacks are easy and inexpensive.

- Follow-ups. Telephone surveys also make it much easier to *recontact* respondents if initial findings indicate that a new variable is required. Recontacting is problematic with face-to-face interviews (although it can be done by telephone if the interviewer gets a name and phone number at the end of the interview). It is impossible in questionnaire surveys with anonymous respondents.

CASE EXAMPLE

A researcher was hired to conduct a study for a large corporation. Increasing numbers of scientific and technical personnel were refusing transfers to other parts of the country, even though a refusal could hinder future promotion. During the course of telephone interviews the researcher found an unanticipated factor having an important impact. Divorced employees with joint custody of, or access to, their children were reluctant to move because it would mean no longer being able to see them. About a third of the way through the sample the researcher added two questions on child custody and access for divorced or separated respondents. She was able to recall the respondents previously interviewed and get the additional data in 91 percent of the cases.

- Ease of sampling. For consumer surveys of the general population, random sampling of telephone books is easy, although biased. Much of this bias can be eliminated with **random digit dialing (RDD)** techniques (see Box 12.2). Cluster and multistage samples are no longer necessary.

- Administration. Compared to personal interviews, hiring and training telephone interviewers is much easier, since personal appearance and deportment are irrelevant. It is also easier to administer a telephone survey and monitor interviewer performance with research personnel all in one location.

Disadvantages.   Compared to personal interviews, telephone surveys produce slightly higher nonresponse rates, especially for the elderly and poorly educated (Schuman and Kalton, 1985) and young adults (Thornberry, 1987). People may suspect the caller is selling something and hang up. Item nonresponse rates are also somewhat greater.

Telephone surveys also produce unrepresentative samples. Since women are more likely to answer the telephone than men, telephone surveys will underrepresent males unless care is taken in the design to counter this effect. During the times that major sports events are televised, the overrepresentation of women can be substantial.

BOX 12.2
FOCUS ON RESEARCH
Random Digit Dialing for Telephone Surveys

For surveys of the general population, the telephone book makes a poor sampling frame. Many telephone numbers are now unlisted, especially for higher status individuals and families, so undercoverage and selection bias are significant.

Random digit dialing (RDD) overcomes the limitation of telephone books. Beginning with a list of area codes and active exchanges (the first three digits of a North American telephone number indicate the exchange), you can randomly select four-digit numbers to obtain complete random telephone numbers. These numbers include both listed and unlisted telephones, as well as commercial and business establishments. Using RDD reduces undercoverage to those individuals and families who do not have a telephone, now less than 10 percent of the adult population.

Despite its advantages, some bias remains when RDD is used. Telephone ownership is less among lower status and younger individuals, and homes with two or more telephone lines are overrepresented. In addition, RDD cannot distinguish between residential and commercial numbers.

The combination of RDD with CATI systems makes possible powerful software that will randomly select numbers and drop exchanges if they have too many nonresidential (i.e., business and commercial) numbers.

Another problem is restrictions on question content and format. Complex questions are difficult to ask over the telephone. Closed questions with many response categories are either precluded or must be converted to a set of subquestions, since the respondent can't see the list of options. Respondents feel less comfortable with telephone than personal interviews (Groves and Kahn, 1979). In particular, sensitive and threatening questions are more problematic because of less rapport between respondent and interviewer. However, respondents are more likely to report some things (such as health problems) in telephone than in face-to-face interviews (Thornberry, 1987).

Telephone interviews are time limited. Because of the lack of an interviewer's presence to maintain interest and motivation, and the inability to pause (like a questionnaire), consumer survey telephone interviews are generally limited to about 15 minutes. This means that the number of variables is curtailed, and certain peripheral control variables may have to be excluded. (Interviews for internal business research may be longer if respondent interest and commitment are high and can be maintained.)

An additional problem is less control over the measurement situation compared to personal interviews. Because respondents provide little nonverbal feedback to the interviewer, it is more difficult to assess respondent states such as boredom, resentment, and reluctance. Respondents are more likely to hang up before the end of a telephone interview than they are to terminate a personal one, unless the topic is very salient to the respondent. In addition, respondents may consult with others to get answers to questions.

Some of these problems can be overcome by following up the telephone interview with a mailed questionnaire.

CONDUCTING QUESTIONNAIRE SURVEYS

Chapter 9 described in detail how to construct individual questions and design a questionnaire. Here we consider other aspects of a questionnaire survey: distribution and collection procedures, the cover letter, and steps you can take to improve response rates. As well as the general objectives of research validity and efficient use of resources, these aspects are directed toward two specific objectives:

- Minimizing nonresponse: cases missing because of "throwaways" and "leave-until-laters."

- Reducing measurement error: both unreliability and bias.

The first task is to get the questionnaire to the respondents in an effective and cost-efficient way and in a manner that will not harm the response rate.

Distribution and Collection Procedures

Questionnaires can be distributed many ways, not just by mail. These methods entail different costs and generate different response rates.

- Mail to home or workplace. Response is improved when the envelope is addressed to a specific individual by name.

- Deliver to respondent's home, with the completed questionnaire to be returned by mail or picked up. Research and experience suggest that calling in person to deliver (and pick up) the questionnaire, instead of mailing it, maximizes response rates. Response rates are higher when you indicate the pickup day (e.g., "this coming Wednesday"). This option is expensive, but often feasible for volunteer organizations with willing members.

- Hand out in person at the workplace or other public location (e.g., a survey is handed to employees at their work stations by the researcher or by supervisors or is handed out at the entrance to the plant as employees arrive or leave). Response rates tend to be low: it's too easy to discard the questionnaire, and respondents usually don't have time to look at it (and get interested) at the time they get it.

- Place stacks of questionnaires in strategic places for passersby to help themselves. As well as low response rates, this method suffers from the other disadvantages of self-selection sampling.

- Include the questionnaire with purchases, as a magazine insert, or printed on product warranty registration cards. Response rates vary, but tend to be low.

- Administer to a group of respondents gathered in a room for the purpose, under the supervision of a researcher. **Group administration** guarantees high response rates if you can get the individuals you want into the room. It also reduces measurement error, since respondents' questions can be answered.

(The problem of confidential returns [respondent's identity known] is discussed later in the chapter.)

The Cover Letter

The cover letter tells respondents what your survey is about, answers their questions, and should quell their misgivings. It should maximize response rates and motivate respondents to answer questions completely and accurately.

Contents.   Following Dillman (1978), the contents of the letter should

- State the purpose of the study and emphasize its importance (and for whom it's important—will it have any direct or indirect benefit for the respondent? For a group the respondent belongs to? For society generally?)

- Indicate how the respondent was selected, and why his or her response is needed. For example,

   Your name was chosen as part of a scientific random sample, so your participation is important for the overall results to be accurate.

- If possible, promise confidentiality or anonymity.

- Emphasize the simplicity of answering the questionnaire. You might also mention the estimated time it will take (based on pretesting, not the researcher's hunch). If your pretests show variability in the time it takes for completion, give a range (e.g., 15 to 20 minutes), which doesn't look quite as daunting as just "20 minutes."

- Mention the incentive for participation (if any).

- Give a suggested deadline date for completing and returning the questionnaire.

- Mention how the respondent may get a copy of the results (if applicable).

- Give a contact name and telephone number for any questions the respondent might have.

- Thank the respondent.

- It often helps to add a postscript suggesting that the respondent take the time "right now" to fill out the questionnaire.

SUGGESTION

Don't try to save on mailing costs by using too light a paper. It will tear more easily, leading respondents to throw it out rather than return a torn questionnaire. If printed on both sides, respondents may have trouble reading it because the print shows through.

Form.   To increase its readability, the cover letter must be short (one page maximum). If possible, each paragraph should contain just two or three sentences, with blank lines between paragraphs. (See the example in Appendix D.) Considering the list of cover letter contents and the need for brevity, you can see why writing effective cover letters is somewhat of an art.

Response rates are usually highest when the cover letter is short and looks personal, is typed (but not right justified), and is signed in ballpoint on a soft surface so the pen makes a visible impression.

Increasing Response Rates

Questionnaire response rates vary from about 10 percent for some political and marketing surveys to over 90 percent for salient topics in a group with strong self-identification. Overall a "typical" response rate is about 50 percent; a "good" one is 60 percent to 70 percent. A low response rate always carries the danger of extensive nonresponse bias.

Nonresponse occurs two ways:

• The respondent begins the questionnaire but quits partway through. This kind of nonresponse can be reduced by careful question wording and instrument design as discussed in Chapter 9.

• The respondent doesn't answer at all. This kind of nonresponse is overcome by creating a favorable initial impression through prior contact, the envelope, cover letter, and layout of the questionnaire.

A considerable amount of research (much of it by market researchers) has been conducted on factors that lead to high response rates (e.g., Goyder, 1982; Pressley, 1985; also see Kanuk and Berenson, 1975, and Heberlein and Baumgartner, 1978, for reviews). There is also some evidence that the general public responds to different factors than do businesses and other organizations (Pressley, 1978).

The results of some of this research are summarized here. The techniques are discussed in the approximate order in which the respondent encounters them.

Target Population.   One factor beyond the control of researchers, because it is dictated by the research problem, is the nature of the target population. Research suggests poorer response rates for lower socioeconomic status groups, the elderly, nonwhites, members of the armed forces, and men in general.

Prenotification.   A telephone call in advance of a mailed questionnaire can bring a significant improvement in response rate. The effect is less with mailed prenotification. It appears to make no difference whether prenotification is by postcard or letter.

Mailing Date.   Questionnaires should be mailed to arrive on Tuesday, Wednesday, or Thursday. They should not be sent out in the summer or near holidays.

Arrival Envelope.   Response rates are higher with a handwritten rather than typed address, and a postage stamp rather then metered mail. Certified or registered mail and special delivery bring higher response rates than first class, especially when used for follow-up reminders. Use a personal name on the envelope. Envelopes with windows tend to be mistaken for bills or solicitations and should be avoided.

Sponsorship.   Government sponsorship increases the response rate; identification of a market research firm decreases it.

Salience.   Response rates improve substantially when (1) the respondent is identified as a member of some particular group, rather than just a member of the general public, and (2) the questionnaire addresses an issue of importance to that group. (Response rates may be even higher when the researcher is also a member of the same group.) Salience is second in importance only to follow-ups in affecting response rates.

Incentives.   Researchers often use incentives to reward respondents for completing a questionnaire. The most obvious incentives are monetary. For example, a questionnaire survey of personnel managers used a cover letter with two quarters glued to it. Following an idea discussed by Pressley (1985), the researcher included the following paragraph in the cover letter:

> *We recognize that 50¢ would only compensate you for a few seconds of your time. However, we would like you to use this token of our appreciation to help pay for a cup of coffee while you fill out this brief questionnaire.*

Surveys have used a wide variety of nonmonetary incentives, including trading stamps, pencils, ballpoint pens, lottery tickets, and product samples. The incentive should be appropriate to the sample. A questionnaire survey of book club members attached to the cover letter a tea bag in an individual packet. A survey of students attached a return stamp to the cover letter with a paper clip. The letter suggested that if the respondent used campus mail to return the questionnaire, the student could keep the stamp for his or her own use.

It appears that incentives work because of their symbolic, rather than their actual, value. An incentive suggests that the researcher is aware of, and appreciates, the imposition the questionnaire might cause.

Offer of Survey Results.   Despite the value that researchers attach to them, the offer to reveal survey results has not been found to improve response rates (although it may if the results are salient to respondents). However, if you anticipate follow-up or further surveys, respondents who

SUGGESTION

When you want to attach an incentive to a questionnaire or cover letter, rubber-based glue seems to work best. It is less likely to tear the questionnaire than staples and easier on automatic mail-sorting machinery than paper clips.

request results voluntarily supply their names and addresses and are a good pool of future respondents. For consumer surveys, particularly, these cases have shown some interest and can be used for more in-depth research. They are not, however, likely to be a representative sample.

Overall Appearance.   The questionnaire must be easy to read. The type must be easily legible (don't photo-reduce to less than 15 characters per inch). Avoid dark colored paper and thin paper that tears or shows through. Make sure that questions are not crowded and there is plenty of blank space around each one.

The appearance of crowding can be reduced by using blank space instead of lines for open-ended answers, unless they are very short write-ins (e.g., year of birth; number of branch plants). Use boxes or brackets rather than lines for check answers.

Size of Paper.   Standard letter-size paper can get buried in a pile of similar-size papers. A slightly unusual paper size will make this less likely. Legal-size paper is a readily available option. Questionnaires in booklet form look important and may get earlier attention.

Color of Paper.   Some research shows that green gives higher response rates than white. Yellow is known for its impact on the optic nerves. Questionnaires on yellow paper may be harder to ignore, thus leading to higher response rates.

Preliminaries.   The top of the first page should show a title describing what the research is about. It should be interesting enough to capture attention. The title may indicate what group is involved (respondents should be easily able to identify themselves as members of the group), it may emphasize that the study is confidential, or it may stress an interesting issue. Keep in mind that the title will influence the respondent's frame of reference.

Also include at the top an assurance of confidentiality or anonymity. Use the appropriate term. *Confidentiality* means you know the respondent's identity but won't divulge the information; *anonymity* means that even the researcher doesn't know the respondent's identity.

Include any general instruction about how questions are to be answered. For example,

PLEASE CHECK <u>ONE</u> ANSWER PER QUESTION UNLESS OTHERWISE INSTRUCTED.

Initial Questions.   Unlike interviews, questionnaires should never begin with open-ended questions that require much thought. Such questions will dismay respondents about the time and effort the questionnaire will require and lead them to discard it. Instead, begin with factual questions that are easy to answer. Make sure the initial questions are clearly relevant to the survey topic.

SUGGESTION

Commercial survey firms generally use booklets rather than stapled pages. This format looks more professional, an important factor in consumer surveys. Booklets also make page turning in an interview slightly less awkward. However, consider the higher cost of designing and printing booklets compared to stapled sheets. Keep in mind that desktop publishing software for your microcomputer can reduce these costs substantially and produce a very professional-looking survey instrument.

Question Wording and Form.   Here are some suggestions to prevent respondents' quitting in frustration or boredom:

- In consumer surveys, since commitment is usually low, keep the interview or questionnaire interesting, perhaps with visual material. Avoid the boredom of a long string of similar questions and response formats, such as lengthy attitude scales.

- Use closing questions to get personal and demographic data such as age, gender, and income. Other awkward or embarrassing questions should also be saved for the end in most questionnaires. The assumption is that respondents who have invested their time will not break off with the end in sight. Even though the respondent can readily tell that the end is near, insert a bridge that indicates why personal data questions are relevant and necessary.

- It is common practice to use the final question to ask for general opinions and comments. The number and content of these comments can be a useful indicator of the respondent's involvement with the topic.

- The final line of a questionnaire should thank the respondent.

Question Numbering.   Questions must be numbered. However, if there are many questions, divide the questionnaire into sections and start each section with "1." You don't want to dismay respondents who immediately check the final page to see how many questions there are.

Questionnaire Length.   Although research results are ambiguous, in general the longer the questionnaire, the lower the response rate. However, the maximum acceptable length of a questionnaire depends on the importance of the topic to the respondent. A questionnaire for a organizational informant on a topic of significance for the organization might take more than an hour with no loss of respondents; a consumer survey should take no more than 12 to 15 minutes. If the topic is not particularly salient to the respondent, Sudman and Bradburn (1982) recommend a maximum of two to four pages.

To make a questionnaire appear short, print on both the front and back of each page. Do not crowd questions or response categories to keep the number of pages to a minimum; it makes the questionnaire look both unprofessional and complicated. Use legal-size paper if you can fit all questions on one page without crowding. Alternatively, photo-reduce the print slightly, but, as we said, not to less than 15 characters per inch.

Return Envelope.   A regular postage stamp leads to higher response rates than a machine stamp or a business reply envelope. The stamp suggests the investment in time and money the researcher is making and the researcher's expectation that the questionnaire will be returned.

Follow-Ups.   Follow-up reminders are the most effective way of raising response rates. Most survey experts now recommend two follow-ups, the first usually a postcard, the second a letter with another copy of the questionnaire. A third follow-up doesn't seem to have much effect.

The timing of reminders is important; if the period between contacts is too long, respondents may forget whether they've done the questionnaire, or it may be thrown out. Many researchers leave a week to ten days between contacts.

Follow-up notification should be addressed to specific respondents when returns can be identified and you know which cases haven't yet responded. If replies are anonymous, however, you must send a general follow-up to all cases in the sample. The issue with general reminders is whether to include another copy of the questionnaire. There is some evidence that a second copy of the questionnaire is not significantly more effective than just a reminder (Heberlein and Baumgartner, 1978). However, the second copy will be used in instances where the original questionnaire has been lost or was never delivered. The danger is that you'll get two questionnaires from some respondents, which will add to the sample bias by giving extra weight to those respondents. (Nonetheless, the gain in response rate probably overcomes the loss in bias.)

In any case every reminder, general or targeted, should contain a phrase such as, "If you have recently returned the questionnaire, please accept our thanks and disregard this notice."

CONDUCTING INTERVIEW SURVEYS

Chapter 9 discussed the construction of interview questions and the layout of the interview schedule. We now deal with other aspects of the interview situation: how to contact respondents and how to introduce and conduct the interview.

For both personal and telephone interviewing, the major concerns underlying these aspects are research validity, the cost-benefit ratio of the research, and the familiar objectives of

- Maximizing response rates (by obtaining the respondent's initial agreement to the interview and ensuring that the interview is completed).

- Minimizing measurement error (both unreliability and bias).

Contact Procedures

Survey researchers use three major contact procedures for interviews:

- "Cold" contacts: the interviewer contacts respondents at their homes or offices by calling in person (for a personal interview) or telephoning (for a telephone survey). If the time is inconvenient, the interviewer arranges a time to call back. At the same time, the interviewer tries to get answers to any *screening* questions to prevent an unnecessary callback in case no person at the location or telephone number fits the target population. The cold contact procedure is least expensive, but produces the highest refusal rates.

- The researcher makes a prenotification telephone call to alert the respondent to the interviewer's coming visit or telephone call. The caller asks screening questions, and if the respondent is in the target population, schedules a specific time for the interview. To save costs, prenotification calls can be made by noninterviewer personnel.

- The researcher sends a prenotification postcard or letter informing the respondent of the upcoming interview visit or call. The card or letter may invite the respondent to telephone for an appointment or it may be followed by a telephone call from the researcher. The caller will ask screening questions and, if appropriate, make an appointment.

In general, costs go up with the number of prior contacts, but refusal rates decline.

  Timing the Contact. For at-home telephone surveys of the general population, slightly less than one answered call in five will lead to a completed interview. To improve the odds, call from five to nine in the evening. The best days are Mondays to Wednesdays; Saturday all day and Sunday afternoon and evening are also good. It appears to be a good strategy to call back a refusal about a week later; many can be converted into completed interviews.

Introducing the Survey

  Internal business research seldom involves unscheduled personal or telephone interviews. However, unscheduled cold contact interviews are common in consumer surveys. In these interviews the first few moments of contact are crucial. The introduction must gain respondent cooperation and reduce fears that the study is a disguised attempt to sell something, to proselytize, or to get inside the home for some dubious purpose.

  The introductory statement should include

- The interviewer's name (and the respondent's, unless replies are to be anonymous).

- The purpose of the call: an interview.

- The topic of the interview. The more salient the topic to the potential respondent, the more likely he or she will agree to the interview.

You may also decide to mention the following points in the introductory statement:

SUGGESTION

If screening (to find cases in the target population) is complicated, save the time of wasted interviews by using an initial telephone contact both to ask the screening questions and to schedule an appointment.

- The sponsor or survey organization. Response rates improve with government sponsorship. Most interviewers working for marketing research and polling firms don't mention a commercial client or sponsor, even if asked.

- What incentives the interviewer is offering, if any.

The statement should be kept short; anything over 20 to 25 seconds will start to raise suspicions about what you're trying to hide.

Answer respondents' questions about the study, including the probable length of time it will take (based on pretest results). Sudman and Bradburn (1982) recommend the following response:

Most interviews last about____minutes; it depends on how much you have to say.

If asked, "Why me?" be prepared to state, briefly, that the respondent was chosen as part of a scientific random sample, and thus the respondent's answers are important for the study to be accurate. Difficult or more complex questions can sometimes be deflected by promising to have them answered in a follow-up telephone call or letter from the project manager.

Personal Interviews.

For personal interviews, the appearance and manner of the interviewer is very important, since it conveys to the respondent about as much information as the introductory statement. For interviewer's clothing, a good strategy is to strike a balance between informality and formality one level "higher" than what respondents themselves would wear for arranging a bank loan. Another way of putting it is to match the community standards of business dress.

A problem for interviewers calling at homes is not to look like a salesperson or someone distributing other material. Avoid briefcases and attaché cases; use a clipboard instead. This makes it clear that you are carrying only papers, not product samples. It may be useful to show the respondent a *letter of introduction* (with letterhead). This is a particularly good strategy when the letterhead identifies the sponsor as an educational institution, government agency, or other relatively prestigious organization.

Telephone Interviews.

Telephone interviewers are often mistaken for sales callers. The tone and content of the interviewer's introductory statement must provide reassurance; interviewers may have to spend a few more seconds convincing respondents that the study is genuine.

An alternative is to use prenotification by mail to overcome respondents' suspicions. In this case, the caller refers to the postcard or letter. Of course, if the person answering the telephone didn't see or hear about the prenotification, the problem remains.

Pretest your introduction, and make sure it conforms to patterns of local culture. In some communities, for example, first names are expected; but in Canada, for example, the use of first names by strangers often generates suspicion and hostility.

Conducting the Interview

Good interviewing is a combination of interpersonal skills, training, and experience. Here are some suggestions for making interviews easier for new and experienced interviewers alike.

Choosing Interviewers. Interviewers' race and gender can sometimes have an undesired effect on respondents' answers. Racial and gender differences have an impact for questions about issues related to the characteristic (such as racial attitudes or antifeminist sentiments). These differences also affect answers when respondents want to present a favorable image of themselves. Where there are no obvious differences, or the issues are irrelevant, respondents assume that interviewers hold opinions similar to their own.

The Interview Schedule. Select the largest size of paper that an interviewer can handle comfortably and fit onto a clipboard. Use both sides of each page, but don't try to crowd questions too much to save paper. Respondents worried about the length of an interview are encouraged when they see interviewers turning pages fairly regularly.

The Beginning. One or two open-ended questions at the beginning of an interview help create a rapport with the respondent and increase his or her commitment to the interview. They give the respondent a chance to express feelings and opinions. At the same time, they give the interviewer an opportunity to show that he or she is genuinely interested in what the respondent has to say and is not being critical or evaluating the respondent's remarks.

Opening questions should be easy to answer and general in focus. They should reassure the respondent that he or she will have little difficulty answering the coming questions. Avoid questions that might be embarrassing or to which respondents might not know the answer. Opening questions should also be clearly relevant to the subject of the study. Factual questions generally meet these objectives better than attitude questions. An exception is attitude questions on topics about which everyone has an opinion, such as food prices.

Maintaining Motivation and Data Quality. Once the interview is underway, the interviewer's objectives are to prevent a premature end to the interview and to get the best quality data possible.

To sustain the respondent's interest and motivation, keep in mind that respondents react both to the questions and to the interviewer. Experienced interviewers adopt a pleasant conversational manner that builds rapport and reassures the respondent that he or she will not be embarrassed or judged. Remove the threat of being unable to recall past behavior by prefacing questions with "Do you happen to know . . . ?" or "Can you recall offhand . . . ?" Also include "I don't know" as an answer category (Sudman and Bradburn, 1982).

To ensure data quality, experienced interviewers read each question as written (to minimize measurement error) and record answers to open ques-

SUGGESTION

Attach a **face sheet** to each interview schedule. The face sheet contains questions for the interviewer to complete, before and after the interview. For example,

- Information relevant to the final stage of field sampling (such as number of adults in the household)

- Information that might help assess whether response bias is a problem, such as type and size of home, evidence of children, nature of neighborhood, and so on

- Information on the number and timing of callbacks

- The respondent's telephone number for verification purposes

- Information to assess interviewer performance, such as time to complete interview, whether others were physically present during the interview, and what distractions were present (e.g., television or radio)

However, don't get carried away and burden interviewers with requests for more information than you will make use of.

BOX 12.3
MOVING SOUND: A CONTINUING CASE

Part Ten: Interview Rehearsals

"OK, pretend I've just walked up the steps into the bus."

"All right. Ahem. Excuse me, I'm with Moving Sound, and I wonder if I could just have a minute of your time."

"Hold the clipboard up so they can see it. Less threatening."

"All right. We're doing a short survey of customers . . ."

"No, wait. They might not be customers if they haven't bought anything yet, or it's their first visit. Better make that 'people who drop by today.' "

"We're doing a short survey of people who drop in today. Is this your first visit to the Moving Sound bus?"

Pete and George are on site devising the script for the mini-interviews. After a couple of minutes, Pete finishes the interview.

"So if you'll take the questionnaire home, fill it out and mail it back in this prepaid envelope, we'll enter your name in a draw for two free CDs of your choice. Three people who drop in today will win. Thanks again for your time, and enjoy shopping."

"That sounds pretty good, Pete. One important thing is not to speak too fast. And don't worry about being nervous. You'll get over it quickly. You'll probably start enjoying it."

"I think I can manage it. The instructions and routine are pretty clear."

"And I'll give you a hand training the other three interviewers. We do that on Tuesday, right?"

"Right. Tuesday at noon. Hamburgers are on me."

tions verbatim, or as close to verbatim as possible. When the respondent doesn't understand a question, the interviewer repeats it. Where an answer is ambiguous or suggests that the respondent is using an inappropriate frame of reference, interviewers probe to get accurate answers. Good probes are neutral—they don't suggest an evaluation of the respondent's answer, nor do they suggest that the interviewer is looking for a particular answer. They are also natural and conversational. (Reread the section on probing in Chapter 9.)

Inexperienced interviewers often read questions too quickly and don't give respondents enough time to think through their answers to more complex questions (Converse and Presser, 1986). Good interviewers pace themselves to avoid creating an impression of necessary haste. (In telephone interviews, even knowing that the call is long distance can pressure the respondent to hurry.) Rehearsals and practice are important (see Box 12.3).

Avoid burdening interviewers with the task of coding open questions during the interview. Save the coding for editors and coders. Complex skip patterns can also confuse interviewers and lead to accidental item nonresponse. Pretesting with interviewers can help identify potential skip pattern problems.

Interviewers must learn and practice how to remove distractions such as radio and television, how to discourage friends and relatives from sitting in on the interview, and how to handle interruptions. Further information on the strategy, techniques, and tactics of interviewing can be found in texts such as Gorden (1975).

Interview Length.   If an interview is too long, the potential respondent may refuse or break off the interview before completion. A common rule of thumb is that most personal interviews should last no more than an hour and telephone interviews no more than 15 minutes, *unless* there are other factors (such as a salient topic or incentives) to encourage participation and maintain interest.

Ending the Interview.   Interview schedules generally save personal demographic, sensitive, and potentially embarrassing questions until the end. One exception to this rule is a demographic question asked at the beginning for screening purposes. Another is long interviews. It is a mistake to wait until the respondent is fatigued before asking difficult questions. Instead, include them when rapport and trust have been established. Use pretests to find the best placement.

For interviews the use of a bridge to closing questions is useful and often necessary for restoring interest and getting accurate demographic and background data.

> *Finally, here are a few questions to ensure that our sample has a good cross-section of Americans (or Canadians or Californians or Albertans or Bostonians—select a region with which the respondent likely identifies).*

> *These final few questions will allow us to combine your answers with those of other similar participants.*

End with a request for general comments and opinions, followed by a thank you.

Personal Interviews.   In face-to-face interviews, the researcher must be sensitive to the possibility that a respondent may not be able to read well enough to handle a response card. To avoid embarrassing respondents, the first response card should be handed to the respondent while remarking,

> *Perhaps this card can help you with your answer. It lists the different answers you might give.*

This gives the respondent an opportunity to decline the response card. If he or she does, the interviewer should be sensitive to illiteracy or language problems. He or she should take time to read the response categories slowly and clearly, repeating them as necessary.

Taping an interview sounds like a good idea for neophyte interviewers, but the problems of getting the respondent's agreement, batteries, breakdowns, and changing tapes during sensitive questions are burdensome. Listening to the tapes is time consuming, and transcribing them can be fairly expensive. In

BOX 12.4
RESEARCH SKILLS

Interviewing with a Tape Recorder

If you decide to use a tape recorder, get the respondent's permission in as matter-of-fact manner as possible. Present the recording as something that is done routinely. Keep the explanation short, and move immediately to the interview. Use an introduction something like the following (adapted from Gorden, 1975):

(AS YOU SET IT UP . . .) We always record the interview so that the information will be accurate. I listen to it and type up the relevant material so that the tape can be used over *again. Shall we get started? (SHORT PAUSE) Now then, my first question is . . .*

Put the recorder on the floor out of sight of the respondent, so he or she isn't bothered by the sight of rotating spools or cassette spindles. Take care to place the microphone on a soft surface, facing more toward the respondent than to you and out of the direct line of sight. (Respondents will normally get used to the microphone very quickly and ignore it for the rest of the interview, as long as it doesn't move and doesn't make noise.)

most cases tape recording is not worth the trouble. Nevertheless, in-depth unstructured interviews may be recorded because of the prevalence of open-ended questions. Likewise, tape-recorded interviews are invaluable for training purposes and for monitoring improvements. See Box 12.4.

Interviewers should be careful of their nonverbal behavior. For example, fidgeting while the respondent ponders a question can create the impression that the interview is moving too slowly. Facial expressions can suggest that a response was unexpected or unwelcome.

The very last step is often a request for a telephone number and a name so that the interview can be validated. It is wise to part on good terms, in case a follow-up telephone call is needed to clarify some answer.

Telephone Interviews. One of the most important strategies for reducing nonresponse rates is to get through the first two minutes of the telephone interview. Keep the first few questions interesting, short, and fairly easy to answer. Save questions with more than two or three response categories for later in the interview.

The major problem confronting telephone interviewers is lack of control over the interview situation. Distractions such as radio and television can lead to measurement error and increased unreliability if respondents don't hear a question clearly or don't give much thought to their answers. If you hear background distraction, give respondents an opportunity to turn it off or move to another extension.

Another problem that telephone interviewers face is the pause to write down an answer. Respondents, unable to see what the interviewer is doing, may continue to talk and wander off topic. On the other hand, if the interviewer asks them to wait while he or she writes down an answer, the respondents' attention may wane. The best solution is to develop a personal shorthand to record answers and to use as many closed-ended questions as possible.

SURVEY ISSUES AND PROBLEMS

Now we discuss some of the issues and problems faced in survey research. Precoding addresses the cost problem, and pretesting the data quality problem. Other topics addressed here are coping with refusals, respondent identification (placing identifying information on questionnaires), and the problems of surveying organizational informants. We end with a consideration of ethical issues raised whenever people are asked about their feelings and behaviors.

Precoding

One of the major time-saving devices in survey instrument layout is to utilize precoding. This practice makes it possible to keypunch data into the computer directly from the interview schedule or questionnaire, avoiding the intermediate step of coding forms. See Box 12.5.

Pretesting Surveys

Chapter 8 discussed the pretesting of measures in general terms. We now examine some issues particularly relevant to pretesting in surveys.

Surveys require pretesting of (1) question form and content, (2) the instrument as a whole, and (3) survey procedures. Two kinds of field pretests are useful:

- A "participating" pretest in which respondents know that they're in a trial run and are invited to comment on the questions, instrument, and procedures (Converse and Presser, 1986).

- A regular pretest that duplicates as closely as possible the conditions and respondents you expect to find in the field (Box 12.6).

Question Content.   Check question content to ensure that measurement error is kept to a minimum. This includes validity, reliability, and bias. Use the criteria discussed in Chapter 9: clarity, specificity, appropriate language, emphasis, simplicity, brevity, neutrality, and relevance.

A very useful pretesting technique is to give respondents alternate wordings for the same question. Ask what difference the wordings make to their interpretation of and answer to the question.

BOX 12.5
RESEARCH SKILLS

Precoding Closed-Ended Questions

For data analysis, each answer to a question is converted to a number or code (e.g., for a question about union membership, "No" = 0 and "Yes" = 1). Prior to data analysis, the researcher constructs the coding rules and records them in a codebook. (Codebook preparation is discussed in Chapter 13.)

The normal coding procedure is that coders read each completed questionnaire or interview and enter the appropriate code numbers on coding sheets. These sheets are then given to keypunchers for data entry.

However, *precoding* bypasses the coding procedure for closed-ended questions. The codes that correspond to each possible answer are printed directly on the questionnaire or interview. Keypunchers enter the designated code number directly from the instrument. If an answer is ambiguous or open-ended, an editor writes the correct code directly on the instrument prior to data entry.

Precoding can be done two ways. For either option, print the data matrix column number(s) corresponding to each question on the far right side of the page. This helps keypunchers put the codes in the correct columns. (This step is not necessary if keypunchers use data entry software that enters codes by question number or variable name, such as SPSS/PC+ Data Entry.)

1. Print the code numbers next to the response categories. Respondents circle the appropriate number. Keypunchers enter the circled number.

How do you feel about your job?   (22)

(PLEASE CIRCLE THE NUMBER BESIDE THE ANSWER CLOSEST TO YOUR FEELINGS)

very satisfied	5
somewhat satisfied	4
so-so	3
somewhat dissatisfied	2
very dissatisfied	1
no opinion	9

Note that the code numbers don't have to appear in sequence from "1" up. In this example they correspond naturally to the amount of satisfaction.

2. Alternatively, print the code numbers next to the check boxes. Keypunchers enter the number next to the checked box.

How do you feel about your job?   (22)

very satisfied	[ ]$_5$
somewhat satisfied	[ ]$_4$
so-so	[ ]$_3$
somewhat dissatisfied	[ ]$_2$
very dissatisfied	[ ]$_1$
no opinion	[ ]$_9$

As shown in this example, the numbers for a questionnaire are small so that respondents aren't confused. It also helps to add a note at the beginning of the questionnaire stating that the numbers are for administrative purposes only and should be ignored.

Question Form. Also check that the form of each question enhances understanding and readability and minimizes recording errors. You may have to reorder the items in a response format or break a long question into two sentences.

BOX 12.6
CAMPBELL SWITCH: A CONTINUING CASE

Part Fifteen: Pretesting

"Say, George, you're quite the cook!" Roberta takes another large bite of muffin. "What did you say was in this?"

George beams. "Kelp. Kelp and bran."

Roberta pales and gags slightly.

"They should really keep us going," George adds. "Now, we were talking about who's going to pretest our survey. How about I try it on a few people here at the office, and you try some outsiders. Maybe some of your friends at the squash club."

Roberta gives a muffled groan.

"Well, if you don't like that, we could switch. The important thing is to try the form on someone who doesn't know anything about the plant."

Roberta waves her arms wildly.

"OK, I'll do the outsiders. And since time is short, I think after that we should go directly to a few employees."

Roberta swallows. "Kelp? Kelp?" she asks incredulously.

"Good, isn't it? But help me with this. Which employees should we pretest the questionnaire on? I don't think that we should try it at Ajax. It's a small plant, and anyway everyone there is really sensitive about this thing."

Roberta takes a gulp of coffee. "Whew! I don't believe it!"

"You don't think they're sensitive about all this?"

"That's not what I meant. But you're right. So the solution is to pretest it here. Concord is a much bigger plant, we've got over 1,500 employees here. Let's find out from Ryan which department here has had some trouble recently, and we'll pretest there."

"Say, that sounds good. I'm seeing Ryan later this morning and I'll check with him. Now let's go over the pretesting procedures."

"Fine, George. But next time, don't give me a muffin I haven't pretested."

Instrument.   The layout of the instrument as a whole (questionnaire or interview schedule) should also be checked during pretesting. Is it easy to read or too cluttered? Do earlier questions provide inappropriate frames of reference for later ones? Is the instrument too long or too boring to maintain respondents' interest and commitment? Are the skip patterns obvious and clear?

Procedures and Process.   Finally, pay attention to the entire measurement process, from introduction to conclusion. Look for unanticipated problems. Do interviewers use screening questions properly? Are respondents reasonably clear about the purpose of the research and the anonymity or confidentiality of their responses? At the end, do they feel satisfied with the experience? Time how long it takes respondents to finish the interview or questionnaire.

Pretesting Questionnaires.   For the participating pretest, have respondents complete the questionnaire while you sit nearby. Encourage them to think out loud about the questions as they answer them. Take notes in the margins of your own copy of the instrument. If you cannot be present, ask respondents to write their reactions to items on the questionnaire itself.

Your distribution and collection procedures may also require pretesting if you use other than mail-out and mail-back methods.

Pretesting Interviews. Check the entire interview process, paying particular attention to how answers are recorded. Do interviewers need spare pencils? Are the clipboards too long or too short? Is the tape recorder obtrusive or picking up too much background noise? Do you need to add probe reminders for certain questions?

Interviewers are often required to carry out the last stage of a multistage sampling design while in the field. For example, if lists of employees at selected McDonald's restaurants are not centrally available, interviewers will have to make a random selection of employees from a list supplied on the spot by each restaurant manager. These *field sampling* procedures must be pretested to ensure that they run smoothly, the instructions are clear, interviewers know how to list cases and use their random number tables (or other random selection devices), and substitutions are kept to a minimum.

For the participating pretest, follow each question with a probe to elicit the respondent's interpretation of the question and frame of reference. Sudman and Bradburn (1982) suggest,

What did you think we meant when we asked that question?

(This technique is similar to the random probes discussed in Chapter 9.)

Note respondent's reactions: interest, fatigue, boredom, or hostility. At the end, ask what the interview was like and what they thought of it. This postinterview debriefing will elicit more frank opinions if carried out by someone other than the original interviewer.

Each pretest interviewer should conduct several test interviews (four or five as a minimum) to avoid undue emphasis on one particular and unrepresentative experience. Have interviewers make lots of comments in the margins as they work their way through the pretest.

Nonresponse Bias

Among the general population, refusal rates for surveys have increased substantially in the past few years.

- Response rates for personal interview surveys of the general population are now normally around 70 percent, and considerably less in urban areas.

- Response rates for general population questionnaires can be as low as 10 percent.

Together with the problem of noncontacts (e.g., respondents who have moved, are away on vacation, have left their jobs), the growing tendency to refuse an interview or questionnaire presents a sizable threat of nonresponse bias.

Replacement Cases.

When researchers using personal or telephone interviews can't contact a sample person or can't persuade one to participate, they often add another respondent to the sample in order to maintain the desired sample size and to compensate for possible nonresponse bias. However, the process of adding a replacement case is more complicated than it seems, since it often doesn't eliminate the nonresponse bias.

To see why, imagine a survey of a firm's employees, half of whom are women. You initially try for a sample of 64. When contacted, men agree to take part, but half the women decline because of family and other responsibilities. Your first achieved sample consists of 32 males, 16 females, and 16 refusals (all female). You randomly draw another 16 employees (half are women). Of these, once again half the women and none of the men decline, for a second achieved sample of 40 males, 20 females, and 4 refusals. If you continue, the most likely sample you end up with is 43 males and 21 females, a far cry from their equal proportions in the population. The nonresponse bias persists, *even though you randomly drew replacement cases.*

Similarly, a replacement procedure that seems at first a commonsense way of reducing nonresponse may actually contribute to nonresponse bias. For example, if an employee isn't available to be interviewed, selecting a replacement from among nearby employees in the same department will bias the sample by underrepresenting employees who are more likely to be absent. The reasons for the absence may be relevant to your research; such employees may be more likely to be ill or to be suspended for disciplinary reasons, for example. Even drawing the name of a replacement employee randomly will also result in an underrepresentation of the type of missed employee.

A better procedure is to select a replacement that matches as closely as possible the refusal or noncontact case. This means that interviewers must get as much information as possible about such cases: age, gender, employment status, occupation, income, and other relevant variables.

However, you still don't know if you're matching on variables related to the nonresponse bias. For example, you may match replacements on gender, age, education, and income, but if the refusal is related to ethnic background, you'll still suffer the nonresponse bias—fewer cases with certain ethnic backgrounds.

Researchers who increase the sample size of a questionnaire survey to reduce nonresponse bias are making the same mistake. Increases to sample size can only overcome random nonresponse and reduce sampling error. They do *not* repair nonresponse bias.

The most acceptable procedure for reducing nonresponse bias is to *try to secure data from (or about) each case in the initial sample.* This includes carefully planning the initial contact, arranging for callbacks and reminders, and making participation as painless as possible. For questionnaires, use the techniques just described to maximize participation. For interviews, pay attention to the initial contact and the measurement operation, and fine-tune it to encourage cooperation and reduce refusals. If respondents cannot be contacted on the first attempt, try the now standard procedure of a minimum of three or four callbacks at different times of day on different days of the week.

Timing.   For both questionnaires and interview surveys, use common sense in timing the survey; consider the work, holiday, and budget cycles of respondents. Don't send out questionnaires to managers at the end of the fiscal year; don't survey employees during periods of heavy overtime or when a strike may be pending. Don't survey anyone close to or during holidays.

Assessing Nonresponse Bias.   An important step for the survey researcher who wants to combat nonresponse bias is to estimate its extent and how much it threatens external validity. Box 12.7 discusses this question; actual details for evaluating sample representativeness are given in Chapter 14.

ADVANCED TOPIC

Analyzing Late Returns.   An alternative procedure is to assume that respondents who return their questionnaires late are more like refusals than those who return them early. Therefore, you can get a rough idea of the extent and nature of nonresponse bias by comparing early with later returns. By coding the date received for each case, you can regress potentially biased variables on time to see whether any trends show up in the data.

The problems with this procedure are the neglect of noncontacts and the weakness of the initial assumption. It is possible that refusers are qualitatively different from both those who return questionnaires promptly and those who delay. The technique is probably more valid when the researcher has used follow-ups and reminders (as long as the questionnaire doesn't evoke a lot of hostility).

Confidentiality and Respondent Identification

Researchers often want questionnaires returned in a way that maintains confidentiality but not anonymity. In other words, the researcher needs to know who the questionnaire is from, but doesn't want others to be able to get this information. Reasons for confidential respondent identification include

- Sending targeted reminders to those who have not returned questionnaires.

- Matching questionnaire data with information from other data sources.

BOX 12.7
RESEARCH SKILLS

Estimating Nonresponse Bias

The extent of nonresponse bias should be estimated whenever possible, since you can then take steps to counteract it or, at the least, qualify your conclusions. Nonresponse bias in interview surveys can often be reasonably well estimated. Questionnaire surveys present more difficulties.

INTERVIEW SURVEYS

If the field interviewer can obtain some information about nonresponding cases, researchers can often assess the threat of nonresponse bias. For each refusal and noncontact, the interviewer notes or asks about demographic and other relevant characteristics, and perhaps even the reasons for refusal.

- The residence may show signs of the presence of children, and the dwelling unit and neighborhood will allow rough estimates of income.
- Other members of the family, or even neighbors, may be able to provide basic information.
- In other cases it may be feasible to telephone refusal cases to get demographic or other relevant data related to nonresponse.

As long as interviewers record the same information for every completed interview, these data can be analyzed to determine whether there are any systematic differences between respondents and nonrespondents. Researchers using interview surveys can also follow the same procedure recommended for questionnaire surveys.

QUESTIONNAIRE SURVEYS

The best alternative for researchers using questionnaires is the following procedure:

1. Estimate what variables relevant to the study might be associated with nonresponse, for example, ethnic background or race, employment status, or organization size.
2. Wherever possible, obtain the frequency distributions in the target population for these variables and for basic demographic characteristics. Census documents are a good source of demographic information; payroll records provide information about employees; industry associations often collect information about firms.
3. Include in the questionnaire one or more items to gather the *same* information.
4. When data gathering is complete, compare distributions of the achieved sample and the target population on these variables. The extent of the differences is an indicator of nonresponse bias.
5. If the discrepancy seems to be relevant to the topic of the research, you can adjust the sample to give more weight to the responses of cases in underrepresented groups. (Details of such weighting are given in Chapter 14.)

One major problem with this method is that it is often difficult to obtain information about the target population to compare with the sample, particularly if the target population is not defined in common demographic terms. For example, there is no easy way to determine the gender ratio of purchasers of frozen fish.

Another is that even if the achieved sample appears representative for the characteristics you have tested, you can't be certain that it isn't biased on other unmeasured characteristics of importance to the research. Similarly, knowing the nonresponse bias on one variable does not mean that similar levels of bias exist for other variables. Nevertheless, some evidence that a sample is representative is better than none, and some indication of *how* it is unrepresentative should help the researcher to add appropriate limitations to the conclusions.

Identification Methods. There are several methods for making respondent identifications. The most straightforward is to enter the respondent's name on the questionnaire itself.

CASE EXAMPLE

A study of collective bargaining relationships mailed questionnaires to union and management informants. Names and addresses were obtained through prior telephone calls to each employer and then to the appropriate union local representing its employees. Because of the importance of matching union and management and having each respondent discuss the same round of negotiations, it was decided to affix to each questionnaire a label with the name and address of the respondent, the name of the company and the union local, and the year and month of settlement.

This procedure, however, may upset or alarm some respondents and reduce response rates, particularly in employee surveys. Some employees may not trust their supervisor with a questionnaire, even in a sealed envelope. One solution is to have respondents return them to the researcher by public or office mail rather than through the supervisor.

Another technique is to assign a code number to each respondent and enter the code on the questionnaire. The bottom of the last page is least obtrusive; the top of the first page is most convenient for the researcher. Most respondents are not troubled by such codes, since they suggest that care is being taken to keep their identities confidential.

If you only want to send targeted reminders, a third option is to ask respondents to return both the unidentified questionnaire and an identifying card. To emphasize anonymity, ask respondents to mail the stamped response card separately from the questionnaire. Some cards will be returned without questionnaires and vice versa, but the technique is better than no identification of respondents.

CASE EXAMPLE

A mailed questionnaire survey combined the identification of respondents with an incentive. With each questionnaire a small card was included. On one side was a name and address label (identical to the one on the envelope in which the questionnaire was sent to the respondent). On the other was printed,

> *Here is my completed questionnaire.*
> *Please enter my name in the draw for*
> *free passes to Canada's Wonderland*
> *Amusement Park.*

In the cover letter, respondents were instructed to return the card either with the questionnaire or in a separate envelope if they wished. From among the returned cards ten would be drawn and the recipients would receive free passes to a major amusement park. From her original sample list the researcher checked off the names from returned cards to determine to whom to send reminders.

Research suggests that response rates for general population surveys are not significantly affected by respondent identification on the questionnaire (although it might affect the actual content of responses for sensitive questions). However, there is some indication that questionnaire surveys of organization informants have lower response rates when questionnaires show respondent codes. This is particularly true when the code number is written instead of typed, perhaps because the writing looks more obvious or less professional.

Covert Identification. If you don't want respondent identification to be apparent, there are several covert ways of identifying questionnaires. One is to mark the edges of the paper lightly with a felt marker. Such marks are hard to notice. There are fourteen easily identified mark positions on each sheet (three along the top and bottom; four on each side). Treating the positions as a binary code (mark or no mark) allows slightly over 16,000 unique markings. Other techniques include invisible ink and codes disguised as other numbers (e.g., embedding the number in the phrase "Return to Room Number . . .").

Any identification procedure raises the ethical question of potential harm to respondents, as well as legal problems concerning the divulging of personal information. Before you use it, you must check the legal requirements in your jurisdiction and consider ways to protect respondents' identities and the consequences if your methods become known. See Box 12.8.

Surveying Organizational Informants

Business researchers often use questionnaires or interviews to obtain information about departments or other administrative subunits from strategically placed members. The researcher's principal problem is to choose the best informant from each unit.

BOX 12.8

RESEARCH ETHICS

Three Ethical Issues in Surveys

1. Informed Consent. The principle of *informed consent* is important to survey ethics. Respondents have a right to know the content or topic of your survey and the right to refuse to participate if they object to its true purpose.

If informed consent is not possible because knowledge of the study's purpose might bias responses, a disguised purpose is acceptable provided you adhere to the principle of *accepted risk* (as described in Chapter 1). Employees expect and accept that employers should know their home addresses and social security numbers; they do not accept that it is the employers' (or anyone's) business to know their sexual habits and religious beliefs, unless they choose to make them known.

Beware, however, of overemphasizing the ethical obligations. Elaborate descriptions of the research purpose and the opportunities for refusing to participate raise unfounded suspicions and fears. A worthwhile middle ground advocated by Singer (1978) is to include in the introduction a brief statement such as,

> *Naturally, this interview is totally voluntary, and if you don't want to answer a particular question, just tell me and we'll pass over it.*

There is no corresponding common practice in questionnaire surveys, but the pressures to participate are very much weaker, so the problem of right to refuse is seldom an issue.

2. Confidentiality and Anonymity. Having promised confidentiality (or anonymity), make sure that you keep that promise. Ensure that data are not available to unauthorized persons and that they are not misused.

Questionnaires (or identifying codes) should be kept safely locked up when not in use. If necessary, remove identifying information by using code or identification numbers, and guard any papers linking numbers to respondents. At the end of the study, this linking information should be destroyed. This doesn't mean, of course, that the data have to be destroyed, just so long as the identifying information is.

Guarding respondent identities is particularly important for repeated-measure surveys, such as panel designs, where identifying information is essential and data may be retained for several years.

3. Contact Effects. Researchers conducting personal or telephone interviews have direct contact with the individuals who are ultimately the sources of data. (For questionnaire surveys the contact is more indirect.) This direct contact raises the issues of invasion of respondents' privacy and the anxiety provoked by sensitive questions.

Some respondents find stressful the invasion of privacy that an interview represents. Unlike questionnaires, which they can simply discard, an interviewer is a real person the respondent has to deal with. The interviewer exerts social pressure solely by his or her presence (in person or on the telephone).

To avoid surprise and embarrassment, interviewers must prepare respondents for the questions they are going to ask. They must also explain the necessity of asking for personal and private information, such as family income. The respondent's option of declining to answer these or any questions must be made clear to avoid unnecessary pressure.

Researchers should emulate the injunction given to medical students: Above all, do no harm! The measurement operation must leave respondents in no worse condition than they were initially. Questions that raise anxiety levels (e.g., about socially deviant behavior such as industrial sabotage or unpleasant personal experiences such as unemployment) must be handled with care. If possible, hire a psychologist for half a day to train interviewers in rudimentary therapy to know when to let respondents talk to relieve anxiety, and when and how to gracefully postpone or terminate interviews to avoid harming respondents.

Locating Informants. Good informants meet two criteria:

- They have access to the necessary information.

- They are sufficiently motivated to gather and provide that information.

To select informants, learn enough about each unit to be able to identify strategically located positions. Normally the higher their positions in their units, the more data informants can provide. However, high-level informants may not be in a position to describe the typical perceptions or feelings of lower level members. If necessary, use prenotification telephone calls to locate the best informants, and then send them the questionnaire or schedule an interview.

To motivate informants, provide them with information about the study, its purpose, and its sponsor. Point out how the topic might be of interest and the findings useful to the informant and his or her unit. Ensure that survey questions are pertinent to the research topic and unnecessary or irrelevant questions are deleted or skipped.

Measurement Mode. Another problem in surveys of organizational informants is the choice of measurement mode. Compared to questionnaires, personal interviews make it more difficult for informants to decline requests for information. On the other hand, it is awkward to interrupt an interview (personal or telephone) while the respondent looks up an answer to your question. Decide on measurement mode on the basis of how much record checking you want the informants to do (e.g., production records) and how readily accessible the records are likely to be.

Some suggestions:

- In an interview, use a few early questions to establish that you're talking to the right person, that is, one with access to the information you want.

- In an questionnaire, ask for the informant's position in the organization in order to assess his or her quality as a data source.

- For both questionnaires and interviews, arrange to telephone later for further information should the need arise.

- Sudman and Bradburn (1982) suggest that the threat to the informant of appearing ignorant can be reduced by prefacing factual questions with,

Do you happen to know . . .

Can you recall, offhand . . .

- For data questions (e.g., number of female employees; turnover rate; sales figures) use open-ended questions rather than categories. This produces more accurate data and avoids position bias.

Multiple Informants. At some increase in costs, you can improve the reliability of responses by surveying two or three informants from each organization or unit. Combine their answers to get your measures. If you uncover major discrepancies, recontact the respondents for clarification, or otherwise judge each case on an individual basis. Try to determine which respondent is in the best position to know, and which seems to have provided the more complete and accurate data. For some variables, you may have to average the answers.

Ethical Issues

Because data is obtained directly from individuals, surveys encounter ethical problems to a greater degree than available data studies and of a different nature from field experiments. In particular, three ethical issues require attention: informed consent, confidentiality and anonymity, and contact effects. All three are discussed in Box 12.8.

■ *The Lighter Side of Research*

Public opinion and the weather are equally hard to predict, and equally changeable.

—Anonymous

Market survey: An opportunity to spend hundreds of hours and thousands of dollars to find out that there is very little you can do, except perhaps to conduct another survey.

Employee survey: A means of discovering that employees won't tell you what you most need to know.

Summary

The three types of surveys (questionnaire, personal interview, and telephone interview) differ in important respects. Questionnaires are the cheapest and are particularly good for sensitive questions and information the respondent has to look up. Personal interviews are best for complex topics and for research needing high response rates. Telephone interviews are the choice when time is short. Computer-assisted telephone interview systems allow researchers to carry out telephone surveys very quickly and to use complicated question and skip patterns.

Questionnaires, personal interviews, and telephone interviews are prone to different kinds of errors. Questionnaire studies are highest on measurement error and nonresponse bias (refusals and noncontacts). Personal interviews tend to be highest in sampling error. Telephone interviews are most likely to be affected by unmeasured variables, particularly uncontrolled variation affecting the dependent variable.

Questionnaires can be distributed by mail, in person, by self-selection, with products or magazines, or administered to groups of respondents. The cover letter is an important part of the questionnaire. It must tell respondents what the survey is about and answer their questions while motivating respondents to complete the questionnaire and answer questions completely and accurately. The two most important ways of increasing questionnaire response rates are reminders and making the topic salient to respondents.

Interview surveys can contact respondents cold or use preliminary telephone calls or mailings. The introduction to the survey and (for personal interviews) the appearance of the interviewer are important for reducing nonresponse and motivating respondents. Interviews should begin with simple open-ended questions to help interviewers build rapport and trust.

Precoding is an important technique for reducing survey costs. Pretesting is vital for reducing measurement error and nonresponse. Pretests should be conducted with both participating and regular respondents and should include question form and content, the overall instrument, and other survey procedures.

Where Are We Now?

This completes our examination of measurement and data-gathering methodologies. In the fourth and final section of the text we turn to the question of what to do with the data we've gathered: data preparation, analysis, and reporting.

Discussion Issues and Assignments

1. Devise three research plans and designs using each of the three major methodologies to test the following idea: "Those professors most vulnerable to having courses canceled for lack of student interest (which would mean their teaching other courses they found less interesting) are most likely to develop 'sexy' course titles or offer other inducements to maintain sufficiently high enrollments."

2. Look through marketing, accounting, or other business or organizational research journals, and find two examples of research reports based on available data. Determine whether, and how, this research could have been carried out with a survey or field experiment methodology.

3. Contact several marketing or consumer research firms, and ask for copies of the materials they use to train telephone or personal interviewers. Compare how well their training procedures appear to deal with measurement error problems and missing data problems.

4. If you wanted to survey your fellow students about their grades in various courses and how those grades might be related to career plans, which type of survey would you use, and why?

5. Conduct three in-depth, unstructured interviews of other students (preferably ones with whom you are unacquainted). Discover what factors and feelings underlie their choice of optional courses. Before the interviews, construct a rough interview schedule of the topics you want to cover. Decide how you want to record their answers. Afterward, compare your findings with those of others in the class.

6. Using the questionnaire designed to gather student opinions on "The best methods for assessing student performance and assigning grades" (question 5 in Chapter 9), vary two factors thought to affect response rates (paper color or size, appeal to help fellow students in their research, distribution method [hand out in class or at the door as students leave the class], return method, questionnaire length). Compare the return rates. Which of your two factors has the most impact on rates?

Further Reading

Dillman, D. A. 1978. *Mail and Telephone Surveys: The Total Design Method.* New York: Wiley-Interscience.

> Dillman's work covers survey procedures from the point of view of maximizing response rates and data quality. Lots of practical advice.

Gorden, R. L. 1975. *Interviewing: Strategies, Techniques, and Tactics.* Homewood, IL: Dorsey.

> This is an excellent review of methods for interviewing based on a theoretical model of the interview as dyadic communication.

Groves, R. M., and R. L. Kahn. 1979. *Surveys by Telephone: A National Comparison with Personal Interviews.* New York: Academic Press.

> The classic comparison of these two survey alternatives. Very useful if you're using either type of interview.

Miller, D. C. 1991. *Handbook of Research Design and Social Measurement* (5th ed.). Newbury Park, CA: Sage.

> Latest edition of a classic resource for survey research. Miller covers all facets of a survey project.

Rossi, P. H., J. D. Wright, and A. B. Anderson. 1983. *Handbook of Survey Research.* New York: Academic Press.

> An excellent source for more advanced reading on a wide variety of topics related to survey research, including measurement and sampling, administering the data collection, and analysis.

PART FOUR

Data Analysis and Reporting

The techniques of preparing and analyzing data and reporting the findings and recommendations.

CHAPTER 13

Data Preparation

CHAPTER OBJECTIVES

- What happens once the raw data start arriving on your desk?
- How is nonnumeric information converted to numbers?
- How are data entered into your computer?
- What checks can you make for data quality?

CHAPTER OUTLINE

DATA ADMINISTRATION
THE CODEBOOK
EDITING AND CODING
DATA ENTRY
DATA CLEANING

*A*s data begin to accumulate, newcomers to research commonly feel both excitement and dismay. It's rewarding to see all those questionnaires or available data collection forms (or even that diskette containing financial information on corporate mergers!)—these are the results of your design and data-gathering efforts. But what do you do with them? Where do statistics come in? What do you test, and how? What do you do with the results?

Chapters 13 through 18 deal with these questions. They lay out a step-by-step systematic procedure for organizing and analyzing data to produce a report of valid and relevant results in the shortest possible time.

The six chapters divide data analysis into three steps:

- Data preparation

- Preliminary and descriptive analysis

- Analysis of relationships

This chapter discusses the first stage. Chapters 14 and 15 deal with the second step: preliminary and descriptive analysis. The analysis of relationships is covered in Chapters 16 and 17, while chapter 18 ties it all together in the final report.

Before we turn to the particulars of data preparation, it's worthwhile taking a look at the major research tool you'll be using in this stage of your research: your computer. Large organizations may have a mainframe computer that many users share, or perhaps departments have their own mini mainframe. However, in the last few years individual microcomputers have become increasingly important in business research.

As noted in Chapter 1, this increasing use of microcomputers in the office has led many managers to undertake their own in-house research projects. Managers typically begin by using their micros for such tasks as accounting and payroll, spreadsheets, database management, sales and inventory control, and word processing. As they grow used to doing their own computing, they look for new tasks for these tools and turn to business research.

The trend to in-house business research is also due to new developments in user-friendly statistical analysis software for microcomputers. Some of these packages have enormous power and convenience features previously available only on large mainframe computers. (A package is a set of programs that run a variety of statistical procedures and has the capacity for merging and aggregating data files.)

Business research on micros offers time and convenience. Because mainframe computing facilities tend to be centralized, access for small-scale, informal business research projects is often inconvenient and limited. There is usually paperwork to complete and approvals to obtain, as well as a time lag between requesting a job and receiving the results. Personal microcomputers are much more accessible, and the paperwork required to get results is minimal or nonexistent. Results are available in seconds or minutes, rather than days or weeks.

A second advantage is that the analysis can be integrated with other programs. Data can be fed in from database and spreadsheet files. Statistical results and tables can be transferred to a word processing program or graphics package for editing into reports. (All the examples of computer output in this text have been edited with a word processor; see Figure 13.3 on page 484 for an example.)

A further advantage is ease and flexibility. Good statistical packages can be run *interactively*. Thus instead of submitting a batch job and waiting for the results before running the next program, the user is in conversational communication with the computer, can enter one command at a time, and can get an immediate response. Furthermore, the best packages provide extensive documentation that offers instruction in both the use of the software and statistics. Some packages include an on-line help facility, which uses the computer itself to answer the user's questions and provide help.

As a result of these features, managers are finding that they and their assistants can carry out their own business research projects, including the data analysis.

In addition to your computer, you'll need a statistical software package to carry out the data analysis (see Box 13.1).

The data analysis examples in this text were carried out with SPSS/PC + and STATPAC GOLD. (The first is a large and powerful statistical package for microcomputers, with many features of specific interest to the business user. The second is a smaller and less expensive package that is still flexible and user friendly.)

DATA ADMINISTRATION

Whatever your methodology, data preparation begins with the collected raw data sitting in front of you. Typically, they consist of one or more of the following:

- A diskette or computer data tape containing available data

- A pile of completed interview schedules

- A stack of returned questionnaires

- A heap of data collection forms with information from researcher observations or available data sources

Alternatively, your data may already be in your computer as a database or spreadsheet, or you can transfer them there directly through telephone lines or a local area network.

BOX 13.1
FOCUS ON RESEARCH

Selecting Statistical Software

The microcomputer software available for statistical analysis differs sharply from what was available a few years ago. No longer are these packages designed only for the statistically sophisticated scientific user. Current software packages make it possible to analyze data in a range of ways, from the simple to the highly refined and complex. The documentation is written so that you don't need a great deal of statistical or computing experience.

Over 200 separate statistics packages are available for microcomputers. The software you select should meet most or all of the following criteria:

1. It offers a range of statistical procedures, including the ones you feel you are most likely to use. (Check Chapters 15, 16, and 17.)

2. Documentation explains how to use both the software and the statistical procedures and is easy to use (an extensive index is a great help).

3. Package includes an on-line help facility.

4. Package includes an on-line tutorial.

5. Documentation includes many examples of the output results of statistical procedures.

6. Package has its own editing system for writing and changing commands.

7. It can import data from other software files, such as spreadsheets and database programs.

8. Printing of results can be tailored to provide camera-ready copy for reports. It should also have graphics capabilities to translate results to bar charts, line graphs, and so on.

9. Procedures can be executed interactively.

10. Package allows you to match and merge multiple files (especially useful when your data are coming from two or more sources, for example, personnel and payroll).

11. Procedures allow you to analyze questions with multiple responses (for example, "Which three of the following statements best describe your job? . . .").

Software that meets these criteria is likely to be particularly useful for business research. Other factors to consider include the speed and cost of the software. Programs that work with a math coprocessor chip run more quickly. Prices range from a few hundred dollars to over $2,000 for a complete package.

(For further information see Schervish, 1988, and the review articles that appear regularly in microcomputer publications.)

To prepare these data for computer analysis involves some or all of the following nine tasks:

1. Screen the cases.

2. Assign an identification number to each case.

3. Make the logbook entry.

4. Do the initial check.

5. Prepare codebook.

6. Edit.

7. Code.

8. Enter data into computer.

9. Verify and clean the data.

The first three steps are administrative. The fourth is a quality control measure. These four steps should be carried out as soon as each case is complete. The remaining five are all concerned with the transition from paper to computer. The data preparation phase ends with clean data in the computer, ready for analysis.

Available data studies usually omit the first four steps, and field experiments the first three. Surveys may require all nine.

Screening

In a questionnaire survey, your sample may contain cases that lie outside your target population if your sampling frame doesn't correspond exactly with the group you want. For example, you want regular employees but your sample also contains employees still on a 90-day initial probationary period. The questionnaire will contain a *screening question* to help you identify inapplicable cases. Screen out these cases as soon as possible. Don't waste time correcting them or entering their data into the computer.

Common sense and planning ahead make questionnaire screening easier. For example, if you want to reject questionnaires from respondents younger than age 20 or older than 65, it helps to have the year of birth screening question in an easily accessible place, such as the top of the last page.

In interview surveys and available data studies, screening normally takes place as the data are gathered or, in the case of computer data sets, as part of preliminary computer analysis. In field experiments, screening out inapplicable cases is normally part of the case selection procedure.

ID Numbers

Each case must have a unique identification number (ID). For surveys, add an ID number to each case after you've screened it. Available data often come with their own ID numbers; field experiments usually assign ID numbers as the data are collected.

ID numbers are the link between the computer data and the raw data. You'll need them for several purposes:

- If data cleaning uncovers cases with unusual or invalid codes, you'll need the ID to get back to the questionnaire or data collection form for checking.

- Selecting subsamples from your sample for reliability tests.

- Choosing a few cases to test recodes and newly computed variables.

ID numbers also help to protect data source confidentiality in case unauthorized persons access your computer files.

Numbering. ID numbering should start at 01 or 001 or 0001 (depending on the total number of cases you have). When you have distinct groups, subsamples, or strata, a useful practice is to add a digit to the beginning of the ID to indicate which subsample or sample stratum a case comes from. For example, all cases from the sample of hostile takeovers begin with the number "1" (e.g., 1001, 1002, etc.), and cases from the sample of friendly mergers begin with "2." As you sort or thumb though the cases, this will make it easy to separate them into groups or samples.

In panel and pooled time-series designs, it is useful to add "measurement time" digits to the end of the case ID to identify each observation of each case. For example, with 12 different cases each measured annually from 1942 to 1989, ID numbers for observations of the third case would be 0342, 0343, 0344, . . . 0389.

Existing Computer Files. When data are to be transferred directly from computer to computer, omitting the paper stage, cases may already have unique identification numbers (for example, personnel or employee numbers). If so, transfer those numbers, as well as the other variables, and use them as IDs. If there are no such identifiers, you may be able to use your statistical software to assign an ID to each case automatically.

Logbook Entry

Surveys with identifiable respondents use a logbook to record which questionnaires have been returned or interviews completed. Available data studies and field experiments seldom require logbooks. The logbook indicates which cases require reminders or callbacks.

Initial Check

As soon as possible, carry out an initial check of each case. If you find errors, you may still be able to get back to the data source to correct the mistake or resolve the ambiguity. In particular, look for data that seem to be unreasonable (e.g., a birthdate of 1896), missing data, illegible words, and marks that can't be interpreted.

Available Data. Data transferred from files and records should be checked over before you leave the data site. A quick scan of your data-gathering forms will show you values that appear to be out of the ordinary and marks that you cannot decipher. Data forms should also be checked (by a different person, if possible) after screening, identifying, and logging.

SUGGESTION

If questionnaires or interviews consist of two or more sheets stapled together, mark the ID in felt-tip pen in the top left-hand corner, close to the staple. Store the questionnaires with the stapled corner uppermost. This will make it much easier to find the case you want as you thumb through a stack of them.

SUGGESTION

If you use computer-printed labels for mailing the questionnaires, print a duplicate list of the labels and use it as a logbook. This makes it easy to mark off questionnaires as they are returned, so that you can send reminders out as needed.

SUGGESTION

Make a flow chart of how to handle questionnaires when they are returned from a mail survey. For example,
  Open envelope.

  Staple together loose questionnaire sheets. Staple any notes, letters or other accompanying material to the questionnaire.

Check confidential code and note return in logbook.

Check screening questions and whether key questions answered.
  If screened out, put in "Not Usable" box.
  If more than 3 key questions unanswered, put in "Not Usable" box.

If usable, enter ID number (in sequence) on top left corner. Pass to editor's box.

Edit, and clip code form to questionnaire.
  Note new editing decisions, with case number, in codebook.
  If respondent requests copy of results, note on sample list "A."

Pass to coders' box.
And so on . . .

Interviews.   If you have interviewers in the field or on the telephone, try to check their interviews that night or the next day. Field directors or project managers should look over each interview schedule for completeness, legibility, and unusual responses. If important questions are unanswered, ask the interviewer and, if necessary, recontact the respondent. This is also a good time to call back a sample of respondents to verify that they were properly interviewed. Even when interviewees are anonymous, those interviewers producing problem cases should be alerted to the difficulty.

Questionnaires.   If respondents are known or asked to identify themselves, they can be recontacted for clarification if the initial check uncovers missing or ambiguous answers. However, if responses are anonymous, you may leave all checking for the editing stage.

Field Experiments.   Check the data as soon as possible after they are gathered (questionnaires, researcher observation, available data).

THE CODEBOOK

The next step in data preparation for *all* methodologies is to draft the codebook. The codebook is your guide to the data in the computer. You'll need it for cleaning the data and carrying out your analysis. It should be with you whenever you sit down for a session at the computer.

Codebooks range from a single sheet of paper for small studies using available data to large and elaborate documents for major surveys. The codebook has two general functions:

- It tells you what data is stored in the computer.

- If you use a **raw data file** (a computer file containing only numeric data), it tells you where in the file each piece of information is stored. Otherwise, it tells you how to access the data you want.

Codebooks also contain other information you'll find necessary and useful for your data analysis. *A good codebook is essential for efficient data analysis.*

Codebook Contents

For each variable, a codebook usually gives the following information:

- The *variable* (e.g., "size of department")

- The *variable acronym* (e.g., DEPTSIZE)

- The *column number(s)* in which values for this variable will be entered (only necessary for data read from a *raw data file*).

- The *codes* for values of a category variable or *rules* for a quantitative variable.

- The code(s) for *missing values*

Data Source.   Many researchers include information in the codebook about the source of the data for each variable (e.g., "question 7" or "personnel files"). Sometimes the exact question wording from the questionnaire or interview is included. This is very useful in helping to interpret unexpected results and saves the time otherwise spent finding a copy of the questionnaire when you're at the computer. It is also extremely helpful if other researchers are likely to use the data later for secondary analysis.

Administrative Variables.   Codebooks also provide for variables with administrative information on each case. Depending on the size and complexity of your project, you may want to code some or all of the following information as variables in your data file:

- Identification number for the case (essential).

- The line numbers for that case when data for each case are entered on more than one line. The first line for each case is coded "1," the second "2," and so on.

- Which subsample the case belongs to.

- Date available data transferred or questionnaire received or interview conducted or observations made.

- For surveys:
  number of reminders or follow-ups.
  variables representing the interviewer's perceptions of the interview and the respondent.
  interviewer identity.

- Editor identity.

- Coder identity.

- Keypuncher (data entry) identity.

Normally, the first variable is the ID number, followed by other administrative variables, followed by the actual data variables.

Administrative variables are useful in tracking down errors in the data preparation stage. They can also provide information helpful in assessing nonresponse bias. It is *essential* that subsamples be identifiable if the design includes a nonproportional stratified sample (although if they are identified as part of the ID number, a separate administrative variable is not needed).

Box 13.2 shows the first page from the Campbell Switch example codebook.

SUGGESTION

For surveys, put a blank copy of the questionnaire or interview in a three-ring binder and use it as your codebook. Write in the variable (if different from the question), its acronym, codes, missing value codes, and column numbers.

SUGGESTION

To help guide your data analysis, include in your codebook your statement of the research problem and the specific research questions.

BOX 13.2
CAMPBELL SWITCH: A CONTINUING CASE
Part Sixteen: The Codebook

George: Here's my draft for the codebook.
Let me get your reactions by 3 P.M. See you
later!—Rob

CODEBOOK: CAMPBELL SWITCH STUDY

Notes:
Missing values 9 (99, 999, etc.) unless otherwise indicated.
Not applicable variables left blank.
Data from records and files: columns 5 to 45.
Data from observations and questionnaires: cols. 46 to 87.
One record per case.

Variable	Codes	Cols.
ID	(assigned)	1–3
EDITOR	1 Newman	4
	2 Wright	
	INFORMATION FROM PERSONNEL FILE	
PLANT	1 Concord	5
	2 Ajax	
HIRED	Year first hired by Campbell Switch: code last 2 digits	6–7
JOB	Job classification number: all 4 digits	8–11
	(Skill level to be recoded from this variable)	
GENDER	1 Female	12
	2 Male	
BIRTH	Year of birth: last two digits	13–14
QUITDATE	Date of termination (yymmdd)	15–20
	If still employed, leave blank	
AJAX	0 Never worked at Ajax	21
	1 Shifted to Ajax at start-up	
	2 Shifted to Ajax since start-up	
ABSENT	Number of days absent (Feb 01 to May 31)	22–23
TRANSFER	0 No transfer requests	24
	1 Requested transfer Ajax to Concord	
	2 . . . within Ajax	
	3 . . . Concord to Ajax	
	4 . . . within Concord	
	If more than one, code latest . . .	

Variable Acronym

Most statistical software programs require a short name or acronym for each variable. This is the name you'll use to access that variable when you run specific statistical procedures. Normally it can be no longer than eight characters, and there are usually certain characters that can't be included, or that can't be the first character in a variable acronym. Some typical examples are as follows:

VARIABLE	ACRONYM
Age	AGE
Group size	GPSIZE
Question one	VARQ1
Marital status	MARSTAT (or MARITALS or MSTATUS, etc.)
Natural log of the size of the organization	LNORGSIZ

Column Numbers

This information is necessary only when the statistical software reads a *raw data file* (instead of importing data from other software or having data entered though the statistical software itself). The computer treats the raw data file as a data matrix. The codebook indicates in which columns of the data matrix each variable is to be found (e.g., "Gender" in column 7, "Hourly Wage" in columns 8 to 12). Make sure you assign enough columns to handle the largest value. For example, if you are recording annual income, you'll likely need six columns in case one or more persons has an annual income in six figures.

For example, reexamine the Campbell Switch codebook in Box 13.2. The top left-hand corner of the corresponding data matrix might look like this:

```
00122834068255       0021 . . .

00222744068251900322 1001 . . .

00311854068249       0000 . . .

. . .

. . .

. . .
```

Each line holds the data for one case (employee). Each column or group of columns is a variable. Using the codebook, you can interpret the numbers in the data matrix. (Try it!)

Computer Records. When data are entered into the computer, each line of the data matrix usually becomes one **record** in the computer's *raw data file.* A computer monitor will display your raw data file in data matrix form. Since most monitors show only 80 characters in a line at one time, if the line is long you must scroll right or left (as well as down and up) to cover the entire matrix.

Sometimes researchers store data in 80-character records (known as "card-image" format). This practice originates from the days when computers read data from cardboard punch cards that could hold only 80 columns. If you

In a computer, a **record** is a predetermined number of characters in sequence. The computer treats each line of data in the data matrix as a separate record.

use card-image format, any line over 80 characters long has to be broken into two or more records.

Decimals. Check your software to see how it handles decimal places. Better statistical packages provide an option for letting the computer insert decimal points, so there is no need to enter them or to leave a column for them as long as you enter the appropriate number of digits. For example, wage rates coded as 1147 and 920 can be automatically converted to 11.47 and 9.20 for statistical analysis.

Free-Format Coding. The coding format just described is known as *fixed format.* It always places each variable in the same column for each case, and the numbers for each variable always line up in vertical columns. For example, in a particular data matrix, "gender" is always found in column 44 and age in columns 46 and 47.

An option available in some statistical packages is to use *free-format* coding (sometimes called "freefield format"). This type of data entry ignores column numbers; the data are entered in a long row with only a special character (called a *delimiter*) to separate the variables or fields. (A *field* is one or more columns occupied by a single variable.) Common delimiters between fields are commas or one or more blanks.

Because free-format coding ignores column numbers, the variables don't necessarily line up vertically. For example, the data file matrix for five cases and four variables (age, hourly wage rate, charitable contributions, bonus points) might look like this under the different formats:

FIXED FORMAT	FREE FORMAT: BLANK DELIMITER	FREE FORMAT: COMMA DELIMITER
2610.43125 175	26 10.43 125 175	26,10.43,125,175,
4715.213242482	47 15.21 324 2482	47,15.21,324,2482,
3212.89 901669	32 12.89 90 1669	32,12.89,90,1669,
24 8.16 0 844	24 8.16 0 844	24,8.16,0,844,
3911.48150 563	39 11.48 150 563	39,11.48,150,563

As you can see, the number of blanks between variables in free-format data makes no difference.

To make a raw data file matrix easier to read, use fixed format with a blank between each variable:

26 10.43 125   175

47 15.21 324 2482

32 12.89 90 1669

SUGGESTION

If you are using a rank ordinal variable, include an extra two columns to deal with ties. One will be for a decimal point, the other for a decimal digit. Then code each tied case as the average of the tied ranks. For example, if the 12th and 13th cases are tied, code each as "12.5"; assign the next case the rank code "14." If cases 27, 28, and 29 are tied, code each as "28"; code the following case as "30." Four cases tied between 7 and 10 are each coded "8.5."

24 8. 16   0 844

39 11.48 150 563

Data can be entered more quickly in free format, but if a variable is accidentally skipped, the wrong value will be read for all variables and cases from that point on. In general, fixed format is preferred unless there are only a few variables.

Codes

Codes are the numerical values entered into the computer to represent your data. The codebook summarizes the rules for translating the information in your raw data to the appropriate number or value for the data file.

For *quantitative and rank ordinal measures* these rules are very straightforward. For example,

- The variable "Year of Birth" is coded as two digits representing the last two digits of the respondent's birth year. Thus 1956 is coded as "56."

- The rank assigned to a case (rank ordinal measure) is its code.

For *category measures* (nominal, category ordinal, or dichotomous), the rules simply indicate which number will represent which category.

- The variable "Gender" is coded so that "Male" = "0" and "Female" = "1."

- The 5-category variable "Satisfaction with Supervisor" is coded from "1" representing "Not at all satisfied" to "5" representing "Highly satisfied."

For some category variables, the categories will not yet have been chosen. This will be true for

- Open-ended questions in interviews and questionnaires.

- Available data in which information is recorded on the data collection sheets as found in the files (e.g., employees' job titles).

These categories must be specified before the data can be coded. (See Box 13.3 and Box 8.4 in Chapter 8.)

Numbers or Letters? As well as numeric variables coded only as numbers, most statistical software will also accept *string variables*—combinations of letters, numbers, and certain other characters. Such codes are called *alphanumeric.* Which should you use and when?

Some information (such as respondent's name and address) obviously has to be coded alphanumeric. For other variables, the advantages of numeric

BOX 13.3
RESEARCH SKILLS
Coding Open-Ended Questions

Open-ended questions require particular attention. Since you usually prepare the codebook before all the data are collected, you cannot anticipate all possible responses. This means you cannot establish codes for all possible answers. To overcome this problem, researchers use two procedures.

1. Broad Category Codes. Initially define broad categories in the codebook. Leave the specific codes for editors to define as they edit the questionnaires or interviews. For example, initial broad codes for the open-ended question "What do you like best about your work?" are

10–19   answers related to co-workers

20–29   answers related to content of work and intrinsic benefits

30–39   answers related to wages, benefits, and extrinsic rewards

40–49   answers related to supervision or autonomy

50–69   other answers

99   no answer

As editors go through the questionnaires, they would further define categories, such as,

11   good friends, friendly, get along with co-workers

12   things in common with co-workers (religion, politics, etc.)

13   respect for skills, abilities of co-workers

14   co-workers are nonsmokers and so on.

2. Codes Based on a Subsample. Select a sample of questionnaires (at least 20, more if the question is complicated), and use it to develop categories for coding based on what these respondents report. (Pretest results are very useful for this purpose.) Leave some unspecified codes as extras so that if necessary you can add further categories as the editing progresses.

Multiple Responses. Open-ended questions (such that those that ask "Why?") may yield two or more responses. The most convenient way to handle these questions is to decide beforehand the maximum number of reasons or comments to code (usually no more than five). Then specify five variables (e.g., "First Reason" to "Fifth Reason") and code each one, using blanks for unused variables. (Check Box 13.4)

"Other" Category Responses. An "Other" write-in response category (in an otherwise closed response format) is also an open-ended question. Develop codes for the four or five most likely responses, and leave additional blank codes in the codebook to write in other codes as they occur during your editing.

Finally, remember that coding categories must be mutually exclusive. However, the exhaustive rule can be relaxed for open-ended questions if you develop the categories as editing proceeds. You'll likely find that your sample doesn't include all possibilities, so there is no need to have categories for responses that don't appear.

codes include greater flexibility in the use of multivariate statistics. In some instances you may have to recode alphanumeric to numeric in order to perform certain statistical tests. Using numeric codes in the first place can save time (even though the computer does the conversion for you).

The advantage of alphanumeric is that it helps coders. Letters save time and reduce coding errors. For example, it is easier to remember to code males as "M" than as "1." On the whole, most researchers prefer numeric codes for all variables likely to be used in statistical tests. Other information is coded alphanumeric.

Coding Conventions.   To make coding easier and less prone to errors, some coding conventions have emerged over the years. They include the following:

- Dichotomous variables: when a variable has two categories, the values "0" and "1" are often used as follows:

0	"no," "off," "not used, mentioned, or chosen"
1	"yes," "on," "used, mentioned, or chosen"

(The 0, 1 configuration is particularly useful if you plan to use regression analysis. Dichotomous variables can be used as dummy variables without further recoding. See Chapter 17.)

- Higher category values indicate greater amounts or levels of some characteristic.

- For category and quantitative variables, the values 8, 9, 98, 99, and so on, are reserved for missing value codes.

Coding Dates.   In many studies, researchers often want to code beginning and ending dates and then use these dates to calculate the duration of time periods (e.g., the duration of a trading suspension). Before deciding on a coding format, check your statistical software to see if there is a special function for handling time and converting date codes to duration measures. For example, in SPSS/PC+ the YRMODA (year-month-day) function operates by converting each date to number of days since the beginning of the Gregorian calendar. Thus the difference between two dates is easily converted to number of days (or months, or years).

To use this function (or a similar function in your statistical software), code year, month, and day as three separate variables. For example,

Year suspension began	YRHIRE	cols 14-15
Month suspension began	MOHIRE	16-17
Day suspension began	DAHIRE	18-19

Do the same for the variables reflecting the end of the time period.

SUGGESTION

To reduce survey coding errors and speed up coding of category variables, simply assign "1" to the first response category in each question, "2" to the second, and so on, regardless of content. Leave blanks to indicate that a question was not answered. After data are entered, use the computer to recode the values to conventional codes (e.g., so that a "5" on a scale of 1 to 5 represents the highest or strongest value).

Missing Value Codes

A *missing value* means that a particular case is missing information on a particular variable. The information may be unreadable, an item nonresponse, unavailable for some other reason, or missing because the question or variable is irrelevant for that case. For example, "Do you hold a position in your union local?" is irrelevant if an employee's workplace is not unionized.

For any variable with missing values for one or more cases, you need to designate at least one unique code to indicate that data are missing. This code signals the computer to ignore a missing value case when performing counts and calculations. There are several ways to code missing values.

A common procedure is to use a blank. Most statistical packages automatically treat blanks as missing values. (Before you use blanks, however, check your statistical software. Some packages convert blanks to zeros. Also, if your data are in free format with blanks as delimiters, you can't use blanks to indicate missing values.)

Another convention is to use the number "9" to represent missing values (as long as "9" isn't the code for a legitimate value or category for the variable). For multiple-column variables, nines are used in all columns of the variable ("99," "999," etc.). Other options are the digit "0" or the letter "M."

In some instances you may want to identify more than one type of missing information for a variable. For example,

SUGGESTION

Because the codebook serves as a guide to the data, photocopy extra copies and keep them in a secure place. You may want to carry out secondary analysis of the data in the future as part of some other project. For this reason, the data and codebook should almost never be discarded. You can easily store the raw data in diskette form in a binder containing the codebook.

8	"Don't know"
9	"Did not answer"
blank	Instrument nonresponse (useful when data comes from more than one data source)

Multiple missing value codes that distinguish item nonresponse from an irrelevant or a nonapplicable item or a "don't know" answer allow you to look for characteristics associated with item nonresponse. This helps in assessing item nonresponse bias. Similarly, you can check for instrument nonresponse bias when data come from self-report sources plus one or more other sources (such as available data, outside observer, or informant).

Codebook Problems

Two kinds of questions or data present special codebook problems: questions to which a respondent can give more than one legitimate answer (see Box 13.4) and data with repeated measures of the same cases (see Box 13.5).

BOX 13.4
RESEARCH SKILLS
Coding Multiple-Response Questions

For some questionnaire and interview items, a respondent may provide more than one answer. There are two types of multiple-response questions.

- The first uses a *"yes/no" checklist of categories*. For example, "Which of the following events occurred during your last strike?" followed by a list of events such as picket line violence, police called, injunction sought, and so on. Respondents check off as many categories as apply.
- The second type involves *rank-ordering a list of items*. For example, "Which are the most important factors you consider in promoting foremen? Please rank the three most important, using "1" for the most important, "2" for the second, and "3" for the third most important," followed by a list of options such as age, productivity of crew, breadth of experience, and so on.

There are two ways to code answers to multiple-response questions.

1. Each *response category* is treated as a separate variable and coded according to whether it was checked (usually "0" for no check, "1" for checked), or what rank it received ("1" for first, "2" for second, and so on). This option is best when respondents make a large number of choices, since it requires as many variables as there are response categories.

2. Each *choice* is treated as a separate variable and coded according to the category selected for that choice. For example, if respondents are asked to rank the three most important categories, the question could be coded as three variables: "First Choice," "Second Choice," "Third Choice." This option only applies to ranked or preference lists and is best when the maximum number of actual choices is small.

A problem arises in the analysis of these groups of variables. For example, if you want to know what proportion of all *choices* were of a certain type (rather than what proportion of *respondents* made a certain kind of choice), you'll have to do a certain amount of programming. To save you time, some statistical packages have special routines for analyzing multiple-response questions. Check your software.

EDITING AND CODING

Once the rules of translating the data to numbers are established and recorded in your codebook, the work of actually converting data to numbers can begin. This involves two steps: editing and coding. Editing and coding are necessary for

Data collection forms for available data and researcher observations

Questionnaires

Interviews

BOX 13.5
RESEARCH SKILLS
Coding Repeated Measures

In general, the following conventions handle different types of repeated-measure data. However, check your data entry and statistical software for any special requirements.

- For *before-after* and *panel designs*, each repeated measure requires a new *variable*. To make analysis easier, choose variable names that reflect the measurement time point, for example,

Sales before training program	PRESALES
Sales after training program	PSTSALES
Job satisfaction at time 1	JOBSAT1
Job satisfaction at time 2	JOBSAT2
Job satisfaction at time 3	JOBSAT3

- For *time series and interrupted time series,* each repeated measure is normally treated as a separate case or *observation* (as discussed in Chapter 5). Thus each measurement time point adds another row to the data matrix.
- For a *pooled time series* (more than one case), each combination of case and measurement time adds another observation (row). The normal way of entering this kind of data is as follows:

Row of data for case one at time 1
case one at time 2
case one at time 3

. . . .

case one at time t
case two at time 1
case two at time 2
case two at time 3

. . . .

case two at time t
case three at time 1
case three at time 2
case three at time 3

. . . .
. . . .

case n at time t

If easier, you may choose to enter the data for all cases at time 1, then all cases for time 2, and so on. If you keep the case and time identification variables at the beginning of each line, you'll find it easier to keep track of where you are in coding and data entry.

If data are imported from other computer files, editing and coding are normally not necessary.

Editing

The overall purpose of editing is to prepare data for coding. Each questionnaire, interview, or data collection form should be edited. Editors normally correct information on the questionnaire or form itself. This additional information is then used by the coders.

Editing can begin as soon as the codebook has been drafted and 10 or 20 cases are available. In order to achieve consistency, it is a good idea to keep a record of editing decisions on blank pages added to the codebook. Also record the cases affected by each decision, in the event that you later revise the decision.

Editing accomplishes four specific purposes: resolving ambiguities, coding open-ended questions, supplying missing information where possible, and adding administrative information.

Resolving Ambiguities.   The editor's major task is to resolve ambiguous answers or information, especially in questionnaires. For example, a respondent checks two mutually inconsistent response categories. The editor checks through the questionnaire for other information, including comments and marks in the margins that might indicate which is the wrong answer. Suggestions for editing ambiguities are discussed in Box 13.6.

Open-Ended Responses.   A second task for editors is to interpret answers to open-ended questions and indicate which code the coder should use. The more skilled the coders, the more this function can be entrusted to them. However, editors normally take responsibility for developing the codes for open-ended questions as questionnaires or interviews are processed.

Missing Information.   Editors may make educated guesses for missing information on the basis of other information in the case. For example, a respondent's gender can sometimes be strongly inferred from answers to other questions. When the correct answer is unclear (and respondents' attitudes are always uncertain), editors normally leave the variable as "missing."

Conversely, if a respondent or interviewer has failed to follow a skip pattern and has answered questions that clearly *should* be skipped, the editor converts those responses to the appropriate missing value codes. For example, if a consumer who never drinks wine answers questions about wine preferences, the editor should delete those responses and substitute missing value codes.

Administrative Variables.   Some editors also code administrative variables. They may note this information in any of three ways:

- On the questionnaire or interview itself (typically across the top of the first page)

- For large projects, on a specially prepared face sheet attached to the front of each completed instrument

- Directly on a coding form

The alternative is to leave administrative data up to the coder. Obviously, coders and keypunchers have to add their own identity codes if these are to be recorded.

An example of a questionnaire page with editor's comments and decisions

SUGGESTION

If the coder is entering codes on the right-hand margin of a questionnaire or interview, the editor's comments should be kept to the left-hand margin. The editor should use a colored pen or pencil different from the data collector's or respondent's and the coder's (e.g., green or red).

BOX 13.6
RESEARCH SKILLS

Editing Ambiguous Data

For *inconsistent and illogical responses* when the correct answer is obvious, make the necessary change. For example, a plant with only one union is extremely unlikely to have had 44 legal strikes in the past year, although it may have had a strike lasting 44 days. Use your judgment. (You must be familiar with both the objectives of the research and the nature of the sample.)

Otherwise, change data to "missing" if they are clearly inconsistent with what else is known. For example, an employee working at one plant cannot claim to hold a job that exists only at another plant. Depending on what other information you can find, one or both of the inconsistent variables must be coded "missing."

Another type of consistency for which editors are responsible is *rates and units*. If a respondent answers a question about wages in dollars per hour, instead of per week, translate the response to the relevant rate. Similarly, if distance to work is asked in miles but given in kilometers or blocks, convert the response to the appropriate unit.

Other answers may be abbreviated, smudged, or written in the wrong place. In each instance judge how to interpret the mark, and if possible convert it to usable data.

In the case of *truly ambiguous responses* that other information does not resolve, such as double-checked questions, the editor has three options:

1. Code the question as "missing data." This is safe, but it discards useful information.

2. Take advantage of the fact that the question may still provide *some* information (if a respondent checks two of five categories, we know three categories he or she *didn't* check). To use this partial information, resolve the discrepancy randomly, using a coin or die to select one of the chosen responses. This option prevents systematic bias (but adds to the random noise for that variable). It also prevents too great a loss of cases because of missing data, which can be important in a small sample.

3. Code conservatively *against* your hypothesis or the relationship you expect to find. Select the option you least expect, given other information about the case. This introduces a conservative systematic bias into your data and reduces the chances of drawing falsely positive conclusions about relationships.

for the coder is shown in Figure 13.1. In the figure, the editor's decisions, which would normally be written in red or some other color to distinguish them from the respondent's marks, are typed in uppercase in the margins. (To explain these decisions, the figure shows rationales for the editor's decisions added in parentheses.)

Coding

The basic purpose of coding is to prepare data for entry into the computer. Coders convert the information from data collection forms, questionnaires, or interviews into numbers (or letters or other symbols), ready for data entry.

13. Does your organization run or use any training programs?
   (CHECK ONE RESPONSE)

   [✓] Yes   [ ] No   (SKIP TO QUESTION 14)

   Are they available . . .   (CHECK ONE RESPONSE)

   [ ] To full-time employees only

   CODE ———— [✓] To full-time and part-time employees, on the same basis

   [ ] To full-time and part-time employees, but not on the
   same basis   (PLEASE EXPLAIN:)

   IGNORE
   (explanation
   not consistent
   with third
   category)
      As long as they are recommended

      by supervisor

   [✗] Other   (PLEASE EXPLAIN:)

   IGNORE
   (a check mark
   "corrected"
   to an "X")

   Does this policy derive in whole or in part from one or more
   collective agreements?

   [ ] Yes   [ ] No ————————————— MV = b̶
   (code as a blank
   to indicate item
   nonresponse)
   (The symbol
   consisting of
   the letter "l"
   over the letter
   "b" means
   "blank")

14. Is job security in your organization related to:

	For Full-Timers	For Part-Timers
Seniority	[✓]	[ ]
Merit	[ ]	[ ]
Not applicable; we have no policy	[ ]	[✓]
Other (PLEASE EXPLAIN:)	([ ])	[ ]

Based on job classification

CODE
(comment appears
to be an additional
basis for job
security, but only
for full-timers.)

15. Does this policy derive in whole or in part from one or more
   collective agreements?

   [✓] Yes   [ ] No

FIGURE 13.1 Example of Editing

There are a variety of ways to code raw data, as described in Box 13.7. Figure 13.2 is an example of a customized coding form. When coders run into problems they should refer them back to the editor for a decision.

Available Data.   Researchers using available data from files and records can save time and reduce errors by combining the data collection step with editing and coding. Quantitative variables present no problem; the numbers transferred from the available sources normally need no coding. For category variables, however, try to do the coding on site. For example, instead of writing employees' job classifications on the data collection form, write in the appropriate code for the classification.

This procedure requires fairly skilled people to collect data, since they have to make editing and coding decisions on the spot. It also means that you'll have to develop the coding categories prior to data collection and design the data collection form so that it can be easily read by data entry personnel.

If coding cannot be combined with data collection (perhaps because some coding decisions are too difficult), you can still design the data collection form so that it can also serve as the coding form from which data are entered directly into the computer. Leave space for category variable codes to be entered by an editor. Also leave room for the case ID number and other administrative variables to be written in later.

Computed Variables.   It is tempting to have coders make calculations for new variables, such as adding numbers of male and female employees to get total work force size. However, you are better off entering the raw data (number of male and number of female employees) and getting the computer to calculate the total. This saves time, reduces errors, and gives you the original numbers if you need them later for your analysis.

DATA ENTRY

If your data are already in a computer (for example, in a financial spreadsheet or personnel database), you have only to get your statistical software to read those data. However, if your data are in questionnaires, interviews, or data collection sheets, the information must be entered into the computer. Data entry is normally performed by keypunching, or keying in the data at a terminal consisting of a keyboard and a video screen. (This process is sometimes called "data capture.")

Entry Options with Microcomputers

With a microcomputer, you have a choice of four options for your data entry procedure. The first two produce a raw data file, the third results in data

BOX 13.7
FOCUS ON RESEARCH

Coding Procedures: Raw Data to Computer

Coding is the link between raw data and the numbers in the computer. Researchers have four major options for coding raw data.

1. Standard coding forms. The old-fashioned way is to write the numbers on standard printed coding forms: sheets ruled into 80 columns and 30 rows. (The 80-column format originated in the days when information was fed to computers through punched cards that had room for 80 columns of numbers.)

If your variables require more than 80 columns, each case will require two or more lines (records). Add a variable at the start of each line to identify the *record number* for the case: code "2" for the second line for each case, "3" for the third, and so on.

2. *Customized coding forms.* A common practice today is to use coding forms specifically designed for each project. These forms contain information (e.g., question numbers, variable names, column numbers) to help coders keep track of their place and thus reduce coding errors. Customized coding forms make it possible to use a single record for each case. Be sure to check your statistical software to see the maximum record length it will read. (For example, SPSS/PC+ will accept records up to 1,024 columns and STATPAC up to 5,000.) Also check your data entry method to find the maximum number of columns you can use in a single record. (For example, if you use word processing software to enter your data into the computer, the line length you can type is likely to be limited.)

Prepare a master coding form and then photocopy or print as many as needed. You may use a separate coding sheet for each case, which can then be clipped to its questionnaire. Alternatively, you can save paper by using the same sheet to record data for several cases. Figure 13.2 shows a coding form for a major project with over 400 variables.

Note that the record length is 573 columns.

Customized coding forms reduce coding error and require only one record per case. When your variables require more than 80 columns, this makes it easier to check data visually on your computer screen, since each line has the same format and variables will line up in vertical columns. The major disadvantage is that most monitors or terminal screens cannot show more than 80 columns of data without scrolling sideways.

3. *Coding on the instrument.* This option does away with coding forms altogether. Coders write the code numbers on the questionnaire or data collection form itself. Questionnaires, interviews, and data collection forms can be designed to leave space for such coding, which is normally done in one of two places:

- Across the top or bottom of each questionnaire page (or alternatively across the top or bottom of the first page if the questionnaire is short).

- In a column down the right-hand side of the questionnaire page. Some researchers include boxes or lines on the right-hand side of the page for coders to write in code numbers.

This option somewhat reduces clerical errors, since data are coded close to the raw information rather than on a separate sheet, and errors are easier to spot. However, it requires more time for data entry, especially when the numbers are in vertical columns instead of horizontal rows. Also, the paper you have to take to the computer for data entry will be much bulkier if the questionnaire is lengthy. This option is probably best for surveys with relatively few variables (e.g., a two- or three-page questionnaire) or for available data studies.

4. *Precoded questionnaires.* Precoded questionnaires and interview schedules substantially reduce both clerical errors and time. For all category variables, the code numbers corresponding to each category are printed on the questionnaire itself. The respondent circles the number representing his or her answer. (See Box 12.5 in Chapter 12.)

One variation is to print the numbers beside the corresponding answer check boxes. Another is to omit the numbers from the questionnaire but print them on clear acetate sheets (many photocopiers will do this). Keypunchers then overlay the appropriate sheet on each page to see what codes to enter in which columns. (For most populations this isn't necessary. Most people aren't confused by the precode numbers if you take sufficient care in laying out the questionnaire.)

The major advantage of precoding is that no coding is required: keypunchers enter the appropriate numbers directly from the questionnaire or form, and editors write in the code numbers of open-ended and ambiguous responses.

directly in the statistical software, and the fourth uses other software to enter data.

- *Word processing.* Most word processing programs allow you to create and correct a raw data file. This file can then be exported as an ASCII file.[1] Your statistical software package then reads the ASCII raw data file for your statistical analysis. Be sure to check whether the width (number of columns) you need can be handled by the word processing package. Remove margins so that the first character appears in column 1.

- *Commercial data entry.* The easiest way to enter data is to hire a commercial data entry firm to do it for you. You give them your code sheets or coded forms or questionnaires; they'll return a diskette with the data in the format you wish (usually an ASCII file for microcomputer use). The cost of commercial data entry varies with the nature of your data. It is cheapest (and fastest) with standard 80-column coding forms. It can be approximately three to four times as expensive to enter data directly from questionnaires with margin coding.

- *Statistical software.* Some statistical software packages have provisions for keying in raw data and correcting it.[2] Routines especially for data entry can be extremely useful and often incorporate data-checking features.

- *Database and spreadsheet packages.* Database and spreadsheet software packages are an alternative way of entering data. Many statistical software packages will *import* data files directly from such programs.

Data Entry with Mainframe Computers

If you plan to analyze your data on a mainframe, as opposed to a microcomputer, there are three principal ways of entering data.

---

[1]ASCII characters are those commonly used in microcomputers; they are not the computer language codes used in mainframes.

[2]For example, this can be done in SPSS/PC+ with the Data Entry option or with a BEGIN DATA command. In STATPAC, there are three options for entering data using the statistical software.

SIC CODE SHEET

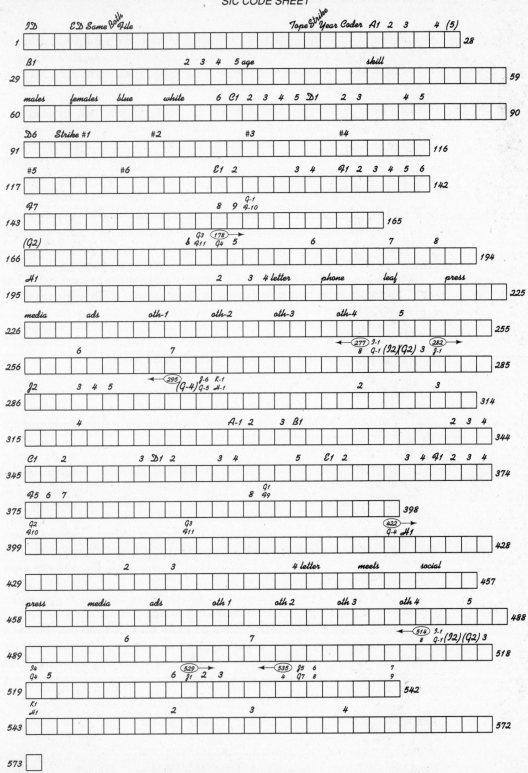

FIGURE 13.2 Example of a Customized Coding Form

- *Direct entry.* The operating system editor you use to write commands for the computer will normally allow you to enter and correct a raw data file. Be sure to check the maximum line length that your system will permit to see whether you can keep each case on a single line.

- *Commercial data entry.* Commercial firms will keypunch data for entry to a mainframe as a raw data file. The firm will provide the data on either a magnetic tape or a diskette that can be read into your mainframe system, or they may be able to transfer the raw data file to your mainframe by telephone line. You can then use the mainframe system editor to correct your data during the cleaning phase.

- *Send from micro.* With this option, you create the raw data file on your micro and then transfer it to the mainframe over a telephone line, using a modem and the appropriate software (such as KERMIT). The transmission software converts your micro's ASCII output into a computer language the mainframe can use. You can either use the mainframe system to correct the data file during data cleaning or make the changes on your micro and retransmit the corrected raw data file.

Importing Data from Other Computer Files

In business research, available data studies often import data from existing computer files (such as spreadsheet or database files). The problems are how to (1) transform the data to a format your statistical software can use and (2) transmit the data to your own microcomputer.

If your statistical package will accept the available data directly, no change of format is necessary. Otherwise, export the available data to an ASCII file, and then import that ASCII file to your statistical package.

Transferring the file itself is fairly easy. One way is simply to copy the data you want to a diskette and then read it into your own computer. For larger files (such as the large commercial database files used in financial research), you may have to download over telephone lines. If the file is extremely large, you won't be able to import the file easily. In this case, carry out analysis on a mainframe computer.

If all the data you want are in just one file, just copy the variables you want from the available source to a new data file (which you can then convert to ASCII format if necessary). Where two or more files are involved, they will have to be merged. This will require a common identifier variable for each case in each file (such as a personnel number). Merging can be done with database software or with some statistics packages.

Verifying

Verification is a procedure that checks for data entry errors in raw data files. Common errors are sixes that look like zeros and sevens that look like

BOX 13.8

RESEARCH SKILLS

Manual Data Verification

If you enter data into a raw data file, here is a procedure for manually verifying to find keypunching errors:

1. Get a printout of the raw data file. This is called a *data listing*. If possible, print each case (record) on a separate line. This may be difficult or impossible if your record length is greater than the number of characters your printer will print in a row. (In condensed form, many printers have a limit of around 132. Wide carriage printers can print more, but also have limits.)

If you can't get all the variables on a single line, try several listings, each with as many variables as will fit on a line. The alternative is a listing that wraps the record, that is, continues to print a record on the next line, taking as many lines as nec-

essary to accommodate the longer line of the data file. Wrapped lines are difficult to read for manual verification.

If you cannot get a listing, try verifying the data from your computer screen. This, however, is a fairly cumbersome procedure. If your software permits, use the cursor and scale lines to help you keep your place.

2. Once you have the data listing (or the visual display on screen), verify manually by having one person read the numbers from the coding forms while another follows the printout or screen. Always read *from* the source most likely to be ambiguous, that is, the coding forms, questionnaire, or interview schedule. Take turns to avoid fatigue.

3. Circle or underline errors in red, so that you can easily find entries that need correction.

ones or twos. Commercial firms verify data by reentering the entire data set using special equipment that signals whenever the second entry doesn't exactly match the first. The data entry operator then compares the two entries and the coding form to see which is the correct character.

A second option is to use *manual verification*. This requires the help of a patient friend (see Box 13.8). Manual verification is thorough but time consuming.

Studies have shown that a relatively small percentage of errors are due to data entry, particularly if the keypunching is done by someone with typing skills. For this reason, business researchers who don't use commercial data entry firms often skip manual verification and go directly to the data-cleaning stage.

SUGGESTION

If you plan to verify your data manually, leave an empty column between variable fields. This will make it much easier to read the values for specific variables from your data listing.

DATA CLEANING

Once the raw data file is in the computer, the researcher cleans it to remove coding and other errors. *All data, from surveys, available sources, or data collection forms, should be cleaned.* Only then can you carry out data analysis with confidence in your results.

Coders are prone to the same errors that affect data entry personnel: misreading sixes for zeros, and so on. Coders may miss inconsistent answers as well. If a researcher doesn't verify the data entry, the cleaning process will also pick up some, but not all, of the data entry errors.

Preparing for Computer Runs

The check for coding errors requires computer runs using statistical software. However, before you can do these runs, your statistical software must read the data. Your computer not only has to read the numbers, but it also has to know what meanings to assign to them—which numbers are which variables, what are the missing value codes, and so on. If you use the statistical software to enter the data, the computer already has the necessary *data definition* information that tells it how to treat the information. However, data definition requires extra steps for raw data files and imported data.

Raw Data Files. If you're using a raw data file, you must give the computer information about the raw data file matrix. Your statistical software needs this data definition or "data dictionary" information in order to carry out statistical calculations. In particular, it must know

- Whether data is fixed format, and if so in what column(s) each variable is found.

- The acronym that identifies each variable.

- Whether a variable's values are numeric (numbers only) or a combination of letters and numbers (alphanumeric).

- Whether and where to insert decimal points.

- For each variable, the values you have assigned (if any) to indicate missing data.

- For some software: the total number of cases.

You may also want to provide the computer with other information to appear on printouts of statistical results:

- The complete name (label) for each variable

- The label for each category of a category variable

- The title of your project

Usually this is handled by software commands. Most software packages combine the raw data file and the data definition information to create a special **processing file** (called "systems file," "data set," "input file," etc.) for the computer to analyze. Using a processing file saves the computer a great deal of time compared to using a raw data file.

Imported Data. If you're importing spreadsheet or database data, some of the data definition information will also be imported. The rest you must now add using statistical software commands. Check your software documentation to see what the statistical package imports along with the data.

Once the data have been read by the statistical software package, the researcher runs statistical routines to find *illegitimate* and *illogical codes,* both the result of coding errors. Once the researcher knows which variables have erroneous values, additional runs locate which cases have the errors. Corrections can be made two ways:

SUGGESTION

Never erase your raw data file or your file of data definition information until the project is finished! If you accidentally delete cases or variables from the processing file, you'll need these files to create a new processing file.

- To the raw data file, if there is one, after which a "clean" processing file is created. (An exception is data entry software such as DATA ENTRY II, which can be programmed to check your data file for illegitimate and illogical codes as you enter the data. You can then make corrections immediately. The same feature is available with CATI software in telephone interviewing. For these procedures, cleaning takes place at the same time as data entry and the processing file is automatically corrected.)

- To the processing file itself, using commands in the statistical software that recode or redefine data. This is preferable when data have been imported from spreadsheets or databases, or entered through the statistics software.

Illegitimate Codes

Illegitimate codes are values of category variables not defined in the codebook. (They are sometimes called "wild" codes). For example, if gender is coded "1" for males, "2" for females, and blank for missing value, a code of "7" is illegitimate and probably the result of a data entry or coding error.

The steps for finding and correcting illegitimate codes are as follows:

- Run a *frequency distribution* for each category variable, and check the resulting distribution with the codebook.

- If the frequency distribution shows one or more illegitimate codes, run a *list* to find the ID numbers of the cases with the illegitimate codes. (In most statistical packages this is easily carried out with a conditional command such as "IF," "SELECT IF," or "PROCESS IF.")

- Armed with this information, consult the coding form or original questionnaire, interview, or data collection form to find the correct value.

- Revise the raw data file and/or the processing file.

Figure 13.3 displays the output from two runs to locate and identify cases with illegitimate codes. The first run is a frequency distribution of the variable "travel mode" showing that two cases have an illegitimate "8" code. The second is the output from a list run identifying the ID numbers of the cases with the illegitimate "8" code.

FIGURE 13.3
Cleaning: Example
of Runs to Identify
an Illegitimate Code

```
                    FIRST RUN:  FREQUENCY DISTRIBUTION

Commands (STATPAC):  FREQUENCIES MODE
                     OPTIONS TF=E

Results:


              Travel Mode                    Number  Percent  Cumulative
---------------------------------------      ------  -------  ----------

              1 = Walk                           8    2.2 %       2.2 %
              2 = Bicycle                       17    4.6 %       6.8 %
              3 = Bus                          130   35.5 %      42.3 %
              4 = Car                          206   56.0 %      98.6 %
              5 = Other                          3    0.8 %      99.5 %
              8 =                                2    0.5 %     100.0 %
                                             ------  -------    -------
              Total                           366  100.0 %     100.0 %


              Missing cases = 2
              Response percent =  99.5 %



                    SECOND RUN:  LIST ILLEGITIMATE CASES

Commands (STATPAC):      IF MODE=8 THEN SELECT
                         LIST MODE ID

Results:


MODE     ID

-----------

8        97
8        123
```

The researcher then returns to the questionnaires or data collection forms for case numbers 97 and 123 to find the correct code for the variable "travel mode." The correction is then made to the raw data file or through the statistical software.

At the same time you check for illegitimate codes, also look for suspicious frequency distributions. In particular, examine whether too many or too few cases share the same value. For example, if only 1 department out of 54 reports an "average" level of turnover, check for a systematic coding error.

Illogical Codes

An illogical code for a case is one that represents an inconsistency in the data for that case. This kind of coding error always involves two (or more) variables. For example, a respondent is coded as answering "No" to a question asking whether the workplace is unionized, and "3" to a question asking for number of union meetings of the employee's local attended in the past three months. The two responses are illogical, and the researcher must resolve the inconsistency.

Like illegitimate codes, this type of checking is limited to category variables. However, researchers may temporarily recode a quantitative variable to a category one in order to check for illogical responses. For example, a researcher recodes "income" into five categories to see whether reported income is consistent with occupational category.

The steps for locating and correcting illogical codes are as follows:

- Run a *cross-tabulation* of the two variables, noting which cells of the resulting table should logically be empty. For example, the cell that represents unskilled laborers earning more than $60,000 per year should have no cases in it.

- If some cases fall into these illogical cells, run a *list* to obtain their ID numbers.

- Consult the coding form or original questionnaire or data collection form to find the correct values.

- Correct the raw data file and/or the processing file.

Figure 13.4 shows a likely data entry error in the output from a cross-tabulation of "mode of transportation" by "distance from residence to work." The results show one highly unlikely case: a person living more than 10 miles from work who regularly walks. The figure also shows the output from a list run identifying the ID number (304) of the case with the illogical code. The researcher then consults the original interview or available data to see if there is an error and what the correct values should be.

■ *The Lighter Side of Research*

Overheard: A researcher overwhelmed with coding errors remarks, "For some people, cleanliness is next to godliness, but for me, cleanliness is next to impossible!"

—paraphrase of the Charles Schultz character Pigpen

Data Cleaning: A purification ritual, following which the researcher blithely acts as if all measurement errors had been eliminated from the data.

SUGGESTION

To help you keep track of cases in your analysis, for each variable enter in the codebook the number of "missing data" cases for that variable. This will help you solve problems of "disappearing cases" that occasionally crop up when you begin your analysis of relationships.

SUGGESTION

When you do cross-tabs for illogical codes, have the computer include (rather than skip) cases with missing values. This will help you find cases that logically should have responses but are erroneously coded as nonresponses.

FIGURE 13.4
Cleaning: Example
of Runs to Identify
an Illogical Code

FIRST RUN: CROSSTABULATION

Commands (SPSS/PC+): CROSSTABS /TABLES MODE BY DISTANCE /OPTIONS 1.

Results:

Crosstabulation: MODE   Travel Mode
                  By DISTANCE Distance to Work

DISTANCE-> MODE	Count	Less than 1	1 to 3	3 to 10	More than 10	Missing	Row Total
		1	2	3	4	9	
1 Walk		7			1		8 / 2.2
2 Bicycle		11	6				17 / 4.6
3 Bus		3	18	80	29		130 / 35.3
4 Car		4	9	99	94		206 / 56.0
5 Other			2	1			3 / .8
9 Missing		1		1	1	1	4 / 1.1
Column Total		26 / 7.1	35 / 9.5	181 / 49.2	125 / 34.0	1 / .3	368 / 100.0

Number of Missing Observations =   0

SECOND RUN: LIST

Commands (SPSS/PC+):   IF (MODE EQ 1 AND DISTANCE EQ 4) TEMP = 1.
                         PROCESS IF (TEMP EQ 1).
                         LIST /VARIABLES ID MODE DISTANCE.
Results:

ID MODE DISTANCE

304   1   4

Number of cases read =   1   Number of cases listed =   1

Summary

This chapter covers data preparation: the steps between data gathering and data analysis. Not all methodologies require all the steps we described.

The first step is to screen each collected case to ensure that it is valid, that is, falls within the target population. Each valid case is then assigned an ID number. If the project is a large one or involves follow-up contacts with data sources, administrative information about the case may be recorded in a logbook.

Following these administrative steps, the researcher begins to check the data. An initial check is often made as soon as each questionnaire, interview schedule, or data-gathering form is collected or received. The next check is carried out as the case is prepared for entry into the computer. This preparation involves four steps: preparing a codebook that describes the nature of the raw data file in the computer, editing the case, coding it, and actual data entry.

The codebook contains information on each variable including its acronym, the columns containing the data for that variable, and codes for its categories and missing values. The codebook may also contain information on the source of data for each variable. In addition, it specifies various administrative variables, including the ID number for each case.

Each questionnaire, interview schedule, or data form is edited to prepare it for coding. Editing is the second checking stage. The editor's job is to resolve ambiguities, code open-ended responses, fill in missing information wherever possible, and add administrative variable information.

The coder converts the information in each questionnaire or data form to numbers to prepare it for data entry. Coding can be done on standard or customized forms or on the questionnaire or data form itself. Precoded questionnaires eliminate much of the data-coding step.

Following editing and coding, data are entered into the computer as a raw data file or through the statistical software itself. Available data can be imported directly from spreadsheets or database programs. Sometimes data entry includes verification to check for entry errors.

The fourth and final check is data cleaning. Cleaning checks for coding errors and other discrepancies in the data. The researcher uses statistical runs to look for illegitimate and illogical codes.

Where Are We Now?

When data preparations are complete, you have a clean processing file representing the results of your problem specification, research design, and data gathering. You are now ready to begin data analysis to answer your specific research questions. For business and other specific applied research, this begins with preliminary and descriptive analysis.

Discussion Issues and Assignments

1. Contact a marketing or consumer research firm. Find out how they edit, code, and enter data from surveys and from field experiments. How does the firm balance the competing demands of time and accuracy?

2. Plan how you would prepare the data gathered from the student survey discussed in question 5, Chapter 9, and question 6, Chapter 12. What administrative variables would you include? Would you use fixed or free format? How would you code missing data? Prepare the codebook.

3. Edit, code, and clean the data relevant to the previous question. Do you think you caught all the errors? How much time and effort did it take? What would you do differently if you did it again?

4. Find a student doing a survey as part of a sociology course (there should be several on campus at any given time). Ask how he or she plans to prepare and analyze the data. Volunteer to plan the data preparation for him or her and construct the codebook (get the approval of the student's instructor first). If you have time, edit, code, enter, and clean the data. Consult with the student about codes for open-ended questions.

5. Ask a faculty member for some old raw data (questionnaires, interviews, or data collection forms). Plan the data preparation, do the initial checks, prepare the codebook, and edit, code, clean, and enter a dozen cases. Evaluate your data preparation in terms of time and accuracy. Also evaluate the original data-gathering instrument: how did it affect your time and accuracy?

6. The raw data matrix on page 465 contains an illogical code. Find it.

7. The financial pages of your daily newspaper contain information on stocks, bonds, commodities, and a host of other business-related matters. Select five variables, and design a codebook for coding this information. Make one of the variables nonquantitative (e.g., whether a firm is mentioned in the business news or the nature of the news about a particular industry).

Further Reading

Karweit, N., and E. D. Myers, Jr. 1983. "Computers in Survey Research." Chapter 11 in P. H. Rossi, J. D. Wright, and A. B. Anderson. 1983. *Handbook of Survey Research.* New York: Academic Press.

    A more advanced discussion of some of the techniques of preparing data for computer analysis.

Norusis, M. 1986. *The SPSS Guide to Data Analysis.* Chicago: SPSS.

    A good introduction to the basics of data preparation, particularly for those planning to use a mainframe computer and SPSS-X software.

Warwick, D. P., and C. A. Lininger. 1975. *The Sample Survey: Theory and Practice.* New York: McGraw-Hill.

    Warwick and Lininger provide a wealth of practical advice for data preparation, particularly coding, for surveys.

CHAPTER 14

Preliminary Data Analysis

CHAPTER OBJECTIVES

- What checks do you perform *before* carrying out data analysis?
- What problems might you find that would distort data analysis, and how can they be corrected?
- What data modifications are likely before further analysis can be carried out?

CHAPTER OUTLINE

t helps to think of data analysis taking place in three stages, each with a particular objective.

1. *Preliminary analysis* (this chapter) checks your data and constructs new variables. *All research requires at least some preliminary analysis.*

2. *Descriptive and univariate analysis* (Chapter 15) estimates population characteristics for descriptive research and summarizes sample characteristics for other kinds of research. It also tests hypotheses about population characteristics.

3. *Relationship analysis* (Chapters 16 and 17) explores the relationships among variables and differences among groups.[1]

PRELIMINARY ANALYSIS

The purpose of preliminary analysis is to prepare your data for descriptive and relationship analysis. Preliminary analysis includes a series of checks to ensure that your conclusions about relationships will not be invalid because of peculiarities in the data. It includes weighting and sample checks, distribution checks, and measurement checks. It also involves the computation of new variables from your existing ones, including scales and indexes.

When these checks and computations are complete, you'll be ready to proceed with descriptive and univariate analysis and the investigation of relationships in your data. To skip preliminary analysis is to risk research errors and faulty conclusions and recommendations. The ethical aspects of preliminary analysis are discussed in Box 14.1.

SUGGESTION

It is important that, should you accidentally lose your computer's processing file, you can quickly use the raw data file to reconstruct it and continue with data analysis. *Keep a log of your preliminary analysis computing.* Record each variable you recode or compute and how you did it. Record each case you correct or drop.

WEIGHTING AND SAMPLE CHECKS

If your research involves sampling, especially nonproportional, you first need to perform weighting and sample checks.

• Adjust subsamples from *nonproportional stratified sampling* so you can carry out further data analysis.

• Is the sample sufficiently representative? Is there evidence of nonresponse bias?

---

[1]The analysis of group differences is also an analysis of relationships: the groups differ on an initial variable (e.g., whether they've heard a radio commercial), which is related to some other variable representing the effect of that initial difference (e.g., cola purchases).

BOX 14.1
RESEARCH ETHICS

Preliminary Analysis Checks

In applied research, preliminary analysis checks are more than prudence and caution. They represent an ethical obligation on the part of the researcher.

The purpose of the checks is to ensure research validity, in particular that anomalies in the data do not lead to erroneous conclusions about the existence or strength of a relationship. An organization's policies, practices, investment decisions, structural reorganization, or other actions may depend on research results. The livelihood of the organization and its employees or members may be at stake. In such circumstances, it would be unethical for a researcher to offer recommendations based on findings that had not been subjected to preliminary analysis checks.

Among the different checks, the issue of when to drop outlier cases raises the most ethical questions. In general, it is not ethical to drop cases, transform variables, or select relationship tests in a way calculated to improve the results. Researchers follow relatively strict professional guidelines about these and related research practices.

These procedures help achieve and verify sample representativeness, that is, how well the sample reflects the target population.

Weighting Nonproportional Stratified Samples

Surveys that use nonproportional stratified samples intentionally oversample some groups and undersample others. This means that, relative to their proportions in the target population, some groups are overrepresented in the overall sample and others are underrepresented.

Before you proceed with other checks or data analysis, you must restore the relative proportion of cases in your sample to that in the target population. This procedure is called *weighting*. It is required whenever you use a *nonproportional stratified sample* and analyze the sample as a whole (rather than compare subsamples or investigate only one subsample at a time).

You must increase the number of undersampled cases so that their percentage of your total sample is the same as their percentage in the target population. At the same time, your weighting procedure must not increase the total sample size, since a larger sample might falsely indicate significant relationships where there are none.

The solution is simultaneously to increase the undersampled cases by *upweighting* and to decrease the oversampled cases by *downweighting*.

To weight your sample, follow these steps:

Weighting involves multiplying each case by a factor so that some cases count more than others. It is used with nonproportional sampling to return each subsample's proportion of the total sample to its corresponding proportion in the population.

1. Determine the proportion of each group or subsample in the target population.

2. Determine the proportion of each group or subsample in the achieved sample.

3. Calculate the weighting factor for each subsample group i as follows:

$$\text{Weight Factor}_i = \frac{\text{(target population proportion of group } i)}{\text{(achieved sample proportion of group } i)}$$

4. Weight each case in subsample group i by the subsample's weighting factor. Your statistical package will have a routine to accomplish this.

Weighting is not required if you have only one sample or use the same sampling fraction for all subsamples (a proportional sample). Even if your sample is nonproportional, weighting is not required for all your analysis; analysis should be carried out on the *unweighted* sample

- When you analyze each subsample *one at a time* (for example, checking the correlation between age and productivity within each subsample separately). This will allow you to take advantage of more cases and better precision in your estimates.

- When you *statistically compare two or more subsample groups* (for example, a test of the difference in average age across subsamples).

However, all other analysis using nonproportional samples must be carried out using weighted cases.

CASE EXAMPLE

A researcher studying employment equity samples a corporation's hiring decisions over the past ten years. In all, 865 decisions involved line manager positions, and 122 were to fill staff positions. Her initial sample is 110 (55 from each group). Her achieved sample consists of the 101 decisions for which she found adequate records: 53 line positions and 48 staff positions. The target population proportions for line and staff positions are .88 and .12, respectively; the corresponding achieved sample proportions are .52 and .48. She weights each line manager case in her sample by multiplying it by the weighting factor .88/.52, and each staff case by the weighting factor .12/.48. The result is a weighted sample of 89.7 line manager decision cases (upweighted from the 53 in the original sample) and 12.0 staff decision cases (downweighted from the original 48). The total weighted sample size is 101.7, very close to the original sample size of 101.

Sample Check

Once any necessary weighting has been carried out, check for sample representativeness. If 76 percent of the population of accounting projects involves a certain treatment of intangible assets, so should the sample. But does it? Often we can't tell, because the population figure to compare with isn't available. But rather than trust to luck, we can check, tentatively, just how representative our sample is. The procedure is identical to that for assessing nonresponse bias in questionnaires (Chapter 12, Box 12.7):

1. Select some characteristic for which you have information about both the target population and the sample. (Often such information just isn't available; it certainly isn't likely to be available for the key and primary variables in our research, so we often settle for other descriptive characteristics, or [for people] demographic characteristics, such as age or gender.)

2. Compute the mean or proportion of that characteristic in the sample.

3. Compare it with the mean or proportion of the same characteristic in the population.

We can help this check along with some prior planning. First, investigate just what population characteristics are available. Then, include those characteristics as variables in your data gathering.

A sample check is useful even when you enumerate the entire target population. If any more than just a few cases are missing, the check will compare your achieved sample with the target population and warn you of any potential missing cases bias.

> *Nonrepresentativeness.* A nonrepresentative sample is a problem because it may (1) limit the overall external validity of your conclusions and (2) reduce the internal validity of conclusions about relationships among variables through missing cases bias. What do you do if a sample check reveals a substantial difference between population and sample?

- The simplest option is to note the difference and qualify your conclusions accordingly.

- One further step is actually to investigate for the possible effects of missing cases bias in your supplementary analysis.

- A third possibility is to draw an additional sample and combine it with the original. In this additional sample, make every effort to get data from cases having characteristics associated with nonresponse or missing cases in the original sample.

Beware: it is tempting to attempt to correct an unrepresentative sample by *upweighting* the cases that are underrepresented on the test characteristic, using the same methods as for weighting nonproportional stratified samples. If you're short of male consumers, you could just make each one count more! This option must be exercised with extreme caution, however. If you adjust for one characteristic, you may unknowingly distort other characteristics.

Even worse is the situation in which the sample is nonrepresentative not because of the chance factors in random sampling, but because cases of a

SUGGESTION

For *external* research sample checks, try census and other government documents. Check with your college or university library or your local reference library. For *internal research,* ask. Departments such as sales, personnel, payroll, or production may have summary figures for the target population you're interested in.

certain kind were less likely to be included (i.e., systematic missing cases bias). Thus older respondents are more likely to refuse interviews, busy people are less likely to complete questionnaires, and sloppy and poorly run departments are less likely to provide production and performance data. Upweighting when you have missing cases bias can lead to distorted results, particularly when the characteristic associated with noninclusion in the sample is also related to your dependent variable. For example, if busy female managers are less likely to be absent than other managers, and less likely to answer a questionnaire, your conclusions about relationships between gender and absenteeism will be distorted if you upweight the female cases.[2]

DISTRIBUTION CHECKS

For each variable in your research, each case takes one of several possible values. Thus for "gender," cases may be male or female; for "share price," cases may range from zero to hundreds of dollars. The dispersion of cases over a variable's values constitutes the **distribution** of a variable. Because certain distributions can create data analysis problems, all methodologies—available data, field experiments, and surveys—require distribution checks. They are particularly important in available data studies when the researcher is less familiar with the data. Distribution checks answer the following questions:

• Does each variable have enough variation to be useful?

• Is the shape of the variable's distribution likely to violate statistical assumptions and distort the results of relationship analysis?

• Are there any extreme cases that might distort the results of relationship analysis?

Examining Distributions

Distribution checks make use of frequency distributions, graphics, and statistical measures of distribution characteristics. Table 14.1 summarizes the most useful graphics and statistics for distribution checks. Most statistical packages permit you to calculate most or all of them.

Category Variables. A **frequency distribution** table shows how many cases have each value or are in each category. For example, in a sample of bankruptcies, the category variable "type of bankruptcy" is distributed as

---

[2]Note that the weighting procedure in the case example automatically incorporated weighting to cover missing cases as well as for the nonproportional sampling. If you believe that this might introduce errors into your analysis, calculate the weighting factors using the initial sample proportion instead of the achieved sample proportion.

TABLE 14.1 ■ GRAPHICS AND STATISTICS FOR DISTRIBUTION CHECKS

Type of Variable	Graphic Display	Statistic
Nominal	Bar chart in order of decreasing frequency	Percentage frequency distribution
Dichotomous	Bar chart	Percentage frequency distribution
Category ordinal	Bar chart	Percentage frequency distribution
Rank ordinal	—	Percentage frequency distribution*
Quantitative	Histogram Box plot	Mean and median (compare) Skewness Interquartile range
Time-series variable	Time-series plot Sequential box plot Correlogram (autocorrelation function)	Durbin-Watson d Correlogram ρ

*This will show you which ranks have ties. Warning: the computer output will require many pages if there are a large number of cases.

follows: "personal" 104 and "business" 43. Useful graphics include bar charts, pie charts, and column charts (see Figure 14.1 and Chapter 18). There are no widely accepted statistics that summarize the distribution for category variables.

Quantitative Variables. To assess the distribution of a quantitative variable, examine a histogram or box plot and calculate the coefficient of skewness.

A **histogram** groups the many values of a quantitative variable into about 12 to 20 categories. For example, labor costs might be grouped as follows: zero to $200,000, $200,001 to $400,000, $400,001 to $600,000, and so on. It then displays graphically the relative number of cases in each category and shows the shape of the distribution. A **normal distribution** has a bell shape: many scores in the approximate middle range, a few high, and a few low. The variables "number of hours per week watching television" and "employee hiring-test score" would usually approximate a normal distribution. Other common distributions found in business research are shown in Box 14.2.

Also useful is a **box plot** (see Figure 14.2 on page 499). Box height is an indicator of the variable's variation. Specifically, it is the **interquartile range,** or the distance between the 25th and 75th percentiles. In a box plot, the top

FIGURE 14.1
Examples of
Category Variable
Distributions
(SPSS/PC+
Output)

(a) Frequency Distribution

MARISTAT   Marital Status

Value Label	Value	Frequency	Percent	Valid Percent	Cum Percent
Married	1	222	88.8	91.7	91.7
Widowed/divorced/separated	2	16	6.4	6.6	98.3
Single	3	4	1.6	1.7	100.0
No answer	9	8	3.2	MISSING	
	TOTAL	250	100.0	100.0	

(b) Bar Chart

EDUCATION

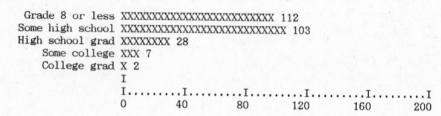

```
      Grade 8 or less  XXXXXXXXXXXXXXXXXXXXXXXXXXXX 112
      Some high school  XXXXXXXXXXXXXXXXXXXXXXXXXX 103
      High school grad  XXXXXXXX 28
          Some college  XXX 7
          College grad  X 2
                        I
                        I........I........I........I........I........I
                        0        40       80       120      160      200
```

25 percent and the bottom 25 percent of cases lie outside the box. Box plots also show the median (a line or asterisk inside the box). The "whiskers" outside the box indicate the distance to the most extreme case within 1.5 times the interquartile range from the end of the box. Any other cases lying beyond the ends of each whisker are also shown.

The **coefficient of skewness** measures how uneven the distribution of cases is on either side of the mean (see Box 14.2). Negative skewness means more cases trailing away in the lower value tail of the distribution; positive means more in the higher.

Sufficient Variation

Any variable that doesn't vary much will be of little use in explaining the variation in other variables because it cannot *covary* with anything else.

Category Variables. For category variables, inspect the frequency distribution. What proportion of cases fall into the largest category? As a rough rule of thumb, if over 85 percent of the cases fall into one category, the variable will be of limited use. If over 90 percent are in the dominant category, the variable definitely has insufficient variation.

Remedy. At this stage, there's nothing you can do to overcome insufficient variation in a category variable. The only option is to drop the variable from the analysis and report the distribution (e.g., "A total of 97 percent of the

---

SUGGESTION

Printing a bar chart for each category variable will make the check for sufficient variation easier. For nominal variables, specify a bar chart with categories in order of decreasing frequency.

BOX 14.2
FOCUS ON RESEARCH

Common Frequency Distributions Found in Business Research

The quantitative variables most commonly used in business research take one of six frequency distribution shapes.

- *Normal:* This is the familiar bell-shaped distribution with many cases near the mean and increasingly fewer at values more distant from the mean. Monthly sales figures for a firm over a two-year period would likely show this shape. This is the most desirable distribution shape; it meets the assumption of a normal sampling distribution required for many statistical tests.
- *Skewed Normal:* This is a bell-shaped distribution with extra cases trailing off to the right or left. It

is perhaps the most common distribution in business research. For example, police salaries across municipalities show negative skewness (to the left) because there are some communities that pay police significantly lower salaries. Employee ages within a firm tend to be skewed positively (to the right) because there are some employees considerably older than the others.
- *Declining:* This shape shows large numbers of cases with small values of the variable, and fewer cases as the values increase. It can be either concave or convex. The frequency distribution of length of strikes (in days) in an industry over a one-year period shows the concave shape.

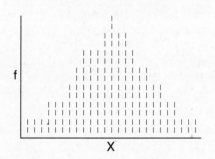

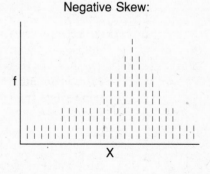

Negative Skew:

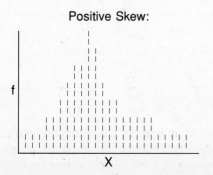

Positive Skew:

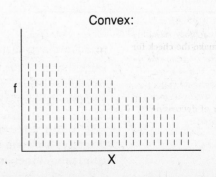

Convex:

Concave:

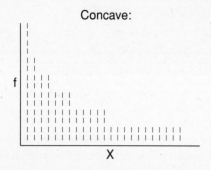

• *Increasing:* This shape shows few cases at low values, but more cases as the values of the variable increase. It, too, can be either concave or convex. This frequency distribution occurs when a variable has a specific ceiling, such as a proportion of female employees in firms.

Concave:

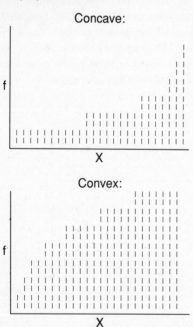

Convex:

• *Uniform:* This distribution shows approximately equal numbers of cases at all values of the variable. The price per ounce of many kinds and sizes of breakfast cereal might show approximately this distribution.

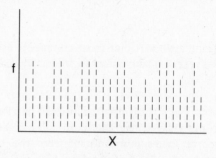

• *Multiple Peaks:* This shape has two or more values at which cases tend to cluster, with fewer cases between the peaks. An example is proportion of firms' employees who are women. Such distributions often indicate the combination of two or more subgroups. For example, a combined distribution of the wages of skilled and unskilled employees might show two peaks.

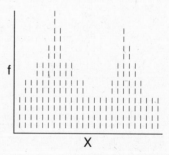

small business bankruptcies involved firms that had no regular accounting procedures").

There are two exceptions to this rule. The first is if the sample size is large enough so that at least 25 cases fall outside the dominant category. That usually leaves enough variation for relationship analysis. The second is if the variable is very important to your analysis (i.e., a primary variable). Chapter 17 discusses how you can use regression analysis to look at the effect of that variable, even if there are only a handful of cases outside the dominant category.

Quantitative Variables.   It is fairly rare to find a quantitative variable with little or no variation. Thus checks for sufficient variation in quantitative variables are generally omitted. (Note that rank ordinal variables, by their nature and the fact that they have few ties, always have variation.)

Distribution Shape

The shape of a variable's distribution may affect the validity of statistical tests and measures.

Category Variables.   Most relationship tests and measures used with category variables are **nonparametric**; that is, they do not require assumptions about the shape of the variables' distributions. However, some are *margin sensitive:* they give distorted results when the distribution is severely nonuniform (a distribution is **uniform** when there are approximately equal numbers of cases in each category). If some categories have very few cases, the result of the relationship test may be unreliable (see Chapter 16).

To check the distribution of a category variable, examine a frequency distribution or a bar chart. Examples are shown in Figure 14.1. There is no rule for deciding when a category variable has a nonuniform frequency distribution; instead, inspect a bar chart for noticeable valleys. Both of the variables in Figure 14.1 clearly have severely nonuniform distributions.

Remedy.   Improve a severe nonuniform distribution by carefully combining sparse categories with each other or with larger ones to make the distribution more uniform. **Collapsing** is the procedure of combining two or more categories into one (e.g., "semiskilled" and "unskilled" into "non-

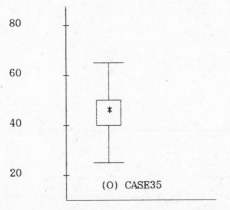

FIGURE 14.2
Example of a Box Plot (This box plot shows a fairly normal distribution with one outlier, case number 35)

Variable	TRANSACT	Average number of broker transactions
N of Cases	60.00	

Symbol Key: * – Median   (O) – Outlier   (E) – Extreme

skilled") or grouping cases into categories (e.g., "ages 18–23," 24–30," etc.).

1. Category Variables. A researcher may collapse a category variable for several reasons:

- To obtain a more even distribution and avoid misleading statistical results.

- To combine theoretically similar categories in order to make results more easily read and understood.

- To reduce the number of categories temporarily (this is useful as a temporary measure in certain kinds of multivariate analysis, as described in Chapter 17).

The choice of which categories to combine is normally based on two criteria:

- Uniform distribution: to achieve approximately equal-sized categories.

- Logic: some categories fit together in the context of the research problem.

Theoretically, any two or more *nominal* measure categories can be combined; for *category ordinal* measures, the categories to be combined must be adjacent in order to preserve the category ordering. For example, the five categories

Strongly agree
Agree
Neutral
Disagree
Strongly disagree

could be collapsed to

Agree or strongly agree
Neutral, disagree, or strongly disagree

but not to

Strongly agree or strongly disagree
Agree
Neutral or disagree

For example, for the first variable in Figure 14.1, the second and third categories should be combined. For the second variable, all those with high school graduation or better should be combined into a single category.

Overcollapsing should be avoided. In fact, it is best not to collapse unless the reasons are compelling. Collapsing into fewer categories loses information, results in less sensitive measures, and can distort measures of relationships.

2. *Quantitative Variables.* Quantitative variables are sometimes collapsed into ordinal categories for the following reasons:

- Temporarily for cleaning illogical codes. For example, age is collapsed into two categories—below and above voting age—to find illogical codes for the question, "How did you vote?"

- Temporarily for use in some kinds of multivariate analysis.

- When managers are more comfortable with tables than other forms of results. Collapsing for this reason is often used in descriptive research.

The choice of *cutting points* separating categories can be made on any of the following six criteria:

- Division points with some theoretical or commonsense importance (such as ages of life-cycle changes or legal voting age)

- Natural breaks in the distribution such as would be found if there were multiple peaks (see Box 14.2)

- Cutting points used in other research, so you can compare distributions (e.g., the age categories used in census documents)

- Categories with equal numbers of cases (e.g., median, quartiles, quintiles, etc.)

- Categories with equal range (such as 5-year age categories)

- Cutting points that are round numbers (e.g., ages 20–29, 30–39, etc.)

Converting quantitative data into categories should be avoided wherever possible because of the enormous loss of information. In general, try to use between five and ten categories when collapsing quantitative variables. The more categories, the less information is lost. Reducing a quantitative variable to eight categories loses about 30 percent of the information; to two categories loses about 70 percent (Bryson and Phillips, 1974). In addition, the calculation of measures of central tendency and variability is less accurate if carried out on collapsed data; these calculations should be performed on the uncollapsed information.

Quantitative Variables.   Certain statistical tests for quantitative variables assume a normal distribution. If this assumption is not met, the results of the tests can be distorted. The easiest way to check whether a quantitative variable is normally distributed is to examine a histogram. Some statistics packages superimpose a normal curve on the histogram with the same mean and standard deviation as your sample. This makes it easier to judge how close to normal the distribution is.

Also compare the variable's mean and median; if they are approximately the same, the variable is probably, but not necessarily, roughly normal in distribution. If the differences are moderate, the distribution is somewhat skewed (the number of cases in one tail is greater than the other). If the differences are substantial, then the distribution is likely to be far from normal. Finally, as a general rule of thumb, a roughly normal distribution with a coefficient of skewness greater than 1.0 (or less than -1.0) may require transformation if the sample size is small.

Fortunately, the normality assumption is fairly **robust** in statistical tests. It can be violated, sometimes quite drastically, without undue harm to the results. However, if a distribution is far from normal (substantially skewed or multipeaked), the results of statistical tests may be unreliable. (For more details, check Chapters 16 and 17.)

Remedy. If an important variable is nonnormal and your statistical test assumes normality, the remedy is to **transform** the variable to bring it closer to a normal curve shape. See Box 14.3 for a discussion of common transformations. Which is best depends on the degree of skewness in the variable and is determined by trial and error.

Outliers

An **outlier** is a case that lies at one extreme end or the other of the distribution of a variable, separated from the rest of the cases more than is likely in a normal distribution.

The third distribution check, for outliers, applies only to quantitative variables. An outlier can seriously distort your results. For example, a single extreme case can affect the mean so that it is no longer a good measure of central tendency. If the nine employees of a small firm earn monthly salaries of $1,500 each and the manager makes $20,000 a month, the mean salary is $3,350, which isn't typical of any employee. Similarly, an outlier may seriously distort a relationship test because that one case strongly influences the test results. (Such a case is said to have high **leverage**.) Outliers can affect all relationship tests. Consequently they cannot be ignored *even if you have a large sample.*

The outlier check is carried out only after data have been transformed to correct problem distributions, since a transformation may move an apparent outlier much closer to the rest of the data. Run histograms and look for cases well separated from the main body of data. Also check the cases with lowest and highest values. (Some statistics programs and regression diagnostics routines identify outliers for you.) In general terms, anything further than three standard deviations from the mean can be considered a potential outlier.

Remedy. If you find a value substantially distant from the rest of the distribution, take the following three steps:

1. Investigate whether that case is a measurement, coding, or data entry error, and correct it as required.

2. If the value is not an error, check to see whether the outlier has a substantial effect on your results. Run descriptive statistics with and without the case;

BOX 14.3
RESEARCH SKILLS
Transforming Variables

The logic behind transformation is to alter the data by removing the effect of some naturally occurring process that results in a skewed distribution. Constant growth rates are one example; other processes that result in skewed distributions are competition for scarce resources, which shows up in such indicators as net worth of a company (a few do very well, most do less well) and mortality (people and firms are more likely to perish or drop out as some characteristic, such as age, increases). Therefore, cases that seem to be extreme become, after transformation, part of a more normal distribution.

We don't have to know the underlying process in order to use transformations. The immediate objective is to find the transformation that brings the bulk of the data into a nearly normal distribution. Any remaining outliers can then be examined separately.

Distributions Skewed Right. The most common skewness is to the right (positive skew): Variables such as size of firm, employee ages, wages, monthly sales, and consumer savings often take this form. To correct distributions skewed right, a number of transformations can be used. (All assume no negative values; if your data have negative values, add a constant to each value to make them all positive.) In order of strength (the degree to which they correct for skewness), they are

Square root	$\sqrt{X}$
Log	$L_{10}(X)$ or $Ln(X)$
or log of value + one[1]	$L_{10}(X+1)$ or $Ln(X+1)$
Negative reciprocal root	$-1/\sqrt{X}$
Negative reciprocal	$-1/X$

For positively skewed data, begin with a logarithmic transformation. It will correct most distribution

[1] Use this form of logarithmic transformation when values are close to zero, since the log of zero is undefined.

problems and is the most common transformation. It is also effective for time-series data that show a fairly constant rate of growth. It transforms these nonlinear series to linear ones.

Distributions Skewed Left. Skewness in this direction is less common, but still occurs in business research. To correct a distribution that is skewed left (and assuming all values are positive), try the following transformations in order of strength:

Squared	X^2
Cubed	X^3
Biquadratic	X^4

Choosing a Transformation. Selecting a transformation for a single sample is usually not very difficult, since computers can easily generate the histograms and statistics that allow us to compare transformations. The task becomes more difficult if several comparison samples, each with a separate distribution, have to be transformed (all, of course, with the same transformation). It helps to keep in mind the following criteria, in order of importance:

1. Select the transformation that provides the most symmetry for the middle half of the cases, that is, those between the first and third quartiles.

2. If the first criterion is met, choose the transformation that achieves symmetry in the outer quarters of the distribution, that is, in the first and fourth quartiles.

3. If the first and second criteria are met, choose the transformation that results in the fewest outliers.

Exceptions. The transformations described here will not work for uniform distributions or those with two or more peaks or clusters. The best tactic with such distributions is to look for a factor that will break down the sample into two or more subgroups, each with a more regular distribution. This breakdown factor often becomes a moderating variable in multivariate analysis. Similarly, declining distributions in which the peak occurs at the zero point (i.e., most cases have none of the characteristic) are also difficult to transform, although they can sometimes be treated as extreme examples of positively skewed distributions.

Improving Measures. As well as for correcting skewed distributions, researchers transform variables to create measures that more accurately reflect intended concepts. As discussed in Chapter 8, many factors such as age, wages, and firm size are transformed to take into account that the *measure* does not have a linear relationship with the *concept.* Most of these transformations are logarithmic.

check the variable's relationship to your dependent variable with and without the case. Compare your results.

3. If it affects results, check to see whether it is a unique case in other respects than the variable you are checking. To do this, list its ID number, locate the raw data, and check other characteristics. (To avoid listing all your cases, ask the computer to select only those cases above (or below) a given point on the variable in question; find an appropriate point by referring to the histogram.)

SUGGESTION

If you contemplate dropping one or more outliers, carry out your analysis both with and without those cases and, if they are substantially different, report *both* results. If you do so, also describe the ways in which the outliers are different from the other cases, that is, their extreme characteristics.

If the outlier affects results, but no other variables for that case are outliers, follow option a or b. If other variables indicate that the case is truly unique in several respects, follow option c:

a. The first and preferred option is to *transform* the variable's distribution so that the outlier is brought closer to the mean. This option is available only if the variable has not already been transformed.

b. Change the value for that particular case to a "missing value" code. This retains the case, but removes it from analysis of that particular variable so it cannot unduly influence results. For example, if you are studying CEOs and find one aged 87, and the rest are between 34 and 62 with a mean age of 54 and a standard deviation of 5.2, you might find that the outlier would be so different in other respects from other cases that its presence would distort your conclusions involving that variable.

c. The third option, and last resort, is to drop the entire case. This should only be done if it appears to be different from other cases in many important characteristics, and these differences have "theoretical" implications that suggest this case is not in your intended target population. In other words, extremely atypical cases can and should be dropped as long as you can justify dropping them. If the 87-year-old CEO in the example was the only one in your sample who also owned the firm, you would be justified in treating that case as theoretically different and dropping it.

Remember that dropping an outlier is serious and should only be done when you understand *why* it is different from other cases.

MEASUREMENT CHECKS

Following sample checks and adjustments, researchers check the quality of their measures, particularly for important and multiple-item measures. Measurement checks answer these two questions:

- Are the measures sufficiently *valid* and *reliable* to use?

- Is there evidence of *item nonresponse bias*?

For example if, in a questionnaire to accountants about their reporting practices, you included reversed versions of the same question or response format (to check for equivalence reliability and position or acquiescence bias), this is the stage at which to compute the correlation between the two items.

Measurement Validity

Good measures are both reliable and valid. A valid measure is one which reflects or captures the concept of interest to the researcher. Checks for validity fall into two categories: *theoretical* and *empirical.* Theoretical validity (face and content validity) is a matter of judgment and can be checked at any time (preferably prior to data gathering). However, since empirical validity (criterion and construct validity) requires that you actually have the data ready for analysis, it is part of your preliminary analysis. Normally researchers check only a few variables for empirical validity: key and primary variables, plus indexes and scales.

Criterion Validity. This type of empirical validity examines the relationship between the variable to be checked (often a scale) and a criterion variable. For both *concurrent* and *predictive* validity, a strong relationship between criterion and variable increases confidence in the validity of your measure. If the relationship is weak, then your conclusions about that variable will have to be qualified, since it is not picking up the concept you intended. (Note that criterion validity is often checked with just a subsample of your data for which the criterion is gathered.) See Chapter 16 for bivariate measures of association to use for criterion validity checks, as well as the other checks we describe later that involve correlations.

Construct Validity. These validity checks examine hypothesized relationships between the variable to be checked and other variables in your study. *Convergent validity* checks relationships you expect to be reasonably strong. For example, if a measure of safety consciousness based on answers to a series of attitudinal questions correlates strongly with employee's accident records, your confidence in the validity of your measure is increased. Likewise, if you develop a measure of how accountants handle variable manufacturing costs for certain new manufacturing processes and find that the measure does not correlate with rate of return as you expected, you would likely revise or abandon the measure. Checks for *discriminant validity* are the opposite: you expect and hypothesize a *lack* of relationship between the variable to be checked and some other.[3]

With multiple-item measures, researchers also check interitem construct validity to determine whether more than one theoretical construct is represented in the items. The normal technique is to use *factor analysis* to determine whether there is a single underlying construct (see Box 14.4).

Reliability

Reliability is checked in two general ways: stability and equivalence. *Stability* is normally assessed by the test-retest method: checking the relationship between two applications of the measure at different times. The higher the correlation, the greater the reliability. Stability assessments encounter a number of difficulties and for that reason are not as useful as equivalence-based checks. However, they are the only way to assess reliability for single-item measures, and they lend themselves to repeated-measure experimental designs. When there is a control or comparison group, use it to test reliability, since one expects (or hopes for) little or no change there. If a test-retest shows low reliability in a single-item measure, conclusions may have to be qualified.

Equivalence checks of reliability are limited to multiple-item scale measures. (This section deals with existing multiple-item scales; for the construction of new scales, see the section on scale and index construction.) The underlying idea is to examine the relationships among the items.[3] If the items correlate highly they are equivalent measures of the underlying concept and the overall measure is therefore reliable. If an equivalence check shows low reliability, researchers normally delete one or more items to improve reliability.

The two most common procedures for checking the reliability of multiple-item measures are split-half and internal consistency.

Split-Half Reliability Checks. When a number of items are used to measure the variable, one way to assess reliability is to divide the set of items in two arbitrarily, construct a scale from each half, and determine the correlation between the scales. This **split-half** method, as it is called, estimates reliability with the following equation (to compensate for the fact that the scale you will actually use is twice as long as each half, and therefore more reliable than either half):

$$REL = (2\ r)\ /\ (1\ +\ r)$$

[3]Note that for multiple-item measures, both validity and reliability involve looking at relationships among the items. The difference is subtle. Validity checks look for *patterns* of relationships and underlying factors to see if they correspond to the concepts you had in mind for the measure. Reliability checks ignore what the items actually measure, but investigate whether they measure the same thing by examining the *degree* of relationships among the items. But since an index usually combines two or more fairly disparate items, unlike an attitude scale which normally measures a single underlying concept, there is little point in trying to assess the reliability of an index by examining interitem correlations.

BOX 14.4
RESEARCH SKILLS

Factor Analysis

USES

- To see which variables in a set are closely related to one another, that is, to find the pattern of correlations among the variables.
- To determine measurement validity in index and scale construction.

CONCEPT

The idea is to reduce a larger number of variables to a minimum number of latent factors, each of which represents a different concept or dimension in the data. From a correlation matrix, factor analysis creates a linear combination of the variables (a factor) that best explains their joint variance; this first factor is followed by other orthogonal linear combinations, each succeeding factor explaining the variance remaining after prior factors have explained all they can. Factors are then rotated to maximize their correlations with some variables and minimize them with others, in order to make the factors more easily interpretable.

CHECKS

- For outliers that might distort correlation coefficients.
- Whether correlations are sufficiently high for factor analysis to be useful (Bartlett's test of sphericity and the Kaiser-Meyer-Olkin test).
- That variables have approximately normal distributions.

OUTPUT

- Loadings: the correlations between each variable and each of the factors (for orthogonal factors).

Loadings and correlations are somewhat different if oblique rotations are used.
- Eigenvalues: estimates of the amount of variance explained by each factor. Useful in deciding how many factors to include. One rule of thumb is to keep all factors with an eigenvalue greater than one. Otherwise, use a *scree plot* to help you decide the number of factors.
- Communalities: estimates of the proportion of variance in each variable explained by the factors. Useful in deciding which variables, if any, should be dropped from the analysis.

VARIATIONS

Principal components analysis stops short of rotating the factors: the principal components are the unrotated orthogonal factors. They are generally more difficult to interpret. The technique is not as frequently used in business research. Principal components also refers to the method of extracting the initial factors. Alternative methods include maximum likelihood and unweighted least squares.

Most factor analysis is exploratory. *Confirmatory* factor analysis is used to test prior hypotheses about the interrelationships of variables.

COMMENTS

- When factors are rotated to improve interpretability, a nonorthogonal (oblique) rotation is normally better for most business research, since there is little necessity for assuming that the factors must be independent of one another.
- Factor analysis will not work satisfactorily with small samples.
- There is no simple significance test for factors.
- Missing values: for small and moderate size sam-

ples avoid reducing the number of cases too much: use pairwise deletion or estimate values for cases that otherwise would be dropped.

- In factor analysis for measurement validity checks, use a scree plot of eigenvalues to assess the number of factors underlying the items, and use oblique rotations to get the most interpretable factors. Unless specifically constructed with intended subscales, a scale should have only one factor.

- For category items, you can use *latent structure analysis* in place of factor analysis (which assumes quantitative variables).

For example, if two halves correlate at .75, the estimated reliability for your scale would be .86. (Most researchers strive for scale reliabilities of .85 or better.)

Internal Consistency Checks. An alternative approach, better than the split-half method, examines the relationships among all items simultaneously, rather than just relying on a single arbitrary division of the scale into two halves. **Cronbach's alpha** is the most frequently used consistency measure (Box 14.5).

Interrater Reliability. This equivalence check for reliability is used when two or more coders or interviewers make decisions about interpreting information or coding data. Checks for interrater (or intercoder) reliability are usually based on correlations between the coders' scores on a common set of cases. With a minimum of 20 cases, the correlation should be .85 or higher. If the codes are categories (e.g., two raters evaluate the financial health of 133 firms on a four-point scale), use a PRE measure of association (see Chapter 16) and look for values of .70 or better. The sooner in a project you carry out interrater reliability checks, the sooner you can make corrections to improve data reliability.

Missing Data and Item Nonresponse Bias

Missing data refers to cases with incomplete information, that is, data are present for only some of the variables. This measurement check looks for both (1) the extent of missing data in general and (2) missing data that suggests the presence of item nonresponse bias. (When the entire case is missing, the corresponding problem is missing cases bias; see the discussion of sample checks earlier.)

Missing data can be a serious problem in multivariate analysis, particularly if there are relatively few (less than 100) cases. It is a problem that cannot be ignored, but no matter how you deal with it, you encounter some risks. The problem of item nonresponse bias is more critical in descriptive and prediction research, which attempt to estimate population characteristics. However, this kind of bias can also distort conclusions about causal effects in explanatory and evaluation research.

BOX 14.5
RESEARCH SKILLS

Chronbach's Alpha

USES

Item analysis: assessing the reliability of an additive scale, that is, a scale in which the total score is the sum of scores on a set of individual items.

CONCEPT

Cronbach's alpha is an internal consistency measure of reliability. The idea is to determine the average covariance among pairs of items in the scale. The higher this average, the more the items correlate with one another, and thus the greater the internal consistency and reliability.

VARIATION

Some software provides, for each item, the value of alpha if that item were to be deleted from the scale. This information is particularly useful if you are constructing a scale out of a larger number of items, rather than just checking the reliability of an existing scale.

COMMENTS

The value of alpha ranges between zero and one (although it can be negative if correlations among the items are not all positive). A value of .85 or better is usually taken to represent sufficient reliability. Values less than .70 mean the measure is suspect. In general, alpha will be greater the larger the interitem correlations or the more items in the measure.

Assessing. Unfortunately, the lack of data means that you cannot assess item nonresponse bias directly. However, there is an indirect way of checking by looking at other variables that might be associated with nonresponse. Steps for carrying out this check are described in Box 14.6 (see page 512).

CASE EXAMPLE

In a survey of airline flight attendants' attitudes toward mandatory drug testing, the researcher noticed that a fairly large number of respondents scrawled on their questionnaires and refused to provide demographic information. They also were less likely to answer questions about the extent of marijuana use and their use of prescription drugs. In an analysis of item nonresponse bias, the researcher found that these respondents were *more* likely to support mandatory drug testing in the workplace. She then concluded that estimates of marijuana use among her respondents were probably too high, given that those who supported mandatory drug testing were probably less likely to use it. She also concluded that the attendants who didn't respond to the particular items were very angry about drug use by their co-workers and were offended by the questions asking about their own use of marijuana and prescription drugs.

Remedies.   The next step is to remedy the situation. Unfortunately, little is known about the effects of different ways of dealing with missing data. At the very least you should identify the extent and nature of any item nonresponse bias, and use it to qualify your conclusions or help explain unexpected results.

ADVANCED TOPIC

Options for handling missing data include the following:

- *Listwise deletion.* Dropping a case with any missing data is acceptable if the sample is large and missing cases bias is not a problem. Otherwise, this option will seriously reduce the number of cases and can distort conclusions in the presence of item nonresponse bias.

- *Pairwise deletion.* The second option makes use of all possible pairs of cases when calculating the bivariate correlations on which multivariate analysis is based. For example, if variable X is missing data for seven cases while variables Y and Z have complete data for all 100 cases, the correlations involving X will be based on 93 cases; the Y-Z correlation is based on all 100. The problem here is that sometimes this produces anomalies in the statistics that lead to faulty conclusions. The problem is less acute the larger the sample.

- *Substitute the mean.* The third option is to substitute the mean value for the variable. This is a conservative procedure, but it also decreases the size of correlations. If you have to substitute the mean of a variable in several cases, the loss of research power can be substantial. A refinement is to substitute not the overall mean, but the mean for other cases with similar characteristics.

- *Substitute a predicted value.* The fourth option is to substitute a predicted value based on a multiple regression of variables and cases with complete data. In other words, the variable with the missing value(s) is treated as the dependent variable. This option requires more time and effort, but it does make use of all available information. One drawback is that it tends to produce data points close to the regression line, thus making your data look better than they really are.

The best strategy is to try two or three options and compare the results you get. If the results are similar, you can be more confident that missing cases are not producing misleading analysis. Note that none of these will remedy item nonresponse bias, for which the only solutions are indirect, as illustrated in the preceding case example.

COMPUTING NEW VARIABLES

The final, and often the biggest, task in preliminary analysis is to compute the new variables needed for analysis. This step includes recodes of existing variables, computation of composite variables that combine two or more original variables, construction of new scales and indexes, and the computation of gain scores. This is also the point at which structural variables, computed from lower level data sets, would be added to your computer file. All computations should be checked (see Box 14.7).

Recodes

Researchers frequently find it necessary to recode variables for consistency and better analysis. Such recoding includes collapsing categories, reversed codes, dummy variable recodes, and ranking scale recodes.

Reversed Codes. To avoid confusion during analysis, category variables should be coded logically so that the greater the value, the more of some quality. For example, a rating question with five categories from "Like very much" to "Don't like at all" might be coded 1 to 5 for data entry convenience. This variable should be recoded so that the higher the value, the greater the degree of liking. A simple formula for reverse coding is

$$\text{NEWVAR} = (n + 1) - \text{OLDVAR}$$

where NEWVAR is the acronym for the new variable, OLDVAR is the old variable, and n is the number of categories.

Dummy Variables. Regression analysis, the most common statistical technique in business research, requires that nominal variables be recoded to dichotomous dummy variables. For convenience, name the new variable after the category coded "1."

If you have a *dichotomous* variable (such as firm ownership: private or public) recode it to "0" and "1." The new variable would be called either PUBLIC or PRIVATE depending on which category was coded "1."

Recode any nominal variable with *three or more categories* to a series of dummy variables, each representing the presence or absence of a category.

BOX 14.6
RESEARCH SKILLS

Assessing Item Nonresponse Bias

Following are four steps for estimating the existence and extent of item nonresponse bias in a variable.

1. Run frequency distributions to identify those variables with a disproportionate number of missing value cases. (For example, imagine that in a survey of 250 employees, 27 gave no answer to a question asking whether they had ever considered early retirement. The variable with the next highest number of missing answers had only 7 missing values.)

2. Think of factors (for which you have measures) that might be associated with nonresponse for the variables with many missing cases. (For example, it could be that *older* employees who actually are considering early retirement might not want their employer to know about it and might therefore have left the question unanswered. The variable possibly associated with missing data is "age.")

3. If the associated variable is *quantitative*, calculate its mean for both the missing and the nonmissing groups. (Temporarily recode the variable with the missing values into a new variable with two categories: "missing" and "nonmissing.") Check with a t-test using a fairly high level of alpha, such as .15. If the differences are significant, then item nonresponse bias is a definite possibility. (In our example, the average age of the "missing" group is 51.4 and for the "nonmissing" group is 48.2, but the difference is not significant at the .15 level.)

4. If the associated factor is a *category variable*, recode as in step 3 and cross-tabulate to calculate the proportion of missing cases in each category of the factor. Check with a chi-square test at a .15 alpha level. Again, significant differences indicate a definite possibility of item nonresponse bias. (In our example, 5.5 percent of female employees left the question unanswered; 12.3 percent of males did, with a difference significant at the .15 level.)

Thus, in a study of equipment downtime, the variable WORKSITE with four categories (Ajax, Brant, Cochran, and Dundas, originally coded "1" to "4") would be recoded to four new dummy variables:

AJAX   = 1 if equipment failure occurred at the Ajax work site
         = 0 otherwise

BRANT   = 1 if failure at the Brant work site
         = 0 otherwise

COCHRAN = 1 if failure at the Cochran work site
         = 0 otherwise

DUNDAS   = 1 if failure at the Dundas work site
         = 0 otherwise

Thus an incidence of equipment failure leading to downtime at Dundas, originally coded as "4" for the variable WORKSITE, would produce dummy variable codes of "0" for AJAX, BRANT, and COCHRAN, and "1" for DUNDAS. (Regression analysis requires that one of these categories be

BOX 14.7
MOVING SOUND: A CONTINUING CASE

Part Eleven: Constructing New Variables

"This is fun! It's a lot like the mainframe software we used back in business school." Peter is proudly showing George some of the preliminary analysis he's carrying out for the project. "Sharon got this micro for accounting and inventory, and there's plenty of room for the new statistical software too."

"And you're doing the analysis?"

"Well, Bill from the stock room is actually operating the computer. I'm just telling him what to run."

"And who did the data entry?"

"Well, we were going to send it out, but I convinced Sharon we could save money if Bill took care of it. It wasn't hard, either, with the special software they have. Did some of the cleaning automatically."

"And the editing and coding?"

"Bill again. But I took care of the tough editing decisions."

"And was it Bill who dug up the available data on sales and stuff?"

"Right. How'd you guess?"

"I think I smell someone painting a fence. You haven't been reading *Tom Sawyer*, have you? Never mind. What's this composite variable you wanted to ask me about?"

"Well, we have the variable 'sales' and 'town population' and 'campus population'—number of students on campus. If I create a new variable, 'sales per population,' do I use town population or campus population as the denominator?"

"Go with campus population. It's a better measure of your target marketing group."

"And I have three categories for the weather variable: better than average, average, and worse than average. What do I do with it?"

"Convert two to dummy variables, and pick one, say 'worse than average,' for the reference category."

"OK. And how do I test this formula I worked out for that question which asks them to rank their favorite kinds of music? You know, I have to assign ranks to the unranked choices, like 'country music.'" He gives George a nudge in the ribs.

"The best way is to ask the computer to list the first ten or twenty cases. Ask for the original variables, plus your new variables. Then do the calculations by hand, and check whether your results match the new variables."

"Sounds easy enough."

"It is. Data analysis is mostly just common sense. And by the way, you'll get a better feel for what's going on if you do the runs yourself. Your software works interactively, you know. It's not like those batch jobs you did on the mainframe. Don't be afraid to get your hands in the data. A little fence paint never hurt anyone."

"Huh?"

dropped from the regression equation to serve as the "reference" category. Thus you need only recode dummy variables for all but one of the categories in the original nominal variable.)

Category ordinal variables are generally not converted to dummy variables because this loses the ordering information in the variable. (See Chapter 17 for alternatives.)

Ranking Scale Recodes. Ranking scale questions ask respondents to rank-order a list of items. For example, department heads might be asked to rank the most difficult budgeting problems their department faces, choosing from a list of 11 options. Treat each option as a *separate variable,* with a value indicating what rank it received. Thus if a respondent ranks the option "unanticipated equipment repairs" second, this variable is coded as "2."

Some researchers go further and group the items to reduce the number of variables. The grouping is either

- On some *theoretical* basis using the researcher's judgment (e.g., "unanticipated equipment repairs" and "underestimated supplies usage" are judged to belong to the same group), or

- On some *empirical* basis using a statistical procedure such as factor analysis to discover which options "go together" (e.g., ranks for "unanticipated equipment repairs" and "temporary secretarial staff costs" correlate highly).

Each group is assigned the average of the rankings the respondent gave the group options.

Composite Variables

Unlike recodes that convert one variable into one or more new variables, composite variables are those constructed from two or more original variables. They include proportions, rates, counts, and elapsed time variables.

Proportions and Rates. Preliminary analysis often involves this kind of calculation, particularly for available data studies. For example, if you have two variables representing the number of male and female employees in each of 54 departments, you'll likely need to convert these data to a new variable, proportion of females (or males), in order to take into account the fact that departments are not all the same size.

The same principle is used for defining rates. For example, if you have two variables representing number of bankruptcies in each state, and each state's population, you can calculate the number of bankruptcies per 100,000 population by dividing number of bankruptcies by state population and multiplying by 100,000.

If your unit of analysis is a group, department, or other aggregate that varies in size, failure to convert data to proportions and rates will produce distorted results. Variables such as number of accidents, total hours of overtime worked, expenses over budget, number of machinery failures, and similar characteristics will inevitably correlate highly with one another because they all correlate with size. Converting these variables to standardized measures (per person) will overcome the problem.

Counts. The number of times something occurs or is mentioned is often a useful composite variable. For example, this is a convenient way of handling responses to a question using a grouped ranking response scale.

CASE EXAMPLE

A researcher surveyed a sample of brokers to determine what personal and firm factors led them to recommend certain types of stocks. He asked respondents to rate the potential of each of 74 stocks as "great," "modest," or "little." The researcher also wanted a general measure of each broker's optimism about the market in general. To compute this new variable, he counted the number of stocks each respondent rated "great." The result was a new quantitative variable ranging from "0" (no stocks rated "great") to "74" (all rated "great"). The researcher then checked the distribution of the new variable to look for normality and outliers.

Counts are also useful in analyzing open-ended general comment questions in surveys. Code each separate remark as "positive," "negative," or "neutral." Then count the number of negative comments made by each respondent to get an indicator of his or her feelings about the overall topic. Even better, count all comments, and compute the proportion that are negative.

Elapsed Time Computations.   Variables representing elapsed time are important in business research and are generally computed as the difference between two "event" dates (e.g., the beginning and end of a period of production downtime or the date of placing a supplies order and the date of delivery). As long as the event dates are coded as "year, month, day," many statistical packages have special routines or functions to convert dates to elapsed days, months, or years (as noted in Chapter 13).

The same routines can also compute the time from some event to the present, such as the length of time a product has been on the market. Simply designate some date (such as the first day of data gathering) as the "present," and apply the routine.

Scale and Index Construction

Scales and indexes are composite variables, since they represent new variables constructed from a set of separate items. The normal procedure is to select from the items you originally measured the subset that produces the scale or index with the greatest reliability and validity.

Scale Construction.   Imagine that your questionnaire data include 15 attitudinal items asking about union activities on two dimensions—job protection and benefits. You want to construct from these items a scale of "union satisfaction." This involves two steps: (1) selecting which of the 15 items make the best scale (called **item analysis**) and (2) combining them into a single variable.

The first step is to check the validity and reliability of your items. For validity, follow the procedures just suggested for measurement validity checks.

Assume you have tried to tap two different dimensions of union satisfaction. By examining the results of a factor analysis, you can check to see how many factors or dimensions you have and whether they correspond to the two you want to measure. As a result of this analysis, you might discard some of the items as irrelevant.

The next part of item analysis is to examine the reliability of the remaining items. Reliability checks for existing scales were described earlier. Here we are discussing the use of reliability checks for the construction of a *new* scale. However, the procedure is the same: use Chronbach's alpha to look for internal consistency among items. Again, you may discard one or more items because of inconsistency. In particular, drop items that seem to have a substantial downward effect on the level of alpha. If the two intended dimensions of your scale are relatively unrelated (which the validity check will tell you), you should assess separately the reliability of the subset of items pertaining to each dimension.

The second step, combining the items, is discussed in Box 14.8.

Index Construction.   Imagine that from available secondary data you want to construct an index of the workplace climate consisting of a combination of the noise level, the absenteeism rate, the turnover rate, and the number of accidents.

The first step is to check the validity of the index. If there are five or more items you can try a factor analysis (see Box 14.4). Otherwise limit your check to an inspection of the correlation matrix of items. Keep in mind that, because this is an index, you are not expecting high interitem correlations (and in fact very high correlations would indicate redundant items). Compare the correlations (or number of factors) with what you expected when you assembled the items. Delete any items that seem not to be capturing aspects of the concept you want.

The second step is to combine the items (reliability is normally not an issue for indexes, since they intentionally tap different dimensions of a concept). This may involve *weighting* the items differently to reflect your assumptions about their relative importance to the overall concept. For example, you may decide that noise level is three times and absenteeism is four times as important as turnover and number of accidents in contributing to workplace climate. See Box 14.8.

Gain Scores

Panel designs and experimental pretest-posttest designs utilize repeated measures of a variable. To handle these measures, a common solution has been to calculate the **gain score** for each case, the difference between its pretest and posttest values or between two waves of a panel. The gain score represents the gain, or change in each case, for example, the change in sales across 35 marketing regions following an advertising program.

A major problem with the use of gain scores is that the gain is often

BOX 14.8
RESEARCH SKILLS

Combining Scale or Index Items

Once item analysis is complete, the final step in constructing a scale or index is to weight and combine the individual items into a new variable.

Scales. Scale items are usually attitudinal questions with the same response scale format, similar wording, and coded from 1 to N (number of response categories). The following steps will result in a scale that also ranges from 1 to N and gives each item in the scale the same weight:

1. Recode reversed item variables to get consistent ordering. The highest value (e.g., "5" on a five-point scale) should represent the highest level of the characteristic or attitude for each item.

2. Compute a new variable equal to the sum of the item variables.

3. Divide the new variable by the number of items.

Thus the scores for a scale of union attitudes, based on 12 five-point scales, would range from "1" (all responses equal "1") to "5" (all responses equal "5").

Indexes. For indexes, you are often dealing with factors measured on different units. In the text example, noise is a subjective rating from 1 (low) to 7 (high). Absenteeism rates vary from .00 to .19 and turnover from .00 to .12. The number of reported accidents varies from 3 to 57. Thus procedures for index construction must take into account these differences. Use the following steps to obtain an index ranging from 1 to 10:

1. Recode items as necessary so that each has a consistent ordering.

2. Consider whether one or more of the items should be transformed to obtain a more normal distribution or to better reflect the relationship between measure and underlying concept. (For example, the log of number of employees is a better measure of firm size than just "number of employees.")

3. Convert each item to a common scale of 0 to 10. First, subtract (or add) the minimum value so that the lowest possible score is zero. Second, divide by one-ninth of the new maximum value so that the maximum is 9. Third, add one so that the new variable ranges from 1 to 10. For example, the number of accidents ranges from 3 to 57. It is converted as follows:

$$\text{NEWVAR} = [(\text{OLDVAR} - 3)/6.0] + 1$$

4. If items are to be weighted differently, multiply by the weighting factors.

5. Sum the items, and divide the sum by the total of the weighting factors (the weighting factor for an unweighted item is "1"). For example, the workplace climate index with the weighting given in the text example would be

$$\text{CLIMATE} = [3(\text{NOISE}) + 4(\text{ABSENTEEISM}) + \text{TURNOVER} + \text{ACCIDENTS}]/9$$

Because the assignment of weights is somewhat arbitrary and is akin to adding apples and oranges, you should avoid extreme differences in weights wherever possible. (A more refined index can be obtained by using as weights the regression coefficients you obtain by regressing the rest of the items on one chosen at random. For most business research, however, the gain is not worth the effort or the assumptions about item distributions required for this procedure.)

correlated with the pretest score or original value. For example, regions that show high levels of sales on the pretest show higher levels of gain. Thus higher gain scores might simply be an artifact of higher pretest scores. As we discuss in Chapter 17, multivariate analysis alternatives to gain scores produce results with greater internal validity.

PRELIMINARY ANALYSIS OF TIME SERIES

Time-series designs require a somewhat different set of preliminary checks (trend, seasonal cycles, autocorrelation, and homogeneity of variance) and new variable computations (lagged and leading variables). The specific procedures depend on which type of time series you have, but in all types time is included as a second, independent variable.

Types of Time Series

Time-series designs involve the use of data gathered at more than one time point or period. As discussed in Chapter 4, there are four different types of time-series designs: trend, concomitant, interrupted, and pooled.

- *Trend* time series involves one variable (e.g., number of mergers and acquisitions per month) and one case (e.g., the United States). It is commonly found in descriptive research. The principle objective is to describe the trend and cycles underlying the data, gain insight into what has happened in the past, and extrapolate to the future.

- *Concomitant* time series involves one case and two or more variables. The researcher is usually interested in the relationship between a dependent variable and one or more independents. The variables may represent continuous series of changing circumstances (such as monthly sales), discrete events (such as strikes), or onetime changes (such as new employment legislation).

- *Interrupted* time series also involves one case and two or more variables. However, the primary independent variable is a manipulated change (such as a new hiring policy) that usually occurs near the middle of the series.

- *Pooled* time series is any of the preceding three types with more than one case. Normally there are no more than a dozen cases; if there are many cases and few time points, you have a panel design, a version of repeated-measures designs. (Panel design data are generally analyzed quite differently from time series.)

With respect to the preliminary analysis checks described earlier, all these designs should employ measurement checks for validity, reliability, and nonresponse bias where appropriate.

Problems.   Time-series data often violate the assumptions underlying relationship tests (see Chapter 17). The major consequence is that estimates of population characteristics and relationships often appear to be much more precise than they should be. Less often, the estimates themselves are *biased* (too high or too low). For these reasons, it is important to check time-series data in preliminary analysis. In particular, researchers try to correct for the effects of trend, seasonality, autocorrelation, and changes in the variance of a variable over time. Outliers and nonlinearity can also lead to distorted conclusions.

Trend and Seasonality Problems

Trend is a consistent upward or downward drift in observations over time; labor costs and the proportion of population in rural areas both show trend. It is a problem for all time series except trend time series, which specifically examines trends.

Trend is a problem because it can seriously distort conclusions about the relationships between variables. Any time two variables both change in a relatively consistent fashion over time, even for different reasons (e.g., the consumer price index increases and age-specific death rates decrease), simple measures of relationship will show a correlation *due solely to trend,* even though there is no true cause-and-effect relationship between the variables. "Time" acts as an extraneous variable creating a spurious correlation between other variables.

A simple demonstration of the trend problem is shown in Figure 14.3. The graph shows how two variables "A" and "B" change over time. The two variables show almost no relationship. However, if you rotate this book so that the dashed lines become the horizontal and vertical axes (which is analogous to adding trend to each variable), it is clear that the correlation between the variables increases. As one goes up, the other tends to rise as well. These two variables are now correlated solely as a result of trend.

Seasonal cycles (e.g., higher levels of a variable in the summer, lower in winter) can also exaggerate a relationship. They may also obscure longer term changes (a problem in trend series analysis) and introduce variation that reduces the precision of population estimates.

Detection.   Check for trend and seasonality with a **time plot.** Time plots simply plot a dependent variable against time (as in Figure 14.5 on page 525). They are extremely important in preliminary analysis of time-series data—the equivalent of frequency distributions, bar charts, and histograms for

FIGURE 14.3
Illustration of
Correlation Due
Solely to Trend

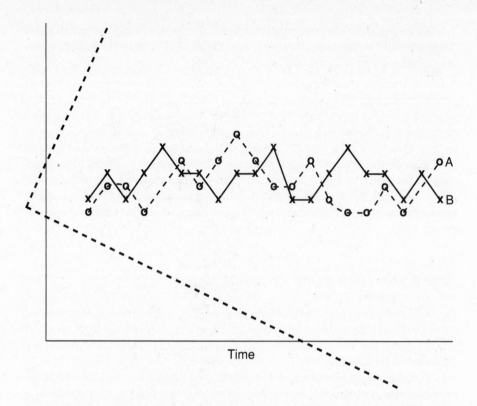

Time

non-time-series variables. It is sometimes useful to add a **trend line** to the time plot (as in Figure 14.5).[4]

Other means of examining trend include smoothing functions and sequential box plots. **Smoothing functions** remove seasonality and some of the random fluctuations in the data so that you can see any trend more clearly. **Sequential box plots** consist of a series of box plots for consecutive sets of observations. Whichever procedure you use, check for both linear and nonlinear trends.

Solutions. Because of its effects on measures of relationship, trend must always be dealt with in all but trend-analysis time series. The general approach is to identify the trend and seasonality and remove it from the data statistically or mathematically.

- If you have 50 observations or more, the statistical approach of choice is ARIMA ("Box-Jenkins") modeling. This procedure (1) models the effects of autocorrelation, trend and seasonality, and random disturbances and (2) uses the model to "remove" these effects from the data.

[4]The trend line is produced by *regression analysis,* which generates the straight line that best fits the data. Regression analysis is vital to time series. More on regression can be found in Chapters 16 and 17.

- Another statistical solution is to add a "time" variable to the multivariate analysis. Similarly, three seasonal dummy variables will remove seasonality.

- Mathematically the researcher can remove trend by transforming the data (usually with a log or exponential transformation). This is the most effective way of dealing with nonlinear trend.

- Another mathematical treatment for trend is to *difference* the variable (see Box 14.9). Seasonal differencing can reduce or remove seasonal cycles from the data.

After each attempt, be sure to recheck the time plot to see whether trend has been removed.

Autocorrelation

Another problem that threatens internal and external validity in time-series analysis is autocorrelation (also known as "serial correlation").

Autocorrelation occurs because observations from the same case taken close together in time will be more alike than observations further apart. Monthly sales, quarterly production costs, people, firms, and other types of cases tend to be alike from one measurement time to the next because of inertia or the lingering effects of events. For example, the Canadian dollar exchange rate one week tends to be fairly close to the rate the following week. Thus over a period of weeks the rate slowly rises or falls, but the correlations between successive weeks are positive and fairly substantial.

Autocorrelation may also be negative. For example, if absenteeism is high one day it may be very low the next, as other employees feel obliged to show up, even with coughs and colds, in order to get the work done. However, because absenteeism is low the second day, on the third those same employees may feel justified in staying home, since there now seem to be plenty of people around to share the extra work their absence creates. Once again, successive observations are correlated.

Like trend, autocorrelation is useful in *trend analysis,* since it makes prediction of future values easier. However, it is a problem for interrupted, concomitant, and pooled time series. It violates a basic assumption of most multivariate analysis: independent observations. Figure 14.4 shows what happens. The assumption of independent observations implies that values of a variable should fluctuate randomly on either side of the trend line. However, with autocorrelation the data points remain on one side of the "true" trend line for many observations, only slowly moving to the other side over a long period of time. As a result, a trend line calculated using standard techniques will often show a different slope than the "true" trend line, and the variation among observations will be sharply reduced. The problem often becomes worse as the time between observations decreases.

Autocorrelation occurs when adjacent observations in a time-series variable are correlated, that is, they are more like one another than would happen by chance. In other words, the variable is correlated with itself.

BOX 14.9
RESEARCH SKILLS
Differencing a Time Series

Trend, autocorrelation, and seasonality are problems in concomitant, interrupted, and pooled time series. Differencing is a relatively simple technique for attacking these problems and obtaining a *stationary series* (one without a systematic increase or decrease in the level of the series). It is based on the assumption that each observation is affected by the previous (or several previous) observations, and it tries to remove that effect.

The method is simple: for a variable with trend, from each observation *subtract the value of the previous observation.* The result is a "first-order differenced" series. For example, the time series for a variable is

7 9 8 9 11 12 11 14 13 13 15 16 15 18 10

The trend is obvious. When differenced, the series becomes

2 −1 1 2 1 −1 3 1 0 2 1 −1 3 2

There is no longer any trend. Note, however, that the number of observations is reduced by one.

If a differenced series still shows trend or autocorrelation, you can repeat the operation to obtain a "second-order" series (i.e., the trend is quadratic

rather than linear). You will almost never have to use a higher order of differencing.

Seasonal Differencing. If your series show seasonal fluctuations, these too can be reduced by differencing. The technique here is to subtract from each observation the previous observation from the *same season.* For example, consider the following quarterly data:

7 9 10 8 8 10 10 7 8 9 8 6 8 9 7 7

The seasonal fluctuations are again obvious. When seasonally differenced by subtracting from each observation the observation four positions previous, the series is

1 1 0 −1 0 −1 −2 −1 0 0 −1 1

The seasonal component has now been removed from the data. Notice that the number of observations has been reduced by four (the number of seasons).

Many statistical packages have a routine that will carry out differencing for you. The alternative is to carry out your differencing manually or write a short program to compute differenced values.

Over the long run, errors in estimating the slope of the trend line cancel out. However, the reduced variation leads to *overestimates* of the precision of slope estimates. Without correction, the amount of confidence we place in our estimates is too optimistic. In concomitant time series, we often conclude that we have statistically significant relationships when we do not.

Descriptive and prediction research require precise estimates of population characteristics; explanatory and evaluation research only seek to identify causal relationships. Because precision is vital for the former, autocorrelation is a major concern. For explanatory and evaluation research, trend is a greater problem than autocorrelation. Nonetheless, it is a problem that should not be overlooked, particularly in business research.

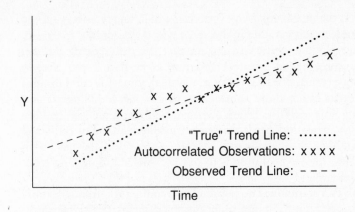

FIGURE 14.4 The Autocorrelation Problem

Detection. It is often difficult to determine autocorrelation from time plots, but it doesn't hurt to look. Plot the variable after removing trend, and look for a smooth curve of observations that slowly weaves back and forth across the trend line (positive autocorrelation) or a spiky sawtooth curve (negative autocorrelation).

Researchers also use statistical measures of autocorrelation. Two tests for the presence of autocorrelation are

- The **Durbin-Watson** test, which produces the statistic d. The value of d ranges from 0 to 4; the closer it is to 2.0, the less autocorrelation. (Check an advanced statistics text for significance tables of d to interpret your results.) Note that this test cannot be used if a previous (lagged) value of the dependent variable is included as an independent.

- The **autocorrelation function,** which indicates the degree to which one observation is dependent on preceding ones. The autocorrelation function is a series of correlations between observations and the immediately preceding ones, those two "steps" back, those three "steps" back, and so on. Each step represents a lag, so that the correlations are calculated for lag 1, lag 2, lag 3, and so on. (The *correlograms* produced by statistical packages also provide useful information for ARIMA techniques designed to remove autocorrelation.)

(Seasonality in a variable can also be detected by examining the correlogram of residuals when the variable is regressed on time—observations in the same season [e.g., autumn] tend to be correlated.)

Good statistical routines will provide or allow you to estimate the value of ρ, an indicator of the degree of autocorrelation. As a rule of thumb, autocorrelation is present if ρ in the autocorrelation function is greater than .30, and you should not use OLS regression for time series. Instead, use an alternative regression technique, such as generalized least squares or pseudo-GLS. Details about these procedures and other aspects of regression techniques for time series can be found in Ostrom (1978) and Kennedy (1979). Some statistical packages contain special routines for handling concomitant and interrupted time series with autocorrelation.

Solutions.   If the number of observations is small, one relatively simple solution is to difference each variable in the same way we described for trend. This solution requires some caution to ensure that the differencing doesn't overcorrect and produce negative autocorrelation. Note that if you already differenced to remove trend, this step is not available to you. A second option, and one that produces much more satisfactory results for concomitant and pooled concomitant time series, is to use a special regression analysis routine that corrects for autocorrelation. Such options are available in major statistical packages. If the number of observations is large, as is often the case with financial or sales data, the best solution is to use the ARIMA modeling technique we mentioned earlier.

Autocorrelation can sometimes be reduced by avoiding too frequent measurement. Don't be tempted to obtain more observations by taking measurements from smaller and smaller periods. The result is often a high degree of autocorrelation. The longer the period between measurement time points, the more change you are likely to find in a variable and the less autocorrelation.

Homogeneity of Variance

One of the assumptions for using regression methods in time series (as well as other relationships) is that the variance in the dependent variable doesn't change substantially over time (or over other independent variables). In other words, the average difference between adjacent observations should not increase or decrease with time. If this is not the case, the data are said to show *nonhomogeneous variance* (also known as heteroscedasticity).

Violation of this assumption is most critical in prediction research. It means that the precision of estimates of slope is less than it should be and that in a small sample the estimate itself may be considerably off.

Detection.   Nonhomogeneous variance can be seen most readily by inspecting a time plot. See Figure 14.5. If the vertical distance between points seems substantially larger at one end of the time dimension than the other (as in part "B" of the figure) the variance may be nonhomogeneous. If your statistics package has them, you could carry out further tests (with residual plots) to confirm the nonhomogeneous variance.

Solution.   There are two standard ways of dealing with nonhomogeneous variance. One is to transform the data. Typical transformations are those discussed earlier in Box 14.3. Inspect the time plot after each transformation to see which one most reduces the nonhomogeneous variance.

The second solution, *weighted least squares,* is simple to understand, but computationally complex. The negative effects of the large variance would be reduced if you could get the regression analysis to pay less attention to observations with large error terms, that is, large distances from the trend (regression) line. This is what weighted least squares does.

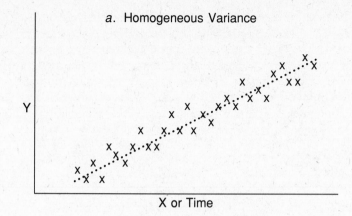

a. Homogeneous Variance

Y

X or Time

FIGURE 14.5
Nonhomogeneous
Variance

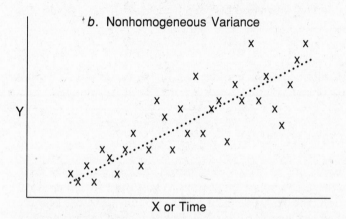

b. Nonhomogeneous Variance

Y

X or Time

Outliers and Nonlinearity

An *outlier* is an observation far from the trend line that may represent either faulty measurement or a unique situation (for example, a highly publicized drug-tampering incident may have produced a sharp but temporary decline in sales of a pain-relief medication). In either case, the outlier might distort the results of your analysis. See Figure 14.6. As the figure shows, the trend line is substantially flatter without the outlier case.

Time-series outliers are most easily detected with time plots. Deal with them as suggested earlier for cross-sectional data: either transform the variable or drop an observation you can demonstrate to be truly unique on theoretical grounds. In either instance, compare your results with and without the correction.

A nonlinear trend line occurs when a series increases (or decreases) at an increasing rate. A time plot shows the characteristic ever-increasing upward (or downward) slope. This condition can generally be corrected by differencing the series *twice,* as described in Box 14.9. Alternative solutions include (1) transforming the variable to make it linear (usually a log transformation is

FIGURE 14.6
Example of
Distortion Due to an
Outlier

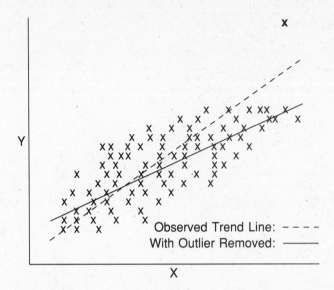

sufficient) and then differencing to remove the linear trend and (2) using nonlinear regression. Transformation is the simplest of these solutions.

Lagged and Leading Variables

A **lagged** variable is one in which each observation includes a variable whose value is taken from a *preceding* time period. A **leading** variable is one in which each observation takes its value from a *following* time. The use of these variables was described in Chapter 5; here we discuss how to compute them.

While these variables can be coded manually (insert the value from the preceding [lagged] or following [leading] observation), it is easier to record each variable in its own observation time and then ask the computer to move specific variables forward or backward. As well as saving time and avoiding clerical errors, this option allows you to vary the amount of lag or lead (moving observations more than one time period) and check the effect of different lag or lead times. Many statistical packages will carry out these operations for you. If your software will not move values forward (leading), you can accomplish the same result by lagging all the variables but the one you want to lead.

You will have missing values for the cases at the beginning of your observations for lagged variables and at the end of your observations for leading variables, unless you can find these values in other data and add them to your raw data or processing file.

■ *The Lighter Side of Research*

It is ironic that the earliest use of statistics and probabilities was to calculate gambling odds, while today businesses use statistics to take the gamble *out* of their decision making.

Summary

This chapter described the tasks involved in preliminary data analysis. Preliminary analysis checks your data for problems that might distort further analysis, constructs scales, indexes, and other variables, and in general prepares your data for further analysis.

The specific tasks of *preliminary analysis,* in the recommended order, are as follows:

- Weight nonproportional stratified samples.

- Check sample for representativeness.

- Check category variables for sufficient variation: drop problem variables.

- Check category variables for uniform distribution: collapse problem variables.

- Check quantitative variables for normal distribution: transform if necessary.

- Check quantitative variables for outliers: transform variable, convert to missing value, or drop case.

- Check for criterion validity where appropriate.

- Check construct validity with other variables.

- Check interitem construct validity for multiple-item measures.

- Check test-retest reliability where appropriate.

- Check interrater reliability where appropriate.

- Check reliability of established multiple-item scales.

- Check variables with many missing cases for item nonresponse bias; try several remedies (listwise and pairwise deletion, substitute mean, regression estimates).

- Recode category variables for consistency and dummy variables.

- Construct composite variables for proportions, rates, and counts.

- Compute elapsed time variables from date variables.

- Construct and test new scales and indexes.

- Add structural variables to data set.

- Compute gain scores if needed.

In addition, for *time-series* data:

- Check time series for trend and seasonality.

- Check time series for autocorrelation.

- Check time series for homogeneity of variance.
- Compute lagged and leading variables as needed.

Where Are We Now?

At this point, you have checked your data thoroughly and can be reasonably sure that any conclusions you draw from this point on are not likely to be distorted because of data peculiarities. You have also recoded variables or prepared new ones you'll need for your analysis. The next step is to undertake descriptive and univariate analysis.

Discussion Issues and Assignments

1. Chain grocery stores in your area opened last Sunday in defiance of Sunday shopping laws that prohibit stores above a certain size from opening. The government is threatening legal action. The council representing these larger stores needs to gauge public opinion before deciding whether to fight the injunction and continue to stay open this coming Sunday. They come to you asking for a public opinion survey with results within 48 hours. You decide on a telephone survey of 300 randomly selected households in a nonproportional stratified sample. You have data on household characteristics, major shopper characteristics, grocery shopping patterns, and opinions about Sunday shopping. The data were entered into your computer at the time of each interview using a CATI system and cleaned for illegal codes only. You have five hours until your deadline. With all your staff working, running statistical routines and writing simultaneously, you know that you will be able to accomplish only partial preliminary analysis. (1) Which preliminary analysis checks do you decide to do? (2) If the data have not been cleaned at all, which preliminary analysis do you carry out? If your decisions depends on other factors, what are they and how do they affect your decisions?

2. Preliminary analysis of data for a marketing study of demand for additional services (such as enlargements, extra prints, and cropping) at photo-processing outlets shows that Fairbanks, Alaska, is an extreme outlier. Under what circumstances would you drop it from your sample of cities?

3. Ask faculty members for copies of old data sets (preferably raw data sets or processing files on tape or diskettes). Carry out preliminary analysis checks, and recode and compute new variables.

4. A study of managers in a brewing company obtained the following achieved samples in six subsamples:

1. upper level male managers	41 of 52	(population)
2. upper level female managers	3 of 3	
3. mid-level male managers	75 of 91	

4. mid-level female managers   15 of 17

5. lower level male managers   98 of 227

6. lower level female managers   75 of 82

Only subsample 5 was sampled (initial sample size = 125); all the others were enumerated. What weights would you apply to each subsample before proceeding with analysis?

Further Reading

Bryson, K. R., and D. R. Phillips. 1974. "Method for Classifying Interval-Scale and Ordinal-Scale Data." Chapter 4 in D. R. Heise (ed.), *Sociological Methodology 1975.* San Francisco: Jossey-Bass.

> A method for collapsing quantitative data into categories that minimizes the loss of information.

Norusis, M. J. 1986. *The SPSS Guide to Data Analysis.* Chicago: SPSS.

> A good guide to writing programs for data manipulation and analysis on a mainframe computer using SPSS-X.

Sutton, Robert I. 1989. "Reactions of Nonparticipants as Additional Rather than Missing Data: Opportunities for Organizational Research." *Human Relations* 42:423–439.

> Sutton suggests interesting ways of gathering and analyzing information about nonrespondents, both those outside the initial sample and those who refuse to participate.

Tabachnick, B. G., and L. S. Fidell. 1989. *Using Multivariate Statistics* (2nd ed.). New York: HarperCollins.

> An easily understood guide to missing data difficulties and other data problems. Very useful for anyone contemplating multivariate analysis.

CHAPTER 15

Descriptive and Univariate Analysis

CHAPTER OBJECTIVES

- Which descriptive statistics provide information about the typical case in the sample?
- How can we estimate sample and population characteristics?
- How do we test hypotheses about population characteristics?

CHAPTER OUTLINE

DESCRIBING THE SAMPLE AND DEPENDENT VARIABLE
BREAKDOWNS
POPULATION ESTIMATES
HYPOTHESIS TESTING

nce preliminary analysis is out of the way, researchers carry out *descriptive and univariate analysis.*[1] This analysis involves several tasks:

- Describing the typical case in the sample. This gives both researcher and audience a feeling for the kind of persons, groups, organizations, events, or objects to be analyzed. For example, if the unit of analysis is persons, report typical demographic characteristics such as average age and proportion male. For a study of bank failures, you might report average size and distribution by geographic region.

- For explanatory research, examining the key dependent variable. This is the focus of the research—what it seeks to explain.

- For descriptive research, estimating characteristics about the population.

DESCRIBING THE SAMPLE AND DEPENDENT VARIABLE

Descriptive analysis of the sample and dependent variable answers the following questions:

- What does the typical case look like? *(central tendency)*

- How typical is the typical case? *(variation)*

- What's the overall picture of the dependent variable the research is trying to explain?

These questions mark the beginning of our statistical analysis (see Box 15.1). Since the answers to these questions involve the entire sample, computations are based on *weighted* cases. Since they have only one case (or a few pooled cases), time-series designs generally omit sample descriptions, but often include descriptive analysis of the dependent variable.

Central Tendency

Measures of central tendency provide a portrait of the typical case: the average time to process an order, the median age of a car renter, the most

[1]Don't confuse descriptive analysis with *descriptive statistics*. Descriptive analysis depicts sample (or population) characteristics. Descriptive statistics are those involving no sampling distribution. See Appendix A for a discussion of descriptive and inferential statistics.

BOX 15.1
FOCUS ON RESEARCH

Statistics Texts

A good statistics text will complement the discussion of data analysis in this and the following chapters. Experienced researchers keep a collection of favorite texts to consult for matters on which memory has dimmed, and for the unusual and obscure points that crop up from time to time. We particularly like the following:

Blalock, *Social Statistics*

Clark and Clark, *A Statistics Primer for Managers*

Glass and Hopkins, *Statistical Methods in Education and Psychology*

Kennedy, *A Guide to Econometrics*

Tabachnick and Fidell, *Using Multivariate Statistics*

common meat purchase in supermarkets, the mean commodity price over the past year. Because there is no single measure of central tendency for all variables, you must select the most appropriate measure, taking into account the variable's level of measurement and its distribution.

Category Variables.   For nominal-level and dichotomous variables the most useful measure of central tendency is the **mode,** the category with the most cases. For category ordinal variables, the category containing the **median** case is also useful. The median is the middle case; when rank-ordered, half the cases lie above (and the other half below) it. It lies at the 50th *percentile:* 50 percent of the cases have equal or lower values. There is no measure of central tendency for rank ordinal variables (in which each case has a separate, unique rank).

Quantitative Variables.   For quantitative variables the *mean* (the arithmetic average) is the most common statistic of central tendency. However, if a variable's distribution is strongly skewed or there are a few extreme outliers in one tail of the distribution, the median is more useful. For example, a sample of six firms with sales increases of 2, 2, 3, 4, 5, and 18 percent produces a mean sales increase rate of 5.7 percent, which is certainly not typical of the sample. The median of 3.5 percent is more typical of the sample cases. For distributions with many cases "tied" at the same value (such as students' ages in years), the mode is also a useful measure of central tendency, since it indicates which value of the variable is shared by the most cases.

While assessing the central tendency of any variable, always check its distribution to see whether it is **multimodal** (cases are clustered into two or more peaks). A single central tendency measure for a multimodal distribution is often misleading; a better measure is to indicate the modal values at which cases tend to cluster or peak.

Weighted Average.   When the unit of analysis is a higher level combination of other units (such as groups or firms composed of individual employ-

BOX 15.2

RESEARCH SKILLS

Calculating Weighted Averages

A weighted average adjusts each case by the proportion of subunits it contains. For example, to determine the weighted average rate of profit in a sample of photo-finishing firms, multiply each firm's profit rate by the proportion of employees working at that firm. (The proportion is the number of employees at the firm divided by the total number of employees in all firms in the sample.) The rates of large firms contribute more to the weighted average, and the rates of smaller firms have less impact.

The weighted average is

$$6 \times (12/97) + 8 \times (14/97) + 9 \times (8/97) + 10 \times (63/97) = 9.2\%$$

By comparison, the unweighted mean for the four firms is 8.2 percent. The weighted mean attaches more importance to the rate of profit in the largest firm.

Firm	Rate of Profit	Number of Employees
A	6%	12
B	8%	14
C	9%	8
D	10%	63
		Total: 97

ees), a **weighted average** may be a more useful indication of central tendency for quantitative variables, especially when cases vary in size or importance. A weighted average attaches more weight to larger or more important cases. See Box 15.2.

Variability

Measures of variability indicate just how typical the typical case is, and thus how much faith can be placed in the measure of central tendency. They indicate whether there is a great deal of difference among the cases or whether they are all pretty much alike. The greater the variability, the less typical of all cases is the central tendency value.

Category Variables. There is no widely accepted measure of variability for category variables. Check a bar chart or frequency distribution to see the degree to which all cases are concentrated in one category.

Quantitative Variables. The simplest measure of variability for quantitative variables is the **range** (highest value minus lowest). However, it is very sensitive to a single extreme value, since it takes into account only two cases in the entire sample.

SUGGESTION

For most explanatory and evaluation research, you need only report ranges to indicate variation in the sample description variables. However, you should report standard deviations for the dependent variable.

A better range-related measure is the **quartile deviation:** one-half of the difference between the first and third quartiles. The first quartile is the value of the 25th percentile—one-quarter of the cases lie below it. Similarly, the third quartile is the value below which three-quarters of the cases lie. The quartile deviation is also called the *semi-interquartile range.*

The most commonly used measure of variability is the **standard deviation.** Its major advantage is that it takes all cases into account, not just the extremes or the quartiles. It is based on the average of each case's distance from the mean. The distances are squared, so that larger distances count more, and the result is reduced by taking its square root. The formula for *sample* standard deviation is

$$s = \sqrt{\frac{\Sigma_i \; (X_i - \overline{X})^2}{n}}$$

where X_i is the value of X for the ith case, $\overline{X}$ is the mean, and n is the sample size.

This formula calculates the standard deviation of the sample cases. The formula for an *unbiased* estimate of the *population* standard deviation is slightly different:

$$s = \sqrt{\frac{\Sigma_i \; (X_i - \overline{X})^2}{n - 1}}$$

We have more to say about population estimates later on.

The *square* of the standard deviation is called the *variance;* the variance of a variable is an important concept in multivariate analysis.

Standard Scores.   The standard deviation is expressed in the same *units of measure* as the mean. For example, the variable "age" has a mean in years, and its standard deviation is also expressed in years. Thus you can calculate for any case how many standard deviations it lies from the mean. If the mean age is 22, and the standard deviation is 4 years, a person with age 28 is one-and-a-half standard deviations from the mean. Similarly the age 14 is two standard deviations below the mean. This calculation can be carried out for each case. The result is called the **standardized,** or **Z-scores.** Negative Z-scores indicate the case lies Z standard deviations below the mean. The mean of a standardized variable is zero.

BREAKDOWNS

Often researchers want to provide sample descriptions for particular subgroups of cases. These summary statistics are called breakdowns. In marketing research, for example, brand preference is normally reported overall and separately for males and females. This distinction allows the reader to make more informed decisions and to concentrate on the categories of most interest.

- In *descriptive research,* provide breakdowns of the key variables (e.g., purchases) by important demographic variables such as gender, age category, income, and region.

- In *evaluation research,* show breakdowns of demographic or other basic characteristics of your sample *by experimental group* (e.g., the average age and gender composition of treatment and comparison groups).

- In *explanatory research,* furnish breakdowns of demographic or basic characteristics *by subsample* (e.g., average age of CEO in subsamples of public and private firms).

Computer mapping graphics offer a particularly useful form of breakdowns for descriptive research. Statistical packages or special microcomputer software can generate maps that indicate the levels of a category variable by geographical area. This form of breakdown is very easy to read; see Figure 15.1 for an example.

The **breakdown** of a variable is its mean or proportion for each of the subgroups within the overall sample.

SUGGESTION

Avoid too many breakdowns in evaluation and explanatory research. Keep in mind that most subsample differences will be discussed when you deal with the specific research questions.

POPULATION ESTIMATES

Population estimates are an important part of descriptive research. They require inferential statistics, since they draw conclusions about the target population on the basis of a sample. They involve two components: (1) moving

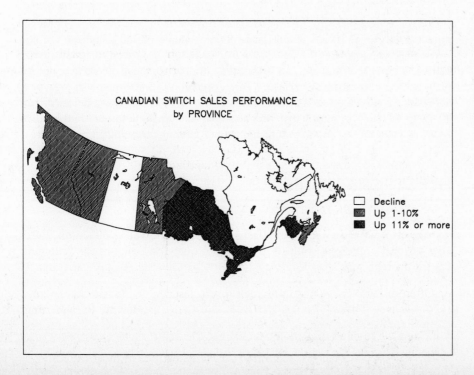

FIGURE 15.1
Computer Mapping for Breakdowns (This figure was produced using SPSS/PC+ and Ashton-Tate Map-Master)

CANADIAN SWITCH SALES PERFORMANCE
by PROVINCE

☐ Decline
▨ Up 1-10%
■ Up 11% or more

from information about the sample to estimates of the population and (2) estimating the accuracy of those estimates. (The remaining material in this chapter builds on the introduction to sampling theory and inferential statistics in Appendix A.)

Population estimates, such as the proportion of the adult population buying your firm's brand of disposable diapers and the average age of the diaper buyer in the population, are simply the means and proportions of your sample. These estimates are *unbiased* (the mean of their sampling distribution equals the population parameter; see Appendix A).

Descriptive research (with its need for highly accurate estimates) generally includes *estimates of the accuracy of its population estimates.* (For example, if 28 percent of a sample of customers report unsatisfactory delivery times, how accurate is this as an estimate of the proportion of all customers dissatisfied with delivery times?) Such estimates involve **confidence intervals,** which are a way of indicating the chance that an estimate is *wrong.* (Procedures for calculating confidence intervals are given in the "Sample Example" of Appendix A.) The more important the decisions based on the research, the greater the need for confidence intervals. This is especially true when money is being committed to new products or large advertising campaigns on the basis of your results. For example, before commissioning a new television commercial showing multichild families, a marketing executive will want to know how much confidence to place in your estimate that 63 percent of all disposable diaper purchasers have two or more children.

CASE EXAMPLE

A researcher was hired by a union to assess how its members felt on a number of potential bargaining issues. She drew a random sample of 650 members and surveyed their opinions. Because the union leadership was prepared to commit strike funds to obtain action on certain issues, they wanted to know the accuracy of the results. An excerpt from her report: "The proportion of union members in favor of negotiating a flextime work clause is 74.8%, with a 95% confidence interval from 70.6% to 79.0%. This means that with a sample such as the one used in this study, 74.8% is accurate within 4.2 percentage points 19 times out of 20."

HYPOTHESIS TESTING

Descriptive research, particularly in quality control applications, often goes beyond population estimates to answer questions such as the following: "Is the average admitting interview time at City General Hospital less than 12 minutes?" These kinds of questions involve testing *hypotheses* about the population characteristic. The hypotheses take two forms:

• Testing whether a population characteristic is *greater than* (or *less than*) some specified value

- Testing whether a population characteristic is *equal to* some specified value

Both kinds of hypothesis testing make use of the same information you need for population estimates: a sample mean (or proportion) and a sample standard deviation from a random sample. Both also use the sampling distribution to allow you to calculate the probability of the true population characteristic falling within some range of values.

The three steps in hypothesis testing are as follows:

1. Specify the research hypothesis and null hypothesis.

2. Select an alpha level for probability of a Type I error.

3. Calculate the critical region for rejecting the null hypothesis, and determine whether the null hypothesis is rejected.

Research and Null Hypotheses

The first step is to specify your research hypothesis and your null hypothesis. The **research hypothesis** (designated H) is a statement usually expressing the existence of some difference between some desired standard or norm and the true population value; the **null hypothesis** (designated H_0) is the opposite statement that no difference exists. Here are examples of the two kinds of hypotheses:

Guidelines stipulate that the average hospital admission interview should require less than 12 minutes. Hospital management suspects that interviews are taking too long.

H: "The mean admission interview time is 12 minutes or more."
H_0: "The mean admission interview time is consistent with the guidelines, that is, less than 12 minutes."

The publisher of a text recommends a selling price of $45.80. However, the publisher suspects that bookstores are not adhering to this figure.

H: "The average selling price of this text is not the recommended sales price of $45.80."

H_0: "The average selling price of this text is the recommended price, $45.80."

Type I and Type II Errors

The logic of hypothesis testing is to begin with the assumption that the null hypothesis is correct and to see whether the evidence is strong enough to reject it. Thus you begin by assuming that the population value is the value specified in the null hypothesis (or greater or less than this value, as indicated in the null hypothesis). When you draw a sample, its mean may be different from this value (or range of values) only because of sampling error. However, as we saw earlier for the precision of population estimates, the probability of a divergent sample mean grows less the further it is from the population (or sampling distribution) mean—there are fewer possible samples of size n with such means to be drawn. If this probability is too small to be believable, you reject the original assumption that the population value is the one specified in the null hypothesis.

You may mistakenly reject a null hypothesis which is true, in other words, wrongly conclude that the research hypothesis is the correct one. This kind of mistake is called a **Type I error.** Conversely, you may mistakenly accept a null hypothesis which is false. This is a **Type II error.** The two types are inversely related: the less the chance of a Type I error, the greater the chance of Type II. In hypothesis testing, researchers are generally more concerned with Type I errors.

The second step in testing your hypothesis is to decide what chance of Type I error you are willing to accept. (This is analogous to asking how far from the sampling distribution mean would your sample mean have to be before you conclude that the sampling distribution mean is not the value in the null hypothesis.) By convention, researchers select probabilities of .10, .05, .01, or .001 that a Type I error may occur. This probability is called the **alpha** level of the hypothesis test. The more costly a Type I error, the smaller alpha the researcher selects. However, researchers avoid too stringent an alpha level because the chance of a Type II error would become unacceptably large.

Critical Region

The third step is to decide what values of a sample mean you would interpret as convincing enough to persuade you to reject the null hypothesis. In other words, how different from the hypothesized standard or convention must your sample mean be to convince you that more than sampling error is involved, that is, that there is a true difference between what you want and what's actually out there?

These values constitute the **critical region** of the sampling distribution. A sample mean in the critical region means that you reject the null hypothesis. Establishing a critical region requires three steps: (1) selecting the appropriate sampling distribution, (2) selecting a one- or two-tailed test, and (3) calculating the critical region values.

Sampling Distribution. If your sample is fairly large (as a rough rule of thumb, anything over 100), you can assume that the sampling distribution of sample means will be normal in shape. This means that you can use the well-known properties of normal curves to calculate critical region values. On the other hand, if your sample is smaller, you should use Student's t distribution, which has a shape that changes with the size of your sample.

One- or Two-Tailed Test. Next, decide whether your null hypothesis implies a critical region divided into two parts. In the first of our two examples, only mean interview times somewhat above 12 minutes would lead you to reject the null hypothesis. Thus the critical region in the first example is located in only one end of the sampling distribution. The hypothesis test is *one-tailed.* In the second example, an average selling price for the text either much below or much above $45.80 would lead you to reject the null hypothesis. This means that the critical region is found at *both* ends of the sampling distribution. An hypothesis test with a two-part critical region is called a *two-tailed* test—each tail of the sampling distribution contains part of the critical region.

Critical Region Values. Once you know which alpha level you want, which sampling distribution you are using (normal or Student's t), and whether your test is one- or two-tailed, you can determine which values of the sample mean constitute the critical region and would lead to your rejecting the null hypothesis.

Critical Values for a Normal Distribution. If you are using a normal distribution, find a table of "areas under the normal curve" (Appendix B). Your alpha probability corresponds to *the proportion of the area under the normal curve* in one or both tails of the distribution. Thus, for a one-tailed test and an alpha of .01, you want to find the distance from the mean at which the remaining area under the curve is 1 percent of the total area. Similarly, for a two-tailed test and an alpha of .05, you want to find the distance from the mean in each tail at which the remaining area under the curve is half of .05, or .025 of the total area under the normal curve.

The table gives distances from the mean in Z standard error units. For each distance, there is a corresponding area under the curve. Estimate the standard error of the sampling distribution from the standard deviation of your sample. Then, to use the table:

- First find the area under the curve that corresponds to your chosen alpha level (or half the level if your test is two-tailed). This may involve subtracting your alpha value from .5 (representing the total area under half the curve).

- Next, find the corresponding distance from the mean in Z standard error units.

For example, for a two-tailed test and an alpha of .05, the probability limit of the critical region for each tail is half the area under the curve minus half the alpha probability, or .5 − .025 = .475. According to the table, the corresponding distance from the mean for this probability is 1.96 standard errors. Thus the critical region is any sample mean greater than 1.96 standard errors from the mean in either direction.

For the first example (which requires a one-tailed test), the table gives a Z value of 2.33 standard errors for the boundary of the critical region for a one-tailed alpha level of .01. Thus the critical value for rejecting the null hypothesis is any sample mean more than 2.33 standard errors greater than the hypothesized mean of 12 minutes.

Suppose that, from a random sample of 144 interviews, you find a mean interview time of 12.4 minutes with a sample standard deviation of 3.6 minutes. In order to determine the actual critical region, you must convert the standard error units to actual values of the variable and add and/or subtract them from your sample mean. In the example, the sample standard deviation is 3.6 minutes. Use the following formula to estimate the standard error from the sample standard deviation:

$$SE = \frac{s}{\sqrt{(n-1)}}$$

With a sample size of 144, the standard error is .30 minutes. Thus the critical region is any sample mean greater than $2.33 \times .30 = .70$ minutes greater than the hypothesized mean, or $12 + .70 = 12.70$ minutes.

Finally, determine whether the sample mean falls within the critical region. Since the actual sample mean is only 12.4 minutes, accept the null hypothesis that the mean time for admission interviews is 12 minutes or less. (For practice, calculate what your decision would be if you used a .05 alpha level, which gives a Z value of 1.65 for a one-tailed test.)

Critical Values for Student's t Distribution.

With small samples and the t distribution, calculate critical values in terms of the t statistic, rather than in actual values of the variable the hypothesis deals with. First consult a t-distribution table (Appendix B) to find the critical values of t for your hypothesis test. Because the shape of the t distribution varies with sample size, you must also know the *degrees of freedom* in your sample. (The degrees of freedom is equivalent to one less than the sample size.) For each alpha level and degrees of freedom, the table gives a critical value of t. For example, for a one-tailed test, an alpha of .05, and 29 degrees of freedom (sample size of 30), the critical values of t are those greater than 1.699. Any sample value of t (or absolute value of the sample t if you use a two-tailed test) greater than the table value means the null hypothesis should be rejected.

Once you have the critical value of t, calculate the sample value of t:

$$t = \frac{\overline{X} - \mu}{\dfrac{s}{\sqrt{n-1}}}$$

where μ is the population value specified in the hypothesis.

Finally, compare the two to see whether the sample t value falls within the critical region. Imagine that you collect data from a sample of 45 bookstores, and find a mean selling price of $48.55, with a simple standard deviation of $2.40. With the population value $\mu = \$45.80$, a two-tailed test is required since higher *or* lower selling prices will lead to a rejection of the null hypothesis. Using an alpha of .01, the critical values of t are those greater than 2.704 or less than -2.704. The sample mean of $48.55 produces a t value of 7.60, large enough to result in a rejection of the null hypothesis, and a conclusion that the text is not selling at the publisher's recommended price.

■ *The Lighter Side of Research*

I always find that statistics are hard to swallow and impossible to digest. The only one I can ever remember is that if all the people who go to sleep in church were laid end to end they would be a lot more comfortable.

—Mrs. Robert A. Taft

Summary

This chapter has examined descriptive and univariate analysis. This type of analysis, which examines variables one at a time, summarizes demographic or other basic characteristics of samples using measures of central tendency and variation. Breakdowns provide these characteristics for subsamples. Descriptive analysis also includes an examination of the dependent variable on which the research focuses.

Another important component of descriptive analysis, particularly for descriptive research, is estimates of population characteristics and tests of the estimate's precision, using confidence intervals. Finally, descriptive analysis tests hypotheses about population characteristics.

Where Are We Now?

All the preliminaries have been completed and sample and population characteristics described or estimated. For descriptive research, all that remains is to write up the report. For prediction, evaluation, and explanatory research, you are now ready to get to the real heart of your data, analyzing the relationships. That's the topic of the next two chapters.

Discussion Issues and Assignments

1. Select six case examples of research projects from earlier chapters, and indicate which measures of central tendency and dispersion for what variables would be most appropriate in descriptive analysis.

2. Think of a variable and situation in which you would report, as part of the descriptive analysis, all three measures of central tendency: mode, median, and mean.

3. For the following variables, indicate which measures of central tendency and variation are most appropriate: CEO annual income, firm return on investment, highest academic degree, proportion of faulty chip returns (by month), unemployment rate, gender, disposable income, type of work shift (day, afternoon, etc.), rating of business opportunities (7-point scale).

4. You are interested in the grades assigned to students by the instructors in a set of business courses in your college. Under what circumstances would you use a weighted average?

5. Select a random sample of 20 page numbers from this text. Then count the number of words on each page. Calculate the range, interquartile range, and standard deviation of page word counts. Discuss the advantages and disadvantages of each.

6. Calculate the Z-scores for the 20 pages in your sample from question 5. Calculate the mean and standard deviation of these scores.

Further Reading

Clark, John J., and Margaret T. Clark. 1983. *A Statistics Primer for Managers.* New York: Free Press.

    This very useful text discusses a variety of measures of central tendency and variation of use in business research, including geometric and harmonic means.

CHAPTER 16

Relationships and Group Differences: Bivariate Analysis

CHAPTER OBJECTIVES

- Which relationships does a researcher investigate?
- What can bivariate analysis tell us?
- How is association measured?
- What's the difference between tests for significance and association?
- What can a bivariate analysis check for?

CHAPTER OUTLINE

BASICS OF BIVARIATE ANALYSIS
BIVARIATE ASSOCIATION
MEASURES OF ASSOCIATION FOR CATEGORY VARIABLES
MEASURES OF ASSOCIATION FOR RANKED ORDINAL VARIABLES
MEASURES OF ASSOCIATION FOR QUANTITATIVE VARIABLES
STATISTICAL SIGNIFICANCE
COMMON SIGNIFICANCE TESTS
BIVARIATE CHECKS

O nce preliminary, descriptive, and univariate analyses are completed, the researcher turns to the investigation of relationships. This is when you're likely to hear the newcomer to research muttering questions like

Does this require a significance test?

What multivariate statistics does *this* research question need?

What's a *partial correlation*?

What does this result mean?

Arrrrrgh!

For many, analysis of relationships is where the terrors of stats phobia and analysis anxiety take hold! To help you avoid these unpleasant afflictions, this and the following chapter are designed to make your encounter with data analysis as pleasant and fruitful as possible.

- Although the chapters deal with statistics, there are no derivations and few formulas (consult a statistics text for the derivation and calculation of each test statistic). Instead, we focus on the underlying *idea* behind each statistical test.

- Second, we highlight the *logic* of your analysis, considering, in light of your research questions, *what* you need to test and *why*. Calculating a statistic without knowing why is likely to lead to mistaken conclusions and inappropriate recommendations. It also induces an especially tempting vice: overanalysis.

- Third, we recognize that researchers today use statistical software packages. Thus we emphasize the choice of statistical technique, the assumptions required, and how to interpret your computer's output.

This chapter begins the discussion of analyzing relationships and group differences. It deals with bivariate analysis involving only two variables at a time. Chapter 17 considers multivariate analysis.

BASICS OF BIVARIATE ANALYSIS

Bivariate analysis is the typical starting point of relationship analysis for evaluation and explanatory research. It isn't required in descriptive research, which involves no relationships, and it is usually omitted in prediction research, which normally goes directly from preliminary to multivariate analysis.

Bivariate analysis has two objectives:

- To examine the *overall* relationship between a dependent and independent variable (with no other variables controlled).

- To check for data problems that might distort multivariate analysis.

But before you begin analysis, you have to decide which relationships to examine out of the many possibilities in your data.

The Research Questions

If your data set contains N variables, there are $N(N - 1)/2$ different two-variable relationships you could test (ignoring causal direction) and many more involving three or more variables. Even with only ten variables, there are over a thousand possibilities! Since you can't test them all, which ones do you analyze?

The answer is simple: your specific research questions (see Chapter 2) guide your data analysis. In business research, the specific research questions replace the research hypotheses found in basic and academic research.[1] In more formal terms, each research question specifying a primary relationship (linking a primary to a key variable) represents a *research hypothesis* to be tested.

Avoid the temptations of overanalysis ("Wouldn't it be interesting to see if . . . ?"). It wastes resources and time and sidetracks you from the real purpose of your research. This can be fatal for inexperienced researchers, who may end up with irrelevant results and recommendations.

BIVARIATE ASSOCIATION

The first assessment of a relationship is to determine the bivariate association. Association tells us the strength or importance of a relationship between two variables. For example, inventory and productivity are strongly associated if the larger the inventory, generally the greater the productivity. If one of the variables identifies groups, such as "gender" (male and female employees) or "plant" (Ajax, Bolton, Como), association tells us *how different the groups are* with respect to the other variable. Thus, if the productivity of the Ajax plant is greater than the Bolton plant, which in turn is greater than the Como plant, productivity is associated with plant.

Association can vary in strength from none (age is unrelated to productivity) to perfect (each additional year of age always brings an increase in productivity, and the increase is the same each year). In causal terms, association measures *effect size:* the effect an independent has on a dependent variable. Bivariate association is your initial estimate of each independent variable's importance.

Association can be measured approximately by visual inspection (eyeball-

SUGGESTION

Let your data analysis be driven by your specific research questions. Take a copy of the questions to your computer terminal when you do your analysis. It will serve as a useful guide to what you're supposed to do, and more important, what you don't have to do! Underline the key and primary dependent and independent variables, which will help identify the relationships you want to examine at the bivariate stage.

Association (also called *correlation* and *covariation*) is the degree to which two variables systematically change together (covary), either across cases or within the same case over repeated measures.

---

[1]However, we keep the *null hypotheses,* which are important components of statistical tests.

ing the data) and more accurately by using a specific statistical measure of association. It helps to use both.

Visualize the Relationship

To get an initial feel for each bivariate relationship, examine a visual picture (see Figure 16.1). Inspect the following:

- *Cross-tabulations* ("cross-tabs") when both variables are category. Inspect the cell numbers and percentages to get an idea of the overall pattern.

- *Scatterplots* when both variables are rank ordinal or quantitative. Look at the general shape of the data points and check for points that lie outside the main cluster (see Box 16.1).

- *Group box plots* when one variable is category and the other is rank ordinal or quantitative (frequently the situation in experimental designs). Use one box for each category group. Check medians, box heights, length of "whiskers," and outliers.

Examples of all three are shown in Figure 16.1. We have more to say about these specific examples later. With practice, you'll be able to get a rough idea of the extent and form of a relationship and whether there are likely to be problems with the data when it comes time for multivariate analysis.

Once you have a graphic picture of a bivariate relationship, the next step is to use one or more statistical measures of association.

Two Interpretations for Measures of Association

The most useful measures of association have simple interpretations, so it is not necessary to rely totally on phrases such as "moderate," "substantial," and "relatively weak." The two general ways of interpreting association are (1) proportional reduction of error **(PRE)** or proportion of variance explained **(PVE)** and (2) effect of unit change (slope).

PRE and PVE Interpretations of Association Strength. Several category measures of association indicate the proportional reduction of error: the *proportion by which prediction of one variable can be improved (prediction errors reduced) by knowing the value of the other.* If you know one characteristic of a consumer (e.g., gender), how much better can you predict the other (e.g., attitude toward a particular product) than if you didn't know the person's gender? A coefficient of 0.0 indicates that knowing gender doesn't help reduce your prediction errors at all; a coefficient of .50 indicates that you can reduce your errors in predicting attitudes by 50 percent if you know the consumer's gender; a coefficient of 1.0 indicates that you can reduce your prediction errors entirely: gender and attitude are perfectly correlated so that knowing one tells you the other with certainty.

The general formula for PRE measures is

$$\frac{\left(\begin{array}{c}\text{prediction errors in Y}\\ \text{without knowing X}\end{array}\right) - \left(\begin{array}{c}\text{prediction errors in Y}\\ \text{after knowing X}\end{array}\right)}{(\text{prediction errors in Y without knowing X})}$$

(a) Crosstabulation for Two Category Variables

FIGURE 16.1
Visualizing
Relationships

Crosstabulation: PRODUCT Dept Productivity
                  By PLANT Plant Location

PLANT_>	Count Col Pct	Ajax 1	Concord 2	Row Total
PRODUCT				
V. Good	1.0	7 / 26.9	4 / 16.0	11 / 21.6
Good	2.0	4 / 15.4	9 / 36.0	13 / 25.5
Fair	3.0	7 / 26.9	9 / 36.0	16 / 31.4
Poor	4.0	8 / 30.8	3 / 12.0	11 / 21.6
Column Total		26 / 51.0	25 / 49.0	51 / 100.0

(b) Box Plots for Category and Quantitative Variables

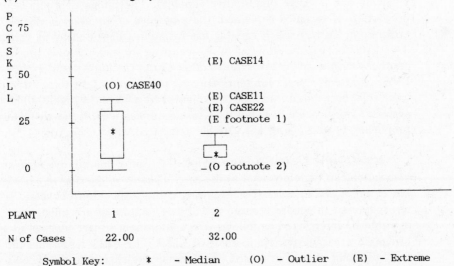

PLANT	1	2
N of Cases	22.00	32.00

Symbol Key: * – Median (O) – Outlier (E) – Extreme

Boxplot footnotes denote the following:

1) CASE39, CASE63

2) CASE20, CASE28, CASE55

(Figure 16.1 continued)

(c) Scatterplot for Two Quantitative Variables

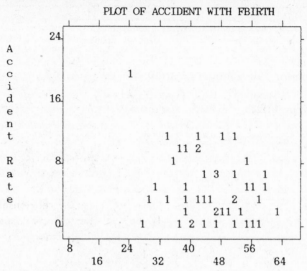

PLOT OF ACCIDENT WITH FBIRTH

Foreman's Year of birth

48 cases plotted.

Output produced by SPSS/PC+ software.

     An equivalent interpretation is frequently used for measures of association involving one or more quantitative variables. These measures represent the proportion of variance explained: the *proportion of variation in one variable explained by another.* Each variable has variation (measured by its variance). This variation can be thought of as occurring for two reasons: that due to another variable, and the rest due to other causes (including random noise). A PVE measure of association represents the proportion of the total variation in a variable that is accounted for or explained by a second variable. (The term *explained* as used here does not have causal implications. It merely means the proportion of variance in one variable associated with another.)

    Effect of a Unit Change (Slope).   Some quantitative measures of association can be interpreted as the *effect a change of one unit in one variable has on the second variable.* For example, if the association between "size of newspaper ad in square inches" and "sales" results in a coefficient of 122, it would be interpreted as follows: Each additional square inch of ad space brings an average increase in sales of $122. The $122 represents the "effect" of a unit change in ad size. The greater the change in the second variable, the stronger the association. Unlike PRE or PVE measures, unit change measures depend on the units of measure of the variables. Thus the coefficient of 122 would be different if ad size were measured in centimeters or sales in pounds sterling.

BOX 16.1
RESEARCH SKILLS
Reading Scatterplots

A scatterplot (also called scattergram) shows how two quantitative (or ranked ordinal) variables are related. By convention, the dependent variable takes the vertical axis and the independent variable the horizontal axis. The position of each dot, or case, is determined by its values on the two variables (see Figure 16.1 for an example). If your software will do so, it is useful to have the OLS regression line superimposed on the plot—its slope is a measure of association.

Look for the following:

- Whether the points indicate any pattern. (If overall shape is oval and tilted, variables are related.)
- Whether the oval is tilted to the left (negative relationship) or right (positive), and how much. The more tilt, the stronger the relationship.
- How narrow the oval is. The narrower, the stronger the relationship.
- Whether the oval appears straight or curved. If curved, it's a nonlinear relationship.

MEASURES OF ASSOCIATION FOR CATEGORY VARIABLES[2]

Researchers almost always examine relationships between category variables in a cross-tabulation ("cross-tab" or *contingency*) table. They then percentage the table and calculate one or more other measures of association.

Cross-Tabulations

The basic parts of a cross-tab table include cells, row and column totals, and identifying labels. The *cells* show the number of cases for each combination of the variables' categories. For example, in Figure 16.2 showing the relationship between employee gender and preference for collective agreement benefits among a sample of 190 employees, a total of 13 males prefer dental over other benefits. The column totals at the bottom are the univariate distribution of the variable "gender" (71 females, 119 males). Similarly, the row totals on the right are the distribution of "benefit preferences." These column and row totals are called the *marginals* of the table.

[2]Actually, you can use any statistical measure or test you like with data from any level of measurement, since the numbers themselves don't know what they mean or where they come from. The numbers are simply numbers. However, the issue you must face is whether the numbers fit the *assumptions* of your test or measure. Such assumptions include, for example, independent measures with normal distributions and homogeneous variance (Gaito, 1980). The validity of your *interpretation* of the test results rests on whether assumptions were violated, not on the level of measurement. The connection is this: data from higher levels of measurement are more likely to meet these assumptions than those from lower levels.

(a) Crosstabulation for Two Category Variables

Crosstabulation: BENEFIT   Employee's Benefit Preference
By SEX   Gender of Employee

BENEFIT	SEX_> Count	Female	Male	Row Total
Medical		20	59	79
Dental		6	13	19
Pension		20	25	45
Holidays		20	11	31
Job Post		5	11	3
Column Total		71 37.4	119 62.6	190 100.0

(b) Scatterplot for Two Quantitative Variables

Crosstabulation: BENEFIT   Employee's Benefit Preference
By SEX   Gender of Employee

BENEFIT	SEX_> Count	Female	Male	Row Total
Medical		20 28.2	59 49.6	79 41.6
Dental		6 8.5	13 10.9	19 10.0
Pension		20 28.2	25 21.0	45 23.7
Holidays		20 28.2	11 9.2	31 16.3
Job Post		5 7.0	11 9.2	3 1.6
Column Total		71 37.4	119 62.6	190 100.0

Percentaging Tables

It isn't always easy to see from the cell numbers the extent of association between two variables. However, percentaging a table produces *percentage differences,* a simple and easily understood measure of association. The basic procedure is to calculate percentages in one direction of the table, and then to calculate one or more percentage differences in the other direction. Follow the steps in Box 16.2 and Figure 16.2.

A major drawback with percentaging to measure association is that, as the numbers of rows and columns increases, a single percentage difference no longer captures the relationship. With larger tables, many differences would be required, and the measure is no longer straightforward. The solution is to turn to measures of association that reduce *any* table to a single measure.

BOX 16.2
RESEARCH SKILLS

Percentaging a Cross-Tabulation

1. Calculate percentages *within categories of the independent variable,* using each category total as the base. (If you percentage the wrong way your results will be wrong.) In the example in Figure 16.2, first calculate the percentages of females preferring each of the benefit options, using the total number of females (71) as the base. For example, 28.2 percent of females (20 out of 71) prefer medical benefits, 8.5 percent prefer dental, and so on. Then repeat the procedure for males, the other category of the independent variable "gender." The correctly percentaged table is shown in part (b) of Figure 16.2. (Notice that each of the margins is also percentaged for you.)

2. Select a *reference category* of the dependent vari-

able. This is usually the most important category and the one about which you wish to draw conclusions. In the example, if you were most interested in which employees choose pension plan improvements, you would use that as the reference category.

3. Calculate the *percentage difference* for the reference category by comparing percentages in the *opposite direction* from the one in which you percentaged the table. In the example, since percentaging was vertical, the comparisons and calculations of percentage differences would be horizontal. Thus, while 28.2 percent of female employees want pension benefits, only 21.0 percent of males feel likewise. The percentage difference is 7.2 percent.

Other Measures of Association for Cross-Tabs

There are many different measures of association to represent the strength of the relationship between two category variables in a cross-tabulation. In order to select the most appropriate for your purpose, compare them on the following five properties.

1. Ordinality. Certain measures of association are sensitive only to ordinal association; use them whenever both variables have ordinal category measures. If you don't, your results may falsely indicate a high level of association. (As discussed later, an exception is the comparison of both nonordinal and ordinal measures of association, such as *gamma* and *lambda,* to detect nonlinearity.) Note that dichotomous variables can almost always be treated as ordinal.

2. Margin sensitivity. The margins of a cross-tabulation are the frequency distributions of each of the variables. Some measures of association are sensitive to uneven margin distributions: if some categories of one variable have very few cases, the results of these measures are likely to be distorted.

3. Maximum and minimum values. In the most convenient measures of association, the value zero represents no association, 1.0 is perfect association, and for two ordinal variables − 1.0 is perfect negative association. For measures without this range, interpretation and comparison of results is difficult, since you must calculate each time what the maximum (or minimum) value of the measure might be for a particular cross-tabulation.

4. *Symmetry.* A symmetric measure is one in which the two variables can be treated interchangeably; there is no need to identify one as the dependent variable. On the other hand, an asymmetric measure will give two different results, depending on which of the two variables you treat as dependent. (Percentage differences are asymmetric, since they depend on the direction in which you calculate the percentages.) For relationships with assumed causal direction, asymmetric measures of association are more accurate.

5. *Ease of interpretation.* Measures of association that have PRE (proportional reduction of error) interpretations are preferred, other properties being equal.

Percentage differences can be used with both nominal and ordinal category variables, are margin sensitive when the reference category has few cases, range from −100% to +100 percent, are asymmetric, and are easily interpreted. Other common measures of association for category variables are discussed below. Measures with major limitations, such as phi (applies only to 2 × 2 tables), tau-b (limited to square tables), and the contingency coefficient (upper limit varies with the size of the table), are not included.

Nonordinal Measures.

Cramer's V: Based on chi-square (a significance test of whether two variables are independent, discussed later), adjusted for sample size. Requires same assumptions as chi-square: (1) random sample, (2) multinominal distribution, (3) expected cell frequencies greater than 3. Minimal margin sensitivity. Range 0 to 1. Symmetric. No simple interpretation.

Lambda: Based on reduction of errors in predicting one variable from the other. Margin sensitive. Range 0 to 1. Asymmetric (symmetric version is mean of the two asymmetric values). PRE interpretation. A value of zero does not necessarily indicate the two variables are independent.

Ordinal Measures.

Gamma: Based on consistent and inconsistent orderings of pairs of cases, but ignores tied pairs. High margin sensitivity. Range −1 to +1. Symmetric. PRE interpretation. Warning: value may be substantially higher than what would be obtained using other measures of association. Also, gamma becomes artificially inflated as the number of categories decreases.

Kendall's tau-c: Based on consistent and inconsistent ordered pairs, but does not ignore tied pairs. High margin sensitivity. Range −1 to +1. Symmetric. No simple interpretation.

Somer's d: Based on consistent and inconsistent pairs, adjusting for ties in each variable separately. Some margin sensitivity. Range −1 to +1. Asymmetric. PRE interpretation.

Among these three, gamma is often preferred (because of its PRE interpretation) unless there are relatively few categories in one or both of the variables, in which case tau-c or d are better measures and less inflated than gamma. However, if you are concerned with questions of causality and can specify a dependent variable, Somer's d is preferred because it is asymmetric.

MEASURES OF ASSOCIATION FOR RANKED ORDINAL VARIABLES

Ranked ordinal measurement involves assigning each separate case a unique rank on a variable.[3] There are two major measures of association for pairs of such variables.

Spearman's rho: Based on the differences in ranks in the two variables. Range −1 to +1. Symmetrical. Measure can be interpreted as the Pearson correlation coefficient based on rank scores of the two variables. Thus the square of rho has a PVE interpretation.

Kendall's tau: Based on consistent and inconsistent orderings of pairs of cases. Range −1 to +1. Symmetrical. PRE interpretation as improvement in predicting rankings of one variable based on knowledge of rankings of the other.

Of the two, rho is preferred, since it makes use of the extent of the difference in ranks, where tau only notes for each case which variable ranks higher, or whether they are tied. However, a recent article by Ord (1982) suggests that tau has an advantage when not all cases in the sample are ranked. Ord's article illustrates this advantage with the following example.

CASE EXAMPLE

An advertising agency asked respondents, "What's the most outstanding TV commercial you've seen in the past few weeks?" The tabulation of answers each year results in the top 25 advertisers (e.g., Miller Lite, Ford, Bell Systems). The question is whether there is an association between the rankings in one year and those in the following year. (Note that the unit of analysis here is the advertiser, not the respondent, and the two variables are "Overall Rank in Year One" and "Overall Rank in Year Two.") Ord suggests that tau has an advantage over rho, since it can utilize more information. Rho can only be applied if an advertiser shows up in both lists; tau can be applied as long as an advertiser shows up in at least one list. All you need assume is that a missing advertiser had an overall ranking lower than 25.

---

[3]Do not confuse ranked ordinal variables with survey questions in which respondents are asked to rank a set of N options, such as preferred sources for seeking help with work-related problems. The latter are really category ordinal measures with each option a separate variable and each possible ranking, 1 through to N, a separate category.

MEASURES OF ASSOCIATION FOR QUANTITATIVE VARIABLES

The measures of association depend on whether one or both variables are quantitative.

Association Between Two Quantitative Variables

These measures of association have the following properties: all pick up ordinality but not nonlinearity, minimum value is zero, and all have PVE or unit change (slope) interpretations. Not all are symmetric.

Regression coefficient b: Based on the *slope* of the least-squares regression line when Y regressed on X. (This is the straight line in a scatterplot, drawn from one end of the oval of points to the other, which comes closest to all the points. It minimizes the sum of the square of the vertical distances between each point and the line.) No range restriction: may take any value, depending on what units the variables are measured in. Asymmetric. Unit change interpretation. Because its value depends on variables' units of measure, coefficients from different variables cannot be directly compared unless they are dummy variables.

Standardized regression coefficient (beta): Same as *b*, but calculated from standardized variables (transformed to a mean of zero, standard deviation of one). No range restriction. Asymmetric. Unit change interpretation. Since all units are standard deviations, coefficients from different variables can be compared.

Correlation coefficient r: Also called the Pearson correlation coefficient. Based on both the slope of the least-squares regression line and the dispersion of values of X about the line. Range -1 to $+1$. Symmetric. The square of *r*, denoted R^2, is called the *coefficient of determination* and has a PVE interpretation. Because *r* has no unit of measurement, correlations involving different variables can be compared directly.

Researchers sometimes debate the relative advantages of these two measures of association (O'Grady, 1982, and Box 16.3).

Association Between Quantitative and Category Variables

The simplest measure of association is differences of means across the categories: the larger the differences, the stronger the association. Other more rigorous measures of association are products of analysis of variance (ANOVA) and discriminant analysis.

BOX 16.3
MOVING SOUND: A CONTINUING CASE

Part Twelve: Correlation or Regression?

"George! It's me, Pete. I'm sitting at my computer, and it's too easy! I can get everything. Problem is, I don't know what to do with it."

"I take it you're into the data analysis?"

"Yes. The questionnaires. But here's my question. Do I use regressions or correlations for my bivariate analysis? Or do they give me exactly the same thing?"

"Good questions, and the answer to the last one is 'No.' Since correlations are influenced by the dispersion of cases about the regression line, and regression coefficients are not, you can get a situation in which the regression coefficient is high but the correlation coefficient low."

"OK, I understand that. But which one do I use?"

"Well, some researchers prefer regression to measure association because random measurement errors can contribute to variance and give you lower correlation coefficients, but measurement error won't affect the slope. They count on significance tests as indicators of dispersion. Other researchers prefer correlations because they can easily be compared across variables to give relative importance or effect size."

"That doesn't answer the question!"

"That's because there isn't a simple answer. My advice for analyzing relationships is to run and report both. That gives you maximum information about relationships in the data."

"Will do. And this software makes it easy. Whatever did they do before micros?"

Eta: A product of an ANOVA multiple classification analysis (MCA). Based on the ratio of explained to total sum of squares. Range 0 to 1. Asymmetric: the category variable is the independent. The square of eta is called the *correlation ratio* and has a PVE interpretation.

Discriminant function coefficient: A product of discriminant analysis (used when the category variable is the dependent—however, many researchers, unfamiliar with discriminant analysis, use ANOVA and eta regardless of which is the dependent). These coefficients are comparable to the regression coefficient in regression analysis. May take any value. Asymmetric. Unit change interpretation. For dependent variables with more than two categories, more than one coefficient may be required to indicate the association. (See the description of discriminant analysis in Chapter 17.)

The choice of a measure depends on three criteria:

- Whether the data meet the assumptions required by the measure (e.g., level of measurement)

- The properties of the measure (maximum value, margin sensitivity, symmetry)

- Whether the measure can be easily interpreted

STATISTICAL SIGNIFICANCE

Once the association between two variables is known, researchers normally apply a **significance test** whenever the research design involves randomness. Significance tests are the third application of inferential statistics. Unlike the other two, population estimates and hypothesis tests (see Chapter 15), they involve relationships rather than population characteristics. Significance tests answer two questions:

- In research using random samples they check whether a relationship could have been found solely because of the chance factors involved in sampling, that is, sampling error. If not, then the results can be generalized to the target population.

- In true experiments with random assignment they check whether group differences could have occurred because of random assignment error instead of the manipulation. If not, then this alternative explanation can be ruled out, increasing internal validity.

This section first discusses the logic and use of significance tests. It then turns to three problems and issues involving statistical significance: degrees of freedom, sample size, and the alpha problem.

A relationship is **statistically significant** if the probability of its occurring by chance (as a result of random sampling error or random assignment error) is found to be less than a predetermined alpha level.

The Logic of Significance Tests

The logic of significance testing is to propose a null hypothesis that no relationship exists (i.e., any apparent relationship is due to sampling or assignment error), and then see whether the data allow you to reject that hypothesis. Like the calculation of confidence intervals and hypothesis tests, significance tests are based on sampling distributions (but of test statistics, not sample means) and probabilities. The basic procedure is to calculate a special statistic (the three most widely used are chi-square, F, and Student's t) for which the sampling distribution is known, and then see if its value exceeds a specific critical level. If it does, you can reject the null hypothesis and conclude that the relationship is statistically significant. Most microcomputer statistical packages will carry out the calculations and comparisons for you.

The critical level is determined by selecting a probability level *(alpha)* representing the chance of a Type I error. Rejecting a true null hypothesis is a Type I error—you conclude that a relationship exists when it doesn't. Deciding that there is no relationship when in fact there is constitutes a Type II error.

In general, researchers are more concerned about Type I than Type II errors. However, the less the chance of a Type I error, the greater the chance of a Type II error. Researchers try to select alpha levels sufficiently low to reduce the chance of Type I error and high enough so they will not overlook significant relationships. Conventionally, the four alpha levels (or

BOX 16.4
RESEARCH SKILLS

Selecting a Significance Level

The legitimate use of statistical tests requires that you select a significance level *before* you see the data. In other words, decide beforehand what probability of Type I error (alpha) you can accept. Your alpha decision should take into account the following factors:

- The cost of a Type I error. If it's a multimillion dollar decision, be safe with a smaller alpha. On the other hand, if you want more research power to uncover relatively weak effects, use a larger alpha.
- The size of your sample. Since sampling error is larger with smaller samples, you may want to be more lenient (larger alpha) with small samples, other matters being equal, in order to avoid low research power.
- Is it a reversed hypothesis? Normally, we expect that a relationship exists, so our null hypothesis is that there is *no* relationship. On occasion we expect that there is no difference between two groups, so our null hypothesis is that there *is* a significant difference. In these situations, to maintain a conservative test we use a much larger level of alpha, often .20, .25, or .30. (What we are doing is trying to select a smaller probability of a Type II error, but these errors are very difficult to calculate. A rough equivalent is a larger level of alpha.)

"significance levels") used in increasing order of stringency are .10, .05, .01, and .001 (see Box 16.4). The choice of alpha should be made *before* any tests are conducted.

A second determinant of the critical level is whether a test is one-tailed or two-tailed, that is, whether the critical region is divided between both ends of the sampling distribution. A one-tailed test is appropriate whenever the researcher expects a relationship to have a particular direction (positive or negative). This is the most common situation in business research. On the other hand, if research is exploratory and no direction is assumed, a two-tailed test is required.

Researchers debate the issue of using significance tests with enumerations (instead of samples), as discussed in Box 16.5.

Degrees of Freedom

The sampling distributions of significance test statistics take different shapes depending on the **degrees of freedom** in the sample.

The degrees of freedom is the number of cases or observations that are free to vary, *given what you know about the sample.* For example, if you have three cases and know nothing else, the three may take *any* combination of values. However, if you calculate (or know) their mean, this calculation uses up a degree of freedom—it imposes an arithmetic restriction on the data. Since the sum of the values divided by the number of cases equals the mean, once you

BOX 16.5
RESEARCH ISSUES

Significance Tests and Enumerations

Researchers disagree over whether it is legitimate to use statistical tests of significance when the data represent a population rather than a sample.

The "No" side researchers claim that, since tests of significance test whether a finding based on a sample holds for a population (as opposed to occurring by chance through sampling error) and are based on the sampling distribution, they shouldn't be used when there isn't a random sample, and thus no sampling error (Morrison and Henkel, 1970).

The "Yes" side researchers hold that tests of significance represent a way of ruling out an alternative explanation for a relationship related to measurement misclassification: that it is a result of chance. If, in other words, a random classification would have produced the same degree of relationship (Blalock, 1979), then there is little reason to suppose that a true relationship exists.

The "No" position involves issues of external validity: we can't test for valid generalization when there is no larger population to generalize to. The "Yes" position, on the other hand, concerns internal validity: ruling out the alternative explanation that an observed relationship occurs through chance alone.

The resolution of this dispute is to recognize that researchers use randomness in two different situations: random sampling (mostly in surveys) and random assignment (in true experiments). Any use of a significance test is really a test for sampling error or assignment error. Could the observed results have happened as a result of an unusual sample or assignment of cases?

This suggests that significance tests are appropriate for *random sampling* and *random assignment* designs. It is *not* necessary for an experiment to employ a random sample for a significance test to be appropriate.

Beyond these two circumstances, the use of significance tests is only suggestive. For example, economists using income data from an enumeration and testing whether a regression coefficient is significantly different from zero are in effect asking, *"If these data were from a sample, could this particular coefficient likely have happened by chance?"* If such usage helps economists understand their results, well and good, but they must avoid the mistake of using significance tests as if they measured effect size.

---

calculate the mean only *two* values are free to vary. In other words, you can determine all three values if you know the mean plus two of the values. (Try this: if the mean is 6, and two of three values are 4 and 5, what's the third value?) Thus calculating a mean leaves $n - 1$ degrees of freedom in a sample of n cases.

Degrees of freedom is useful because it represents the exact correction that must be applied to sample size in order to calculate an unbiased estimate of many population characteristics and significance test statistics. For example, while the numerator of the formula for *sample* standard deviation contains the term n, the corresponding term for the estimate of the population standard deviation is $n - 1$. This correction is necessary because the formula for standard deviation contains the term $\overline{X}$, the mean, which uses up a degree of freedom in the sample. (Note that the sample mean itself is an unbiased estimate of the population mean and needs no correction to degrees of freedom.)

Significance and Sample Size

The significance of a relationship depends on its strength of association. However, significance tests are also based on sampling distributions, so the larger a sample (the more degrees of freedom), the smaller the standard error and the more likely a relationship is to be significant. One way to ensure that relationships are not a result of chance is to use larger samples or experimental conditions. However, sample size does not affect measures of association. Thus you *cannot* draw conclusions about the strength of association based on a significance test, since significance reflects both association and sample size.

The Alpha Problem: Multiple Tests

Carrying out many significance tests on the same data (but with different sets of variables each time) presents the possibility of biasing your results in the direction of finding a significant relationship where none exists (a Type I error). This difficulty is known as the *alpha problem*.

The problem comes about this way. If you select an alpha level of .05, you expect that 1 time out of 20 you will make a Type I error and reject a null hypothesis that you ought to accept. However, as you run more and more tests, the chances of doing exactly that increase. Inevitably, you will conclude that, among some set of variables, there is a relationship when there really isn't.

To reduce the alpha problem,

- Avoid vacuum cleaner analysis, examining all possible relationships. Concentrate on the relationships in your specific research questions.

- Use statistical tests that incorporate many comparisons at once (such as ANOVA in place of multiple t-tests).

- Choose a more stringent level of alpha (.01 instead of .05, or .001 instead of .01)[4]

- Calculate the number of significant findings you would expect by chance. If the number of significant relationships is greater than this, you can have more confidence in your findings.

Note that the alpha problem is compounded if a researcher runs all possible bivariate combinations, examines their measures of association, and applies significance tests *only* to those that appear substantial. The interpretation of the significance test is likely to be faulty. For example, if you have 20 relationships and select the largest for a significance test at the .05 alpha level, the true level of significance, because you selected the relationship to be tested, is closer to .64 (Selvin, 1958).

[4]Consult a statistics text such as Glass and Hopkins (1984) for procedures to adjust significance levels when using families of significance tests on related variables.

Significance or Association?

Some research reports emphasize tests of association (such as gamma and the correlation coefficient r), and others concentrate on tests of statistical significance (such as chi-square, t-tests, and ANOVA). In some circumstances bivariate tests may show that a relationship is significant but weak, or alternatively that it is insignificant but strong. The newcomer to research legitimately asks, "Are both association and significance equally important? If not, why not?"

The answer depends on three factors: (1) research objectives, (2) the importance of generalizing, and (3) sample size.

Research Objectives.   Different disciplines have come to emphasize different objectives, and these objectives have affected the traditional choice between association and significance tests in each discipline. Psychologists conducting controlled laboratory experiments with manipulated variables and random assignment have traditionally used ANOVA, a test of significance. For them, significance tests answer the question of whether an effect could have occurred by chance through random assignment error. The actual strength of a relationship is less important in laboratory research because it depends so heavily on the nature of the manipulation and the control of extraneous variables, rather than some intrinsic quality of the independent variable.

Survey researchers, on the other hand, have been more interested in the strength of relationships. They want to discover the relatively more important causes. In addition, significance is less salient because with large survey samples almost any relationship will be statistically significant, even if it is relatively weak.

Economists traditionally look at t-test (or F-test) measures of significance for the coefficients in regression equations. They rely on the size of the coefficient itself as a measure of effect strength, although since coefficients are seldom comparable across variables they look to significance tests for intervariable comparisons.

Importance of Generalizing.   Consider the difference between business and organization research. Business research results are normally generalized to a very specific target population whose size and elements are known. In this case, significance tests are important, since external validity is crucial. For example, pilot project results may lead to a program's being implemented throughout the corporation.

For organization research, however, the population is vague. The purpose of the research is to discover something about how organizations *in general* work. In this case, measures of association assume more importance relative to measures of significance (Selvin, 1958).

Sample Size. Larger samples decrease the standard error, an essential component of significance tests. As a result, increases in sample size make it more likely that an effect of any given size will be statistically significant. However, sample size has no effect on measures of association. The implication is that for very small samples (approximately 30 or less for nonexperimental designs to 10 or less for experimental designs) and very large samples (500 or more), relying solely on tests of significance is likely to be misleading. In both cases we also need to know the strength of the association.

- For a small sample, if we get a substantial measure of association we will want to pay attention, even though the relationship may not be statistically significant. The data suggest that the relationship might be significant if a larger sample were gathered.

- For a large sample, if we get statistical significance we still might not want to pay too much attention to the relationship if the strength of association is low. The data suggest that the relationship is trivial and would not have been significant in a smaller sample.

In short, here are some guidelines for the use of tests of association and significance in business research:

- Small sample: Emphasize association over significance.

- Medium-size sample: Look at both.

- Large sample: Emphasize association over significance.

For most research, it makes sense to check for association first and then to test for significance. However, in experiments researchers may conduct significance tests before (or even instead of) examining effect size, for the reasons mentioned earlier.

COMMON SIGNIFICANCE TESTS

This section summarizes briefly the characteristics of common significance test statistics. We begin with a discussion of test properties.

Significance Test Properties

Three properties are important when you choose a significance test: power, whether it is parametric, and robustness.

Power of a Statistical Test.   An important aspect of any statistical test of significance is its power—its ability to avoid Type II error. (Recall that a Type II error occurs when you accept a null hypothesis that should be rejected. In other words, you decide that there is no relationship when there really is one.)

Where β (beta) designates the probability of a Type II error, the **power** of a test is formally defined as $1 - β$.

Actual values of β in any given situation are usually difficult to calculate. However, statistical tests themselves vary in their power. Thus you can reduce Type II errors by using more powerful statistical tests.

Unfortunately, it is not easy to rank significance tests in terms of their power. The power of a test depends on the sample size, and the gain in power as size increases varies from test to test. However, in general parametric tests have greater power than nonparametric tests. If both a parametric and nonparametric test are feasible for a given relationship, the parametric test is preferred.

Parametric and Nonparametric Tests.   The term *parametric* is used to describe any significance test that requires assumptions of normality, such as the t-test and F-test. *Nonparametric* significance tests (such as chi-square and the Mann-Whitney test) don't require an assumption of normality.

For a nontransformable variable (uniform distributions, those with several peaks, and declining distributions that peak at the zero point), try both nonparametric tests based on rank ordinal scores and parametric tests. If the results of both parametric and nonparametric tests are fairly similar, you can go ahead and use the more powerful parametric tests.

Parametric significance tests involving group differences (such as ANOVA, t-tests, and discriminant analysis) assume that the *sampling distribution* of the test statistic is normally distributed. Since large samples have normal sampling distributions no matter what the sample distribution (following the central limit theorem), this assumption can be ignored with sample sizes over 100, and experiments with about 30 in each condition. On the other hand, significance tests for factor analysis and regression assume that the *variables* (only the dependent variable for regression) are normally distributed. Since sample size doesn't affect variable normality, researchers routinely test for normality with these procedures.

Researchers with small samples and nonnormal distributions are thus faced with the trade-off between a parametric test with greater power and a nonparametric test that does not violate assumptions about the sample or sampling distribution.

Note that rank ordinal variables have, by definition, uniform distributions. Except in the case of ties, there is only one case assigned to each rank. However, as long as there are 20 or more cases, parametric tests should work with rank ordinal data (Tabachnick and Fidell, 1989).

The **robustness** of a statistical test, with respect to a particular assumption, is its ability to give reliable conclusions despite violation of that assumption.

Robustness.   Statistical tests vary in how sensitive they are to violations of their assumptions. Obviously, robustness (defined at left) is a desirable quality in a test. The more robust, the less you need be concerned about violating assumptions and distorting measures of significance. Note, however, that robustness is assumption specific: a test may be quite robust with respect to one assumption, but very sensitive to violations of another.

Summary of Significance Tests

Box 16.6 gives basic information about some of the more common tests of significance. In general, the stricter the assumptions, the more power a test has. Thus, while you could use a chi-square test by grouping quantitative data, this is normally not advisable because of the loss of power and information this would involve.

Unlike measures of association, the researcher usually has little choice among significance tests, since convention or the nature of the data dictate which is used with a particular statistical procedure (e.g., F-tests in analysis of variance, chi-square tests with nominal data).

BIVARIATE CHECKS

Bivariate relationships can reveal potential problems that might produce misleading results. In particular, check important bivariate relationships for ordinality or linearity, joint outliers, and homogeneity of variance. Failure to meet these conditions may result in distorted measures of association or tests of significance.

Ordinality and Linearity

The most important check in bivariate relationships is whether a relationship is nonordinal or nonlinear. (Note that this test does not apply to relationships with one or two nominal variables.)

A relationship involving two ordinal variables (or one ordinal and one quantitative) has *ordinality* if it has a consistent direction, positive or negative. A relationship is positive if both variables increase together, negative if as one increases the other decreases. However, if a relationship changes direction, with one or more peaks or valleys, it is nonordinal. For example, if retail investors avoid both stocks ranked highly favorable and those ranked as highly unfavorable by brokers, and prefer those stocks ranked "uncertain," the relationship between preference and ranking is nonordinal.

A relationship involving two quantitative variables is *linear* if the trend line that best fits the data points is straight; otherwise it is a curvilinear relationship.

In business research, many relationships are nonordinal or nonlinear. Bivariate measures of association do not pick up such relationships. Small deviations from ordinality and linearity are not a problem, but substantial departures will result in distorted (usually underestimated) measures of association and significance. Similarly, the *mathematical function* expressing algebrai-

SUGGESTION

If you are uncertain to what extent an important assumption has been violated, use both a parametric and nonparametric test. If the results are consistently similar, then report the more powerful parametric test and mention the results of your comparison. If the results are different, report each statistic and suggest for the reader which might be the preferable one and the possible error involved in accepting it.

BOX 16.6
FOCUS ON RESEARCH
The Major Significance Tests

Chi-Square: Used to test whether two category variables are statistically independent. Also useful for curve fitting and for testing the goodness-of-fit of observed with expected distributions.

Assumptions: Nonparametric. Independent random samples.

Comments: Sample size should be relatively large. If expected frequencies in more than 20 percent of the cells are small (2 or less), use a correction for continuity, or collapse categories. If the sample size for a 2 × 2 table is small, use Fisher's exact test instead.

Fisher's Exact Test: Used as a test of significance for whether two dichotomous variables are statistically independent when sample size is too small for a chi-square test.

Assumptions: Nonparametric. Independent random samples.

Comments: One-tailed test (direction of relationship predicted). If not, double the significance level (e.g., from .01 to .02). Based on the hypergeometric distribution. It is somewhat more conservative than the chi-square test (i.e., it is slightly more difficult to reject the null hypothesis).

Student's t-Test: Used to test for difference of means between two groups. Often used to test significance of regression coefficients (i.e., testing the null hypothesis that the coefficients are equal to zero).

Assumptions: Parametric. Normal sampling distribution (robust for large n). Independent random samples.

Comments: When more than two groups are involved, F-tests in ANOVA are preferred to avoid the alpha problem. In regression, only the distribution of the dependent variable need be normal.

F-Test: Used to test for difference of means among two or more groups in ANOVA and its variations. Also used to test significance of regression coefficients in place of t-tests and to test for homogeneity of variance. In general, it is the basic test used with the general linear model underlying most multivariate analysis.

Assumptions: Parametric. Independent random sampling (or assignment). Normal population distribution of dependent variable (moderately robust). Normal sampling distribution of dependent variable about values of the independent variable(s) (or a joint normal distribution). (Robust for larger subsample sizes.) Variances about values of the independent variable(s) are equal (moderately robust).

Comments: The F statistic is calculated from a ratio. The numerator is affected by the amount of variance in the dependent variable explained by the independent variable(s); the denominator is affected by the unexplained variance in the dependent variable. Each F-test involves two different degrees of freedom, one for the numerator and one for the denominator. The critical value of F depends on these degrees of freedom.

Mann-Whitney Test: Used as a nonparametric substitute for ANOVA when subsample sizes are small and population is not normally distributed. It tests for differences in the distributions of two samples (not just their means).

Assumptions: Nonparametric. Two independent random samples.

Comments: This test is only one of several that can be used in place of ANOVA F-tests for significant differences between groups when t-test or F-test assumptions are clearly not met. The runs test and the Kolmogorov-Smirnov are others. In most, but not all instances, the Mann-Whitney is more powerful than the alternatives. Blalock (1979) regards this test as a relatively powerful nonparametric alternative to the t-test.

Others: Many measures of association (e.g., the Pearson correlation coefficient and some ordinal measures of association) have related tests of statistical significance. These tests usually examine the null hypothesis that the level of association is zero.

cally the relationship between two quantitative variables, with coefficients estimated using regression analysis, will be inaccurate if the relationship is nonlinear.

The problem then reduces to two questions: (1) is there a nonordinal or nonlinear relationship, and, (2) if so, what's a better measure of the true degree of relationship?

Two Category Ordinal Variables. To detect nonordinality, examine the cross-tabulation with categories percentaged correctly to see whether a clear nonordinal relationship is present. Sometimes this is difficult to see, particularly in tables with more than two rows and two columns. To help you decide, (1) check the pattern of percentages in the highest and lowest categories of the dependent variable, and (2) check the pattern of the largest *(modal)* percentages in each category of the independent variable. Figure 16.3 illustrates the tactic, using the variables "item cost" (independent) and "item inventory" (dependent).

FIGURE 16.3
Ordinal and Nonordinal Relationships with
Category Ordinal Variables

Level of Item Inventory (in %) by Item Cost

(a) Mostly Ordinal		Low	Item Cost Medium	High
Level of Inventory	High	65%	15%	20%
	Medium	20	70	20
	Low	15	15	60
		(194)	(312)	(110)

(b) Nonordinal (U-shaped)		Low	Item Cost Medium	High
Level of Inventory	High	65%	15%	60%
	Medium	20	15	20
	Low	15	70	20
		(194)	(312)	(110)

(c) Partly Ordinal		Low	Item Cost Medium	High
Level of Inventory	High	65%	75%	20%
	Medium	20	15	20
	Low	15	15	60
		(194)	(312)	(110)

- The "high inventory" dependent variable category in table (a) of Figure 16.3 shows the percentages 65%, 15%, 20%, which is not quite ordinal. However, the modal percentages (in boldface) in "item cost" independent variable categories (65%, 70%, 60%) show a clear ordinal trend. This table appears to be largely ordinal. An ordinal measure of association would be appropriate and would indicate a very strong relationship.

- In table (b) the "high inventory" category shows 65%, 15%, 60%, clearly nonordinal. The pattern of modal "item cost" percentages shows a U-shaped pattern. An ordinal measure of association here would indicate an extremely weak relationship, although there is clearly a strong *nonordinal* one (medium-cost items are much more likely to have low inventory levels).

- In table (c) the "high inventory" category shows 65%, 75%, 20%—which we can call partly ordinal because the 10% difference in the first two is too small to be considered. The modal "item cost" percentages show a partial ordinal trend. Low and medium-cost items are much alike, and only high cost items differ in inventory levels. Since there is no strong nonordinal relationship, an ordinal measure of association would be appropriate and would show a moderate level of association.

SUGGESTION

A nonordinal relationship may be hard to detect with four or more categories of the dependent variable. After percentaging, circle the one or two highest percentages within each category of the independent variable, and look for an emerging pattern. It will help to collapse temporarily the dependent variable to three categories with as uniform a distribution as possible.

The cross-tab in Figure 16.1a shows a nonordinal relationship between plant location and department productivity rating. The Ajax plant has the higher proportion of both "very good" and "poor" departments.

To confirm the presence of nonordinality, compare an ordinal-level and a nominal-level measure of association (e.g., lambda and gamma). Because it is independent of the order of categories, the nominal measure will pick up any relationship. The ordinal measure, however, will only pick up an ordinal relationship. Thus, if the first is substantially greater than the second, you have a nonordinal relationship. An alternative is to calculate and compare the correlation coefficient r and eta for the table. If nonlinearity is present, eta will be substantially larger than r. (Keep in mind that it is the relative difference between r and eta that matters. Do not use these statistics as measures of association for category ordinal variables.)

Category Ordinal and Quantitative. To detect nonordinality, examine group box plots, particularly group means and medians, to see whether there is a consistent upward or downward trend across groups. Deviations in groups with relatively few cases can be ignored. This procedure will also work with a category ordinal and a rank ordinal variable.

To confirm, run an ANOVA with polynomial contrasts. Quadratic polynomials should be sufficient. If the contrasts are significant, the relationship is nonordinal.

Two Rank Ordinal Variables. Check for nonordinality with a scatterplot. To confirm, temporarily collapse the independent variable into categories, and run an ANOVA test as just described for a category ordinal and quantitative variable.

Two Quantitative Variables. Look for nonlinearity in a scatterplot. The most frequent nonlinearity in business research is a curve that begins steeply but slowly flattens out, as shown in Figure 16.4. If the data points are too scattered to make the trend clear, temporarily collapse the independent variable into categories and treat it as a category ordinal variable. Run group box plots.

This same temporary collapsing of the independent variable can provide a confirmatory check for linearity. Compare the correlation coefficient r (for the uncollapsed variable) with eta (from an ANOVA using the collapsed variable). If eta is noticeably greater than r, nonlinearity is present.

Note that even if the scatterplot for your data shows a linear relationship, you cannot be certain that at much higher (or lower) values of the independent variable than you have, the relationship is still linear. For example, a sample of firms ranging in size between 12 and 228 employees shows a linear relationship of size and employee morale. However, the real effect of size may die out after a thousand or so employees, so the curve flattens out after that point. Thus caution is always required if you generalize to higher or lower values of the independent variable than those in your sample.

Remedies. There are no simple techniques for measuring association in nonordinal relationships. The simplest solution is to substitute measures for nominal-level variables, collapsing quantitative variables to categories.

However, if a relationship between two quantitative variables is nonlinear, association is fairly simple to assess. The most common solution is to transform one of the variables. Try the data transformations discussed in chapter 14. An alternative for nonlinear but ordinal relationships is to treat the varia-

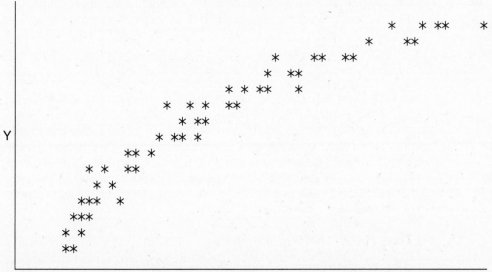

FIGURE 16.4 The Most Frequent Type of Nonlinear Relationship in Business Research

bles as rank ordinal and use a nonparametric measure of association such as Spearman's rank-order correlation coefficient. A third alternative is to run ordinary regression with additional terms to pick up the nonlinearity (see Chapter 17). A more complicated alternative is to run nonlinear regression.

Joint Outliers

A second check, for relationships between two quantitative variables, is to examine the scatterplot for joint outliers. For example, Figure 16.5 shows a case that lies outside the main cluster of cases, but is not an outlier with respect to the univariate distribution of either the X or Y variable. (The scatterplot in Figure 16.1b shows a joint outlier in the upper left-hand corner. It would also be a univariate outlier on the "accident rate" variable.)

Joint outliers are a problem because they can distort measures of association. This happens because they have disproportionate *leverage* compared to other cases: their influence on the statistical result is much greater than that of other cases closer to the trend line. One outlier can noticeably affect the regression line slope in a small sample of cases.

Remedies. A joint outlier must be treated with caution. Transformation is a solution, but it often introduces nonlinearity into the relationship. Dropping the outlier is suspect because the results so clearly improve measures of association and significance. The most cautious treatment is to keep it in the analysis, but examine it as a special case. If truly unique in ways that make it

A **joint outlier** is a case that lies substantially outside a bivariate or multivariate distribution, but is not necessarily an outlier for any of the variables' univariate distributions.

FIGURE 16.5
Example of a Joint Outlier That Is Not a Univariate Outlier for Either Variable

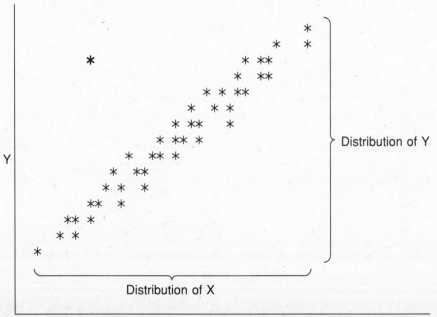

theoretically inappropriate for your analysis, a joint outlier may be dropped. If you do so, report results both with and without the outlier.

ADVANCED TOPIC

Homogeneity of Variance

A third check, for any relationship involving a quantitative variable, is for homogeneity of variance. Many statistical tests of significance assume that variance in the dependent variable is similar across values of the independent. This means that as X increases, the *range* of values in Y doesn't change dramatically. Failure to meet this assumption can lead to distorted significance test results and smaller correlations.

Detection. For *a category and a quantitative* variable, box plots will indicate whether variances are homogeneous. The box plots in Figure 16.1c show nonhomogeneous variance. The box height (interquartile range) for "percentage of skilled employees (by department)" is considerably greater in plant 1 than plant 2. For *two quantitative* variables, inspect the scatterplot to see whether the spread of data points about the trend line increases or decreases with X. Reexamine Figure 14.5.

There are statistical routines for detecting nonhomogeneous variance. One is a plot of regression residuals against the independent variable. Regression and ANOVA routines usually contain other tests for homogeneity of variance. Consult your software documentation.

Remedy. Normally, the assumption of homogeneous variance is quite robust and can be violated to a modest degree without threatening results. However, if the departures are substantial, particularly if the group sizes in an ANOVA are substantially different, you must either reduce the nonhomogeneity or use nonparametric tests. A common remedy is to apply a logarithmic transformation to the dependent variable when both means and variance increase across categories.

Another technique analogous to reducing nonhomogeneity is to use weighted least-squares regression. This procedure treats error terms differently depending on the value of the independent variables.

■ *The Lighter Side of Research*

Statistical analysis: Mysterious, sometimes bizarre, manipulations performed upon the collected data of an experiment in order to obscure the fact that the results have no generalizable meaning for humanity. Commonly, computers are used, lending an additional air of unreality to the proceedings. (Woodman, 1979)

Summary

The analysis of relationships among variables is the essence of most business research. Relationship analysis begins with a review of the relationships in your research questions, followed by bivariate analysis of primary relationships (involving key and primary dependent and independent variables). As well as providing initial estimates of the effects of independent variables, bivariate analysis checks for data problems that might distort multivariate analysis. In particular, researchers look for nonlinearity or nonordinality, joint outliers, and nonhomogeneous variance, using both statistical tests and graphic aids: cross-tabs, scatterplots, and box plots.

Where Are We Now?

Once bivariate analysis and checks have been finished, the researcher has a rough idea of the answer to each specific research question (except those involving three or more variables together). The next step is to check whether those answers hold up under multivariate analysis, when the effects of other variables are taken into account.

Discussion Issues and Assignments

1. Locate a cleaned data set (with a codebook) on which you and other members of the class can practice. Designate a quantitative and a category dependent variable, and a series of quantitative, category ordinal, and nominal independent variables. Choose bivariate measures of association and determine the nature of association between ten pairs of variables.

2. On the same data set, select and run tests of statistical significance. Are such tests appropriate for all your variable pairs?

3. On the same data set, run bivariate analysis checks for linearity, homogeneity of variance, and joint outliers. Try to correct any problems you find. Compare your problems and corrections with those of the other students. Did they define the same situations as problems? Did they try the same corrections? Discuss any differences.

4. For each of five pairs of category variables, calculate as many measures of association as your software will allow. Rank-order the magnitudes of the results within each variable pair, and then compare across pairs. Which measures give generally higher values? Which are less stable (i.e., fluctuate more)?

5. Select 25 pages of this text at random, and calculate for each these two variables: number of words and number of sentences. Use your computer software to calculate the correlation and regression coefficients, trying both words and sentences as the dependent variable. Also calculate significance tests. Add a joint outlier case (make it up), and recalculate the measures of association and the significance tests. Discuss any differences.

6. For the same data used in question 5, convert the measure of each variable to ranked ordinal. Compute nonparametric measures of association and significance. What differences does the ordinal ranking make? Calculate correlation and regression coefficients on the ordinal rankings, and compare with the results of question 5.

Further Reading

Henkel, Ramon E. 1976. *Tests of Significance.* Beverly Hills: Sage.

> A review of the basic methods and issues in the use of significance tests.

Knoke, David, and Peter J. Burke. 1980. *Log-Linear Models.* Beverly Hills: Sage.

> A good readable introduction to the use of this method in determining relationships among category variables. It is the only major alternative to cross-tabulations.

Liebetrau, Albert M. 1983. *Measures of Association.* Beverly Hills: Sage.

> This work covers most of the commonly used measures of association for nominal, ordinal, and quantitative data.

Morrison, Denton E., and Ramon E. Henkel. 1970. *The Significance Test Controversy.* Chicago: Aldine.

> A readable and now classic introduction to the major issues in what has continued to be a series of debates on the use of significance tests.

Rosnow, R. L., and R. Rosenthal. 1989. "Statistical Procedures and the Justification of Knowledge in Psychological Science." *American Psychologist* 44:1276–1284.

> A good discussion of recent issues in statistical and methodological problems, including significance tests, effect sizes, and Type I and Type II error.

CHAPTER 17

Relationships and Group Differences: Multivariate Analysis

CHAPTER OBJECTIVES

- What are the varieties of multivariate analysis, and what do they do?
- How do we build forecasting and selection prediction models?
- How do we determine the importance of each variable in evaluation and explanatory research?
- How can data from repeated-measure and time-series designs be analyzed?
- What can we do when we find unexpected results?

CHAPTER OUTLINE

ultivariate analysis is essential for today's business research. Consider the following research questions:

- "How much more productive is an employee likely to be who scores 50 points higher on the dexterity test, controlling for age and gender?" *(prediction research, nonexperimental design)*

- "How great an impact did the new investment software have on monthly brokerage fees, compared to other factors?" *(evaluation research, quasi-experimental design)*

- "Which location factors produce more walk-in sales: easy parking, other stores nearby, or store frontage?" *(explanatory research, nonexperimental design)*

- "In order to target advertising most effectively, we need to know how many different types of customers we have out there." *(explanatory research, nonexperimental design)*

Informed answers and useful recommendations for questions such as these require multivariate analysis, because it provides superior estimates in prediction research and much more accurate indications of a variable's real effect in evaluation and explanatory research (see Box 17.1).

TYPES OF MULTIVARIATE ANALYSIS

Multivariate analysis is the examination of relationships involving more than two variables.[1] There are two broad kinds of multivariate statistics used in business research:

- *Dependence relationships*. The researcher seeks to discover how one or more dependent variables is affected by two or more independent variables.

- *Interdependence relationships*. These techniques examine the underlying structure among variables (or cases) without specifying any of them as dependent variables.

Within dependence relationships, the inclusion of more than one independent variable achieves two important ends: (1) determining the *joint effect* of a

[1]The term *multivariate* has two meanings among researchers. For some it means situations with two or more independent variables; for others (particularly psychologists) it is limited to situations with two or more *dependent* variables. The former is the usage we adopt here.

BOX 17.1
RESEARCH ETHICS
The Ethics of Multivariate Analysis

When it comes to data analysis, ethical concerns largely revolve around the issue of accepted research practice. The researcher must balance the amount of analysis against the interests of the organization or client. In particular, researchers face the question of whether to carry out multivariate analysis.

In the past, a researcher might have argued that multivariate analysis was too time consuming for the benefits it brought and monopolized too much valuable computer time. However that argument does not stand up today. With the statistical software now available and the proliferation of microcomputers, multivariate analysis is readily available and relatively simple. It is not just expected, but required.

The failure to carry it out produces misleading conclusions about the roles played by certain variables. For example, a variable that appears to be vital at the bivariate level may turn out to be spurious in multivariate analysis. Misleading conclusions in turn

lead to less effective and sometimes harmful recommendations.

Interestingly, multivariate analysis today is almost *too* easy! Researchers who don't know the assumptions, limitations, and appropriate uses of the various multivariate techniques can also produce mistaken conclusions and dubious recommendations. While few of us are statistical experts, we do have an ethical responsibility to know what we're doing, and more important, to know what *not* to do.

Multivariate analysis is a powerful tool, but it must be wielded with care. Business researchers have an ethical obligation both to their organizations and to the profession to conduct appropriate multivariate analysis in keeping with the data, as well as the financial and time limitations of their projects. If a satisfactory level of multivariate analysis is not possible, the researcher has an obligation to point this out, together with the weaknesses it implies for specific conclusions and recommendations.

number of independent variables acting together on a dependent and (2) measuring the *unique effect* of each of several independent variables on a dependent.

- *Prediction model building* finds the set of independent variables that most efficiently predicts the dependent variable. It relies heavily on measures of joint effect and is all that's required for forecasting or selection prediction research.

- *Explanatory and evaluation research* go further to examine the unique effect of each independent variable on a dependent and to compare these effects. A variable's unique effect is an indication of its importance as a cause of the dependent variable.

The Logic of Multivariate Analysis

The rationale for multivariate analysis is that it allows researchers to statistically control for certain variables while examining the effects of others. This can be extremely important when, as is often the case in business research, control through research design (selection of comparison groups and samples) is imperfect or impossible. The benefit of statistical control is that when two independent variables (a primary X and a control variable C) are both related to a dependent variable Y, we get a better idea of the importance of X if we statistically control for C. (Of course, to do so we must have measures for all three variables.)

The logic behind statistical control is simple. First, we calculate the effect of C on X. Then we subtract this effect from X. Third, we measure the association between the adjusted X and Y.[2] The result is a measure of association between X and Y controlling for C. We call it the *unique effect* of X. Most multivariate statistical procedures employ this type of control.

Figure 17.1 shows symbolically how this works. Each variable is represented by a circle. The circle is that variable's variation. The overlap of two circles indicates that those variables covary. The greater the overlap, the greater their covariation (association). The overlap area represents the variation in the dependent variable explained by an independent variable.

Multivariate Analysis and Significance Tests.   Figure 17.1a shows a dependent variable Y and three independent variables: X and two control variables C_1 and C_2. Each of the independent variables overlaps with the dependent variable Y.

We can think of the statistical significance of X as the ratio of the amount of variation in Y that X explains (the overlap area of X and Y) to the variation in Y left unexplained (the rest of Y). If no other variables are controlled, the unexplained area of Y is everything except the overlap with X. However, if other variables are controlled, they take away some of the variation in Y that X doesn't explain. Therefore the significance of X may increase because the unexplained portion of Y decreases. Thus it is generally easier to detect statistically significant relationships when other independent variables are statistically controlled. This is how multivariate analysis increases research power.

Interrelated Independent Variables and Effect Size.   Often control variables are related to both the dependent variable and to the independent variable X. Figure 17.1b shows this more complicated situation: both control variables C_1 and C_2 are related to X as well as Y and overlap with both. This means that some of the covariation of X with Y is shared by C_1 and C_2. This *shared covariation* is shown by the darkly shaded areas.

Now consider this problem: What is the effect size of X, that is, the variation in Y that is explained by X? If we include the shared covariation portions, we are exaggerating the effect of X by ignoring the input of C_1 and C_2. For example, the variable X may appear to cause Y, but the effect may really be C_1 working "through" X.

The solution that researchers usually adopt is to *count only the unshared*

---

[2]An alternative procedure is to adjust *both* X and Y by removing the effects of other independent variables from both.

FIGURE 17.1
Statistical Control in
Multivariate Analysis

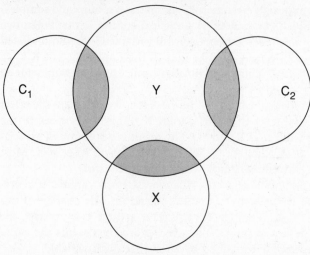

(*a*) Unrelated Independent Variables

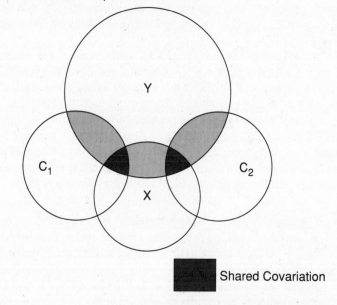

(*b*) Interrelated Independent Variables

Shared Covariation

covariation. This produces a measure of the unique effect of X on Y. It is the proportion of the dependent variable's variation accounted for *solely* by X. We get the unique effect of an independent variable when we control for other independent variables in multivariate analysis.

The balance of this chapter discusses the use, rather than the calculation and derivation, of multivariate techniques. It offers suggestions about which techniques to use in different situations. Table 17.1 summarizes the multivariate techniques for dependence relationships most useful in business research.

FORECASTING AND SELECTION MODELS

Forecasting and selection *prediction research* use multivariate analysis to construct and test prediction models. For both forecasting and selection prediction, the researcher's task is to choose from among a set of possible predictors (independent variables) those that best predict a selected criterion (dependent variable). These are the variables that make up the *prediction model*. For example, from data on *existing* retail outlets, the researcher generates the following prediction model for the success of an outlet:

$$Y = -120 + 7X_1 + 4X_2 + 3X_3$$

where:

　　Y　is predicted average monthly sales, in thousands
　　X_1 is store frontage in feet
　　X_2 is number of other retail businesses within 50 yards
　　X_3 is number of parking spaces within 100 yards.

The researcher now predicts the expected monthly sales of a potential new outlet location with 20-foot frontage, 10 other business within 50 yards, and 25 parking spaces within 100 yards. Using the prediction model, the new site is predicted to have monthly sales averaging $135,000.

Normally the researcher has a variety of possible predictors to select from (chosen in the design portion of the research and measured in the data-gathering phase). Note that predictors are not assumed to have any causal relationship with the dependent variable. *Causal relationships are neither important nor necessary for accurate forecasting or selection prediction.*

Model Building Techniques

The statistical procedures for model building are generally based on *stepwise regression* analysis. (Multiple regression and its variations are described in Boxes 17.2 and 17.3.) Stepwise regression takes the independent variables one at a time, starting with the variable most strongly related to the dependent variable, and constructs a set of prediction models. Each succeeding model has one more variable than the last. The procedure ends when either all available variables have been used, or none of the unused variables can improve the prediction of the dependent variable.

TABLE 17.1 ■ MULTIVARIATE STATISTICAL PROCEDURES FOR DEPENDENCE RELATIONSHIPS

Dependent Variable	Independent Variables (IVs)	Recommended Procedure
Quantitative	*Mostly quantitative:*	
	• All quantitative IVs	Standard regression; stepwise for forecasting and selection models
	• Includes some nominal or dichotomous IVs	Regression with dummy variables
	• Includes some category ordinal IVs	Regression treating category ordinals as quantitative (best if five or more categories)
	Mostly category:	
	• All nominal or dichotomous IVs	Analysis of variance (with regression option)
	• Includes a few quantitative IVs	Analysis of covariance
	• Includes a few category ordinal IVs	Analysis of variance with trend (polynomial contrasts)
Category Ordinal		Treat the category ordinal as a quantitative dependent variable (especially if five or more categories) and proceed as above.
Dichotomous or Nominal	Quantitative IVs	Logit (logistic) regression or discriminant analysis (especially for selection prediction models)

T A B L E   1 7 . 1 *(Continued)*

Dependent Variable	Independent Variables (IVs)	Recommended Procedure
	Mix of quantitative and category IVs	Logit regression with dummy variables or discriminant analysis
	All dichotomous or nominal IVs	Highly unlikely, but check an advanced statistics test for log linear analysis
Rank Order	Treat as quantitative as long as there are at least 20 cases.	

These are the steps:

• The first variable (the one most strongly related to the dependent) explains as much of the variation in the dependent variable as it can.

• Among the remaining variables, the procedure tests to see which is most strongly related to the dependent. This variable is then added to the prediction model to see what additional variation it can explain.

• A third variable (most strongly related of those remaining) is then added to pick up whatever it can of the remaining variation, and so on.

Measures of Joint Effect

Measures of *joint effect* tell us how much impact all the independent variables acting *together* (jointly) have on the dependent variable. Prediction research relies heavily on measures of joint effect for building forecasting and selection prediction models. As we see, joint effect measures are also important in evaluation and explanatory research, but for different purposes.

In prediction models, after each variable is added, the stepwise regression routine measures the joint effect of the variables now in the model. The measure used is the *coefficient of determination* (the squared multiple correlation), represented by the symbol R^2. R^2 is equivalent to the proportion of variation in the dependent variable explained by all the independent variables in the model acting jointly. Even if some other technique than regression is used (for example, discriminant analysis), the researcher relies on a measure of the joint effect of the variables in the model (see Table 17.2).

BOX 17.2

RESEARCH SKILLS

Using Multiple Regression

Multiple regression is probably the most frequently used statistical procedure in business research. It examines the effects of quantitative or category independent variables on a quantitative dependent.

Concept: There are two related ways of thinking about how multiple regression works: (1) it finds the linear combination of independent variables that best estimates the relationships of independent variables to the dependent, or (2) it finds the line, plane, or surface that minimizes the sum of the squared differences between the data points and the surface. (This is the meaning of "least squares" in ordinary least-squares (OLS) regression. See Box 17.3 for alternatives to OLS.)

Assumptions: Normally distributed dependent variable; homogeneity of variance in dependent variable; linear relationships. There are several ways of expressing the assumptions necessary for significance tests and accurate measures of effect in regression analysis. The following is one set, phrased in terms of the error terms:

- Expected value of error terms is zero.
- Error terms are uncorrelated with independent variables. (This is the most crucial assumption. It is justified if the unmeasured causes of Y are "numerous, singly unimportant, and not highly inter-related" or "unrelated to X in situations where one or two omitted factors predominate," Blalock, 1979:197).
- Error terms are normally distributed about values of the dependent variable.
- Variance in error terms is constant about values of the dependent variable.

These assumptions are met by a multivariate normal distribution with random sampling (independent cases).

Checks: For multicollinearity, examine the correlation matrix and the *tolerance* of each variable (tolerance indicates how strongly an independent variable is related to other independents). Good statistical packages provide a variety of other *regression diagnostics* to check how much assumptions are violated.

Measures of Joint Effect: Examine R^2 (the *coefficient of multiple determination*). Note that R^2 is only a measure of *linear* association; two variables may have an R^2 of zero but have a strong curvilinear relationship. For prediction models, the adjusted R^2 is a better indication of joint effect, since it corrects for the number of independent variables. Simply adding more independents will almost always increase the value of R^2. For prediction research, then, researchers find the model that maximizes the adjusted R^2. For statistical significance of the entire model, most software provides an F-test.

Measures of Unique Effect:

- The *partial regression coefficient* indicates the slope or unit change effect of a variable. It tells how much change in the dependent variable you will get with a single unit change in the independent. For example, a coefficient of 184.66 tells you that for each additional year of technical training (the independent variable), an employee's monthly salary (the dependent variable) increases by about $185. (Use t- or F-tests of significance to see if the slope is significantly different from zero.)
- *Part correlations* (also called semipartial correlations) and *partial correlations* correspond to bivariate correlation coefficients. Part correlations, when squared, represent the proportion of *all* the variation in the dependent accounted for by a variable; squared partial correlations represent the proportion of the *explained* variation in the dependent accounted for by the variable. Researchers generally prefer part correlations as a measure of effect size. (A significance test will

indicate whether correlation coefficients are significantly different from zero.)

Measures of Relative Effect: Compare (1) partial correlations, (2) part correlations, (3) standardized regression coefficients (betas), or (4) the hierarchical gain in R^2 (when variables are entered in order of causal priority).

Comments:

- When the dependent variable is logged (the resulting regression equation is called *semilogarithmic*), the regression coefficients can be interpreted as the *proportional* change in Y given a unit change in X. For example, if the dependent variable is "log of unit sales," the coefficient for the independent variable "hours of training" can be interpreted as the proportionate increase in sales for each additional hour of training. (There are limitations to this interpretation, however. For example, it cannot be used for dummy variables. See Thornton and Innes, 1989.)
- The assumption of independent observations needed for significance tests requires that residuals be random in whatever order or subsets the cases are in; there must be no "pattern" in the residuals. Autocorrelation in time series is the most common violation of this assumption.
- The number of cases (observations) should be, ideally, about 20 times the number of variables. This can be lowered to a minimum of 5 times if (1) the dependent variable is not skewed, (2) the degree of association between dependent and independents is moderate or better, and (3) measurement error is minimal (Tabachnick and Fidell, 1989).

- If the independent variables are all interrelated, they may all show relatively low unique effects because of the large amount of shared covariation. However, the R^2 for the total regression equation will be high. To detect this, examine both the R^2 and the bivariate correlations, which should both be high.
- Convert category independent variables to *dummy variables* (except when you treat a category ordinal variable as quantitative). For each category variable (1) select a "reference" category against which the effects of other categories will be compared, (2) create a new "dummy" variable for each remaining category, coded "1" if the case falls in that category, "0" otherwise. (3) Interpret the dummy variable regression coefficients as the effect of that particular category compared to the reference category. For category variables with three or more categories (thus represented by two or more dummy variables), a measure of unique effect can be obtained by entering all the dummies together as a block and observing the change in R^2.
- When an independent variable is not linear, use regression with polynomial terms. This is equivalent to adding new variables to pick up the nonlinearity in the relationship. In most instances, you will only need the X^2 term. (Only in rare cases will the X^3 term be necessary.) Actually, it is simpler to carry out the regression with a second variable Z defined as the square of X. This quadratic equation gives a parabolic curve. Parabolas will fit a wide variety of nonlinear relationships (Stolzenberg and Land, 1983).

Selecting the Best Model

The problem for the researcher is deciding when to stop the process, or, more technically, which of the many models represents the best prediction. It might seem that the one with the most variables, or the highest R^2, is the logical choice. After all, each additional predictor improves the prediction just a little bit more, even though the amount of improvement declines at each stage. For example, a selection model that accounts for 50 percent of the variation in

BOX 17.3

FOCUS ON RESEARCH

Variations of Regression Analysis

The major question in multivariate analysis is what to do when two (or more) independents are interrelated, as well as related to the dependent. How is their shared explanation of the dependent to be handled? Three regression variations handle shared covariation among independents in different ways:

- *Standard* regression ignores shared covariation in measures of the unique effect of separate variables, but includes it in the measure of the variables' joint effect. It is used in most regression analysis.
- *Stepwise* regression assigns the shared covariation to the independent variable with the stronger covariation with the dependent variable. Use this variation for building forecasting and selection prediction models.
- *Hierarchical* regression is a method in which the researcher's assumptions about causal ordering (the order in which variables "enter" the regression equation) determine to which variable the shared covariation is assigned. This variation is useful for causal modeling. (See the appendix following this chapter.)

Other variations concern what to do when the dependent variable isn't quantitative, is restricted in some way, or has other problems, or the research problem calls for more than one dependent variable to be examined simultaneously. Consult your software documentation and an advanced statistics text for more information about these variations:

Logit (logistic) regression is used when the dependent variable is a dichotomy or nominal category variable. The statistical tests are based on the log likelihood of a fitted model. Logit coefficients are more difficult to interpret than those of OLS regression. An alternative to use with a dichotomous dependent variable is the *linear probability* model, simply OLS regression.

Tobit analysis is useful as an alternative to nonparametric techniques based on ranks when the dependent variable is nonnormal because of many cases clustered at one extreme end (e.g., number of days absent in past month—most employees will have "none").

Probit analysis is the technique of choice when the dependent variable is a probability and thus restricted to the range of zero to one.

Two-stage least squares is a good solution to the autocorrelation problem in time-series regression analysis when a previous value of the dependent variable is treated as an independent. This approach is also useful for models with reciprocal causality (X causes Y and vice versa).

Weighted least squares is useful when variances in the error term are correlated with independent variables (nonhomogeneous variance). The use of OLS regression will not produce biased estimates of population parameters, but the precision of those estimates will be less than with weighted least squares.

Canonical correlation is a variation of multiple regression that handles multiple dependent variables.

monthly sales in existing outlets is better than one that accounts for only 45 percent. However, although each additional variable adds to the predictive power of the model, it also imposes costs.

- As the number of variables increases, the quality of the prediction becomes *artificially better* simply because the number of cases in the sample is limited.

TABLE 17.2■ MULTIVARIATE ANALYSIS MEASURES OF UNIQUE, JOINT, AND RELATIVE EFFECTS

	Multiple Regression	Analysis of Variance and Covariance	Discriminant Analysis
Unique Effect	Regression coefficient or partial or semipartial correlation	Betas from Multiple Classification Analysis (MCA)	Standardized discriminant function coefficients
Joint Effect	Coefficient of determination (R^2)	Omega squared or R^2 from MCA	Square of the canonical correlation
Relative Effect	Compare standardized regression coefficients (unstandardized for dummy variables) or partial or semipartial correlations	Compare betas from MCA	Compare standardized discriminant function coefficients

This condition is called **overfitting**; the model fit the data too well, so that results can't be generalized beyond the specific sample of cases used to generate the model. Ultimately, with as many variables as cases, you could predict each case in your sample perfectly. However, this would be highly misleading, since the sample you use to generate the prediction model is not the same as the population in which you'll apply the model.

• Applying a model with many predictors is more costly in terms of time and data-gathering effort. For example, a selection model based on a job applicant's education level, years of prior experience, and a test score is easier to apply than one that also considers three other test scores, four additional demographic factors, and seven measures of prior experience.

To avoid these problems, researchers assess the quality of each prediction model not with R^2, but with an *adjusted R^2*, which corrects the value of R^2 to take into account the number of predictors in the model and the sample size. After a certain point, when the contribution of each additional predictor to the model is minimal, the values of the adjusted R^2 begin to decline. This is the point at which researchers often decide they have the best prediction model. Although somewhat arbitrary, it is often treated as the point at which the costs to accuracy are balanced by the costs of using a larger prediction model.

Note that this procedure is entirely *empirical*. The data themselves decide which variables will appear in the model. There is no theoretical input on the part of the researcher (except in choosing the original potential predictor variables), nor is there any question of causality. In fact the coefficients of predictors in a prediction model can give quite misleading impressions of both the direction and size of causal impact. For this reason, stepwise techniques should *never* be used in evaluation and explanatory research, where recommendations rely on knowing the unique effect of each variable.

MULTIVARIATE ANALYSIS OF UNIQUE EFFECTS

Evaluation and explanatory research use multivariate analysis to estimate the unique effects of each of several variables on a particular dependent variable.[3] In evaluation research, attention focuses on the manipulated variable representing the program, policy, or action to be evaluated. In explanatory research, the researcher's interest is usually on a much larger number of variables. In both cases, additional independent variables are included as statistical controls.[4]

From Bivariate to Multivariate

The first estimate of an independent variable's importance is provided by its bivariate association with the dependent variable. However, bivariate association makes a poor estimate of importance for three reasons:

- Besides X, typically many other variables also cause Y. The noise produced by these other variables makes it difficult to detect a statistically significant effect of X. Unless this noise is reduced using *control variables* and multivariate techniques, we will miss many important relationships by relying on bivariate measures.

- Very often other independent variables, as well as being related to Y (the dependent), are also related to X. Thus X shares covariation in Y with these variables. This can lead to *spuriousness* and *confounding effects*, which bivariate analysis alone cannot detect. In addition, shared covariation because of relationships among independent variables produces overestimates (and sometimes underestimates) of X's importance.

[3]Researchers interpret measures of unique effect as representing not just the importance, but also the "causal" impact of the variables. True causal analysis, however, involves additional assumptions on the part of the researcher (see the appendix at the end of this chapter).
[4]A word of terminological caution: economists often refer to their regression models as "prediction equations." However, what they are actually doing is closer to a test of unique effects and causal hypotheses than to forecasting or selection prediction. See Cook and Campbell (1979) for a cogent discussion of the differences between using regression for prediction and for causal analysis.

- A variable's effects may differ from one situation to another or from one group to another. These *third "moderating" variable* effects cannot be picked up with bivariate analysis, nor can *interaction effects* involving two independent variables.

Interaction effects and control, moderating, spurious, and confounding variables are all discussed in Chapter 5. Because of the limitations of bivariate measures, researchers use multivariate analysis to deal with these variables.

Table 17.2 indicates which measures of unique effect are produced by different multivariate techniques. For example, in standard regression analysis, this information is provided by several statistics: partial regression coefficients, part correlations, and partial correlations (see Box 17.2 and Box 17.4). The corresponding measures for analysis of variance and discriminant analysis are shown in Boxes 17.5 and 17.6.

Unique Effects and Bivariate Association

Researchers gain important information about the interrelationships among independent variables by comparing a variable's unique effect in multivariate analysis with the corresponding bivariate measure of effect size (no other variables controlled). Table 17.3 summarizes how to interpret these comparisons. In particular, the comparison provides information about spurious, confounding, intervening, and suppressor variables.

Spurious, Confounding and Intervening Effects. Spurious and confounding relationships involve extraneous variables which make it appear that X and Y are causally related. Intervening variables mediate the X-Y relationship. When any of these other variables are controlled, its relationships with X and Y are removed. What we see then is the unique effect, the "true" adjusted relationship between X and Y (ignoring other extraneous factors not included in the multivariate analysis).

If the unique effect vanishes, you can conclude that what appeared to be a bivariate relationship is spuriously produced or mediated by one of the control variables. If the unique effect is somewhat smaller, but still present, the original relationship was only partly spurious or mediated. The extraneous or intervening variable(s) and X share covariation in Y. On the other hand, if the unique effect remains about the same, then there is (among the variables in the analysis) no extraneous or mediating variable.

Suppressor Effects. If a comparison of unique effect and bivariate association shows the unique effect to be *larger,* the culprit is a suppressor effect.

A suppressor effect works this way. Two original variables X and Y and a suppressor variable S are combined in a pattern of relationships so that the sign of the X-S-Y relationship (positive or negative) is opposite to the sign of the X-Y relationship. The possible patterns that lead to suppressor effects are

A **suppressor variable** is related to both an independent variable X and a dependent variable Y in a way that makes the bivariate X-Y relationship appear weak or nonexistent.

BOX 17.4

CAMPBELL SWITCH: A CONTINUING CASE

Part Seventeen: Unique Effect Measures

"Hey! Did you hear the good news?"

"The analysis is finished?"

"No. Andrews!"

"Andrews is doing the analysis?"

"No, Andrews is being transferred to the coast. I may get his office."

"Won't you hate to leave your cozy little closet?"

George glares at Roberta and dumps a small stack of computer output on her desk. "What about these?"

"What's the problem?"

"I've got three different measures of unique effect: partial regression coefficient, partial correlation, and part correlation."

"We call that a semipartial correlation. But I bet you're wondering which one to use."

"Exactly. I know how they're defined, and roughly how they're calculated, but I don't know which one to concentrate on."

"What I've found most useful is to think of both the relationship involved and how the results might be used. Let's see." She scans the top sheet. "Here's a regression with 'number of times late' as the dependent variable, and one of your independents is age. Another one is Ajax."

"That's the dummy variable for 'plant.' Ajax is coded '1.' "

"For that variable, you want to know mostly how much of the variation it explains. I like to report squared semipartials for that. They indicate the amount of the total variation you're explaining. The

squared partial is just the proportion of the 'explained' variance the variable explains. It depends too much on what unmeasured variables you've omitted from the analysis. The squared semipartial is less sensitive to specification errors."

"So why ever calculate partials?"

"They're useful to compare with bivariate correlations when you want to remove specific extraneous factors or suppressor variables, since they remove the effect of the controlled variable from both X and Y."

"And semipartial correlations only remove it from X! So you compare zero order with partial correlations, but use semipartials to measure effect size."

"That's roughly it."

"And regression coefficients?"

"I like to report those too as effect sizes, since they're less sensitive to the 'noise' variation. They also give the reader a more understandable idea of the effect of a variable. Let's see here. Oh, here it is. Based on the slopes, you'd report that the average effect of being at the Ajax plant is 4.3 more days late for work."

"But each year of age gives only .0004 more days."

"And that's another point. I'd only report the slope when there's some relationship worth talking about."

"So what about marital status?"

The discussion of effect size measures continues.

---

shown in Figure 17.2. Note that in every case the suppressor variable S is related to both X and Y. The S-X relationship need not be a causal one; the suppressor variable only has to covary with X. When S is uncontrolled, the bivariate association includes the variation due to S (just as in spurious relationships). Because of the differences in their direction, the two relationships cancel each other out, and the result is that the net variation (the bivariate association) is smaller than the unique effect of X. When S is controlled in

BOX 17.5

RESEARCH SKILLS

Using Analysis of Variance

Analysis of variance (ANOVA) and its variations are used in experimental, and often in quasi-experimental, designs. ANOVA assesses the effect of a few category variables (including manipulations representing experimental conditions) on a quantitative dependent variable. The independent category variables are called *factors* and normally represent different subgroups or subsamples.

Concept: ANOVA divides up ("partitions") the variance in the dependent variable and attributes it to (1) independent variable factors, (2) interactions among factors, or (3) noise (within-cell variation) due to other influences.

Assumptions: Homogeneity of variance across conditions; normal populations or distribution of errors (both very robust assumptions); independent samples or independence of errors (not robust).

Checks: Check for homogeneity of variance with a separate F-test. Consult your statistical software for ways of testing other assumptions.

Measures of Joint Effect: When cell n's are equal, eta squared (or omega squared) values can be summed to get the joint effect. Some multiple classification analysis (MCA) routines produce an R^2 that will give a joint effect when cell sizes are unequal. For statistical significance of the entire model, examine the F-test results.

Measures of Unique Effect: From MCA, examine etas or betas (equivalent to standardized regression coefficients) for each independent variable. For the sample alone, use the sample correlation ratio instead of eta. Omega squared can be used to measure effect size when cell sizes are equal. An alternative is the intraclass correlation coefficient. An F-test of a ratio of explained and unexplained variance indicates whether each variable is statistically significant.

Measures of Relative Effect: Compare etas or betas from MCA.

Variations: Analysis of covariance (ANCOVA) adds one or more quantitative independent variables

(called *covariates*) to the analysis. Multiple analysis of variance (MANOVA and MANCOVA) is used when the dependent variable is a multiple-item measure such as a scale or index.

Comments:

- Using ANOVA in quasi-experimental designs (most pilot projects and evaluation studies) generally produces unequal cell sizes. Unequal n's permit independent variables to be related (sharing covariance with the dependent variable), and make the assumption of homogeneity of variance more critical. Special steps must be taken in partitioning the variance. The following options are available:
  - Use regression analysis with dummy variables instead of ANOVA.
  - Use multiple classification analysis (Blalock, 1979).
  - Use *hierarchical* partitioning, in which shared covariation is assigned to factors in an order specified by the researcher.
  - Use *regression* partitioning, in which, as in standard regression, the variance attributed to each factor is what is left over after all other factors and covariates have been adjusted for.
- As well as merely establishing that the groups differ, you can use *a priori* contrasts to test ideas about differences between specific groups. This is useful, for example, if you expect two groups to be similar and both to be different from a third group.
- When an independent variable is category ordinal (rather than nominal) use a polynomial contrast to check whether the relationship is ordinal.
- For repeated-measure designs, analysis of covariance is often used with the pretest score treated as a quantitative covariate.

BOX 17.6
RESEARCH SKILLS

Using Discriminant Analysis

Discriminant analysis is useful when the research problem is to find the "causes" or correlates of membership in already established groups, such as subscribers and nonsubscribers to a newsmagazine. It examines the effects of category and quantitative independent variables on a category dependent variable representing the groups. (It is the reverse of MANOVA, which examines the consequences of being in different, often manipulated, groups. A category independent variable of MANOVA becomes the dependent [groups whose membership is to be predicted] in discriminant analysis.)

Concept: Discriminant analysis finds the linear function of independent predictor variables (the discriminant function), which maximizes the differences in group means. These variables predict or determine which group a case will belong to. With a dependent variable having three or more categories, more than one discriminant function may be necessary to distinguish the groups satisfactorily. Each function will best discriminate one or more different groups from the others. In this instance, a classification function for each group produces a score for each case, and cases are assigned to the group for which their classification score is greatest.

Assumptions: The assumptions required for F-tests in ANOVA generally hold true for discriminant analysis as well. These assumptions are less robust the smaller the sample size, in particular the smallest group subsample size: random sample, multivariate normal sampling distribution (not robust for outliers), equal covariance matrices, and linearity.

Checks: Check for multivariate outliers, since discriminant analysis is sensitive to them, even for larger samples.

Measures of Joint Effect: Proportion of cases correctly classified (is it better than chance?); square of the canonical correlation (PVE interpretation) for each discriminant function. Significance test (chi-square) of overall prediction for each discriminant function (does it classify groups better than chance alone would?).

Measures of Unique Effect: Unstandardized discriminant function coefficients; discriminant function coefficients in hierarchical discriminant analysis. F-tests for statistical significance of predictor variables.

Measures of Relative Effect: Compare standardized discriminant function coefficients.

Variations: Discriminant functions may be nonlinear.

Comments:

- The prediction research "prediction model" equivalent of discriminant analysis is concerned only with finding the best discriminating function, ignoring which variables it contains and what their coefficients are. For explanatory and evaluation projects, however, business researchers will want to analyze the relationships between predictors and the dependent variable.

- A bivariate measure of a predictor variable's effect can be obtained by comparing the group means for that variable.

- The smallest group should contain substantially more cases than there are predictor variables to avoid overfitting.

- If you use nonproportional stratified samples, specify appropriate *a priori* probabilities of classifying cases. (These would normally be the true proportion of each group in the population.)

- If your dependent variable groups would be created by arbitrarily collapsing quantitative data (such as "high" and "low" credit risk loan applicants on the basis of number of payments late or missed), use regression rather than discriminant analysis. However, if the groups are "real" (such as those who defaulted on loans and those who did not), discriminant analysis is appropriate.

TABLE 17.3 ■ INTERPRETING COMPARISONS OF BIVARIATE AND UNIQUE EFFECTS

Compared to Bivariate Effect, the Unique Effect of X . . .	Interpretation
Stays the same.	Other independents related only weakly or not at all to X.
Decreases somewhat.	Shared covariation with other independents.
Decreases almost to zero.	Another independent is creating a spurious or confounded or mediated bivariate relationship.
Increases.	Another independent is exerting a suppressor effect.

multivariate analysis, its variation (and the X-S-Y relationship) is eliminated and the unique effect of X appears.

Note that multivariate analysis doesn't tell you which of the other independents is the suppressor variable. To discover this, you have to try them all out, one at a time. Also note that the only difference between extraneous and suppressor variables is that the three two-variable relationships are all positive (or one positive) in the former, and all negative (or one negative) in the case of suppressor effects.

CASE EXAMPLE

A researcher examining the productivity of telephone operators in Northwestern Telephone, a small regional company, was surprised to find that experience was relatively unrelated to productivity (bivariate $r = .14$). Since other researchers had found strong experience-productivity linkages in other settings, she thought that perhaps a suppressor variable might be working. Multivariate analysis of her data showed that "job satisfaction" was indeed acting as a suppressor variable. The satisfaction variable was positively related to productivity, but negatively related to experience (more experienced operators were evidently dissatisfied with working conditions). Thus experience had a negative effect on productivity through covariation with job satisfaction, but a positive unique effect. The two contrasting effects produced no relationship between seniority and productivity when job satisfaction was left uncontrolled. When it was controlled, the partial correlation between experience and productivity rose to .39.

On occasion a suppressor variable may lead to a dramatic change in sign for a relationship.

FIGURE 17.2
Relationship
Combinations That
Produce Suppressor
Effects

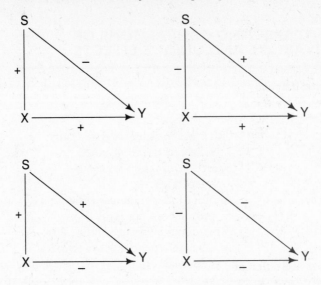

CASE EXAMPLE

A midwestern university researcher conducted a survey of firms to find ways of improving employees' job satisfaction. His initial bivariate results showed that a *lower* average wage appeared to cause a *higher* average level of job satisfaction. However, this surprising and counterintuitive relationship was found to be due to a suppressor variable, "size of firm." Firm size affected both wage levels (smaller firms can't afford to pay as much) and job satisfaction (employees tend to be more satisfied in small firms). Thus the observed covariation between average wage and average job satisfaction was largely influenced by the shared covariation with firm size, which swamped the smaller unique effect of wages on job satisfaction.

Keep in mind that controlling for other variables does not take care of all the problems of measuring a variable's importance. Difficulties in design, measurement, and sampling can all lead to distorted measures of unique effect, even when other variables are controlled, as discussed in Box 17.7.

Relative Effects

Researchers doing evaluation or explanatory projects are interested in more than the unique effects of their key or primary independent variables. Often they want to be able to compare the importance of two or more variables. A consumer researcher may want to know whether package size or color has a greater effect on sales.

The relative importance of two or more variables can be assessed by comparing their correlation-based measures of unique effect. Slope-based

BOX 17.7

FOCUS ON RESEARCH

Other Problems in Multivariate Analysis for Effect Size

The omission from your research design of an important independent variable (**specification error**) can distort measures of other variables' importance. If the omitted variable were to be included, the coefficients of other variables might change drastically. Unfortunately, it is impossible to tell beforehand what effect an omitted variable might have.

The quality of the *measurement* of the variable will affect any estimate of the size of its relationship with the dependent variable. A poorly measured variable will bring more noise to the relationship, reduce the covariation of the variables, and underestimate the independent variable's importance.

A variable for which the *sample is truncated* will show a smaller relationship because of the limited range of possible covariation with the dependent variable. This will lead to an underestimation of the variable's importance in the population (although not within your sample).

measures are inappropriate because they are not metric free. (For example, the size of a partial regression coefficient depends on the unit of measure of the variable, such as equity value in dollars, yen, or pounds sterling.) However, if the variables are standardized (to means of zero, standard deviations of 1.0), the regression coefficients (now called "betas") are comparable.

In addition, the variables for which importance is to be compared must have been measured equally well, and none should be artificially weakened as a result of a truncated sample (or alternatively, each should be equally truncated) (Cooper and Richardson, 1986). Failure to observe these two conditions will unfairly tip the scales in favor of the better measured or less truncated variable. (This point echoes a caution suggested in earlier chapters: compared to mistakes in sampling and choice of data analysis techniques, poor measurement is by far the greatest problem facing business researchers.)

Joint Effects

As we saw earlier, the joint impact of all independent variables in the analysis on the dependent is essential for building forecasting and selection prediction models. However, measures of joint effect also have a use in evaluation and explanatory research. If the joint effect is much lower than expected, it means that important causes have probably been omitted from the analysis *(specification error)*. If so, conclusions about the variables *in* the model may be wrong ("biased"). If the unmeasured variable were added, it might change the size of some other variable's unique effect or might even reverse the direction of its unique relationship with the dependent variable. Table 17.2 indicates measures of joint effect for different statistical techniques (for example, R^2).

For cross-sectional designs, typical values of R^2 are .30 to .40 when persons are the unit of analysis; values for aggregate units of analysis are often a bit lower. For time-series designs R^2 values are typically much greater, between .80 and .95, since each unit serves as its own control, thus reducing enormously the number of uncontrolled factors in the data. If you find an R^2 value much below these, you should be concerned about specification error or poor measurement.

Interacting Variables in Multivariate Analysis

To check for expected interacting variables (those mentioned in your research questions), the general procedure in regression analysis is to use separate analyses for each category of a *moderating variable* and multiplicative terms for *interaction effects*. (Analysis of variance automatically incorporates tests for interactions among factors.)

Moderating Variables.   The question is whether one or more independent variables have different effects in one group compared to others. For example, are the factors that produce successful product launches different for food products and drug products? Here, "type of product" is the moderating variable to be tested. Similarly, in one industry the success rate of franchise operations (Y) may be highly related to cash flow (X); in another industry the relationship is relatively weak. The moderating variable is "industry."

Normally there is little interest in the unique effect of a moderating variable: the issue is whether it moderates the effects of another variable. The procedure is as follows:

- Collapse the potential moderating variable into two or three categories (if it is not already a category variable).

- Run separate multivariate analyses for the cases in each category, taking care to omit the moderating variable from these analyses.

Then compare the results. Use measures of association rather than significance tests to compare across categories. (Most researchers prefer regression coefficients to correlation coefficients because they are less affected by variance in the dependent variable.) Because significance is sensitive to the number of cases being analyzed, and because you are likely to have different numbers of cases in each category of the moderating variable, results would be misleading. (However, you can use a significance test in each partial to determine whether any association is statistically significant.) Some variables may have different unique effects across groups. (With regression analysis, the slopes of some variables may be different across groups, or the intercept terms may be different.) If differences are substantial, a moderating effect exists.

CASE EXAMPLE

Under the prompting of impending pay-equity regulations, a researcher in Southern Software, a medium-size white-collar firm, was assigned the task of examining the determinants of employee's income and whether they were different for males and females in the organization. The determinants included in the study were job, education, training, experience, marital status, career orientation, and department size as well as gender. The researcher ran two analyses: one for the 88 males in the study, another for the 198 females. The results showed that the regression coefficients for the effects of job, education, training, and career orientation were much the same in the two regressions. However, the coefficients were markedly different for experience (much lower for females), marital status (being married mattered much more for females), and department size (much lower coefficient for females). He concluded that gender moderated the effects of these three factors in determining income.

If you find a substantial moderating effect, you must be cautious about interpreting the rest of your results. The safest procedure is to carry out completely separate analyses for the two (or more) subgroups for which an important variable operates differently. If you do not, and continue to analyze the entire sample as a single group, you are in effect averaging the results over the categories of the moderating variable. This may lead to weak results or distorted conclusions (see Blalock, 1979:365).

Interaction Effects. The problem is to test whether two variables have a joint nonadditive effect on the dependent variable. For example, does the combination of small firm size and being in the retail industry produce a substantially greater probability of tax accounting problems?

The simplest procedure is to include in the analysis both variables plus a *cross-product* term consisting of the product of the two variables, such as in this equation:

$$Y = a + b_1 X_1 + b_2 X_2 + b_3 X_1 X_2 + b_4 X_3$$

If the cross-product term coefficient (b_3) is substantial, then the two variables interact in affecting Y. Unfortunately this procedure will pick up only multiplicative interaction and ignore other types of nonadditivity, but it is the only simple procedure available and is sufficient for most business research.

CASE EXAMPLE

A researcher for Subarro, a manufacturer of motorcycles, was checking the benefits of advertising. His sample consisted of 65 retail locations in the Northeast, for which he gathered data about advertising expenditures, customer flows, numbers of sales staff, sales, and other variables. He found (1) advertising served initially to bring more potential customers into each location and (2) the bivariate correlation coefficient between potential customers (the count of people actually in the store) and sales was .56. However, under multivariate analysis the partial correlation between potential customers and sales dropped to .17. After trying several alternative models, the researcher discovered an interesting finding: potential customers interacted with numbers of sales staff in producing increased sales. When a cross-product interaction term was added to the regression, it showed a substantial unique effect (partial correlation of .42). The researcher concluded that it required a combination of advertising and more sales staff to increase sales. Without the sales staff, the greater number of potential customers produced by the advertising did not translate into increased sales. He recommended a combination of targeted advertising and part-time sales staff.

MULTIVARIATE ANALYSIS FOR REPEATED-MEASURE DESIGNS

Repeated-measure designs are those in which a group of cases are measured several times. In such designs, each additional measure of a case is treated as an additional variable. The most common of these designs are pretest-posttest experiments and panel design surveys.

The multivariate analysis of data from repeated-measure designs is complicated by the nonindependence of variables. For example, an individual's job satisfaction at time 1 is usually going to be fairly similar to his or her job satisfaction at time 2. This nonindependence violates an important assumption of multivariate statistics and can distort conclusions. The statistical procedures we suggest vary in how well they deal with this problem. Sometimes the optimal techniques are fairly sophisticated and beyond the scope of this text. What we recommend is not always the best available option, but is adequate for most business research projects.

Pretest-Posttest Designs

These are experimental designs involving one or more dependent variable measures before and after a manipulation. Pretest-posttest designs are common in pilot projects and evaluation studies. Their analysis involves four kinds of key and primary variables.

- The *pretest result* on the key dependent variable (e.g., sales performance, absenteeism incidents). There may be two or more pretests. This is usually (and ideally) a quantitative variable.

- The *posttest result* (or results if there are multiple posttests). Ideally the same measure as the pretest variable. (In business research, subjects are seldom given two or more different treatments, so although these are repeated-measure designs, they involve only measures before and after a single treatment rather than the multiple treatments of within-subject designs.)

- The category variable that indicates whether a case belongs to a *treatment or comparison group* (or which of several treatment groups). If there is no comparison group this variable will be absent from the analysis, and a different procedure is required as described later.

- *Control variables,* such as age and job category. These are normally measured at the time of the (first) pretest.

Bivariate Checks.   Check for homogeneity of variance in the dependent variable across groups and across time (pretest and posttest for each group). If multiple pretests and posttests are evenly spaced, a check for linearity may also be useful, especially in the comparison group. Because of the manipulation, the treatment group may not show linearity.

Multivariate Alternatives to Gain Scores.   In the past, a common procedure has been to calculate the gain score (posttest minus pretest) and use it as the dependent variable. This practice creates problems because of the threats to internal validity it fails to rule out (Reichardt, 1979). In particular, gain scores are frequently correlated with the pretest level.

Alternative procedures involve the use of the posttest as a dependent and the pretest as a control variable. The "adjusted" posttest scores, when pretest scores are controlled, are known as *residual gain scores,* and their correlation with the pretest is zero. This can be achieved in analysis of covariance (ANCOVA) by including the pretest as a covariate, and in regression by including the pretest as a control variable. In both cases, the analysis can include other independent variables as well.[5]

No Comparison Group.   Sometimes a researcher has no alternative but a pretest and posttest measure of the dependent variable in a treatment group, with no comparison group available. If at all possible, such designs should be turned into interrupted pooled time series by including a series of pretest and posttest measures. Failing that, the only option is a repeated measures or "matched" t-test with degrees of freedom reduced to take into account the nonindependence of observations. Note that control variables play no role in this analysis except as potential moderating variables—apply the t-test to subgroups of the sample to see if the change is greater for some groups than others.

[5]For a good and highly readable discussion of statistical procedures for these designs, consult Reichardt (1979).

CASE EXAMPLE

The head office of White-Lewis Manufacturing instituted a no-smoking policy to cover all personnel. A researcher was assigned to evaluate the effects of the policy, particularly on absenteeism and morale. No comparison group was available, but by using matched t-tests, the researcher was able to show that absenteeism decreased, morale did not change, and tardiness increased following the policy implementation. The researcher then tested gender and smoking behavior as moderating variables. The change in absenteeism was greater among male than among female employees. With respect to morale, the researcher found higher levels among nonsmokers and lower among smokers.

Panel Designs

These nonexperimental repeated-measure designs often have a substantial number of cases and usually use two to four successive waves of surveys. They are usually associated with explanatory research.

The major difference in data analysis between panel designs and ordinary cross-sectional data is that panel data allow you to investigate lagged relationships. For example, if the relationship between advertising and sales is of

FIGURE 17.3
Lagged Correlations, Autocorrelations, and Synchronous Correlations in a Panel Design

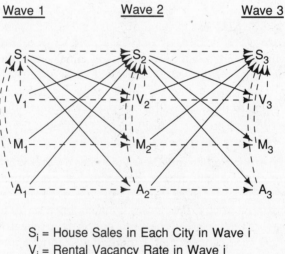

S_i = House Sales in Each City in Wave i
V_i = Rental Vacancy Rate in Wave i
M_i = Mortgage Rate in Wave i
A_i = Advertising Expenses in Wave i

————▶ Cross-lagged Correlations
- - - -▶ Autocorrelations and Synchronous Correlations

interest, since both advertising and sales are measured for each case several times, the lagged relationship involves advertising at one time and sales at a subsequent time. (These designs may also include comparison samples similar to comparison samples in cross-sectional designs. Add a category independent variable to indicate to which sample a case belongs.)

Bivariate Checks. The bivariate checks for panel data include the same nonlinearity, outliers, and homogeneity of variance tests suggested earlier for cross-sectional data. First carry out the checks separately within each wave. Then repeat the tests on lagged relationships involving key and primary variables.

Bivariate and Multivariate Analysis. An example of panel data variables and the relationships among them is shown in Figure 17.3. The research seeks to discover whether advertising affects housing sales, controlling for rental vacancy rate and mortgage rate. (The data are gathered from 54 cities in three successive quarters and adjusted to remove seasonal influences.) The analysis should ideally take into account all three types of relationships: lagged, autocorrelation, and synchronous correlation.

There are a number of ways of approaching the analysis of panel data. Two of the simplest are gain scores and cross-lagged correlations.

Gain Scores. At first glance, the use of gain scores seems to be a logical method for analyzing panel data. For example, the change in house sales from time 1 to time 2 $(S_2 - S_1)$ might be regressed on the three independent variables measured at time 1. However, gain scores are often misleading because the gain is frequently correlated with the level of the initial score (the same problem faced in pretest-posttest designs).

Cross-Lagged Correlations. Another technique is to compare *cross-lagged* correlations. For example, the correlation between advertising at time 1 and sales at time 2 is compared with the corresponding correlation between sales at time 1 and advertising at time 2. (Other variables could be added as controls in two regression equations.) If one correlation is substantially greater than the other, a causal relationship for that correlation is inferred on the grounds that time-order supports only one of the two correlations.

This technique also has problems. Differences in the stability of autocorrelations in the same variable from wave to wave (e.g., S_1-S_2, S_2-S_3) as well as differences in the synchronous correlations among variables within the same wave (e.g., A_1-S_1, A_2-S_2) can distort results. More sophisticated applications of cross-lagged correlations that take into account these autocorrelations and synchronous correlations do not entirely remove the problems (Cook and Campbell, 1979).

MULTIVARIATE ANALYSIS FOR TIME SERIES

This section considers multivariate relationship analysis for three kinds of time-series data: concomitant, interrupted, and pooled. (Trend time series does not involve multivariate analysis—it is descriptive research that leads to projections of population characteristics.) Regression analysis (and its variations) is the most common statistical technique used with time series. However, its application to time series is seldom straightforward. The researcher often has to deal with the problems of trend and cycles, autocorrelation, and homogeneity of variance.[6]

Concomitant Time Series

Concomitant time series involves the relationships among two or more variables. The fact that the data are time series is normally secondary—the focus is on the relationships, not changes over time. Thus in concomitant time series, time is normally not included as a variable except for purposes of detrending all variables. The researcher then has the choice of proceeding with relatively simple and straightforward statistical approaches or more complicated techniques that deal with more of the problems that time series entail.

The simplest approach is to use bivariate and multivariate methods with no special provisions for time series—in other words, to treat each observation as if it were a case. An alternative approach is to make use of the information on the time order of observations to help shed light on causality. This involves lagged variables, normally in regression with the dependent variable measured at a later time point. For example, to test the effects of advertising budget, release of new product lines, and competitors' advertising on sales, regress sales for one month on the three variables measured the preceding month. This would result in one fewer observation than time periods because of the lagging. You may also try different lag periods. If, for example, you believe that advertising for services (such as TV repairs) has a reputation effect that doesn't show up until consumers need the service, try lagging the dependent variable two or three months or more.

Third, causal inferences can be strengthened by comparing unique effects from cross-lagged regressions (for example, monthly budget analyzed with the *preceding* month's sales) and unlagged regressions (each month's advertising budget with the same month's sales). However, the cross-correlation approach can lead to errors in conclusions because of the less-than-perfect reliability of measures and "feedback" effects because of causality in both directions.

---

[6]For pooled interrupted time series, some methodologists recommend that when the number of observations is small the researcher use MANOVA tests for changes in the slope and level of the dependent variable as a result of the manipulation (Fox, 1984).

A fourth and better alternative, if your statistical software has it, is to use one of the special regression routines for autocorrelated time-series data.

Interrupted Time Series

This kind of time series results from an experimental or quasi-experimental design in which an independent variable is manipulated at some point during the series. Thus changes over time are of central interest. For example, weekly product sales are recorded for the ten weeks before and after introduction of a new package design. The issue of interest is whether the intervention has had an effect. The question for bivariate analysis is whether a before-and-after difference exists in the dependent variable. Multivariate analysis determines whether any difference is a result of the manipulation or can be explained by other factors.

First examine a time plot of the dependent variable for before-after differences, in particular

- A change in the level of the dependent variable.

- A change in the slope or rate of increase in the variable.

- A change in both level and slope.

Examples of these types are shown in Figure 17.4. The horizontal axis represents time, and the letter M indicates the point of manipulation. (Sometimes plots have to be smoothed in order for changes to be readily seen. Most computer packages that handle time series include a smoothing utility, most commonly a moving average.)

Test the conclusions you draw from the time plot using the regression equation:

$$Y = a + b_1 M + b_2 T + b_3 MT$$

In this equation, M represents the manipulation (coded zero up to the manipulation point and one thereafter), and T represents time periods. The term MT is a cross-product of manipulation and time.

- If the coefficient b_1 is statistically significant or the corresponding partial correlation is substantial, the intercept has changed at the point of manipulation, thus moving the line "higher."

- If the coefficient b_3 is statistically significant or the corresponding partial correlation is substantial, the slope has changed.

Multivariate Analysis. Add control variables by inserting new terms into the regression equation. If your design includes a comparison no-

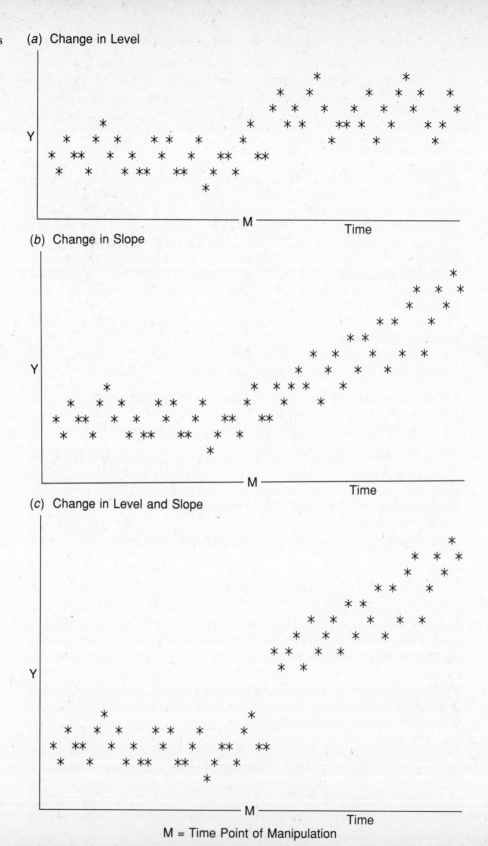

FIGURE 17.4 Types of Before-After Changes in Interrupted Time Series

(a) Change in Level

Y

M

Time

(b) Change in Slope

Y

M

Time

(c) Change in Level and Slope

Y

M

Time

M = Time Point of Manipulation

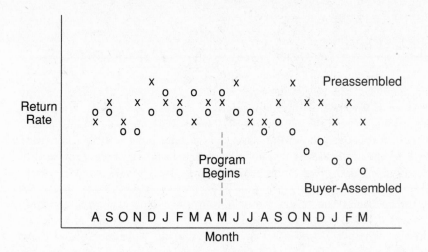

FIGURE 17.5
Quality Control
Program and Return
Rates for
Preassembled and
Buyer-Assembled
Bicycles

treatment group, calculate a separate regression for those observations and compare slopes and intercepts for the M and MT terms. Also compare groups visually in an *overlay plot* (see Figure 17.5). The figure compares return rates of defective preassembled and buyer-assembled bicycles before and after the implementation of a new quality control program. The plot suggests that the program had the most impact on returns of buyer-assembled bicycles.

Autocorrelation will lead to errors in assessing whether the intervention has made a statistically significant difference—your conclusions are likely to be too optimistic. (This problem can be overcome by using a special regression routine that deals with autocorrelation. More sophisticated techniques for interrupted time series are beyond the scope of this text.)

Pooled Time Series

Pooled time-series designs, either concomitant or interrupted, involve a number of cases (usually a dozen or less) measured over a number of time periods. For simple bivariate analysis, it helps to aggregate the cases at each time point in order to produce a single time plot for all cases. The real issue is how to treat the additional data points in multivariate analysis, since the observations are not independent.

The simplest solution is to ignore the nonindependence problem and simply use ordinary regression. This is often good enough for determining important variables in explanatory research and determining in rough terms whether a manipulation has had the intended effect. A better solution is to add an additional dummy for each case (minus one) and each time period (minus one). This option requires a greater number of observations, since it can add a considerable number of variables to the analysis.

MULTIVARIATE ANALYSIS OF INTERDEPENDENCE

On occasion the researcher will want to investigate the relationships among sets of variables without specifying a dependent variable. Two such procedures were described in Chapter 14: Chronbach's alpha and factor analysis. The former is used in item analysis to select the most reliable scale from among a set of variables. Factor analysis is used in empirical analyses of validity to determine whether more than one underlying concept is included in a scale or index.

At other times, the researcher will want to examine the relationships among sets of cases. This procedure, called **cluster analysis,** is useful in determining whether all the cases in the sample can be grouped into a few simple categories in which cases within a category are more alike than cases across categories. For example, a researcher might want to see whether all retail brokerage transactions can be grouped into a small number of categories, so that sales staff can be assigned by category of customer. The use of cluster analysis is described in Box 17.8.

SUPPLEMENTARY ANALYSIS

After multivariate analysis, carry out **supplementary analysis** to explore any anomalies and unexpected results in your findings:

- Relationships that were reversed in direction from what you expected.

- Relationships that were not as strong as you expected.

The idea is to think up, and then test, possible explanations for the unexpected findings. It requires that researchers be inventive, original, imaginative, and creative. Supplementary analysis may add important qualifications to your conclusions or may suggest the need for follow-up research.

Note the limitations of supplementary analysis. Because it is conducted *after the fact* and is exploratory in nature, it cannot produce conclusions about relationships in your data. Its purpose is to *generate* potential explanations for why the unexpected occurred. Confirmatory testing is necessarily left for further research, since it is not legitimate to use the same data set both to generate and to test hypotheses.

Unexpected Direction

It isn't uncommon to find the direction of a relationship reversed from what was expected. Before you make recommendations based on such a sur-

BOX 17.8
RESEARCH SKILLS

Using Cluster Analysis

Cluster analysis identifies the number and nature of relatively homogeneous groups of cases on the basis of their values on selected variables, so that cases within a group are similar, and different from cases in other groups.

Concept: One of several available methods is used to measure distance between cases. These distances (in n-dimensional space, where n is the number of clustering variables) are used to group the cases into clusters, starting with the two closest cases. The procedure works iteratively, usually starting with as many clusters as cases, and ending with a single cluster containing all cases (or alternatively, starting with one and ending with many). The objective is to identify the stage that provides optimal clustering.

Checks: Select variables carefully, since they determine the nature of group differences. In particular, decide which variables you want most to be reflected in differences among clusters and the variables for which differences don't matter as much. Either weight the latter to contribute less to cluster distances, or drop them from the analysis.

Output: The *cluster coefficient* shows, at each stage, how different are the two clusters (and/or cases) being combined at that stage. This is useful in deciding the optimal number of clusters—stop when differences are large. Much the same information is shown graphically in a *dendrogram*.

Variations: Although normally considered in terms of cases, cluster analysis can also be used to cluster *variables* into homogeneous groups. The difference between this and factor analysis is that the latter includes variables negatively related to a factor, whereas cluster analysis of variables can be limited to positive correlations.

Comments:

- Since most variables will be measured in different units (department budgets in dollars, size in number of employees, productivity rating on a ten-point scale, etc.), variables should be standardized before cluster analysis.
- If the number of cases is not large, an *icicle plot* is a useful way of seeing how the clustering proceeds. If there are many cases, examine only the last two dozen or so steps.

prising finding, make an effort to account for it. Tackle such situations by considering the following possibilities:

- The relationship might be spurious, or confounded with another variable not included in the analysis. Find or create a proxy measure for the possible extraneous variable, and rerun the analysis including it. With luck, you'll find a suitable measure already in your data. Otherwise, you'll have to hunt for a proxy variable and do the best you can.

- A suppressor effect might be responsible. Find or create a proxy measure for the suspected suppressor variable, and rerun your analysis.

CASE EXAMPLE

A consulting firm examining absenteeism in a postal service found that, contrary to expectations, delivery persons using vehicles had higher absenteeism rates than those delivering mail on foot. In their supplementary analysis, the researchers conjectured two possible explanations for this relationship, one spurious and one an intervening variable: (1) vehicle delivery persons were more likely to be assigned to postal divisions in large urban centers where absenteeism is generally higher (spurious), and (2) temperature changes getting into and out of their vehicles made vehicle persons more prone to illness (suppressor variable). They tested the first possibility by controlling for urban or rural postal divisions and reexamining the relationship between mode of delivery and absenteeism. The second was tested by comparing the relationship for absenteeism incidents during the winter months (when temperature changes would be greater) and summer absenteeism.

Weak or No Relationship

Failure to find expected relationships is relatively common in business research. This failure is often a result of one or more of four conditions: unreliable measures, nonresponse bias, suppressor effects, and moderating variables. (Other explanations, such as curvilinear relationships, have presumably been eliminated during the preliminary analysis and bivariate checks.)

Unreliable Measures. Measures with high levels of random measurement error will often produce data with so much variation that an existing relationship cannot be detected. This is particularly so for correlation measures based on covariance, such as r. Two checks should help to suggest whether measurement error is at the root of your failure to find an expected relationship.

- Compare the correlation coefficient r and the regression coefficient b. These two measures of association are sensitive to different aspects of the relationship (see Chapter 16). In particular, if r is very weak, but b is substantially different from zero, it is likely because of excessive variation in the relationship, which in turn suggests random measurement error (low reliability).[7]

- Check the relationship of the independent variable with another independent with which you expect it to be related, using the same comparison of correlation and regression coefficients. For example, if you expected a high relationship between brand name recognition and sales, and failed to get it, check the measure of brand name recognition by examining its relationship with exposure to advertising. Again, a substantial slope and a low correlation coefficient suggest the problem may lie with measurement error.

Nonresponse Bias. Nonresponse bias can produce a relationship weaker (or stronger) than expected. If this problem seems likely, reexamine your sample check to see if either variable might be associated with systematic nonresponse. If so, try to find a third variable associated with nonresponse.

[7]Note that the regression coefficient is *not* likely to be statistically significant (since this would require greater reliability in the measure), only that its magnitude may be substantial.

Typically such a variable is related to being too busy to respond or fearing that response might lead to some problem or disadvantage.

Attempt to get a proxy measure for this new variable. Then, for just those cases with values related to nonresponse (e.g., "busier" or "fearful of responding"), reanalyze the data. As long as you have at least a modest number of the less-likely-to-respond cases in this category, you should get a more accurate idea of what the true relationship would be if you had no nonresponse bias.

CASE EXAMPLE

A personnel director surveyed lower and middle-level managers in Southcal Instrumentation Company about their satisfaction with the competence of their support staff. Of 125 questionnaires distributed, 98 were returned. He found that women managers were less likely to be happy with their staff. This result surprised the personnel director, since other indications from his preliminary investigation suggested that the support staff of female managers were if anything *more* likely to be satisfied with their manager, and supervisor-employee satisfaction is usually reciprocal.

Reexamining his sample check, the director noticed that female managers were underrepresented in the sample (response rates of 96 percent for male managers, 53 percent for female), raising the possibility of systematic bias in the relationship between manager's gender and evaluation of support staff. He decided to see whether busy female managers might be both less likely to respond to his survey and more favorable in their evaluations of support staff. As a proxy measure of how busy a manager is, he used the answers to a question asking how many evenings a month a manager had worked past six o'clock, and collapsed the variable to two categories with a cutting point close to the median response (54 managers more busy; 44 less busy). He noted that female managers were underrepresented in the "busy" category.

He then reanalyzed the data separately for the busier and less busy managers. The results for the busier managers showed a higher level of satisfaction with support staff for female managers. For less busy managers, women were slightly more likely to be dissatisfied. The personnel director tentatively concluded that the original relationship between manager's gender and evaluations of support staff was a consequence of nonresponse bias: busier female managers were less likely to respond to the survey than either busier males or less busy females. They also had higher levels of satisfaction with their support staff.

Supplementary analysis of nonresponse bias is only tentative. An alternative explanation that fits the case example data equally well is that female managers are, in fact, less busy than males (i.e., less likely to work past six o'clock) and that nonresponse rates for female managers are not related to being busy. Supplementary analysis only indicates that the relationship *might* have been altered (and in what manner) because of nonresponse bias.

Suppressor Effects. A unique effect may be less than expected because a suppressor variable was not included in the analysis. Most likely a potential suppressor variable was not measured. The only solution is to find, among the variables, one that comes closest to a proxy for a possible suppressor and try it out. In particular, you are checking to see whether a relationship between two variables increases substantially in magnitude when the third variable is controlled. The results are hardly likely to be definitive, but they may be enough for you to suggest in your report what is actually occurring in the data.

Moderating Variables. A moderating variable may be responsible for an unexpectedly weak relationship. Overall effect size can be diminished because a relationship has opposite directions in two different groups or is largely limited to a certain group. For example, if the relationship between age and buying patterns isn't as strong as expected, check gender as a moderating variable. Perhaps the effect occurs only for women or is perhaps reversed by gender (e.g., females buy small quantities frequently; males buy large quantities infrequently).

Bivariate scatterplots are often useful in checking for moderating variables in supplementary analysis. Two different groups, in one of which the two variables are related while in the other there is no relationship, may produce a bivariate scatterplot like that in Figure 17.6a. The variability in Y increases sharply as X increases. Alternatively, two groups in which a relationship has opposite signs may produce a scatterplot like the one in Figure 17.6b. The variability in the dependent is greater at both extremes of the independent variable. Note that such plots don't indicate just what the moderating variable might be; they only suggest that one might be active.

If your scatterplots suggest the possibility of a moderating variable, try to think what it might be, and then try overlay plots with likely candidates as the third variable (collapsed to two categories), such as that in Figure 17.5. Overlay plots use different characters or symbols to represent the data points of the different categories.

CASE EXAMPLE

A study of salary determinants in Atlantic Electronics, a large organization selling electronic products in its own chain of outlets, revealed that among store and office staff and managers, levels of seniority were unrelated to salary. Supplementary analysis showed a moderating variable effect: among males, the relationship between seniority and salaries was positive, and among females, negative. Further supplementary analysis showed the cause of this reversal for female employees. Until recently, the firm had hired women almost exclusively for low-level secretarial and clerical jobs with low salaries. Many of these employees had long years of service with the firm. Only recently, the company had hired women for higher level managerial jobs at higher salaries. As a result, for women, greater levels of seniority were associated with lower salaries.

a. Relationship in One Group, Not in Other

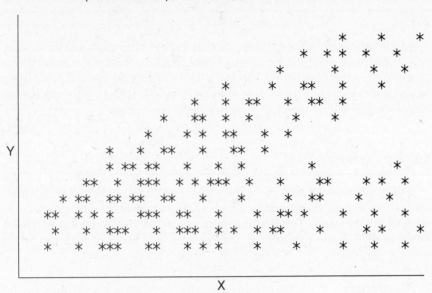

FIGURE 17.6
Supplementary
Analysis:
Scatterplots
Suggesting
Moderating
Variables

b. Opposite Relationships in Two Different Groups

The researcher uncovered the moderating variable by examining scatterplots, which showed a likely moderating effect of two relationships working in opposite directions (highest variance in salaries at low and high levels of seniority). She then tried a number of possible factors until she discovered gender to be the moderating variable. The explanation was tested by rerunning the analysis separately for managerial jobs and for secretarial and clerical jobs.

OTHER ANALYSIS ISSUES AND PROBLEMS

Multivariate analysis encounters a wide variety of problems. This section deals briefly with some of the more common in business research: multicollinearity, small samples, sparse categories in an important variable, and using a scale or index as your dependent variable. See also Box 17.9 for the debate about treating ordinal variables as quantitative measures.

Multicollinearity

Multicollinearity occurs when relationships among independent variables are very strong. It inflates the standard errors associated with estimates of slopes and makes tests of their significance unreliable. It also reduces measures of unique effect and may hinder the matrix operations required for multivariate analysis.

Diagnosis. Check a *correlation matrix* of bivariate correlations among the independent variables. High values (.90 or more) indicate that multicollinearity might be a problem. (However, if three or more variables together produce multicollinearity through linear combination, the correlation matrix may not indicate the problem.) Also check the *tolerance* of each variable; low tolerance indicates that a variable can be strongly predicted by some combination of other independent variables.

Solutions. To avoid the effects of multicollinearity:

- For two highly related variables, retain the variable with the greatest theoretical importance for the research and drop the other.

- Treat the highly related variables as a single block. In this instance, the change in R^2 can be used as a measure of the effect of the block variables together.

- Moderate multicollinearity can be ignored if the problem variables are only very weakly related to the dependent variable.

Small Samples

The major problem with a small sample is that the sampling distribution for a variable is unlikely to be normal if the population isn't. This violates an assumption underlying most parametric tests of statistical significance. Fortunately, this assumption is fairly robust, but for extreme nonnormality, transform the variable (as discussed in Chapter 14).

A second problem occurs when there aren't enough cases in the sample for multivariate analysis. As a rough rule of thumb, the number of cases should be

BOX 17.9
RESEARCH ISSUES

Treating Category Ordinal Variables as Quantitative

Whether as dependent or independent variables, multivariate techniques for handling ranked and category ordinal variables are awkward. An alternative technique is to treat such variables as quantitative measures. There is relatively little risk in treating a ranked ordinal variable as quantitative, particularly when the sample or subsample size is 25 or more. A category ordinal variable with five or more categories is probably worth the risk of treating as a quantitative variable, especially with sample or subsample sizes of 100 or more. Research simulations suggest that this practice produces acceptably low levels of

bias and loss of precision (Johnson and Creech, 1983).

These procedures are a matter of some debate (since such variables don't have normal distributions and thus strictly speaking can't be used for parametric tests). However, the errors are so small and the gains in using the more powerful parametric statistical tests are so great that the practice is justified for most business research. Only if the cost of a wrong conclusion is very great should a more conservative approach be adopted.

a minimum of four to five times the number of independent variables and ideally 20 times the number of variables (Tabachnick and Fidell, 1989). Violations of this requirement result in **overfitting:** the data fit the regression line too well, and estimates of effect size and significance cannot be trusted.

A quick and dirty remedy for too few cases and too many independent variables is to carry out your analysis two or three times with different sets of variables, and then combine only the variables with substantial effect sizes in a final model. The following procedure will help to minimize the main problem with this remedy—specification error.

- First, inspect the correlation matrix of independent variables. Divide the variables into groups so that variables in different groups are *not* related although variables within the same group may be. Try to have the maximum number of variables in a group about one-fifth to one-tenth the number of cases.

- Perform your multivariate analysis separately with each group of variables.

- From each group, select the variables having the strongest association with the dependent variable, and repeat the multivariate analysis with this final set of variables.

Sparse Categories in an Important Variable

Sometimes the researcher is faced with too few cases in one particular category of an important category independent variable. For example, if a firm wants to know the effect of regional differences on grocery store sales, but one region has only four stores, that category is too sparse to have much confidence in the results of bivariate or multivariate analysis, and the standard errors are likely to be too large to demonstrate any significant effect.

An alternative technique makes use of the additional information conveyed by the relationships of other variables to the dependent variable. Carry out multivariate analysis *without* the cases in that category and *without* the variable involved. (In the example, this would mean dropping the variable "region" and the four stores from the analysis.) Then use the resulting regression coefficients and the values of the other variables for the four cases to predict the value of the dependent variable in each of the cases in the sparse category. Compare those results with the actual values. If the actual values are consistently higher (or lower) than the predicted, you can tentatively conclude that the effect of that category, compared to the other(s), is to increase (or decrease) the dependent variable.

Scales and Indexes as Dependent Variables

From time to time research designs involve a set of separate but related dependent variables, such as employees' absenteeism, tardiness, and productivity ratings, all aspects of "employee performance." To treat all dependents at once requires canonical correlation or multivariate analysis of variance (or covariance).

However, when the dependent variable is a multiple-item *scale* or *index*, you may be able to use techniques that apply to single dependent variables, such as regression analysis. For a *Likert-type scale*, carry out item analysis on the scale to achieve a satisfactory level of reliability, then treat the scale score as the dependent variable. This reduces the dependent variables to a single measure. For a *ranking scale, check scale*, or *index*, there are four options for treating the multiple dependent variables:

- Analyze all items simultaneously with MANOVA or canonical correlation. This assumes that there is a single dimension underlying the scale or index items.

- Group the items into several unidimensional subscales on an a priori theoretical basis, sum each subscale's items to a single score, and analyze each subscale separately. The objective is a small number of unrelated dependent variables, each capturing a different dimension.

- Group the items empirically. Use factor analysis to see if items cluster. If they do, determine each respondent's mean subscore for each cluster, and treat each cluster as a separate dependent variable.

- Treat each item as a separate dependent variable. This is the only acceptable procedure when there is no justifiable way of grouping items.

■ *The Lighter Side of Research*

Mean: How a researcher might feel after seeing very high skewness in an important dependent variable.

Median: Statistical analysis that falls somewhere between rare and well done: looks finished on the outside but underdone when you get into it.

Standard deviation: The all-too-common analysis of research questions irrelevant to the project's overall objective.

Summary

Following bivariate analysis and checks, carry out multivariate analysis. For forecasting and selection models in prediction research, use stepwise regression to find the best model (highest adjusted R^2). For evaluation and explanatory research, multivariate analysis provides unique effect measures of each independent variable's importance. Researchers also use multivariate measures of joint effects to assess whether important variables may be missing from their analysis. Repeated-measure and time-series designs require special multivariate treatments.

All researchers should consider supplementary analysis to try to account for unexpected findings or nonfindings. The chapter discusses techniques for examining relationships in which the direction is unexpected or association is found to be unexpectedly weak.

Where Are We Now?

At the end of your supplementary analysis, your data analysis is complete. You have drawn statistical conclusions relevant to your research questions and have investigated any unexpected results. The final stage is to convert the findings to conclusions and recommendations and to report them. This is the topic of the final chapter.

Discussion Issues and Assignments

1. Using the data set from question 1 of Chapter 16, draft a set of research questions and divide them up so that no two students' variables completely overlap. Calculate unique effects for five variables. Compare the unique effects of any variables common to two or more students. Discuss why there might be differences. How much is due to differences in the selection of control variables?

2. Which multivariate technique would be most appropriate in each of the following research scenarios? What measures of unique, relative, and joint effect would you examine?

a. You have data on 14 monthly economic indicators (GNP, unemployment, etc.) for the past five years. You want to predict the share price of Mattel in forthcoming months.

b. You want to find if stocks listed on the New York Stock Exchange can be grouped into categories of stocks similar in terms of high and low trading price over the past 52 weeks, the stock's annual dividend, the difference between high and low prices in the most recent day of trading, the change in price from the previous day, the volume of trading, and the price/earnings ratio.

c. You want to know whether the seven variables in item b represent a single underlying dimension.

d. The undergraduate admissions committee of your college asks you to help them predict which applicants are most likely to succeed in your program. Among the variables on which they have information are previous academic record, performance on standardized tests, ratings of letters of recommendation (on a 7-point scale), appearance of the applicant's application form (on a 5-point scale), how well thought out the applicant's future career plans are (on a 7-point scale), and participation in extracurricular activities (on a 6-point scale). They also know the performance in the college's program (grade point average) of 244 previous students.

e. The same committee asks you to determine which factors are more important to success in the program, so they can offer remedial work in relevant areas of the curriculum. As well as the variables in the previous question, they have information (from a questionnaire) on study habits, course load, major, test-writing skills, essay-writing skills, analytical skills, and demographic variables (age, gender, parents' occupations and income, number and ages of siblings).

f. The same committee wants to know what factors seem to cause some students to major in humanities, others in sciences, and still others in social sciences.

g. Last year, half the incoming class were assigned sophomore and senior students as advisors; the other half were assigned faculty advisors. The college administration wants to know what differences, if any, this made in students' performance in their freshman year.

ADVANCED TOPIC

3. Without dropping or adding variables, revise the causal model sketch in the gender-salary case example in the appendix that follows in light of your own knowledge or experience. How does your version of the relationships between these variables compare with others?

4. Find a research article in a business research journal. List the variables reported in the article, and sketch a likely causal model. Then check the findings and decide whether the reported results are consistent with your model. Specify what additional analysis you would have to undertake in order to test your causal model.

Further Reading

Cook, T. D., and D. T. Campbell. 1979. *Quasi-Experimentation: Design & Analysis Issues for Field Settings.* Boston: Houghton Mifflin.

> See Chapter 6 for a very accessible discussion of the statistical analysis of interrupted time series.

Kennedy, P. 1979. *A Guide to Econometrics.* Oxford: Martin Robertson.

> A very readable account of autocorrelation and other problems and issues in time-series data.

Ostrom, Charles, Jr. 1978. *Time Series Analysis: Regression Techniques.* Beverly Hills: Sage.

> A good introduction to a complex topic.

Sharma, S., R. M. Durand, and G. A. Oded. 1981. "Identification and Analysis of Moderator Variables." *Journal of Marketing Research* 18:291–300.

> An interesting perspective on a topic too often ignored.

Stolzenberg, Ross M., and Kenneth C. Land. 1983. "Causal Modeling and Survey Research." Chapter 15 in Peter H. Rossi, James D. Wright, and Andy B. Anderson (eds.), *Handbook of Survey Research.* Orlando: Academic Press.

> A good introduction to causal modeling and its role in research.

Tabachnick, B. G., and L. S. Fidell. 1989. *Using Multivariate Statistics* (2nd ed.). New York: Harper & Row.

> A delightful and painless treatment of multivariate analysis for the statistically impaired.

APPENDIX TO CHAPTER 17

Causal Modeling

Up to now, we've described the use of multivariate techniques to identify the **unique effects** of independent variables. This approach meets the three criteria of causality discussed in Chapter 3: time order, covariation, and nonspuriousness (when potential extraneous variables are measured and controlled). However, in many circumstances it is possible to obtain a more complete picture of the causal relationships among variables. This activity is called **causal modeling** and is performed with path analysis or structural equation models.

- Causal modeling provides a better estimate of a variable's true **causal effect.** This can be quite different from the variable's unique effect. Information about causal effects leads to more relevant conclusions and more useful recommendations.

- The disadvantage of causal modeling is the time it takes. Researchers must be more familiar with their variables and must spend more time exploring potential causal structures. It also requires additional assumptions.

It is important not to confuse the terms *multivariate analysis* and *causal analysis*. Multivariate analysis refers to a group of statistical techniques for handling three or more variables at a time. Causal analysis is the researcher's attempt, using multivariate techniques, to find the causal relationships among variables in the data. It requires the researcher to make theoretical assumptions that the data *cannot* test (such as the time ordering of two variables). Thus you can think of causal analysis as the combination of multivariate techniques *plus* the researcher's theoretical assumptions.

DIRECT AND INDIRECT EFFECTS

An important idea in causal modeling is the distinction between *direct* and *indirect effects* among measured variables. A direct effect exists when one variable exerts a direct causal impact on another. An indirect effect exists when the causal path between two variables goes through one or more intervening variables. Consider the variables in Figure 17.7. This model assumes that the relationship between interest rates and investment in new technology has both a direct and an indirect path. The latter occurs when high interest rates lead to a decrease in expected market growth, which in turn leads to decisions not to invest.

Note that effects are direct or indirect *only with respect to the variables actually measured*. Adding a new intervening variable, for example, could change a direct effect to an indirect one.

PATHS AND EFFECT MEASURES

Between any independent X and dependent variable Y, four different types of paths can exist. These are illustrated in Figure 17.8.

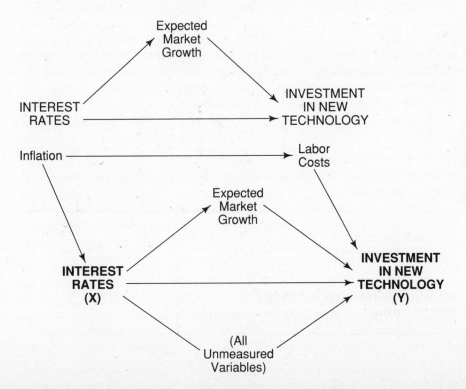

FIGURE 17.7 Direct and Indirect Effects

FIGURE 17.8 Examples of Different Paths Linking X and Y

- *Direct causal path* (interest rates and investment)

- *Indirect causal path* through intervening variables (expected market growth)

- *Indirect noncausal path* (through inflation and labor costs). (It is noncausal because it works "backward": interest rates are assumed here not to cause inflation, but rather the reverse.)

- *Indirect unmeasured paths* (causal and noncausal, through other unmeasured variables linking interest rates and investment)

Different measures of a variable's effect incorporate different sets of paths:

- A *bivariate* measure of association for X-Y includes *all possible paths relating the two variables, causal or not,* including all paths through unmeasured variables. Because it includes the noncausal paths, it *exaggerates* the true causal effect of X.

- The *unique effect* includes only the direct causal path and paths through unmeasured variables. Because it omits the indirect causal paths, it *underestimates* the true causal effect of X. (This is the shared covariance ignored in multiple regression.)

- The *causal effect* includes both direct and indirect causal paths and unmeasured paths. It omits the noncausal paths. This is what causal modeling produces.

Standard multivariate analysis treats all independent variables equivalently. Intervening variables are not distinguished from indirect causes. For example, in the sketch below, work-group cohesion (X) doesn't affect group productivity (Y) directly, but operates indirectly through group pressure on members to maintain group productivity norms (V). The result is that although the bivariate X—Y association is substantial, the unique effect of X is zero, while the unique effect of V is considerable.

$$X \to V \to Y$$

A recommendation based only on unique effects would be misleading. In other words, unique effect measures may be too restrictive and may miss the real or ultimate causes of Y.

Note that even the causal effect measure is imperfect, because it necessarily includes the effect of X through noncausal paths involving unmeasured intervening variables. However, as more of such variables are included in the research, this error decreases.

MEASURING CAUSAL EFFECTS WITH STRUCTURAL EQUATION MODELS

The term *structural equation models* refers to a variety of approaches used to represent the causal structure among a set of variables. The models may have one equation, or several; they may involve only measured variables or include unobserved latent variables; their parameters may or may not be similar to regression parameters in terms of how they can be interpreted; they may include nonrecursive relationships in which two variables may each cause the other.

Measuring the causal effect of an independent variable with structural equations requires four stages.

Stage One. First make assumptions about the causal structure of the variables in the research. In particular, you must assume which variables are *endogenous* (i.e., determined at least in part by other variables in the model) and which are *exogenous* (determined solely by variables outside the model). The result is an hypothesized causal model.

Stage Two. Produce a set of simultaneous structural equations which express variables as functions of other variables. There is one equation for each endogenous variable, in which it is the dependent variable. Exogenous variables are included in equations only as independent variables. The equations incorporate the researcher's assumptions about which linkages exist among variables.

For example, a researcher proposes four variables with linkages and causal ordering as shown in Figure 17.9a. (Arrows indicate presumed causality. Use lines without arrowheads to indicate noncausal covariation.) This model has

(*a*) Hypothesized Model

FIGURE I7.9 Causal Modeling

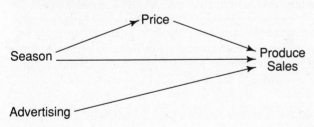

(*b*) Saturated Model

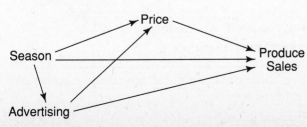

two endogenous variables, price and sales. It translates into the following structural equations:

$$\text{Sales} = b_1 \text{ Price} + b_2 \text{ Season} + b_3 \text{ Advertising}$$
$$\text{Price} = b_4 \text{ Season}$$

where the b terms represent coefficients.

Stage Three. Run each of these equations and estimate the coefficients. Check each term's coefficient. If it is small, or not significantly different from zero, modify the model by dropping the link between the variable involved and the endogenous variable.

The two most common structural equation techniques for estimating coefficients are path analysis and LISREL. Path analysis involves an equation for each endogenous variable in the model. The coefficients of a path model are estimated from standardized regression coefficients. The major difference in LISREL is its explicit consideration in the model of unmeasured latent variables.

Stage Four. Once the intervening variables in the model have been tested and confirmed, use a *hierarchical* multivariate technique to assess the causal effect of a variable:

- First, enter all variables causally prior to X and those not causally linked to X into the statistical model to explain as much of the variation in Y, the dependent variable, as they can.

- Second, add X to the analysis. (Note: *All variables but Y causally dependent on X are omitted from the analysis.*) Then determine what contribution X adds to the proportion of explained variance in Y. Measure effect size using *change* in total variation in Y explained (such as change in R^2) or a measure of the unique effect of X (e.g., in regression use the regression coefficient or a partial or semipartial correlation). See Table 17.4.

An alternative procedure is to use causal modeling to infer the linkages, rather than relying on the researcher's assumptions. This requires two stages. First, with the appropriate causal ordering assumptions, test a model with all possible linkages (the *saturated model,* shown in Figure 17.9b). This model produces these equations:

$$\text{Sales} = b_1 \text{ Price} + b_2 \text{ Season} + b_3 \text{ Advertising}$$
$$\text{Price} = b_4 \text{ Season} + b_5 \text{ Advertising}$$
$$\text{Advertising} = b_6 \text{ Season}$$

Run these equations. Drop those coefficients that are small or statistically insignificant, leaving the inferred model.

TABLE 17.4■ **MEASURES OF CAUSAL EFFECT IN CAUSAL MODELING**

Technique	Measure of Causal Effect
Regression	Change in R^2 or Hierarchical measure of any unique effect
Analysis of Variance and Covariance	Change in omega squared or Hierarchical measure of beta (from Multiple Classification Analysis)
Discriminant Analysis	Change in canonical correlation squared or Hierarchical measure of standardized discriminant function coefficient

CASE EXAMPLE

A researcher was interested in studying the effects of gender on salary in the offices of Northeast Union Security, an insurance company. In the 12 offices in 5 different regions across Canada, women had only been hired in significant numbers in the last decade, and as a result they were fewer of them in high-status positions. The researcher assumed the following (simplified) causal model involving six variables:

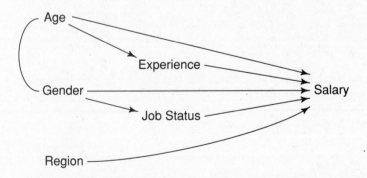

(Lines with arrows represent assumed causal relationships. Those without arrows indicate noncausal covariation.) The researcher found the bivariate association (eta from a one-way analysis of variance) between gender and salary was .39. Eta squared gives an indication of the variable's bivariate importance: gender accounts for 15.2 percent of the variation in salary.

To assess the unique effect of gender, the researcher used standard regression with all five variables entered. He then examined the coefficient of the dummy variable for gender, as well as its squared semipartial correlation. This indicated the average result (in annual salary) of being a woman in the organization (a salary difference of −$1,288), and how much of the variation in salary was attributable to the direct effect of gender (5.4 percent).

The researcher reasoned that gender may have indirect as well as direct (unique) effects on salary, particularly through job status. Causal analysis confirmed the researcher's model. To assess the real causal effect of gender, the researcher ran a hierarchical regression. The first equation contained the variables age, experience, and region. The second added gender. He then examined the regression coefficient for gender (−$4,292) and its squared semipartial correlation (9.8 percent). These results suggested a causal effect of gender on salary somewhere between the effect suggested by bivariate association and the measure of unique effects.

Finally, the researcher wanted to know the relative effects of gender and experience. To compare unique effects, he returned to the standard regression and compared the squared semipartial correlations of each variable. The results were .054 for gender and .230 for experience. To compare causal effects, he used the same result for experience (since no variable in the causal model is dependent on it) and the causal effect obtained earlier for gender. He concluded that women in the organization suffered some salary bias, even taking into account the fact that they tended to have been hired later than males and that much of the salary discrimination occurred because women were given lower status jobs. He further concluded that the effect of gender on salary is one-quarter to one-half the effect of experience.

CHAPTER 18

Conclusions, Recommendations, and Reporting

CHAPTER OBJECTIVES

- What are the different parts that make up a research report?
- How should a report be organized?
- What writing styles are appropriate?
- Where should findings and conclusions be placed?
- How are recommendations drawn from findings and conclusions?
- What's different about progress and interim reports? Oral reports?
- How do you report bad news?

CHAPTER OUTLINE

REPORT DECISIONS
CONTENT: THE SECTIONS OF A RESEARCH REPORT
ORGANIZATION AND STYLE
WRITING UP THE FINDINGS AND CONCLUSIONS
DRAFTING RECOMMENDATIONS
REPORT VARIATIONS AND PROBLEMS

good research report is more than icing on the cake; it *is* the cake! All the work spent in problem formulation, design, data gathering, and analysis is lost if results are ignored because they haven't been communicated clearly and concisely. Too often good research is underutilized because the people to whom it is reported can't make sense of the jargon, find the conclusions too limited and qualified, or see the recommendations as irrelevant or unfeasible. The final task of the researcher, then, is to produce a good report.

This chapter doesn't follow the logical order of findings, conclusions, recommendations, and report. Instead, the report is front and center. There is a reason for this. Effective research requires that you keep your bottom-line product in mind at all times. That product is your report. Your entire research effort is directed toward producing a report with valid findings and relevant recommendations. Thus our suggestion about when to write. We return to this theme later. In the meantime, we begin with some planning decisions involving the content, organization, and style of your report. First, note that business researchers produce four types of reports:

SUGGESTION

Keep your report in mind as you do the research. Plan to write sections as early as you can—don't wait until everything else is done!

- *Formal reports:* longer, cover more topics, and contain more technical and other complex details. Typical for large and important projects.

- *Informal reports:* shorter, cover fewer topics, and include less technical detail and complexity. Typical of small in-house projects.

- *Interim reports:* describe the current stage of research and perhaps some preliminary findings. Their purpose is to reassure the reader that the research is proceeding satisfactorily and perhaps to give an inkling of the most likely results to come.

- *Oral reports:* range from short summaries to full-length briefings with supporting documentation and audiovisual aids.

The first two types are covered in detail throughout the chapter. We discuss interim and oral reports toward the end.

REPORT DECISIONS

Before you begin writing the report, you have to make decisions on the following three issues:

- *Content:* the topics or parts of the report and the amount of detail in each part. Reports range from informal one- or two-page memos of findings and conclusions to lengthy and detailed documents describing background, procedures, and other topics.

- *Organization:* the arrangement of the parts. Unlike academic writing, business research reports tend not to follow the problem-methods-findings order of topics.

- *Style:* how formal or informal the writing style. First person? Third person? Active or passive voice? Bullets and boldface?

Each of these decisions will be affected by the following three factors:

- The nature of the *audience* which will read (or listen to) your report

- The *importance* of the problem your research deals with

- Your *purpose* in presenting the report

We begin with a look at the determining factors of audience, importance, and purpose, and then see how they affect the content, organization, and style of your report.

The Audience

Content, organization, and style should suit your audience. Readers may include one or more of the following groups of business managers, organization officials, or other employees or individuals:

- *Board of directors and upper level managers.* They have little time to digest more than the basic recommendations of your research and a brief summary of the problem background and research methodology.

- *"Client" upper level managers* who defined the initial organization problem and parameters and approved the resources to carry out the research. They know much more about the problem.

- *Affected middle managers* who will have to implement the recommendations if approved. They're concerned with the feasibility of your recommendations.

- *Other middle managers.* They will want to know the reason for the research and your conclusions. Your recommendations may affect indirectly their operations.

- *Affected lower level managers, supervisors, and foremen.* They need to have some idea of why changes are taking place and the implications for their own responsibilities.

- *Experts familiar with the problem* who have experience and knowledge of the specific problem or situation that gave rise to the study. They will want to know what information you gathered, where you got your data, and your specific findings.

- *Research experts* who will want to know about your design decisions, data-gathering procedures, and statistical analysis. They're concerned with the validity of your conclusions and recommendations.

- *Employees* who were interviewed or supplied data or were otherwise involved in the research at various stages and who will want to know if their contributions have been accurately portrayed or distorted.

- *Potentially hostile individuals and groups* who will want to know if there's anything in your report they should know about or be prepared to counter, or who worry that your recommendations may adversely affect their position in the organization, or who may actively oppose your recommendations.

- *Outside individuals and groups* external to the organization, but who have an interest in its decisions and actions.

These groups have different needs with respect to the content of a research report. Because your audience likely includes several of them, you must decide how to reconcile their competing demands.

This task is made easier by the fact that most business research is reported only internally; reports are seldom circulated outside the organization. Further, internal circulation is often very limited. Compare this with policy research, in which report readers include experts in the field, politicians, public service personnel, lobbyists, interest groups, voters, and taxpayers. Because of the limited audience, business research reports are generally somewhat easier to write than reports for other kinds of applied research.

SUGGESTION

For a wide and varied audience, consider two or three versions of the report that differ in content and style. For example, submit the full version of the formal report to upper level personnel. Issue a condensed version for wider distribution to lower levels of the organization. Edit this version for distribution outside the organization.

Importance of the Problem

Content, organization, and style of a report are also affected by the problem it analyzes. Small everyday problems such as office no-smoking policies and evaluations of software purchases have only minor significance for the organization as a whole. However, new products or endeavors, mergers, and major expenditures often involve issues fundamental to the success, and even survival, of the organization. The more important the issue, the more detail a research report includes and the more formal its style.

Not surprisingly, researchers often overestimate the importance of their work. As a result, their research reports may be too large and too formal for the problem. On the other hand, underestimating the significance of an issue suggests that the researcher is unaware of what matters in the organization! As we see here, you can organize the content of your report to overcome this dilemma.

Your Purpose

Researchers may have different motives in writing a report. At one extreme they seek only to *provide information*. Their reports are written to give decision makers the facts they need to make informed decisions. They contain no recommendations, but leave the reader to infer them from the findings and conclusions. The researcher is disinterested and neutral. At the other extreme are researchers whose objective is *advocacy* of some decision or action. They write the report to influence the decision or action the readers will take. In the middle are researchers who not only provide information, but also *offer recommendations*. They may evaluate the likely outcomes of several options.

In business research, most reports are somewhat closer to the information than the advocacy position. Reports of descriptive research, in particular, tend to be purely informational. However, reports that strongly argue for some particular position are not uncommon.

The advocacy approach has two particular problems. First, it is often incompatible with unbiased, objective research. Researchers with an ax to grind may overlook contradictory findings and weak relationships. Conclusions may have only weak support; recommendations may be less than fully valid. Second, even if the researcher advocates a position only after the research is finished (so findings and conclusions are unbiased), readers will tend to discount recommendations if the researcher seems prejudiced toward one particular option.

A common variation of the advocacy approach occurs when a key decision maker in the audience is biased toward one particular option before the research is carried out. The researcher may advocate alternative options that the research suggests will have better outcomes. As we see, report organization can help overcome readers' biases.

CONTENT: THE SECTIONS OF A RESEARCH REPORT

Each research report, long or short, formal or informal, written or oral, contains at least some the following sections (shown in typical order):

Front Matter

Summary

Conclusions and Recommendations

Introduction or Background or Objectives

Literature Survey

Methodology and Procedures

The Sample

Policy or Program

Findings and Conclusions

End Matter

Appendices

Many reports omit one or more of these sections or combine two or three into a single section.

Content Decisions

The most important factor determining which of these parts to include in your report is the audience that will read it. Problem importance and your own objectives also play a role. You should provide more information

- The higher the reader's organizational level. (Even though high-level managers may not have time to read it, they may delegate someone to report its implications.)

- The more the reader is affected by the organization problem or question the report addresses, or the more he or she is affected by the recommendations, or the more he or she would be involved in implementing recommendations.

- The more important the problem in terms of the organization's success and survival.

- The more you wish to advocate certain actions or recommendations.

If one or more of these criteria represent a majority of your most important readers, include all or nearly all of the parts just listed. A good rule of thumb is to provide *enough information for another researcher to replicate your study.* On the other hand, for lower level readers not directly concerned by the issue, and for problems of minor importance for which you may make recommendations but have no vested interest in seeing them adopted, a report could include only

Summary

Conclusions and Recommendations

Background

Appendices:

  Methodology

  Sample and Major Findings

At the extreme, a one- or two-page memo might be enough. Very short informal reports are useful in the following circumstances:

- The research problem is small in scope, perhaps only a single department in the organization. Thus the distribution of the report will be limited.

- You want to write an interim or progress report, or a report on the exploratory phase of research.

If your audience is varied, it is wise to adapt the content to the most important reader, keeping in mind that you must supply enough technical information (in appendices) for the needs of other researchers and personnel close to the problem.

Front Matter

Front matter consists of the covering letter or letter of transmittal, routing page, title page, and tables of contents for the text, for tables or charts, and for figures or illustrations. The more formal the report, the more front matter. Shorter informal reports may omit all but the title page.

Cover Letter or Letter of Transmittal. Very often a letter accompanies the submission of a report. Cover letters are common in internal research and with shorter informal reports. Letters of transmittal (which indicate that the accompanying report fulfills the researcher's contractual obligations) are found in more formal reports, particularly when an organization commissions research from an outside agency or consultant.

Both cover and transmittal letters summarize the purpose of the study, give the terms of reference and details of the authorization under which the research was carried out, and touch on the major conclusions and recommendations. A letter of transmittal usually follows the title page; a covering letter is usually clipped to the front of the report. (In very formal reports a copy of the original letter of authorization may follow the letter of transmittal.)

Routing Page. When a report is confidential, or important for only a small number of persons in the organization, a routing page may be attached to a report to indicate to whom it is being circulated. Normally, however, this is done not by the researcher, but by the person who initiated the research and who decides which other individuals in the organization should have a look at the results.

Title Page. The title page should include the title, the name of the principal researchers, the date of submission, and the person or organization to whom the report is submitted. For external research, the title page also contains the name of the firm that did the research.

Titles should be specific and brief. They should include the key variable and the research population and suggest the general purpose of the research (descriptive, prediction, evaluation, or explanatory). For example,

Descriptive: Sales of Wheelbarrows and
                 Garden Tools by Season in
                 the Mid-Atlantic Region

Prediction: The Outlook for Wage Increases in
                 the Next Three Rounds of Bargaining
                 at International Copper

Evaluation: An Evaluation of
                 the "Personal Absenteeism Monitoring"
                 (PAM) Program
                 at the Boulder, Colorado, Plant

Explanatory: Cash Flow Problems and
                 Accounting Procedures at
                 United Ajax

Table of Contents. Tables of contents require two decisions: whether to include one and how detailed to make it. Your decisions should be based on the length and technical complexity of your report, its audience, and common sense. It helps to remember that the table of contents serves two functions.

• It gives the reader a preview of what the report includes.

• It helps the reader locate information of particular interest.

A reader can preview a short report (less than ten pages) by quickly leafing through it. Longer reports need a table of contents so the reader can see what's inside. Similarly, if the report contains a lot of technical information, technically minded readers will find a table of contents useful when they reread it for additional detail. If you also include lists of tables and figures (again for readers seeking details), put each list on a separate page.

Include section headings and page numbers. For a lengthy report, include both headings and subheadings. For pagination and other details, consult a style manual (such as Turabian, 1973, or Northey, 1986).

Summary

The summary, also called the Synopsis or the Executive Summary, is written last. In content it is an abstract of the background and objectives of the research, general methodology, findings and conclusions, and recommendations. Very few of your readers will have the time, motivation, or expertise to read your report cover to cover. Many will read only the summary; in some instances that's all that will be circulated. The guiding principle is that someone moderately familiar with research procedures and the organization should be able to understand quickly the reason for the research, the results and recommendations, and how they were arrived at.

Summaries are concise. They often make use of point form to highlight important matter and seldom contain illustrative aids. This brevity requires more care than in other sections of the report—highly concise writing is always more difficult.

In general, the higher up in the organization the report is to go, the briefer the summary (because those at the top have more demands on their time). Reports for top management or organization officials should be summarized in one page. Otherwise, summaries may be two or three pages long, never more.

Conclusions and Recommendations

At this point, let's distinguish among three different parts of your research report: findings, conclusions, and recommendations.

• *Findings* are the numbers that describe the sample and represent the results of statistical tests and procedures. (For example, "Sales in the New England region are up 4.5 percent, in the Mid-Atlantic region up 5.6 percent, and in the South Atlantic region down 3.4 percent. The correlation between district sales and district manager's experience is .58 in the 17 districts of the South Atlantic region, but only .14 in the 37 districts in the other two regions.")

• *Conclusions* are based on your findings. They are what you infer about differences among groups and relationships among variables. (For example, "The new sales incentive program appears to be working in New England and Mid-Atlantic regions, in that inexperienced managers are also getting high levels of sales. The program is having less effect in the South Atlantic districts.")

• *Recommendations* are the actions you suggest based on the conclusions you have reached. (For example, "A new sales training program should be targeted to less experienced district managers in the South Atlantic region, where it appears that community standing has a larger effect on performance. The new program should be directed toward helping managers raise their community profiles and status.")

Conclusions are the link between findings and recommendations. This raises the question of where to put them in the report. Some researchers prefer to put them with the findings, others with the recommendations. Here are two solutions:

• If the report is short and informal, combine findings, conclusions, and recommendations into a single section.

• For a formal report, present your conclusions in two separate sections. Early in the report present conclusions and recommendations together. Then later include your conclusions in the section on findings. Thus your logic in drawing conclusions from findings will be readily apparent, and readers who skip the findings (and many will) will encounter conclusions in the recommendations.[1]

[1]Note that neither of these arrangements is used in reports of basic research, where findings are reported separately from conclusions, which are presented in a Discussion section of the report or article.

Because reporting findings and drafting recommendations are major tasks in report writing, we discuss each in detail later in a separate section.

Introduction, Background, Objectives

This section of a report may be identified as Introduction, Background, or Objectives. Its purpose is to state and explain (1) the organization problem that led to the research and (2) the specific research questions the report attempts to answer. It includes background on the scope or breadth of the problem, generally expressed as the individuals or groups to which the results are intended to apply. (In some cases this section also contains a mention of the approval or authorization for the research, if not covered in a letter of transmittal.) Ideally this section should motivate readers and spark their interest in how the researcher managed to come up with an answer to the intriguing and important questions he or she faced.

If the report is intended only for those close to the problem, this section can be very short, as little as a paragraph or two. An informal report will normally devote a page or two to this section, with perhaps a table or figure to illustrate the seriousness of the problem or urgency of the question. For a formal report, this section may be many pages long, with a lengthy and detailed description of the problem. It may even be divided into three separate sections.

Literature Survey

Full literature reviews are very rare in reports of business research. Nonetheless, there are times when an audience might wish to know what related work has been done, particularly of a general applied nature, with relevance to the current situation. For example, a project evaluating a particular marketing technique might include a review of relevant literature in the appropriate journals reporting applied marketing research.

Methodology and Procedure

This section of the report summarizes and explains the research design (including sampling design) and data-gathering procedures, including manipulations, random assignment, comparison groups, data-gathering instruments for surveys and available data studies, and information about research personnel employed in the study. It should also include a discussion of precautions taken to ensure data quality. It may also include a project chronology describing when each step was taken.

For many studies, this section also includes details about the measures used for primary and key variables. Particularly in evaluation research, readers will want to know how the impacts of programs or policies were evaluated and whether measures are sensitive and make intuitive sense. Reports of reliability and validity tests for key and primary variables also belong here.

Because it is usually read only by those with some expertise, it often contains more detailed and technical information than other sections of the report. Often parts of this section (for example, a detailed description of sampling design and procedures) or even all of it are included as an appendix rather than in the body of the report.

The Sample

As a prelude to the findings, this section reports (1) descriptive analysis of the demographic characteristics of the sample, (2) analysis of sample representativeness, and (3) the distribution and central tendency of the key variable. This section usually stands alone in medium to lengthy research reports and is combined with the research findings in smaller reports.

Demographic Characteristics. For prediction, evaluation, and explanatory research, readers will want to know the general characteristics of the sample or population from which you obtained your data. This requirement is usually met with a summary of the demographic characteristics of your cases. If the unit of analysis is individual persons, you would typically report

- Proportion of women.

- Average age and the range (or standard deviation) of ages.

- Frequency distribution of locations (regions, cities, plants, or other geographic identifiers).

- Other demographic characteristics relevant to the research (e.g., average education, median income, etc.).

You may also include breakdowns by subsamples or demographic variables (for example, average age by gender or region).

Comparable summary statistics for organizations or organizational units would be size, gender ratio, location, and industry. For example, with departments in an organization as the unit of analysis, you might give the average size and standard deviation, the proportion with a production function, and the average, minimum, and maximum gender ratios among departments.

In prediction research it is particularly important to identify the sample on which the prediction model is based, so that if it is applied to other populations the extent of generalizability can be assessed. For example, a model predicting the productivity of an all-male work force may have less applicability to a mixed force.

Sample Representativeness. For surveys and available data samples, this section presents your analysis of the representativeness of your sample and discusses any problems with low response rates and missing cases bias.

If the response rate to a survey varies across subsamples, discuss possible reasons for the differences and how they might affect the accuracy of your conclusions about group differences. Include any supplementary analysis you did on this issue. Try to account for differences in response rates; for example, is one group of respondents intrinsically less interested in the topic than another? Were different procedures or personnel used? Did the timing of the data gathering (such as holidays and vacations) produce the differences?

Key Variable.   This section provides information about the distribution of the major variable of interest. In prediction and explanatory research this is the dependent variable; it tells the reader just what variation you're going to try to predict or explain. For example, if the research problem is absenteeism, you would report the mean levels of absenteeism and some indication of variation (such as range or standard deviation). In evaluation research, this portion is normally omitted, since the key variable representing the program or policy being evaluated has a separate section of the report all its own.

Policy or Program

In evaluation studies and pilot projects, this section describes in detail the program, policy, action, or practice being evaluated. Report the numbers of cases in the treatment and comparison groups and how comparison groups were selected. Include any tests for the prior equivalence of these groups. For example, in evaluating a training program, you would report

- How many employees took the program.
- How many are in the comparison group.
- The nature of the manipulation (the training program), its duration, and how employees were selected for training.
- Any information indicating similarities or differences in treatment and comparison groups regarding performance levels prior to the training.

In shorter reports combine this section with the discussion of methodology.

Findings and Conclusions

The findings are the meat of the report; it is also the part that gives new researchers the most problems. Because of their importance, we discuss the findings and conclusions later in a separate section.

At this time, however, one important point needs to be made. Even with the most efficient data analysis, much more is analyzed than is reported. The researcher's problem is to divide the wheat from the chaff and then to select the most important and relevant wheat. Your objective is to feed, not stuff, your reader!

End Matter

This section of a research report includes endnotes and, if required, either references or a bibliography (more likely in longer, more formal reports).

The choice between endnotes and footnotes should be based on audience needs. Both contain parenthetical information that expands on material in the text. If many readers are likely to want to see this information, use footnotes, since they are much more readily accessible. However if the material is likely to be of interest to only a small proportion of readers, avoid the clutter and provide endnotes.

Note the difference between References and Bibliography. The former is a list of the works specifically cited in the report, whereas a bibliography also includes items that were not cited but are relevant to the report.

Appendices

Appendices provide technical details and supplementary information that is too complex or detailed for the text. They typically include accounts of the sampling design, examples of data-gathering documents, and descriptions of unusual methodological or data analysis techniques. Other possible appendix material includes descriptions of the data (such as lists of the firms surveyed or the documents consulted), summary tables and statistics, correlation matrices, and tables of regression coefficients. If you refer to variables by their computer acronyms, also include a table of variables and their acronyms.

Writing Schedule

A habit we learn in college courses is to write reports only after all the research is complete. However, in business research this practice is inefficient. A far more useful procedure is to write the report *as you do the research*. This strategy offers several important advantages:

- It saves time. You can write portions of the report during lulls in the research, especially while waiting for questionnaires to be returned or interviews to be completed.

- It helps prevent overanalysis. As you write, you see what information you need next, and you carry out *only* the analysis necessary to provide it. (We'll see that this is particularly important in writing up the findings.)

- It encourages supplementary analysis. As you discuss the findings, puzzling and unexpected situations are more readily apparent. Now is the time to carry out the supplementary data analysis. Don't wait until later: data may have been removed from the computer, there may be no time left, or programmers may not be available. The question doesn't get answered and an important recommendation may be missed.

SUGGESTION

In business research reports, do not use footnotes for references. This style, with *op. cit., ibid.,* and other Latin abbreviations, is more appropriate to the humanities than to applied research. Instead, use a social science style (as in this text).

• It helps avoid straying off the subject. If you write as you conduct the research, you'll keep in mind the ultimate product (your report), and you'll focus on the research problem and specific research questions.

Box 18.1 suggests a writing schedule for the parts typically found in a business research report.

ORGANIZATION AND STYLE

The previous pages have dealt with the content of your report: which of the possible sections to include and what to put into them. We now turn to the overall organization of the sections and the writing style you use to report your research.

Format: The Order of Parts

The various parts of a research report do not always follow the same order. The ordering is governed primarily by your purpose (information or advocacy), although the nature of your audience and the importance of the problem also play a role. In general, researchers choose between two types of format: logical and order-of-interest.

The Logical Format. This format arranges sections in temporal or logical order, the order in which decisions are made and research is carried out. It typically results in this order:

Summary

Introduction, Background, Objectives

Literature Survey

Methodology and Procedures

The Sample

Policy or Program

Findings

Conclusions

Recommendations

Appendices

The logical format is relatively rare in business research. However, it is useful when the principal audience will be hostile or skeptical, or when the

BOX 18.1
RESEARCH SKILLS

Scheduling the Report Writing

To be efficient, write each section as soon as possible, which means in some cases before you begin the data gathering and data analysis!

- *Introduction, Background, Objectives:* Write this section as soon as design decisions have been made and you get go-ahead approval for the project. Take as much as possible (with revisions) from the proposal.
- *Literature Survey:* Same as above.
- *Methodology and Procedures:* Write up the methodology as soon as the design and data-gathering decisions have been made. Add further information later about methodological problems that arose in the course of the research (for example, a large proportion of nonresponses to your questionnaire may have necessitated an unplanned telephone follow-up, or supplementary available data had to be obtained from another source to cover unexpected missing data).

- *Appendices—Data Gathering and Analysis:* Include copies of data-gathering instruments and procedures as soon as they're developed. Similarly, write lists of data sources as soon as they're known. Write up the appendices on methodological techniques as you carry them out. Add tables as you run them and work them into the text of the findings.
- *The Sample:* Write the sample section as soon as you finish your descriptive analysis.
- *Findings and Conclusions:* The most effective time to write the findings and conclusions section is as you carry out the data analysis.

The following sections are all that should be left by the time you finish your computer runs:

- *Conclusions and Recommendations*
- *Summary, Front and End Matter*

---

researcher adopts an advocacy position for a particular recommendation. The logical order should lead the reader slowly toward inevitable conclusions, rather than beginning with recommendations to which he or she objects. If a summary is included, it too should reflect this order.

If your purpose is to win over a reluctant audience, then you should also pay attention to the order in which you present specific conclusions. Given a set of conclusions that support your point, present them in the following order: strongest, third strongest, fourth, fifth, and so on, ending with the second strongest. (This technique takes advantage of the extra weight readers attach to first and last points in a list.)

The Order-of-Interest Format.   This format arranges sections in the order of their interest or importance to the reader and is the most common format in business research. It begins with a brief summary of the research. This is immediately followed by the bottom-line information in more detail: the conclusions and recommendations. Only then does the report describe the background of the organization problem and the situation that led up to the research. The results follow. A literature survey, if there is one, is often relegated to the appendix along with the methodology and, for evaluation research, a description of the program or policy manipulation.

This format is particularly useful when the reader is more interested in the results and recommendations than how they were arrived at. The underlying objective is to provide at each step the information the reader would like to know next.

Ambiguous Problem Importance.   If you are uncertain about the importance of the organization problem or the research, err on the side of including more detail (i.e., more parts), but assign more of them to the appendices. Thus the information is available for those who want or need it, but in an unobtrusive way.

Writing Style

Like other expository writing, research reports should be clear and concise. Buy and use a style manual for suggestions (the best known is Strunk and White, *The Elements of Style,* 1979). Box 18.2 summarizes a number of points to keep in mind as you write.

Vague Writing.   Try to be specific when writing a business research report. One recurring problem is failure to interpret the numerical results of analysis. You must tell the reader specifically what the numbers mean.

Poor: *"The correlation is .48 between manager education and assessment favorableness."*

Better: *". . . This means that managers with higher levels of education tend to give performance assessment reviews with higher ratings."*

SUGGESTION

Jot down on a 3 × 5-inch card the three or four most important improvements you need to make in your expository writing (e.g., "avoid passive voice"). Tape it to the wall over your desk.

A second problem is presenting results for no apparent reason. To avoid this, always give a reason for the information you're providing. Let the readers know why they should want to know what you're telling them. (One simple way to achieve this is to use the specific research questions as headings or subheadings in the report.)

A third vague writing problem is insufficient detail when discussing limitations to a conclusion (such as a nonrepresentative sample, a nonnormal distribution, or too small a sample). It isn't enough to remark that "results should be treated with caution." Be specific. Tell the reader what errors are likely and in what degree.

Formality.   Research report style may range from the highly informal to the somewhat formal. Formal reports, compared to informal communications, have more of the following characteristics:

BOX 18.2
RESEARCH SKILLS
Writing Style

Keep these general style suggestions in mind as you write:

- **Words:**
  Short and clear. Find the *right* word for what you want to say. Don't use variable acronyms (e.g., NUMKIDS, MOSPOS) in the text, tables, or graphics (although they can be used in large summary tables in the appendices).
- **Phrases and ideas:**
  Keep them simple. Reword until the underlying idea is clear.

- **Sentences:**
  Vary the length, but remember short is better than long.
  Avoid the passive voice.
  Don't overuse the verb "to be."
- **Paragraphs:**
  Strive for paragraph unity—restrict it to one idea.
  Keep the sentence subjects consistent throughout the paragraph.
  Avoid lengthy paragraphs.
  Use point form for a succession of items or ideas.

Headings and subheadings

Table of contents

Footnotes or endnotes

References or bibliography

More use of passive voice

Third person instead of first

Less use of point form

Note that formal writing does not mean long-winded or stuffy. It should be just as clear and concise as informal writing.

Your choice of how formal to make your report is dictated by four considerations:

- Your style should be consistent with organizational practices and traditions. If short informal memos are the way it's done, keep reports short and informal. If formal reports are the tradition, use that style and format.

- Other matters being equal, the higher in the organization the most important reader of your report, the more you will probably lean to formal writing (unless organizational culture dictates otherwise).

BOX 18.3
RESEARCH SKILLS
Presenting Numbers in Reports

These conventions will make your report easier to read and avoid misleading readers.

Significant Digits. Too many digits imply a higher degree of accuracy than you actually have (don't report a correlation of .2245 based on a sample of 122). Too few don't give the reader enough information.

- For a percentage or most other statistics, the number of significant digits should reflect the number of cases used in generating the figure and the quality of the measure. A rough rule of thumb is

Less than 100 cases:	two significant digits
100 to 999:	two or three
1,000 or more:	three or four

- For means and standard deviations these limits are more flexible and depend in part on the variable. The mean age in years could be three significant digits (including a decimal) if you have over 100 cases; mean annual income could be rounded to three significant digits to make comparisons easier ("The mean is $22,300 for females and $26,400 for males") or presented using all five digits (e.g., "The average annual salary is $26,359").
- Measures of correlation and association are traditionally reported to only two decimal places. Three are sometimes used if the number of cases is over 1,000. No leading zero is required, since readers know that correlations have a 1.0 maximum.
- If you are comparing statistics or percentages across samples or across tables, use the *same number of decimal places,* even though this means that some figures will have more than three significant digits. ("The chi-square values for the three tables are 4.92, 12.85, and 1.22, respectively.")

Rounding Fives. There is sometimes confusion about how to round when the digit to be dropped is a 5, such as .665 to be rounded to two digits. (Note that .6651 presents no problem; it is rounded to .66 always.) Recheck Box 8.2 for statistical rounding procedures.

Percentages. Use a percent sign for informal reports; the word *percent* for more formal ones. The correct term when there is no preceding number is *percentage* ("The percentage appears small, however . . ."). If the percentage figure is less than one insert a leading zero to let the reader know it isn't a typo (e.g., "Of the males, 0.22% preferred Brand X"). In tables, use the % sign only in the first row of a column of percentages.

Readability. Try to avoid beginning a sentence with a number; if you must, then spell it out. Likewise, avoid ending with a number, particularly a decimal (e.g., ". . . shown to be 28.2. However, . . .").

- The more important the problem, or the more novel your recommendations, the more formal the report.

- Considerations of your own personal style and taste. These will affect the degree of formality with which you are comfortable.

Numbers. The question of how to deal with numbers raises problems for many writers. Box 18.3 discusses some of the conventions for reporting numbers in the text and in tables and graphics.

Writing. Very few of us are skilled enough to write a polished report at one sitting. We suggest you follow these five stages for report writing.

1. Write the initial draft for *content and comprehensiveness*. (Ideally, this should pull together the sections you have been writing all along, prior to and during data analysis.) Try to get in everything that should be said. Don't worry about organization or style at this stage, and don't revise. Begin with a simple introduction that will guide your writing of the following material, then at the end rewrite the introduction.

2. *Check for accuracy* and errors of fact. Rewrite as necessary.

3. Rewrite for *organization*. Strive for a logical flow of ideas, subsections, and sections. Put yourself in the position of the reader—what would he or she want to know next?

4. Rewrite for *style*. Check your choice of words, your sentence length and form, and paragraph unity.

5. *Proofread* for content, organization, and style. Include the details: punctuation, spelling, consistent underlining of headings, pagination, and so on. Correct as necessary.

Presentation

The presentation of your report—its layout and appearance—should follow both organizational practice and general conventions. The following are some general points to keep in mind:

- Pages should not look crowded. Use wide margins and adequate spacing between paragraphs and sections.

- Unless the report is fairly formal, make liberal use of point form to convey a series of ideas.

- Use bullets, boldface, or boxes to highlight important conclusions and recommendations.

- Use lots of headings and subheadings to tell your reader what each section is about.

- Avoid right justification unless you have a proportional spacing printer. The wide gaps between words look awkward.

- Use spiral binding. It looks tidy, helps keep the report from falling apart if it is handed around, and lies flat. Protect the report with a clear plastic cover.

WRITING UP THE FINDINGS AND CONCLUSIONS

We dealt earlier with the problem of where to put conclusions (solution: with *both* findings and recommendations). Other issues that researchers face in writing up their findings and conclusions are as follows:

- How should the reporting of findings be organized?

- How much should I say?

- When should I use a table or graphic?

- Where and how do I report statistical tests?

Although there are no hard and fast rules, and researchers tend to adopt variations they feel most comfortable with, the following suggestions will make this section of your report both easier to write and to read.

Your goal is a report in which the discussion of findings and conclusions seems to flow logically and effortlessly. With some care, you can avoid frustrating readers with findings presented in no apparent logical order and a jumble of seemingly unrelated results. This confusion is a potential danger with any research involving more than four or five variables. To avoid it, use or adapt the following suggestions:

- Report the descriptive analysis of population or sample demographic characteristics in the Sample section.

- In explanatory research, report the univariate analysis (central tendency and variation) of the key dependent variable in the Sample section. This tells the reader *what aspects of that sample or population you want to explain.* (In evaluation research, univariate analysis of the key independent variable is described in the Policy or Program section.)

- Report both (1) univariate analysis of other primary independent variables and (2) relationship analysis in a series of subsections in the Findings and Conclusions section.

The following pages describe how to organize your univariate and relationship findings in a logical series of subsections. We first examine how to divide Findings and Conclusions into subsections; we next examine what to discuss in each subsection.

Organizing the Section

The most effective way to organize your Findings and Conclusions is to use subsections corresponding to each of your specific research questions. If, as suggested, you included these questions in the Introduction (or Background or Objectives), their reappearance in Findings and Conclusions ties your results to the purpose of the research. The reader can clearly see how you addressed each research question and what the answer to each question is. You can even use the research questions themselves as the subheadings for the subsections.

Typically there is a specific research question for each primary variable or set of primary variables. For explanatory research, the primary variables reflect potential major causes of the key dependent variable. For evaluation research, they represent potential consequences of a program or policy. In prediction research, they are the potential predictors in a forecasting or selection model. Use a different subsection for each research question (or for each primary variable).

The order of subsections should be logical. Use either of the following orders:

- Importance to the organization, beginning with the most important primary variable or research question and ending with the least.

- Temporal or causal priority, beginning with the most causally prior primary variables (e.g., characteristics individuals have from birth) and ending with those closest to the dependent variable (e.g., current attitudes or recent behaviors). This is most useful in conjunction with causal modeling (see the appendix at the end of Chapter 17).

Note that neither ordering is based on your key variable(s), but rather on primary variables presumed to be *related* to the key variable. Note also that there are no subsections corresponding to control variables, just as there are no specific research questions that deal only with control variables. This is consistent with their function in the research, which is only to make clearer the role of the other, more important, primary factors. If you want to report the joint effect of all the variables together, add a final section titled something like, "Combined Effects of the Independent Variables" and report the R^2 values or comparable measures of joint effect.

SUGGESTION

Write up your results *as you do your computing.* For all your analysis, ask yourself, "How and where will this fit into the report?" If you're not sure, think twice about doing that particular analysis!

CASE EXAMPLE

In an explanatory study of the causes of spray painting machine breakdowns, the research report organized the Findings and Conclusions section with the following subheadings: "Machine Overheating" (the most likely cause according to management), "Ambient Temperature and Humidity," "Faulty Materials," "Faulty Employee Procedures," and "Line Voltage Fluctuations."

CASE EXAMPLE

An evaluation research study examined the effects of restructuring the engineering department. The research report organized findings and conclusions into three subsections, representing the three major consequences of the restructuring: "Productivity," "Employee Morale," and "Interdepartmental Relations."

An advantage of this organization is that it helps prevent overanalysis. You report only what's pertinent to the specific research questions and focus on the primary relationships implied or stated in the questions.

Organization Within Subsections

Each subsection of the Findings and Conclusions deals with a specific research question or primary variable (or related set of primary variables). For evaluation and explanatory research, use the following organization within each subsection:

- Present univariate statistics (central tendency, variation) for the primary variable.

- If there are univariate or joint outliers or other distribution problems, identify them and discuss how you handled them. If you conducted the analysis with and without the outliers, compare the results for the rest of the analysis in the subsection.

- State the bivariate relationship between the primary and key variables.

- Give the unique effects of the variable as determined by your multivariate analysis. If an interaction effect is to be tested (for example, with a cross-product term in the regression), report that result as well.

- Compare bivariate and unique effects and discuss as required (e.g., if spurious, or if a suppressor effect is evident).

- If a moderator variable is expected, give the results of that analysis (for example, separate regressions for each category of the moderating variable).

- Add any supplementary analysis required to make clear the role of the variable(s) and to account for any puzzling findings, such as the lack of an expected relationship.

- End each subsection with the conclusions you reach about the role of the variable (and answer to the specific research question). Add any limitations to your conclusions. See Box 18.4.

CASE EXAMPLE

An evaluation project examined the effect on productivity of a new method of calculating productivity bonus payments in 14 mines of a large mining firm. It included the specific research question, "Has the new procedure affected rates of wildcat strikes, slowdowns, or sabotage?" (Other questions dealt with absenteeism, turnover, tardiness, and several measures of productivity.) In the final report, the subsection dealing with this question started with an overall description of current levels of wildcats, slowdowns, and sabotage. This was followed by a discussion of the bivariate relationships between the procedure change and each primary variable (i.e., the before-after difference): no change for strikes, moderate increase for slowdowns and sabotage.

The report then gave the multivariate results of the unique effects of the change on each variable, controlling for a number of demographic and organizational independent variables. The results: still no change for strikes, slight increase in slowdowns and sabotage. The results of an interaction effect (a cross-product term combining each of the three primary variables with a dummy variable for "forthcoming union elections" were then reported: no interaction effect. Bivariate and unique effects were compared.

At this point a moderating variable (surface or underground operation) was tested with separate results for each category. The results showed substantial increases in slowdowns and sabotage in surface operations, but no changes in underground sites. The subsection then reported some supplementary analysis of the surface-underground difference. The subsection ended with four general conclusions that the researcher drew from these findings and a qualification based on questionable measurement of sabotage incidents.

Writing and Computing.

This organization of Findings and Conclusions can also guide your computing. Carry out your computer analysis step by step for each subsection, writing up the results as you get them.

- As soon as you have finished the computing necessary for the topics in the Sample section (sample description, sample representativeness, key variable univariate analysis), start the computing you need for Findings and Conclusions.

- Do the computing for each research question in turn. With microcomputers, it is no longer necessary to submit large batch jobs that combine many different analyses.

- Within each research question, run univariate, bivariate, multivariate, and moderating variable analysis in turn. As you get the results, write them up, a paragraph (or more) for each. Finish off with any supplementary analysis required.

- Start writing each paragraph *before* you actually have the results! This will force you to think clearly about just what you need to run, and why. This ensures that you do as much analysis as you need and no more. It may be helpful, prior to analysis, to make up a dummy table for each relationship or a list of the correlation coefficients or other statistics you will need.

SUGGESTION

Don't use the terms *bivariate* or *multivariate* in your report unless readers are likely to understand the procedures of data analysis. Instead, talk in more concrete terms about each variable and specific research question.

SUGGESTION

When you write up your findings, keep a copy of your codebook handy to verify what the numbers mean (for example, whether a relationship is positive or negative) and where the data came from (e.g., questionnaire wording).

A **dummy table** is a table without the numbers: it has the title, headings, and everything else. Its purpose is to make sure you carry out the computer runs needed to get the numbers to complete the table.

BOX 18.4

MOVING SOUND: A CONTINUING CASE

Part Thirteen: Research Report Excerpt

. . .
TO: Sharon
FROM: Peter
DATE: April 23
RE: TV COMMERCIAL PILOT PROJECT

Here are the results of our pilot project re. the TV commercial. Basically, it works, but not everywhere and not for everybody. Nevertheless, I recommend we run it at all our locations, but combine it with college paper advertising in some situations. Details follow.

Background: The idea for a commercial first came up because of . . .
Methodology: We ran the commercial for three weeks in two locations, Buffalo and Blacksburg. We looked at sales before and during the run, and at responses to 275 interviews and 256 questionnaires . . .
Findings: Here are the results for the following seven research questions. (I've put details in parentheses since you said you wanted to see the stats.). . .
   3. Who Saw the Commercial? Among those interviewed at the buses, we found that age and student status, but not gender, made a difference in who remembered the commercial. The average age of interviewees was 23.1 and ranged from 14 to 62 (an outlier, but kept in the analysis). The median was 22 years.

For the 122 who said they had seen the commercial (and recalled some content), the average was 19.9 years. By comparison, the age was 25.6 for those who hadn't seen it or couldn't recall any content.

Although this difference is substantial and significant (in a t-test at the .05 level; eta squared of .13), multivariate analysis controlling for other factors, including music preferences, showed a smaller unique effect of age (squared semipartial correlation of .04). It appears that age is related to music preferences, which in turn seems to affect both who saw the commercial and remembered it. Age alone has only a minor effect.

With respect to student status, of the interviewees 78 percent were students enrolled in high school (32 percent) or college (46 percent). . . .

It seems clear that the commercial is reaching those individuals we want it to. . . .

Descriptive and Prediction Research.   Organizing your findings is less problematic for descriptive and prediction research. For descriptive, discuss each key variable in a separate subsection, together with any breakdowns and conclusions pertaining to that variable. In many instances the discussions will be sufficiently short so that separate subsections are not required.

For prediction research, a single section generally reports the results of multivariate analysis: which variables are in the forecasting or selection model and the joint impact of variables in the model. Univariate and bivariate results are occasionally presented, but discussions of interaction terms, moderator variables, and supplementary analysis are rare.

What to Include

Each computer run produces a great many numbers. Which of these go into the report? Which should be presented in figures or tables? Which can be safely ignored?

Use this guiding principle: the numbers you report, and where, should match the technical competence of your audience. In general, the less competent your most important readers, the more you should relegate numbers to tables and appendices. However, almost everybody understands means and percentages, and you should always include these in your report where relevant.

Chapters 16 and 17 discuss bivariate measures of association and statistical significance, and multivariate techniques. First, select the measure or technique appropriate to your data (its measurement level or the data assumptions it meets), and then select the measures of association, significance, unique, relative, or joint effects recommended in these chapters. To help your readers, consider these suggestions:

- Comparisons across groups or over time are more easily seen with graphics (see Box 18.5). Base the group comparisons on means or percentages.

- Include a summary table of multivariate results showing all independent variables, primary (or key) and control. (If you have more than one primary or key dependent variable, include a summary table for each.) Such tables are particularly useful for reporting significance tests.

- Make sure that you report somewhere the number of cases on which each finding is based, particularly significance tests. Normally these numbers are not included in the text but placed in tables.

- Keep significance levels unobtrusive by using asterisks to indicate levels of significance and a legend at the foot of the table, for example, "* = significant at the .05 level."[2]

Tests of Assumptions. These tests are important for technical audiences, for they justify your conclusions. Place this technical material in footnotes or an appendix. For example, a footnote might read, "Tests showed no appreciable levels of autocorrelation"; the appendix would present the result of a Durbin-Watson test and a significance test of the Durbin-Watson statistic.

Limitations to the Conclusions. If conditions or circumstances that limit your conclusions apply to most of your findings (such as low re-

SUGGESTION

In matching content to audience, keep in mind the distinction between (1) *interpreting* your conclusions and (2) *justifying* your conclusions. The first is important for all audiences, particularly managers not well versed in research methods and statistics. The second is only important for research-knowledgeable readers.

SUGGESTION

Add an appendix for the nonstatistical reader that describes the nature of the statistical tests you use and how to interpret the results of those tests.

[2]Don't use two or three different significance levels (e.g., .05, .01, .001) as a substitute for measures of strength of association. Instead, report appropriate measures of effect, and use a single significance level throughout the report (unless you actually change your willingness to encounter a Type I error or need a more powerful test of significance).

BOX 18.5
FOCUS ON RESEARCH
Using Graphics in Research Reports

Graphics are very useful in business research reports, and with the variety of good microcomputer software to produce them, their use is growing rapidly. Graphics convey your findings at a glance and make comparisons easy to see. Unlike tables, good graphics do not contain a lot of information; cluttered figures are probably worse than no graphics at all. Similarly, they do not need interpreting in the text to the same extent that tables do. However, each graphic must contain a title, appropriate labeling, and, where necessary, footnotes, explanatory notes, and an acknowledgment of sources.

Types of Graphics. In addition to the plots and graphs used in analyzing and representing relationships, business researchers can choose from among a variety of graphics to report results. Examples of common graphics are shown in Figure 18.1 (a map chart example can be found in Chapter 15, Figure 15.1).

Pie and column charts both show the relative sizes or proportions of categories. One hundred percent stratum charts show changing proportions.

Bar charts are useful for comparing discrete categories of a variable or change over time in a category variable. Addition of a second variable produces a stacked or multiple bar chart. A 100 percent bar chart shows stacked proportions, with the height of the bars held constant.

Histograms show the distribution of a quantitative variable by collapsing the variable into a large number of categories, each of which is represented by a bar (like a bar chart) except that the bars touch.

Line graphs are most commonly used to show change in a single variable over time. By convention, the horizontal axis is used for time, the vertical axis is the variable. Multiple-line graphs are useful for comparing the change in two or more groups (particularly helpful in explaining moderator effects).

Stratum charts show how category sizes change over time. One hundred percent stratum charts do the same for category proportions.

Map charts use different markings or colors to indicate category (or the level of a grouped mean or proportion) by region. For example, red might indicate regions with average strike rates higher than .15, blue lower than .05, and white those in between.

Each of these graphics can be modified to emphasize the subject matter of the comparison. For example, corporations routinely use pie charts represented as coins with segments exploded outward to indicate corporate income from various categories or how income is dispersed. Similarly, bar charts are often shown as stacks of coins or objects representing a firm's product, such as shipping crates or drums.

sponse rates, nonresponse bias, or the ecological fallacy of drawing conclusions at levels other than the unit of analysis), report these in a summary subsection at the end of your Findings and Conclusions. However, if the limitation applies only to a particular independent variable (because of unreadable documents, poor question wording, or a truncated sample), discuss it in the appropriate subsection.

Tables and Graphics

Tables save space by including large amounts of information in an easily accessible form. However, you cannot rely on tables alone to do your work for you. They must be discussed and interpreted in the text in order to ensure that the reader gets the point you intended to make. Box 18.6 discusses the parts of a table.

Here are some suggestions for using tables:

- The body of your report should contain only highly relevant tables (involving key and primary variables) with a moderate number of cells or numbers; very complex tables should be put into the appendix.

- You will save space and make the text easier to read by reporting significance test results and the N's on which tests are based in tables rather than in the text.

- For percentaged cross-tabulations you must give the base on which each percentage is calculated.

- Dollar and percent signs should appear only in the first row and for the row of totals at the bottom of a table. If there are both positive and negative values, avoid clutter by using only minus signs; all other values will be read as positive.

- The easiest way to discuss a cross-tabulation in the text is (1) select the most important category of the *dependent* variable according to the research problem (e.g., percentage of accounts underbudgeted rather than overbudgeted), then (2) compare that category across categories of the *independent* variable (e.g., by academic department). Do not discuss all categories of the dependent variable.

For example, "Table 7 shows that, of all departments, Economics had the highest proportion of underbudgeted accounts at 42 percent; the least underbudgeting occurred in Anthropology and Chemistry, which had none. The differences across departments are substantial (eta = .45) and statistically significant at the .05 level." (For a less sophisticated audience the second sentence should be omitted, with the eta and significance level [and F value with degrees of freedom] reported only at the foot of the table.)

- When constructing tables with nominal variables, don't include the value you assigned each category, such as "0" for males and "1" for females. These numbers have only symbolic meaning; use instead the value labels

FIGURE 18.1
Examples of
Graphics and Their
Use

(a) Pie Chart

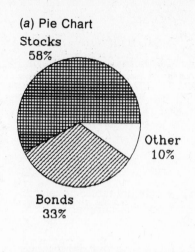

(b) Column Chart

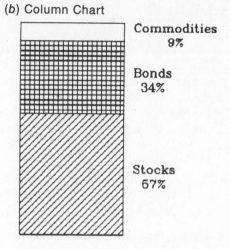

(c) Bar Chart

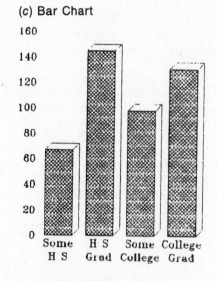

(d) Stacked Bar Chart

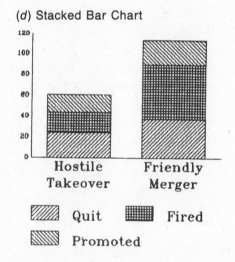

(e) 100% Bar Chart

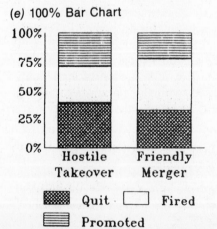

(f) Multiple Bar Chart

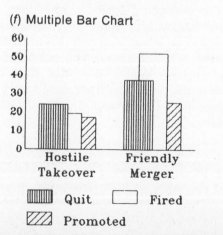

(g) Histogram

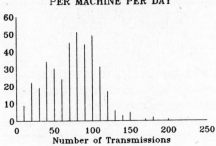

(h) Line Graph

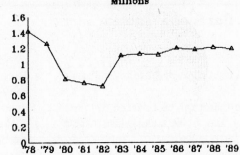

(i) Multiple Line Graph

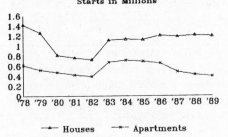

(j) Stratum Chart

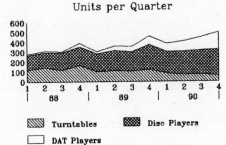

(k) 100% Stratum Chart

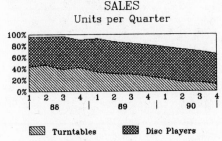

Figures produced with Harvard
Graphics option of SPSS/PC+.

"male" and "female." Similarly, you may omit the numbers for ordinal
categories if appropriate word labels are available.

- As well as the individual tables for each of the important relationships you
  want to show, include a summary table of the association and significance of
  these relationships.

BOX 18.6
FOCUS ON RESEARCH

Parts of a Table

Each table has at least some of the following parts:

- *Table number* (so that it can be referred to in the text and listed in the list of tables). Use Arabic rather than Roman numerals.
- *Title.* The title should indicate the variables found in the table and the time period, sample, or subsample it applies to (if not the same throughout the section). It should also make clear, if necessary, the nature of the number found in each cell of the table (e.g., a percentage, a sales figure in thousands of dollars, a consumer price index). Within these constraints, find a title that is as short as possible.
- *Box head or column head.* This is the identification of the tables' columns. By convention, this is usually (but not always) the categories of the independent variable in cross-tabulation tables.

- *Stubhead.* This identifies the rows of the table. By convention, it is usually categories of the dependent variable in cross-tabulations.
- *Summary statistics.* If the table involves just one relationship, or a small number of partial relationships, these are placed at the foot of the table and provide information about measures of association and tests of significance. If the table reports a number of relationships, this information is normally included in a column (or row) of the table.
- *Footnotes and explanatory notes.* They explain limitations and inclusions and symbols used for significance levels or other purposes.
- *Sources.* The source(s) of the data should be given whenever a table is taken from secondary sources, rather than from information collected and analyzed by the researcher.

Graphics such as bar charts, pie charts, and line graphs are extremely useful for conveying certain kinds of information (see Box 18.5). However, be careful because it is easier to provide misleading impressions with graphics than in text or in tables (see Box 18.7).

Statistical Procedures

Statistics involves numbers. Your job is to interpret these numbers for your reader. In doing so, keep two points in mind:

- Too many numbers produce numbness.

- Every number needs a comparison number.

As a rough rule of thumb, the less statistically knowledgeable your audience, the fewer numbers in the text. At the extreme, only include those numbers that point readers to the appropriate place in a table to ensure that they see the comparison you want to make.

No number makes sense by itself. A comparison number or scale has to be implicit or specified. For example, if you read that a relationship has a "scrunch" value of 2.88, the information alone means nothing until you know that "scrunch" values range from zero to three, and anything over two means an impact of earthquake proportions. Thus you must provide comparisons for the numbers, interpret them, and signal when a particular finding should be paid attention.

Where to Report Results? For any statistical result, you must choose whether to report it in the text, in a table, in a graphic, in the appendix, or at all. As we already noted, numbers in the text should be limited, particularly for readers with less statistical sophistication. Tables are generally a good place to report statistical tests. If there are many tests, a summary table is an excellent way to handle them. Graphics can generally handle only simple information and are normally limited to univariate distributions and bivariate comparisons. Seldom do they contain relationship statistics.

Here are some suggestions for reporting statistical tests:

- When a quantitative variable's distribution is skewed, give the median as well as the mean.

- For category variables, there is usually little reason to report means or medians. Instead, show the distribution in a frequency distribution or bar chart. If necessary, point out the modal category in the text.

- For category ordinal variables: if unipolar, present the percentage of cases in the most important end category or combine the two or three categories at that end. If the scale is bipolar, you have a choice of reporting the most relevant end category or categories, or you may want to report categories or combinations of categories at both ends. For example, researchers normally report the percentage agreeing in a Likert-type scale ("Strongly agree" plus "Agree"), but many researchers would report both ends of a seven-point satisfaction scale. They might indicate the percentages highly satisfied ("Extremely" and "Highly") combined and the percentages highly dissatisfied (the corresponding categories at the other end of the scale).

- If you report both association and significance tests for surveys, there is logic in presenting measures of association *before* measures of significance. The first indicates the size of an effect in the sample, the second indicates whether it could have occurred by chance. The order can be reversed for true experiments; significance indicates whether there is an effect at all (or whether it is assignment error) and association then indicates how large it is (which is less important in experiments).

- In explanatory research, it is often useful to include in the appendix a summary table that shows, for the independent variables:

Names and acronyms, both primary and control

Overall means or proportions

BOX 18.7
RESEARCH ETHICS
Misuse of Graphics

Because of their visual impact and apparent simplicity, graphics are susceptible to misinterpretation and misuse. Researchers have an ethical obligation to ensure that their graphics don't present a false impression.

Among the ways this can happen are inappropriate or omitted categories in pie charts; nonzero origins in line graphs, stratum charts, and bar charts; and inappropriate scales in line graphs and stratum charts.

* *Omitting one or more categories* from a pie chart will give a misleading impression of the absolute size of the remaining categories. Similarly, dividing a natural category into many small subcategories can downplay its importance.

* *Nonzero Origins.* Vertical axes that do not start from a zero origin will produce steeper lines and much more dramatic differences among groups. They can make relatively insignificant increases and differences look like major gains. On the other hand, a nonzero origin can save space and in some cases is the only possible alternative. In such instances, use a zigzag in the line representing the vertical axis just above the origin to clearly signal what you're doing.

* *Inappropriate scales* in line graphs and stratum charts can also give a misleading impression. A compressed horizontal scale or stretched vertical scale will make change look much more dramatic. Charts with one scale in logarithmic form (called

(a) Zero Origin

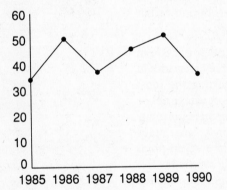

(b) Nonzero Origin

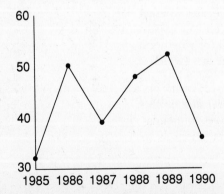

(a) Standard Scales

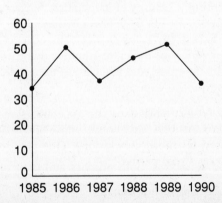

(box continues)

(Box 18.7 continued)

semilogarithmic scales) are good for examining rates of change, but are easily misinterpreted by the average reader. Uneven time periods on the horizontal axis can also distort the impression of change.

(*b*) Compressed Vertical Scale

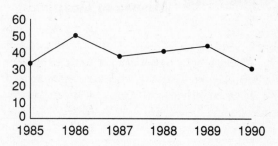

When there are comparison groups or subsamples, the mean or proportion by group

Bivariate measure of association with the dependent variable

For the primary independent variables, unique effects

Level of statistical significance (using asterisks)

- For ranked choice measures, report cumulative counts in a table. Give the number of first choices for each option, the sum of first and second choices, and the sum of first, second, and third. This gives a more accurate picture of the options' relative importance than merely showing separately the number of first, second, and third choices. It also avoids the error of attaching too much weight to a large number of second or third choices and saves the reader the effort of trying to add the numbers.

DRAFTING RECOMMENDATIONS

Newcomers to business research often underestimate the difficulty involved in drafting recommendations. Before we consider the reasons for the difficulty, let's examine the criteria for good recommendations: validity, relevance, and feasibility.

- From the researcher's point of view, a *valid* recommendation is one that is supported by the conclusions. This is usually a straightforward matter of checking recommendations against conclusions. Keep in mind that limitations to conclusions (e.g., nonresponse bias) also apply to the recommendations based on those conclusions. One way to deal with limitations is to recommend a trial period.[3]

[3]For pilot projects, your recommendations are valid only for the particular program or policy tested. Remind readers that significant changes to the program or policy may make your recommendations invalid.

BOX 18.8
RESEARCH ETHICS

Recommendations

Whatever you recommend is likely to have an effect, or otherwise you wouldn't recommend it. (Even recommending the status quo affects an organization and its members or employees.) As a researcher, you cannot avoid responsibility for the ethical, legal, or moral consequences of your recommendations, even though it is not up to you to implement them. For that reason, now is a good time to ask yourself, of each recommendation, what its consequences might be.

- Is this recommendation likely to harm those from whom data was gathered or who otherwise took part in the research? If so, is this harm within the limits of *accepted risk?*

- Is the recommendation likely to cause harm to others not involved in the research? If so, is the harm within the limits of accepted risk?

- Does this recommendation violate generally accepted community standards of conduct?

(Return to Chapter 1 for a more extensive discussion of research ethics and the test of accepted risk.)

- From the organization's point of view, a *relevant* recommendation addresses the underlying organizational problem. It isn't cosmetic, and it isn't limited to some tangential issue.

- A *feasible* recommendation is one that doesn't require time, money, or personnel resources to implement beyond what the problem warrants. In other words, the cure must not be worse than the disease! It also takes into account the likelihood of opposition within the organization to the recommendation's adoption.

Not all research requires recommendations. Descriptive and prediction research normally don't, nor might an evaluation research project that only seeks to determine how much of an impact some program or action has had. However, most explanatory research requires some attention to recommendations, since it is undertaken to address a problem facing the organization. Similarly, much evaluation research ends with a recommendation to continue, expand, or end a program, policy, or pilot project. In some circumstances an organization specifically asks that no recommendations accompany the report. If you're in doubt, clarify this point as you investigate the organizational problem and specify the research problem. Recommendations raise questions of business research ethics. See Box 18.8.

We now discuss types of recommendations and why this step of the research is often difficult. We then turn to some suggestions for overcoming these problems. Finally, we consider a useful practice in business research—involving management in drafting the recommendations.

Types of Recommendations

There are four different kinds of recommendations a researcher can make. Listed in order of increasing cautiousness, they are as follows:

- *Action:* The researcher unequivocally recommends a specific action or decision. Ideally, the report also discusses why alternative actions are not recommended.

- *Comparison of actions:* Rather than a single action, the researcher reports several alternative actions the organization might undertake and assesses the strengths and weaknesses of each as suggested by the research results, without selecting one particular action.

- *Information:* Instead of actions, the researcher recommends factors to be taken into account in the organization's decision making on a particular topic. This stance offers the report as a source of information for the use of decision makers, rather than specific suggestions for organizational action.

- *Further research:* The researcher admits that the research does not point clearly to any actions or alternatives and recommends that further study be undertaken.

A report may also recommend actions designed to provide better information about the situation. For example, researchers will sometimes recommend regular data gathering in order to facilitate future or ongoing analysis of the effects of some action or to monitor a situation for potential problems to enable a quick response. If the research uncovers a new organization problem, the report might recommend its examination in future research.

Recommendation Problems

Drafting recommendations is often problematic because (1) it is more subjective than objective, (2) it often requires generalizing beyond the study, and (3) it requires knowledge of the organization.

Subjectivity.   Recommendations seldom follow logically and unambiguously from findings and conclusions. For example, you conclude that certain accounting practices appear to be the reason for cash flow problems. Change is clearly needed, but *what* change? The researcher's problem is to bridge this gap between conclusions and recommendations (see Box 18.9). As Lazarsfeld and Reitz (1975) point out, the researcher does this with a combination of guesses and creative thinking. The researcher also needs as much information as possible about the organization and its environment.

A related difficulty is that organizations tend to think in terms of distinct categories: Plan A or Plan B, yes or no, sell or keep, hire or not. The world, however, tends to operate on continuous dimensions, so the problem for the

BOX 18.9

CAMPBELL SWITCH: A CONTINUING CASE

Part Eighteen: Research Report Excerpt

. . .

CONCLUSIONS AND RECOMMENDATIONS

Analysis of the available data indicate that the turnover and absenteeism problems, the requests for transfer back to the Concord plant, and the newly uncovered lateness problems are much more likely to occur among older and more experienced skilled employees at the new Ajax plant. Compared to age, seniority, experience, and skill, other factors showed relatively minor effects.

Observation and available data indicate that these individuals are now overwhelmingly working in homogeneous work groups of senior skilled employees like themselves. Observation also suggests that there are very different social patterns in these groups compared to the more heterogeneous groups in the Concord plant. These differences have to do with the deference and informal authority granted to the senior employees by their juniors in work groups at the Concord plant.

We believe that the problem group of employees feels deprived of the perks of high status, higher skill levels, and more experience compared to younger employees with less seniority in the same work group.

Recognizing that the Ajax plant was specifically staffed with skilled and experienced employees in order to achieve full productivity more quickly and recognizing that the strategy is now leading to productivity declines due to the problems previously identified,

We recommend

That further hiring at, or transfers to, the Ajax plant emphasize younger, less skilled, and less experienced employees.

We further recommend that

These new employees be integrated into work teams with the older, more skilled and experienced employees.

. . .

researcher is to determine (subjectively) the critical point between making one recommendation or another. For example, if a correlation between productivity and job structure is .4, is this enough to warrant a recommendation for change?

Generalizing.   Recommendations require generalizing from the research findings for a specific set of cases or observations:

- To other groups or parts of the organization or perhaps the entire organization (or its potential clients and customers).

- To at least the near future and possibly several years or even a decade or more. You must assume that the causes you have found will continue to be important causes in this future.

- To policy and program actions that represent somewhat different variables than those in the research. In the case of pilot projects, almost never is the implemented policy or program identical to the tested one.

   Knowing the Organization. Without knowing the organization, the researcher cannot make an effective leap between conclusions and recommendations and cannot generalize with confidence. The researcher needs information about overall organization goals and culture; the potentially competing goals and cultures of subgroups within the organization; organizational resources; its present and likely future financial and competitive environment; structural, personnel, and economic constraints; the costs of different options; and the likelihood of their successful implementation.

   The best general approach to solving these problems is, for each recommendation, to draft a set of competing options and then compare them for validity, relevance, and feasibility.

Generating Creative Recommendations

   How do you get that creative spark that bridges the conclusions-recommendations gap? One way is to ask yourself which of the following sets of alternatives the research conclusions point to:

- Change *people* (behavior, attitudes, performance), or change the *organization* (organization structure or processes or technology)?

- At what place should the change be implemented? Are there vital points at which change would be most effective? Which group? What stage in the production processes (of goods or services)?

- When is change most likely to be effective? In calendar time? In production cycles?

Other techniques that may help include lateral thinking, brainstorming with others familiar with the situation, and letting the matter stew for several days in the back of your mind.

Relevant and Feasible Recommendations

   To be useful, recommendations must address the real organization problem. To ensure relevance, ask these questions of your potential recommendations:

- Is the recommendation relevant to the organization's initial problem? Does it address the real underlying issue?

- Is the recommendation likely to be effective? Will it change the situation enough to alter the level of the key or primary dependent variable?

- Will the recommended action have a lasting impact or will it likely only be a temporary improvement?

- What are the long-term effects of the recommended action likely to be?

- What side effects and unanticipated consequences might there be that lead to new problems?

- What feedback effects might there be that give rise to processes that lead to a continuation of the old problem?

- What interaction effects might there be that neutralize the action in some circumstances? Are these moderating factors political? Structural?

Any set of recommendations is a compromise between what the conclusions dictate and the constraints (financial and political) of the organization. Here is a set of questions you can ask yourself to help arrive at feasible recommendations:

- Is the recommendation practical? Is it too expensive to implement? Too time consuming? Does it require too many personnel? Would it have to overcome too much opposition within the organization?

- What are the costs and benefits of implementing the recommendation? (Include side effects as well as main effects and long-term as well as short-term effects.)

- What political ramifications will the recommendations have? Who will gain, and who might lose (power, privilege, status, autonomy, money—consider both tangibles and intangibles)?

One of the most difficult issues for researchers is anticipating opposition. Recommendations almost always involve change, and most individuals and organizations have a natural resistance to change. Change is threatening and arouses anxiety; many individuals have a stake in the status quo. The researcher cannot merely make the most logical recommendations and then ignore the realities of implementation.

Involving Management

One of the requirements for good recommendations is information about the organization. And who knows the organization more than managers? It is often useful to involve one or more managers in the recommendations (but not those who are part of the organization problem and thus might have their judgment affected).

The manager will be able to suggest what actions are totally unfeasible and to help with an analysis of the potential costs and benefits of alternative options. He or she will help you take into account the political climate inside the organization and anticipate how certain conclusions or recommendations may be received. Management input will also help with an assessment of both short- and long-term implications of your recommendations, and perhaps advise on legal and ethical issues that the recommendations may involve.

Collaboration on recommendations also ensures that both parties' interests are protected. The researcher wants recommendations that accurately reflect the findings and conclusions. The manager wants recommendations that are relevant and feasible and are unambiguous and readily translated into organizational action. Communication between manager and researcher at this stage can improve the cost effectiveness of the research enormously.

REPORT VARIATIONS AND PROBLEMS

Business researchers often submit interim reports and present their results orally. This section discusses briefly both these kinds of reporting. In addition, it deals with three common reporting problems: no results, bad news, and interference.

Before we turn to these issues, however, it is important to keep in mind that, once the report is out, matters are often largely out of your hands. No matter how good or bad the results may appear to you, you can never be sure how they are going to be used.

CASE EXAMPLE

Sommer and Nelson (1985) report a follow-up study to examine how the findings of an earlier study were utilized. The initial study was designed to gather information that would help the establishment and spread of farmers' markets in California. In comparing farmers' markets with commercial supermarkets, the researchers gathered data from farmers, customers, and market managers with interviews and questionnaires. These data were supplemented by observation of marketing behavior, price comparisons, and even flavor tests and analyses of residues. The authors made their findings widely available in a series of articles in trade periodicals concerned with farming and direct marketing, as well as reports to the farmers' market organizations taking part in the study. In the follow-up, they found that their initial results were not much used by market managers to improve their farmers' market performance. Instead, they were used in external dealings with city officials and for advertising purposes.

Progress and Interim Reports

In business research, progress reports and interim reports tend to be short and informal. The question of what to include is best addressed by considering what the reader wants to know. This reader is often a manager seeking reassurance that work is on schedule, research budgets are under control, and that no major problems have occurred that threaten the likelihood of getting relevant and feasible recommendations on time.

A useful format for such reports is to borrow from the original proposal and to show how work is progressing on each of the tasks discussed in the proposal. There is no need to go over the reasons for and background to the research or its methodology.

Oral Reports

Oral presentations of results are quite different from the content, organization, and style of business research reports. In fact, following the format of a research report is probably a good way to guarantee a restless audience. In content, resign yourself to conveying much less information than the typical report. In organization, the best practice is to treat the oral report like a speech, following the old three-part dictum: "Tell them what you're going to tell them, tell them, then tell them what you told them." In style, match the degree of formality to the situation. At one extreme is a meeting of the board of directors; at the other is a lunch-hour chat about the findings.

Here are a few suggestions to help you prepare and deliver an oral report of research results.

- Start with a dramatic illustration of the initial problem. This will gain attention and motivate the audience to be curious about the solution.

- Be careful about handouts and illustrations. They will attract lots of attention and perhaps focus audience interest on the wrong issues or side issues. The more detailed they are, the more likely this is to happen. (Also, this information takes time to assimilate. If it's too complicated, you'll lose your audience who will still be trying to figure out the material while you've moved on to the next point.)

- As long as you keep them simple, slides, overhead projectors and other audiovisual aids such as posters, flip charts, and samples can help to reinforce the points you want to make.

- A good idea, if using an overhead, is to distribute copies of each screen to the audience as a handout. This will allow them to add their own notes and take the handouts away with them.

- Especially useful for presentations of research results is the equipment to project computer screen images. This hardware is used in conjunction with an overhead projector and will allow you to show tables, charts, and other computer images. Caution: prepare the files you want to show beforehand, and edit out the unnecessary detail. Note that these systems allow you to call up results (or perform the statistical runs on the spot) to answer questions from your audience, but make sure you practice if you're going to try this.

- Anticipate questions and prepare answers beforehand. Handling questions well is important. Your work will be judged partly on how you present information and respond to questions.

- Follow the rules of good speech making. Don't memorize, and don't read from your notes. Rehearse to check for speed, volume, movement, and tone of voice. Don't go overtime, and always allow more time for audience reaction and questions than you think it will take.

No Results

If you fail to find an expected relationship, your report must discuss why. Consider these two reasons: (1) methodological flaws prevented you from finding the true relationship, or (2) the relationship really doesn't exist. While this discussion can never be conclusive, you should be able to comment on the likelihood of one or the other as a potential explanation of null results.

There are two likely sources of methodological flaws: poor measurement or data, and missing variables. Neither poor measures nor unreliable data can effectively pick up a weak relationship. Check for the following symptoms: N's are too small, the sample shows nonresponse bias, individual questions show response bias, question categories are too insensitive, or the sample is truncated. Another test is to examine a relationship (between two independent variables) that you *know* exists. If you can't find it, then the problem is likely to be the data. There is no solution for this problem except to repeat the study or gather better data.

The second methodological flaw is missing variables or specification error. It may be that the real, or most important, causes weren't measured. Check to see whether the total variation in the dependent variable explained by your primary independent and control variables is substantially less than 25 percent.[4] If so, the principal causes are not in the analysis. You might recommend further research concentrating on the most likely other causes.

> **SUGGESTION**
>
> Include in the appendix or summary a list of the factors that were found *not* to have an effect.

CASE EXAMPLE

A student researcher carried out a study of absenteeism in an auto parts plant which, because of the reluctance of the personnel manager to alienate plant foremen, omitted variables measuring management style. The researcher included demographic characteristics, seniority, working conditions, transportation patterns, and job characteristics as primary variables. She found that none of her primary variables were substantially related to absenteeism. She concluded that the causes most likely lay with the major unmeasured variables having to do with style of supervision and how absenteeism was handled by foremen.

[4]For time series, the variation explained should be greater than 75 percent.

Fortunately, in business research knowing that a factor is not an important causal influence may be very important news for the organization. This information could save time and money otherwise invested in actions that are unlikely to produce results.

Bearing Bad Tidings

No one likes to bring bad news, but business researchers find themselves in that position from time to time. Here are some suggestions for dealing with bad news in your report.

- Use an ounce of prevention. If your initial investigation of the problem suggests that the results may be unfavorable, make sure management understands this possibility. Discussing it at that time can prevent the difficulty of unpleasant surprises at the reporting stage.

- If descriptive research shows that the current situation is poor, suggest what the causes might be. Offer a short proposal for research to examine them more closely and make recommendations.

- If forecasting prediction research suggests trouble ahead, make clear the basis on which the forecast is made, and suggest a solution. Indicate what specific factors contribute most to the unfavorable prediction and what would have to change to alter the forecast.

- If evaluation research finds no effects, or negative ones, for an otherwise popular program, practice, or policy, provide an analysis of intervening variables to explain why, and suggest what might be done to make a difference. Above all, make sure that the negative results are not an artifact of measurement or design problems.

- If explanatory research suggests that the only viable solution to a problem requires a decision that management doesn't want to make, make sure your report presents clearly the conclusions that lead to that recommendation. Also discuss why alternative steps won't achieve the desired result. Finally, estimate how, when, and to what degree the situation would improve if the recommended changes were to be made. This might involve some supplementary analysis with a prediction model.

Interference

Interference usually involves an attempt to suppress or modify certain conclusions. It is distinct from the consultation and collaboration with management that leads to relevant and feasible recommendations. Although it probably happens fairly rarely, interference can be a real problem when you are carrying out the research for your immediate superior and the interference comes from someone higher up the organizational ladder. The trade-off is sometimes stark: employment security and advancement versus professional and business ethics.

- Interference is best handled by anticipation. Forewarn managers of the possibility of negative findings, and try to avoid unpleasant surprises.

- Make sure that the report is as balanced as is reasonable. Don't concentrate solely on the negative. Recommend ways of improving a poor situation.

- Broaden your audience, and make sure they know who else knows about the results. Interference solely to protect one individual's interests at the expense of the organization is less likely to be tolerated by others.

Unfortunately, office politics being what they are, any research has the potential for upsetting someone. At the extreme your report may become a personal and political rather than a research issue. If so, you face some hard questions for which there are no easy answers. Are there other powerful people in the organization who will support you? Should you capitulate and take it as a hard lesson learned and resolve to avoid similar situations in the future? Should you bail out (of the department with a transfer, or out of the organization by securing a job somewhere else)? It may help to reconsider the ethical questions raised in Chapter 1.

■ *The Lighter Side of Research*

Do not put your faith in what statistics say until you have carefully considered what they do not say.

—William W. Watt

He uses statistics as a drunken man uses lampposts—for support rather than illumination.

—Andrew Lang

Summary

Business researchers use four different types of reports: formal, informal, interim, and oral. Their content, organization, and style are affected by three major factors: audience, importance of the problem, and whether the researcher wishes to be neutral or to advocate a particular action or recommendation.

The content of a report consists of a number of sections: Front Matter, Summary, Conclusions and Recommendations, Introduction or Background or Objectives, Literature Survey, Methodology and Procedures, The Sample, Policy or Program, Findings and Conclusions, End Matter, and Appendices.

The more formal the report, the more of these sections it is likely to contain. The organization of sections follows two general patterns: the logical and the order-of-importance. Writing style varies in formality, but should always be clear and concise.

Findings and conclusions are best organized by subsections corresponding to specific research questions. Within each subsection, proceed from a univariate description of the independent variable to bivariate and multivariate analysis. Conclude each subsection with supplementary analysis, conclusions, and a discussion of any limitations to which the conclusions are subject. Use tables and graphics to save space and make your points more vivid.

Recommendations are difficult to draft because of the subjectivity involved and the generalization and information required. To draft valid, relevant, and feasible recommendations, make sure they relate to valid conclusions, and consult with management about issues of feasibility and relevance.

If you find no results, look for methodological flaws that might account for the lack of findings. Try to forestall the problems of reporting bad news and interference in your research by forewarning your audience of possible negative results.

Where Are We Now?

You've finished. You've now followed the business research process through from the initial problem to recommendations for fixing it. There are two further steps you can take to increase your business research skills. One is to carry out real research projects. The second is to increase your facility with statistics and statistical computer packages. And above all, never lose sight of the fact that the end of business research is better business. Better research is the tool!

Discussion Issues and Assignments

1. In Chapter 2, Box 2.1 is Tom Harper's memo to the general manager, outlining a list of specific research questions. In what order would you suggest that Tom report his findings on these questions in his report?
2. Check newspapers and newsmagazines to find vague or misleading graphics. Indicate how you would correct them.
3. Locate a research report (ask professors who do consulting work).
   a. Try to rewrite a page to see if you can improve the style.
   b. Examine the overall organization. Reshuffle the parts as if you were writing to advocate a particular position.
   c. Consider which sections of those described in this chapter are missing from the report. Discuss why.
   d. How are the findings organized? Could the organization be improved?
   e. Examine the balance of data (tables, statistical tests) between the body of the report and the appendices. For what kind of audience would you divide it differently?

f. What kind of recommendations does the report suggest? Reword them to recommendations of another kind.

Further Reading

Lazarsfeld, P., and J. Reitz. 1975. *An Introduction to Applied Sociology.* New York: Elsevier.

> Chapter 5 contains very useful material on the process of working out recommendations.

Northey, Margot. 1986. *Impact: A Guide to Business Communication.* Scarborough, Ontario: Prentice-Hall.

> A very handy introduction to business writing. Chapters 9, 10, and 11 deal with informal and formal reports and oral presentations.

Strunk, William, Jr., and E. B. White. 1979. *The Elements of Style* (3rd ed.). New York: Macmillan.

> The classic guide to good writing. Both enjoyable and indispensable.

Wainer, Howard, and David Thissen. 1988. "Plotting in the Modern World: Statistics Packages and Good Graphics." *Chance* 1:10–20.

> A good review of the graphics available for statistical computing as well as examples of good and bad uses of figures and graphs.

APPENDIX A

An Introduction to Sampling Theory and Inferential Statistics

This appendix provides a short introduction to the basics of sampling and inferential statistics. By means of an extended example, it illustrates the following concepts: population, sample, estimate, sampling error, sampling distribution, standard error, confidence interval, and precision. It also demonstrates the effect of sample size and sample stratification on sampling error.

A SAMPLE EXAMPLE

A researcher wants to know how many days, on average, each employee of a very small firm was absent last year. He also wants to know how precise his estimate is.

Population

The researcher's work force *target population* consists of six employees, identified as A, B, C, D, E, and F. You know, although the researcher does not, how many days each employee has been absent:

Employee:	A	B	C	D	E	F
Days Absent:	1	3	3	5	7	9

You can therefore calculate the mean of "days absent" for the population:

$$\overline{X} = \frac{1 + 3 + 3 + 5 + 7 + 9}{6} = 4.67$$

The researcher, of course, doesn't know this.

Sample

To estimate the population mean for "days absent," the researcher draws a random *sample* of size two from the population of employees. He randomly chooses employees C and F, measures their absences, and calculates the mean days absent for his sample:

$$\overline{X} = \frac{3 + 9}{2} = 6.00$$

This sample mean becomes his *estimate* of the population mean. (It can be shown that the sample mean is the best (unbiased) estimate of the population mean.) The researcher has now answered one of his questions: he has an estimate of the population mean of number of days absent: 6.00.

Sampling Error

The next question is, How accurate is this estimate? You, the reader, can tell immediately: the difference between the researcher's estimate and the true population value is 6.00 − 4.67 = 1.33. However, the researcher doesn't know this. Instead, he must estimate the accuracy of his estimate. *How he goes about doing this is at the heart of inferential statistics.*

First, consider *why* the researcher's estimate has any error at all. Assuming no measurement error, the error in his estimate is due solely to *the chance involved in drawing a random sample.* Some samples (such as employees B and E) would give a highly accurate estimate; others (such as A and C) would give a very misleading one. This kind of error is called *sampling error:* it's the likelihood of drawing one of the unrepresentative samples.

We can now restate our researcher's problem. To estimate the precision of his population estimate of "days absent," he needs to know the chance of his drawing a bad sample, that is, the sampling error. (Keep in the back of your mind a second question: How can the researcher reduce the sampling error in order to improve his estimate of the population? We return to this later on when we look at sample size and sample stratification.)

Sampling Distribution

Before we can answer the researcher's question about the accuracy of his estimate, we must look a little more closely at sampling error. It occurs because of the particular sample the researcher randomly chose. If he had selected employees A and E, his estimate (the sample mean) would have been 4.0; if he had selected B and C, it would have been 3.0. In fact, there are 15 possible samples of size two he could have chosen (sampling without replacement). These samples, and their sample means, are as follows:

SAMPLE	VALUES	SAMPLE MEAN
A B	1, 3	2.0
A C	1, 3	2.0
A D	1, 5	3.0
A E	1, 7	4.0
A F	1, 9	5.0
B C	3, 3	3.0
B D	3, 5	4.0
B E	3, 7	5.0
B F	3, 9	6.0
C D	3, 5	4.0
C E	3, 7	5.0
C F	3, 9	6.0
D E	5, 7	6.0
D F	5, 9	7.0
E F	7, 9	8.0

As you can see (and remember that the researcher cannot), the researcher's estimate of the population mean (the sample mean) could have been as little as 2.0, or as high as 8.0, depending on which particular sample he drew.

The histogram showing the distribution of these sample means looks like this:

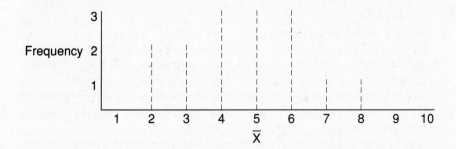

This distribution of the means of all possible samples (of size two) is very useful: its shape gives an idea of how many good and bad samples the researcher *could have* selected. In other words, it shows the sampling error of the researcher's sample. Most of the 15 possible samples would have produced a mean between 4 and 6. Only two samples would have given a mean as low as

2, and only one a mean as high as 8. (Note that other variables, such as age, would have different sampling distributions.)

This distribution allows you (but not the researcher) to calculate the probability of a poor sample, that is, one that is far from the population mean. The probability of a sample mean of two is $2/15$; the probability of a sample mean of eight is $1/15$. (The researcher can't calculate these probabilities because he doesn't know the days absent of each person in the population—only in his sample.)

This useful distribution of the means of all possible samples is called the *sampling distribution*. In practice, researchers never actually calculate it, since they never collect all possible samples. All they collect is data from one sample. (Do not confuse the sampling distribution with the distribution of the sample, which is determined from the data actually collected.)

As well as indicating by its shape how much sampling error the researcher might have, the sampling distribution has another useful feature: it can be shown that its mean is identical to the mean of the population, 4.67. (Try it out for yourself.) We make use of this feature in a moment.

The problem of estimating the sampling error now becomes a question of how to summarize information about the shape of the sampling distribution, since the sampling distribution indicates the probability that the researcher would draw a poor sample. In other words, how many possible samples would give estimates a long way from the mean of the sampling distribution?

Standard Error

The **standard error** of a variable is the standard deviation of the sampling distribution of means of that variable from all possible samples of size *n*. The lower the standard error, the lower the sampling error and the more accurate the population estimates of the variable (the higher the *precision*).

Intuitively you can see that if the sampling distribution were less spread out, sampling error would be low. No matter what sample our researcher chose, its mean wouldn't be far from the mean of the sampling distribution, and thus the population mean. On the other hand, if it were very spread out, then his chance of selecting a poor sample (and thus a poor estimate) would be much greater. There would be more possible samples with means far from the sampling distribution mean.

This suggests that the characteristic of the sampling distribution that is of most use in determining sampling error is its variation, or how spread out it is. This variation is conveniently measured by the distribution's *standard deviation*. The higher the standard deviation, the more spread out the distribution, and the more likely the researcher is to draw a sample with a mean far from the true population mean.

We give a special name to the standard deviation of the sampling distribution: the **standard error.** It is used as a measure of sampling error. You can easily calculate the standard error of our example sampling distribution: 1.70 (check it yourself). The poor researcher, however, cannot, since he doesn't have the sampling distribution. But he can try to *estimate* the sampling distribution's standard error.

Estimating the Standard Error

Up to this point, you can see how convenient the researcher's life would be if he only knew the sampling distribution. Its mean is equal to the population mean, and its standard error tells something about how likely he is to have a poor sample (sampling error). Unfortunately, the real sampling distribution is never known.

However, he can estimate the sampling distribution mean and standard error.

• The best (unbiased) estimate of the sampling distribution mean (and thus the population mean) is the sample mean. In general, *the sample mean or proportion is the best estimate of the population mean or proportion.*

• The best (unbiased) estimate of the standard error is the standard deviation of the sample divided by the square root of the sample size minus one:

$$SE = \frac{s}{\sqrt{(n-1)}}$$

where *n* is the sample size.

The researcher has already calculated his sample mean and used it to *estimate* the population mean. He now calculates the standard deviation of his sample:

$$s = \sqrt{\frac{\Sigma_i\,(X_i - \overline{X})^2}{n}} = 3.00$$

He then uses this, with the preceding formula, to *estimate* the standard error of the sampling distribution. (Confirm that the estimated standard error is 3.0 in his two-employee sample.) He is now in a position to say something about the accuracy of his population estimate.

Before we see how he does this, let's just review where we are:

• You can use a sample not only to estimate a population mean (or proportion), but also to estimate the precision of your estimate! This simple fact underlies all inferential statistics.

• It will help to clarify things if you keep in mind the four separate distributions:

   1. The *population* of cases, the mean of which you want to estimate with known precision.

   2. The *sampling distribution* of the means of all possible samples of size *n*. This is never calculated. It is the theoretical link between the population and your sample.

3. The *estimated sampling distribution,* the mean and standard error of which you calculate from . . .

4. The *sample* (of *n* cases) you actually draw, the mean and standard deviation of which you can readily calculate.

- The researcher *knows*
  Sample mean (6.00)
  Sample standard deviation (3.00)

- The researcher *has estimated*
  Mean of the sampling distribution and population (6.00)
  Standard error of the sampling distribution (3.00)

Precision, Confidence Intervals, and Probabilities

The researcher now wants to say, in more exact terms, just how precise he believes is his estimate of the population mean. To indicate **precision,** researchers use statements of the following form: "The probability is P that the true population mean lies within A units of X." In other words, *the combination of a probability and the width of a range around the population estimate provides the statement of the precision of that estimate.* The range around the estimate is called a confidence interval.

> **A confidence interval** is a range, on either side of the estimated mean, within which the researcher believes the true population mean falls with a certain probability.

Researchers express the width of confidence intervals in standard errors from the sampling distribution mean. (In the example, the estimated mean is 6.0 and the estimated standard error is 3.0. Thus a confidence interval two standard errors wide would lie between 3.0 and 9.0; a confidence interval four standard errors wide would lie between 0.0 and 12.0.)

We now have the confidence interval range. How do we get the probability that a point falls within that range? To do this, we make use of the **normal distribution.**

Statisticians have shown that as the sample size grows larger, *every* sampling distribution of sample means approaches the shape of the normal curve, *regardless* of the shape of the population distribution. This is fortunate, because we know from other statisticians who have studied the properties of normal curves that any point has a certain probability of falling a certain distance from the mean. This distance is given in standard deviations. The probability is the proportion the area under the curve from the mean to the point represents of all the area under the curve. Thus, for example, the probability that a point will fall between the mean and two standard deviations above the mean is .4773. That is, the area under the curve from the mean to the +2 standard deviation point is 47.73 percent of the total area under the curve.

Researchers use tables of normal curve probabilities to find the probability that a point will be within a given distance (in standard deviations) from the mean of a normal distribution (see Appendix B). Applying this to the *sampling distribution,* researchers calculate *the probability that a sample of the size they use falls within a given number of standard errors of the mean of the sampling distribution.*

For example, if the estimated mean of a sampling distribution is 50, and the estimated standard error is 5, the researcher can calculate the probability of getting a sample with a mean between 40 and 60, that is, within two standard errors of the estimated mean. This probability is .9546.

Of course, the researcher's actual sample mean is 50. But he knows (or can estimate) that his sample mean (and thus the estimated population mean) *might have been* anywhere between 40 and 60 with a 95 percent probability.

Typically researchers select confidence intervals with probabilities of either .90 or .95, and then consult tables to see how many standard errors wide the confidence interval must be to reflect this probability of containing the population mean. The table of normal curve probabilities (Appendix B) indicates a probability of .95 that a point will lie within 1.96 standard deviations on either side of the mean. (With small samples, replace 1.96 with the appropriate value from the t distribution table in Appendix B.)

Back in our example, the researcher calculates that, since the estimated population mean is 6.0 days absent and the estimated standard error is 3.0 days, then the probability is .95 that the population mean falls within the confidence interval ranging from $6 - 1.96(3.0)$ to $6 + 1.96(3.0)$, or 0.12 to 11.88. This range is the *95% confidence interval* for the estimated mean days absent of the population. It indicates the estimated precision of the researcher's estimate. The researcher's confidence interval is interpreted this way: if he drew 20 separate and independent samples of size two, in 19 of them the true population mean would fall within the calculated 95% confidence interval of 0.12 days to 11.88 days.

The researcher has now answered his two questions: he has a population estimate, and he has an estimate of the precision of his estimate. He did it all with just the mean and standard deviation of his sample!

Sample Size Effects

But now the researcher is asking another question: How could he get a more accurate estimate of the population mean of "days absent"? With his sample of size two, the 95% confidence interval is quite wide (about zero to 12 days). His estimate of 6 days isn't very precise.

It should now be clear that the smaller the standard error of the sampling distribution, the smaller the confidence interval will be. Thus smaller standard errors mean greater *precision*. But how can the researcher reduce the sampling error in order to improve the precision of his population estimate? The answer is that our researcher can do two things: increase sample size or stratify the sample. Let us see first how sample size affects the standard error of sampling distributions.

Suppose the researcher increases his sample size to three. There are now 20 possible samples of size 3 (sampling without replacement). To save space, here are the sample means for the first five and the last:

SAMPLE	VALUES	SAMPLE MEAN
A B C	1, 3, 3	2.3
A B D	1, 3, 5	3.0
A B E	1, 3, 7	3.7
A B F	1, 3, 9	4.3
A C D	1, 3, 5	3.0
. . . .		
D E F	5, 7, 9	7.0

The histogram showing this sample distribution looks like this:

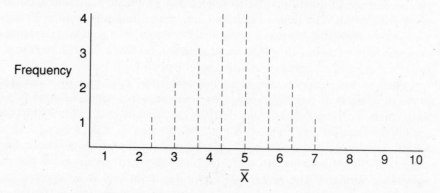

The mean of this sampling distribution is 4.67. As we'd expect, this is the same as the mean of the sampling distribution of samples of size two and identical to the population mean. The actual standard error is 1.20, substantially less than the 1.70 standard error for the sampling distribution of samples of size two. Compare the shapes of the two sampling distributions. Notice how this one appears to be more compact and less spread out. The worst samples of size three would have more accurate means than the worst samples of size two.

This example demonstrates that, as sample size increases, standard error (and thus sampling error) declines. The amount of this decline can be seen from the formula (approximate) relating standard error to population standard deviation:

$$SE = \frac{\sigma}{\sqrt{n}}$$

Since the population standard deviation (σ) remains constant, it is apparent that as *n* increases, SE decreases.

Furthermore, because SE is related to the square root of *n*, in order to cut the standard error in half, the researcher would have to increase the sample size fourfold. Thus reducing sampling error by increasing sample size has diminishing returns. Each additional 100 cases reduces the sampling error successively less. This is why, after a point, increasing sample size in order to reduce sampling error becomes just too expensive. But there are other ways to reduce sampling error, among them using a stratified sample.

Stratified Samples

Suppose that employees A, B, and C work in one plant, and D, E, and F work in another. As you can see, employees in the first plant tend to have fewer days absent. While you know this, the researcher can only guess it. On the basis of his hunch that plant is related to days absent, he decides to stratify his sample by plant. He draws a sample of total size two, this time taking one employee randomly from each plant.

Look what happens to the sampling distribution. The result of stratifying the sample is to reduce the number of possible samples from 15 to 9:

SAMPLE	VALUES	SAMPLE MEAN
A D	1, 5	3.0
A E	1, 7	4.0
A F	1, 9	5.0
B D	3, 5	4.0
B E	3, 7	5.0
B F	3, 9	6.0
C D	3, 5	4.0
C E	3, 7	5.0
C F	3, 9	6.0

The histogram showing this sampling distribution looks like this:

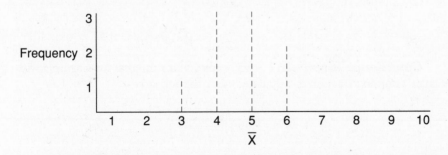

The mean is still 4.67, but this time the standard error has dropped to 0.94 from 1.70. Clearly, stratifying the sample lowered the sampling error significantly. It did this by *deleting the most unrepresentative possible samples.* (Check by comparing the original list of 15 possible samples of size two with the 9 above.)

Stratification reduces sampling error when (1) the strata are relatively homogeneous, compared to the population, and (2) different from one another in terms of the stratification variable ("days absent" in this example). The example meets both criteria: in the first plant, the days absent were 1, 3, and 3; in the second, 5, 7, and 9.

Suppose the researcher had decided to stratify on gender instead of plant. Employees A, C, and F are females; B, D, and E are males. As you can see, the two strata are far from homogeneous. Females are absent 1, 3, and 9 days; males are absent 3, 5, and 7 days. The means of the two groups are not very different.

The standard error for this stratified sample is 1.89, which is larger than the standard error for the unstratified sample, 1.70. Thus stratifying on a variable for which the cases in each stratum are not somewhat homogeneous may provide no reduction at all in sampling error.

To summarize, the concept of sampling distribution helps make clear the effect on the standard error (the measure of sampling error) of (1) increases in sampling size and (2) stratifying on variables that are homogeneous within strata. We end with a discussion of the finite population correction, sometimes applied to confidence intervals, hypothesis tests, and significance tests.

Finite Population Correction

The finite population correction was mentioned in Box 7.4 in Chapter 7. Here we discuss details of its calculation and use.

If the sampling fraction is greater than 20 percent (10 percent when you need more precise estimates), you should apply the **finite population correction** to your calculations of confidence intervals, hypothesis tests (Chapter 15), and significance tests (Chapter 16). Failure to apply the correction will result in confidence estimates that are too conservative.

To apply the correction, first determine f, the sampling fraction, and then multiply the standard deviation (or standard error) by the term

$$\sqrt{1 - f}$$

Confidence Intervals. A 95% confidence interval for a sample with a large sampling fraction is calculated with the formula

$$\overline{X} \pm 1.96 \left(\frac{s\sqrt{1 - f}}{\sqrt{n - 1}} \right)$$

For example, if you sampled 135 machinery orders out of a population of 366 and found a mean of 4.3 postinstallation adjustments, with a standard deviation of 2.7, your 95% confidence interval is 3.9 to 4.7 using the finite population correction. It would be 3.8 to 4.8 without the correction. Note that with the correction, the confidence interval is somewhat smaller, and thus the estimate more precise.

Estimates involving proportions involve an identical adjustment: multiply the estimate of the standard error (the square root of $p(1-p)/n$) by the finite population correction:

$$p \pm 1.96\sqrt{1-f}\left(\sqrt{\frac{p(1-p)}{n}}\right)$$

For example, the 95% confidence interval for the proportion of management teams reporting "satisfaction" with a week-long training seminar, with the sample proportion satisfied at .76, a sample size of 110, and a population of 249, is .70 to .82.

Hypothesis Testing.   To see whether the population mean or proportion is equivalent to (or greater or less than) a particular standard value, use the finite population correction when the sampling fraction is large.

If in the hospital example (see p. 540) the population of admission interviews was only 500, the sample size of 144 would give a sampling fraction of .288 and a finite population correction of .844. Adding this term to the calculations produces a new critical region: .59 minutes above the hypothesized standard value, or any value greater than 12.59 minutes. The effect is to increase the size of the critical region in which the null hypothesis can be rejected.

Significance Tests.   The procedure is the same with tests of statistical significance. Multiply estimates of standard deviation (or standard error) by the finite population correction term.

APPENDIX B

Statistical Tables

09188	20097	32825	39527	04220	86304	83389	87374	64278	58044
90045	85497	51981	50654	94938	81997	91870	76150	68476	64659
73189	50207	47677	26269	62290	64464	27124	67018	41361	82760
75768	76490	20971	87749	90429	12272	95375	05871	93823	43178
54016	44056	66281	31003	00682	27398	20714	53295	07706	17813
08358	69910	78542	42785	13661	58873	04618	97553	31223	08420
28306	03264	81333	10591	40510	07893	32604	60475	94119	01840
53840	86233	81594	13628	51215	90290	28466	68795	77762	20791
91757	53741	61613	62269	50263	90212	55781	76514	83483	47055
89415	92694	00397	58391	12607	17646	48949	72306	94541	37408
77513	03820	86864	29901	68414	82774	51908	13980	72893	55507
19502	37174	69979	20288	55210	29773	74287	75251	65344	67415
21818	59313	93278	81757	05686	73156	07082	85046	31853	38452
51474	66499	68107	23621	94049	91345	42836	09191	08007	45449
99559	68331	62535	24170	69777	12830	74819	78142	43860	72834
33713	48007	93584	72869	51926	64721	58303	29822	93174	93972
85274	86893	11303	22970	28834	34137	73515	90400	71148	43643
84133	89640	44035	52166	73852	70091	61222	60561	62327	18423
56732	16234	17395	96131	10123	91622	85496	57560	81604	18880
65138	56806	87648	85261	34313	65861	45875	21069	85644	47277
38001	02176	81719	11711	71602	92937	74219	64049	65584	49698
37402	96397	01304	77586	56271	10086	47324	62605	40030	37438
97125	40348	87083	31417	21815	39250	75237	62047	15501	29578
21826	41134	47143	34072	64638	85902	49139	06441	03856	54552
73135	42742	95719	09035	85794	74296	08789	88156	64691	19202
07638	77929	03061	18072	96207	44156	23821	99538	04713	66994
60528	83441	07954	19814	59175	23695	05533	52139	61212	06455
83596	35655	06958	92983	05128	09719	77433	53783	92301	50498
10850	62746	99599	10507	13499	06319	53075	71839	06410	19362
39820	98952	43622	63147	64421	80814	43800	09351	31024	73167

59580	06478	75569	78800	88835	54486	23768	06156	04111	08408
38508	07341	23793	48763	90822	97022	17719	04207	95954	49953
30692	70668	94688	16127	56196	80091	82067	63400	05462	69200
65443	95659	18288	27437	49632	24041	08337	65676	96299	90836
27267	50264	13192	72294	07477	44606	17985	48911	97341	30358
91307	06991	19072	24210	36699	53728	28825	35793	28976	66252
68434	94688	84473	13622	62126	98408	12843	82590	09815	93146
48908	15877	54745	24591	35700	04754	83824	52692	54130	55160
06913	45197	42672	78601	11883	09528	63011	98901	14974	40344
10455	16019	14210	33712	91342	37821	88325	80851	43667	70883
12883	97343	65027	61184	04285	01392	17974	15077	90712	26769
21778	30976	38807	36961	31649	42096	63281	02023	08816	47449
19523	59515	65122	59659	86283	68258	69572	13798	16435	91529
67245	52670	35583	16563	79246	86686	76463	34222	26655	90802
60584	47377	07500	37992	45134	26529	26760	83637	41326	44344
53853	41377	36066	94850	58838	73859	49364	73331	96240	43642
24637	38736	74384	89342	52623	07992	12369	18601	03742	83873
83080	12451	38992	22815	07759	51777	97377	27585	51972	37867
16444	24334	36151	99073	27493	70939	85130	32552	54846	54759
60790	18157	57178	65762	11161	78576	45819	52979	65130	04860
59467	58309	87834	57213	37510	33689	01259	62486	56320	46265
73452	17619	56421	40725	23439	41701	93223	41682	45026	47505
27635	56293	91700	04391	67317	89604	73020	69853	61517	51207
86040	02596	01655	09918	45161	00222	54577	74821	47335	08582
52403	94255	26351	46527	68224	90183	85057	72310	34963	83462
49465	46581	61499	04844	94626	02963	41482	83879	44942	63915
94365	92560	12363	30246	02086	75036	88620	91088	67691	67762
34261	08769	91830	23313	18256	28850	37639	92748	57791	71328
37110	66538	39318	15626	44324	82827	08782	65960	58167	01305
83950	45424	72453	19444	68219	64733	94088	62006	89985	36936

61630	97966	76537	46467	30942	07479	67971	14558	22458	35148
01929	17165	12037	74558	16250	71750	55546	29693	94984	37782
41659	39098	23982	29899	71594	77979	54477	13764	17315	72893
32031	39608	75992	73445	01317	50525	87313	45191	30214	19769
90043	93478	58044	06949	31176	88370	50274	83987	45316	38551
79418	14322	91065	07841	36130	86602	10659	40859	00964	71577
85447	61079	96910	72906	07361	84338	34114	52096	66715	51091
86219	81115	49625	48799	89485	24855	13684	68433	70595	70102
71712	88559	92476	32903	68009	58417	87962	11787	16644	72964
29776	63075	13270	84758	49560	10317	28778	23006	31036	84906
81488	17340	74154	42801	27917	89792	62604	62234	13124	76471
51667	37589	87147	24743	48023	06325	79794	35889	13255	04925
99004	70322	60832	76636	56907	56534	72615	46288	36788	93196
68656	66492	35933	52293	47953	95495	95304	50009	83464	28608
38074	74083	09337	07965	65047	36871	59015	21769	30398	44855
01020	80680	59328	08712	48190	45332	27284	31287	66011	09376
86379	74508	33579	77114	92955	23085	92824	03054	25242	16322
48498	09938	44420	13484	52319	58875	02012	88591	52500	95795
41800	95363	54142	17482	32705	60564	12505	40954	46174	64130
63026	96712	79883	39225	52653	69549	36693	59822	22684	31661
88298	15489	16030	42480	15372	38781	71995	77438	91161	10192
07839	62735	99218	25624	02547	27445	69187	55749	32322	15504
73298	51108	48717	92926	75705	89787	96114	99902	37749	96305
12829	70474	00838	50385	91711	80370	56504	56857	80906	09018
76569	61072	48568	36491	22587	44363	39592	61546	90181	37348
41665	41339	62106	44203	06732	76111	79840	67999	32231	76869
58652	49983	01669	27464	79553	52855	25988	18087	38052	17529
13607	00657	76173	43357	77334	24140	53860	02906	89863	44651
55715	26203	65933	51087	98234	40625	45545	63563	89148	82581
04110	66683	99001	09796	47349	65003	66524	81970	71262	14479

31300	08681	58068	44115	40064	77879	23965	69019	73985	19453
26225	97543	37044	07494	85778	35345	61115	92498	49737	64599
07158	82763	25072	38478	57782	75291	62155	52056	04786	11585
71251	25572	79771	93328	66927	54069	58752	26624	50463	77361
29991	96526	02820	91659	12818	96356	49499	01507	40223	09171
83642	21057	02677	09367	38097	16100	19355	06120	15378	56559
69167	30235	06767	66323	78294	14916	19124	88044	16673	66102
86018	29406	75415	22038	27056	26906	25867	14751	92380	30434
44114	06026	79553	55091	41212	95385	37882	46864	54717	97038
53805	64150	70915	63127	41288	63695	38192	72437	75075	18570
03474	76025	97043	33834	44638	54040	82797	00545	38159	16089
35870	89158	55864	98078	50563	36492	10994	85909	09018	19252
73887	67928	60045	70782	11937	04074	53814	46621	52577	94853
45968	73667	65062	73306	76045	78649	91654	53958	96537	95542
67622	54579	17279	67440	56441	20681	64011	52226	96618	32831
60664	67547	39523	02043	59748	01887	69229	94653	99271	98164
62155	09234	47367	13047	06364	35064	10073	06793	80248	29009
44969	11129	17139	79630	89772	26921	56949	23465	30036	17173
82459	96218	60768	76417	24405	18710	68887	82394	69729	82503
40873	41590	67255	30757	09657	91881	34578	09511	05417	58953
18532	10721	22029	48524	47778	00881	83489	03464	57462	97459
86689	39755	39547	00740	36666	07993	31671	86304	12970	73402
52849	31652	79655	11250	18463	57518	20306	25301	01374	51208
33298	87662	61849	60923	68685	69411	39266	80320	34844	89416
81569	83651	35795	40168	33501	01042	58931	03892	85188	74740
85476	23790	33842	89565	53359	25579	59049	62394	72435	12457
21904	18370	97035	57905	09581	91227	92754	37760	01411	07440
87175	88318	63242	85960	56690	12618	30493	11569	73723	07448
58830	00157	65814	21118	22140	73793	57855	81830	06795	13183
12625	30635	56429	73216	12342	36722	83886	96828	82870	90954

97614	02370	42160	73370	11944	49067	59452	80495	43911	46712
17033	68037	41963	03874	44856	82985	57453	84358	16120	04454
76624	00405	62369	55080	61880	51270	87807	10653	36894	70850
35660	00234	14705	93418	94084	82856	25384	71555	56754	78315
18291	91656	98079	52384	43306	65205	75903	58701	99496	50048
33557	87793	90857	10143	46726	84284	43635	41213	83845	70986
91408	80220	05728	68890	46577	21152	43759	43301	93661	97252
50106	10099	13722	18572	44024	00351	18173	23717	85114	85998
57782	63951	53723	86853	63851	79430	49181	46386	69666	55743
76162	71724	40028	94786	34457	16906	90040	30789	40281	94697
96584	81907	04055	53990	66397	80579	42517	78181	39251	09467
67097	95523	66568	63632	71048	15581	39904	75774	77495	75994
29911	65690	41178	47712	70355	16998	56025	05230	10093	71495
34784	70950	54680	57811	53782	39145	36829	85342	40406	35883
45668	03459	29870	78252	70088	70621	67153	05737	40933	91075
93335	86853	15860	81167	91259	16118	52401	83593	84474	02423
75608	39646	90871	70284	82100	96032	05115	63678	02225	88087
58581	44364	57468	21539	13042	64150	63754	05210	87644	54114
64013	63562	41388	32397	74152	23982	71982	71700	33026	66477
47838	46712	39848	35083	65927	97868	11067	76771	71799	43836
41014	97025	93225	08511	63096	26628	73012	12543	76269	99708
02629	49845	73677	19193	14924	57236	95564	15010	59667	73773
78515	02624	99744	13585	33746	58771	94785	62628	99585	11363
80832	59979	09444	78700	02596	85984	69438	16913	96475	93283
18625	77086	45911	39746	64722	39938	43930	54619	00302	50384
02738	75714	75249	95439	80714	52555	47266	96190	78750	94973
83669	16479	53163	48071	28000	45011	26733	67132	83362	84162
43028	08415	27236	52651	89059	64844	80910	01676	91752	57815
26264	03415	57532	29981	61200	96036	62600	20068	56530	38487
08432	89514	26883	69165	97237	22361	55276	39902	95927	82190

Source: Rand Corporation, *A Million Random Digits with 100,000 Normal Deviates.* (Glencoe, IL: Free Press, 1955).

TABLE B.2 ■ AREA UNDER THE NORMAL CURVE[a]

z	.00	.01	.02	.03	.04	.05	.06	.07	.08	.09
0.0	.0000	.0040	.0080	.0120	.0160	.0199	.0239	.0279	.0319	.0359
0.1	.0398	.0438	.0478	.0517	.0557	.0596	.0636	.0675	.0714	.0753
0.2	.0793	.0832	.0871	.0910	.0948	.0987	.1026	.1064	.1103	.1141
0.3	.1179	.1217	.1255	.1293	.1331	.1368	.1406	.1443	.1480	.1517
0.4	.1554	.1591	.1628	.1664	.1700	.1736	.1772	.1808	.1844	.1879
0.5	.1915	.1950	.1985	.2019	.2054	.2088	.2123	.2157	.2190	.2224
0.6	.2257	.2291	.2324	.2357	.2389	.2422	.2454	.2486	.2517	.2549
0.7	.2580	.2611	.2642	.2673	.2704	.2734	.2764	.2794	.2823	.2852
0.8	.2881	.2910	.2939	.2967	.2995	.3023	.3051	.3078	.3106	.3133
0.9	.3159	.3186	.3212	.3238	.3264	.3289	.3315	.3340	.3365	.3389
1.0	.3413	.3438	.3461	.3485	.3508	.3531	.3554	.3577	.3599	.3621
1.1	.3643	.3665	.3686	.3708	.3729	.3749	.3770	.3790	.3810	.3830
1.2	.3849	.3869	.3888	.3907	.3925	.3944	.3962	.3980	.3997	.4015
1.3	.4032	.4049	.4066	.4082	.4099	.4115	.4131	.4147	.4162	.4177
1.4	.4192	.4207	.4222	.4236	.4251	.4265	.4279	.4292	.4306	.4319
1.5	.4332	.4345	.4357	.4370	.4382	.4394	.4406	.4418	.4429	.4441
1.6	.4452	.4463	.4474	.4484	.4495	.4505	.4515	.4525	.4535	.4545
1.7	.4554	.4564	.4573	.4582	.4591	.4599	.4608	.4616	.4625	.4633
1.8	.4641	.4649	.4656	.4664	.4671	.4678	.4686	.4693	.4699	.4706
1.9	.4713	.4719	.4726	.4732	.4738	.4744	.4750	.4756	.4761	.4767
2.0	.4772	.4778	.4783	.4788	.4793	.4798	.4803	.4808	.4812	.4817
2.1	.4821	.4826	.4830	.4834	.4838	.4842	.4846	.4850	.4854	.4857
2.2	.4861	.4864	.4868	.4871	.4875	.4878	.4881	.4884	.4887	.4890
2.3	.4893	.4896	.4898	.4901	.4904	.4906	.4909	.4911	.4913	.4916
2.4	.4918	.4920	.4922	.4925	.4927	.4929	.4931	.4932	.4934	.4936
2.5	.4938	.4940	.4941	.4943	.4945	.4946	.4948	.4949	.4951	.4952

z	.00	.01	.02	.03	.04	.05	.06	.07	.08	.09
2.6	.4953	.4955	.4956	.4957	.4959	.4960	.4961	.4962	.4963	.4964
2.7	.4965	.4966	.4967	.4968	.4969	.4970	.4971	.4972	.4973	.4974
2.8	.4974	.4975	.4976	.4977	.4977	.4978	.4979	.4979	.4980	.4981
2.9	.4981	.4982	.4982	.4983	.4984	.4984	.4985	.4985	.4986	.4986
3.0	.4987	.4987	.4987	.4988	.4988	.4989	.4989	.4989	.4990	.4990

[a]Distance from mean in z standard deviations. Area is proportion of total area under curve, e.g.: the probability of falling between the mean and 1.55 standard deviations above the mean equals the proportion of the area under the curve in this region, which equals .4394.

Source: Abridged from Table I of *Statistical Tables and Formulas* by A. Hald (New York: John Wiley & Sons, Inc., 1952). Reproduced by permission of A. Hald and the publishers, John Wiley & Sons, Inc. Copyright © 1952 by John Wiley & Sons, Inc.

TABLE B.3 ■ DISTRIBUTION OF STUDENT'S t

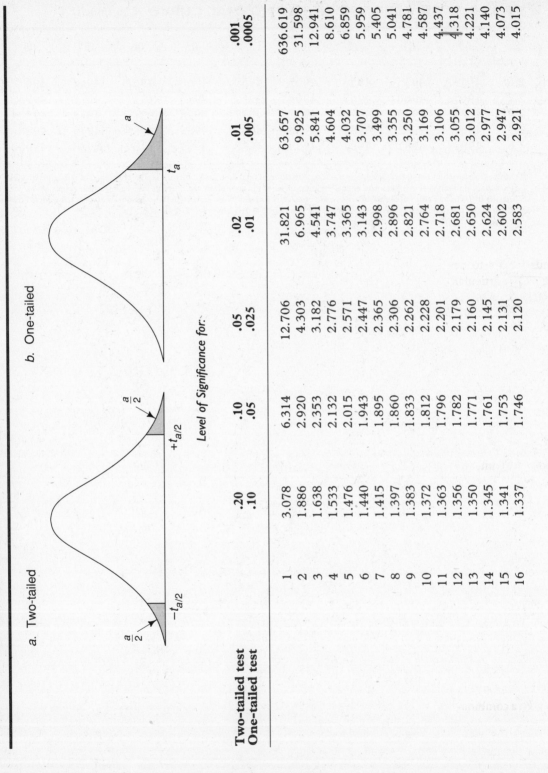

a. Two-tailed

b. One-tailed

	.20 .10	.10 .05	.05 .025	.02 .01	.01 .005	.001 .0005
	Level of Significance for:					
Two-tailed test	.20	.10	.05	.02	.01	.001
One-tailed test	.10	.05	.025	.01	.005	.0005
1	3.078	6.314	12.706	31.821	63.657	636.619
2	1.886	2.920	4.303	6.965	9.925	31.598
3	1.638	2.353	3.182	4.541	5.841	12.941
4	1.533	2.132	2.776	3.747	4.604	8.610
5	1.476	2.015	2.571	3.365	4.032	6.859
6	1.440	1.943	2.447	3.143	3.707	5.959
7	1.415	1.895	2.365	2.998	3.499	5.405
8	1.397	1.860	2.306	2.896	3.355	5.041
9	1.383	1.833	2.262	2.821	3.250	4.781
10	1.372	1.812	2.228	2.764	3.169	4.587
11	1.363	1.796	2.201	2.718	3.106	4.437
12	1.356	1.782	2.179	2.681	3.055	4.318
13	1.350	1.771	2.160	2.650	3.012	4.221
14	1.345	1.761	2.145	2.624	2.977	4.140
15	1.341	1.753	2.131	2.602	2.947	4.073
16	1.337	1.746	2.120	2.583	2.921	4.015

TABLE B.3 ■ DISTRIBUTION OF STUDENT'S t (Continued)

Level of Significance for:

	Two-tailed test	.20	.10	.05	.02	.01	.001
	One-tailed test	.10	.05	.025	.01	.005	.0005
17		1.333	1.740	2.110	2.567	2.898	3.965
18		1.330	1.734	2.101	2.552	2.878	3.922
19		1.328	1.729	2.093	2.539	2.861	3.883
20		1.325	1.725	2.086	2.528	2.845	3.850
21		1.323	1.721	2.080	2.518	2.831	3.819
22		1.321	1.717	2.074	2.508	2.819	3.792
23		1.319	1.714	2.069	2.500	2.807	3.767
24		1.318	1.711	2.064	2.492	2.797	3.745
25		1.316	1.708	2.060	2.485	2.787	3.725
26		1.315	1.706	2.056	2.479	2.779	3.707
27		1.314	1.703	2.052	2.473	2.771	3.690
28		1.313	1.701	2.048	2.467	2.763	3.674
29		1.311	1.699	2.045	2.462	2.756	3.659
30		1.310	1.697	2.042	2.457	2.750	3.646
40		1.303	1.684	2.021	2.423	2.704	3.551
60		1.296	1.671	2.000	2.390	2.660	3.460
120		1.289	1.658	1.980	2.358	2.617	3.373
∞		1.282	1.645	1.960	2.326	2.576	3.291

Source: Adapted from Table III of Fisher & Yates: *Statistical Tables for Biological, Agricultural and Medical Research,* published by Longman Group UK Ltd. London (1974) 6th edition. Previously published by Oliver & Boyd Ltd. Edinburgh; reproduced by permission of the authors and publishers.

Suggested Questions and Response Categories for Demographic and Other Variables in Survey Studies

The wordings and categories suggested here are appropriate for survey business research (questionnaires or interviews). They may also provide categories for available data studies. Adapt them as necessary to meet your particular needs.[1]

Where different categories or response formats are required, "I" refers to an interview format; "Q" refers to the questionnaire format.

Age

I: In what year were you born? 19_____
Q: Year of birth? 19_____

Marital Status

Married or living together	1
Widowed	2
Divorced or separated	3
Never married	4

Gender

Male	1
Female	2

---

[1]These suggested wordings are adapted from a number of sources, including research conducted by the author and his students and the Social Science Research Council (1975).

Region *(Continental U.S.A.)*

New England	1
Middle Atlantic	2
East North-Central	3
West North-Central	4
South Atlantic	5
East South-Central	6
West South-Central	7
Mountain	8
Pacific	9

Region *(Canada)*

British Columbia	1
Prairie provinces	2
Ontario	3
Quebec	4
Atlantic provinces	5
Territories	6

Education

1: What is the highest grade or year you finished in regular school or college?

COLLEGE = 13 to 16
GRADUATE STUDY = 17
ENTER TWO-DIGIT CODE: —— ——

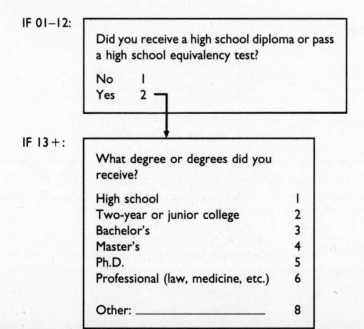

IF 01–12:

Did you receive a high school diploma or pass a high school equivalency test?

No   1
Yes   2

IF 13+:

What degree or degrees did you receive?

High school	1
Two-year or junior college	2
Bachelor's	3
Master's	4
Ph.D.	5
Professional (law, medicine, etc.)	6
Other: _____	8

Q: What is the highest grade or year you finished in regular school or college?

Less than grade 8	1
Grade 8	2
Grades 9 to 11	3
Grade 12	4
Grade 13 (Canada only)	5
Some college or university	6
Two-year college degree	7
Four-year college degree	8
Some postgraduate work	9
Professional degree	10
Master's or Ph.D. degree	11
Other: _____	12

Training

I: Besides your regular schooling, have you ever attended any other kind of school for six months or more, such as vocational training?

No   1
Yes   2

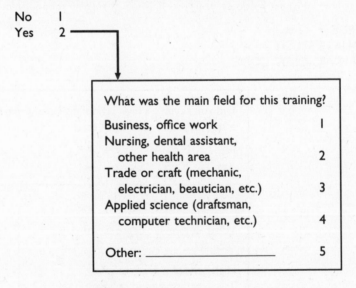

What was the main field for this training?	
Business, office work	1
Nursing, dental assistant, other health area	2
Trade or craft (mechanic, electrician, beautician, etc.)	3
Applied science (draftsman, computer technician, etc.)	4
Other: _____	5

Q: Besides your regular schooling, have you ever attended any other kind of school, such as vocational training, for six months or more?

CHECK ANY THAT APPLY.
[same categories as above]

Employment Status

I: Are you now working at a paying job, doing unpaid work, unemployed, going
to school, or retired?

Has a paying job	I
Has an unpaid job, family business	2
Keeping house, child rearing	3
Unemployed	4
At school	5
Retired	6
Disabled, too ill to work	7
Other: _____	8

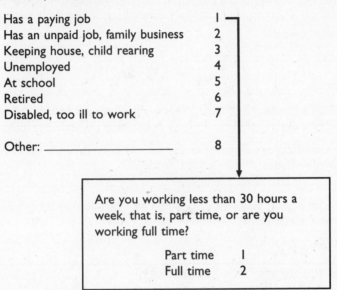

Are you working less than 30 hours a
week, that is, part time, or are you
working full time?

Part time	I
Full time	2

Q: Are you now working at a paying job?

Keeping house, child rearing	I
Unemployed at present	2
At school	3
Retired	4
Disabled, too ill to work	5
Work at an unpaid job or family business	6
Have a job, but not working now (e.g., temporary layoff)	7
Work at a paying job	8
Other: _____	9

Are you working full time, or working
less than 30 hours a week, that is, part
time?

Full time	I
Part time	2

Industry

There are widely accepted *industry* codes. For the United States, use the Bureau of the Census Standard Industrial Classification (SIC) codes. Statistics Canada also has a set of industrial codes. Two-digit codes are sufficient for most business research.

Occupation

I: What kind of work do you do? What is your main occupation called?

_____

Tell me a little more about what you actually do in that job. What are some of your main duties?

_____

What kind of business or industry is that in? What do they do or make at the place where you work?

_____

Q: Please describe your main occupation.

Title:

Kind of work you do:

Kind of business or industry:

Alternatively, you can use a set of response categories and ask the respondent to select the one that represents his or her occupation.

How would you classify your occupation, the kind of work you regularly do?

There are a wide variety of occupation lists; the most detailed is the U.S. Bureau of the Census classification. The best strategy is to use a set of categories that reflects the *dimension* relevant to your research problem. Examples of such dimensions are content of work (hands/head, people/things, unskilled/semiskilled/skilled, blue collar/white collar), industry, social status of job, responsibility of job, amount of training or education required by job, and amount of management or supervision the job entails.

Unfortunately, there is no single widely accepted list of occupations for any of these dimensions. Because most lists incorporate two or more dimensions, researchers have to adapt or create lists that suit their needs. Here are three typical lists; revise them as needed to suit your target population:

List A

Farmer or
  fisherman
Laborer
Retail sales
Wholesale and
  other sales
Service worker
Skilled service
  occupation
Clerical worker
Machine operator
  or driver
Skilled trade
Supervisor
Technician
Manager or owner
Professional

List B

Clerical and general
  office work
Sales occupation
Service occupation
Farming, fishing,
  mining, forestry
Manual laborer
Skilled or semi-
  skilled trades
Transportation
First-level
  supervisor
Teaching
Scientific and
  technical
Social and artistic
Executive, managerial,
  and related
Housewife
Professional

List C

Technician
Skilled crafts
Service worker
All other blue-collar
  occupations
Teachers, accountants,
  nurses, and similar
  occupations
Sales and clerical
Supervisor or foreman
Manager
Physician, lawyer,
  dentist, architect,
  etc.
Business owner

Union Membership

I: Are you a member of a labor union?
    Yes   I
    No   2

Even though you are not a member, do
you happen to know whether a labor
union bargains with management on your
behalf?

            Yes   I
            No   2
            Don't know   9

Do you know whether *any* workers at
your place of work are unionized?

            Yes   I
            No   2
            Don't know   9

Q: Are you a member of a trade union?

    Yes   I

    No   2

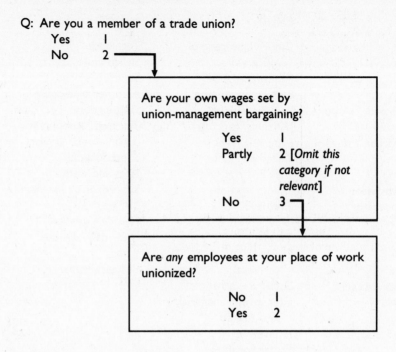

Are your own wages set by union-management bargaining?

        Yes   I

        Partly   2 [*Omit this category if not relevant*]

        No   3

Are *any* employees at your place of work unionized?

        No   I

        Yes   2

Income

Tailor the response categories for income questions to fit the target population. If they also correspond to categories in existing sources of income data, you can compare distributions to judge whether your sample is representative.

I: HAND CARD TO RESPONDENT. Would you please tell me the letter on the card that best represents your total family income in 19____before taxes? This should include wages and salaries, net income from business or farm, pensions, dividends, interest, rent, and any other money income received by all those people in the household who are related to you.

ENTER TWO-DIGIT CODE: ____ ____

A.	Under $4,000	01
B.	$4,000 to 5,999	02
C.	$6,000 to 7,999	03
D.	$8,000 to 9,999	04
E.	$10,000 to 11,999	05
F.	$12,000 to 13,999	06
G.	$14,000 to 15,999	07
H.	$16,000 to 17,999	08
I.	$18,000 to 19,999	09
J.	$20,000 to 24,999	10
K.	$25,000 to 29,999	11
L.	$30,000 to 34,999	12
M.	$35,000 to 39,999	13

N. $40,000 to 49,999	14
O. $50,000 and over	15
Refused	98
Don't Know	99

Q: What was your approximate total family income from all sources, before taxes, in 19____? *PLEASE CIRCLE THE CORRESPONDING NUMBER.* [same categories as above]

Transportation

When asking transportation questions, note that choice might be seasonal (e.g., bus in winter, bicycle in summer), and that transportation between two given points may involve more than one mode.

Bus or streetcar	1
Subway, El, LRT	2
Train	3
Private car	4
Car pool	5
Taxi	6
Bicycle	7
Walk	8
Other: _____	9

APPENDIX D

Examples: Cover Letter, Questionnaire, and Data-Gathering Form

The data-gathering instruments in this appendix are from two business research studies carried out by students for client organizations.

The questionnaire was used by a team of three students to survey employees in several locations of a major corporation. The objective of the study was to assess the effectiveness of the company's training center. The survey represented part of the project. The survey design involved three groups: employees who had taken a specific course, employees who had taken a different course (to test for placebo effects), and employees who had taken no course. This version of the questionnaire is addressed to employees who had taken a selling skills course. It also asks about negotiating skills—a course the respondents had not taken. (Identifying information has been removed from both cover letter and questionnaire.)

The data-gathering form is from an available data study examining absenteeism and performance and how they relate to employee appraisal data. The researcher gathered data from three different files: payroll, personnel, and operations. The first two were kept in the 12 plants selected for the study; the third was centrally located. The data collection form shown here is for data from the employee's personnel file. The form was designed after examining actual samples of the material in the files, taking into account the order of the information. For all three sources, the researcher took precautions to safeguard confidentiality and ensured that the data-gathering did not violate any statutes concerning confidential employee information.

Centre for Industrial Relations

University of Toronto TORONTO ONTARIO M5S 1A1

FIGURE D.I
Examples of a Cover
Letter and
Questionnaire

January 18, 19XX

Dear XXXXXXXXXX Employee,

What do you think of the training offered by the Organization
Effectiveness Centre (Training Centre) in XXXXXXXXXXXXX?

Given the importance of training in a person's development,
XXXXXXXXXX feels that the time has come to evaluate the
effectiveness of the training it offers you through the Centre.

This questionnaire is part of an independent research study being
carried out by students of the University of Toronto's Master's
in Industrial Relations program. You have been pre-selected to
participate in this study. The success of the research depends
on <u>your</u> participation. Your responses will remain strictly
confidential; <u>no one from within XXXXXX will ever see your</u>
<u>completed questionnaires</u> (including XXXXXXXXXXXXX, one of the
students conducting this study and an employee of XXXXXXXXXXXX).
The results of the study will be available to the company in
early May, 1990. Please note, only summary tables will be
provided. If you are interested in examining the results, you
should contact XXXXXXXXXX at (XXX) XXX-XXXX.

Please read the instructions carefully and answer all the
questions to the best of your ability. We would appreciate it if
you would return your questionnaire by **FEBRUARY 16, 19XX**, in the
stamped pre-addressed envelope which has been provided to you.

Thank you very much for your help.

Sincerely,

XXXXXXXXXXXX, XXXXXXXXXXX, and XXXXXXXXXXXX

P.S. Why not take half an hour and complete the questionnaire
     now? If you have any questions while completing the survey,
     please feel free to contact XXXXXXXXXX at (XXX) XXX-XXXX
     during working hours.

123 St. George Street   Toronto Ontario Canada   M5S 1A1   *(Figure D.1 continues)*

(Figure D.1 continued)

OPINIONS AND ATTITUDES

Definitions:

"supervisor" - the individual to whom you report directly
"senior management" - all managers above your immediate supervisor
"work group" - the people you work with every day, or if you
are a supervisor, those people whom you supervise
"company" - XXXXXXXXXXXXXXXXXXX
"OE Centre" - Organization Effectiveness Centre (Training
Centre in XXXXXXXXXX)

Look for instructions which will tell you which questions may be skipped.
Remember, your responses will be treated with strict confidentiality.

1.   I am aware that the OE Centre in XXXXXXXXXX offers training courses.

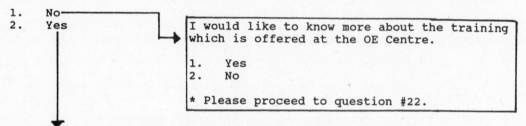

     1.   No
     2.   Yes

         I would like to know more about the training
         which is offered at the OE Centre.

         1.   Yes
         2.   No

         * Please proceed to question #22.

2.   I am aware that the OE Centre provides training and development
      resources on-site for individual business needs.

     1.   Yes
     2.   No

3.   I have taken a course offered by the OE Centre within the past 12
      months.

     1.   Yes
     2.   No ──────────────▶ If No, please proceed to question #22.

Here are some questions about your general feelings regarding the training
offered by the OE Centre:

		Strongly Disagree	Tend to Disagree	Tend to Agree	Strongly Agree	Not applicable/ Don't Know
4.	I am satisfied with the quality of the training offered by the OE Centre.	1	2	3	4	9

		Strongly Disagree	Tend to Disagree	Tend to Agree	Strongly Agree	Not applicable/ Don't Know
5.	I feel that the training courses offered by the OE Centre:					
	- are relevant to my job.	1	2	3	4	9
	- are useful on my job.	1	2	3	4	9
	- help me perform my job better.	1	2	3	4	9
6.	The training provided by the OE Centre is not related to the work I do.	1	2	3	4	9
7a)	The training offered by the OE Centre helps my business/function fulfil its goals.	1	2	3	4	9
b)	The training offered by the OE Centre is important enough to justify its costs.	1	2	3	4	9

Please think back to when you took the Selling Skills course when answering the following questions:

		Strongly Disagree	Tend to Disagree	Tend to Agree	Strongly Agree	Not applicable/ Don't Know
8.	I enjoyed the Selling Skills course.	1	2	3	4	9
9.	The Selling Skills course was:					
	- valuable to me on my job	1	2	3	4	9
	- practical	1	2	3	4	9
	- relevant	1	2	3	4	9
10.	During the course, I was given the opportunity to practice the new skills I learned.	1	2	3	4	9

(Figure D.1 continues)

(Figure D.1 continued)

	Strongly Disagree	Tend to Disagree	Tend to Agree	Strongly Agree	Not applicable/ Don't Know
11. I feel that the atmosphere of the course made it easy to learn what I was supposed to learn.	1	2	3	4	9

12. I asked my supervisor if I could attend the Selling Skills course.

    1.   Yes
    2.   No

	Strongly Disagree	Tend to Disagree	Tend to Agree	Strongly Agree	Not applicable/ Don't Know
13. The instructor for the Selling Skills course:					
- was well prepared	1	2	3	4	9
- was helpful	1	2	3	4	9
- presented material clearly	1	2	3	4	9
- helped me apply the skills to my job	1	2	3	4	9
- was dynamic and enthusiastic	1	2	3	4	9
- encouraged participation	1	2	3	4	9
- provided enough feedback	1	2	3	4	9
- made good use of visual aids	1	2	3	4	9

14. I had received training in selling skills within 12 months prior to attending the Selling Skills course.

    1.   Yes ─────────────────────▶ ┌───┐
    2.   No   │ I enjoyed that prior course (choose one):   │
                                     │ 1. more than the Selling Skills course   │
                                     │ 2. less than the Selling Skills course   │
                                     │ 3. about the same as the Selling Skills   │
                                     │   course   │
                                     └───┘

15. **The Selling Skills course was (choose one):**

    1.   too long
    2.   too short
    3.   about right

16. **I remember much of what I learned in the Selling Skills course.**

    1.   Yes
    2.   No

17. **I often apply what I learned from the Selling Skills course on the job.**

    1.   Yes
    2.   No ────────▶ | If No, please skip to question 19. |

	Strongly Disagree	Tend to Disagree	Tend to Agree	Strongly Agree	Not applicable/ Don't Know
18. When I apply what I learned, I am rewarded by: - my supervisor	1	2	3	4	9
- XXXXXXXXXX	1	2	3	4	9
19. I am encouraged to use new skills on the job: - by my supervisor	1	2	3	4	9
- by my work group	1	2	3	4	9

20. **I would like to take another course from the OE Centre's training program.**

    1.   Yes
    2.   No

21. **I would recommend the Selling Skills course to others.**

    1.   Yes
    2.   No

(Figure D.1 continues)

(Figure D.1 continued)

Sometimes people have to learn and use certain skills for their jobs. At the same time, there are other skills which are not important for their jobs. Please answer the following questions regardless of whether the skills form part of your actual job description:

	Not at All	Not very Well	Well	Very Well	Extremely Well
22a) How well would you say you understand the following:					
- the ways to successfully develop professional relationships with customers	1	2	3	4	5
- how to successfully close a sale	1	2	3	4	5
- how to help a customer achieve his/her objectives through the use of XXX products	1	2	3	4	5
- the distinction between servicing the customer and selling the product	1	2	3	4	5

	Not at All	Not very Often	Often	Very Often	Always
b) How often would you say you do the following on the job:					
- develop professional relationships with the customer	1	2	3	4	5
- successfully close sales	1	2	3	4	5
- help the customer achieve his/her objectives through the use of XXX products	1	2	3	4	5
- emphasize customer service more than selling the product	1	2	3	4	5

Sometimes people have to learn and use certain skills for their jobs. At the same time, there are other skills which are not important for their jobs. Please answer the following questions regardless of whether the skills form part of your actual job description:

	Not at All	Not very Well	Well	Very Well	Extremely Well
23a) How well would you say you understand the following:					
- the major strategies, tactics, tips and techniques for negotiating	1	2	3	4	5
- how to communicate well while negotiating	1	2	3	4	5
- how to get the most from your concessions					
- how to avoid mistakes in negotiations	1	2	3	4	5
- the ethics of negotiation	1	2	3	4	5

	Not at All	Not very Often	Often	Very Often	Always
b) How often would you say you do the following on the job:					
- prepare for negotiations	1	2	3	4	5
- communicate while negotiating	1	2	3	4	5
- apply the strategies, tactics, tips and techniques for negotiating	1	2	3	4	5
- get the most from your concessions	1	2	3	4	5
- practice ethical negotiations	1	2	3	4	5

(Figure D.1 continues)

(Figure D.1 continued)

The following questions are aimed at understanding how you feel about training and how you perceive the Company feels about training:

	Strongly Disagree	Tend to Disagree	Tend to Agree	Strongly Agree	Not applicable/ Don't Know
24. I feel training is important:					
- for an employee's personal development	1	2	3	4	9
- for the Company to emphasize	1	2	3	4	9
25. Given the current and future economic situation the Company finds itself in, I feel the Company puts enough of its emphasis on training.	1	2	3	4	9

26. I am aware of my training needs.

   1.   Yes
   2.   No

27a) My supervisor is aware of my training needs.

   1.   Yes
   2.   No

  b) My supervisor discusses my training needs with me.

   1.   Yes
   2.   No

	Strongly Disagree	Tend to Disagree	Tend to Agree	Strongly Agree	Not applicable/ Don't Know
28. By sending employees for training, the Company shows that it cares for their development.	1	2	3	4	9
29. Going to training courses provides people with a good opportunity to interact with others.	1	2	3	4	9

	Strongly Disagree	Tend to Disagree	Tend to Agree	Strongly Agree	Not applicable/ Don't Know
30. I would participate in some training courses at the OE Centre to get away from my job for a while.	1	2	3	4	9

The following are some questions about your attitudes toward your job, your supervisor, your work group and XXXXXXXXXXXXXX as a whole. Remember, all your responses will be treated confidentially:

	Strongly Disagree	Tend to Disagree	Tend to Agree	Strongly Agree	Not applicable/ Don't Know
31. I enjoy my job.	1	2	3	4	9
32. I am challenged in my job.	1	2	3	4	9
33. I am confident about my ability to do my job.	1	2	3	4	9
34. My salary fails to adequately meet my economic needs.	1	2	3	4	9
35. My job adequately meets my personal needs.	1	2	3	4	9
36. I am expected to do too much on my job.	1	2	3	4	9
37. I feel secure in my job.	1	2	3	4	9
38. Compared with people in similar jobs at other companies, my job situation (ie. pay, benefits, working conditions) is good.	1	2	3	4	9
39. I have an opportunity to grow in my job.	1	2	3	4	9
40. Considering everything, I am satisfied with my job.	1	2	3	4	9

(Figure D.1 continues)

(Figure D.1 continued)

	Strongly Disagree	Tend to Disagree	Tend to Agree	Strongly Agree	Not applicable/ Don't Know
41. Morale could be higher in my work group at the present time.	1	2	3	4	9
42. There is a real sense of teamwork among me and my work group.	1	2	3	4	9
43. I get along well with my coworkers.	1	2	3	4	9
44. I have confidence and trust in my supervisor.	1	2	3	4	9
45. My supervisor gives me regular feedback about my performance.	1	2	3	4	9
46. My supervisor encourages me to develop myself on the job.	1	2	3	4	9
47. Within the next 12 months, it is likely that I will leave XXXXXXXXXXXX to take another job.	1	2	3	4	9
48. Over the past 6 months, there has been a significant negative change in:					
- my job conditions (ie. decrease in pay, demotion)	1	2	3	4	9
- my personal life (ie. death in the family, illness, divorce).	1	2	3	4	9
49. Now that I have worked for XXXXXXXXXXX I would still choose to work here if faced with the same decision again.	1	2	3	4	9
50. I am proud to work for XXXXXXXXXXXX.	1	2	3	4	9

	Strongly Disagree	Tend to Disagree	Tend to Agree	Strongly Agree	Not applicable/ Don't Know
51. I have a feeling of loyalty towards XXXXXXXXXXXX.	1	2	3	4	9
52. I hope to build my future with XXXXXXXXXXXX.	1	2	3	4	9
53. Compared to other companies I know about, XXXXXXX XXXXX is a good place to work.	1	2	3	4	9
54. I have a clear understanding of the goals of my business/ functional area.	1	2	3	4	9
55. I am encouraged by the direction I see XXXXXXXXXXXX taking today.	1	2	3	4	9

If you have any additional comments about how the training offered by the OE Centre or XXXXXXXXXXXXXX as a whole can be improved upon, please write them in the space below.

(Figure D.1 continues)

(Figure D.1 continued)

FACTUAL INFORMATION

Please answer the following questions by circling or filling in the appropriate response.

Your responses will be treated <u>confidentially</u>. No one from within XXXXXXXX will have access to completed questionnaires.

While we have some data about you, these background questions ensure that this research study is representative of all XXXXXXXXXXXXXXX employees.

1.   What is your sex?

    1.   Male
    2.   Female

2.   What is your year of birth?   19 ____

3.   What is your first/preferred language?

    1.   English
    2.   French

4.   What is the highest grade or year you finished in regular school or college/university?

1.	less than grade 8	6.	community college graduate
2.	grade 8 to 11	7.	university graduate
3.	grade 12	8.	some post-graduate
4.	grade 13	9.	graduate degree
5.	some college/university		

5.   Do you have a professional designation (eg. CMA, CA, P. Eng.)?

    1.   Yes
    2.   No

6.   How long have you been an employee of XXXXXXXXXXX?

    _____ years, _____ months

7.   Where do you work?

1.	XXXXXXXX	5.	Other Ontario
2.	XXXXXXXX	6.	BC, Alta, Sask, Man
3.	XXXXXXXX	7.	NB, NS, Nfld
4.	XXXXXXXX	8.	Quebec

8.   **What business do you work in?**

1. XXXXXXXX		9. XXXXXXXX	
2. Medical Systems		10. XXXXXXXX	
3. Motors and Drives		11. **Meter Controls**	
4. XX Capital		12. **Silicones**	
5. Aerospace		13. **Plastics**	
6. Functional (Pooled Finance, Legal, etc.)		14. XXXXXXXX	
		15. **Lighting**	
7. Info Services		16. **Mobile**	
8. Computer Services			

9.   **What is your current position level/grade?**

Level/Grade _____
[   ]   Don't know/unassigned
[   ]   XXXXXXXX

10.   **What is your current functional work assignment?**

1.	Manufacturing	4.	Marketing/Sales
2.	Research/Development/ Applications Engineering	5.	Finance
3.	Service/Installation/ Repair Engineering	6.	Relations or other (Legal, etc.)
		7.	Clerical

11.   **What type of job do you have:**

1.   Individual Contributor/Specialist
2.   Manager
3.   Foreman/Forewoman
4.   Other

Thank you very much for your participation. Please seal and mail your questionnaire in the pre-addressed and postage paid envelope provided.

Points to Note

- Although the students sent out the cover letter on the university letterhead, they make it clear in the text that the study is being carried out for the employer. Not to do so would be unethical.

- The cover letter uses both boldface and underlining for emphasis.

- The P.S. in the cover letter asks respondents to complete it immediately. It also provides two other points of information: the approximate time required and a phone number for questions.

- Important terms are defined for respondents at the beginning of the questionnaire.

- Response categories have been precoded.

- Skip patterns are made more clear with the use of boxes and arrows.

- Bridge sentences are provided in bold.

FIGURE D.2
Personnel File Data
Collection Form

Personnel File Data

PERSONNEL #: __ __ __ __ __

Checked? [ ]

CODER CODE: _____

Collection Date: _____

Plant: _____ CODE: __ __

Ee Name: _____

SEX (F = 0,   M = 1): __

BIRTHDATE: m __ __   y __ __

Marital Status: _____ CODE: __ __

NUMBER OF DEPENDENTS (INCLUDING SPOUSE): __

DATE OF HIRE: m __ __   y __ __

Job: _____ CODE: __ __ __

Department: _____ CODE: __ __

DATE OF START IN PRESENT JOB CATEGORY: m __ __   y __ __

DATE OF LAST APPRAISAL: m __ __   y __ __

APPRAISAL RATINGS: (a) __ (b) __ (c) __ (d) __ (e) __ (f) __

Appraisal Comments: CODES: __ __ __ __ __

Appraiser (right-justify initials; 9 = illegible letter): __ __ __

Coder's Comments:

Points to Note

- Using data from an employee's personnel file raises both ethical and legal questions. Some jurisdictions require employee approval for certain uses of this information. *Check beforehand!*

- The lines are right-justified so that codes are all on the far right-hand side of the page. This makes it easier to see what information is missing and reduces data entry errors.

- The researcher used uppercase for the information actually to be entered into the computer, lowercase for other information.

- Collection dates are important administrative information in case there are major problems or changes to the data midway through the collection period.

- Rather than entering the contextual variables (plant size, location, etc.) on each sheet, the researcher saved time by using the computer and IF commands to enter these variables (e.g., IF [PLANT = 12] SIZE = 124).

- As well as copies of this form, the coder took the project codebook to the data-gathering site with codes for "plant," "marital status," "job title," "department," and "appraisal comments."

- The researcher allowed for coding the content of the first five comments on the most recent appraisal.

- The researcher coded the initials of the appraiser, rather than names, since preliminary examination of the data revealed that in about one-third of the cases, appraisals were initialed rather than signed.

APPENDIX E

Planning and Running a Research Project

This appendix offers suggestions for administering a business research project. It covers (1) who should do the research, (2) research planning, (3) the research proposal, and (4) project administration.

Your decisions in each of these areas are affected by the research situation, in particular its constraints. These constraints consist of restrictions on time, money, personnel, data access (individuals, groups, files, records), and political considerations (e.g., a newly appointed vice president is concerned that research activity itself might create problems he or she doesn't feel able to handle yet). Before you begin research planning, it's a good idea to list the obvious and potential constraints affecting your research. Keep them in mind as you plan and design the project. Avoid unpleasant surprises later on!

WHO DOES THE RESEARCH?

Your choices are to *make* the research (do it in-house) or *buy* it (hire outside consultants or vendors). Your decision about internal or external researchers will depend on the following points:

- The in-house research option is almost always the cheapest. Exception: it may take you more time and money to develop efficient measures for some sensitive topic than to use a vendor who has already conducted research on the topic.

- With internal researchers, you'll be better able to keep track of the design, data gathering, and data analysis. As a result, you'll be better able to assess the validity of the research conclusions.

- Internal researchers will need less time to investigate the organization problem. On the other hand, their findings and impressions will be colored by familiarity, assumptions, and past experiences. External researchers may be able to shed new light on a problem situation. In addition, experience with other projects and organizations may provide added insight in their recommendations.

- With in-house personnel, research skills are often limited. A reputable consulting firm or vendor is more likely to be up to date on methods and analysis techniques. Research validity is thus likely to be higher if you buy the research from the right source.

- The larger or more complex the project and the more important the strategic decisions riding on the results, the more you should consider a reputable consulting firm with proven performance.

- The more sensitive the research, the more you may want an external firm to handle it. Particularly if internal organization politics are involved, the final conclusions and recommendations will be seen as more neutral and credible if consultants carry out the research. Similarly, external researchers are less subject to internal political pressures (but keep in mind their desire for future contracts!). On the other hand, if the subject matter is highly confidential (as is sometimes the case for marketing research with new product lines), in-house research is less likely to result in leaks.

- External firms vary widely in their ability to do high-quality research. Impressive-looking reports with eye-catching covers, quality paper, and expensive binding are no guarantee that the conclusions are valid and the recommendations relevant. The most expensive-looking report can contain nothing more than a few descriptive-level recommendations and incomplete, shoddy, or almost no multivariate analysis. Before you use a firm, ask your industry contacts for their experiences, and ask each bidder for copies of recent nonconfidential reports. Find out exactly who will be doing your work: will they subcontract it out to someone whose ability is in doubt?

- The procedures for securing external researchers vary widely. At one extreme, informal contacts often lead to a contract; at the other, the firm needing the research formally contacts selected research vendors with a Request for Proposal (RFP), inviting them to submit bids for the research project specified in the RFP.

- An intermediate solution to the internal-external decision is to contract out only certain parts of the research, such as design, data collection, or data analysis.

- If the decision is to proceed in-house, you may have a third option. Some organizations maintain a department designed to provide research services to other organization units. You may be able to use this in-house department, as opposed to conducting the research solely with your own immediate personnel and resources. Apply the same criteria and questions you would ask of external research consultants.

In any event, a good relationship between manager and researcher, whether in-house or external, is vital for best results. Close contact is essential at both the initial and end stages of the research process.

RESEARCH PLANNING

Research planning refers to the estimation of time, personnel, money, and other resources necessary for carrying out a project. Like most other aspects of business research, research planning can range from quick and dirty to elaborate and detailed. Your choice will depend on the importance of the research problem and what you need. Early on in any project, you may require go-ahead approval to design the research. For this approval, approximate time and cost estimates will suffice. For a full-fledged proposal, however, planning will have to be much more exact and detailed.

- Prior to detailed planning you should have written specific research questions. Also note, as explicitly as possible, the general purpose of the research, key variable(s), primary variables, and research boundaries. This information will drive your planning and research decisions, and you should refer to it whenever you have a problem or decision to make. Keep it in the codebook.

- Also make note of the design decisions as you make them: unit of analysis, basic and specific type of design, data sources, target population, and sample type and size. Keep them in mind as you plan the research.

Matrix Method of Planning and Costing

A very convenient way of planning a research project is to use the matrix method. The matrix is a table that divides the project into distinct tasks and specifies the resource requirements for each task. Each task occupies a row of the matrix; each requirement is represented by a column.

The Tasks. Following is a general list of the tasks a project might include:

1. Administration: a category often underestimated. It includes time spent on the following activities: getting the project planned, approved, and started; writing proposals and securing funds; buying or renting necessary supplies, equipment, and materials; getting access to data or research sites; securing support services (data entry, statistical analysis, word processing); and paying bills and handling budgets.

2. Hiring and training personnel: for a small project, include with administration. For a larger project, this can be a major task.

3. Investigating the organization problem: may require interviews, observation, examination of past reports, travel.

4. Review of literature and existing information: examining related and similar research for (1) variables and relationships you might include and (2) useful designs, instruments, or measures. May involve library time.

5. Specifying the research problem: type of research, key and primary variables, research boundaries, specific research questions.

6. Design decisions: may require investigation of potential data sources and comparison samples or groups.

7. Preparing and testing instruments and procedures, including trial runs and pretests: if the project uses available data, it may require trips to check sources and secure samples or getting data tapes from government or other organizations. Questionnaires, interview schedules, and data collection forms have to be printed.

8. Drawing the sample: requires a sampling frame and procedures. Lists may have to be photocopied, and travel may be involved to get them. Alternatively, sampling frame procedures may have to be tried on site.

9. Gathering data: normally requires a number of subtasks, depending on the methodology used (survey, experiment, available data). For example, the tasks for mailed questionnaires include stuffing envelopes, attaching stamps, mailing, and screening, logging, and numbering returns. Tasks for interview surveys include contacts, callbacks, appointments, follow-up phone calls, and the actual interview.

10. Data checking, editing, and coding. (The time for this task is almost always underestimated!)

11. Data entry.

12. Writing and entering data definition information (to create the statistical software's processing file).

13. Data cleaning.

14. Preliminary and descriptive analysis.

15. Bivariate, multivariate, and supplementary analysis.

16. Drafting conclusions and recommendations: this may involve meetings with managers.

17. Preparing and distributing final report.

The Resource Requirements.

For each task, specify the following resource requirements in separate columns of the matrix:

- *Personnel:* Specify (a) skills needed, (b) required number of persons with each skill, (c) nature and amount of training required, (d) cost per person per hour (or day) for each skill level. Keep in mind that interviewers and editors may need fairly detailed training.

- *Travel:* where, time required, costs for accommodation, transportation, parking, meals, personal services (e.g., laundry).

- *Equipment and Documents:* nature, quantity, costs. Include here the cost of data obtained from other sources and transferred by tape, diskette, or phone line, or in document form.

- *Supplies and Materials:* nature, quantity, costs.

- *Services:* for example, typing, photocopying, printing, telephone, translation, courier, fax, consulting, data entry, programming, computer analysis (mainframe connect time, storage, processing, and printing charges). Include costs of each service.

- *Time:* Estimate task and subtask time in hours for small projects, days for larger ones. (1) Estimate the actual number of hours or days for each task and subtask. (As a rough rule of thumb in calculating task times, take the estimated minimum time required to perform each task and *double* it!) (2) Estimate the starting and finishing dates.

- *Money:* Add the costs for each task. Sum these subtotals to get overall cost of the project. Also sum the separate columns to get subtotal costs for personnel, travel, equipment and documents, supplies and materials, and services.

Here are examples of some of the items that might appear in your planning matrix:

- Under administration equipment: a filing cabinet.
- Under administration supplies: file folders are a must.
- Under data entry supplies: floppy disks, a diskette storage box.
- Under sampling documents: a book with table of random numbers.

- Under data-gathering supplies, for a questionnaire survey: envelopes, paper, staples, postage stamps.

Work Schedule

Based on your time estimates, draw up a work schedule for each task. For anything larger than a minor project, use a simple *Gantt chart*. On graph paper list each task in a column on the left-hand side. Mark the horizontal axis in time units from the beginning date to the planned end date of the project. Then, for each task, draw a horizontal line starting at the date at which the task begins and ending when the task should finish. The length of each task line will depend on the duration of that task. You'll be able to see at a glance which tasks must logically follow others (for example, data gathering must follow sampling) and which can overlap (for example, editing and coding can begin while data gathering is still underway). (See Figure E.1 for a typical Gantt chart.)

THE RESEARCH PROPOSAL

The form and content of a research proposal depend on a variety of factors. Some projects need only a short informal proposal; others will require a full and detailed account of what is to be done, why, how, at what cost, and with what final result. In general, the larger and more important the project, the more detailed the proposal. Proposals from external researchers and consultants also tend to be more detailed than those from in-house researchers. The form and content also depend on the urgency of the problem, whose approval is needed for money, and whose approval is needed for access to data or data sources. As a rule of thumb, the higher in the organization such approval is granted, the more formal the proposal.

A formal detailed proposal contains most or all of the following information, in approximately this order:

- Description of organization problem
- Outline of objectives and general research problem, together with specific research questions
- Rationale for the research; expected results and their benefits (may include utility analysis)
- Any contributions from past reports, existing research literature
- Design decisions

FIGURE E.1 A Gantt
Chart for Scheduling
a Mail Survey

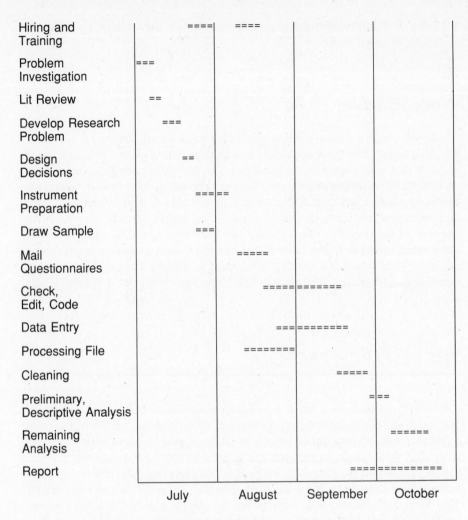

- Sampling and data-gathering procedures
- Descriptions of variables and measures
- Examples of data-gathering instruments
- Budget and financial arrangements
- Personnel required and other resource usage; impact on organization (e.g., interruptions to production for interviews)
- Work and reporting schedule

An informal proposal will be much shorter and less detailed and may omit entirely the literature search, descriptions of measures, examples of data-gathering instruments, and budget and work schedule information. At its shortest, the proposal may take the form of a one- or two-page memo or even a verbal description of the proposed project.

In some cases, the approval process occurs in two stages: (1) early approval to proceed with a major proposal, based on a description of the organization problem and a statement of the research problem, and (2) approval based on a detailed research proposal.

PROJECT ADMINISTRATION

Administering a research project involves a variety of tasks. Both common sense and a concern for data quality will help you manage your project to a successful completion. Chapters 10, 11, and 12 offer specific suggestions for available data studies, experiments, and surveys, respectively. Here are some more general suggestions:

- If you are running a moderately sized or larger project while carrying out other management duties, it is extremely useful to appoint an assistant with full-time responsibility for the project. Otherwise, many of the small details, decisions, and tasks required for high-quality research will be delayed or overlooked. In general, a full-time research administrator is well worth the cost.

- Consider the use of desktop publishing software for the preparation of questionnaires and cover letters. Ordinary word processing packages should be more than adequate for other research forms, including interview schedules, data collection forms, codebooks, and editing instructions.

- Make use of micro software packages for project management (such as Harvard Total Project Manager).

- Keep a log of research decisions you make. When a new problem occurs, check the log in order to make a consistent decision.

Recruiting and Training Personnel

Although a single individual can carry out almost any project alone (and many students do), and available data research often needs only one person, some survey and experimental projects benefit by having additional personnel. In particular, surveys involve more subtasks than experiments or available data studies and require more research help. Especially when data are gathered by interviews, additional personnel help you avoid a prolonged data collection phase.

Of course, the more personnel involved, the more administrative time and skills are required. One substantial investment is the time spent recruiting and training research personnel, particularly interviewers, editors, and coders.

Recruiting.   Interviewers should be hired on the basis of experience and self-presentation. Appropriate dress and deportment are obviously important for securing respondents' cooperation, maintaining their interest, and motivating them to provide accurate reliable information. For telephone interviews appearance is immaterial, but voice and manner are critical. Interviewers must also be able to think quickly on their feet and adapt to the variety of situations they are likely to encounter in the field. The same qualities are important for individuals who help administer group questionnaires for pilot projects and other experimental studies.

Your most capable and experienced staff should be assigned to editing. This task requires intimate familiarity with both the objectives of the research and data analysis procedures. Editors make important decisions about data that will have substantial effects on the validity of the research. If you employ a full-time research administrator, this individual could also assume editing duties for a moderately sized project.

Coders should have good clerical skills. Their most important requirement is low error rates. Try to minimize the number of judgments coders are responsible for. In particular, the better the editing, the fewer decisions coders have to make. (In small projects, the same individual can carry out both editing and coding.) Similar qualities are important for the individuals who gather secondary data from existing files and transfer them to data collection forms.

Training.   Good training reduces measurement error. Poor training will often result in noisy data. The closer that research personnel work to the data source, the more important their training. All personnel should be told, and reminded, that you're serious about the confidentiality (or anonymity) of data.

Interviewer training is the most critical and the most time consuming. Aside from learning how to select respondents, make contacts and callbacks, probe responses, and follow skip patterns on their interview schedules, interviewers must learn a variety of interpersonal skills. For example, they should be trained to postpone interviews with obviously tired or distracted respondents. They must learn how to remove distractions, noise, and other impediments to error-free measurement. In particular, interviewers working in the respondents' homes should know how to turn off television sets and politely usher other persons from the room.

- Prepare a background statement to accompany each difficult or problem question that indicates what the question is getting at. This will help interviewers know when they have a satisfactory answer and when they need to probe.

- Interviewers must be trained to handle skip patterns smoothly. One way to do this is to present them with a set of profiles of respondents and then ask which questions should be asked of that person (Converse and Presser, 1986).

Monitoring the Data Collection

Monitor data collection to ensure both good sample and data quality. Tired, frustrated, or overzealous researchers have been known to interview friends or enter totally fictitious information on data collection forms in the comfort of their own living rooms!

Some forms of data collection are easy to monitor, such as telephone interviewing with a CATI system. Others, such as field observation, are far removed from project administrators and more susceptible to researcher cheating. Try to build a check system into the data collection process. At the least, ask researchers to specify the date, time, and place of data collection activity.

Data cleaning can also be an important form of monitoring. In general, for interviews and available data sources, start data cleaning as soon as a dozen or so cases are available. This will help you identify any problems while there may still be time to correct them. Make sure that ID codes for the interviewer (or other data gatherer), editor, and coder are included in the administrative data for each case. This will help you track down, and fix, faulty data handling.

Field Interviews.   An important part of monitoring and controlling field interviews is to have interviewers fill out face sheet reports attached to their completed interviews. These face sheet reports contain information about the respondent and the interview situation. Such information can be very useful for making sense of editing problems, helping to interpret unanticipated results, and reducing nonresponse in future interviews and studies.

These face sheet reports should note

- A record of attempted contacts.

- Problems encountered during contact attempts and the interview itself.

- Visible characteristics of the respondent, group (e.g., family), or organization that might be coded and analyzed to evaluate nonresponse bias.

- Information about the respondent's reactions to the interview (e.g., cooperative, enthusiastic, nervous, forgetful, suspicious, hostile).

- Date, day, and time of the interview and where it took place (e.g., living room, office, conference room).

- Whether others were present (who?); any interruptions.

- A callback telephone number.

Interviewers should get the name and telephone number of each respondent, so that a random sample can be called back to ensure that the interview took place. At the same time, respondents can be asked if there were any problems with the interview, if they felt uncomfortable, or if they had other difficulties. In asking for names and telephone numbers, interviewers can make it clear that the purpose of the call is to check on the *interviewer,* not the respondent. When necessary, this call can be combined with checks for ambiguous answers or missing information uncovered by editing. To check on interviewers, marketing and public opinion research firms will often validate as many as 10 percent of the respondents.

Give individual feedback to each interviewer as the research progresses. Mention specific questions they're doing particularly well, and discuss items with which they're having problems. Review what the problem questions are trying to measure and what probes might help to get the information. Make sure you listen to what they say: it might lead to useful advice for other interviewers on the project.

Telephone Interviews.   The interviewer should note each telephone number on an interview face sheet so that a sample of interviews can be verified. Such monitoring is much easier if a CATI system is used; the supervisor can actually listen in on an interview and watch on his or her own monitor the responses being entered by the interviewer.

Debriefing Interviewers.   In addition to monitoring face sheets, you can learn much of benefit (especially for future projects) by meeting with interviewers as a group regularly during and after the project, and having them discuss their experiences and impressions with one another.

GLOSSARY

Accepted risk An ethical test: the researcher should avoid probable and plausible damage to individuals and organizations beyond the risks they normally accept in the course of work and everyday life.

Achieved sample The cases about which the researcher actually obtains sufficient information for analysis.

Acquiescence A response set in which respondents tend to agree to questionnaire or interview items, regardless of wording.

Aggregate data Data gathered from a higher-level unit of analysis than the unit the researcher wants to draw conclusions about. Aggregate data are usually from an aggregate, but sometimes from a body of individuals.

Aggregation bias The error of assuming that causal relationships found with aggregate data are true at the lower-level unit of analysis.

Alpha level The researcher's choice of acceptable probability of a Type I error. Typically .10, .05, .01, or .001 depending on the cost of an error.

Alphanumeric codes Alphabetic and other nonnumeric characters used to code data. Particularly important in **string** variables, such as names and addresses.

Alpha problem Multiple significance tests, which increase the chance of a Type I error.

Anchored response options On a numeric rating scale question, the response options that are labeled (usually the end points).

ANOVA (ANalysis Of VAriance) A multivariate technique for a quantitative dependent variable and a few category independent variables.

Antecedent variation Existing variation in the independent variable, through manipulation by the researcher or naturally occurring variation across cases or observations. A prerequisite in all research designs.

Association A relationship between two variables that vary together so that as values of one change, values of the other systematically change. The degree of association is a measure of effect size.

Autocorrelation In time series, a condition in which adjacent observations are correlated rather than independent. The value at one time is affected by the value at a previous time.

Autocorrelation function In time series, procedure that measures the correlation between observations at different degrees of time difference.

Available data Information generated or gathered by other persons or agencies for their own purposes.

Bar chart A graphic that shows the distribution of a category variable.

Basic design The fundamental distinction among research designs. The three basic designs (true, quasi-, and nonexperimental) differ on whether a variable is manipulated, and whether cases are randomly assigned to groups.

Bias Systematic errors in measurement, sampling, or estimates that produce distortions predominantly in one direction.

Bipolar attitude question Presents both views of the opposite sides of an issue by means of wording or response categories.

Blind treatments Experiments in which participants are unaware of which level of the manipulated variable they receive. In **double-blind** treatments, neither participants nor the researchers they interact with know the level.

Blocked design In experiments, the addition of two or more nonmanipulable independent variables. Each category of the nonmanipulable variable constitutes a block.

Box plot A graphic showing the distribution and central tendency of a quantitative variable.

The box height corresponds to the interquartile range.

Breakdowns Means or proportions presented separately for demographic or geographic categories, such as sex or region.

Bridge In a questionnaire or interview, a short statement to inform the respondent of a change in topic for the following questions.

Business research A practical, applied-research tool for obtaining the information that organizations need to answer questions and solve business problems.

Case study Intensive examination of a single instance of a phenomenon of interest, such as a factory or a leveraged buyout. Often used in exploratory stages of research.

Category variable A variable measured at the dichotomous, nominal, or category ordinal level.

CATI systems Hardware and software for computer-assisted telephone interviewing.

Causal modeling Statistical analysis using assumptions about the causal priority of variables, and testing causal structures among the variables.

Chronbach's alpha A measure of scale reliability that examines all item interrelationships simultaneously.

Closed format question Provides specific categories for the respondent's answer, one or more of which the respondent selects.

Cluster analysis A multivariate technique that identifies, with respect to a set of variables, the number and nature of relatively homogeneous groups of cases.

Cluster sample A probability sample in which cases are grouped into naturally occurring clusters, and the clusters are sampled with equal probability of being chosen.

Codes The numerical values that represent data, particularly for category variables. In some cases, alphabetic or other non-numeric characters are used.

Cohort A group of cases (usually persons) going through the same stage of an experience at the same time. The class of 1995 is a cohort.

Collapsing Reducing the number of categories in a category variable by combining categories.

Comparison group In a quasi-experiment, the term applied to the cases to be compared to the treatment group. Generally does not involve random assignment. An experiment may involve more than one comparison group.

Concept A broad and abstract idea about some meaningful attribute of objects, persons, groups, organizations, aggregates, or events. Theories relate concepts; for research, concepts are represented by variables.

Concomitant time series Time series with more than one variable, in which the focus is on the relationships among variables rather than trends.

Concurrent validity A type of criterion validity assessment in which the criterion is measured at the same time as the measure being assessed.

Confidence interval A range on either side of the estimated mean within which the researcher believes the true population mean falls with a stated probability of error (alpha level). Researchers often use a 95% confidence interval.

Confounded variables Two independent variables that covary so that it is impossible to determine which is the cause of a dependent variable. In an experiment, a confounding event is called a **history effect** when it affects all conditions, and **local history** when it affects only one condition.

Construct validity Checking statistically whether a multiple-item measure has one (sometimes more) underlying dimension consistent with the desired concept, and whether the measure relates as expected to other variables measured with known high validity.

Contamination Participants tell others of a study's procedures and purpose, thus affecting the behavior of subsequent participants, or participants in other experimental conditions.

Content analysis Procedures for systematically converting written text to numerical variables for quantitative data analysis.

Content validity The researcher judges to what extent a multiple-item measure reflects all possible meanings and aspects of a concept.

Contextual variable An attribute representing the context or circumstance of a case, common to a subset of cases, such as the exchange rate the day of a financial transaction, common to all transactions that day.

Control group In a true experiment, the group of cases that is not subjected to the new policy, program, or practice. Formed by random assignment.

Convenience sample The researcher selects any cases conveniently at hand.

Correlates Variables between which a correlation exists, with neither variable identified as the independent or dependent.

Correlation *See also* **Association.** If both variables increase together, the correlation is positive; if one increases as the other decreases, the correlation is negative.

Covariation *See* **Association.**

Criterion validity Assessing measurement validity by checking the measure against a criterion that exactly represents the intended concept.

Criterion variable In an experiment, another term for the dependent variable.

Critical region In univariate hypothesis testing, the range of values within which the researcher is willing to accept that the null hypothesis is rejected.

Cross-sectional design Data gathered at a single measurement time point. Compare with **longitudinal design.**

Data listing A computer printout of a raw data file.

Data matrix An array of research data in numerical form, in which each row is a separate case, and each variable is one or more columns. The information gathered by the researcher fills the body of the matrix.

Debriefing In research using deception, disclosing its nature and giving participants an explanation of both the study's true purpose and why deception was necessary.

Degrees of freedom The number of elements in a sample free to vary, equal to the number of cases or observations minus the number of known parameters (such as the sample mean).

Demand effects Participants in research act or answer questions in ways that they think the researcher wants. Particularly a problem in experiments, in which they are known as **demand characteristics.**

Descriptive analysis Estimates population characteristics for descriptive research and summarizes sample characteristics for other kinds of research.

Descriptive statistics Statistical procedures, such as measures of association, which do not infer population characteristics from a sample, that is, do not require inferential statistics.

Diary survey Respondents are given diary forms or booklets covering a specific period of time, and are asked to fill in the relevant information.

Differencing An arithmetic technique for reducing trend and autocorrelation in a time series by subtracting from each observation the preceding value.

Direct effect In a research model, the anticipated causal effect of an independent variable with no intervening variable.

Discriminant analysis A multivariate technique for determining which independent variables best account for the distribution of cases in a category-dependent variable.

Distribution For any variable, the dispersion of cases over the values of that variable.

Double-barreled question A question that erroneously incorporates two different questions.

Downweighting Adjusting samples to make them representative by having oversampled cases count less in the analysis.

Dummy table A table with title, headings, and labels, but no numbers. Used to plan data analysis.

Dummy variable Dichotomous variable coded "0" (indicating absence of an attribute) and "1" (presence). Used in regression analysis.

Durbin–Watson test A statistical test for the presence of autocorrelation in time series.

Effect size The degree of effect an independent has on a dependent variable.

Efficiency The precision of a sample relative to its size.

Empirical validity An objective approach, using research data, to assessing measurement validity. It includes criterion and construct validity.

Enumeration Gathering data from all elements in the target population.

Evaluation study Assessment of an existing program, policy, or practice.

Experimenter bias Researchers' behavior that affects the behavior and responses of participants.

Exploratory research Unstructured research that examines the nature and dimensions of a phenomenon, often prior to explanatory research.

External research Research using information from cases (usually individuals such as customers) outside an organization.

External validity Conclusions about facts or relationships have external validity when they can be validly generalized from a sample of cases to the target population.

Extraneous variable One related to both a dependent Y and independent variable X in such a way that it produces covariation between them. However the X–Y relationship is spurious, not causal.

Face sheet A page attached to the front of an interview schedule. It contains questions about the respondent and interview situation for the interviewer to complete.

Face validity The researcher judges whether, on the face of it, a measure reflects an intended concept.

Factor analysis A statistical procedure to find which variables are closely related to one another. Used to determine measurement validity in index and scale construction.

Factorial design In experiments, adding one or more additional manipulated independent variables. In a *fully crossed* factorial design, experimental conditions consist of each possible combination of independent variable categories.

Field In a data matrix, one or more columns assigned to a particular variable.

Field experiment An experiment carried out in a naturally occurring situation, usually to test the effect of one or two manipulated variables. Includes pilot projects and evaluation studies.

Field sampling Carrying out the sampling procedure in the field, just prior to data gathering. Common in the final stages of multistage sample surveys.

Filter question Identifies respondents for whom one or more following questions are not applicable, so such respondents can skip those questions.

Finite population correction The square root of the unsampled proportion of the target population. Applied to inferential statistics calculations to correct for the use of sampling without replacement when the sampling fraction is large, since sampling *with* replacement is assumed by sampling theory.

Fixed format Coding scheme for a raw data file in which each variable is always in the same column or columns. Compare **free format.**

Focus group With the guidance of a group leader, selected participants discuss their reactions and feelings about a product, service, or type of situation of interest to a client. Clients often watch focus groups through one-way mirrors.

Forecasting prediction A type of prediction research used to estimate future levels of some factor, such as sales or inventories. It is based on present and past information, and estimates of related future conditions.

Formative evaluation Examines the process by which a program or policy operates to achieve desired effects, often through nonsystematic observation or unstructured in-depth interviews. Frequently carried out in the early stages of the policy or program.

Free format A coding scheme for raw data in which special delimiter characters (usually blanks or commas) separate variables. Thus a particular column is not always assigned to the same variable. Compare **fixed format.**

Frequency distribution A table showing the number and percentages of cases having each value of a variable.

Funneling Questions in questionnaires and interviews are ordered from the most general to the most specific.

Gain scores In repeated-measure studies, the difference between a case's pretest and posttest measures.

Gantt chart A chart with lines showing the start and finish dates for each stage of a project; very useful for research planning.

Generalization The application of research results to cases or situations beyond those specifically examined in the research.

Group administration For questionnaires, having a group of individuals gather in one place and complete the questionnaire under the supervision of a researcher.

Histogram A graphic that shows the distribution of a quantitative variable.

Homogeneous variance In many statistical procedures, an assumption that variance in the dependent variable does not change substantially over values of the independent variables.

Hypothesis The researcher's prediction of an expected relationship or value.

Identifier variable For each case, a unique identification number used in each of two or more data sources so that data about each case from the different sources can be matched.

Import To have your statistical software read data from a spreadsheet or database file, or a data file written in ASCII characters.

Independence Two variables are independent when knowledge of one doesn't help to predict the other; two cases are independent when selecting one for a sample doesn't affect the other's probability of selection.

Index A measure consisting of a series of items representing two or more different variables, combined to represent an overall concept.

Indirect effect In a research model, the anticipated causal effect of an independent variable working through a specified intervening variable.

Inferential statistics Statistical tests that lead to conclusions about a target population based

on a random sample and the concept of sampling distribution.

Informant A respondent who provides information about a body or relationship of which he or she is a member.

Informed consent Disclosing research objectives to participants, and giving them an opportunity to decline without penalty.

Initial sample The sample drawn from the sampling frame; the cases about which you try to obtain information. Compare with **achieved sample.**

Instrumentation effects Effects due to changes to measuring procedures or instruments in mid-study. An alternative explanation threatening internal validity.

Intact group In an experiment, a preexisting group that is assigned to one condition as a whole, without random assignment of group members. Any similarities or relationships among group members violate the assumption of independent cases.

Interaction effect Two independent variables combine in a nonadditive manner to cause a dependent variable.

Internal research Research conducted with a population inside the organization.

Internal validity Conclusions about facts and relationships pertaining to the cases actually analyzed have internal validity when they are accurate and have few plausible alternative explanations.

Interquartile range A measure of dispersion; the distance between the 25th and 75th percentiles of a quantitative variable.

Interrater reliability The extent to which two or more researchers measuring the same cases and variables come up with identical results.

Interrupted time series A type of quasi-experimental design; time series with a manipulated change, usually near the middle of the series.

Intervening variable A third variable located temporally and causally between an independent and a dependent variable. It suggests a causal process linking the other two variables.

Item analysis Statistical analysis to determine which items of a multiple-item scale should be dropped in order to improve the scale's reliability.

Item nonresponse bias Information about a variable is missing for certain cases that are systematically different from others in the sample.

Joint effect The effect of a set of independent variables on a dependent variable. Very important in selection and forecasting prediction. Compare **unique effect.**

Joint outlier A case substantially outside a bivariate or multivariate distribution, but not necessarily an outlier for any univariate distribution. Joint outliers can distort the results of multivariate analysis.

Judgment sample Using his or her own judgment, the researcher selects apparently typical cases. If the researcher relies on experts to suggest cases, it is called an **expert sample.**

Key variable The variable central to the research problem; a dependent variable in prediction and explanatory research, an independent variable (the program or policy being evaluated) in evaluation research.

Lagged variable In time series, represents a case attribute at some previous measurement time point.

Leading question An item phrased to influence the respondent to make a particular answer.

Leading variable In time series, represents a case attribute at some subsequent measurement time point.

Level of analysis The scope of the unit of analysis. Individuals are a lower level of analysis; organizations are higher because a set of individuals makes up each organization; geographical regions are higher yet.

Level of measurement The properties of numbers assigned to cases as part of the measurement operation, ranging from nominal (purely symbolic) to ratio (all the attributes of the common number system).

Leverage The influence a single case has on the results of statistical analysis. Outliers can distort results if they have high leverage.

Linearity In relationships, the property that the trend line which best fits the data points is straight, rather than curvilinear. Most tests of association and significance assume linear relationships.

Loaded question An item worded with emotional phrases or biased response categories, thus likely producing biased answers.

Local history In an experiment, a confounding event that affects cases in only one condition, and is thus an alternative explanation reducing internal validity.

Longitudinal design Data gathered at two or more measurement time points.

Marginals The row and column totals of a cross-tabulation table. They give the frequency distributions of the two variables in the table.

Maturation A threat to internal validity in designs with multiple measurement points. Between measures, cases develop in some natural way that is mistaken for the consequence of an experimental manipulation.

Mean The arithmetic average of a variable; a measure of central tendency.

Measurement bias The measured value of a variable is systematically distorted in one direction from the "true" value of a variable.

Measurement error The difference between the "true" value and the measured value of a variable.

Measurement validity The extent to which a measure reflects the concept of interest to the researcher.

Median The value marking the midpoint of a variable's frequency distribution. Fifty percent of the cases have equal or greater values. A measure of central tendency.

Mediating variable *See* **Intervening variable.**

Missing value A special code (often blanks or 9s) to indicate that for a particular case, the value of a particular variable is missing. This allows the computer to skip that case when doing computations involving that variable.

Mode The value with the most cases in a variable's frequency distribution. A measure of central tendency.

Moderating variable Affects the degree or form of the relationship between an independent and dependent variable.

Mortality The nonrandom loss of cases over time in an experiment or other design with multiple measurement time points. **Systematic mortality** involves cases with certain characteristics. **Differential mortality** involves cases in one condition more than others.

Multicollinearity A problem in multivariate analysis when two or more independent variables are highly correlated.

Multimodal A frequency distribution with two or more distinct peaks.

Multistage sample Like a cluster sample except cases in the chosen clusters are then sampled. Thus sampling occurs at two or more stages. Usually based on geographic divisions of the target population (e.g., sample states, then counties, municipalities, blocks, dwelling units, and residents).

Natural experiment Quasi-experiment in which the manipulation occurs by chance, such as a snowstorm or natural disaster.

Nonparametric Statistical tests and measures that require no assumptions about the shape of the variables' distributions.

Nonprobability sample Nonrandom procedures produce a sample in which the probability of a given case being selected is unknown, and may be zero. Thus the sampling error is unknown and precision cannot be estimated.

Nonproportional stratified sample Subgroups (strata) in the target population are sampled with different sampling fractions. Often small groups are oversampled to facilitate comparisons across groups.

Nonresponse bias In a survey, systematic underrepresentation of certain types of cases because of refusal or inability to participate, or the researcher's inability to contact the case.

Normal distribution A commonly found frequency distribution with an approximate bell shape. It is often assumed for inferential statistics.

Null hypothesis The statement actually tested statistically, expressing the absence of a relationship or no difference between desired standard and actual population value. Compare with **research hypothesis.**

Observation Each separate time a case is measured in a repeated-measures design the result is another observation. The term is mostly used with reference to time series designs. Also, a technique for gathering data.

One-tailed test Univariate hypothesis testing with the critical region entirely within one tail of the sampling distribution, or a significance test in which the researcher predicts the direction of relationship.

Open-format question No response categories are provided. Also called "open-ended" question.

Order effects The wording of preceding questions in questionnaires and interviews affects responses to later questions.

Ordinality In variables, the property that categories can be logically ordered from less to more or smaller to greater. In relationships, the property of consistent direction: as one variable increases, the other systematically either increases *or* decreases.

Outlier A case with an unusually high or low value, compared to other cases. Outliers can produce distorted measures of effect size and statistical significance.

Overfitting Having too many independent variables relative to the number of cases in multivariate analysis; produces artificially good results.

Parametric test A statistical significance test requiring assumptions about the distributions or sampling distributions of the variables; usually that they be normal.

Participant observer An observer who gathers data while taking part in the activity being observed; often (but not necessarily) the other actors are unaware they are being studied.

Periodic A data array or sampling frame list in which every *k*th case has some unique feature. Systematic sampling with a selection interval that is some multiple of *k* will produce a biased sample.

Piggy-backing Adding your questions to someone else's survey.

Pilot project A form of evaluation research in which a new policy, practice, or program is first tried out in a limited situation. The results are evaluated in order to decide whether to proceed with full implementation.

Placebo treatment In an experiment, an irrelevant treatment given to cases in a control or comparison group as an alternative to "no treatment." Used to reduce contamination effects.

Pooled time series A time series design with more than one case (but usually no more than about a dozen).

Position bias Occurs in questionnaires and interviews when the respondent's answer is affected by the positioning of response categories.

Power of a test For a significance test, the capacity to avoid Type II error. Power is defined as 1 minus the probability of Type II error.

PRE (proportional reduction of error) The improvement in predicting which value of a variable a case possesses when the value of a second variable is known. Some measures of association have this interpretation.

Precision The precision of a population estimate is the inverse of the sampling error associated with that estimate.

Precoding Using response category code numbers instead of check boxes on a survey instrument. The interviewer or respondent indicates answers by circling the appropriate numbers. Data entry of those numbers is then done directly from the instrument.

Prediction model An equation in which several independent predictor variables are used to estimate the value of a dependent variable. The outcome of selection or forecasting prediction research.

Predictive validity A type of criterion validity assessment in which the value of the criterion (e.g., bankruptcy) is not known until some time after the measure being assessed (e.g., an index of sales and net earnings) is carried out.

Preliminary analysis Procedures that weight and check data, and compute new variables from existing ones.

Pretest A preliminary evaluation of procedures and measurement operations and instruments in order to make improvements prior to data gathering. Also the measurement of variables prior to an experimental manipulation.

Primary data Data researchers gather for themselves, directly from individuals or through observation. The opposite of available or secondary data.

Primary variable A variable related to the key variable and of major interest to the researcher; predictors and causes in prediction and explanatory research, effects in evaluation research.

Probability sample A sample with random selection so that each case in the target population has a known, nonzero probability of being chosen.

Procedure effect A threat to internal validity caused by faulty research or measurement procedures that distort data. Includes measurement bias, reactive measures, experimenter effects, contamination, testing effects, and Hawthorne effects.

Processing file A file that combines data definition information and the raw data into a single file in a machine language the statistical software can easily work with; produced by many statistical software packages. Also known as systems file, data set, input file, and so on.

PVE (proportion of variance explained) The proportion of variance in one variable accounted for by a second variable. Some measures of association have this interpretation.

Quantitative variable One measured at the interval or ratio level.

Quartile deviation A measure of variability; one-half the distance between the 25th and 75th percentile.

Quota sample A sample obtained by dividing the target population into categories on one or more variables, and assigning quotas to each category proportional to its occurrence in the target population. Interviewers then locate typical re-spondents within each category. Common in market research.

Random digit dialing Techniques in which telephone numbers for a phone survey are generated randomly, to avoid missing unlisted numbers.

Random probe To check measurement validity, the interviewer asks the respondent to amplify his or her answer to a few randomly selected questions.

Random sample *See* **Probability sample.**

Range A measure of variability; the highest value of a variable minus the lowest.

Raw data file A computer file consisting of the numbers that represent your data. Visualize it as a data matrix.

Reactive measures Measures that produce answers or behaviors different from their true values because individuals are aware they are being measured.

Record A predetermined number of characters the computer reads in sequence. In analyzing data, the computer treats each row of data (case) in the data matrix as a separate record. If the lines are very long (i.e., many variables), some researchers prefer to use more than one record per case.

Regression analysis Statistical procedure that measures how well a set of independent variables explains a dependent variable, adjusting for the relationships among the independents. A common technique in business research.

Relationship analysis Analysis of relationships among variables, using both descriptive and inferential statistics.

Reliability Absence of substantial random difference between the measured and true value of a variable.

Repeated-measure design A design involving two or more measurement time points. Useful for assessing trends and reciprocal causality (X causes Y and vice versa).

Representative sample A sample for which the distribution matches the distribution in the target population, for a specified variable.

Research The process of systematically gathering and analyzing information in order to gain knowledge and understanding.

Research errors Aspects of research design, sampling, measurement, or data analysis that reduce research validity.

Research hypothesis A statement expressing a relationship the researcher suspects to be true, or in univariate analysis expressing the existence of some difference between the desired standard and the actual population value. Business researchers often substitute specific research questions. Compare with **null hypothesis.**

Research power The capacity of a design, sample, procedure, or statistical test to find a relationship that actually exists.

Research problem A brief statement of the general purpose, the key variable(s), and the boundaries of the research, usually accompanied by a set of specific research questions.

Research questions Specific questions the research is intended to answer. They imply which relationships among variables the researcher is to examine.

Research relevance The extent to which the research problem produces answers, information, or recommendations relevant to the actual business question, decision, or problem.

Research validity The extent to which findings and conclusions accurately represent what is really happening in the situation. It is composed of internal and external validity and research power.

Response card In interviews, a card on which are printed the response categories for one or more questions. The interviewer hands it to the respondent.

Response data Information gathered from individual self-reports, informants, or observers, using interviews or questionnaires.

Response scale The set of categories from which respondents choose their answers to an item in a questionnaire or interview.

Response set In questionnaires and interviews, the tendency to answer a question in a systematic fashion unrelated to the "true" answer. Includes acquiescence, position bias, and social desirability. Also called **response bias.**

Response unit The unit of measure requested or implied in a questionnaire item, such as length of takeover negotiations in weeks instead of days or months.

Retrospective variables In surveys, questions that ask respondents to recall earlier behaviors, attitudes, or situations. A cheap and error-prone substitute for panel designs.

Robust A statistical test that, when an assumption required for legitimate use of the test is moderately violated, does not produce distorted results. A test may be robust with respect to one assumption (e.g., normal distribution) but not another (e.g., homogeneous variance).

Sample A selected part of a population from which characteristics of the whole are estimated.

Sampling distribution The distribution of the means (or other parameter) of all possible samples of a given size. Never calculated, but represents the theoretical link between sample and population.

Sampling error The error in estimating a population characteristic from a random sample

because of the chance of drawing an unrepresentative sample.

Sampling fraction The ratio of sample size to target population size.

Sampling frame Either a *list* of all cases in the target population from which a sample is selected, or a *procedure* for obtaining a sample of cases from the target population (such as every tenth customer).

Scale A measure consisting of a combination of individual items, each reflecting a different aspect of the same variable.

Scientific method A set of objective, systematic procedures utilizing observable empirical evidence to gain knowledge and understanding.

Screening Discarding cases not in the desired target population. In surveys, screening questions determine whether a respondent is in the target population.

Secondary analysis Analysis of available (secondary) research data originally gathered for a different project and purpose.

Selection interval In systematic sampling, target population size divided by desired sample size, rounded to lowest whole number. Designated i.

Selection prediction A type of prediction research to help managers select from among a set of alternatives, such as job applicants or plant sites. It is generally based on information about present cases.

Self-selection sample Individuals who volunteer to take part in the research.

Semantic differential A multiple-item rating scale in which the respondent evaluates an object or idea on a series of bipolar dimensions, such as good–bad.

Sensitizing measures or procedures Measures that affect participants' subsequent behaviors or responses, producing research error.

Sequential box plots A series of box plots on consecutive sets of time-series observations, used to examine trend.

Shared covariation The portion of variation in a dependent variable jointly explained by two or more independent variables that are related to each other as well as to the dependent variable.

Significance test A statistical test of whether an association could have occurred by chance, through either random sampling error or random assignment error.

Simple random sample Random sample in which each case in the target population has an equal probability of selection.

Skewness The extent to which a variable's distribution has additional cases trailing away on one side of the mean.

Skip pattern The sequence of questions respondents follow as they answer filter questions and follow skip instructions to ignore irrelevant questions.

Smoothing function An arithmetic or mathematical procedure for reducing seasonal and random fluctuations in a time series.

Snowball sample Having located several participants in the target population, the researcher collects data and then asks them to recommend other qualifying individuals to be contacted. Often used to sample respondents with unusual characteristics for which no sampling frame list exists.

Specification error Omitting an important independent variable from multivariate analysis. Can distort results.

Specific research design The particular design chosen for a project, including the number and nature of groups or samples, and the number and spacing of measurement time points.

Split ballot technique Using two different questionnaire versions, randomly distributed, each with response options in a different order, to overcome position-related response bias.

Split-half A procedure for estimating scale reliability by determining the correlation between arbitrarily divided halves of the scale items.

Spontaneous regression A threat to internal validity in designs with multiple measurement points. Because of measurement error or natural processes, cases with extreme values on one measurement are likely to show less extreme values on the subsequent measurement. Can be mistaken for a manipulation effect.

Spurious relationship Appears to be causal, but is actually the result of an extraneous third variable causing both the independent and dependent.

Standard deviation A measure of variability, the square root of the average squared distance of each case from the mean.

Standard error The standard deviation of the sampling distribution. It is a measure of sampling error.

Standardized procedures or measures Procedures or measurement operations that are as identical as possible for all cases.

Standardized variables Variables transformed so that the mean is zero and the standard deviation is one. Also known as **Z-scores.**

Stapel scale A variation of the semantic differential scale, with a single anchored point in the middle of the scale instead of at each end.

Stationary series A time series with no trend or seasonality.

Statistical rounding To avoid bias, numbers ending in "5" are rounded to the nearest even number, not rounded upward.

Stratified sample The target population is divided into groups (strata), and a separate sample is drawn from each. Reduces sampling error.

Structural variables Attributes of cases represented by means, proportions, or ratios of attributes of other cases at a lower level of analysis (e.g., gender ratio of a committee).

Summative evaluation The systematic assessment of the results of a policy or program, to determine whether desired effects have been achieved.

Supplementary analysis Exploratory analysis following multivariate analysis to try to account for unexpected findings and nonfindings.

Suppressor variable A variable S related to both X and Y so that the sign of the X–S–Y relationship is opposite to the sign of the X–Y relationship. This reduces the apparent effect size in a measure of X–Y bivariate association.

Systematic sample After a random start, each ith case is selected from a list or array. Fastest random sampling procedure.

Target population The total set of cases within the research problem boundaries, about which the researcher hopes to draw conclusions.

Telescoping Occurs when respondents recall events as either more recent, or earlier, than they actually occurred.

Test-retest reliability Assessing measurement reliability by comparing a subsequent measurement of the same cases with initial results.

Theoretical validity A subjective approach to assessing measurement validity, including face and content validity.

Time plot In time-series analysis, plot of another variable against time.

Time series A design or data consisting of the same case measured repeatedly at regular intervals.

Transforming Altering a quantitative variable, usually to reduce skewness and make its distribution more normal. The most common transformation in business research is to use the log of a variable.

Treatment group In an experiment, the group of cases given the manipulation (a new policy, program, or practice).

Trend A consistent pattern in observations of a case over time.

Trend line A straight line representing the overall linear trend in a time plot.

Truncated sample A sample that systematically omits certain types of cases (e.g., a sample of new firms may omit those that

have already failed). Often results in attenuated correlations.

Two-tailed test A univariate hypothesis test with the critical region in both tails of the sampling distribution; a significance test in which the researcher does not predict the direction of relationship.

Type I error Wrongly concluding the null hypothesis is false.

Type II error Wrongly concluding the null hypothesis is supported.

Unbiased sample One with low levels of bias due to case selection procedures and to missing cases that are systematically different from obtained cases.

Uniform distribution Distribution of a variable with approximately the same number of cases for each value.

Unique effect The effect of an independent variable on a dependent, taking into account the effects of other independent variables. The effect solely attributable to that independent. Important in evaluation and explanatory research.

Unit of analysis The kind of case about which research gathers data. Can be a person, body of persons, relationship involving persons or bodies, aggregate of persons or bodies, event, or object.

Univariate analysis Analysis of a single variable, including central tendency, variation, and population estimates.

Utility analysis A procedure that systematically, and somewhat subjectively, combines estimates of costs and situation probabilities to help in decision making. Sometimes used to help managers decide whether to carry out a research project. Also called **decision analysis.**

Variance A measure of variability, square of the standard deviation.

Weighted average The mean of a variable with cases weighted according to their size, so that larger cases contribute more to the mean.

Weighted least squares A regression technique that downweights observations with large error terms. It can correct for nonhomogeneous variance.

Weighting cases Multiplying undersampled or oversampled cases to count more (**up-weighting**) or less (**down-weighting**) in the overall sample, as a way of compensating for nonproportional sampling and bringing proportions of cases in the sample up to the population proportions.

BIBLIOGRAPHY

Allport, G. W. 1937. *Personality: A Psychological Interpretation*. New York: Holt.

Andreasen, A. R. 1985. " 'Backward' Market Research." *Harvard Business Review* 63: 176, 180, 182.

American Psychological Association. 1974. *Standards for Educational and Psychological Tests and Manuals*. Washington, DC: American Psychological Association.

Ashenfelter, O., and G. F. Johnson. 1969. "Bargaining Theory, Trade Unions, and Industrial Strike Activity." *American Economic Review* 59: 35–49.

Asher, H. B. 1983. *Causal Modeling* (2nd ed.). Beverly Hills, CA: Sage.

Barnes, P. 1978. "The Effect of a Merger on the Share Price of the Attacker." *Accounting and Business Research* Summer: 162–168.

Barton, A. H. 1958. "Asking the Embarrassing Question." *Public Opinion Quarterly* 22: 66–68.

Bateman, T. S., and G. R. Ferris. 1986. *Methods and Analysis in Organizational Research*. Reston, VA: Reston.

Belsley, D. A., E. Kuh, and R. E. Welsch. 1980. *Regression Diagnostics*. New York: Wiley.

Berk, R. A. 1983. "An Introduction to Sample Selection Bias in Sociological Data." *American Sociological Review* 48: 386–398.

Birnbaum, P. H., and G. Y. Y. Wong. 1985. "Organizational Structure of Multinational Banks in Hong Kong from a Culture-free Perspective." *Administrative Science Quarterly* 30: 262–277.

Blalock, H. M., Jr. 1979. *Social Statistics* (2nd ed.). New York: McGraw-Hill.

Bohrnstedt, G. W. 1983. "Measurement." Chapter 3 in P. H. Rossi, J. D. Wright, and A. B. Anderson (eds.), *Handbook of Survey Research*. Orlando, FL: Academic Press.

Bryson, K. R., and D. R. Phillips. 1974. "Method for Classifying Interval-Scale and Ordinal-Scale Data." Chapter 4 in D. R. Heise (ed.), *Sociological Methodology 1975*. San Francisco: Jossey-Bass.

Campbell, D. T. 1969. "Reforms as Experiments." *The American Psychologist* 24: 409–429.

Campbell, D. T., and D. W. Fiske. 1959. "Convergent and Discriminant Validation by the Multitrait-Multimethod Matrix." *Psychological Bulletin* 56: 81–105.

Campbell, D. T., and J. C. Stanley. 1963. *Experimental and Quasi-Experimental Designs for Research*. Chicago: Rand McNally.

Clark, J. J., and M. T. Clark. 1983. *A Statistics Primer for Managers*. New York: Free Press.

Coale, A. J., and F. F. Stephan. 1962. "The Case of the Indians and the Teen-Age Widows." *Journal of the American Statistical Association* 57: 338–347.

Converse, J. M., and S. Presser. 1986. *Survey Questions*. Beverly Hills, CA: Sage.

Cook, T. D., and D. T. Campbell. 1979. *Quasi-Experimentation: Design and Analysis Issues for Field Settings*. Boston: Houghton Mifflin.

Cooper, W. H., and A. J. Richardson. 1986. "Unfair Comparisons." *Journal of Applied Psychology* 71: 179–184.

Cowles, M. P. 1974. "N = 35: A Rule of Thumb for Psychological Researchers." *Perceptual and Motor Skills* 38: 1135–1138.

DeAngelo, L. E. 1986. "Accounting Numbers as Market Valuation Substitutes: A

Study of Management Buyouts of Public Stockholders." *The Accounting Review* 61: 400–420.

Dillman, D. A. 1978. *Mail and Telephone Surveys: The Total Design Method.* New York: Wiley-Interscience.

Dobbins, G. H., I. M. Lane, and D. D. Steiner. 1988. "A Note on the Role of Laboratory Methodologies in Applied Behavioural Research: Don't Throw Out the Baby with the Bath Water." *Journal of Organizational Behavior* 9: 281–286.

Erickson, B. H., and T. A. Nosanchuk. 1977. *Understanding Data.* Toronto: McGraw-Hill.

Evans, M. G. 1975. "Opportunistic Organizational Research: The Role of Patch-Up Designs." *Academy of Management Journal* 18: 98–108.

Fox, J. 1984. "Detecting Changes of Level and Slope in Repeated-Measures Data." *Sociological Methods and Research* 12: 263–277.

Franke, R. H., and J. D. Kaul. 1978. "The Hawthorne Experiments: First Statistical Interpretation." *American Sociological Review* 43: 623–643.

Frankel, M. 1983. "Sampling Theory." In P. H. Rossi, J. D. Wright, and A. B. Anderson (eds.), *Handbook of Survey Research.* Orlando, FL: Academic Press.

Freedman, J. L., A. S. Levy, R. W. Buchanan, and J. Price. 1972. "Crowding and Human Aggressiveness." *Journal of Experimental Social Psychology* 8: 528–548.

Gaito, J. 1980. "Measurement Scales and Statistics: Resurgence of an Old Misconception." *Psychological Bulletin* 87: 564–567.

Glass, G. V., and K. D. Hopkins. 1984. *Statistical Methods in Education and Psychology* (2nd ed.). Englewood Cliffs, NJ: Prentice-Hall.

Gorden, R. L. 1975. *Interviewing: Strategies, Techniques, and Tactics.* Homewood, IL: Dorsey Press.

Gorn, G. J., and C. B. Weinberg. 1984. "The Impact of Comparative Advertising on Perception and Attitude: Some Positive Findings." *Journal of Consumer Research* 11: 719–727.

Goyder, J. C. 1982. "Further Evidence on Factors Affecting Response Rates to Mailed Questionnaires." *American Sociological Review* 47: 550–553.

Groves, R. M., and R. L. Kahn. 1979. *Surveys by Telephone: A National Comparison with Personal Interviews.* New York: Academic Press.

Grusky, O. 1963. "Managerial Succession and Organizational Effectiveness." *American Journal of Sociology* 69: 21–31.

Heberlein, R. A., and R. Baumgartner. 1978. "Factors Affecting Response Rates to Mailed Questionnaires: A Quantitative Analysis of the Published Literature." *American Sociological Review* 43: 447–462.

Hempel, C. G., and P. Oppenheim. 1960. "Problems of the Concept of General Law." In A. Donato and S. Morgenbesser (eds.), *Philosophy of Science.* Cleveland: Meridian.

Howells, J. M., and P. Brosnan. 1972. "The Ability to Predict Workers' Preferences: A Research Exercise." *Human Relations* 25: 265–281.

Jacob, H. 1984. *Using Published Data: Errors and Remedies.* Beverly Hills, CA: Sage.

Johnson, D. R., and J. C. Creech. 1983. "Ordinal Measures in Multiple Indicator Models: A Simulation Study of Categorization Error." *American Sociological Review* 48: 398–407.

Judd, C. M., E. R. Smith, and L. H. Kidder. 1991. *Research Methods in Social Relations.* New York: Holt, Rinehart and Winston.

Kanuk, L., and C. Berenson. 1975. "Mail Surveys and Response Rates: A Literature Review." *Journal of Marketing Research* 12: 440–453.

Kennedy, P. 1979. *A Guide to Econometrics.* Oxford, England: Martin Robertson.

Kinicki, A. J., and N. S. Bruning. 1982. "The Relationship Between Plant Closings and Employee Behavioral and Attitudinal Consequences." *Proceedings of the American Institute for Decision Sciences* 1: 350–352.

Kipnis, D. 1972. "Does Power Corrupt?" *Journal of Personality and Social Psychology* 2: 33–41.

Kish, L. 1965. *Survey Sampling.* New York: Wiley.

Knocke, D., and P. J. Burke. 1980. *Log-Linear Models.* Beverly Hills, CA: Sage.

Labovitz, S. 1970. "The Assignment of Numbers to Rank Order Categories." *American Sociological Review* 25: 515–524.

———. 1971. "In Defense of Assigning Numbers to Ranks." *American Sociological Review* 26: 521–522.

Langbein, L. I., and A. J. Lichtman. 1978. *Ecological Inference.* Beverly Hills, CA: Sage.

Lawler, E. E., A. M. Mohrman, Jr., S. A. Mohrman, G. E. Ledford, Jr., T. G. Cummings, and associates. 1985. *Doing Research That Is Useful for Theory and Practice.* San Francisco: Jossey-Bass.

Lazarsfeld, P., and J. Reitz. 1975. *An Introduction to Applied Sociology.* New York: Elsevier.

Lieberson, S. 1985. *Making It Count.* Berkeley: University of California Press.

Long, J. S. 1983a. *Confirmatory Factor Analysis: A Preface to LISREL.* Beverly Hills, CA: Sage.

———. 1983b. *Covariance Structure Models: An Introduction to LISREL.* Beverly Hills, CA: Sage.

Luthans, F., and T. R. V. Davis. 1982. "An Idiographic Approach to Organizational Behavior Research: The Use of Single Case Experimental Designs and Direct Measures." *Academy of Management Review* 1: 380–391.

McCall, M. W., Jr., and M. M. Lombardo. 1984. "Using Simulation for Leadership and Management Research: Through the Looking Glass." In T. S. Bateman and G. R. Ferris (eds.), *Method and Analysis in Organizational Research.* Reston, VA: Reston.

McGeveran, W. A., Jr. 1984. "Meditation at the Telephone Company." *Wharton Magazine* 6.

McIver, J. P., and E. G. Carmines. 1981. *Unidimensional Scaling.* Beverly Hills, CA: Sage.

Markus, G. B. 1979. *Analyzing Panel Data.* Beverly Hills, CA: Sage.

Mayer, L. S. 1970. "Comments on 'The Assignment of Numbers to Rank Order Categories'." *American Sociological Review* 25: 916–917.

———. 1971. "A Note on Treating Ordinal Data as Interval Data." *American Sociological Review* 26: 519–520.

Michels, R. 1959. *Political Parties* (orig. ed. 1915). Glencoe, IL: Free Press.

Miller, D. C. 1991. *Handbook of Research Design and Social Measurement* (5th ed.). Newbury Park, CA: Sage.

Mills, D. Q. 1985. "Seniority Versus Ability in Promotion Decisions." *Industrial and Labor Relations Review* 38: 421–425.

Mitchell, M., and J. Jolley. 1988. *Research Design Explained.* New York: Holt, Rinehart and Winston.

Morrison, D. E., and R. E. Henkel. 1970. *The Significance Test Controversy.* Chicago: Aldine.

Mosteller, F., S. E. Fienberg, and R. E. K. Rourke. 1983. *Beginning Statistics with Data Analysis.* Reading, MA: Addison-Wesley.

Nachmias, D., and C. Nachmias. 1976. *Research Methods in the Social Sciences.* New York: St. Martin's Press.

Northey, M. 1986. *Impact: A Guide to Business Communication.* Scarborough, Ontario: Prentice-Hall.

Norusis, M. J. 1986. *The SPSS Guide to Data Analysis.* Chicago: SPSS Inc.

———. 1988. *SPSS/PC+ Advanced Statistics V2.0.* Chicago: SPSS Inc.

O'Grady, K. E. 1982. "Measures of Explained Variance: Cautions and Limitations." *Psychological Bulletin* 92: 766–777.

Ord, K. 1982. "Can 'Top Ten' Lists Be Tested for Correlation?" *Proceedings of the A.I.D.S.* 2: 312–314.

Orne, M. 1962. "On the Social Psychology of the Psychological Experiment: With Particular Reference to Demand Characteristics and Their Implications." *American Psychologist* 17: 776–783.

Ostrom, C., Jr. 1978. *Time Series Analysis: Regression Techniques.* Beverly Hills, CA: Sage.

Payne, S. L. 1951. *The Art of Asking Questions.* Princeton, NJ: Princeton University Press.

Pfanzagl, J. 1968. *Theory of Measurement.* New York: Wiley.

Pressley, M. M. 1978. "Care Needed When Selecting Response Inducements in Mail Surveys of Commercial Populations." *Journal of the Academy of Marketing Science* 6: 333–340.

———. 1985. "A Factor-Interactive Experimental Investigation of Inducing Response to Questionnaires Mailed to Commercial Populations." *1985 AMA Educators' Proceedings.* Chicago: American Management Association.

Price, J. R. 1986. "A Comprehensive Exam for Students in Introductory Psychology." Pages 181–183 in G. C. Ellenbogen (ed.), *Oral Sadism and the Vegetarian Personality.* New York: Ballantine.

Rand Corporation. 1955. *A Million Random Digits with 100,000 Normal Deviates.* New York: Free Press.

Reichardt, C. S. 1979. "The Statistical Analysis of Data from Nonequivalent Group Designs." Chapter 4 in T. D. Cook and D. T. Campbell, *Quasi-Experimentation: Design and Analysis Issues for Field Settings.* Boston: Houghton Mifflin.

Robinson, W. S. 1950. "Ecological Correlations and the Behavior of Individuals." *American Sociological Review* 15: 351–357.

Roethlisberger, F. J., and W. J. Dickson. 1939. *Management and the Worker.* Cambridge, MA: Harvard University Press.

Rosenthal, R., and R. L. Rosnow (eds.). 1969. *Artifact in Behavioral Research.* New York: Academic Press.

———. 1969. "The Volunteer Subject." Pages 61–118 in R. Rosenthal and R. L. Rosnow (eds.), *Artifact in Behavioral Research.* New York: Academic Press.

Satin, A., and W. Shastry. 1983. *Survey Sampling: A Non-Mathematical Guide.* Ottawa: Statistics Canada.

Sawyer, A. G., and A. D. Ball. 1981. "Statistical Power and Effect Size in Marketing Research." *Journal of Marketing Research* 18: 275–290.

Schervish, M. J. 1988. "Personal Crunching." *Chance* 1: 48–51.

Schuman, H., and G. Kalton. 1985. "Survey Methods." Chapter 12 in G. Lindzey and E. Aronson (eds.), *The Handbook of Social Psychology, vol. 1* (3rd ed.). New York: Random House.

Schuman, H., and S. Presser. 1981. *Questions and Answers in Attitude Surveys.* New York: Academic Press.

Schwartz, M. D. 1986. "An Experimental Investigation of Bad Karma and Its Relationship to the Grades of College Students: Schwartz's F.A.K.E.R. Syndrome." Pages 169–175 in G. C. Ellenbogen (ed.), *Oral Sadism and the Vegetarian Personality.* New York: Ballantine.

Scott, C. 1961. "Research on Mail Surveys." *Journal of the Royal Statistical Society* 124: 143–205.

Seashore, S. E., E. E. Lawler III, P. H. Mirvis, and C. Cammann. 1983. *Assessing Organizational Change.* New York: Wiley.

Selvin, H. C. 1958. "A Critique of Tests of Significance in Survey Research." *American Sociological Review* 23: 519–527.

Singer, E. 1978. "Informed Consent: Consequences for Response Rate and Response Quality in Social Surveys." *American Sociological Review* 43: 144–162.

Smith, F. J. 1977. "Work Attitudes as Predictors of Attendance on a Specific Day." *Journal of Applied Psychology* 62: 16–19.

Social Science Research Council. 1975. *Basic Background Items for U.S. Household Surveys.* New York: Social Science Research Council.

Sommer, R., and S. A. Nelson. 1985. "Local Use of Survey Data: Impact of Research Findings on Farmers' Markets." *Human Relations* 38: 233–245.

Staw, B. M. 1975. "Attribution of the 'Causes' of Performance: A General Alternative Interpretation of Cross-Sectional Research on Organizations." *Organizational Behavior and Human Performance* 13: 414–432.

Stolzenberg, R. M., and K. C. Land. 1983. "Causal Modeling and Survey Research." Chapter 15 in P. H. Rossi, J. D. Wright, and A. B. Anderson (eds.), *Handbook of Survey Research.* Orlando, FL: Academic Press.

Strunk, W., Jr., and E. B. White. 1979. *The Elements of Style* (3rd ed.). New York: Macmillan.

Sudman, S. 1976. *Applied Sampling.* New York: Academic Press.

———. 1983. "Applied Sampling." In P. H. Rossi, J. D. Wright, and A. B. Anderson (eds.), *Handbook of Survey Research.* Orlando, FL: Academic Press.

Sudman, S., and N. M. Bradburn. 1982. *Asking Questions: A Practical Guide to Questionnaire Design.* San Francisco: Jossey-Bass.

Sudman, S., and R. Ferber. 1979. *Consumer Panels.* Chicago: American Marketing Association.

Sutton, R. I. 1989. "Reactions of Nonparticipants as Additional Rather Than Missing Data: Opportunities for Organizational Research." *Human Relations* 42: 423–439.

Tabachnick, B. G., and L. S. Fidell. 1989. *Using Multivariate Statistics* (2nd ed.). New York: Harper & Row.

Thornberry, O. 1987. *An Experimental Comparison of Telephone and Personal Health Interview Surveys.* Vital and Health Statistics, Series 2, No. 106. Washington, DC: Public Health Service, National Center for Health Statistics.

Thornton, R. J., and J. T. Innes. 1989. "Interpreting Semilogarithmic Regression Coefficients in Labor Research." *Journal of Labor Research* 10: 443–447.

Tukey, J. W. 1977. *Exploratory Data Analysis,* Reading, MA: Addison-Wesley.

Turabian, K. 1973. *A Manual for Writers* (4th ed.). Chicago: University of Chicago Press.

Van Zelst, R. H. 1952. "Validation of a Sociometric Regrouping Procedure." *Journal of Abnormal and Social Psychology* 47: 299–301.

Walizer, M. H. and P. L. Weiner. 1978. *Research Methods and Analysis: Searching for Relationships.* New York: Harper & Row.

Warwick, D. P. and C. A. Lininger. 1975. *The Sample Survey: Theory and Practice.* New York: McGraw-Hill.

Webb, E. J., D. T. Campbell, R. D. Schwartz, and L. Sechrest. 1966. *Unobtrusive Measures: Nonreactive Research in the Social Sciences.* Chicago: Rand-McNally.

Webster, M. Jr. and J. Kervin. 1971. "Artificiality in Experimental Sociology." *Canadian Review of Sociology and Anthropology* 8:263–272.

Weiss, C. H. 1972. *Evaluation Research.* Englewood Cliffs, N. J.: Prentice-Hall.

Wiseman, F. 1972. "Methodological Bias in Public Opinion Surveys." *Public Opinion Quarterly* 36:105–108.

Woodman, R. W. 1979. "A Devil's Dictionary of Behavioral Science Research Terms." *Academy of Management Review* 4:93–94.

Zinkhan, G. M. and C. R. Martin, Jr. 1983. "Message Characteristics and Audience Characteristics: Predictors of Advertising Response." *Advances in Consumer Research* 10:27–31 (Proceedings of the Association for Consumer Research).

INDEX